Hartley's Foreign Phrases

Stacey International
128 Kensington Church Street
London W8 4BH
Tel: +44 (0)207 221 7166
Fax: +44 (0)207 792 9288
E-mail: info@stacey-international.co.uk
www.stacey-international.co.uk

ISBN: 978-1905299-20-1

CIP Data: A catalogue record for this book is available
from the British Library

Printed and bound by Oriental Press, Dubai

Hartley's Foreign Phrases

J L A Hartley

STACEY INTERNATIONAL

Contents

Preface

The genesis of this book is described in the introduction to the German lexicon.

The first impetus to the compiling of this lexicon [and, thus, as it turned out, of the book itself] was a casual conversation among friends. I mentioned to them that a relative, an autodidact coming from South Africa, had remarked, many years earlier, how strange it was that only two German words had been incorporated into English, 'sobeit' *and* 'albeit'*...*

We friends speculated idly about the actual number of German words and phrases that had been adopted into English and, before many minutes had passed, we were astonished at the number we few could conjure up relying only on memory. We decided, therefore, to go into the matter more deeply and perhaps circulate a word-list. From that simple word-list has developed this present [German] lexicon and, inferentially, the other lexicons in this book.

We friends comprised, in the main, 'those skilled in the art of the dinner-table', imbued with the high principles imparted by Athenaeus in his dramatic piece of that name written at some time after AD 228. Looking back, now, on those *Noctes Ambrosianae – Noctes*, for, though nominally we met for luncheon, very frequently 'we saw the sun down' – I feel both humbled and proud. Those epic events seem to me today to have encapsulated all that Dr Johnson commended when he remarked, 'Sir, it is a great thing to dine with the Canons of Christ-Church.'* Johnson's unfeigned frankness contrasts favourably with Edward Gibbon's atrabilious comment, 'I spent fourteen months at Magdalen College: they proved the fourteen months the most idle and unprofitable of my whole life.' Of 'the Monks of Magdalen', he said, 'their dull and deep potations excused the brisk intemperance of youth.'

Though it would be difficult for me to ascribe any part of our lucubrations to 'the brisk intemperance of youth', yet there was a lightness in our step, and an unspoilt gaiety in our demeanour, which permitted us at every end and turn to ask of the world, 'Dost thou think that, because thou art virtuous, there shall be

* Boswell, *Life*, 20 March 1776

no more cakes and ale?'

It was astonishing that the topic of conversation came so often to be 'words, words, words'. We acknowledged that Thomas Hobbes was right in declaring that 'words are wise men's counters, they do but reckon by them, but they are but the money of fools, that value them by the authority of an Aristotle, a Cicero, or a Thomas [Aquinas], or any other doctor whatsoever, if but a man.' But we rapidly came, also, to the conclusion that, without words, we were as 'the brute beasts that have no understanding'.

Though the predominant reason for the existence of this book is the phenomenal number of words and phrases of foreign extraction in use in the English language, it would not have been written if it had not also been for the immense number of *English* words in English. English-speakers from the earliest days of the language have been conscious of what was called their *wordhord* or 'treasure of speech' – their vocabulary. The subsequent stupendous enrichment of the language owing to the Norman Conquest has been welcomed by the residual and ultimately dominant 'Anglo-Saxon' mother tongue to the extent that most users of the English language are utterly unaware of the debt we owe to French. To a very large extent, we gained an *entire vocabulary* in addition to our native one.

Perhaps because the genius of the language developed in the unconscious recognition that the language was not an insular matter, English-speakers over the centuries seem to have been positively anxious to adopt foreign words. The Renaissance endowed the language with thousands of new words, as was to be entirely expected. The emergence of the natural sciences added further to our *wordhord*. Foreign travel and the growth of the British Empire gave us yet further new words, some truly exotic.

All these newcomers were made welcome. The native spirit of welcoming new words is, I suspect, shared instinctively by the *speakers* of other languages, though their scholars often frustrate that instinct in the cause of linguistic purity. The persistent attitude of *l'Académie Française* is a salutary case in point: in defiance of the trend towards an international language, the Academy sets its face against the use of English words in French. The Academy has been successful in introducing purely French words into, for example, computer usage, so that the French (and the Québecois) say *logiciel* and *informatique* rather than 'hardware' and 'software'. When one considers that the French have adopted tens of thousands of learned and scientific words from Greek, one might be forgiven for suspecting that it is not so much linguistic purity that motivates the French authorities as national touchiness. Those who are committed to an atavistic desire for linguistic purity commonly go the whole hog: Adolf Hitler preferred *Fernschprecher* to *Telefon* and *Fernschreiber* to *Kabel.*

The ease with which we have adopted words from languages other than French is dealt with in the separate introductions to the Sections that follow.

The influence of Latin on English has been profound, particularly when one considers that English is not in any sense a Romance language. But, to varying degrees, that influence has worked on all other modern languages too. In the realm of learning, and especially the physical sciences, Latin has given us not only its own words but has mediated Greek to us in vast quantities. It is utterly impossible to read anything of the modern sciences without in every single sentence stumbling across words with manifestly Greek roots.

Borrowings into English from modern languages have been extremely common during the last three hundred years. Sometimes, of course, new words, such as *kangaroo* and *tsunami*, have been imported to denote novel concepts. At other times, words such as *froideur* have been introduced because 'chilliness' is not sufficiently *nuancé* to exclude purely physical cold. It is almost inevitable that a foreign word, by the time it comes to be used in everyday English, has acquired a refinement – a greater degree of precision – than it enjoyed in its native environment. Although *froideur* is the ordinary French world for 'cold' in the sense that can be established by reading a thermometer, as well as 'chilliness' (in relationships, for example), the word when used in English cannot possibly mean that a thermometer is involved. Thus, the word *froideur* in English has a more precise meaning than the original French word. Likewise, the word *détente* in English is more precise in meaning than it is in French. The list extends to infinity.

Solely from the point of view of pin-point accuracy, our ready adoption of foreign words has immeasurably enriched the language. In respects in which the conventional Englishman tends to be tongue-tied – in discussing sentimental matters, for example – the German language has furnished us with a number of good friends. It is hard to find a native English word for *Sehnsucht*, 'a yearning, wistful longing'. *Schwärmerei* is by no means adequately conveyed by 'a schoolgirl crush'. And *Schadenfreude* remains the *locus classicus*. 'What a fearful thing it is that any language should have a word expressive of the pleasure which men feel at the calamities of others; for the existence of the word bears testimony to the existence of the thing. And yet in more than one [language] such a word is found.' (R. C. Trench, *Study of Words*, 1852.)

English-speakers seem to lack the ability to name emotions. We have no equivalent for the Welsh *hiraeth*: 'homesickness' seems too tame. The Portuguese word *saudade* defies translation except by periphrasis. *Machismo* is a protean word best left in its Hispanic form.

Recent instances of adoptions, probably to be of short-term relevance, have been the Russian words *glasnost* and *perestroika*. From a little earlier, and from Cyprus, we had *enosis*. From Palestine we have had *entifada*.

English-speakers gain in two ways from the uninhibited importation of foreign words: in the first place, a new word with, normally, a high degree of precision is brought into use; and, secondly, the old stock of English words is left intact, but, where near synonyms are imported, the old English words themselves, relieved of the task of conveying the meanings now controlled by the new words, acquire a new and increased precision. We English-speakers are thus two-time winners.

The criteria with regard to foreign phrases, rather than foreign words, are somewhat different. By adopting foreign phrases we are doing no more than accepting this truism: that English-speakers by no means have a monopoly of wit or wisdom.

For many of the foreign phrases included here, it is woefully true to say, with the Italians, *Traduttore, traditore*, 'Translator, traitor': if we translate these phrases, they lose 'a certain something'. That is perhaps not surprising, for the original language is the very language of the *creator* of the thought. Not for nothing do we speak of, 'the *mot juste*'. To say 'the right word' misses 'a certain something' – 'a *je ne sais quoi*'. And it has been proverbial for centuries that *Quidquid latine dictum sit, altum videtur*: 'Whatever is said in Latin seems profound.'

I conclude by acknowledging that this book is highly opinionated. I acknowledge that but I do not apologize for the fact. I trust that those who oppose my stance on whatever issue will believe that they enjoy the same liberty as I do to express personal opinions. I hope that they will choose to promote their own views in the same way that I have.

We logophiles are inherently masochistic. Though the Good Book warns us against over-production, we positively rejoice that 'Of making many books there is no end' and utterly reject the conclusion 'and much study is weariness of the flesh' (*Eccles* 12:12).

Acknowledgements

I am grateful to my collaborators for their valued help in compiling this collection of foreign words and phrases that have been adopted by English-speakers.

For the German Section, my thanks are due to: Sandy Atkinson, Elke and Frank Beckmann, Frederike Beckmann, Dr Michael H Carl, Rosemary and Roy Croft, George Pleischhack, Hélène Hartley, Mark Hartley, Stephen Haskell, William Hosking, Matt Huber, Trevor Martin, Sir Alan Munro, Neil Munro, Dr Gunther Schmigalle and the late Eric Zinnow. Without their valued help (and forbearance), that part of the book could not have been completed.

Neil Munro, Stephen Haskell, Trevor Martin, Michael Carl, the late Eric Zinnow, George Fleischhack and Günther Schmigalle have been particularly productive and particularly patient. There is abundant evidence of their influence throughout the entire Lexicon.

In particular, my old friend Neil Munro's intimate familiarity with the German language and literature – and with the German nation – has been an inestimable boon to me. He has steered me away from many a pitfall, and on an almost daily basis, too. In particular, he has been instrumental, with Michael Carl, in demonstrating to me that I need to draw a distinction between Prince Bismarck's *Blut und Eisen* philosophy and the tendency of German holiday-makers to move other people's towels on the beach.

Dr Michael Carl, Solicitor and *Rechtsanwalt*, has been of great encouragement to me. I thank him more than I can express. He truly manifests all the qualities of the European German.

I am honoured to have had the support of Dr Gunther Schmigalle, of Karlsruhe, during the later part of the compilation of this book. Dr Schmigalle gave me much attention at a time when he was seeing through the press the completion of his critical edition in five volumes of Rubén Darío's *La Caravana Pasa*. I In addition, he continued to aid me after the last of those volumes had been published, during the arduous process of seeing through the press his edition of Darío's *Cronicas Desconocidas*. My gratitude knows no bounds.

Dr Schmigalle and I became acquainted as a result of a correspondence in *The Times Literary Supplement* initiated by a letter of mine protesting about the prevalent habit of dispensing with footnotes and relegating the *apparatus criticus* to end-notes, as though the reader were an octopus. Dr Schmigalle's own policy is to bestow on the reader *as it is needed* the benefit of his knowledge, both wide and profound, of Hispanic and French literature, so that the reader intent on appreciating to the full the unique role of Rubén Darío (Félix Ruben García Sarmiento) in Hispanic letters – as, for instance, the prophet of *modernismo* – need consult no other work of reference. It is all there on Dr Schmigalle's page! In *Cronicas Desconocidas*, for example, there are over a thousand footnotes of invaluable use to the reader.

Dr Schmigalle's help has been given as generously to the French Section as to the others, for his knowledge and appreciation of French life and letters is second to none. And I am bound to add to that accolade another accolade, that his knowledge and appreciation of English – the language and the literature – are extensive and faultless. His fluency in writing English is a marvel!

I have had much help in compiling the French Section. My bilingual wife and children have been a constant source of helpful criticism: to them I offer my unstinting gratitude.

I am extremely grateful to my other collaborators for their valued help in compiling the French Section. Thanks are due to: Sandy Atkinson, Dr Michael H Carl, Rosemary and Roy Croft, Caroline Hamilton, Stephen Haskell, William Hosking, Trevor Martin and Neil Munro. I have mentioned Dr Schmigalle's invaluable contribution to this linguistic department.

I must make a special mention of my indebtedness to my friend of fifty years, Stephen Haskell in the compilation of the French and German Sections. His knowledge of the French language and his appreciation of both French and German literature in its widest acceptation have been of immense help to me, something for which I shall always be most truly thankful. The scope of our catchment area would have been much wider if Stephen Haskell had had his way, such is the stretch of his familiarity with all things French.

I must also mention the immensely important contribution that my old friend Trevor Martin has made to this compilation. His profound scholarship has been immeasurably helpful, particularly in charting a course, as to German history, between a largely laudatory, nineteenth century attitude on the one hand and a largely damning twentieth-century one on the other. I do not think we arrived at a positive conclusion about whether that genie out of the bottle, German Nationalism, was a boon or a curse to mankind, but we acknowledge with gratitude that Neil Munro brokered a peace between the contending camps such that, we all hope, no German reader of this book will have any reason to feel offended.

I must also make mention of Trevor Martin's acerbic wit. Like every good tutor, he spared neither his pupil nor himself. His acerbic wit has, I hope, secured the effect in this book that Dr Johnson looked for in the Duke of Buckingham's play *The Rehearsal.* Talking of the comedy, he said, 'It has not enough wit to keep it sweet.' This was easy: – he therefore caught himself, and pronounced a more rounded sentence: 'It has not vitality enough to preserve it from putrefaction.'

To my many other viva-voce collaborators, who have contributed by many helpful suggestions that have gone into the melting-pot, I offer this sincere blanket thank you.

Abbreviations

In quoting authorities, the principle has been adopted of disregarding the forms in which works of literature are conventionally cast – Parts, Volume, Chapter, Verse, etc – and, instead, to list in purely numerical form the hierarchy implied, as in, for instance, Petronius, *Satyricon*, 119:5, instead of Petronius, *Satyricon*, ch 119, sect 5.

Other examples of this simplified method of citation will make the principle clearer. 'For here we have no continuing city, but we seek one to come': *Hebrews* ch. 13, v. 14 would be cited as *Heb* 13:14. 'Something is rotten in the state of Denmark': *Hamlet*, act 1, sc 4, ln 90 would be cited as *Hamlet* 1:4:90. 'Varium et mutabile semper femina': Virgil, *Aeneid* bk. 4, ln 335 would be cited as *Aeneid* 4:335.

AA	Acts of the Apostles
Ab	Abdias (Obadiah)
Ac	Abacuc (Habakkuk)
Ag	Aggeus (Haggai)
adj	adjective
adv	adverb
Am	Amos
Ap	Apocalypse
AV	Authorized Version
Ba	Baruch
BD	Bel and the Dragon
Bp	Bishop
CC	Canticum Canticorum
CJCP	Chief Justice, Common Pleas
CJKB	Chief Justice, Kings Bench
Ch	Chronicles (Verba Dierum seu Paralipomenon)
Cl	Colossians
Co	Corinthians
Co. Litt.	Coke on Littleton's Treatise on Tenures
Co. Rep.	Coke's Reports (1572-1616)
D Del	Justinian's Digest Delineavit
Dn	Daniel (Danihel)
Dt	Deuteronomy (Deuteronomium)

Dyers	Dyer's Reports, King's Bench, 3 vols (1513-1581)
Eccles	Ecclesiastes
Ecclus	Ecclesiasticus
ed	editor
edn	edition
Es	Esther (Hester)
et seq.	'and following'
e. g.	exempli gratia ('for example')
Ep	Ephesians
Es	Esdras (Ezra)
Ex	Exodus
Ek	Ezekiel
Ez	Ezra (Esdras)
fl	floruit ('he flourished')
Ga	Galatians
Gn	Genesis
Ha	Habakkuk (Abacuc)
Hg	Haggai (Aggeus)
Hb	Hebrews
He	Hester (Esther)
Hi	Hieremias, Threni seu Lamentationei (Jeremiah)
Hz	Hiezechiel
Ho	Hosea (Osee)
ibid	'in the same place'
Ib	Iob (Job)
i. E.	Id est ('that is')
Ih	Iohel (Joel)
In	Ionas (Jonah)
infra	'below' (in the text)
Io	Iosue (Joshua)
Institutes	Justinian's Institutes
Is	Isaiah (Isaias)
Jm	James Jenkins Jenkins's Century Reports (l620-1623)
Jr	Jeremiah (Hieremias)
Jl	Joel (Isohel)
Jo	Joshua (Iosue)
Jb	Job (Iob)
Jn	John

Jh	Jonah (Ionas)
Jd	Jude
Ju	Judges (Iudicum)
Jt	Judith (Iudith)
KJV	King James Version
Kg	Kings (Malachim seu Regum)
L. C.	Lord Chancellor
Lm	Lamentations
Ld	Laodiceans
loc. cit.	loco citato ('in the cited place')
Lv	Leviticus
Lk	Luke
M.R.	Master of the Rolls
Ma	Malachi
Max. Leg.	Bacon's Maxims of the Law
Mc	Maccabees
Mt	Matthew
Mk	Mark
Mi	Micah (Micha)
Na	Nahum (Naum)
Nh	Nehemiah
n	noun
Nm	Numbers (Numeri)
Noy Max.	Noy, Maxims
Ob	Obadiah
Op. cit.	opere citato ('in the cited work')
Os	Osee (Hosea)
pro tanto	'by that much'
PP	Paralipomenon seu Verba Dierum
p.p.	past participle
Pt	Peter
Pl	Philemon
Ph	Philippians
Pinx	pinxit
Plowd.	Plowden's Reports, 2 vols (1550-1580)
PM	Prayer of Manasses
passim	'throughout'
pl	plural

pr.p.	present participle
Ps	Psalms (Psalmi)
pb	proverbs
q.v.	quod vide ('which see')
qq. v.	quae vide ('which see', pl)
Rv	Revelation
RV	Revised Version
Rt	Ruth
Sm	Samuel
Sa	Sapientia
scil	scilicet ('permitted to know')
Sc	sculpsit quaere ('but a doubt is raised')
sic	'thus'
Si	Sirach seu Ecclesiasticus
So	Sofonias
Sr	Saint
supra	'above' (in the text)
Su	Susanna
SS	Song of Solomon
s.v.	sub voce ('under the entry')
Th	Thessalonians
transfd	transferred
Tb	Tobit (Tobias)
Tm	Timothy
Tt	Titus
vb	verb
vern.	Vernon's Reports, Chancery, 2 vols (1680-1719)
viz	videlicet ('permitted to see')
Vg	Vulgate
v.l.	varia lectio
v.ll.	variae lectiones
WS	Wisdom of Solomon (Sapientia)
S3	Song of the Three Children
Zh	Zechariah (Zaccharias)
Ze	Zephaniah (Sophonias)

THE INTERNATIONAL PHONETIC ALPHABET

/ɑ/ as in 'father', 'start' and 'bath'
/æ/ as in 'bat'
/aɪ/ as in 'try'
/aʊ/ as in 'how'
/aʊəɹ/ as in 'sour', 'hour', 'flower'
/ɒ/ as in 'pot' and 'wash'
/ɔː/ as in 'law', 'faught', 'nought'
/ɔɪ/ as in 'boy'
/dʒ/ as in 'age', 'judge', 'soldier'
/ð/ as in 'then', 'there'
/eɪ/ as in 'ace', way', 'steak'
/ə/ as in the first syllable of 'about'
/əʊ/ as in 'no', 'boat', 'know'
/ɛ/ as in 'bed'
/ɛəɹ/ as in 'fair', 'square'
/h/ as in 'Ho!'
/ɪ/ as in 'bid'
/i/ as in 'feet', 'meat', 'replete'
/ɪə/ as in 'serious', 'feared', 'near', 'here'
/l/ as in 'left', 'bell', 'milk'
/ŋ/ as in 'ring', 'sing'
/θ/ as in 'thin', 'thick'
/ɹ/ as in 'north'
/ʃ/ as in 'ship', 'sure', 'station'
/tʃ/ as in 'catch', 'match', 'church'
/u/ as in 'goose'
/ʊ/ as in 'foot', 'good', 'put'
/ʊəɹ/ as in 'door', 'poor'
/ʌ/ as in 'bud'
/ʒ/ as in 'pleasure', 'leisure', 'vision'
/ː/ lengthens the vowel it follows
/ˈ/ indicates where the stress falls
/ˀ/ denotes a glottal stop

French

This Lexicon is the first in a series of relatively concise lists of words and phrases from foreign languages that have been adopted by reasonably well educated English-speakers. English is replete with French words and phrases. We are far from regretting that. John Evelyn said, 'We have hardly any words that do so fully express the French … *naiveté, ennui, bizarre* … let us therefore (as the Romans did the Greek) make as many of these do homage as are like to prove good citizens': *Memoirs*, 1857 edn, III, p 161.

When we started on this French Lexicon, we knew that there would be many more French words and phrases known to English-speakers and used by them than German words and phrases, owing to a number of strong influences, the primary one being the profound impression that French culture made on English-speakers during the period of the Enlightenment. Until 1914, French was *la langue de la diplomatie*, and, indeed, to many, of culture in general. An indication of the predominance of French is furnished by the fact, among many, that the language of conversation of Catherine the Great and of Frederick the Great was not German (or Russian) but French. Frederick the Great prided himself on his French but was not confident (or concerned) about his German.

There is, however, another influence that runs like a hidden stream beneath the surface of the English language, and that is the language known to philologists as Anglo-French or Anglo-Norman. This was the language of the Royal Court in England for some 300 years from the Norman Conquest in 1066. It persisted in legal use for much longer – until 1734, in fact. It was 'the Frensshe of Stratford-atte-Bowe' of Chaucer's well-bred Prioress, of whom the much-travelled Chaucer simply remarks, 'for Frensshe of Paris was to her unknowe'. Francis North (1637-85), the Lord Keeper, when in a hurry, wrote notes for his own use in Law French, for, as his brother Roger said, 'Really the Law is scarcely expressible properly in English'.

Anyone familiar with Anglo French will testify to its efficacy as a means of communication. It has indelibly marked the English language. True, its influence over the centuries on English as it is spoken and written today has been what is perhaps a mixed bag of curses and blessings. It has led to the species of nightmare 'every schoolboy knows', the *faux amis* (*q.v.*), of which there are hundreds in the language, and, of course, to our chaotic spelling (Norman clerks trying to spell Anglo-Saxon words), but at the same time, the language – abhorring synonyms as it does, and preferring to dispose of synonyms by differentiation – has accepted Anglo-French as a means of increasing our vocabulary – our 'wordhord', as our Saxon forefathers called it – so that it is nowadays the envy of the world.

Discerning the connection between a modern English word and its Anglo-Norman ancestor is often a work requiring some patience. In the main, no attempt has been made in this Lexicon to trace the ancestry of those words the English language owes to the Norman Invasion. They are simply too numerous. Such words, French by extraction, are mentioned in this Preface only because they afford an exceptionally effective answer to the question, 'Why are there so many *faux amis* in English?' The primary reason for the presence of this immense contingent of *faux amis* in our language is a dynamic one. There are a great many words, by origin French, that have radically changed meaning over their centuries in England. At the same time, the original French words themselves have very often radically changed *their* meaning in their own homeland.

It is thus that we have so many of these *faux amis*. They are discussed in slightly more detail in the Lexicon, *s.v. faux amis*.

One additional remark is appropriate. In formal English, and in particular in the language of liturgy and the law, doublets, or pairs of words, are very frequently met with. In the Book of Common Prayer one meets 'pray and beseech' and 'rest and quietness', where no distinction can be made between the pairs. In the Law one meets 'save and except', where there is no possibility of a valid distinction's being made. The distinguished legal historian, F. W. Maitland (1850-1906), has added his weight to this explanation: that the ostensible duplication was intended in part to cater for the two linguistic streams in the land, so that, if an 'honest Saxon' didn't understand 'pray', from the French 'prier', he would understand 'beseech', from his native 'seek'. This example demonstrates that it was by no means always the case that the Saxon root prevailed.

Differentiation very frequently nullified the appararent existence of synonymity. The two words 'dove' and 'pigeon' exist in contemporary English. The word derived through Anglo-French, 'pigeon', is the ordinary word for the bird: the word 'dove', from a Germanic root, is reserved for a higher and more august register. Peace-lovers were riled in the sixties by references to Picasso's 'pigeon'.

These differentiations focus attention on what philologists call *register*. The worthy burgesses sitting down in a City of London Livery Company's Hall would be happy with 'Pommes frites' on their menu, but would feel it grossly *below dignitatem* if their Steward put 'Chips' or 'French fries' on their 'Bill of Fare'.

Though we shall not take much account of words that are of remote French origin – those that we owe to Anglo-French – we shall take scrupulous account of French words that have come into the language direct from French, for the very presence of those words in the language is proof that, though we say, 'The Greeks had a word for it', we also say 'le mot juste'.

Translations in this Lexicon are intentionally literal.

The Lexicon

à contre cœur 'Unwillingly, reluctantly, grudgingly'.

à la and **au** (literally, 'to the'). There is some confusion between these two forms. If the expression *à la* is short for *à la mode*, as in à la mode russe ('in the Russian style'), then the gender is fixed in the feminine, in agreement with la mode. The expression is always, for example, 'there were negotiations à la Boris Yeltsin', never 'negotiations au Boris Yeltsin'. Thus one sees, on a menu, 'à la maître d'hôtel', meaning 'à la mode du maître d'hôtel'. *Au* in an adverbial phrase, such as au naturel and *au beurre*, is unrelated to *à la mode*: the preposition and article are governed by the gender of the substantive: for example, *à la crème*, in agreement with the gender of *la crème*, and *au moins*, in agreement with *le moins.*

à la carte Dîner à la carte: 'to dine from a menu giving a range of choices'. *Cf table d'hôte, below.*

à la mode 'In fashion', or, if followed by a name, 'After the style or fashion of…'.

Pronounced /alamɔd/, that is, with a short *o*. For a fuller discussion, see *mode, à la, below.*

à la russe 'In the Russian manner'. For example, *Nous buvons à la russe:* 'We drink in the Russian way' (*scil*, by throwing the drink to the back of the throat).

à l'outrance Literally, 'to the limit'. From *outrer*, originally 'to push to the limit'. In contemporary French the expression is *à outrance.*

> 'There was a famous quarrel, *à l'outrance*, about it': J F Cooper, *Recoll Europe,* I ix 310 (1837). 'Francis II will be called upon to make his choice between casting in his lot with the defenders *à l'outrance* of Gaeta, or making his escape by sea': *Once a Week,* 476/2 20 Oct. 1860.

The word was early naturalized in a slightly different and potentially misleading form.

> 'Come Fate into the Lyst, And champion me to th' vtterance!': Shakespeare, *Macbeth,* III I 72 (1605).

à point In cookery, *un steack est cuit à point s'il est cuit juste assez, entre saignant and bien cuit*; 'a steak is cooked *à point* if it is cooked just enough, between rare and well cooked'.

à propos Broadly meaning 'referring to', from *à* 'to' and *propos,* 'purpose, plan'. In French the words are used adverbially, adjectivally and as a noun.

à rebours 'Against the grain, against the nap (of cloth)'. The expression gained increased currency in England owing to the title of a novel by Joris-Karl Huysmans (1848-1907) entitled *À rebours* (1884). The word was used, however, as a domesticated word from at least the fourteenth century, predominantly in Scotch usage, a souvenir of the Auld Alliance between France and Scotland.

> 'Androcheus … answered hym al at reburs [*v.r.* robours]', R Brunne, *Chron. Wace* (Rolls) 5165 (c1330). 'Þir quhelis... twa aganis twa Sall alwais turne in contrare cours As thingis beand at rebourse', *Sc. Leg. Saints* I. (*Katherine*) 860. *Ibid.* 12652 c

1375. 'Schyre Willame persaywyd then His myschef, and hym send succowris, Ellis had all gane at rebowris'. Wyntoun, *Cron.* IX. viii. 48 c 1425.

abattoir Literally, 'slaughterhouse'. There can be only one reason for the adoption of this French word in place of the native 'slaughterhouse' and that is euphemism. As is so often the case, the French word shocks our sensibilities less than the home-spun word.

accouchement Literally, 'a lying-in, a confinement'. The *OED* says, tersely, 'delivery in childbed'. The derivation is clear enough from the appearance of the word. The reason for the use of the word in English can be ascribed only to euphemism. 'Confinement' was widely used until this present generation. There is still a hospital near Waterloo Station, London, that clearly proclaims itself on its front elevation as a 'lying-in hospital'. The word *accoucheur* was frequently used from approximately the middle of the eighteenth century to approximately the middle of the 19th century to denote a male midwife, albeit with a more elevated status, a status akin to that of a surgeon.

accoutrement[s] Apparel, outfit, equipment, kit. Almost always in the plural: clothes, trappings, equipment. The equipments of a soldier other than arms and uniform. The pronunciation in contemporary England is a hybrid between the French and English pronunciations: /ə'kuːtrəmnt/, rather than the French /akutłəm/ or the traditional, more completely naturalized form /ə'kuːtə[r]mnt/.

adieu Literally, *adieu*, from *à* 'to' and *dieu* 'God', *i.e.* 'I commend you to God!', originally said to the party remaining, as 'Farewell' was said to the party setting forth. Traditionally, the pronunciation in England has been /ə'dju/, though many repertory players would nowadays quail at crying out, 'A Jew!'. Thus, the contemporary English pronunciation tends to imitate the original French /adjœ/, sounding approximately thus: /a'ʤɜː/.

agent provocateur 'An agent employed to induce or incite a suspected person or group to commit an incriminating act': *OED*.

agrément In music most often in the plural. A convenient and abbreviated way of referring to the grace-notes and embellishments that characterize, in particularly, Baroque music. In English, the broad term 'trills' is often used as a short-hand expression for these grace-notes and ornamentations, though, strictly, the word 'trill' is a synonym for 'shake', which is only one of the many ornaments that were ubiquitous in the music of the Baroque era.

'Extraneous episodes, or fashionable divisions, which being the *agrémens* [*sic*], or trimmings, of the times, become antiquated': Charles Burney, *History of Music*, III I 87/1 (1789). '*Agréments*, graces, embellishments, ornaments': J Hiles, *Dictionary of Musical Terms*, p 9 (1871). 'The agrémens [*sic*] used in modern music ... are the acciacatura, appoggiatura, arpeggio, mordent, nachschlag, shake or trill, slide, and turn': Grove, *Dictionary of Music*, I 44/1 (1879).

aide-de-camp 'An officer who assists a general in his military duties, conveying his orders, and procuring him intelligence': *OED*. The plural is *des aides-de-camp*.

aide-mémoire A note created as an aid to the memory, originally used primarily in diplomatic contexts; a memorandum. There are some indications that the French usage is narrowing. For example, the esteemed dictionary *le Petit Robert*, edn of 1970, gives only the following definition: 'Abrégé destiné à soulager la mémoire de l'étudiant en ne lui présentent que l'essentiel des connaissances à assimiler'. The plural is invariable: *des aide-mémoire.*

> '*Examples of Building Construction, intended as an Aide-Memoire for the Professional Man*', (title), H. Laxton (1855). 'No written document on the subject of the British questionnaires, even in the way of an aide memoire, will be handed to the Foreign Secretary': *Westminster Gazette*, 3rd July 1923. 'An agreement reached in 1947 between the BBC, the Government, and the Opposition, and embodied in an *Aide-Mémoire*': *BBC Handbook*, p 23 (1957).

aiguillette[s] The diminutive of *une aiguille*, 'a needle'. The decorative 'ropes' worn on the breast that form part of full-dress military and naval uniform and of some liveries. So called because they terminate in metal points originally applied to assist threading, in the same way that modern shoelaces have metal ends to facilitate threading.

aîné Normally, 'The elder brother or sister'. Also 'the elder of two with the same name'. 'The younger' is *puisné*, from which English 'puny'. The ordinary judges of the High Court are referred to as 'puisne judges', pronounced exactly as 'puny'.

> 'A puisne judge of the High Court of Justice means for the purposes of this Act a judge of the High Court other than the Lord Chancellor, the Lord Chief Justice of England, the Master of the Rolls, the Lord Chief Justice of the Common Pleas, and the Lord Chief Baron': *Act 40 & 41 Vict.* c. 9 §5 (1877).

ambiance In English, 'ambience'. 'Atmosphere' in the figurative sense. The *OED* has the following note: 'The Fr. form *ambiance* is used in *Art* for the arrangement of accessories to support the main effect of a piece'.

amour-propre An assertive self-love anxious to manifest itself and sensitive to causes of offence; 'to have a good opinion of oneself'.

amuse-gueule Broadly, 'amuse-gullet', a term for small savory delicacies served with cocktails. The word *gueule* is the name for the mouth of a dog or other carnivorous animal: hence, the expression *amuse-gueule* is not favoured in polite circles. An alternative, *amuse-bouche*, has been tried but has not found acceptance. See *canapé, below*.

Ancien Régime, l' The French monarchical and feudal system in existence until the Revolution in 1789.

'Angleterre est une nation de boutiquiers, l' 'England is a nation of shopkeepers'. Attributed to Bonaparte by his medical man on St Helena, B. E. O'Meara, *Napoleon in Exile*, vol ii *At St Helena*, p 81 (London, 1822). Bonaparte might have been quoting Pasquale Paoli (1725-1807), a fellow-countryman; if so, he probably said 'sono mercanti': Gaspard Gourgaud (1783-1852, *Journal inédit de Ste-Hélène*, I, 69 (1899)).

Annales, les This influential journal, *les Annales d'histoire économique et sociale,* was founded in 1929 by Lucien Febvre (1878-1956) and Marc Bloch (1886-1944). It promotes the stance taken by historians such as Fernand Braudel and is seen as consistently publishing the most authoritative expressions of the approach to history summed up in the phrase *la longue durée* (*q. v., below*).

apéritif 'An alcoholic drink, taken before a meal, to stimulate the appetite': *OED*. Ultimately from the Latin *aperīre*, 'to open'.

aperçu[s] From *apercevoir,* ' to perceive'. A summary exposition, a conspectus. Also, a revealing, penetrating glimpse; an insight. The second use is almost the only one in English and is most often seen in the plural.

> 'Almost always in the course of each essay there are aperçus of great penetration'. *Times Literary Suppl,* 783/2, 27th December 1957. 'The notes are reminiscent, in their expansive relevance and out-of-the-way aperçus, of the best nineteenth-century editing': *Med. Ævum,* XXXII, 152 (1963).

appui (point d') See the quotation from 1832. Formerly naturalized (/əp'wiː/) but now treated as wholly French (/apɥi/), and also used figuratively and as a term of art in the *manège.* See *point d'appui, below.*

> 'Point of Formation or Appui–Any fixed object or marker upon which a body of troops is directed to commence its formation into line': *Prop. Reg. Instr. Cavalry* iii. 46 3 (1832). 'Horses for the army ought to have a full appui, or firm stay upon the hand': C. James, 'Horsemanship', *Military Dictionary,* p 19 (1816).

'Après nous le déluge'; 'After us the deluge': Madame de Pompadour (1721-64) in Madame du Hausset, *Mémoires,* p 19 (1824).

arbitrage A type of trading in stocks, so as to take advantage of the difference of price at which the same stock may be quoted at the same time in the exchange markets of distant places. [In this sense adopted from mod.F., and usually pronounced ('ɑːbɪtrɑːʒ)]': *OED.*

argot A word of unknown origin signifying the jargon, slang, or peculiar phraseology of a class, originally that of thieves and rogues.

armes blanches, les 'Side-arms', a puzzling expression signifying sabres, *épées,* pistols and other arms carried on the person.

armoire 'A cupboard' or 'closet'; more recently, 'a wardrobe' or 'clothes-closet'.

arrière pensée The words mean, literally, 'behindthought, not 'after-thought'. The French expression means a thought lying behind the ostensible, observable thought. It never means an 'after-thought', a mistake easily made. *Cf l'esprit d'escalier, below.*

arriviste 'One who is bent on 'arriving', *i.e.* on making a good position for himself in the world; a pushing or ambitious person, a self-seeker': *OED.*

art deco or **art déco** (/ar dɛko/ or /ar deko/). An abbreviation of *art décoratif,* 'decorative art', from the name of the exhibition, *l'Exposition Internationale des Arts Décoratifs et Industriels Modernes* held in Paris in 1925. From that, and often with capital initials, the name has been applied subsequently to a style of interior design (furniture, textiles, ceramics, etc), popular in the 1920s and 1930s, characterized by geometrical shapes and harsh colours.

art nouveau (/ar nuvo/), literally, 'new art' (often with capital initials), a style of art developed in the last decade of the 19th century, characterized by the free use of ornament based on organic or foliate forms, often water-lily motifs, and by its flowing (*i.e.,* non-geometrical) lines and curves. (Called *Jugendstil* in Germany.)

aspiration The asterisk in this Lexicon denotes that the initial letter *h* in the relevant word is *aspiré.* That does not mean that the *sound* of the letter *h* is present, but merely that no liaison or elision is made between the word commencing with an *h aspiré* and the definite articles, the indefinite articles and any preceding word. For example, the initial letter of *homard*, 'lobster', is aspirated; thus, one says and writes *le homard*, not *l'homard.*

Almost all the words beginning with an *h aspiré* are of non-Latin origin: that is, they are predominantly of Gaulish or Frankish (Germanic) origin, such as the words *halle* and *hall*, which came into the French language from a Germanic root by quite different means. Two random exceptions to the generalization about the derivations of aspirated words are *héros* and *hierarchie,* which come from Greek. The knowledge of the existence of the rough breathing in these words guaranteed their being classed as aspirated words, but not, of course, to their actually having their initial letters aspirated. The *sounded* aspirate is entirely absent from French, as has been immortalized for all educational levels in England by the television series *'Allo, 'Allo.*

assignat (/asiɲa/) Paper money issued in 1790 by the *Assemblée constituante* on the supposed security of the *biens nationaux*, fundamentally the nationalized property of the Church, and later the property of the Crown. The *assignats* were constantly overissued and by 1796 had become completely worthless.

attaché 'One attached to, connected with, on the staff of, another person or thing; specifically, one attached to the suite of an ambassador': *OED.*

au courant Abreast of affairs; in touch; up to the minute:

au-dessus de la mêlée 'Above the conflict or fray'.

au fait 'In phr. *to be au fait in* or *at*: to be well instructed or 'up to the mark' in, thoroughly conversant with, expert or skilful in. *To put a person au fait of* (= F. *mettre au fait de*): to instruct thoroughly in. Also const. *to*, or (most freq. in recent use) *with*': *OED.*

au fond 'At bottom'; fundamentally; essentially.

au grand sérieux 'In deep or deadly earnest'.

> 'We are not asked to take these narratives *au grand sérieux.* They are rather sketches of the past, illustrating what could have been done, and may be done again by women...' *Notes and Queries* (*Notes on Books*), 10th June, 1893, p. 459.

au pair An odd phrase, used to denote a person, almost always a young female, often a student, living 'on board lodgings' with a family, in receipt of a small wage and helping with the household.

au pied de la lettre Literally, 'to the foot of the letter' but meaning 'to the letter', that is, signifying the word *literally* itself, *verbatim et literatim.* If words are taken *au pied de la lettre,* they are taken literally, not figuratively or metaphorically. The phrase also imports the notion of scrupulously following instructions or directions.

> 'Of course, you will not take everything I have said quite *au pied de la lettre*': Fra. Ollæ*: A Philosophical Trilogy.*

au revoir Literally, 'to re-seeing'. 'Goodbye'.

auteur Literally, 'author'. A specific application of the word has assumed importance in recent years: 'A film director whose personal influence and artistic control over his or her films are so great that he or she may be regarded as their author, and whose films may be regarded collectively as a body of work sharing common themes or techniques and expressing an individual style or vision': *OED*. First recorded in French in *Arts et littérature dans la société contemporaine* 3403 (1936), but later popularized by François Truffaut in *Cahiers du Cinéma* , 26th January 1955, p 26.

avant la lettre 'Before the event'.

> 'In many – perhaps in most – cases what Brugmann, Meillet, and all the other Indo-Europeanists of the older generation called *comparative method* or *comparison between languages* is nothing else than areal [*sic*] linguistics *avant la lettre*': *Word* I. 137 (1945).

baccalauréat The French name for the examination that terminates schooling of a pre-University standard. The English word 'baccalaureate' has for many years denoted the degree of Bachelor of Arts and, more recently, of Science and other specialities. Measures taken to introduce a word such as *baccalaureat* denoting a standard of education much below the baccalaureate as traditionally recognized have met with much resistance, perhaps because of the 'dumbing-down' implicit in these measures. However, the International Baccalaureate has gained considerable acceptance worldwide: it is an international qualification awarded as a result of success in an examination offered by educational institutions in many countries, and is intended to qualify successful candidates for higher education in their own country or abroad.

baccarat A game of cards played between the *banque* and several punters.

> 'There are two forms of *Baccarat*, known respectively as *Baccarat Chemin de Fer* and *Baccarat Banque*': L Hoffmann, *Baccarat*, p 12 (1891).

badinage 'Light trifling raillery or humorous banter': *OED*. *Badinerie:* 'banter'.

bagatelle A trifle; a thing of no importance. The secondary senses, meaning a game played with a ball and cue on a pinboard with a semi-circular end or a similar game sometimes called semi-billiards, are purely English and have no analogue in French.

baguette A long, thin loaf of French bread, of various sizes in different regions.

> 'The baguette ... is the classic French loaf. By law it must weigh 250 grammes': *The Guardian*, p 3/8, 22nd August 1970.

bain-marie A cooking utensil designed to hold a charge of water that is kept just below the boil into which are placed other utensils so as to heat their contents in a gentle fashion. The utensil, 'the bath of Mary', is so called, the celebrated lexicographer Émile Littré thought, from the gentleness of this method of heating.

bal masqué A masked ball.

bal musette A popular dance-hall, often with an accordion band.

ballet 'A theatrical representation, consisting of dancing and pantomime, orginally employed to illustrate dramatically the costumes and manners of other nations, but now for the most part regarded as an artistic exhibition of skill in dancing': *OED*.

ballon d'essai Literally, 'a trial or test balloon'. Figuratively, 'An experimental project or piece of policy put forward to test the feeling or attitude of a person or body of persons; a feeler': *OED*.

baroque A word fraught with difficulty if one views its history. For most of its life it denoted a style of architecture that succeeded the imprecisely defined Classical and Palladian styles. It was typified by such edifices in France as the Palace of Versailles and in England by the Royal Hospitals at Chelsea and Greenwich, and the Church of St Martin's-in-the-Fields. From about 1960, the style of music written just before the Classical period in music ('Pre-classical Music') began to be called *Baroque*, often pronounced with a long *o*. Gradually, during the last twenty-five years of the 20th century, the expression *Baroque music* became the standard way of denoting music written between approximately 1650 and 1750–the dates must remain somewhat flexible and a matter for personal judgement. The word is nowadays pronounced with a short *o*, /ba'rɥk/. (As a matter of interest, its derivation is from the Portuguese for a flawed pearl. As its derivation implies, the application of the word over the years has not been uniformly complimentary.)

> ' ...Baroque (the word which was first applied to art to denote misshapenness)': Keith Millar, *The Times Literary Supplement*, p 10, 13th January 2006.

barouche A four-wheeled carriage having a half-head that can be raised or let down at pleasure, and that seats two couples facing each other. The word is not in fact French, except as a borrowing from English. It is in fact an adaptation into English of a variety of Continental forms. Pronounced /bə'ruːʃ/.

bas bleu A translation of the English *blue-stocking,* meaning exactly the same. For an account of how intellectual ladies in England acquired this name, see the *OED s.v. blue-stocking.*

bas relief 'Low relief'; sculpture or carved work in which the figures project less than one half of their true proportions from the surface on which they are carved. The French expression, pronounced /baʅɛf/, is a calque of the Italian *basso rilievo* (*q.v.* in the Italian Lexicon).

bâton A multi-functional word. The only use of the word that requires a French pronunciation is to name the light stick used by orchestral and choral conductors for beating time. (Perhaps the peculiar mark of a Field Marshal, his baton, might also be pronounced as French. See *Le bâton de Maréchal, below.* The short rod or stick passed from runner to runner in a relay race is always pronounced /'batn/.)

bâtonné Used to describe vegetable cut into 'sticks'. Also used in philately to describe stamp-paper having small ridges or corrugations on its surface, known in the printing trade as *laid* paper, as opposed to smooth paper, which is known as *wove.*

bavardage 'Idle talk, prattle, chattering': *OED. Bavard*: 'A chatterbox'.

BCBG That is, /besebeʒe/, meaning *bon chic bon genre,* 'Good style good manners'. A thinly veiled indication of the speaker's disapproval of the elevated social standing and graces of the subject referred to.

beau Primarily, the French adjective for 'fine, beautiful', in England traditionally pronounced /bu/, as in *Beaulieu* (/'bjuːli/) or, sometimes, /bi/, as in *Beauchamp* (/'biːtʃəm/). Re-imported from French for general use in English in such meanings as 'a dandy', 'a lover or sweetheart', it is always pronounced /bo/. See next.

beau-geste Literally, 'a fine gesture', but in use restricted to a display of magnanimity. (The novel by P. C. Wren, *Beau Geste,* turned into a film in 1939, has as its principal character Michael Geste, known as 'Beau' Geste.)

beau idéal The French meaning is undoubtedly 'The ideal "Beautiful", the word 'Beautiful' being the abstract conception or notion of beauty. The word *beau* is the noun, *idéal* the adjective. But in English, where the adjective usually precedes the noun, the *rôles* are frequently reversed: *beau* is taken as an adjective and *idéal* as a noun, so as to create the concept of 'the highest conceived or conceivable type of beauty or excellence of any kind; that in which one's ideal is realized, the perfect type or model' – used in a sense comparable to *summum bonum*. Inasmuch as the English usage is grammatically correct in French and conveys a useful notion, it is probably best to accept its anomalous presence in English though not in French and accept the occasional puzzled look on French faces.

> 'Wonderfully captivated with the *beau idéal* which they have formed of John Bull': Irving, *Sketch-Book, John Bull* (D) (1820). 'The *beau ideal* of manly beauty': *Gent. Mag.* XCVII. II. 516, 1827. 'The Highlanders came to regard him as the very beaui-déal of a minister': H. Miller *Sch. & Schm.* xxii. 231 (1854).

Beau Ideal was the title of a novel by P. C. Wren in the series featuring Michael Geste as hero: see *Beau Geste, above.*

Belle Époque, la Literally, 'the beautiful age', meaning, in general, a period of high artistic or cultural development, but nowadays used especially of such a supposed period in *fin de siècle* France: *cf fin de siècle, below.*

belles-lettres 'Fine letters, *i.e.* 'literary studies,' parallel to *beaux arts* the 'fine arts'; embracing, according to *Littré*, grammar, rhetoric, and poetry. Elegant or polite literature or literary studies. A vaguely-used term, formerly taken sometimes in the wide sense of 'the humanities', *literæ humaniores*; sometimes in the exact sense in which we now use 'literature'; in the latter use it has come down to the present time, but it is now generally applied (when used at all) to the lighter branches of literature or the æsthetics of literary study': *OED*.

béret A round flat woollen cap worn by the Basque peasantry; also, a clerical *biretta*, and a men's-wear cap named from the *biretta*. Also, a soft, fourcornered cap or beret, formerly worn by the Augustinian canons, similar to the clerical headgear known in England as 'the Canterbury Cap'. Nowadays, the word normally refers to a cap resembling the Basque *béret*, worn by men and women, especially for casual or holiday wear; also, such a cap forming part of the uniforms of the armed services of many nations.

berline A limousine; 'a (luxury) motor car with a compartment for the passengers and a separate compartment for the driver': *OED*. Also used in French to name the interior of a saloon car (US, 'sedan'), and, again in France, as the name for a car with four doors.

bête noire Literally, 'black beast'; figuratively, an insufferable person. A person or thing the bane of a person or of his life; an intolerable person or thing; an object of aversion.

bêtise A foolish, ill-timed remark or action; a piece of folly; an instance of stupidity.

> 'I think it is an *enfantillage*, a *bêtise*, on the part of the Austrian Government': Lady Granville, *Lett.* (1894), I. 406 (1827). 'This *bêtise* of a war has made us all serious': Disraeli, *The Young Duke*, II, II, xix 256 (1831).

bidet '"A vessel on a low, narrow stand, which can be bestridden" (Syd. Soc. Lex.) for bathing purposes. Now usually a shallow oval basin fitted in a bathroom, used for washing the perineum:' *OED*. This definition must rank very high in the hierarchy of dead-pan dictionary definitions. The temptation to refer to the English tourist's conviction that the French are obsessed by foot hygiene has been resisted, and at the same time a venerable, truly archaic past participle, 'bestridden', has been introduced that vies with Evelyn Waugh's use of 'cloven' in *Scoop*: 'I want some cleft sticks, please.'...'We can have some cloven for you, Sir.'

bijou A word of Celtic origins related to finger-rings. Nowadays, a jewel, a trinket; a 'gem' among works of art. Much used attributively. Loosely, also, used as an adjective to imply small, elegant, luxurious (applied especially by estate agents (realtors) to residential accommodation). In the phrase *les bijoux de la famille*, 'the family jewels', the word denotes what in other contexts (and in precisely the same register) might be referred to as 'wedding tackle'. The word *bijou* is enshrined in the hearts of every English schoolboy as one of 'the superlative seven' *Bijou, caillou, chou, genou, hibou, joujou, pou,* all of which make their plurals in *-oux.*

bien pensant Traditionally, in England, the phrase has meant much the same as it has traditionally meant in France, that is to say, 'right-thinking; orthodox, conservative'. See the quotation below from Nancy Mitford. The colloquial remark 'Ça n'est pas tellement catholique' precisely epitomized the normal acceptation of the phrase *bien pensant*. Nowadays, the epithet *bien pensant* conveys almost the contrary impression. The received orthodoxies have radically altered during the latter half of the 20th century, such that what is called 'the soft-Left consensus' as 'emblemed' by Polly Toynbee, of *The Guardian*, is now taken as being the exemplar of right-thinking. It is doubtful whether the term is generally used nowadays in a complimentary sense.

> 'If you are rich, of good family and *bien pensant*': Aldous Huxley, *On Margin* p 113, (1923). 'A Nationalist rising in Spain, which not only M. Maurras but all the French *bien-pensants* supported': *The Times Literary Supplement,* p 622/3 1st October 1938. 'The pitiful, hasty funeral from which the local bien-pensants remain away': *The Listener*, p 209/2, 7th August 1958. 'In her world, Catholic, royalist, *bien pensant*': Nancy Mitford, *Water Beetle, 136 (1962).*

billet-doux 'Sweet-note' A love-letter. Now usually jocular. Properly pronounced /bijɛduː/ but often heard as /bɪlɪd'uː/.

bis A Latin adverb meaning 'twice', used in musical scores to indicate that a phrase or passage is to be repeated. Hence, used by audiences in France and Italy to ask for a repetition. The French word *encore*, as used by English-speaking audiences to ask for a repetition, is never used in that sense by French audiences.

bisque Nowadays, a rich fish soup, particularly one made from lobster, *bisque de homard* (/biːskdəɔmaʁ/) or from crayfish, *bisque d'écrevisse* (/biːskdekʁəviːs/).

bistro[t] A small wine-shop, bar or restaurant. The French spelling is more often with the (silent) *t.* The tendency in France is for the word to mean increasingly a small restaurant rather than a wine-shop. The spelling without the letter *t* tends to emphasize the shift in role from wine-shop to restaurant. *Le Petit Larousse* in its edition of 1972 has only *bistrot* and defines the words thus: '*Pop.* Marchand de vins. Débit de boissons'. The more progressive *Petit Robert,* though in an edition of two years earlier, has '*Bistro* ou *bistrot*: '1° *Pop*. Marchand de vin tenant café ... 2° *Pop*. Café'.

Contrary to saloon-bar wisdom, there is no connection with the identical Russian word for *quick:* anecdotes about French troops in haste in Moscow in 1812 are irrelevant, as are tales of impatient Russian soldiers in Paris in 1815 as part of the Army of Occupation. The derivation of the word is no doubt from the word *bistrouille*, 'bad alcohol, bad alcohol mixed with coffee'. *(*The word *bistro[t]* is not in *Hatzfeld-Darmesteter.)*

bizarre The *OED* defines the word thus: 'At variance with recognized ideas of taste, departing from ordinary style or usage; eccentric, extravagant, whimsical, strange, odd, fantastic'. The Iberian word from which this French word is adapted means 'brave, valorous, courageous', without any sense of oddness. The Spanish and Portuguese word can also mean 'of a soldierly bearing'. The Italian *bizzarro* means 'quarrelsome, argumentative'.

blancmange 'A sweetmeat made of dissolved isinglass or gee boiled with milk, etc., and forming an opaque white jelly; also a preparation of cornflour and milk, with flavouring substances': *OED*. Sometimes called 'milk jelly' or 'milk jello'. A perplexing word, since the French seem to disclaim any knowledge of the dish. An investigation into the etymological career of the word would no doubt be fruitful and absorbing – but profitless, since the dish itself has disappeared from most tables, along with junket (sweetened and flavoured curds) and other nourishing milk products. The philosophical French have an expression for profitless occupations: 'Travailler pour le roi de Prusse', 'to work for the king of Prussia', something as inscrutable as the former appeal of blancmange. (The pronunciation of the word in England has been inveterately fixed for generations as /blə'mɒːndʒ/.)

blasé The past participle of *blaser* 'to exhaust by enjoyment', a modern word declared by *Littre* to be of unknown etymology. Its meaning was initially to be 'exhausted by enjoyment, weary and disgusted with it; used up'. Its impact has been weakened by usage and now tends to mean 'bored or unimpressed through over-familiarity; insensitive, supercilious'. Both *OED* definitions.

bloc 'In Continental politics, a combination of divergent political parties which supports the government in power. Also *transf.*, a combination of persons, groups, parties, or nations formed to foster a particular interest. Also *attrib.*, as in *bloc vote = block vote*': O*ED.*

boche A (French) word for a German.

'Bon appétit!' 'Good appetite! A salutation before eating': *OED*. Much used by English-speakers because there is no English equivalent exhortation.

bon mot 'A clever or witty saying; a witticism; repartee': *OED*.

bon ton 'Good style, good breeding; polite or fashionable society; the fashionable world': *OED*. The *OED* adds 'Archaic', though the phrase is still heard in France and is used by English-speakers.

bon vivant/bon viveur The first is the correct French expression, meaning 'One fond of good living; a gourmand'. *Cf gourmand, below. Bon viveur* is not a French expression.

'Bon voyage!' 'Good journey!'

bonbon A lozenge or other confection made of sugar; a sweetmeat. The French pronunciation is /bɔ̃bɔ̃/ , with both vowels nasalized. The Anglicized pronunciation /bɔnbɔn/ is much more frequently heard in England than the authentic French pronunciation.

bonhomie Good nature; the quality of being a good fellow. Formerly also spelt *bonhommie* but now with only one *m*. So also *bon homme*, /bɔnɔm/, a good fellow.

bonheur-du-jour Literally, 'happiness of the day'. Another odd phrase, signifying an item of furniture as described below.

> 'Small Bureau of the 'Bonheur du Jour' type, in marqueterie of various natural and stained woods' *Provisional Catalogue of Furniture etc in the Wallace Collection,* p283 (1902). 'The writing-table for ladies, known as the *bonheur du jour*, receives a rectangular upper part, the panels of which imitate book backs': H Schmitz, *Encyclopaedia of Furniture,* xxii, p 53 (1926). 'A magnificent Louis XVI black laquer *bonheur-du-jour*, on slightly square, curved and tapering legs': *The Times*, p5/4, 21st May 1955. 'A Hepplewhite bonheur du jour': Advertisement, *The Times,* p 21/5, 7th March 1967.

bonne bouche *Bonne* 'good', and *bouche* 'mouth'. In French, 'A pleasing taste in the mouth' (*Littré*): but in English taken for 'dainty mouthful or morsel' (in French 'morceau qui fait ou donne bonne bouche'). The contemporary English use of the term is equivalent to 'tit-bit'.

boudoir Literally, 'a place to sulk in' from *bouder*, 'to pout or sulk'. A small elegantly-furnished room, where a lady might retire to be alone, or to receive her intimate friends.

bouffant 'Of a hair-style: puffed out; arranged in a swelling or fluffy style. Hence, as a noun, such a hair-style': *OED*. In satirical writing such as is found in *Private Eye*, the adjective *bouffant* applied to a male's hair-style frequently implies homosexuality.

bouillabaisse A Provençal dish of mixed varieties of fish cooked with tomatoes, strongly spiced, served in its own liquor with slices of bread. From Provençal *bouiabaisso*, itself perhaps from *bouillepeis*, 'boil fish'. Sometimes the word is used figuratively to mean a mixture.

> 'It was agreed that if we could find the right premises for a boutique...we would open a shop. It was to be a *bouillabaisse* of clothes and accessories...sweaters, scarves, shifts, hats, jewellery, and peculiar odds and ends': Mary Quant, *Quant by Quant,* p 35 1 (1966).

bouillon Broth; the liquor in which meat or fish is boiled.

boule[s] A French form of bowls, played on rough ground, usually with metal balls. Also in the plural form. See *pétanque*.

boulevard 'A broad street, promenade, or walk, planted with rows of trees. Chiefly applied to streets of this kind in Paris, or to others which it is intended to compare to them. Now frequently (especially in the U.S.), a wide or well laid-out street or avenue': *OED*. In North America, often used for a dual carriageway; an arterial road, main highway, freeway or expressway. (The French word originally meant the horizontal portion of a rampart and is cognate with 'bulwark'; hence the name *boulevard* for the metalled promenades laid out on and using the materials of the demolished fortifications and customs-walls of Paris and other cities.

Applied also to other promenades so constructed.) An Anglicized pronunciation /'bulɪvɑːd/ is widely heard. The French pronunciation is /bulvaʁ/.

boulevardier 'Man about town'.

bouleversement 'A turning upside down; a violent inversion': *OED*.

bouquet A posy; a nosegay; normally somewhat more arranged and formal than a bunch of flowers. Pronounced /buke/. There is no justification for the pronunciation /boːk'eɪː/ – 'boh-kay'.

bourgeois Originally a town-dweller. Later contrasted with the (rougher) country-dweller and the (more polished) aristocrat. Later still, used to denote the mercantile 'shop-keeping' middle class. In recent times used in political controversy as a term of opprobrium. 'In communist or socialist writings: a capitalist; anyone judged to be an exploiter of the proletariat': *OED*.

> 'When I was a boy … *bourgeois* meant "not aristocratic, therefore vulgar." When I was in my twenties this changed … *Bourgeois* began to mean "not proletarian, therefore parasitic, reactionary"': C S Lewis, *Studies in Words,* I, p 21 (1960).

Cf, Il faut épater le bourgeois, below.

boutique 'A small fashion-shop or department that sells ready-to-wear clothes designed by a couturier; a small shop selling 'trend-setting' clothes or other articles, especially for young or fashionable people': *OED*. See the quotation from Mary Quant in the entry *bouillabaisse, above.* By extension, a (usually small) business, not essentially in the fashion sector, offering a highly specialized service or catering to a sophisticated or exclusive clientele.

> 'The boutique investment bank Greenhill is joining the roster of advisers attempting to salvage something from the wreckage of futures broker Refco': *The Daily Telegraph*, 'Business News, 17th October 2005.

brasserie Originally, a brewery. Later, a beer saloon, usually one in which food was served. Nowadays, the name for an extremely popular type of restaurant in which food from an ample but relatively invariable menu is served quickly and inexpensively.

brassière Employed in English to denote the female under-garment used to support the breasts, the French for which is *soutien-gorge*. Both names are euphemisms. The French word *brassière* means a child's sleeved vest or bodice; in the plural, guiding-reins and the straps of a rucksack or knapsack. *Soutien-gorge* means, literally, 'neck-support'.

bric-à-brac Old curiosities of artistic character, knick-knacks, antiquarian odds-and-ends, such as old furniture, plate, china, fans, statuettes, and the like. Pronounced /bricabrac/. Said by *Littré* to be formed after the phrase *de bric et de broc,* 'by hook or by crook'.

brochure Literally, 'a stitched job'. 'A short printed work, of a few leaves merely stitched together; a pamphlet': *OED*. Still recognized as a French word, though thoroughly naturalized as to pronunciation. The French is /broʃy/, the English /'brəʊːʃjə(r).

brouhaha 'A commotion, a to-do, a 'sensation'; hubbub, uproar': *OED*.

> 'I shall never forget the brou-ha-ha … when Cousin Geraldine married into Trade': 'Caryl Brahms' & S. J. Simon, *Trottie True,* vii, p186 (1946).

brusque Somewhat rough or rude in manner; blunt, abrupt. Pronounced /bʁysk/.

buhl from *Boulle,* the name of André-Charles *Boulle* (1642-1732), French cabinet-maker. (*Buhl* appears to be a modern Germanized spelling.) 'Brass, tortoise-shell, or other material, worked into ornamental patterns for inlaying; work inlaid with buhl. Also attrib.': *OED.*

> 'Buhl-work consists of inlaid veneers; and differs from marquetry in being confined to decorative scroll-work': Ure, *Dictionary of the Arts* (1875), *s.v. Buhl.*

bureau An imprecise term. Dr Johnson has for *bureau,* 'A chest of drawers with a writing-board'. In the US and in some parts of Britain, a chest of drawers is called *a bureau.* As specifically designed writing desks emerged in France, their top surfaces, their 'writing boards', were increasingly covered with *bureau,* a coarse woollen stuff akin to baize. In time, the name of the cloth became applied to the writing-desk itself. A similar but more ornamental practice obtains today, whereby desk-tops are covered with leather, most often red, which is gold tooled for decoration. See, in general, *bureau plat, below.*

In some contexts, a bureau can mean a more elaborate desk, with built-in small drawers and slots above the writing level for pens and stationery and with a cover or lid, often at an oblique angle, that can be closed when the bureau is not in use.

By transference, the word *bureau* became a name for where the bureau was used, a synonym for *office.* 'An office, especially for the transaction of public business; a department of public administration. In modern use, an office or business with a specified function; an agency for the co-ordination of related activities, the distribution of information, etc. In this sense the word is chiefly employed when foreign countries are referred to. In the US it occurs in the official titles of certain government offices, whence also in very recent official use in England, as in 'Emigration Bureau', 'Labour Bureau': *OED.* The word, in its acceptation 'office', is now so solidly established in English that it is pedantry or vanity to pronounce it /byro/. It must surely be pronounced /ˈbjʊə(r)əʊ/, or perhaps /bjʊəˈ(r)əʊ/. When applied to the article of furniture, the French pronunciation is used.

In France the *name* of the office of a professional man depends on his profession. See *cabinet/étude, below.*

bureau de change A currency-changing facility.

bureau-plat A simple chest of drawers with its top adapted to writing on, by, for example, the application of leather; a writing-desk that does not have a superstructure and is not, for example, a rolltop desk. See *bureau, above.*

burlesque With the exception of the last-mentioned acceptation, below, there are two general acceptations of the word in current though infrequent use. The older is defined by the *OED* as follows: 'That species of literary composition, or of dramatic representation, which aims at exciting laughter by caricature of the manner or spirit of serious works, or by ludicrous treatment of their subjects; a literary or dramatic work of this kind'. A newer and more common use of the word is defined by the OED as follows: 'Grotesque imitation of what is, or is intended to be, dignified or pathetic, in action, speech, or manner; *concr.* an action or performance which casts ridicule on that which it imitates, or is itself ridiculous as an unsuccessful attempt at serious impressiveness; a mockery'. The word 'satire' has to a large extent taken over the territory of the word 'burlesque' in the two senses above. In the USA, however, the word 'burlesque' is alive in the extended sense 'a theatrical entertainment of a broadly humorous and often earthy character consisting of short turns, and comic skits, and sometimes striptease acts'. See *vaudeville, below.*

'Ça ira' Literally, 'That will come'. It was the refrain of words by a street-singer, Ladré, to a country-dance melody *le Carillon national*, by Bécourt. See Constant Pierre, *Les hymnes et les chansons de la Révolution: aperçu Général et catalogue avec notices historiques, analytiques et bibliographiques*, Paris (1904). It was a popular song of the French Revolution, rivalling only *La Carmagnole (q.v., below)* in popularity. In its original form, it ran:

Ah, ça ira, ça ira, ça ira!
Le peuple en ce jour sans cesse répète
Ah, ça ira, ça ira, ça ira!
Malgré les mutins, tout réussira.

Under the Terror, it became:

Ah, ça ira, ça ira, ça ira!
Les aristocrats à la lanterne
Ah, ça ira, ça ira, ça ira!
Les aristocrat on les pendra.

La lanterne was the lamp-post, from which *les aristocrats* would hang. The singing of the song was prohibited when Bonaparte became First Consul.

cabaret 'A restaurant or night-club in which entertainment is provided as an accompaniment to a meal; also, the entertainment so provided, a floor-show': *OED*. The word is also used for a porcelain tea or coffee service, sometimes accompanied by a small table or tray. In French Canada the word *cabaret* is applied to the tray alone.

cabinet/étude Political use apart, the predominant use of the word *cabinet* in present-day English is to denote 'a case for the safe custody of jewels, or other valuables, letters, documents, etc.; and thus, a repository or case, often itself forming an ornamental piece of furniture, fitted with compartments, drawers, shelves, etc., for the proper preservation and display of a collection of specimens. Also, one containing a radio or television receiver or the like': *OED*. Travellers in France will have noticed that the work-places of doctors and dentists are known as *cabinets* (/cabinɛ/). The less fortunate of those who travel in France might have noticed that the work-places of judges and advocates are also known as *cabinets*. The work-places of notaries and (formerly) *avoués* are known as *études*. A visit to these professionals is a visit *chez le docteur*, etc, not *au docteur*. For the general word for an office, see *bureau, above*.

cabriolet Originally a type of carriage having two wheels, being pulled by a single horse and having a wooden or leather hood and fabric or leather apron to protect the occupants. Later applied to a motorcar having fixed sides and a hood. The word was abbreviated very early to *cab* and exists today in English-speaking countries, but not in France, as a slightly old-fashioned synonym for 'taxi'.

cache A hiding-place, from *cacher*, 'to hide'. In Anglo-American usage, a hole or mound made by American pioneers and Arctic explorers to hide stores of provisions, ammunition, etc, and, nowadays, a small high-speed computer memory into which are placed the most frequently accessed contents of the slower main memory.

cache-sexe 'A covering for the genitals': *OED*.

cachet The contemporary use of *cachet* among English-speakers invokes a figurative seal of approval to an activity, a work of art or literature, or some similar thing. The word derives from *cacher*, 'to conceal', the link with 'approval' being the tenuous one of the personal as distinct from the official seal of a potentate. The *cachet* or 'sign manual' was used, for example, on the *lettres de cachet* of the French Crown whereby subjects might be discreetly exiled or imprisoned.

> 'The journal in which the cachet of fashionable life is to be distinguished': C. Pebody, *Eng. Journalism* xxii. 176 (1882).

cadre In use today only in a military or quasi-military sense. *Littré* pin-points its origin thus: 'l'ensemble des officiers et sous-officiers d'une compagnie'. In modern military administration, the word is used to denote a body of personnel selected for (training for) some specific function. Anglicized and pronounced /ˈcɑːɹdə/. In Left-Wing circles the word *cadre* is sometimes used to denote a political analogue of the military *cadre*. The word was much used in reference to units of young people, among which were the Red Guards, who caused such havoc during the Cultural Revolution in China from 1966 to 1976. (The word also means a *frame*, as in 'picture-frame'.)

café Almost too well known to warrant an appearance. Originally meaning only 'coffee', the word has grown in meaning almost beyond belief. Its pronunciation varies between its most thoroughly acclimatized /kaf/ to a credible imitation of the authentic French pronunciation /kafe/, with, somewhere in the middle, /ˈcafɪ/ and, particularly in the USA, /kafˈeɪː/.

café au lait 'Coffee with milk'. Also used allusively in reference to persons of mixed blood by people who do not consider it a racially loaded expression.

calembour A pun. The word deserves an entry by reason of its supposed derivation, which resembles the derivation of our word 'Spoonerism' (for which, see *contrepêterie, below*). According to Philarète Chasles (1798-1873), quoted by *Littré*, the word is derived from the name of 'the Abbé de Calemberg, a witty personage in German tales'. This fictional character was based on a real person, Pfarrer Wigand von Theben, known as the Pfaff von Kahlenberg, 'Priest of Kahlenberg'. In his fictional embodiment, in the poem *Der Pfaffe vom Kahlenberg* by Phillip Frankfurter (*fl.* 1440-90), he is the perpetrator of numerous pranks. The poem was first printed in 1473. The scenes are set in the reign of Otto the Merry of Austria, who died in 1339.

It needs to be said that the etymology offered by *Hatzfeld-Darmesteter* is utterly different from the preposterous one above.' Peut-être composé de la particle pejorative *calem* et de *bourd* pour *bourde*. Le mot ne deviant d'un usage général que dans la seconde moitié du XVIII siècle.': Hatzfeld & Darmesteter, *Dictionnaire Général de la Langue Française,* Delagrave, Paris (1926), tome 1, p 333: 'Perhaps composed of the pejorative particle *calem* and *falsehood, leg-pull* or *blunder*. The word came into general use only in the second half of the 18th century'.

calque Literally, 'a copy', from *calquer*, 'to trace (a design, etc.)', from Italian *calcare,* from Latin *calc re,* 'to tread' *scil,* 'figuratively, in the footsteps of another'. In linguistics, a loan-translation in which the form or verbal structure of a foreign word or phrase is adopted and translated into the receiving language. For example, *gratte-ciel* is a *calque* of the American 'sky-scraper'.

> '[The Modern English phrase] 'that goes without saying' is a translation-loan of (better, is calqued on) [Modern French]

cela va sans dire': A. S. C. Ross, *Etymology*, 34 (1958).

camaraderie 'Matiness', comradeship; *esprit de corps.*

Cambronne, Mot de 'La Garde meurt, mais ne se rend pas': 'The Guards die but do not surrender'. The *Oxford Dictionary of Quotations* gives the following: 'Attributed to Cambronne [Pierre, Baron de Cambronne, 1770-1842] when called upon to surrender at Waterloo, 1815, but later denied by him. See H. Houssaye, *La Garde meurt et mais ne se rend pas* (1906)'.

'Le Mot', 'the Word' in question, is Cambronne's reputed exasperated response, 'Merde!', after having been urged three times to surrender. The story has gained immense currency since 1862 by virtue of a mention of the supposed incident by Victor Hugo in *Les Misérables*. The English general cried out, according to Victor Hugo, 'Braves Français, rendez-vous!' Cambronne, according to Victor Hugo, replied, 'Merde!' Cambronne himself denied that the incident ever happened, but in 1848 the municipality of his birth and death, Nantes, erected a statue to him that immortalizes the supposed event. As Dr Johnson said, 'In lapidary inscriptions a man is not upon oath': Boswell, *Life*, vol 2, p 407 (1775).

A full account of all aspects of this indestructible legend can be read on the following web-pages:

www.1789-1815.com/wat_mot_cambr.htm
www.1789-1815.com/deleau.htm

camisole 'An underbodice, often embroidered and trimmed with lace': *OED.*

camouflage 'The disguising of any objects used in war, such as camps, guns, ships, by means of paint, smoke-screens, shrubbery, etc., in such a way as to conceal it from the enemy; also, the disguise used in this way': *OED*. The word derives from the noun *camouflet*, meaning, originally, a small mine or charge of powder that one team of sappers and miners would place in the earth between them and the enemy's miners so they might detonate it, after their own tactical withdrawal, and so smother their adversaries. The technique was also applied to the mining of terrain (land-mining): a hole would be drilled with an auger or similar tool and a *camouflet* or the larger *fougasse* would be inserted and then 'disguised' by back-filling and the arrangement of foliage, turf or other matter. Hence, *camouflage*.

canapé A piece of bread or toast, or biscuit, on which are served savouries. Also, 'a sofa', the earlier meaning. The use in catering arises from the resemblance between savoury morsels on toast to persons reclining on sofas. *Hatzfeld-Darmesteter* suggests a derivation from *χωνωπειον*, a mosquito-net: see *s.v. canapé* in *Hatzfeld & Darmesteter, Dictionnaire Général de la Langue Française,* Delagrave, Paris (1926), tome 1, p 341. Classical Latin had *conopeum* (*Lewis & Short*); Mediaeval Latin had *canopeum:* see, *e.g.*, R. E. Latham, *Revised Medieval Latin Word-List* (1965), *s.v. canap-, canav-*. The English word 'canopy' derives from the same source: a *Χωνωπειον* meant, originally, an Egyptian bed that had an integral fine-gauze curtain (a mosquito net). The English language developed the word to stress the *hanging* element; the Romance languages have developed the *bed* element.

canard The *OED*'s note about this word, literally meaning 'duck', is of absorbing interest. 'An extravagant or absurd story circulated to impose on people's credulity; a hoax, a false report. *Littré* says *Canard* for a silly story comes from the old expression 'vendre un canard à moitié' (to half-sell a duck), in which *à moitié* was subsequently suppressed. It is clear that to half-sell a duck is not to sell it at all; hence the sense 'to take in, make a fool of'. In proof of this he cites *bailleur de canards*, deliverer of ducks, utterer of *canards*, of date 1612: [Randle] Cotgrave [*Dictionarie of the French and English Tongues*] 1611, has the fuller *vendeur de canards a moitié*, 'a cousener, guller, cogger; foister, lyer'. Others have referred the word to an absurd fabricated story purporting to illustrate the voracity of ducks, said to have gone the round of the newspapers, and to have been credited by many. As this account has been widely circulated, it is possible that it has contributed to render the word more familiar, and thus more used, in English.'

The *OED* has a note by Sir James Murray: 'I saw the word in print before 1850'.

The most irrepressible satirical magazine in the world is *le Canard Enchaîné,* founded in 1915 by Maurice Maréchal. It adopted the stance and style of the anti-military tracts circulating in the trenches in 1915-16. It is fiercely independent, has never accepted advertisements and enthusiastically denounces corruption and jobbery across the entire spectrum of French life. It is also a spectacular vehicle for the conveyance of that fragile entity, French humour. (The French have no word for *humour* but use the English word, itself derived from the French *humeur*, meaning, in the plural, the bodily fluids that were formerly thought to govern all human physiology – 'the humours'.)

A new meaning of *canard* has recently emerged. An entry in the *Wikipedia* reads: 'In aeronautics, *canard* (French for duck) is a type of fixed-wing aircraft in which the tail plane is ahead of the main lifting surfaces, rather than behind them as in conventional aircraft. The earliest models, such as the Santos-Dumont 14-bis, were seen by observers to resemble a flying duck – hence the name. The term *canard* has also come to mean the tail surface itself, when mounted in that configuration'.

can-can 'A kind of dance made popular at the public balls in Paris, with extravagant and indecent gestures': *OED.* The combination of the music of Jacques Offenbach (1819-80) and the paintings of Henri de Toulouse-Lautrec (1864-1901) have guaranteed the name of this dance a place in the Eternal Pantheon, but it needs to be remembered that, to every Frenchman, this is *le French can-can,* with the word *French* exactly so, in *English.*

cap-à-pie A man is armed *cap-à-pie* if he is armed from head to foot. The modern French terms is *de pied en cap.*

> 'A figure like your father, / Armed at point exactly, cap-a-pe, / Appears before them and with solemn march / Goes slow and stately by them': *Hamlet*, Act I, Sc ii.

carafe 'A glass water-bottle for the table, bedroom, etc. Also, one used at table, etc., for wine; *attrib.*, designating an ordinary wine served in a carafe': *OED.* Sir James Murray reminded us that the word has long been in common use in Scotland. In England it is of later appearance, and is often treated as still French. The difference between the French pronunciation and the anglicized one is insignificant.

carillon The *OED* quotes *Grove*: 'A set of bells so hung and arranged as to be capable of being played upon either by manual action or by machinery'. In general use, the word is Anglicized as /ˈkæɹʌən/ or /kəɹˈʌən/. The French pronunciation is /kaʁijɔ̃/.

Carmagnole, la A popular song at the time of the French Revolution. It vied in popularity with *Ça ira! (q.v., above).* The chorus, *Dansons la Carmagnole,* is set to a commonplace, hackneyed type of melody, but the verse is set to one of the most attractive of all the melodies popular at the end of the eighteenth century.

carrousel In England, a round-about, a merry-go-round. In the US the French word is used. Sometimes spelt *carousel* in English. Properly pronounced /kaɹuzɛl/, not /kaɹusel/, but the second pronunciation is widespread in English-speaking countries.

carte, la and **à la carte** The menu. *Dîner à la carte*: 'to dine from a menu giving a range of choices'. *Cf table d'hôte, below.*

carte blanche Originally, a piece of blank paper on which the recipient was to write the conditions he wished applied to an agreement he was about to enter into. Now, 'a free hand'.

cartouche A representation of a generally oval-shaped panel used to display, for example, the arms of a university press on the spines of books; an oval shape used by popes and noble ecclesiastics to display their arms, the shield being considered inappropriate for a churchman; in hieroglyphics, the oval- or oblong-shaped figures containing representations of divine or royal names and titles, the name *cartouche* having been given to the figure by Jean-François Champollion (1790-1832), the decipherer of Egyptian hieroglyphics. (The French meaning, 'cartridge', is not current in English.)

casserole Originally, in English use, a stew-pan, of metal or earthenware. Now, also a dish prepared in such a utensil, generally braised or roasted. (The quotation below misuses the term 'portmanteau word'. See the entry, *below*, for *portmanteau.*)

> 'A casserole, once upon a time, was a pan with a handle, made in tinned copper, earthenware, enamelled iron or some other heat-resistant material ... In Britain to-day the casserole has become a portmanteau word for any receptacle in a fire-resistant material, with or without a lid, that goes both into the oven and on to the dinner-table': *The Observer,* p 14/4, 17th January 1960.

catafalque 'A stage or platform, erected by way of honour in a church to receive the coffin or effigy of a deceased personage' (*Littré*); 'a temporary structure of carpentry, decorated with painting and sculpture, representing a tomb or cenotaph, and used in funeral ceremonies': [Joseph] (Gwilt [*An Encyclopædia of Architecture, Historical, Theoretical, and Practical* 1842 (1859)]): *OED*. A bier.

catalogue raisonné A descriptive catalogue arranged according to subjects, or branches of subjects; hence, generically or loosely, a classified or methodical list of, for example, paintings on sale or in an exhibition, or of printed books and *incunabula* in a sale.

cause célèbre 'A celebrated legal case; a law-suit that excites much interest': *OED*.

causerie 'Informal talk or discussion, esp. on literary topics; also, a chatty article or paragraph': *OED*.

'C'est magnifique, mais ce n'est pas la guerre': 'It's magnificent, but it isn't war'. Maréchal Pierre Bosquet (1810-61) on the charge of the Light Brigade at Balaclava, 25th October 1854. In Cecil Woodham-Smith, *The Reason Why*, ch 12 (1953).

'C'est pire qu'un crime, c'est une faute' 'It is worse than a crime, it's an error'. Antoine Boulay de la Meurthe (1761-1840), on hearing of the kidnapping and execution of the Duc d'Enghien on 21st March 1804, undoubtedly on the orders of Bonaparte.

'C'est une révolution' On news of the fall of the Bastille, Louis XVI asked, 'C'est une grande révolte?' 'Is it a big revolt?'. 'Non, Sire, c'est und grande révolution' replied the Duc de la Rochefoucauld-Liancourt (1747-1827). See F. Dreyfus, *La Rochefoucauld-Liancourt*, ch 2, sect 3 (1903).

'C'est Vénus toute entière à sa proie attachée' The couplet, from *Phèdre*, I, iii (1677) by Jean Racine (1639-99) runs, 'Ce n'est plus une ardeur dans mes veines cachée: / C'est Vénus toute entière à sa proie attachée': 'It's no longer a burning hidden in my veins: It's Venus entire hooked into her prey'.

'Cet animal est très méchant' In full, 'Cet animal est très méchant, / quand on l'attaque il se defend' 'This animal is wicked/ when one attacks it, it defends itself'. 'Theodore P. K.', in *La Menagerie*, a song of 1868.

chacun à son goût 'Each one to his own taste'. It seems this saying is proverbial, and that it has been for an extremely long time.

chagrin The word ought probably to be classed as completely English as well as French. Its early history is to say the least *improbable*. It was originally, on its introduction into French, the name for a rough animal pelt (for example, the skin from a horse's rump) and of a fabric intended to imitate the roughness of the naturally occurring article. Chagrin had a variety of uses: for example, for smoothing or filing, as sandpaper is used today. Being extremely hard-wearing, the animal form was also used for making watch-cases and spectacle-cases; covering the handles of knives, and covering jewel-cases and travelling boxes. Its fabric form came to be spelt 'shagreen' in England. The roughness of chagrin led to the name's being adopted as a metaphor for the asperities of life, and then for the effect those asperities had on the human spirit, and, ultimately, to 'acute vexation, annoyance, or mortification, arising from disappointment, thwarting, or failure': *OED*. The word has a somewhat different implication in French, as *faire du chagrin a quelqu'un* and *mourir de chagrin* might indicate. The popular song *Plaisir d'amour* contains the line *'Chagrin d'amour dure toute la vie'.*

chaise longue A kind of sofa with a rest for the back at one end only.

> 'The deep, deep peace of the double-bed after the hurly-burly of the *chaise longue*': Mrs Patrick Campbell, on her recent marriage, in Alexander Woolcott, *While Rome Burns*, 'The First Mrs Tanqueray' (1934).

In the USA, sometimes mis-spelt and mispronounced *chaise lounge*.

chamois The European antelope. The name of the animal is nowadays almost exclusively pronounced as French, /Samwa/, though formerly it was pronounced /ˈʃæmɔɪ/ or /ˈʃæmɪ/. The soft leather, the wash-leather, made from various pelts, some split to form skivers, is always pronounced 'shammy leather' (/ˈʃæmɪ ˈlɛðəɹ/).

champagne 'The name of a province of eastern France; hence, a well-known wine of different varieties, white and red, and still or sparkling, made in this district': *OED*. The name is nowadays protected by law and is restricted to those wines made in the defined locality and according to *la Méthode* *champenoise.* The pronunciation of the word in English is always /ʃæpəm 'peɪːn/.

chansonnier A writer or performer of songs, especially satirical songs, in a *cabaret, q. v.*

chaperon/chaperone A person, especially a married or elderly woman, who, for the sake of propriety, accompanied a young unmarried lady in public, as guide and protector. The word *chaperon* means 'a hood or cape'. Little Red Riding Hood is Petite Chaperon Rouge. *Littré* says that the elderly woman protects the younger woman as a hood protects the face. The additional letter *e* frequently seen in English writing is solely owing to the erroneous belief that, chaperons normally being women, a feminine form is needed. The noun is invariable. The pronunciation in English is always /'ʃæpərəʊn/.

char-à-bancs An old fashioned term for a (motor-) coach; in the US, an excursion bus. The original French words mean 'carriage with benches'. These vehicles were much used in England in the early days of motorized transport and were universally called 'sharrabangs' ('ʃærəbæŋz/). Woe betide anyone who attempted /ʃaʁabã/! (The plural is *chars-à bancs.*)

charade A party-game in which words or phrases are represented in silence but by gestures, acting, etc, sometimes syllable by syllable, until they are guessed by the other players. Sometimes the word *charade* is used to disparage an activity as a readily perceived pretence; a travesty: 'It was a mere charade': 'He went through the charade of a public apology'. Pronounced /ʃəɹ'ɑːd/ in England and /ʃər'eɪːd/ in the US.

charcuterie Cold cuts of meat, especially pork, ham, tongue, sausages, *fromage de tête, salade de museau,* etc. Also, a shop that sells items of this kind.

chargé-d'affaires 'A minister who transacts diplomatic business at a foreign court during the temporary absence of the ambassador; also, the representative of a country at a less important foreign court, to which a diplomatist of higher grade is not appointed': *OED.*

charlatan One who pretends to knowledge he does not possess, often applied to quacks. There is no substance in the derivation that has a French king summoning his physician by crying out, 'Charles attend!'. The word has a clearly recorded etymology: *ciarlatore,* Italian for 'a babbler, a patterer, a mountebank', from *ciarlare,* 'to babble, to patter, to act the mountebank', from *ciarla,* 'chat, prattle'.

charlotte russe A dish composed of apple and custard enclosed in a kind of sponge-cake.

châssis 'The base frame of a motor car, with its mechanism, as distinguished from the body or upper part': *OED.* The word is used also for the airframe in an aeroplane (airplane). Despite the presence of the circumflex accent, the pronunciation of the word in present-day France is almost precisely the same as in English, /ʃasi/.

château In principle, 'a castle', but French usage differs somewhat from English usage. For example, what English-speakers would call 'the Palace of Versailles' is called *le Château de Versailles.* A building with mediaeval characteristics such as castellation and machicolation is called *un château fort.* In normal circumstances, the word *palais* denotes a building of less magnificence than a *château.*

The touchstone of royal residence is normally absent from the French use of *palais*. Public buildings sometimes have the name *palais*, as in *Palais de Justice*. (For the pronunciation of *château*, see *Circumflex Accent, above*.)

chauffeur 'A professional or paid driver of a private motor vehicle': *OED*. Originally, the fireman on a (steam-powered) motor vehicle. It is also the name for the fireman on a French steam locomotive. The French name for the engine-driver (train driver) is *le mécanicien*. The French for fireman – that is, a fire-fighter – is *sapeur-pompier*.

chauvinisme Originally, *idolatrie napoléonienne*; from the surname of a veteran soldier of the First Republic and Empire, Nicolas Chauvin of Rochefort, who was wounded 17 times. His demonstrative patriotism and loyalty were celebrated, and at length ridiculed, by his comrades. After the fall of Bonaparte, the name was applied in ridicule to old soldiers of the Empire, who professed an idolatrous admiration for Bonapart's person and acts. Especially popularized as the name of one of the characters in Cogniard's famous vaudeville (*q.v.*), *La Cocarde Tricolore*, 1831 ('Je suis français, je suis Chauvin'); and now applied to any one smitten with an absurd patriotism and enthusiasm for national glory and military ascendancy. The English counterpart is *Jingoism*. The word *chauvinisme* is not applied in French nearly so widely as *chauvinism* is in English, to typify excessive attachment to any ideological cause or prejudice, as in 'female chauvinism', but is ordinarily restricted to French-national patriotism.

chef A (male) head cook.

chef de cabinet A (political minister's) personal private secretary.

chef-d'œuvre A chief piece of work, formerly the work a French apprentice, journeyman or craftsman presented – a condition of his admission to his Guild – as a demonstration of his skill. A masterpiece. Pronounced /ʃedœvʁ(ə)/. Plural: *chefs-d'œuvre*, pronounced identically.

chef-lieu The principal town of a *département*; 'county town'. Pronounced /ʃɛʎœ/ or /ʃɛʎø/ . Plural: *des chefs-lieux* /dɛ ʃɛʎœ/ or /ʃɛʎø/.

chemin de fer 'Railway' or 'railroad'. For the card game, see *baccarat, above*.

chemise A garment: the name has been variously applied at different times; perhaps originally (as still in French and other Romanic languages) the under-garment, usually of linen, both of men and women; a shirt (of a man: *chemisier* of a woman); formerly called 'smock' and 'shift'.Formerly also applied to some under garment distinct from the 'smock', as well as to a priest's alb or surplice (so mediaeval Latin *camisa*); the robe of a herald, etc. In recent use: a dress hanging straight from the shoulders.

'Cherchez la femme' Alexandre Dumas *père* (1802-70) wrote 'Cherchons la femme' *passim* in *Les Mohicans de Paris* (1854-5), attributing the saying, in the form *Cherchez la femme*, to Joseph Fouché (1763-1820), the detestable *Chef de Police* and, later, *Ministre de l'Intérieure* during the *Directoire* and much of Bonaparte's reign. The catch-phrase is used to imply that the key to a problem or mystery is a woman, and that she needs only to be found for the matter to be solved.

chevalier 'knight'.

chevalier d'industrie A surprising euphemism but nonetheless used with telling effect by French writers. A swindler; one who lives by his wits; a promoter of bogus companies; one who runs a 'bucket-shop'.

'Chevalier sans peur et sans reproche' 'A knight without fear and without reproach'. Said of Pierre du Terrain, Chevalier de Bayard (1476-1524) in *Très joyeuse ... histoire du gentil seigneur de Bayart* by Jacques de Mailles, his 'loyal serviteur': Société de l'Histoire de France (ed M. J. Roman); edn Renouard Paris (1878).

chevaux-de-frise Literally, 'horses of Friesland'. A defensive military construction or device employed to check cavalry charges and stop breaches. One of many configurations comprised baulks of timber (*e.g.*, tree-trunks) driven obliquely into the ground, markedly inclining towards the enemy, and sharpened at the upper end so as to impale charging horses. Many English-speaking people will remember the vivid depiction of the placement of *cheveaux-de-frise* in Laurence Olivier's film *Henry V*. Other configurations comprised baulks of timber, laid on the ground, into which had been driven spikes apt to pierce the hooves of horses and to injure and incapacitate fallen men and mounts. The common factor is the presence of spikes, in which respect the *chevaux-de-frise* resemble the present-day police device employed to deflate the tyres of speeding cars, sometimes called in the US 'stop-sticks' and in England 'the stinger'.

The name is much later than the stratagem. According to the *OED*, in their struggles for freedom during the latter half of the 17th century, the Frisians used the construction to remedy their want of cavalry; *cf* the Dutch name *Vriesse ruyters* (Frisian horsemen). In the 17th century *Horse de Freeze* occurs. The descriptions in the quotations below indicate the scope and the longevity of this ingenious manifestation of the art of warfare.

> 'The Count de Serine ... posted his men on the other side, and covered them with Chevaux de Frise fastened together with Chains': *London Gazette* No. 2375/3 (1688). 'Numbers of chevaux de frize were shipt, an instrument to fix in the ground to keep off a body of horse from attacking the foot': Luttrell, *Brief Rel.* II p 520, edn 1857 (1692). '*Chevaux de Frise,* or *Friseland Horse*': J Harris, *Lex Techn, s.v.* 'Fortification' (1704). '*Chevaux de Frise* are large Joists, or pieces of Timber, Ten or Twelve Foot in length, with Six Sides into which are driven a great Number of wooden Pins about Six Foot long, crossing one another, and having their Ends armed with Iron-Points': John Kersey, *Dictionarium Anglo-Brittannicum or a general English dictionary* 1708 (1721). 'The Danes ... had planted themselves ... behind their Chevaux de Frize': . *London Gazette,* No. 4675/1 (1712). 'I shall be very glad to see the chevaux de frise': Wellington in John Gurwood, ed, *The Dispatches of ... the Duke of Wellington 1799–1818* (1834–38) V, p 11 (1810).

Sometimes applied, perhaps fancifully, to a line of spikes, nails or pieces of broken glass fixed along the top of a railing, paling, or wall.

chez Used with (French) personal pronoun or proper name: 'at the house or home of [someone]': *OED*.

chic '"Stylish", in the best fashion and best of taste': *OED*. The essence of *chic* as a concept is almost impossible to define in dispassionate words, hence, no doubt, the indispensable *role* the word plays in English-speaking discussions of fashion. It does not necessarily mean 'in "good" taste', which imports a highly personal criterion. It does not mean 'in the height of fashion'. It does not mean '*comme il faut*'. It does not mean '*bon ton*'. It is perhaps best described by saying that it is the property or quality enjoyed by such women as Coco Chanelle, Princess Grace of Monaco, Audrey Hepburn, Jacqui Onassis and Catherine Deneuve.

The following comment from the *OED's* entry for *chic* will surprise and perplex many: '"Stylish", in the best fashion and best of taste: *adj.* [Not so used in F.]'. It is clear that the French *do* say, for example, 'C'est un quartier chic', and 'C'est un restaurant chic'. It might be that the *OED* is warning us not to dash unhesitatingly into assuming that *chic* necessarily means 'posh'. The comment is certainly delphic.

chiffonier 'A piece of furniture, consisting of a small cupboard with the top made so as to form a sideboard': *OED*. Purely verbal descriptions of items of furniture are frequently uninformative or even deceptive. Unfortunately, those who are conversant with furniture are often too imprecise in their definitions to be of much help to those who consult dictionaries. By origin, the word *chiffonier* meant 'a rag-picker', so, in essence, any item of furniture that provides a repository for snippets of cloth and similar items (buttons, needles, pins, thread and thimbles) ought to qualify as a *chiffonier*. A particular configuration of the *chiffonier* is a table, often fitting into a corner of a room, with a flat working surface and cupboards and small drawers superimposed on the working surface, at working level, apt for the storage of small items used in dressmaking and repair. The name of the item of furniture is fully naturalized: /ʃifəˈniːɹ/.

chignon 'A large coil or hump of hair, usually folded round a pad, which has, at various times (e.g. *c*1780, *c*1870), been worn by women on the nape of the neck or back of the head': *OED*. *Cf postiche, below.*

> 'Nor did she wear a chignon I'd have you all to know /And I met her in the garden where the praties grow': Johnny Patterson: Irish song, *The Garden where the Praties Grow*.

chose jugée 'A matter which has been formally adjudicated and decided and which it is therefore idle or presumptuous to discuss': *OED*.

Chouan A name given to irregular bands who, after 1793, maintained in the west of France a partisan war against the Republic and the first Empire. They also appeared again in 1832. Used also as a polemical name for partisans of the Bourbons. Their name is thought to have been taken from the surname of one of their leaders, Jean Chouan. It is also an older and local form of *chat-huant*, the name of a species of owl. Balzac wrote a novel entitled *Les Chouans* (1829).

cinéma verité 'A film or films which avoid artificiality and have the appearance of real life; the making of such a film; documentary films collectively': *OED*.

cinq-à-sept A reception or cocktail-party 'from five o'clock to seven o'clock'. The expression also denotes the hours a French businessman traditionally spent with his mistress.

circumflex accent A word needs to be said of this diacritical mark. In principle, the accent alters the quantity of the vowel above which it is placed. That is its primary function. It appears in many words that in earlier French has a letter *s* following the vowel. That letter *s* was originally sounded; it *also lengthened the quantity of the vowel it followed.* When the letter *s* ceased to be sounded, the scribes ceased to write the letter but placed the circumflex accent over the vowel to remind readers that the quantity of the vowel was *still* long, despite the absence of the letter *s*. Thus, it is only half the story to say the circumflex accent often indicates an absent *s*. That is true, but it disguises the principle fact – that the vowel over which the circumflex accent is placed is *long*. Nowadays, it scarcely matters with the vowel *a*, since native French-speakers almost universally ignore the distinction between the vowel *a* accented and unaccented by the circumflex. For example, a distinction is almost never made nowadays between *une pâte*, a paste, and *une patte*, the paw of an animal, yet the dictionaries almost uniformly declare in favour of, respectively, /pɑt/ and /pat/. The distinction between the long and short quantities with *o* is, however, still respected: the difference in the sound of, for example, *la cote*, the cost, quota or share, and *la côte*, the side, is profound: /cɔt/ and /cot/. The circumflex accent placed over the vowel *e* produces a sound identical with that of *e* with a grave accent. The circumflex accent makes absolutely no difference to the pronunciations of the vowels *i* and *u*.

citoyen A citizen viewed as a member of a civil community, enjoying its rights and obliged by its duties. A citizen viewed as merely as a city-dweller rather than as a countryman is *citadin*.

claque 'An organized body of hired applauders in a theatre; hence ... a body of subservient followers always ready to applaud their leader': *OED*. From *claque*, a slap or clap of the hand.

cliché In letterpress printing, a stereotype printing-plate; a moulded or cast copy of an original engraving or forme of type. Multiple copies of the original are obtained by stereotyping; hence the figurative use of *cliché* to mean an idea or phrase not new or original but hackneyed. The word is the past participle of a verb *clicher*, a variant of *cliquer*, and is said to derive from the sound (the 'plop') the original printing plate made as it fell on to the pool of molten type-metal in one of the earliest production methods.

clientèle The body of a professional man's clients. Nowadays also used generically for the customers of a wide variety of suppliers.

clique 'A small and exclusive party or set, a narrow coterie or circle: a term of reproach or contempt, applied generally to such as are considered to associate for unworthy or selfish ends, or to small and select bodies who arrogate supreme authority in matters of social status, literature, etc': *OED*. The word is said to derive from the same root as *claque* (*q v*).The *OED* (2nd edn, 1989) remarks that this French word has produced no derivatives in French but has produced many in English, of which it quotes *cliquedom, cliqueless, cliquery, cliquomania* and *cliquomaniac*. So acclimatized has the word become that it has produce the slang word *cliquy*. The root word is often heard mispronounced in England thus: /klɪk/.

cloisonné Divided into compartments: said of enamels produced by a method that relies on putting the coloured powders into compartments before fusing. The raised walls of the compartments are smoothed after firing and present the most noticeable characteristic of *cloisonné* work.

cocotte Originally a child's name for a hen. A prostitute; one of a class of the *demi-monde* of Paris. A small fireproof dish used for cooking and serving an individual portion of food; *en cocotte*, used to designate food thus served, in particular, *un œuf en cocotte* /œ̃n œfɔ̃kokot/, plural *des œufs en cocotte* or *en cocottes*, either pronounced /dεzøkok ot/.

Cognac A French brandy of superior quality distilled from wine from the Cognac region.

coiffeur A hairdresser.

coiffure A 'hairdo'.

comédien[ne] Strictly, an actor or actress who plays in comedies as distinct from tragedies, but the words are much coloured by the English and French tendency to use the words as equivalent to *comic*, the noun. To many there is no significant difference between, for example, a stand-up comic and a stand-up comedian.

comme il faut As it should be: proper(ly); according to etiquette; correct(ly) in deportment or behaviour; in a decent and respectable fashion.

'Comment voulez-vous gouverner un pays qui a deux cents quarante-six variétés de fromage?' 'How would you govern a country that has two hundred and forty-six varieties of cheese?': Général Charles de Gaulle, in Ernest Mignon, *Les Mots du Général*, p 57 (1962).

commode The word has two principal meanings. The first is now historical but is the only word for the phenomenon. In the latter part of the 17th century and the first part of the 18th, women, particularly in France, wore their hair dressed on tall wire frames known as *commodes*. The second meaning is in two parts. The primary meaning of the word *commode*, applied to items of furniture, is 'A piece of furniture with drawers and shelves; in the bedroom, a sort of elaborate chest of drawers, often with a looking-glass, (so in French); in the drawingroom, a large (and generally old-fashioned) kind of chiffonier': *OED*. For *chiffonier*, see *above*. A secondary meaning, which is really a special application of the primary one, is given by the *OED* thus: 'A small article of furniture enclosing a chamber utensil; a close-stool'. In all uses the pronunciation should be /kɔmɔd/, but /kə mouːd/ is often heard for the close-stool, and sometimes for the other items of furniture.

communard 'An adherent of the Commune of Paris of 1871, or of the principles of communalism; a communalism': *OED*. The *OED* adds that *Littré* says that the name is given to the Communards by their adversaries ('Nom donné par les [leurs] adversaires'). However, nothing pejorative remains today in the words *la Commune* and *communard as* used in English as terms of art in history, however much one might deplore the insensate savagery of the Communards. In its secondary sense (see quotation) it is doubtful that the word is used nowadays, even as a technical term.

> 'A Communist is a Socialist ... who wants to have goods in common. A Communard is a person who wishes for an extreme development of local government': Philip G Hamerton, *French and English*, 12A (1889).

communautaire Descriptive of the European Community or, more specifically, descriptive of someone who is in favour of the European Community. Used also as a substantive.

communiqué Literally, 'that which is communicated'. An official announcement or report, especially a report of a meeting or a conference.

> 'An official *communiqué* administering a severe rebuke to the leaders of the Zemstvo movement': *The Spectator*, p 1069/2, 31st December 1904.

compère 'The organizer or general director of a musical or vaudeville entertainment; now especially one whose role in an entertainment on the stage, radio, etc., is to introduce the performers to the audience and provide a linking commentary between the acts': *OED*. Sometimes, 'a master of ceremonies'.

compote Fruit preserved in syrup.

> '*Compote*, fruit stew'd in Sugar, after a manner peculiar to the French': John Evelyn, *De la Quintinie's Compleat gard'ner,* I 91 margin (tr. 1693). 'Cherries ... put into Compotes, half Sugar and Conserves': Bradley, *Family Dictionary,* I. 3 Lij 1(1725).

Also, a dish consisting of fruit salad or stewed fruit, often in or with syrup.

> 'Take out the lemon peel, pour the syrup over the figs, and the compôte [*sic*], when cold, will be ready for table': Mrs Beeton, *Book of Household Management*, §1541 (1861). 'If the compote is not being used for children a little red wine may be added to the syrup when stewing the pears': F. B. Jack, *Good Housekeeping Cookery Book,* p 193 (1925).

concierge 'The person who has charge of the entrance of a building; a janitor, porter': *OED*.

concours d'élégance 'A parade of vehicles in which the entrants are judged according to the elegance of their appearance': *OED*. It is (primarily) the elegance of the vehicles that attracts favourable judgements.

confrère 'A fellow-member of a learned profession, scientific body, or the like. [From mod.F.]': *OED*.

connoisseur A person well acquainted with one or more of the fine arts, and competent to pass a judgement in relation thereto; a critical judge of art or of matters of taste, and, nowadays, of delicacies and wines. Despite the spelling, the word is pronounced /coneskɤ/. (In contemporary French, the word is invariably spelt *connaisseur*.) To pronounce it /conwa'sʝɫ/ is to betray an ignorance of the *use* of the word, since those from whom we should learn about connoisseurship never pronounce it in that way. In speaking of those who sound the letter *t* in the words 'apostle' and 'epistle', H. W. Fowler makes a comment that is highly relevant to the pronunciation /conwa'sʝɫ/: 'Some good people, afraid they may be suspected of not knowing how to spell, say the *t* in self-defence': H. W. Fowler, *Modern English Usage*, p 467 (1926).

We adopted the word *connoisseur* during the period when many words in French now spelt with *-ai* were spelt with *-oi*. For two examples, see the extract from Rousseau's *Confessions* in the entry below for *'Qu'ils mangent de la brioche'*. In a very large number of cases, the spellings with *-oi* and *-ai* were pronounced as though the diphthong had been the simple vowel /e/ – that is, to rhyme with the English word 'way'. In the early days of the French language, the word for 'king' had been pronounced /re/. By 1792, it had come to be pronounced, in virtually all educated circles, as /rwe/. As an act of what we should now call 'political correctness', the pronunciation of the Parisian mob was adopted to a man by the Revolutionaries. Under the Reign of Terror, – almost overnight, in fact – the pronunciation became /rwa/. The pronunciation of *le titi Parisien* (equivalent to the English 'Cockney' for a Londoner) became the accepted pronunciation of *la République*. Trouble arose when Louis XVIII returned to France in 1814. As Ferdinand Brunot (1860-1938) reminds us, 'En 1814, le Roi en rentrant, se rendra ridicule, en disant à l'ancienne mode': *Histoire de la langue française des origines à*

1900, tome X, p 96 (1905-53): 'In 1814, the King, on his return, rendered himself ridiculous by speaking in the old way'.

One of Balzac's characters uses *frait* for *froid*, but Balzac explains of her that 'son language était celui de la vielle cour': *Lys dans la vallée*, p 96. (In French Canada there exists, to this day, a feminine adjective *frette*, for *froide*, 'cold'.) The tenacious persistence of the *ancienne mode* was evidence of its entrenched position in French society. Victor Hugo tells us that even 'the Citizen King', Louis-Philippe, son of the regicide 'Citoyen Égalité', used to refer to 'les Hongrais'. (See *Le Grevisse*, §66 a., in which the authority is given as, 'texte publié par H Guillemin, dans *le Figaro litt* 20 déc 1952'.)

In the tradition song *La Destinée la Rose au Bois* the old pronunciation is retained for the rhymed words *bois, moi, roi* and *soie*, /bwe/, mwe/, rwe/ and swe/.

conservatoire Strictly, the Conservatoire, Paris, but, by extension, the Conservatorium of Leipzig and the several conservatories in Italy: public establishments for special instruction in music and declamation. Sometimes used of similar establishments in England and, in the form 'conservatory', in the USA.

'Console-toi, tu ne me chercherais pas si tu ne m'avais trouvé': Pascal, *Pensées*, (1670, ed L. Braunschvigc, 1909): 'Comfort yourself, you would not seek me if you had not [already] found me'.

consommé Traditionally, a strong broth or soup made by slowly boiling meat for a long time. Nowadays it seems that the word is applied only to clear, thin soups.

contre-coup A counter-blow.

contrepèterie A Spoonerism. *Le Petit Robert* (1970) says, 'Inversion des lettres ou des syllables d'un ensemble de mots spécialement choisis, afin d'obtenir d'autres dont l'assemblage ait également un sens, de préférence burlesque ou grivois': 'Inversion of the letter or syllables of a collection of words specially chosen so as to achieve other arrangements that also have a meaning, for preference amusing or bawdy'.

> '*Femme folle à la messe* pour *femme molle à la fesse*': Rabelais.

contretemps An inopportune occurrence; an untoward accident; an unexpected mishap or hitch, deriving from the same term in fencing, meaning a pass or thrust made at a wrong or inopportune moment.

convenances, les Conventional propriety or usage; the conventional proprieties of life or social intercourse; the conventionalities. See *mariage de convenance, below*.

copain/copine A (male) friend; a (female) friend. There is no form *copaine*.

cor anglais 'English horn'. The tenor oboe.

cordon bleu Literally, 'blue cordon or ribbon', alluding to the sky-blue ribbon worn by the Knights-Grand-Cross of the French Order of the Holy Ghost, the highest order of chivalry under the Bourbon kings; hence extended to other first-class distinctions, such as the Blue Riband prize awarded since the 1860s to the ship that made the fastest transatlantic crossing. (Blue *Ribbon* in the USA). The title 'cordon bleu cook or chef' is a jocular or familiar compliment.

cordon sanitaire A guarded, policed line between infected and uninfected districts, to prevent intercommunication and spread of a disease or pestilence. Nowadays used almost exclusively in a figurative sense.

corps A division of an army, forming a tactical unit; a body of troops regularly organized; a body of men who are assigned to a special service. *Corps Diplomatique*: the body of ambassadors, *attachés*, etc. accredited to a particular Court or capital city. *Corps de ballet*: the dancers in a ballet; the company of ballet-dancers at a theatre.

corsage 'The 'body' of a woman's dress; a bodice (commonly pronounced as French) ... A bouquet worn on the bodice. *U.S*': *OED*. It is probable that most people in England and the USA would now understand the second, not the first, by the word *corsage*, pronounced /kɔʁsɑʒ/.

cortège Originally, a procession of attendants in the train of a personage. Now sometimes used in England for the motorcade following a hearse. Influenced by *cortege funèbre* (*cf Le Petit Robert 1970, s.v. cortège*).

corvée A day's work of unpaid labour due by a vassal to his feudal lord *(la Petite Corvée)*. By extension, the system of forced labour thus exacted. *La Corvée* was extended to the statute labour on the public roads exacted of the French peasants before 1776 (*la Grande Corvée*).

> 'When, in the early part of the [18th] century, the advantages of a good system of high roads began to be perceived by the Government, the convenient idea came into the heads of the more ingenious among the Intendants of imposing for the construction of the roads, a royal or public corvée analogous to that of private feudalism': John Morley, *Critical Miscellanies,* Series II 202 (1877).

coterie This word is a marvellous instance of a word that is at least as much English as it is French, though it clearly has on its face the hallmarks of being an importation from modern French. Its roots and branches are part of the common stock of French and Norman. It links the highest reaches of power and influence to the lowliest and homeliest of words in the language *–cottage*. It nowadays means a group or circle of persons associated together and distinguished from 'outsiders', a 'set', a 'clique'. In English history, it has often implied a select or exclusive circle in Society; a classic instance was 'the Holland House coterie', the influential Whig 'set' that had the *entrée* to the court of the third Lord Holland (1773-1840) at Holland House and were immensely influential in Whig affairs in the early 19th century.

By origin, the word *coterie* implied 'a company of people who live in familiarity, or who work together in a common interest' (*Littré*); originally, 'a certain number of peasants united together to hold land from a lord'; 'companie, societie, association of countrey people' (R. Cotgrave, *Dictionarie of the French and English Tongues*, 1611) from *cotier*, rendering mediaeval Latin *cotrius*, *coterius* 'cottar, tenant of a *cota* or cot'. *Cf* French *cotterie*, 'a base, ignoble, and seruile tenure, or tenement, not held in fee, and yeelding only rent, or if more, but *cens* or *surcens* at most' (Cotgrave). A regular development might have given us 'cottery', (*cf.* 'pots' > 'pottery'); indeed, the word was often spelt 'cotterie' and in *Don Juan (1824)* is three times rhymed with 'lottery':

> I can't exactly trace their rule of right,
> Which hath a little leaning to a lottery.
> I've seen a virtuous woman put down quite
> By the mere combination of a coterie;
> Also a so-so matron boldly fight

> Her way back to the world by dint of plottery,
> And shine the very *Siria* of the spheres,
> Escaping with a few slight, scarless sneers.
> *Canto 13 Stanza LXXXII*

> Why then I'll swear, as poet Wordy swore
> (Because the world won't read him, always snarling),
> That taste is gone, that fame is but a lottery,
> Drawn by the blue-coat misses of a coterie.
> *Canto 4 Stanza CIX*

The third instance perhaps calls into question the *phonetic* reliability of Byron's rhymes. Is there any more excruciating rhyme in English literature than 'lottery' with 'got her, I'?

> A hazy widower turn'd of forty's sure
> (If't is not vain examples to recall)
> To draw a high prize: now, howe'er he got her, I See nought more strange in this than t' other lottery.
> *Canto 12 Stanza XXXIII*

The path to the present-day pronunciation of 'coterie' is relatively easy to follow. One of our most persuasive orthoepists, Dr John Walker (1732-1807) gives a long quantity to the first vowel (*Critical Pronouncing Dictionary*, London 1791), but places the tonic accent on the last syllable. However, that was a shot not too far off the judgement of posterity, since the word 'coterie' is pronounced with the tonic accent on the last syllable by a great many of the predominant English-speaking group, the Americans.

The pronunciation of this *English* word that seems most likely to succeed in England is /ˈkəʊːtərɪ/. The word is no less a French word, however, and, in French, it is pronounced /kɔt[ə]ʁi/ – with a short first vowel and, normally, three syllables.

couchette A Continental railway carriage in which the seats are by design readily convertible into sleeping-berths; also, such a berth.

> 'I booked a *couchette*, which, I am told, is the way Frenchmen always travel. It is a carriage for four, with two berths which open from the wall above the seats. You can lie full length on these, covered with rugs': Evelyn Waugh, *Labels*, p 29 (1930).

couleur locale Added detail given to a literary or artistic subject not intrinsic to the subject-matter itself but intended to fill out the reader's or viewer's appreciation of the scene.

couloir A corridor or lobby; a passage-way. A mountain gulley or gorge. Ruskin, below, argues from the particular to the general.

> '"Couloir" is a good untranslateable Savoyard word for a place down which stones and water fall in storms; it is perhaps deserving of naturalization': John Ruskin, *Modern Painting*, IV V §9. 22 note.

coup d'état 'A sudden and decisive stroke of state policy; specifically a sudden and great change in the government carried out violently or illegally by the ruling power': *OED*.

coup de foudre Literally, 'a stroke of lightning'. A sudden unforeseen occurrence; a revelation; also, love at first sight.

coup de grâce Literally, 'a stroke of grace': a blow by which one condemned or mortally wounded is 'put out of his misery' or dispatched quickly; hence, figuratively, a finishing stroke, one that settles or puts an end to something. Pronounced /kudəgʁɑs/. There is an odd habit in England of pronouncing the phrase without the final sibilant.

coup de théâtre A theatrical hit; a sensational turn or action in a play; any sudden sensational act.

coupe A shallow cup, bowl, or glass. By extension, a mixture of ice-cream and fruit, etc., served in a glass goblet or the like; specifically, *coupe Jacques*.

coupé Literally, 'cut'. A closed two-door motor car, usually with two seats. In USA frequently spelt *coupe* and pronounced /kuːp/.

coupon A word that has many meanings, all stemming from the underlying notion of something cut off, specifically some paper (and probably printed) form to be surrendered in return for some benefit. The word is a fairly modern import from French but has acquired a naturalized pronunciation, /ˈkupɔn/. The French pronunciation is /kupõ/. During the Second World War and the ensuing six years of austerity, coupons were a a feature of life the English could not ignore. Two strange pronunciations became quite common. The first was widespread: /ˈkjuːpɔn/. The second was less widespread but was immeasurable more grating: /ˈkjyːpɔn/.

couturier A male dressmaker or fashion designer.

crampon A small plate of iron set with spikes or points, fastened to the foot to secure a firmer hold in walking over ice or slippery ground, or in climbing a steep slope. Naturalized and pronounced /ˈkræmpən/.

crèche Originally, a public nursery for infants; an institution where the infant children of poor women were taken care of while their mothers were at work, or in hospital, etc. In later and contemporary use, a day nursery for babies and young children.

crème de la crème The *élite*, the very pick of society.

crêpe *Crêpé* means 'crinkled': applied to black fabrics formerly associated with mourning, and to paper used for making, for example, festive decorations and party hats. Specifically, in fashion, *crêpe de Chine*, a white or other coloured fabric made of raw silk.

crétin One of a class of dwarfed and specially deformed idiots found in certain valleys of the Alps and elsewhere. Also in a weakened sense (especially in the indelicate form *crétin des Alpes*): a fool, one who behaves stupidly.

cri de cœur 'A cry from the heart'.

crinoline A fabric comprising a warp of cotton thread and a woof of horse-hair, formerly used *inter alia* for the stiffening of the hooped skirts that eventually acquired that name.

critique An essay or article in criticism of a literary (or more rarely, of an artistic) work; a review. Pronounced approximately as in French since *c* 1815: /kʁɪtˈik/.

croissant A small crescent-shaped roll of bread.

croupier Originally, one who rides behind on the croup (the rump or hind-quarters of the horse, that is, behind the saddle); hence, it seems (from the dictionaries), one who goes halves with a player at cards or dice and stands behind him to assist him; also, a person who stood behind the banker to assist at the obsolete game of basset: and now, with perhaps conscious wit, 'He who rakes in the money at a gaming-table': *OED*. See also *kibitz* in the Yiddish Appendix to the German Lexicon.

croûton 'A small *croût* or 'crust'. A small piece, normally a cube, of toasted or fried bread used to garnish soups and salads.

croquette (From *croquer*, to crunch'.) A ball or mass of rice, potato, or finely minced meat or fish, seasoned and (deep) fried to crispness. Often cylindrical in form.

cuisine Strictly, simply 'the kitchen'; by extension, the entire culinary department or establishment; the manner or style of cooking in practice (*e.g. la nouvelle cuisine)*; in general, what proceeds from the kitchen.

cul-de-sac Literally, 'the neck of a bag'. Much used in England for a street with only one entry/exit, a 'blind alley'. In the US, a dead-end street. The French for such a street is normally *une impasse* or *une voie sans issue*. The English pronunciation of *cul-de-sac* is /ˈkʌldɪsæk/; the French is /kʏdəsak/.

culotte[s] Knee-breeches. See also *sans-culotte* below.

> 'Le bon roi Dagobert/ A mis sa culotte à l'invers': *Old Song.*

curé A parish priest: 'Monsieur le Curé'. A priest without the cure of souls is accorded the courtesy title of *Abbé*, originally meaning 'Abbot'. A monk is known as *Père (Dom* for Benedictines and Carthusians), and a friar is known a *Frère*, with, in all cases in France, surname or Christian name or both.

cy-devant or **ci-devant** Literally, 'heretofore, formerly'. In the early days of the French Revolution, the revolutionaries having abolished aristocracy, there was much confusion about how to identify people. The king, for example, was to be known as Louis Capet, from the name of the Royal House. Since most nobles had territorial titles quite different from their patronymics, the practice arose of continuing to use the familiar titles, but prefixed by *cy-devant*: thus, *le cy-devant Comte de Mirabeau.*

dada, un 'A Hobby horse', both literally and figuratively. The word *dada* is a nursery word for 'horse', exactly equivalent, in the nursery, to 'horsey'. The figurative application in French is exactly and precisely mirrored in English, making the phrase one of the fairly rare instances in English of *un vrai ami* rather than *un faux ami, (q.v. below).*

The application of the word in cultural circles derives from the use of the idiom *être sur son dada*, 'to be on one's hobby-horse', as the title of a review that appeared in Zürich in 1916. The word *Dada* became the badge of the revolutionary, nihilistic movement founded by Tristan Tzara (a Rumanian-born French poet, 1896-1963), Jean Arp, an Alsatian artist known as Hans Arp, (1887-1966), and a German poet Richard Huelsenbeck (1892-1974). The word *Dada* has been applied to an international movement in art and literature, characterized by a repudiation of traditional conventions and reason, and intended to outrage and scandalize. The movement has spawned a myriad of associated forms: for example, *Dadaism, Dadaist and Dadaistic.*

'Dans l'adversité de nos meilleurs amis, nous trouvons toujours quelque chose qui ne nous deplaît pas': Duc de la Rochefoucauld (1613-80), *Réflexions ou Maximes de Morale* (Dutch edn, 1664) maxime 128: 'In the adversity of our best friends, we always find something that is not displeasing to us'. French appears to have no precise equivalent to *Schadenfreude,* having to refer to 'la joie que certains peuvent éprouver face au malheur des autres'. Lucretius (94-55 BC) had said:

> *Suave, mari magno turbantibus aequora ventis*

E terra magnum alterius spectare laborem
Non quia vexari quemquamst iucunda voluptas,
Sed quibus ipse malis careas quia cernere suave est.

De Rerum Natura, 2 1-4.

'Delightful, when the winds are whipping up the waves on the great sea, to look out from the land at the striving of somebody else. Not because it gives pleasure that somebody's in trouble, but because you see the trouble that you yourself are spared'. Gore Vidal has said, 'Whenever a friend succeeds, a little something in me dies': in *The Sunday Times Magazine*, 19th September 1971. Somewhere between those two dates, Dean Trench had said: 'What a fearful thing is it that any language should have a word expressive of the pleasure which men feel at the calamities of others; for the existence of the word bears testimony to the existence of the thing. And yet in more than one [language] such a word is found. In the Greek *επιχαιρεκακια*, in the German, *Schadenfreude*': R. C. Trench, *Study of Words* (ed. 3) ii. 29 (1852). It no doubt redounds to the credit of the French that they have no equivalent of *Schadenfreude*.

(de) bon ton Good style, good breeding; good form; also, polite or fashionable society; the fashionable world. Said by the *OED*, (2nd edn, 1989) to be archaic.

'There was a word, or rather a phrase, in common use among them a century or so gone by, which has fallen into desuetude with us. No one now speaks of *bon ton*.': *Pall Mall Gazette*, 1st August 10/2 1865.

de haut en bas 'From height to lowness, condescendingly as from a lofty position, with an air of affected superiority': *OED*.

'De l'audace, et encore de l'audace, et toujours de l'audace' ; 'Boldness, and again boldness, and always boldness': Georges Jacques Danton (17591794): speech to the Legislative Committee of General Defence, 2nd September 1792, in *Le Moniteur*, 4th September 1792. The *ODQ* cross-references this quotation to a quotation of Lord Chancellor Bacon (1561-1626), 'In civil business, what first? Boldness; what second and third? Boldness. And yet boldness is a child of ignorance and baseness': *Essays*, 'Of Boldness' (1625). Bacon says, also, 'Boldness is an ill keeper of promise': *ibid.*

The word 'audacity' is a good example of a useful word absorbed into English through French that *in usage* differs quite considerably from 'boldness'. Once again we have an example of our anxiety to *differentiate*. Thereby we gain what is effectively a completely new word. 'Audacity' in modern English often (but not always) implies an element of cheek completely absent from 'boldness' (except, perhaps, in Ireland). If we say, 'Such-and-such a person had the audacity to suggest such-and-such a thing', we mean something materially different from if we say, 'Such-and-such a person had the *boldness* to say such-and-such a thing'. (One is constantly reminded of the title of a regular feature in *Readers' Digest*, 'It pays to increase your word-power.)

de nouveau Anew, afresh; from the beginning.

de rigueur Literally, 'of strictness'. Something is *de rigueur* if its observance is rigorously enforced or at least is considered obligatory according to the tenets of certain sections of the community, for example, the dictates of etiquette.

de trop 'Too many'. The meaning is one (or more) too many; in the way; 'Three's a crowd'.

débâcle Increasingly used in England to mean an embarrassing disaster, though its primary meaning, according to the *OED*, (2nd edn, 1989) is 'A sudden breaking up or downfall; a confused rush or rout, a stampede'.

> 'The Brunswickers were routed and had fled..It was a general *débâcle*': Thackeray, *Vanity Fair xxxii*.(1848).

The *OED* quotes as the orginal meaning of the word, 'A breaking up of ice in a river; in *Geol.* a sudden deluge or violent rush of water, which breaks down opposing barriers, and carries before it blocks of stone and other debris'. The English-language edition of Émile Zola's *Le débâcle* published by the Gutenberg Project:

http://www.gutenberg.org/dirs/1/3/8/5/13851/13851.txt has as its title *The Downfall*, but as a supplementary title *The Smash-up*.

R. W. Burchfield, *Fowler's Modern English Usage* (1996), merely comments 'Frequently now written and printed without accents, partly no doubt because of the shortage of special signs on modern daisy wheels and computer keyboards'. In eight short years the daisy-wheel is as dead as the dodo!

débris Originally, the broken-down remains of weathered rock. Now, rubble, 'any similar rubbish formed by destructive operations': *OED*. During the Second World War, the rubble resulting from bomb damage was frequently referred to as *débris*, though it was widely pronounced /də'briː/. The French pronunciation is /debʁi/.

début Originally, the first stroke at billiards. Later, entry into society (*cf débutante* in the dictionaries); the first appearance in public of an actor, actress, or other performer. In English, the word *début* is used, particularly in the USA, as the infinitive of a verb; the past participle of the verb is *debuted*, which is pronounced /'debjuːd/ or, sometimes, /də' bjuːd/. The letter *t* is never pronounced, however anglicized the usage. This English verb has been in use since at least 1830.

> 'He debuted at Naples, about five years ago, and has since performed in the principal theatres of Italy': *Fraser's Magazine* II 52 (1830). 'The moment is a proud one for the debuting youth': F Arthur, *Coparceners*, v 69 (1885).

débutant[e] One who makes his or her *début*.

décalcomanie A method of transferring images to paper, porcelain or similar materials from designs printed on paper or similar material that can, when moistened, be transferred to other surfaces. The 'transfers' themselves, so called in England; called 'decals' in the USA. *Cf calque, above.*

décolleté Of a dress, etc.: cut low round the neck; low-necked. The state of being dressed in clothing that exposes the upper part of the bosom. Pronounced as three syllables: /dekolte/.

dégagé Easy, unconstrained (in manner or address); relaxed; *décontracté*.

> 'I do use to appear a little more dégagé': Sir John Vanburgh, *The Relapse*, IV vi (1697). 'An Air altogether galant and dégagé': Budgell, *The Spectator*, No. 277 (1712).

déjà vu 'An illusory feeling of having previously experienced a present situation; a form of paramnesia': *OED*. The *OED* defines *paramnesia* as, 'Memory that is unreal, illusory, or distorted; *spec.* the phenomenon of *déjà vu*; an instance of this'.

One of the insoluble puzzles of English pronunciation is that the English appear to have become incapable of pronouncing an open *u* sound. That sound has degenerated into *ü,* not hitherto a native sound. Yet, as soon as the opportunity affords of pronouncing the vowel as ü – in *déjà vu* – the nation immediately says 'dayzyah voo' (/deiʒa'vuː/), as though the phrase were *déjà vous*. This is, it seems, an insoluble problem. The strangulation of the open vowel u, /u/, into the constricted sound ü, /y/, is increasing by the day, and is unchecked nowadays: the indulgence granted to 'regional accents' lets everything through, however grotesquely erroneous.

démarche A diplomatic initiative, a political step or proceeding; a development, often a surprising one.

démenti A statement, normally an official one, that gives the lie to some published statement.

demi-monde Literally, the 'half-world', a term coined by Alexander Dumas *fils* to denote 'the class of women of doubtful reputation and social standing, upon the outskirts of 'society': *OED*.

> 'His [Dumas'] *Demi-Monde* is the link between good and bad society … the world of compromised women, a social limbo, the inmates of which … are perpetually struggling to emerge into the paradise of honest and respectable ladies': *Fraser's Magazine,* LI, p 578/1 (1855).

demi-tasse A small coffee-cup; its contents.

demise This word ought not, strictly speaking, to be in this section of the Lexicon but in the Law-French Appendix. Although *desmise, demise* or *démise* are regularly formed feminine nouns from the past participle of *desmettre*, etc, they are not found in Old French but are of extreme frequency in Anglo-French. For more information, see the word in the Law-French Appendix. The word *demise* is a perfectly good modern English word for 'death', albeit somewhat pompous. In all contexts, law and lay, the word *demise* is pronounced /dɪ'maɪːz/.

dénouement or **dénoûment** Literally, 'an unravelling'. Its specific use in English and French is to denote the final unravelling of the complications of the plot in a drama, novel, etc.; the *καταστροφη* in classical drama; the final solution or issue of a complication, difficulty, or mystery.

dépôt The predominant meaning adopted in English derives from the root 'to deposit'. The word *dépôt* has a variety of meaning depending on context, the linking notion being 'a warehouse or storehouse'. In military use alone it might mean a place where military stores are deposited; the head-quarters of a regiment, where supplies are received and from which they are distributed; a station where recruits are assembled and drilled; and a place where soldiers who cannot join their regiments remain (a 'holding unit'). It is also applied to a portion of a regiment that remains at home when the rest are on foreign service. In civilian usage it might mean a coal depot, a grain depot, a furniture depot; in parts of England, the *termini* and garages of trams (streetcars), buses and sometimes trains are known as 'depots'. In addition to the uses above, the word 'depot' is widely applied to railway stations (railroad stations or train stations).

The pronunciation and spelling of the word are contentious subjects. The *OED* (2nd edn, 1989) provides an essay of some length on the word.

> As in the case of other words from modern French, the pronunciation varies widely. The French /depo/, with short *e* and *o* and undefined stress, is foreign to English habits of utterance. The earlier English rendering, as shown by the dictionaries down to 1860-70, was, according to the French historical stress and quantity, or the English conception of it (*cf bureau, château, Tussaud*), /diː'pəʊ/, or, with a conscious effort to reproduce the first vowel in French, /deɪ'pəʊ/, these pronunciations were (1895) still heard, but the stress is now more usually on the first syllable, and the quantity of the *o* doubtful, giving /'dɛpəʊ, 'diːpəʊ/ in England and /'dipəʊ, 'deɪpəʊ / in US (where the word is much more in popular use, and /'diːpɒt, diːpɒt/ are mentioned by Longfellow, Lowell, etc., as popular vulgarisms). The form /'dɛpəʊ/ comes as near the French /depo/ as English analogies admit. The earlier Eng. spelling omitted the accent-marks, and this is now usual; the spelling *depôt* belongs especially to the pronunciation /diːpəʊ/; the actual F. spelling *dépôt* goes together with the attempt to pronounce as in French [*scil*, the adoption of the spelling *dépôt* is seen to replicate the French pronunciation /depo/].

The essay must be judged unsatisfactory. It seems clear that the *OED* is wrong to talk of 'The French /depo/, with short *e* and *o*...'. The *OED*'s own phonetic rendering of the word, (that is, /depo/), demonstrates that the two vowels are, from the point of view of *French* linguistics, unquestionably *long*.

There must also be some doubt about the pronunciations the *OED* gives in this essay. The predominant pronunciation in England is undoubtedly /'dɛpəʊ/: see, for example, *Collins Dictionary of the English Language* (1979). Is there really an alternative? It is possible to spend a whole lifetime in England and never hear /'diːpəʊ/. The historical *résumé* in the essay is perhaps too brief to be accurate: Dr Walker's continuator, Edward Smith (*Critical Pronouncing Dictionary*, London, Edinburgh and New York, 1857) gives only /'depo/, completely without comment. The first vowel is clearly an attempt at reproducing the French: the tonic accent (absent, of course, in the French pronunciation) is clearly on the first syllable.

The powerful influence of spelling, complete with accents – and even with the added influence of foreign travel – has had absolutely no permanent effect on the pronunciation of this word in England. And only very rarely, nowadays, is there any effort precisely to emulate the authentic French pronunciation.

In the USA matters are no less complex. *Merriam-Webster Online* notes as definitions of *depot* the following: a place for storing goods or motor vehicles; a place for the storage of military supplies; a place for the reception and forwarding of military replacements, and a building for railroad or bus passengers or freight. As to pronunciation, *Merriam-Webster* suggests that the military and store-house applications of the word tend to be pronounced /'dɛpəʊ/ and, less often, /'dɪəːpəʊ/; the transportation applications tend to be pronounced /'dɪəːpəʊ/ and sometimes /'dɛpəʊ/.

It seems that we might have to wait some years for usage to determine the exact ground-rules regulating this curiously problematical word.

dernier cri The last word, in, for example, fashion.

dernier ressort The last resort; the ultimate 'court of appeal'.

derrière 'The behind'.

deshabillé, en The state of being partly undressed, or dressed in a negligent or careless style; undress.

détente The easing of strained relations, especially in a political situation.

détour 'A turning or deviation from the direct road; a roundabout or circuitous way, course, or proceeding': *OED*. 'Detour', without the accent, is the normal word in the US for an alternative route that traffic is directed to take.

> 'I was amply recompensed for this *detour*': Sir R C Hoare, *Tour in Ireland* 237 (1807). 'They make wide detours to avoid the spot where he stands in the middle of the pavement': Eugene O'Neill, *Hairy Ape*, 50 (1923).

The expression 'Ça vaut le détour' is always associated with the *Guide Michelin (q.v., below)*.

dicton A saying, maxim or saw. A *dictum*.

'Dieu et mon Droict' or **'Droit'** 'God and my right'. The motto of the Sovereign of Great Britain & Northern Ireland.

'Dieu me pardonnera; c'est son metier'; 'God will pardon me, that's his job': Heinrich Heine (1797-1856). Often ascribed to Voltaire, but said by many anecdotal sources to have been Heine's dying words. It seems Heine's choice of French for his dying words has not been explained.

digestif A spiritous drink taken, in principle, to aid digestion.

dirigisme The philosophy that requires that the state directs and controls all aspects of life, – political, industrial, commercial and social.

diseur/diseuse Literally, 'a talker'. A performer who specializes in monologue. In practice, the word is restricted to female artistes, and virtually to French artistes alone.

> 'She is only a concert-hall singer (or diseuse, to use a newly-coined and specific title)': *Cosmopolitan* XX. 444 (1896).

distrait[e] Having the attention distracted from what is present; absent-minded; also, abstracted. Treated nowadays as a wholly French word. The correct French pronunciation is /distʁɛ, distʁɛt/. Acceptable approximations would be /dis'treɪː, dis'treɪt/.

'Dire Napoléon, dire Buonaparte' See quotation below. 'Dire: Napoléon, ou dire: Buonaparte, cela séparait deux hommes plus qu'un abîme': Victor Hugo, 'L'année 1817', *Les Misérables* III, chap. I: 'Say Napoléon, or say Buonaparte: that separates two men more than an abyss'.

Dom See *curé, above.*

dossier A file-cover and its contents; the entire collection of papers related to a specific subject. The *OED* gives the origin as Latin *dorsum*, 'back', through *dos* 'back', in the sense that a bundle of papers, from their bulging, are likened in appearance 'to a back'. Other authorities suggest that the file-cover was called *un dossier* because it had a label affixed 'to its back'. It is difficult to accept either of these derivations. Traditionally, formal business papers were folded along their major axis, tied with a ribbon and (often) 'pigeonholed'. In the English legal profession to this day, briefs, pleadings and all manner of papers are folded along their major axis and secured with pink ribbon – the origin of 'red tape' – and, in order to protect the papers, a 'back-sheet' is provided (thus called) on which are noted the salient details of the action or matter to which the contents relate. Legal pleadings traditionally appear on one side of the paper only. The back-sheet, too, is written on one side only. It is then flipped over so that its written side faces *down* – faces the desk-top. The rest of the bundle is then placed on top of the back-sheet but, of course, facing *up*. The bundle is then normally securely united by punching, threading, or eyeleting,, or by stapling, and is then folded on its major axis. The back-sheet, at the bottom of the bundle while the bundle is being read, takes the bulk of the wear.

When the bundle is folded along its major (vertical) axis before filing, the legends on the back-sheet are visible, but, so that *all* the detail is visible at a single glance after folding, the detail is written only in the right-hand vertical half, which accounts for the (at first glance) anomalous look of a legal back-sheet.

It is hardly a far cry from paper back-sheets to more durable folders such as the manila folders that are almost universal today. Filing cabinets rendered pigeon-holing increasingly rare and in a positive way discouraged the folding of papers.

> 'In neatly-docketed cabinets round his office stood the *dossiers* of all the criminals with whom he has had anything to do for the past eight years': *Pall Mall Gazette*, 13 June 11/2, 1884 .'A series of *dossiers* by which the record of each workman can be established': H. Belloc, *The Servile State*, ix, 176 (1912).

double entente/double entendre 'A double meaning; a word or phrase having a double sense, especially as used to convey an indelicate meaning': *OED*. The expression *double entente* is current French. The form *double entendre* was at one time spoken French but was of rare occurrence.

douceur Literally, 'sweetness (of, *e.g.*, honey); mildness, gentleness'. Often used as a euphemism for 'sweetener' in the sense 'bribe'. See *pourboire, below*.

> 'The acceptance-in-lieu procedure incorporates tax benefits for owners and a 'douceur' arrangement to encourage them to dispose of their property to public institutions': *National Heritage Fund* (Command Paper 7428, 4 (1979). 'The value of the tax '*douceur*', or sweetener, can easily be outweighed by a higher price from an American institution': *The Listener* 6 Jan. 9/3 (1985). 'The curator may be able to arrange a private treaty sale with the vendor, whereby the Treasury agrees to waive tax and the vendor gets a 25 per cent *douceur*.': *The Times*, 20th October 14/5 1988.

doyen Literally, 'dean'. The senior member of a body. The French word is used for the diplomatist who has been longest *en poste (q. v.)* of the members of the *Corps Diplomatique* accredited to a Court or Capital City. In certain posts the Papal Nuncio is *ex officio* the Doyen. In extended use, the title is honorary or figurative.

> 'Ursula Howells was born in London on September 17 1922 and educated at St Paul's Girls' School, where her father, the musician and composer Herbert Howells, a doyen of English church music, taught music for 26 years': Obituary of Ursula Howells, *The Daily Telegraph*, 1st November 2005.

Dreyfusard 'A defender or supporter of Captain Alfred Dreyfus (1859-1935), a Frenchman of Jewish descent, an officer in the French army, who was convicted of treason in 1894 and declared innocent in 1906': *OED*.

droit de [du] seigneur 'An alleged custom of mediæval times by which the feudal lord might have sexual intercourse with the bride of a vassal on the wedding-night, before she cohabited with her husband': *OED*. That this preposterous notion should still be on the lips of people in the 21st century is a reproach to our standards of education and a slur on our fair-mindedness. For a scholarly exposition of the deplorable travesty of history that characterizes the propagation of this fatuous fable, see Alain Bureau, *Le Droit de Cuissage: La Fabrication d'un Mythe*; Paris: Albin Michel (1995), translated by Lydia G Cochrane, *The Lord's First Night: The Myth of the 'Droit de Cuissage'*; University of Chicago Press (1998).

duvet 'A quilt stuffed with eider-down or swan's-down': *OED*. Not a new word or idea.

> 'There are now to be sold … some duvets for bed covering': Samuel Johnson, *The Idler*, No 40 ¶4 (1758).

eau de Cologne 'A perfume consisting of alcohol and various essential oils, originally (and still very largely) made at Cologne': *OED*. Pronounced as anglicized /əʊdəkələʊːn/ or, as French, /odəkɔlɔɲ/.

éclair 'A small finger-shaped cake made of *choux*-pastry, and filled with any of various kinds of cream': *OED*.

éclaircissement 'A clearing up or revelation of what is obscure or unknown; an explanation… Very common in 18th c.': *OED*. It is sometimes assumed that the French word for 'The Enlightenment' is *l'Éclaircissement*, since that word perfectly conveys what was intended by the movement. In fact, the French term is *l'Âge* or *Siècle des Lumières*, 'the Age or Century of Lights'.

éclat 'Conspicuous success; universal applause, acclamation. Chiefly in phr. *with (great) eclat*': *OED*. Pronounced /ekla/. Fundamentally, the word in this sense means 'burst' or 'outburst', as in 'of acclaim, dissatisfaction, laughter, etc', and, as borrowed and used, 'an outburst of praise, approval, congratulation, etc', but not 'of disapproval, dissent, etc'.

'Écrasez l'infâme!' 'Quoi que vous fassiez, écrasez l'infâme, et aimez qui vous aime', 'Whatever you do, crush the infamy and love those who love you!': Voltaire in a letter to Monsieur d'Alembert, 28th November 1762, in Voltaire Foundation (ed), *Complete Works,* vol 25 (1973). *L'infâme* was, of course, the Catholic Church, to which Voltaire was implacable opposed.

élan Originally, an impetuous rush (of, for example, troops). Derived ultimately from *élancer*, 'to throw a lance' (*Hatzfeld-Darmesteter*). Chiefly abstract in English use, denoting ardour, impetuousness, vivacity, brilliance.

élan vital 'In the philosophy of Henri Bergson (1859-1941), a vital impulse or life force, of which we are aware intuitively; *specifically*, an original impetus of life supposed to have brought about the variations which during the course of evolution produced new species; a creative principle found in all living beings. Hence *generically*, any mysterious vital principle': *OED*.

élite 'The choice part or flower (of society, or of any body or class of persons)': *OED*. The word is a nominal use of the feminine adjective (*partie* or *section* understood) from an obsolete past participle of *élire*, 'to choose or select; to elect'. The contemporary past participle of the verb is *elu*. See *congé d'élire* in the Law French Appendix, *below*.

embarras du choix A superfluity of choices.

'Embarras des Richesses' ('a superfluity of good things'). The title of a play (1726) by the Abbé d'Alleinval (1700-53).

embonpoint A masculine noun meaning plumpness, a well-nourished appearance of body in a complimentary or euphemistic sense. From the phrase *en bon point*. In place of an adjective, the phrase *être en bon point* is used. (The presence of the letter *m* is anomalous, but, since nasalization extinguishes the difference in sound between *m* and *n*, the philologists and lexicographers do not comment on the anomaly.

embouchure Grove's Dictionary of Music (1954 edn) defines *embouchure* as the part of a musical instrument applied to the mouth; the disposition of the lips, tongue and other organs necessary for producing a musical tone. The word is one of the many proofs that, if French has not existed, it would have been necessary to invent it, for, to English-speakers, there is simply no other word for *embouchure* than *embouchure*.

en famille In or with the family, as one of the family, at home; informally.

'En garde!' A warning in fencing and other contexts to be on guard.

en masse In a mass, in bulk.

en passant In passing; glancingly.

en route On route.

enceinte Pregnant.

enclave 'A portion of territory entirely surrounded by foreign dominions': *OED*. The French possessions of Pondicherry, Karaikal, and Mahé were among the foreign *enclaves* in the Indian sub-continent, as were the Portuguese possessions of Goa, Damão and Diu. If the word is considered to be naturalized, it is pronounced /ˈɛnkleɪːv/. If it is considered to have remained purely French, it is pronounced /ɑ̃klav/.

Encyclopédie, l' An immense publishing enterprise, the most ambitious of the entire 18th century. The *Encyclopédie ou Dictionnaire raisonné des Sciences, des Arts, et des Métiers* (1751-1765) embodied and promoted virtually every idea and ideal of the Enlightenment. Launched in 1751 under the tutelage of Jean le Rond d'Alembert (1717-83) and Denis Diderot (1713-84), it was originally intended to be an adaptation for French eyes of Ephraim Chambers's *Cyclopedia* but it grew much beyond the compass of that work of reference. The range of its subject-matter and the depth of knowledge discernible in some of its entries, primarily those of a technical and even scientific nature, elicit wonderment and admiration, even today. So identified did the *Encyclopédie* become with the *Philosophes* (*q.v.*) that the word *Encyclopédiste* became synonymous with *Philosophe*.

> 'The vast undertaking of the Encyclopedia': Edmund Burke, *Reflections on the Revolution in France*, Works, V, 207 (1790).

encore One of the mysteries of language is how English audiences came to ask for a repetition of a musical performance by using the French word *encore* in a way never used by the French in recorded history. See *bis, below*.

enfant terrible A child who embarrasses his elders by untimely remarks; a person who compromises his associates or his party by unorthodox or ill-considered speech or behaviour; loosely, one who acts unconventionally; a 'loose cannon'. The name of a play (*Les Enfants Terribles* ,1929, subsequently filmed) by Jean Cocteau (1889-1963). The name *Les Enfants Terribles* was associated with a series of prints by Sulpice Guillaume Chevalier Gavarni, *dit* Paul Gavarni (1804-1866).

'Enfer, c'est les autres, l' '. From J. P. Sartre's play *Huis-Clos* (1944), sc 5. 'It's the other people who are hell'.

enjambement 'The continuation of a sentence beyond the second line of a couplet. Now also applied less restrictedly to the carrying over of a sentence from one line to the next': *OED.*

> 'It [the couplet] was turned by enjambements into something very like rhythmic prose. George Saintsbury, *Dryden*, 17 (1881). 'I use the term enjambement by itself in its largest sense, that of the running over of the sentence from one line to another. The word is often used by writers on prosody with the narrower force which it originally had, that of the running over of a group of closely joined words': *Transactions of the American Philological Association*, LX 202 (1929).

ennui 'The feeling of mental weariness and dissatisfaction produced by want of occupation, or by lack of interest in present surroundings or employments': *OED*. Increasingly, the word is being used in England as a simple synonym for 'boredom', perhaps to distinguish those who experience *ennui* from the generation that is bored *of* everything, rather than bored *with* everything.

ensemble Most often in the phrase *tout ensemble*, taking all the parts of anything together so that each part is considered only in relation to the whole; the general effect (of a person's appearance, a whole work of art, an entire musical performance, etc.). As a noun, the entire body of performers in, for example, a musical work or theatrical production; also called 'the caste'. Used sometimes in a wider sense, to encompass the non-acting members of the company, as well as 'the caste'.

entente 'Understanding', as used as an abbreviation for the understanding, *l'Entente Cordiale*, arrived at between France and England in 1904 owing in large measure to the sensitivity of Edward VII. Also used in a concrete sense of the treaty organizations between countries emerging from the First World War as a result of *ententes cordiales* freely entered into by those successor states.

> 'The Little Entente (Roumania, Czecho-Slovakia, and Jugo-Slavia)': *The Westminster Gazette*, 23rd January, p 1, 1923.

entr'acte The interval (intermission) between two acts of a play in a theatrical performance; a performance of music, dancing, etc., taking place between the acts.

entre nous Literally, 'between ourselves'. In English usage, a mild warning prefacing a remark that what follows is confidential. Thus, as a noun, a confidential aside.

entrecôte A boned steak cut off the sirloin.

entrée The privilege or right of entrance; the right of admission; originally, the privilege of admission to a royal or other court. For an instance of how this acceptation is alive and in use today, see *coterie* in this Lexicon. Also, a dish until recently served between the fish and the joint, but now, as a result of our changed eating habits, often the main dish of the meal. (*Littré* explains *entrées* as 'mets qui se servent au commencement du repas': 'dishes that are served at the beginning of a meal'.)

entrepreneur The word first became acclimatized in England at the beginning of the 19th century, when it meant, originally, one who directed or managed a public musical institution such as a concert-hall. Shortly after its first reception into English, it came to mean what is now called an *impresario*, one who arranges concerts and musical events, coordinating artistes, their agents, theatre and concert-hall managements and publicity campaigns. The theatrical *entrepreneur* is nowadays always called by the specific name of *impresario.*

The word *entrepreneur* has come, in English-speaking countries, to denote a thrusting, innovative businessman willing to take risks.

entresol A storey (US, 'story'), often of reduced headroom, introduced between the ground floor (US, 'first floor') and the first floor (US, 'second floor'). The motivation for introducing an *entresol* is often the architect's desire to maximize interior space without adversely affecting the aesthetics of the exterior. The Italianate word *mezzanine (q.v. below)* is preferred nowadays in England.

environs Only in the plural in English, though still in the singular in contemporary French: the outskirts, surrounding districts, of a town. In English usage, pronounced /ɛn'vaɪronz/.

épater 'Pour épater le bourgeois': see 'Il faut épater le bourgeois' *below.*

épaulette A strap running from collar to shoulder, sewn at the shoulder end and buttoned at the neck end; part of many uniforms and also of items of hiking, etc, apparel to prevent the (vertical) shoulder-straps of haversacks and rucksacks from sliding off the shoulder. There is an anglicized spelling, epaulet, but it is much less common than the spelling ending *-ette.* The accent is very frequently omitted.

épée 'The sharp-pointed sword used in dueling and (blunted) in fencing': *OED.*

epergne In spite of its appearance, this is not a French word. It looks as though it ought to have been derived from the French *épargner*, 'to be sparing', but in fact the word is unknown to the French. (It means a now-obsolete central ornament for the dinner-table, in more recent years often in a branched form, each branch supporting a small dish for dessert or the like, or a vase for flowers. Pronounced /ɪp'ɛɹːn/.

escalope Thin slices of boneless meat (sometimes of fish), often cut as discs or *medaillons*, prepared in various ways,; a special cut of veal taken from the leg (*escalope de veau*). Pronounced /ɛskalɔp/.

espadrille A canvas shoe with soles of twisted rope, originally worn in the Pyrenees.

esprit de corps 'The regard entertained by the members of a body for the honour and interests of the body as a whole, and of each other as belonging to it': *OED.* Pronounced /ɛspʁidəkɔʁ/.

esprit d'escalier 'A retort or remark that occurs to a person after the opportunity to make it has passed' *OED.* In the US, 'latter-wit'.

> 'The witty response one thinks of only when one has left the drawing-room and is already on the way downstairs, in *Paradoxe sur le Comédien* [by Denis Diderot (1713-

84)]:' *Oxford Dictionary of Quotations*, 4th edn (1992).

esquisse A sketch, a rough design. See *bozetto, modello* and *pensiero* in the Italian Lexicon.

estaminet 'Petit café populaire, (surtout dans le Nord': *Le Petit Robert* (1970): 'A small, popular café, above all in the North [of France]'. 'Emprunté du wallon *estaminet*, d'origine inconnue': *Hatzfeld-Darmesteter* (1926): 'Borrowed from the Walloon, of unknown origin'.

'Étonne-moi!' Sergei Diaghilev (1872-1929) to Jean Cocteau, in Wallace Fowlie (ed), *Journals of Jean Cocteau* (1956) ch 1.

Être surprème, l' 'Le 18 floréal de l'an II [7 mai 1794], la Convention, sur la proposition de Robespierre, avait adopté par acclamation un décret dont l'article 1er était ainsi conçu : «Le peuple français reconnaît l'existence de l' Être Suprême et de l'immortalité de l'âme». L'Assemblée avait ordonné en même temps qu'une fête solennelle à l' Être Suprême serait célébrée le 20 prairial [8 juin]': 'On the 18th floréal of the year II [7th May 1794], the Convention, on the proposition de [Maximilien] Robespierre [1758-1794], adopted by acclamation a decree the first article of which was thus formulated: 'The French people recognize the existence of the Supreme Being and the immortality of the soul'. The Assembly ordered at the same time that a solemn *fête* in honour of the Supreme Being should be celebrated on the 20th of prairial [8th June]'.

The religiosity of Maximilien Robespierre was short-lived: he was executed later in the same year. One wonders whether the mass of the French people adapted their familiar phrase 'C'est le bon Dieu qui t'a puni!' to accord with the spirit of the moving times in which they lived, and murmured, on the news of his death, 'C'est le bon Être Suprème qui t'a puni!'

étude A study (*scil*, a room for study). See also *cabinet, below*.

expertise The fund of skill and knowledge a person builds up in a field of interest. By extension, the word also means (in French but only very rarely in English) an appraisement or report in writing resulting from the application of an expert's *expertise* to a given task.

exposé A public statement or disclosure revealing some (discreditable) information not hitherto known.

> '*The Exposé; or, Napoleone Buonaparte unmasked, in a condensed statement of his career and atrocities*' [title]: P Coxe (1809).

fainéant 'One who does nothing; an idler': *OED*. In English, virtually confined only to allusions to *les rois fainéants*, 'the sluggard kings', a designation applied by historians to the later Merovingians: see *les Rois Fainéants, below*. The word is of interest in itself. Traditionally, it has been derived – *e.g.*, by *Hatzfeld-Darmesteter* (1926) – from *fait*, third person singular present tense of *faire*, 'to do' and *néant*, 'nothing'; in truth, it is 'an etymologizing perversion of Old French *faignant* 'sluggard'': *OED*. The word *faignant* is still heard and seen in France as a vulgarism, sometimes spelt *feignant*, the present participle of *faindre*, 'to skulk', with a range of meanings comprising 'malingerer', 'shirker', 'ne'er-do-well', 'shifty, unreliable type'.

fait, au To be thoroughly conversant with a subject; to be well instructed, expert or skilful in a subject.

fait accompli An accomplished fact; a 'done deed'; an action completed (and irreversible) before affected parties learn of it. The pronunciation is /fɛtacõpli/, not /fetacõpli/:that is, *fait* is pronounced almost to rhyme with English 'get', not to rhyme with English 'gate'. See also *fête*.

farouche Fierce, will or savage; shy, timid or coy; unsociable. A horse that is not easily manageable (for hacking, for example) is said to be *farouche*. The word appears to be a feminine adjective but is in fact invariable.

faute de mieux 'For want of better'.

fauteuil An arm-chair. The word is nowadays accepted as a wholly French word, pronounced /fotœj/. When theatres and railway trains (the Brighton and the Bournemouth Belles, for example) had seats available that were fashioned on arm-chairs, they were often referred to as *fauteilles*, pronounced /'fəʊtɪlz/.

faux 'False'. An adjective much used at present by the fashion trade to denote imitation fur, as in 'with faux-fur collar'. Used by transference and figuratively in other contexts.

faux amis Literally, 'false friends'. Words and phrases in French that in appearance resemble English words and phrases but do not mean the same things. Notorious instances abound. For example, the word *eventuellement* does not mean 'eventually' but 'possibly' or 'if the occasion should arise'. Often these *faux amis* are more insidious by being less obvious. We speak of 'the Fashoda Incident' and by doing so we acknowledge the seriousness of the event. To the French, *un incident* is something of minor importance – the sort of thing described to *Madame la Marquise* by *le valet fidèle* as *un incident*. The number of *faux amis* is very great, but there are no fewer than 39,000 websites on the Internet, accessible by keying *Faux amis,* that deal with the topic from every point of view, including the reasons for the presence of these troublesome phenomena in the English language. Only the more notorious are referred to in this Lexicon.

faux pas Literally, 'a false step'; figuratively, a slip, an action offending good manners; formerly, an act that compromises one's reputation, especially a woman's lapse from virtue.

fête A festival held on a parish's patron-saint's day (rare in England and the US); a bazaar-like occasion to raise money for a charitable cause. The pronunciation in England is at the moment inveterately /feɪt/, but with the increasing popularity of foreign travel there is some cause for optimism that it might revert to its proper French pronunciation, /fɛt/. See *fait accompli, above.*

fête champêtre An outdoor entertainment; a garden party.

fiançailles A betrothal; the first stage of 'trothplighting'; 'getting engaged'. Only in the plural. Pronounced /fiɒ̃saɪj/.

fiancé[e] One who is engaged to be married.

filer à l'anglaise To take French leave; to absent oneself without leave.

fille de joie A prostitute.

'Fils de Saint Louis, montez au ciel' : 'Son of St Louis, ascend to heaven!' Words said to have been addressed to Louis XVI as he mounted the scaffold in 1793. Attributed to Henry Essex Edgeworth of Fairmount, l'Abbé Edgeworth de Firmont (1745-1807), the Anglo-Irish priest who was Louis XVI's confessor in his last hours. He left a detailed account of the king's last hours but declared he was too moved by the events to remember whether or not he spoke these words.

fin de siècle Literally, the end of the (nineteenth) century. The phrase is used attributively to convey the notion that the epoch in question was characteristically advanced, modern, or decadent. (See *La Belle Époque, above.*)

flaire A special aptitude for some skill or *métier*.

flâneur Literally, 'one who strolls'. 'A lounger or saunterer, an idle 'man about town' '. 'There is a Jewish freethinker's saying about Paris – *wie Gott in Frankreich*. Meaning that even God took his holidays in France. Why? Because the French are atheists and among them God himself could be carefree, a *flâneur*, like any tourist': Saul Bellow, *Ravelstein*, p 171 (2000).

fleur-de-lys Nowadays, *fleur de lis*, 'lily-flower', 'flower-de-luce'. The name is principally applied to the heraldic lily, which was probably not originally intended to represent that flower but the iris (*Iris pseudacorus*, the flag or water iris), or, alternatively, the top of a sceptre, of a battle-axe or of some other shafted weapon. The fleur-de-lys was borne on the royal arms of France and also on those of the Kings of England until the Peace of Amiens (1801), when the anachronistic title 'King of France' was abandoned.

When many grouped *fleurs-de-lys* appear in armorial bearings (*Azure fleurs-de-lys or semée*) the charge is known as *France Ancient*. When only three appear (*Azure three fleurs-de-lys or*), the charge is known as *France Modern*. The pronunciation in England is most often /flɟłdə'li/, that is, without the final *s*. The final *s* is pronounced in modern French. The fleur-de-lys is the symbol of the international Scouting movement.

film noir A film of a gloomy or fatalistic character.

> 'It [*sc.* a play] tries to be a parody of a film noir': *The Spectator*, 25th July 1958. 'A school-boy adventure story which turns suddenly and surprisingly into a bleak film noir': *The Times*, 9th May 16/4 1, 1960.

fondu[e] Dishes cooked with emphasis on melted cheese, often with egg and sometimes other ingredients, are said to be *fondu*[*e*].

force majeure Literally, 'superior strength'. Irresistible force or overwhelming power.

> '*Force-majeure*, a French commercial term for unavoidable accidents in the transport of goods, from superior force, the act of God, etc': Simmonds, *Dictionary of Trade*, *s. v.* 'Force majeure' (1858).

forte The feminine adjective meaning 'strong'. The French for someone's strong-point is the masculine adjective *fort* used as a substantive. As so often happens, in taking this word *fort* into English as a substantive we have chosen to add an *e* (*cf locale* and *morale*). In consequence, if we pronounce this word /for/ (as it should be pronounced), we are not pronouncing the word as we have chosen to spell it. If, on the other hand, and following the spelling we have chosen, we pronounce it /fort/, as the French *never* do for the substantive, we are speaking a form of jargon that is very difficult to justify. The pronunciation /'fortɪ/ is very frequently heard these days and in fact the latest edition of the OED (Second Edition, 1989) gives it second place in its pronunciations, the first place going to a pronunciation identical with the numeral 40. The pronunciation /'forte/

is, as it happens, the pronunciation of the *Italian* word for one's strong-point, though that usage is not so particularized as in French: it means any of one's strengths as opposed to one's weaknesses.

There is little prospect of correcting the muddle attaching to this word. It seems best to accept that, in English, the word rhymes with 40 and leave it at that.

Foudroyant, le This word is heavily freighted. It is the present participle of the verb *foudroyer*, 'to strike with or as with lightning', but its place in history is as the name of Nelson's flagship in 1799-1800 in the Bay of Naples, during which tour she captured the last French ship to escape from the Battle of the Nile. The word is pronounced, in its anglicized version, /fu'drɔɪənt/, and, as in French, /fudʁwajɔ̃/. The word had a new lease of life as the name of items of furniture at the end of the 19th century. *HMS Foudroyant* was decommissioned and was due to be broken up. A subscription was raised to save her and restore her, Sir Arthur Conan Doyle being among the subscribers. On 16th June 1897, on what was effectively the maiden voyage of the restored ship, she sank in extremely heavy weather off the coast of Blackpool, Lancashire. The vessel could not be salvaged and was broken up. The timber and copper from the wreck were purchased by the firm of Goodhall, Lamb & Heighway Ltd of Manchester and used for the manufacture of items of furniture and decoration. Items purporting to be made from timber and copper from *Foudroyant* often have a certificate attached to the rear reading:

> **Fletcher's Antique Furniture & the 'Foudroyant' Company Limited.** I hereby certify that the Article sold herewith if of timber is made from timber and if of copper is made of copper obtained from Lord Nelson's Flagship 'Foudroyant' And which Ship was wrecked off Blackpool in the County of Lancaster on the sixteenth Day of June, One Thousand Eight Hundred and Ninety Seven.

A number of items of heavy furniture, typically sideboards, were made from the timbers of *Foudroyant* and were themselves known to the trade and their proud owners as 'foudroyants'.

foyer Literally, focal-point, hearth; by extension, home – 'hearth and home'. From an unattested Late Latin *focarium*, from Latin *focus*, 'hearth, fire-place'. The use of *foyer* as the name for a public room arises thus. Originally, *le foyer* was the green-room in French theatres; now, usually, it is a large room in a theatre, concert-hall, etc., to which the audience may retire during the intervals of the performances. Also, the entrance hall of a hotel, restaurant, theatre, etc. In these usages, the pronunciation preserved, on the whole, a French flavour, /fwɑjeɪ/. During the nineteen thirties and forties, the word was adopted by cinema managements for the concourse between the ticket windows and the entrances to the cinema proper. In that usage, the pronunciation was and is, generally, /'fɔːeɪ/, sometimes /'fɔːɪəɹ/.

fracas A disturbance; a noisy quarrel, row or uproar. The pronunciations are, anglicized, /'frækɑː/, and, closer to the French, /frakɑ/. In the USA, very frequently pronounced /'freɪkəs/. For evidence of a Scotch pronunciation, see the quotation below.

> 'Let other Poets raise a fracas / 'Bout vines, an' wines, an' drunken Bacchus': Robert Burns, *Scotch Drink* 1 (1785).

franc-tireur One of a corps of light infantry, originating in the wars of the French

Revolution, and having an organization distinct from that of the regular army. In other registers, they were 'irregulars' and 'guerrilleros' (see *guerilla* in the Spanish Lexicon), and, in more recent times, 'partisans' and 'maquis'. Under the name *franctireur*, irregulars were the nightmare most feared by every adherent to Clausewitz's principles of war: Carl von Clausewitz (1780–1831), *Vom Kriege* (1832).

'Français, Françaises, je vous ai compris' In a speech at Algiers on 4th June 1958, Charles de Gaulle (1890-1970) said, 'Je vous ai compris': *Discours et Messages*, vol 3, p 15 (1970). The quotation merits inclusion largely because de Gaulle proceeded to dismantle *l'Algérie française*, which was certainly not what *les Français et les Français* in his audience on 4th June 1958 had wished to be understood as wishing.

France profonde, la 'Deepest France'. A term enjoying a period of popularity, denoting the aspects of France furthest from the Metropolis and from modern civilization.

frisson An emotional thrill. Satirized as a stock item in romantic fiction as *un frisson d'extase*.

gamin[e] A neglected boy or (much less often) a neglected girl, left to run about the streets; 'a street Arab'. *Gamine* has acquired the meaning of a boyish-looking girl. Audrey Hepburn in *Breakfast at Tiffany's* had the *gamine* look. It is superfluous to add that *gamine* in this modern sense has nothing to do with deprivation.

garage From *garer*, 'to park'. The almost universal pronunciation in England is now /'gærɑːʒ/ and in the USA /gar'ɑːʒ/. A pronunciation based on the analogy with 'porage' (or 'porridge'), /gærɪʤ/, is often heard in England.

garçon Literally, 'boy' but used without unfavorable reaction in order to summon or refer to a waiter.

garigue or **garrigue** See *maquis, below.*

gauche Lacking ease or grace of manner; awkward, clumsy. (*Gauché* means left-handed.)

gaulliste A follower or admirer of General Charles de Gaulle (1890-1970). A member of the political party de Gaulle founded and led, known, ultimately as the *Union des Démocrates pour la République* (UDR).

Gavroche A street urchin, particularly of Paris, after the name of a *gamin (q.v.)* in Victor Hugo's *Les Misérables*. See *poulbot, below*.

gendarme A soldier in a unit employed on police duties. 'From *gendarme*, a sing. formed from the pl *gens d'armes* men of arms; hence a fresh pl. *gendarmes*. Some confusion between these forms is evident in English writers; in mod.Fr. the spelling *gens d'armes* is restricted to the historic sense': *OED*.

genre Strictly, simply 'kind'; 'sort'; 'style'; in a specialized connotation, a particular style or category of works of art; especially a type of literary work characterized by a particular form, style, or purpose.

gigolo Originally, simply a professional male dancing-partner; by extension, an escort; by further extension, a kept man. Now, especially a young man supported financially by an older woman in return for his attentions. It is hard to gain a full appreciation of the force of the word in French without knowing its derivation – the word is formed, completely popularly, as the masculine correlative of *gigole*, a tall, thin woman, a woman of the streets or public dancehalls.

gilet Originally, a man's waistcoat. In recent months, a new garment has appeared in England with this name. It is a sleeveless jacket with a multiplicity of pockets. It appears to have captured the loyalty of the well-bred 'sharp dressers' and of Sloane Rangers (Preppies).

Gobelins Tapestries made at the state-factory of Gobelins in Paris, so named after its founders.

gourmand and **gourmet** In modern English speech and writing, the word *gourmet* tends to be reserved for those who are discerning in their eating, and *gourmand* for those who go for quantity rather than quality. The distinction is not so marked in French usage. For an enlightened discussion of the subject, see *Fowler's Modern English Usage*, ed R W Burchfield, 3rd edn (1996), *s.v. gourmand, gourmet* (pp 338-9).

goût In its original and purely physical sense, the word denotes the faculty of perceiving and discriminating savours. In a more general and aesthetic sense, the predominant one nowadays, the word denotes the faculty of 'fine-art' appreciation; a connoisseur's individual judgement or predilection in such matters. In addition, the word denotes an acute perception of merit in fashion, design and associated spheres, ranging from furniture and furnishings in general to such wearing apparel as shoes and hats. *Goût* by itself denotes 'good taste'.

Grand Guignol A dramatic entertainment in which short pieces of a sensational or horrific kind are played successively. *Le Grand Guignol* was a theatre in Paris where this type of entertainment was first produced. (The word *Guignol* by itself means a Punch & Judy Show.)

grand mal, le 'General convulsive epilepsy with loss of consciousness; *epilepsis gravior*. Sometimes artificially induced as part of electro-shock treatment': *OED*. *Cf petit mal, le, below*.

grand seigneur 'Great lord', often said derisively of one who adopts airs and graces, who professes claims to noble birth or who spends money in a lordly way.

grand sérieux, au 'In all seriousness'. The construction is 'to treat, take a matter, a person, etc, *au grand sérieux*.

grande horizontale The noun *horizontale* is an old-fashioned but urbane euphemism for 'prostitute'. *Une grande horizontale* was a prostitute with a prestigious *clientèle*.

gros bétards, les A pejorative name for the inhabitants of Great Britain. It is an appellation often triggered off by sight of the International Oval 'GB' on British cars.

gratin, au Dishes are called *au gratin* that have a light crust on their surfaces, now usually formed by a sprinkling of breadcrumbs and/or grated cheese browned in the oven or under the grill.

gratin, le 'The upper crust', *scil*, of society.

Grevisse, le *Le Grevisse* is a remarkable compilation of, arguably, all the rules governing French grammar. Its full title is *Le Bon Usage : Grammaire Française*. It is published by Éditions Duculot, Paris and Louvain-la-Neuve. It was compiled in 1936 by Maurice Grevisse, a Belgian, and, in its 13th edition (1993), it is edited by André Goosse, who is also a Belgian. It runs to 1762 pages. It is safe to say that no real problem associated with French grammar is left undiscussed.

Thorny questions concerning the plurals of compound nouns such as *clin d'œil* are rationally discussed: should the plural be *clins d'œil* or *clins d'yeux*? In favouring the former against writers who say it depends on how many eyes are winking, *le Grevisse* remarks, ' 'Si l'on considère les deux yeux…' , disent les grammairiens, mais il est douteux que les auteur applicant réelement cette distinction': *s.v.* 'Marques du pluriel', § 517, p 811: ' 'If one considers the two eyes…' say the grammarians, but it is doubtful whether the authors really apply that distinction.'

A typical instance of the assurance that *le Grevisse* brings to disputed issues can be seen in the following: 'Dans le composés formés d'un mot invariable et d'un nom, le nom seul prend la marque du pluriel: *Des arriere-boutiques, des haut-parleurs, des non-valeurs, des non-lieux, des quasi-délits. Des à-coups, des après-dîners, des avant-scènes, des en-têtes* (que *Littré* laissait invariable), *des sans-culottes*': 'In the combinations formed from an invariable word and a noun, the noun alone takes the mark of the plural, etc'.

Le Grevisse is far from being a sterile embalming of the French language. On the contrary: it is shot through with shafts of penetrating humanity. 'Vaugelas exigeait *deux arc-en-ciels* et ecrivait luimême: *Ces chef-d'œuvres*. Quel dommage que l'on ait abandonné une règle si simple!': 'Vaugelas insisted on *deux arc-in-ciels* and himself wrote: *Ces chef-d'œuvres*. What a pity one has abandoned so simple a rule!'

> 'Dans *le Grevisse* il y a beaucoup de portes ouverte sur la liberté at la fantaisie, beaucoup de clins d'œil, de signes de connivence': M. Cardinal, *Mots pour le dire* 235 (1975).

grippe Influenza (from *gripper*, 'to seize'.)

gros bataillons, les. 'On dit que Dieu est toujours pour les gros bataillons': Voltaire, *Lettres. À Monsieur d'Alembert*, 28th February 1762: ('It is said that God is always on the side of the big battalions'). The 1992 edition of *The Oxford Dictionary of Quotations* has, 'Dieu n'est pas pour les gros bataillons, mais pour ceux qui tirent le mieux', 'God is not on the side of the heavy battalions, but of the best shots': and cites 'The Picini Notebooks' *ca* 1735-50 in T. Besterman (ed), *Voltaire's Notebooks* (2nd edn, 1968) vol 2, p 547. As supplementary references, it cites '*Cf* Anouilh 23:2, Bussy-Rabutin 164:19'.

gros-point This term has been imported in two senses: *gros point de Venise*, a type of lace worked in bold relief, originally from Venice; and, in more common use, any of a variety of stitches employed in canvas embroidery. *C f petit-point, below.*

guillemets The signs « and » signifying, primarily, a quotation. Employed almost always in the plurel. Named after a printer, Guillaume, who invented these signs. Pronounced /gijmɛ/. The word *guillemets* also denotes quotation marks ('inverted commas'), sometimes called *les guillemets anglais*. In broad principle, reported speech in, for example, novels, is not furnished with *guillemets* but commences with an em (pica) dash and concludes without any specific sign other than a line-break:

> Et après un court moment de réflexion,
> son regard clair se leva encore une fois,
> interrogateur, sur moi:
> –Et si demain vous rencontriez Mme
> Henriette, par example à Nice, au bras de
> ce jeune homme, la salueriez-vous
> encore?
> –Certainement.
> –Et lui parleriez-vous?
> –Certainement.

> Stefan Zweig, *Vingt-quatre heures de la vie d'une femme,* tr Bournac and Hella, le Livre de Poche (1980) 28.

There is no equivalent, with *guillemets,* of the English practice of using single and double inverted commas. If a quotation is included in reported speech commencing with an em dash, it is enclosed between *guillemets*.

habitué One who is in the habit of frequenting a place.

haleine, une longue Literally, 'a long breath'. Used in expressions such as *un travail de longue haleine,* meaning 'a long and arduous effort'.

Hameau, le 'The Hamlet', a pleasure-park in the grounds of the Palace of Versailles modelled on a idealized country village, in which Marie-Antoinette and her intimates imagined themselves to be simple shepherds and shepherdesses.

hangar A covered space for the parking of vehicles and, almost exclusively in English, for the accommodation of aircraft.

hall Really the English word 'hall', imported into French to denote any large room of a public or large private building. Pronounced /ol/. The Parisian market is *Les Halles,* pronounced /le al/.

Hatzfeld et Darmesteter A celebrated etymological dictionary complied by Adolphe von Hatzfeld (1824-88) and Arsène Darmesteter (1846-1900) and published in two volumes between 1890 and 1900. The Germanic sound of the names of these lexicographers conveys a misleading impression. They were Alsatian Jews. After the death of Darmesteter in 1900, André-Antoine Thomas (1857-1935) succeeded him in the work. Thomas' collaboration is recognized in the edition of 1926. The dictionary is an incomparable source of information on the French language, being at the same time both historically precise and accurate and, given its dates of publication, completely modern in its approach. It is notable for its impeccable etymological methodology and for its imitated pronunciation (the lexicographers' own notation is used).

The greater part of the first volume is taken up with a treatment of the formation of the French language. In itself it is a stunning exemplar of how the French language can be – and is – used to maximum effect. The combination of those two qualities of lucidity and limpidity as manifest in this treatment is hard to equal in the entire conspectus of French literature. The authors' treatment of the French language is emblematic of Rivarol's assertion *Ce qui n'est pas clair n'est pas français*. Their essay perfectly justifies the terse assertion of Stendal: *La seule qualité à chercher dans le style est la clarté.*

haut bourgeois The concept of what constitutes membership of *la bourgeoisie* is fraught with perplexity. See *bourgeois, above.* The term *haut bourgeois* is, however, a valid expression of the difference between the general (albeit disparate) interpretations of the Protean word *bourgeois* and the evident existence of a section of society that, though not in any way aristocratic, is plutocratically rich but *very* far removed from shopkeeping. Perhaps the best English translation (that is, translation into the English of England) of *la haute bourgeoisie* would be 'the upper middle classes', the class that still embraces the best educated members of English society – and that still commands the respect of the majority of the population of England. Some people in England might respect, for instance, Billy Bragg, the agit-prop lead-singer of the once noteworthy band *The Red Wedge*, but would immediately move their bank-account if a new manager resembling Billy Bragg were posted into their branch.

haute couture The pinnacle of *couture.* See *couturier, above.*

hauteur Literarily, 'height'. In English, used for 'haughtiness', from the same root.

Heloïse Abelard's mistress. A correspondent has reported having encountered 'Herlouise'.

'Héros pour son valet', in full, 'Il n'y a point de héros pour son valet de chambre': Mme Cornuel in *Lettres de Mlle Aissé à Madame C (1787)*, Letter 13 'De Paris, 1728'. 'No man is a hero to his valet'. The word *héros* is aspirated.

homard, le The lobster. Pronounced /lə omaʁ/.

'Homme malade, l'' 'Nous avons sur les bras un homme malade – un homme gravement malade': 'We have on our hands a sick man – a very sick man'. Reputed to have been said of Turkey, 'the sick man of Europe', by Nicholas I of Russia(1796-1855). There is some conflict about what was actually said, and about who said it. In the second edition (1953) of the *Oxford Dictionary of Quotations*, the reference for this quotation reads '*Parliamentary Papers. Accounts and Papers*, vol lxxi, pt 5. *Eastern Papers*, p 2. *Sir G. H. Seymour to Lord John Russell,* 11th January 1853'. In the fourth edition (1994), the words attributed to Nicholas I are, *only*, 'Turkey is a dying man. We may endeavour to keep him alive, but we shall not succeed. He will, he must, die': In F. Max Müller (ed), *Memoirs of Baron Stockmar* (translated by G. A. M. Müller, 1873) vol 2, p 107.

It is clear that the matter cannot be regarded as completely settled. In a book review published on 8th March 2001 in *The New York Review of Books*, Christophe de Bellaigue wrote:

> I am indebted to Lady de Bellaigue, of the royal archives at Windsor Castle, for providing me with a copy of the letter, written by Sir G. H. Seymour, British envoy to St. Petersburg, in 1853, which has formed the basis of this erroneous attribution. In this letter, which describes a meeting held between Seymour and the Tsar, Nicholas I is reported to have referred to the Ottoman Empire not, as legend has it, as 'the sick man of Europe,' but as a 'man,' who 'has fallen into a state of decrepitude.' *NYRB*, Vol 48, No 4, 8th March 2001.

Christophe de Bellaigue wrote a letter to the Editors of *The New York Review of Books* on 5th July 2001 as follows:

> My thanks to Professor David M. Goldfrank of Georgetown University for putting me at least half right on the origin of the epithet 'the sick man of Europe,' commonly attributed to Tsar Nicholas I with regard to the Ottoman Empire of the mid-nineteenth century ['Turkey's Hidden Past,' *NYR*, March 8]. The source to which I referred when questioning this attribution was a letter written by Sir G. H. Seymour, British envoy to St. Petersburg, to Lord John Russell, on January 22, 1853. In this letter, Seymour reports that the Tsar, in the course of a meeting between the two men, referred to the empire as a 'man' who has fallen into 'a state of decrepitude.'
>
> Professor Goldfrank has guided me to an earlier letter written to Russell by Seymour, in relation to a meeting that had taken place on January 9. In this

> letter, Seymour reports that the Tsar described the Ottoman Empire as 'a sick man – a very sick man.' This leaves us a step closer, but a step short, of 'the sick man of Europe' to which my article referred. *NYRB*, Vol 48, No 11, 5th July 2001.

It seems the matter has rested there. Perhaps this present entry will provoke a renewal of interest.

homme moyen sensuel 'But this whole drama… may best be described as the theatre of the *homme sensual moyen*, the average sensual man, … whose ideal is the free, gay, pleasurable life of Paris': Matthew Arnold, *Irish Essays,* 1882, p 230. It seems that the phrase *homme moyen sensuel* is Arnold's own.

Honi soit qui mal y pense' The motto of the Order of the Garter. Approximately, 'Shame on him who thinks it shame'. The origins of the motto, and indeed of the choice of title itself for the Order, are, in the words of Nancy Mitford's character speaking of the origins of the Radlett family, 'perdues dan les brumes de l'antiquité'. The explanations over the years have been laborious and inconclusive. The following is characteristic.

> In 1349…Edward [III] instituted the Order of the Garter. The origin of this illustrious Order has been much disputed. By some writers it has been ascribed to Richard Coeur de Lion, who is said to have girded a leathern band round the legs of his bravest knights in Palestine. By others it has been asserted that it arose from the word 'garter' having been used as a watchword by Edward at the battle of Cressy. Others again have stoutly maintained that its ringlike form bore mysterious reference to the Round Table. But the popular legend, to which, despite the doubts thrown upon it, credence still attaches, declares its origin to be as follows: Joan, Countess of Salisbury, a beautiful dame, of whom Edward was enamoured, while dancing at a high festival accidentally slipped her garter, of blue embroidered velvet. It was picked up by her royal partner, who, noticing the significant looks of his courtiers on the occasion, used the words to them which afterwards became the motto of the Order, 'Honi soit qui mal y pense', adding that 'in a short time they should see that garter advanced to so high honour and estimation as to account themselves happy to wear it': Wm Harrison Ainsworth, *Windsor Castle,* III ii (1843).

Greimas, A-J, *Dictionnaire de l'ancien français jusqu'au milieu du XIVe siècle* (Paris: Larousse, 1980) ascribes the origin of the motto to the mediaeval poem *Pearl.* For further reading: Henriette Walter, *Honni [sic] soit qui mal y pense,* Éd. Robert Laffont, 2001, p 364.

hors de combat 'Out of the fight'; no longer able to oppose.

hors d'œuvre Literally, 'outside (the) work'. 'An extra dish served as a relish to whet the appetite between the courses of a meal or (more generally) at its commencement': *OED*. The singular and plural are the same

hôtel A large private residence, a town m ansion; a public official residence; *hôtel de ville*, the mansion house of a *maire*, a town hall. *Hôtel-Dieu*, a hospital, recalling the religious origins of these establishments. Nowadays, in England, an establishment for the lodging and entertainment of strangers and travellers, an inn, especially one with pretensions to superiority. The pronunciation in French is sometimes /otɛl/ and sometimes /ɔtɛl/. In English, it is nowadays almost always /həʊ'tɛl/, sometimes /əʊ'tɛl/. Though not recognized by the dictionaries, the pronunciation /ə'tɛl/ is sometimes heard from speakers who use the Received Pronunciation, (*q.v.*).

huis clos Literally, 'closed door'. The noun *huis* comes from the Latin *osmium.* The expression *huisclos* means, literally, 'doors closed' and indicates, for example, 'behind closed doors', in camera, 'a private discussion or viewing of paintings'. In this and similar expressions, the *h* of *huis* is unaspirated.

'Hypocrisie est un hommage...' 'L'hypocrisie est un hommage que le vice rend à la vertu': Duc de la Rochefoucauld (1613-80), *Maximes*, 218 (1678): 'Hypocrisy is the tribute vice pays to virtue'.

'Hypocrite lecteur, – mon semblable, mon frère'; 'Hypocrite reader, – my likeness, – my brother': Charles Baudelaire (1821-67), *Les fleurs du mal* (1857), 'Au lecteur'. Quoted in the first section of T. S. Eliot's *The Waste Land.*

idée fixe Literally, 'a fixed idea'. In some senses, the expression could be a synonym for 'an obsession', but English has found a slot for *idée fixe* that is free from the blame of an obsession. No-one would willingly admit to entertaining an obsession, but almost everyone would cheerfully own to having not a few *idées fixes.*

'Il faut cultiver notre jardin'. In full: 'Cela est bien dit, répondit Candide, mais il faut cultiver notre jardin': Voltaire, *Candide*, ch 30 (1759). Approximately, 'That's all very well, but we mustn't forget to look after our own affairs!'

'Il faut épater le bourgeois': 'One must astonish the bourgeois': attributed to Charles Baudelaire (1821-67), but it seems likely that Baudelaire was quoting his contemporary, Alexandre Privat d'Anglemont (*circa* 1820-59), who had put into the mouth of his character Monsieur Auguste this paean, 'Je les ai épatés, les bourgeois': *Paris Anecdote* (1854), Monselet's edn of 1885, p 76: 'I've astonished them, the bourgeois'. (There is something missing from the English words normally used to translate *épater.* 'Astonish' seems too mild. 'Shock' and 'scandalize' create a falsely moralistic note. Perhaps we can learn something from an older use of the verb *épater*: *épater une verre,* meaning 'to break off the foot or base from a wine-glass'.)

'Il faut manger pour vivre et non pas vivre pour manger': Molière, *L'Avare*, III, i (1669): 'One should eat to live and not live to eat'.

Il faut profiter A common remark: 'We must take advantage [of it – an event, an incident, etc]'.

'Il y a en Angleterre soixante sectes religieuses différentes et une seule sauce' : 'There are in England sixty different religious sects but only one sauce'. Attributed to the Neapolitan diplomatist Francesco Caraccioli (1752-99). See *Notes & Queries*, December 1968.

'Ils ne passeront pas!' 'They shall not pass!' An exclamation used by French soldiers at the defence of Verdun in 1916, variously attributed to Maréchal Henri-Philippe Pétain (1856-1951), 'le Héros de Verdun', and to Général Robert Nivelle (1856-1924). During the Spanish Civil War the Left-Wing forces used the slogan 'No pasarán!': Dolores Ibárruri, 'La Pasionaria' (1895-1989: see the Spanish Lexicon) in a radio broadcast, Madrid, 19th July 1936, in *Speeches and Articles* p 7 (1938).

'Ils n'ont rien appris, ni rien oublié' ; 'They have learnt nothing and forgotten nothing'. Général Charles-François du Perrier

Dumouriez (1739-1823) said of Louis XVIII's Court at the time of the Declaration of Verona, September 1795, 'Les courtisans qui l'entourent n'ont rien oublier et n'ont rien appris': 'The courtiers who surround him have forgotten nothing and learnt nothing': *Examen impartial d'un Écrit intitulé Declaration de Louis XVIII* (1795) p 40. Quoted by Bonaparte, with reference to the returned *émigrés*, in his *Proclamation au Peuple française* of 1st March 1815 on his return from Elba: 'Depuis le peu de mois qu'ils règnent, ils vous ont convaincus qu'ils n'ont rien oublié ni rien appris': 'In the few months that have reigned, they have convinced you that they have forgotten nothing and learnt nothing'. It can, of course, be argued that the ferocity of *la Terreur Blanche* and the implausibility of *la Chambre Introuvable* were lessons learnt solely from the Revolution, for there was nothing an any way comparable under the *Ancien Régime.*

There is a strong oral tradition that Charles-Maurice de Talleyrand-Perigord (1754-1838) said much the same: 'Ils n'ont rien appris, ni rien oublié', which was attributed to Talleyrand by the Chevalier de Panat, January 1796. See A. Sayons (ed), *Mémoires et correspondence de Mallet du Pan,* vol 2, p 196 (1851).

Immortels, les A term often applied to members of l'Académie Française. The name probably derives from the words *À l'Immortalité* engraved on the Academy's first seal. In his novel, *Les Immortals* Alphonse Daudet (1840-1897) fiercely satirizes *les Académiciens.* (A more sardonic interpretation of the title is that *Académiciens* are elected and salaried for life.)

impasse 'A road or way having no outlet; a blind alley, *cul-de-sac.* Also *fig.*, a position from which there is no way of escape': *OED* But in English usage the word *impasse* much more closely adopts the secondary, figurative signification of the word, 'une situation sans issue favorable', or even conveys the notion of a complete standstill or deadlock. See *cul-de-sac, above.*

'Impossible n'est pas français', correctly, *'Ce n'est pas possible, m'écrivez-vous: cela n'est pas français'*: Bonaparte to Comte Le Marois: *Petit dictionnaire des expressions nées de l'histoire,* Tallandier (1993) p 259. See also … *n'est pas français, below.*

'In a room alone' Pascal (1623-62) wrote, 'Tout le malheur des homme vient d'une seule chose, qui est de ne savoir pas demeurer en repos dans une chambre': 'All the misfortunes of men come from one single thing, which is not to know how to be in repose in a room'.

ingénue 'An artless, innocent girl or young woman; also, the representation of such a character on the stage, or the actress who plays the part': *OED.* As with *naïf/naïve (cf, below),* only the feminine form is used in instinctively spoken and written English, though careful persons observe a distinction.

> 'When attacked sometimes, Becky had a knack of adopting a demure ingénue air, under which she was most dangerous': W M Thackeray, *Vanity Fair,* 51, 454 (1848).

insouciance 'Carelessness, indifference, unconcern': *OED.* The use of the word *insouciance* in English when there are the three words given by the *OED* is an object-lesson in why English-speakers are so avid to use French words. As used by English-speakers, *insouciance* implies a degree of carefree nonchalance completely absent from 'carelessness' and 'indifference' and only barely present in 'unconcern'. We thus have an extra word at no expense.

Internationale, l' A revolutionary battle-song composed by Eugène Pottier in 1871 and adopted by French Socialists and subsequently by others.

> '*The Internationale,* the hymn of the Labour movement of the world': Isaac Deutscher, *Stalin*, 12, 491 (1949).

invalid The English word for a sick person has, in England, its final syllable rhyming with 'deed' and, in the US, its final syllable rhyming with 'did'. In both cases the first syllable is now the only one carrying the stress.

'J'accuse!' An outstandingly effective open letter in favour of Alfred Dreyfus from the novelist Émile Zola (1840-1902) to the President of the French Republic was published in *l'Aurore* on 13th January 1898. It ended with several paragraphs inculpating the Army of a number of grave offences, each paragraph beginning 'J'accuse!', whence the name by which this superb piece of journalism has become known to the world.

jalousie 'A blind or shutter made with slats which slope upwards from without, so as to exclude sun and rain, and admit air and some light': *OED*. There is another important objective in installing *jalousies. Hatzfeld-Darmesteter* (1926) has: 'Treillis de bois, de fer, contrevent formé de planchettes parallèles que l'on place devant une fenêtre et derriere lequel on peut voir sans être vu': 'Latticework of wood or iron. A shutter formed of parallel laths that one places in front of a window, behind which one can see without being seen'. *Jalousies* are included in the design of the women's galleries in many Sephardic and Oriental synagogues. (Etymologists tend to shy away from answering the question on every inquirer's lips, 'Why call these shutters or *louvres* by the odd name *jalousies*?' There seems to be no answer.)

jardinière A female gardener, a gardener's wife, a pot or stand for flowers; an ornamental receptacle, pot, or stand for the display of growing flowers within doors, or on a window-sill, balustrade, or other part of a building; also for the display of cut flowers for the decoration of the table. Sometimes, especially in the USA, called 'a planter'.

'Je dis de la prose!' 'Par ma foi! Il y a plus de quarante ans que je dis de la prose sans que j'en susse rien': Monsieur Jourdain in Moliere, *Le Bourgeois Gentilhomme*, II, iv (1671): 'By my faith, for more than forty years I've been speaking prose without realizing it!'

'Je est un autre'; 'I is another'. Arthur Rimbaud (1854-1891) so wrote in a letter to Paul Demeny of 15th May 1871. His very ungrammatical phrase has been compared by some people to the philosophy of Freud (*Das Ich und das Es*). The interpretation of these abstractions is attended by very considerable difficulty. One might say much the same of Pascal's 'Le moi est haïssable' (*q.v., below*), A close study of the works of Blaise Pascal might well induce the reader to conclude that the last thing Pascal *really* thought of himself was that he was hateable. It is an uphill task to persuade people to re-assess Pascal. A good starting-point would be Malcolm Hay, *The Prejudices of Pascal,* Neville Spearman, London: 1962. And there is a degree of banality about Descartes' 'Je pense, donc je suis' – 'Cogito, ergo sum' (*q.v.*) that is paralleled as a platitude only by Pascal's 'L'homme n'est qu'un roseau, le plus faible de la nature; mais c'est un roseau pensant'; 'Man is only a reed, the weakest in Nature, but he is a thinking reed'. It is manifestly absurd to suggest that man is in any sense the weakest of *anything*. Though man might not be a good steward of all he possesses in Nature, there can be no doubt that he is the *strongest* being in nature. The image – the metaphor – of the broken reed served well in Isa 36:6: *Ecce, confidis super baculum harundineum confractum istum super Aegyptum, cui si innisus fuerit homo intrabit in manu eius et perforabit eam; sic Pharao rex Aegypti omnibus qui confidunt in eo*: 'Lo, thou trustest in the staff of this broken reed, on Egypt; whereon if a man lean, it will go into his hand, and pierce it: so is Pharaoh king of Egypt to all that trust in him'. But how can it be said that the metaphor of the reed is viable when there is no conceivable reference to sustaining the walker? Would a *thinking* reed, still handicapped as it would be by its inherent physical weakness, be of any comfort to the walker? Would a *thinking* reed be a viable surrogate for the 'rod and staff' that comfort the sojourner in Ps 23:4 – *Virga tua et baculus tuus ipsa consolabuntur me*: 'Thy rod and thy staff they comfort me'? And if Pascal has *not* chosen to use the reed as a metaphor for something to sustain mankind, then for what reason *has* he chosen it?

Blind to its inappropriateness, Pascal seizes on an image that immediately comes to mind: *Quid existis in desertum videre? Harundinem vento moveri?*: 'What went ye out into the desert to see? A reed shaken with the wind?'. Without regard to the appropriateness of the metaphor, Pascal assures us that, despite our innate frailty, we are 'thinking reeds'. Really? Are we *really* meant to regard that assurance as a penetrating insight into the meaning of life?

Je m'en fichisme 'Couldn't-care-less-ism'. 'Attitude d'indifference envers ce qui devrait intéresser': *le Petit Robert* (1970): 'An attitude of indifference towards what ought to interest one'. A risky locution: the verb *ficher* is here a euphemism.

'Je pense, donc je suis'. Better known among English-speakers in Descartes' own Latin translation, 'Cogito, ergo sum': 'I think, therefore I am'.

> 'Remarquant que cette vérité : Je pense, donc je suis, *cogito, ergo sum*, était si ferme et assurée, que toutes les plus extravagantes suppositions des sophistes n'étaient pas capables de l'ébranler, je jugeai que je pouvais la recevoir sans scrupule comme le premier principe de la philosophie que je cherchais': René Descartes (1596-1650): *Le Discours de la Méthode,* pt 1 (1637). 'Noting that this truth: 'I think, therefore I am', *Cogito, ergo sum,* is so firm and assured that not all the most extravagant suppositions of the sophists were capable of shaking it, I judge that I might receive it without scruple as the first principle of the philosophy I search for'.

Very many will doubt, on first principles, the validity of that contention. Are we thus to assume that idiots do not exist, idiots defined as 'those so deficient in mental or intellectual ability as to be incapable of the ordinary acts of thinking'? We might recall the means by which Dr Johnson convinced Boswell of the implausibility of Bishop Berkeley's tenets (Boswell's *Life*, 6th August, 1763). We might ask the Cartesian to kick an idiot – in the sure and certain knowledge that the idiot would immediately demonstrate to the Cartesian that thinking and existing are by no means interdependent.

Je ne sais quoi 'Chose qu'on ne peut pas définer ou exprimer, bien qu'on en sente nettement l'existence ou les effets'; *le Petit Robert* (1970): 'A thing that one cannot define or explain, though one clearly feels its existence or its effects'.

jeu d'esprit 'A play or playful action in which some cleverness is displayed; now usually, a play of wit in literary composition; a witty or humorous trifle': *OED.*

jeu de mots A play on words; a pun. See *calembour* and *contrepêterie, above.*

jeune premier An actor who plays the part of the principal lover or young hero; the juvenile lead. So *jeune première,* the performer of the corresponding female part.

jeunesse dorée Literally, 'gilded youth'. Historically, a name applied to a group of fashionable counterrevolutionaries formed after the fall of Robespierre; 'now, young people of wealth and fashion': *OED.*

joie de vivre Literally, 'joy of living'. 'A feeling of healthy enjoyment of life; exuberance, high spirits.

> 'He had laughed at Sophie's spiteful jokes, of which the sheer *joie de vivre* had seemed to lessen the bite': Iris Murdoch, *Sacred & Profane Love Machine,* p 96.

jolie laide Literally, 'pretty and ugly'. 'A woman or girl who is attractive in spite of not being pretty': *OED.* A useful term for which there is no possible English equivalent. Pronounced /ʒɔli lɛd/.

> 'One was a beauty or a *jolie-laide* and that was that': Nancy Mitford, *Love in a Cold Climate,* I. viii. 87 (1949).

jongleur In historical contexts, a minstrel; nowadays, in French, a juggler or tumbler. In English, the usage is restricted to a convenient collective name for the mediaeval *troubadours* and *trouvères* who sang in the courts of Europe the wealth of music we are still recovering in the 21st century.

Kir A name for a mixture of dry white wine and *crème de cassis* (a blackcurrant liqueur), served as an *aperitif.* It owes its strange name to the surname of Félix *Kir* (1876-1968), a hero of the Resistance, a canon of Dijon cathedral, and (surprisingly, in a secularist state) *Maire* of Dijon, who is said to have invented the recipe. In fact, the drink had long been known, particularly in the South of France, as *un blanc cassis* (or sometimes as *un blancass*). There seems to be some substance, however, in the tale that *le chanoine* Kir was troubled, in one year of his tour of duty as *Maire* of Dijon, with a gross over-production in the *Dijonnais* of dry white wine and also, at the same time, a gross over-production of blackcurrants. He therefore, it is said, devoted his prodigious energies to popularizing *le blanc cassis.* If this story is substantially true, Kir's marketing flair should not go unnoticed, for the growth in popularity of *le Kir* is unprecedented. It is fortunate that the over-production should have been of blackcurrants and not of the mustard flower that produces *la moutarde de Dijon,* since, otherwise, we might have been drinking a fiery rot-gut compounded of dry white wine and mustard-powder. There was even a ready-made name for such a concoction, *un moutard,* an existing word meaning 'a young lad, a nipper; an urchin; *a brat*'.

The mixture of champagne and *crème de cassis* is called *un Kir royal.*

> 'Around Dijon it [*sc.* Cassis] is used as a popular aperitif, a little Cassis being put in a glass that is then filled with a fairly neutral, dry white wine … Also called kir': Alexis Lachine, *Encyclopaedia of Wines,* p 162 (1967).

'La Révolution dévorât ses enfants' 'Il a été permis de craindre que la Révolution, comme Saturne, dévorât successivement tous ses enfants'; 'It has been permitted to fear that the Revolution, like Saturn, would devour each of her children in turn': in Alphonse de Lamartine, *Histoire des Girondins,* bk 38, ch 20 (1847).

la vie en rose Life as seen through rose-coloured spectacles.

laisser-passer Literally, 'allow to pass'. See the quotation below.

> 'A permit to travel or to enter a particular area': R. G. Feltham, *A Diplomatic Handbook.*, p 178.

laissez-faire Literally, *laissez,* the imperative of laisser, 'to let', and *faire,* ' to do', *i.e.*, 'let (people) do (as they think best)'. A phrase epitomizing the principle that governments should not interfere with the action of individuals, and especially not in industrial affairs and in trade'. *'Laissez faire et laissez passer'* was the maxim of the French free-trade economists of the 18th century; it is usually attributed (*by, e.g., Littré, s.v. laisser,*) to Vincent de Gournay (1712-59), who was an *Intendant du Commerce* and one of the founders, with François Quesnay (1694-1774), of the school of *les Physiocrates*, or *les Économistes*. The motto '*Laissez faire, laissez passer*' is credibly attributed to Gourney, though, anomalously, he left absolutely nothing at all in writing. The doctrines of the (by now international) school of laissez-faire depend essentially on the operation of Adam Smith's 'invisible hand'.

It should be said, also, that the roots of the *laissez-faire* philosophy lie deep in the French character. In 1664 Jean-Baptiste Colbert (1619-83), Louis XIV's great finance minister, invited a number of deputies of commerce to his house to discuss means whereby the government could help commerce. The consensus was, 'Laissez-nous-faire!'; 'Let us alone!': *Mémoires et Journal inédit du Marquis d'Argenson* (edn 1858), vol 5, p 364.

Lalique An adjective used to designate jewellery and decorative glassware by or after the manner of René Lalique (1860-1945), a French designer of jewels and glassware. Sometimes the word with a lower-case initial letter is used to convey the notion, merely, 'after the school of René Lalique', at other times to suggest a spurious attribution.

lamé 'A material consisting of silk or other yarns interwoven with metallic threads': *OED.*

'L'appétit vient en mangeant': 'Appetite comes with eating': François Rabelais (c 1494-1553), *Gargantua*, bk 1, ch 5 (1534).

largesse The *OED* gives the following as its earliest meaning, 'Liberality, bountifulness, munificence', but marks that meaning as *Obsolete*. Nevertheless, those three characteristics remain at the heart of the modern usages of the word *largesse,* as in 'Liberal or bountiful bestowal of gifts; *occas.* lavish expenditure; *concr.* money or other gifts freely bestowed, *e.g.* by a sovereign upon some special occasion of rejoicing or the like': *OED.* 'A generous or plentiful bestowal; something freely bestowed': *OED.* At the root of the word, both literally and figuratively, is the notion of 'broadness' (French, *largeur*). The core meaning is caught in the purely English word 'wideness', as in the popular hymn 'There's a wideness in God's mercy'. (The fully Anglicized spelling 'largess' is less often met with than the French spelling *largesse.*)

Larousse The first edition of Pierre Larousse's *Grand dictionnaire universel du XIXe Siècle* appeared from 1865-90. Since that epoch, *Larousse* has appeared in a number of forms, among them a useful edition with numerous illustrations. This eminent dictionary continues to improve.

layette 'A complete outfit of garments, toilet articles, and bedding for a new-born child': *OED.*

'Le bâton de maréchal' 'Rappelez-vous bien qu'il n'est aucun de vous qui n'ait dans sa giberne le bâton de Maréchal du duc de Reggio; c'est à vous à l'en faire sortir'; 'Remember that there is not one of you who does not carry in his cartridge-pouch the marshal's baton of the Duc de Reggio; it is up to you to bring it forth': Louis XVIII in a speech to the cadets of Saint-Cyr on 9th August 1819, in *le Moniteur universel*, 10th August 1819. The Duc de Reggio whom Louis XVIII was speaking of was Nicolas Charles Oudinot (1769-1851), a courageous commander under Bonaparte but among those who called for his abdication on 4th April 1814. He refused to rally to Bonaparte during the Hundred Days. In recompense, Louis XVIII appointed him Commandant of the *Garde royale* and then of the *Garde nationale de Paris*. In 1839 he was nominated *Grand-Chancelier de la Legion d'Honneur* and in 1842 Governor of *les Invalides*.

The remark is also attributed to Bonaparte (E. Blaze, *La Vie militaire sous l'Empire*, Saint-Cloud, 27 août, 1808).

'Le cœur a ses raisons que la raison ne connaît point'; 'The heart has its reasons that reason knows nothing of': Pascal, *Pensées*, sect 4, no 277 (1670), ed L Brunschvicg, 1909.

'L'état c'est moi' ; 'I am the state': attributed to Louis XIV but no doubt apocryphal. A pronouncement said to have been made before the Parlement de Paris on 13th April 1655; in J. A. Dulaure's *Histoire de Paris*, vol 6, p 298 (1834). In 1792 Maximilien Robespierre (1758-94) said, 'Je ne suis pas ni le courtisan, ni le modérateur, ni le tribun, ni le défenseur du peuple, je suis peuple moi-même': 'I am not the courtier, nor the moderator, nor the tribune, nor the defender of the people, I am the people myself': Speech at the Jacobin Club, 27th April 1792, in G. Laurent (ed), *Le Défenseur de la Constitution*, p 39 (1939).

'Le Congrès ne march pas, il danse': 'The Congress [of Vienna] makes no progress: it dances'. A remark of the Prince de Ligne (1735-1814) to Comte August de La Garde-Chambonas: August de La Garde-Chambonas, *Souvenirs du Congrès de Vienne*, ch 1 (1820).

'L'homme est né libre' 'L'homme est né libre, et partout il est dans les fers'; 'Man is born equal, and is everywhere in chains': Jean-Jacques Rousseau, *Du Contrat social*, ch 1 (1762).

'Le *moi* est haïssable'; 'The *self* is hateful': Pascal, *ibid*, sect 7, no 455. See *'Je est un autre', above.*

'Le silence éternel de ces espaces infinis m'effraie': 'The eternal silence of these infinite spaces [the heavens] terrifies me': Pascal, *ibid*, sect 2, no 206. In view of the invariably favourable mentions that Pascal achieves in English-language publications, it might not be unfair to suggest than, *par contre*, many thousands of mortals are terrified by the ceaseless chat of this irredeemable windbag.

'Les jeux sont faits' Literally, 'the games are made': that is, 'the stakes are set'; in *roulette*, the call made by the *croupier (cf, above)* as the wheel is set in motion. This call is frequently followed by 'Rien ne va plus', 'No more bets'.

'Les sanglots longs' In 1866 Paul Verlaine (1844-96) wrote 'Les sanglots longs / Des violins / De l'automne / Blessent mon cœur / D'un langueur /Monotone': *Chanson d'Automne*: 'The drawn-out sobs of autumn's violins wound my heart with a monotonous languor'. These lines were used in BBC broadcasts to alert the French Resistance to the arrival of D-Day, and were popularized, set to music, by Les Petits Chanteurs à la Croix de Bois.

legerdemain 'Sleight of hand'. This word ought not, by rights, to be in this Lexicon, and that is for two reasons: the first is that it has been an English word since the fourteenth century, and the second is that it has *not* been a French word for almost as long. The French nowadays use *prestidigitation*; the word 'legerdemain' is not even alluded to in *Hatzfeld & Darmesteter* (1926). As an exclusively English word, its pronunciation is /ˈlɛdʒədəmeɪn/.

lettre de cachet See *cacher, above.*

levée From *lever*, 'to lift'. An embankment to prevent the overflow of a river or the incursion of the sea; a word used especially in Louisiana. Almost always without the accent.

> 'The levee, or levy, as it is often written, is the name of the embankment itself': *Encycl. Amer.* I. 197/1 (1883).

The word *levée*, with the accent, meant originally a reception of visitors on rising from bed; a morning assembly held by a prince or person of distinction. In present-day use in England, it means a court or assembly held by the sovereign or his representative, at which men only are received. *Levées* are nowadays held in the early afternoon.

liaison A truly Protean word. It can mean the blending of sauces in cookery; an intimate relationship or connection; an illicit intimacy between a man and a woman; in phonetics, the joining of a final consonant to a following word beginning with a vowel or mute letter *h*. In sung music, a *liaison* is often employed to suppress a short, unimportant syllable in order to facilitate the melody. In a wider sense the term liaison is used in a military context to signify the close connection and co-operation between units, branches, allies, etc., especially during a battle or campaign; this latter usage has produced a perfectly English verb, 'to liaise', conjugated regularly in each mood and through all the tenses. The military application of the word has found a ready acceptance in other spheres, primarily politics and business.

'Liberté, Égalité, Fraternité,'; 'Liberty, Equality, Fraternity'. The motto of the French Revolution, but the sentiment antedates the adoption of the slogan. Setting the fashion for odd resolutions on the Left of politics, the Club des Cordeliers passed a motion on 10th June 1793 urging 'que les propriétaires seront invités...de faire peindre sur la façade de leurs maisons, en gros caractères, ces mots: Unité, indivisibilité de la République, Liberté, Fraternité ou la mort': *Journal de Paris* no 182: 'that the owners... should be invited to have painted on the *façades* of their houses these words: Unity, the indivisibility of the Republic, Liberty, Equality, Fraternity or death': As a sequel, the Revolution developed indigestion from swallowing its children (see 'La Révolution dévorât ses enfants', *above*), and suppressed 'ou la mort' with effect from 1795.

Nicolas-Sébastien Chamfort (1741-94) interpreted 'Fraternity ou la mort' to mean 'Sois mon frère ou je te tue'; 'Be my brother or I'll kill you': in P. R. Anguis (ed), *Oeuvres completes,* vol 1, 'Notice historique sur la Vie et les Écrits de Chamfort', (1824). One can still see, *aere perennius*, in the stone above the portals of many a parish church in France the words *Liberté, Égalité, Fraternité,* incised in implicit compliance with the spirit of this resolution.

lingerie The word derives from *le lin*, 'flax', the plant, from which is made *le linge*, 'linen'. Its modern sense comprises ladies' underwear in general. It is pronounced as in French, /lɛ̃ʒʁi/. The prevalent pronunciation in the USA, /ˈlɑndʒəreɪ/, would be appropriate only if the word were spelt *lingeré.*

liqueur The word is applied to a wide range of strong alcoholic liquors sweetened and flavoured with aromatic substances. Pronounced /likœʁ/. The best Anglicized pronunciation, /lɪˈkør/, is very close to the authentic French, though the acceptable alternative /lɪkˈjøɹ/ is often heard.

littérateur 'A literary man, a writer of literary or critical works': *OED.*

Littré From 1859-72 Émile Littré saw through the press his monumental *Dictionnaire de la langue française* – 'perhaps the greatest dictionary ever compiled by one man': *The Oxford Companion to French Literature,* Clarendon Press, edn 1969, citing the *Encyclopaedia Britannica,* edn 1911, 'the Scholars' Edition'. A supplement to *Littré* appeared in 1877. See also *Larousse, above.*

longue durée, la A phrase of considerable importance in the study of history, coined by Fernand Braudel (1902-85). It epitomizes the interests and methods of the *Annales* (*q.v., above*) school of historical study. Throughout his life, the French historian championed the multiplicity of time, and the pressing need for historians to look beyond 'social time' or *l'histoire événementielle,* the history of events, in order to embrace *la longue durée,* the slower moving structures and cycles of centuries. His three historical time-scales were *la longue durée* (comprising the broadest picture-painting – of climatic, demographic and agrarian changes); *la conjuncture* (the medium term, comprising social, economic and institutional trends) and, last (to Braudel, the least significant), *l'événement* (comprising what he considered was the largely superficial succession of political and military events).

longueurs, les A phrase dear to generations of literary critics long dead. In a feline way, tedious passages were known as *des longueurs.* So frequently was the phrase encountered that Harrap's *New Shorter French and English Dictionary* (edn 1974), a substantial work despite its name, gave as a good specimen phrase, exemplifying the use of *longueur,* the following 'Roman où il y a des longeurs'. (One is tempted to add, in a tit-for-tat feline way, [*sic*], to drawn the reader's attention to the fact that that word *longueurs* is mis-spelt as *longeurs* in this entry of *Harrap's.*)

lorgnette/lorgnon A *lorgnette* is a pair of eye-glasses held in the hand, usually by a long metal, ivory, or tortoise-shell handle. The word can also mean, in earlier use, a single (monocular) opera-glass. A *lorgnon* might mean binocular opera-glasses, or perhaps a lorgnette: usage was imprecise even in the days when such items were in use.

> 'The General … took up his Opera-glass – the double-barrelled lorgnon was not invented in those days': W M Thackeray, *Vanity Fair,* 29 (1848).

louche In its primary meaning in everyday French speech, *louche* means, 'squinting', but it has many other meanings too. Of explanations or schemes, it can mean 'oblique' or 'not straightforward'. Of human beings it most often means 'shifty and disreputable'. Of places, it can mean 'unsavoury, unsalubrious'. Of wine, it can mean 'lacking in transparency, cloudy'. Of illumination, it can mean 'sickly, weak, feeble'. Guy de Maupassant (1850-93) has, 'Patron d'une banque louche, directeur d'un journal suspect'. Georges Duhamel (1884-1966) has, 'Des vices cachés, un passé louche'. The etymology of the word is turbid.

It derives from *lusca*, the feminine of *luscus*, a one-eyed man. (The Latin for one who squints is *strabo*.) Why the derivation should have been through the distaff side one cannot explain. The word has existed only in feminine form throughout the development of French, and was applied to females only for a long period of time. It is still feminine in form though it is nowadays invariable in practice. That is, there is no adjective *louch*: *louche* serves to qualify both genders. (When, with *absinthe*, water is dripped over a cube of sugar held in a slotted spoon made for the purpose into the neat absinthe, the result is a milky greenish liquid. The liquid is then said to be *louche*.)

luxe/luxury This entry exists merely to remind readers that the French for 'luxury' is *luxe*. The word *luxure* means 'lust'. The phrase *de luxe* is a good mnemonic. (The phrase *de luxe* is pronounced /də lyks/.)

lycée The name given in France to a secondary school maintained by the State, in contradistinction to a *collège* or secondary school maintained by a municipality or by a religious group. In specific terms, *un college libre* is a private educational establishment, often owned, staffed and run by a religious organization. No doubt the term *collège libre* would apply also if ever secularist groups were obliged to fund their own schools.

macabre 'Gruesome, ghoulish, grim'. Probably best known, as a word consciously recognized as French, in the phrase *La Danse macabre*, referring to *La Danse macabre* in G minor, Op. 40 by Camille Saint-Saëns. In other contexts, and pronounced /'məkɑbɹ/, the word is regarded as completely English, conjuring up the notion of a morbid, unhealthy fixation with death, abnormally susceptible to or characterized by gloomy or unwholesome thoughts and feelings.

macédoine A French feminine adjective meaning, simply, Macedonian. Its first recorded use was in 1740, to mean a mixture or medley of things. It nowadays denotes a mixture of vegetables, very often cubed, and sometimes a mixture of fruit, though rarely. Neither is an especially Macedonian dish. It is unclear why this adjective implying a Macedonian thing of the feminine gender should be used as a noun standing for things not in any way related to Macedonia. The suggestion that it refers to the diversity of peoples in the Macedonian empire of Alexander the Great has not been established.

'Mais où sont les neiges d'antan?': 'But where are the snows of yester-year?': François Villon (b 1431), *Le Grand Testament, Ballade des Dames du Temps Jadis* ('The Grand Testament, Ballade of the Ladies of Bygone Times'). *Jadis* is pronounced either /ʒadis/ or /ʒɑdis/.

maître d'hôtel Literally, 'master of the hôtel [private town-house]; butler'. Nowadays, a head waiter, often of a superior sort. *Maître d'hôtel* butter is butter seasoned with fresh parsley and lemon juice, usually served with grilled foods. *Maître d'hôtel* sauce, from *sauce à la maître d'hôtel* (1803), is a white sauce based on seasoned butter, fresh parsley, and lemon juice.

maladroit 'Lacking in adroitness or dexterity; awkward, bungling, clumsy, inept': *OED*. The word has been in use for centuries as an English word, with an English pronunciation. The French acceptation of the word still comprises the range of physical clumsiness – the range of meanings given by the *OED* – but since the early 17th century has also conveyed the notion of habitual tactlessness, of a lack of the social graces, etc. It seems to be the case in contemporary English that 'maladroit' is now reserved for the figurative sense only.

malaise 'An uncomfortable sense of imperfect health': *OED*. Frequently applied figuratively to the state of health of, for example, society or a given community. Improperly used to mean 'unease' or 'uneasiness'. Pronounced /mə'leɪz/, /mæl'eɪz/ or /malɛz/, not /malez/ – in other words, not 'mal-ease'.

mamelles, le deux mamelles de la France. 'Labourage et pâturage sont les deux mamelles de la France'. A declaration of Maximilien de Béthune, Baron de Rosny, later Duc de Sully (1559-1641), expressive of one of his fundamental beliefs as minister of Henri IV.

manège 'An enclosed space for the training of horses and the practice of horsemanship; a riding school. The movements in which a horse is trained in a riding school; the art or practice of training and managing horses; horsemanship' *OED*.

mange-tout A variety of pea, *Pisum sativum*, variety *macrocarpon*, producing pods that have no fibrous inner layer or film. Pods and peas are eaten whole while still technically unripe. May be eaten raw in a salad. Also called 'the mange-tout pea'; formerly called 'the sugar-pea' in England. Normally called 'the snow pea' in most of the US.

manqué 'Lacking'. Nowadays, used chiefly to describe a person who has failed to achieve a role, profession, etc., to which he aspires or is suited, in the following type of construction: 'He's a crooner *manqué*'. There is a widespread impression that the (soldiers') word 'manky', meaning unsatisfactory in one way or another, is an adoption of *manqué* dating from the First World War. However, judging from the published evidence, that appears not to be a well founded impression. In its draft revision dated September 2000 of its entry *Manky*, for which it gives as a definition, 'bad, inferior, defective; dirty, disgusting, unpleasant', the *OED* dates its use from only 1958. At least, it records as its first published use the year 1958. Many will recall the widespread use of the word much earlier than that. In 1950 it was already well established among soldiers, with no suggestion of its having been a neologism. (There is a Northern English dialectal word *manky* meaning, of children, 'naughty', or, of a horse 'skittish', and also various Scotch forms that derive from extremely ancient roots, the link between all these words being the notion of deficiency in some respect or other.)

maquette A small preliminary sketch, or wax or clay model, from which a work (usually in sculpture) is elaborated. In graphic-art usage, a 'rough', a 'visual'. See also *esquisse, above*, and *bozzetto*, *modello* and *pensiero* in the Italian Lexicon.

Maquis 'The French resistance movement formed during the German occupation of 1940-5; (usu. in *pl.*) a member of this movement. Also *fig.* and in extended use with reference to similar movements in other countries': *OED*. The word means, primarily, the type of scrubland that characterizes much of Corsica, into the remoter parts of which those escaping the law would flee. The Corsican word is *macchia*. Gallicized as *maquis,* the word has been adopted for similar tracts of vegetation in Southern France and, as a term of art, elsewhere. A native French word for comparable vegetation is *garigue* or *garrigue,* and, in the USA, the Spanish word *chaparral* is used.

Mardi Gras Literally, 'fat Tuesday', Shrove Tuesday, the day before Ash Wednesday, the beginning of Lent. So called because perishable types of food that would be 'given up for Lent' would be consumed. Mardi Gras was the last day of Carnival, which word itself implies the lifting or taking away of meat from the diet during the forty days of Lent. Pronounced, in French, /maʁdigʁa/ and, in English, /ˈmɑːdɪgrɑː/.

mariage blanc 'An unconsummated marriage': *OED*.

mariage de convenance 'A marriage arranged or contracted from motives of convenience, mutual advantage, or expediency (as opposed to love or sexual attraction)': *OED*. See *les convenances, above*.

Marianne The personification of the French Republic, usually portrayed as a female figure wearing a Phrygian cap. Thus, a *sobriquet* (*q.v.*) of the French Republic itself.

marivaudage Exaggerated sentiment expressed in affected language, after the style of Pierre Carlet de Chamblain de Marivaux (1688-1763); a verbose and affected style.

> 'Crébillon is entirely out of fashion, and Marivaux a proverb: *marivauder*, and *marivaudage* are established terms for being prolix and tiresome': Horace Walpole, Letter 19 Nov. in *Correspondence,* (1948), XIII, 144 (1765).

marmite 'A cooking pot of metal or (now usually) of earthenware': *OED*. Pronounced /maʁmit/. Also, in England, a proprietary name for a savoury paste, pronounced /mɑːmait/, made from yeast and vegetable extracts. The product was originally advertised for enriching soups and stews; its packaging has borne the device of a cooking pot since manufacture began in 1902.

marron glacé 'A chestnut preserved in and coated with sugar or syrup, as a sweet': *OED*.

Marseillaise, La A French revolutionary marching song written and composed by Claude Joseph Rouget de Lisle, a military engineer in the Rhine army on the declaration of war against Austria in 1792. Initially popularized by the volunteer army units marching from Marseilles to Paris, and adopted as the French national anthem in 1795. Pronounced as French, /maʁsɛjɛz/.

massage 'The rubbing, kneading, or percussion of the muscles and joints of the body with the hands, usually performed by one person on another, esp. to relieve tension or pain; an instance of this': *OED*. Increasingly in use figuratively to mean 'to alter statistics for partisan purposes'. The pronunciation in England normally has the tonic accent on the first syllable; in the USA the accent is normally on the second syllable.

matériel Pronounced /mateʁjɛl/. Originally and still chiefly in military use: the equipment, supplies, etc., used by an army, navy, or other organization, as distinguished from the personnel or body of people employed. In the international vocabulary of civil engineering, the word means 'plant and equipment'.

matinée Formerly, an entertainment presented in the morning or (in later use) at any time of the day before the evening; nowadays, exclusively an afternoon performance at a theatre or cinema. Pronounced /ˈmætɪneɪː/.

Maurists, the *La congregation de Saint-Maur*, a community of Benedictine monks founded in 1618. The Congegation quickly established, under its first superior-general, Dom Grégoire Tarisse OSB, a reputation for learning and literary industry. That reputation was augmented year by year until the Revolution. The chief house of the Maurists was at the Abbey of Saint-Germain-des-Prés. Dom Jean Mabillon OSB (1631-

1707) and Dom Bernard de Montfaucon OSB (1655-1741) were among the distinguished scholars to have been members of this congregation.

mayonnaise A thick, creamy sauce consisting of egg yolks emulsified with oil and seasoned with salt, pepper, vinegar, and (usually) mustard, used as a cold dressing or accompaniment for salad, eggs, fish, etc, or as the base for other sauces. Also with distinguishing words such as *garlic*, *herb*, *mustard*, etc. Normally pronounced in English /meɪjəˈneɪːz/, though there is a noticeable tendency among travelling English people to make an effort to pronounce the word as the French do, /majɔnɛz/. (On the derivation of *mayonnaise* there is no end of controversy and no sign of consensus. No etymology so far proposed has any significant merit. The most breathtakingly absurd derivation appears in *Brewer's Dictionary of Phrase & Fable,* 14th edn (1989); 'A sauce made with pepper, salt, oil, vinegar, the yolk of egg, etc, beaten up together. When the Duc de Richelieu captured Port Mahon, Minorca, in 1756, he demanded food on landing; in the absence of a prepared meal, his chef took whatever he could find – hence the orginal form *mahonnaise*.' In the first place, there is no evidence that the Duc de Richelieu or his cook had anything to do with the sauce. In the second place, if 'the cupboard was bare', what did the Duke have with his 'mahonnaise'? In the third place, how do we account for the delay of over fifty years after the fall of Minorca before the form *mahonnaise* appears? And, lastly, how do we account for the co-existence of the forms *mayonese, magnonese*, and *bayonnaise* side-by-side with the form that eventually won out? (A number of dictionaries have tentatively cited the Port Mahon derivation, including the *New English Dictionary* of 1906, the earlier name of the *OED*. The draft revision of the entry *mayonnaise* dated March 2001 withdraws the derivation but is frankly unable persuasively to postulate any other.)

mélange 'A mixture, combination, or blend; a collection of heterogeneous items or elements; a hotchpotch, a medley': *OED*.

> 'I did not tell him that I thought they [*sc.* Keystone Comedies] were a crude mélange of rough and tumble': *Charles Chaplin, My Autobiography*, ix, p 146 (1964).

ménage 'A domestic establishment, or its members collectively; a household, a home. In later use also: the parties involved in a romantic or sexual relationship regarded as forming a domestic establishment; the relationship itself': *OED*. Popularized in *ménage à trois*.

> 'I long to ... see you in your *ménage*, which I cannot express in English, because we have no word for it': Samuel Romilly, in *Life Sir S. Romilly* edn. 3, I. 297 (1842).

mentalité 'The attitude of a person or group of people to the world and their conception of their place within it': *OED*. There does not appear to be any significant difference between that definition and the *OED's* definite of the undoubted English word *mentality*: 'Mental character or disposition; the characteristic attitude of mind or way of thinking of a person, social group, etc. Freq. with modifying word'. There is, however, a curiosity about the word. A note in a draft revised entry for *mentalité* published by the *OED Online in* September 2001 reads: 'The French word is normally taken as a loan from English, although the English word is not well attested before 1840: ...*Cf* Italian *mentalità* (1846, denoting the essential constituent of the mind), Spanish *mentalidad* (20th cent.), German *Mentalität* (c 1912), Dutch *mentaliteit*, all from French'.

Fowler (*Modern English Usage*, 1937) roundly condemns the word *mentality*. He suggests a dozen words fitter for the purpose and dismisses mentality (and by inference *mentalité*, which he does not notice) as 'truly superfluous'. However, it has to be conceded that there is room for the word in the language if we use it in, for example, the way in which the author of the following example uses it:

> If we think of a historical period as defined by what the French have usefully designated a mentalité – a shared set of attitudes, practices and beliefs – then periods end when one *mentalité* gives way to another. Something like this happened in 1962, when Abstract Expressionism came to an end – not necessarily because the movement was internally exhausted but because a new artistic *mentalité* was in place. And these *mentalités* tend to rewrite the history of art in their own image. So Marcel Duchamp and John Cage, who would at best have been marginal to the Modernist aesthetic to which Abstract Expressionism subscribed, became the generative figures of the new period. Picasso, who had cast so daunting a shadow over Modernist artistic practice, was now esteemed primarily for having invented collage. Not everyone, of course, crossed the boundary into the new *mentalité* at once. There were many in the art world – artists as well as critics – who continued to frame the meaning of art in terms of the *mentalité* in which they had grown up': Arthur C Danto, *The Nation*, 29th March 1999.

menu 'A list of the dishes to be served at a meal, or which are available in a restaurant, etc.; a card on which such a list is written or printed, a bill of fare. Also: the food available or to be served at a meal or in a restaurant': *OED*. The word comes ultimately from the same Latin root as *minute*, meaning 'small'. *Hatzfeld-Darmesteter* provides the link by saying that the menu gives the *details* of the meal. The pronunciation in English is solely /ˈmɛɲuː/. The French is /məny/.

meringue 'A light mixture of stiffly beaten egg whites and sugar, baked until crisp; a shell or other item of confectionery made of this mixture, typically decorated or filled with whipped cream. In some recipes, esp. when meringue is used as a topping, cooking of the mixture is stopped before it is completely crisp': *OED*. The pronunciation is completely anglicized: /məˈræŋɡ/. The French pronunciation is /məʁɛ̃g/.

mésalliance 'A union between two people that is thought to be unsuitable or inappropriate; *esp.* a marriage with a person of a lower social position': *OED*. This notion of *mésalliance* was for many years so much a part of the social structure of England that the word was completely anglicized, to 'misalliance'. However, changing social patterns have rendered the concept obsolete and opened the door for the return of *mésalliance* as a delicate euphemism. The word is pronounced only as in French, with a befitting range of delicate pronuntiations: /mɛzaljɒ̃s/, /mɛzaliɒ̃s/ or /mɛzaʎɒ̃s/.

'Messieurs les anglais/français, tirez les premiers!' 'Gentlemen the English/French, fire the first!' For many years there has been a story circulating about a supposed exchange of gallantries immediately before the Battle of Fontenoy (1745) in which one side or the other offered the other side the first shot. Neither France nor England has been able to establish which side played the gentlemen, though it is abundantly plain that someone must have done so – or, rather, *failed* to have done so, since the battle undoubtedly commenced. Voltaire added his own authority to the story, though Voltaire's status as a historian is open to grave doubt, which Edward Gibbon had no hesitation in proclaiming.

Those wishing to investigate might well start with a visit to this web-site:

> http://vdaucourt.free.fr/Auteroche/Auteroche.htm

A fair but somewhat anglophile account of the Battle of Fontenoy is given in Winston Churchill's *History of the English Speaking Peoples*, Vol 3, p 107.

Perhaps the account of the incident by Lord Charles Hay, the commander of the 1st Battalion (Grenadier) Guards, is the most authentic account we have. Lord Charles wrote to his father, the Marquess of Tweedale, immediately after the battle and makes no mention of the episode that has grown into a fable. F. H. Skrine, *Fontenoy* (1906) says, 'Lord Charles Hay stepped to the front of his battalion and saluted with his hat. Then he took out a pocket-flask and ironically drank to their health, shouting, 'We are the English Guards, and hope you will stand till we come up to you, and not swim the Scheldt as you did the Main at Dettingen''.

We have, also, to remember that Fontenoy was one of the Maréchal de Saxe's greatest victories.

métayage 'A system of land tenure in which the farmer pays a certain proportion (usually half) of the produce to the landowner as rent, and the owner provides (a part of) the stock and seed. Also more generally: any form of sharecropping': *OED*.

> 'Thus there came into favour a system of 'share farming' (in Europe better known as metayage)': A José, *Australia, Human and Economic*, 262 (1932).

metier 'Originally: an occupation, a profession. Subsequently usually in extended use: a field or department of activity in which a person has special skill or ability; one's *forte*': *OED*.

mezzanine See *entresol, below*.

Michelin, le Guide The proprietary name for any of various touring guides (originally to France, later also to other countries) produced by the Michelin company.

midinette 'A French, esp. a Parisian, shop girl; *esp.* a milliner's assistant. In extended use: a fashionable but empty-headed young girl': *OED*. The etymology of this word deserves an excursus, drawn from a revised *OED* entry dated March 2002. The word derives from a nonce-word in a caption to a drawing in *Le Journal Amusant* of 17th May 1890 naming the archetypal shop-girl by a combination of the words *midi* 'midday'and *dinette* 'snack meal', with reference to the short breaks the girls took at lunchtime.

The word *dinette* also denotes a child's plaything, a doll's dinner-party.

Mieux est l'ennemi du bien, le ('The best is the enemy of the good'.) Voltaire, *Contes 'La Begueule'* though in his earlier *Dictionnaire Philosophique*, article 'Art dramatique'(ed 1770), he quotes an Italian proverb, 'Le meglio è l'inimico del bene'.

mignon Small, neat; perfectly formed; prettily small and delicate. Once anglicized but nowadays pronounced as French, /miɲ ɔ̃/, in particular in *filet mignon*, a slice cut from the small end of the tenderloin of beef.

migraine 'A severe headache which characteristically affects only one side of the head and is typically preceded or accompanied by visual or other neurological disturbances and is associated with nausea and vomiting': *OED*. Only two of a number of pronunciations are in common use today, /ˈmiːgreɪn/ and /ˈmaɪːgreɪn/. It seems likely that the latter will oust the former.

milieu 'An environment; surroundings, especially social surroundings…a group of people with a shared (cultural) outlook; a social class or set': *OED*.

minute A 'minute steak' is a steak thin enough to be cooked 'in a minute'. Hence, the pronunciation of *minute* is as for the unit of time.

mise en bouche A slightly artificial name for small confections served between courses in a meal. Unlike sorbets, they are savoury in nature, and are often a vehicle for demonstrating the chef's *expertise*. It has been suggested in recent weeks that *mise en bouche* might be more acceptable to polite society than the animal associations of *amuse-gueule* (*q.v.*).

mise en scène The staging of a play; the scenery and properties of a stage production; the stage setting; the set; the 'production' in general. Also, figuratively (see quotation), the setting, surroundings, or background of any event or action. 'The producer' is *le metteur en scène*.

> ' …also, the curious *mise-en-scène* contributed to my memory: it was after midnight in Paris in the bar of the Boeuf-sur-le-Toit…': Truman Capote, *Answered Prayers: The Unfinished Novel*, edn 1987, p 58.

miséricorde Literally, 'pity, compassion'. A narrow shelf projecting from the underside of a hinged seat in a choir stall, on which the occupant of the stall might half-sit while in principle standing during Divine Service. This word has been in use in English since the twelfth century, but is still regarded as being a French word, a common occurrence when the modern French remains substantially the same as the French we adopted. Pronounced /mɪˈzɛːrɪkɔːrd/ in England, with a strong tonic accent on the second syllable. In the USA, often pronounced with the tonic accent on the first syllable.

Mistral, le The strong, cold, north-westerly wind that blows down the Rhône valley and southern France into the Mediterranean, mainly in Winter and early Spring, considered by some to be invigorating. The word had at one time acquired the status of being naturalized, particularly in scientific (meteorological) contexts, but the increasing opportunities of travel have returned the word to denizen rather than native status, with the consequence that it is nowadays almost uniformly pronounced /lə mistʁal/.

mitrailleuse The name given to the French machine-gun brought into use in the Franco-Prussian War (1870). The name derives ultimately from the small shot fired by artillery from canisters or cases. This shot was grimly called *mitraille*, the name of the smallest coin current in the Low Countries. The word *mitraille* is cognate with our word 'mite', as in 'the widow's mite' (*Mk* 12:42).

mode, à la The French phrase has been used primarily in two senses in English. The first is 'In the fashion, according to the fashion', as in 'This is very much *à la mode* these days', though, in fact, the phrase is no longer in keeping with modern ways of speaking. In that usage, the phrase has 'passed its sell-by date'. In a second usage, as in *à la mode de maître d'hôtel,* it is still very much alive. It ought to be noted, however, that the phrase *à la mode,* by itself, is not in any way restricted to fashion or high living. It is an ordinary, plain, workaday phrase. It is present in one of the simplest French nursery-rhymes:

> Savez-vous planter les choux
> À la mode, à la mode,
> Savez-vous planter les choux
> À la mode de chez nous?

'Moi?' An arch exclamation frequently uttered by Miss Piggy, a glove-and-rod puppet created by James Maury Henson (1936-90) in *Sesame Street* and *The Muppet Show.* By her 'faux'-coy use of French, she demonstrated her cosmopolitan 'cool'.

moiré An adjective implying that the subject demonstrates a watered-silk effect. In scientific contexts, the word is used to denote an interference pattern similar to that produced by the manufacturing process combining heat and pressure that produces the fabric known as 'watered silk'. Nowadays almost universally pronounced /'mwareɪ/ by English-speakers.

'Mon centre cède, ma droite recule, situation excellente, j'attaque' 'My centre is giving way, my right is retreating, situation excellent, I am attacking'. From a message sent by Maréchal Ferdinand Foch (1851-1929) during the first Battle of the Marne, September 1914, in R. Recouly, *Foch*, ch 6 (1919).

moral/morale 'The mental or emotional state (with regard to confidence, hope, enthusiasm, etc.) of a person or group engaged in some activity; degree of contentment with one's lot or situation': *OED.* The spelling *morale* is an expedient unconsciously adopted by English-speakers to imitate in writing the French pronunciation, /moral/ rather than /'mɒrəl/.

morgue Nowadays, a slightly dramatic name for a mortuary, much more popular in the USA than in England. The originally meaning of the word *morgue* denoted a haughty look on the face, as on the faces of gaolers (jailers) who received unidentified corpses in one of the old prisons of Paris, whence the word became the name for the space in which the corpses were stored pending identification, and from there to the place where, nowadays, corpses are hygienically stored pending legal disposal.

mot juste 'The precisely appropriate word or expression': *OED.* The undoubted fact that every English-speaker instinctively recognizes the expression *le mot juste* and admits its validity is the best evidence that English-speakers *need* French. That innate, utterly instinctive recognition is the most powerful influence behind the complete bewilderment experienced by English-speakers at the categorical refusal of *l'Académie française* to admit an equivalent free trade from English into French.

motif A (usually recurrent) feature of an artistic composition, including such activities as embroidery and lace-making, especially a distinctive or salient one; the structural principle or dominant idea of a work; an object or group of objects forming a distinct element of a design; any small design or symbol. Also: a particular type of subject for artistic treatment. In music, used often as an abbreviation of the German term *Leitmotiv.* The word should not be applied in such instances as 'the profit motif', where 'motive' is the correct choice.

moue 'A pouting expression, often conveying (mock) annoyance or distaste, or used flirtatiously': *OED.* The word was earlier fully naturalized as 'mow', as in 'mock and mow', but nowadays is viewed as completely French and pronounced /mu:/.

mousseline Originally, French for 'muslin'. By extension, perhaps through the use of muslin in cookery (for filtration and the making of moulds, icing-nozzles, etc.), now applied in the kitchen as well as to clothing and furnishings. See the quotation below.

> '*Mousseline sauce.* Hollandaise sauce to which beaten egg white or whipped cream has been added, giving a frothy effect': *Good Housekeeping Home Encyclopedia*,. (ed. 4) 562/1 (1956). '*Mousses* are poached in a mould the contents of which are sufficient for a number of people, whereas *mousselines* are spoon-moulded *quenelles*, shaped like eggs': G. A. Escoffier, *Guide to Modern Cookery* II. xv. 469 (1907).

musette 'Any of various kinds of small bagpipes; especially a bellows-blown bagpipe of exquisite design, popular at the French court in the 17th and early 18th centuries; a type of oboe developed from the chanter of a *musette*; an organ stop so named from its tone, thought to resemble the tone of a musette; an item of (US) military equipment, a 'musette bag'.

naïf /naïve 'Originally: natural and unaffected; artless; innocent. Later also: showing a lack of experience, judgement, or wisdom; credulous, gullible': *OED*. As with *ingénu/ingénue (cf, above)*, only the feminine form is used in instinctively spoken and written English, though careful persons observe a distinction between the genders.

navette The primary sense of the word *navette* is 'shuttle', though the original meaning was (the root of) the vegetable rape, which is related to the comestible turnip, *le navet*. *La navette* has a bullet-shaped root, which led to the adoption of the word *navette* when the shuttle was popularized. The fact that the shuttle moves to and fro between two points led to adoption of the word *navette* for a shuttle-service of vehicles between points, and is now also used for specific vehicles performing such a service, as with a people-carrier or courtesy-car running regularly between an airport and a hôtel.

née Literally, 'born', prefixing a woman's maiden name, as in 'Mrs John Smith, *née* Jones'.

negligé 'A woman's light dressing-gown, *esp.* one made of flimsy, semi-transparent fabric trimmed with ruffles, lace, etc.; (also) a night-gown': *OED*.

...n'est pas français *Ce qui n'est pas clair n'est pas français:* Antoine de Rivarol (1753-1801) *Discours sur l'Universalité de la Langue Française* (1784): 'What is not clear is not French'. See also *Impossible n'est pas français, above.*

'Nez de Cléopâtre, le'. 'Le nez de Cléopâtre: s'il eût été plus court, toute la face de la terre aurait changé': 'If the nose of Cleopatra had been shorter, the whole face of the earth would have changed'. Pascal, *Pensées* (1670), ii, 162.

niche A recess into which, for example, a statue is placed, the most common meaning until recent years. Also, though rarely, an animal's lair. By far the most common use of the word nowadays is to denote 'a place or position suited to or intended for the character, capabilities, status, etc., of a person or thing': *OED*. Much used in modern marketing, as in 'a niche product', to mean a product that has its own unique place in the market.

The pronunciation of the word has undergone a radical transformation in less than a single generation. The *Online OED*, September 2003, has the following note:

> N.E.D. (1907) [the *New English Dictionary*, the earlier name for the OED] gives only the pronunciation /nɪtʃ/ and the pronunciation /niːʃ/ is apparently not recorded before this date. H. Michaelis & D. Jones *Phonetic Dictionary of the Eng. Lang.* (1913), and all editions of D. Jones *English Pronouncing Dictionary* up to and including the fourteenth edition (1977) give /nɪtʃ/ as the typical pronunciation and /niːʃ/ as an alternative pronunciation. The fifteenth edition (1991) gives /niːʃ/ in British English and /nɪtʃ/ in US English.

It seems likely that the great increase in foreign travel, prepared for by language courses, has led to the adoption, after years of neglect, of the original French pronunciation of *niche*.

'Ni saint, ni romain, ni empire' In 1756 Voltaire wrote: 'Ce corps qui s'appelait et qui s'appelle encore le saint empire romain n'etait en aucun manière ni saint, ni romain, ni empire': *Essai sur l'histoire générale et sur les mœurs et l'esprit des nations*, ch 70 (1756): 'This body that is called and still calls itself the Holy Roman Empire was not in any sense holy, or roman, or an empire'.

noblesse oblige Literally, 'nobility obliges', a phrase meaning that noble ancestry constrains one to honourable behaviour; privilege entails responsibility.

> 'Noblesse oblige': Duc de Lévis (1764-1830), 'Morale; Maximes et Préceptes No 73', *Maximes et Réflexions*, (edn 1812). 'To be sure, if 'noblesse oblige', royalty must do so still more': F. A. Kemble, Letter, 1st August 1837, *Records of Later Life* (1882). 'When someone excused coarseness...on the ground of genius, he said, 'That is an error: *Noblesse oblige*.'': G. K. Chesterton, *Robert Browning*, v 11 (1903).

Noël The feast of Christmas; Christmastide. Not in standard use in English as the name of Christmas, though sometimes used in anglicized greetings based on French models and as an alternative spelling for the anglicized 'Nowell'. The word *Noël* is the standard word for a French Christmas carol. In that usage, so spelt, and pronounced as French, /nɔɛl/.

noisette The hazelnut. The word is also used adjectivally in the names of desserts containing the nut. Also, a small round piece of meat, especially a cut of lamb or mutton taken from the rib or loin. Usually in the plural. The term *casse-noisette* is used, as well as *casse-noix*, for nutcrackers for all varieties of nut. *Un menton en casse-noisette* denotes 'a Hapsburg chin'.

nom de guerre Literally, 'war name'. A name assumed by or assigned to a person engaged in an enterprise, for example (formerly) courtship, publication, or espionage, in order to conceal his true identity. *Cf, nom de plume, below.*

> 'I have adopted a *nom de guerre*, as allowing me a freer scope': Washington Irving, *Life & Letters*, (1864) II. 369 (1829).

nom de plume Literally, '[quill]-pen name'. A usage almost entirely restricted to English-speakers and meaning *nom-de-guerre, q.v., above*. In recent years, some French writers have adopted this intuitive term.

'Non, je ne regrette rien' 'No, I regret nothing'. The refrain from Edith Piaf's most popular song.

nonchalant Literally and by derivation, 'not to be warm, 'fired up' or zealous'. Pronounced as French, /nɔ̃ʃalɑ̃/.

nonpareil 'Without peer'. In this sense pronounced as French, /nɔ̃paʁɛj/. The pronunciation of the old typographical term 'nonpareil', for a size of type (6 points), larger than ruby and smaller than emerald (in the USA, larger than agate and smaller than minion) is /'nɔnpəreil:/, but the word is (or was) often very slackly pronounced.

nostalgie de la boue, la A line taken from a play, *Le Mariage d'Olympe*, act 1, sc 1, 1855, by Émile Augier (1820-89):

> MARQUIS: Mettez un canard sur un lac au milieu des cygnes, vous verrez qu'il regrettera sa mare et finira par y retourner.
>
> MONTRICHARD: La nostalgie de la boue!
>
> MARQUIS: Put a duck on a lake in the midst of swans and you'll see that he'll miss his pond and end up by returning to it.
>
> MONTRICHARD: Nostalgia for the mud!
>
> *Le Mariage d'Olympe*, act 1, sc 1, (1855).

'Nous avons changé tout cela'; 'We have changed all that': The exchange in *Le Médecin malgré lui,* II, iv (1667) goes:

> *Géronte:* Il me semble que vous les placez autrement qu'ils ne sont: que le cœur est du côté gauche, et le foie du côté droit.
>
> *Scanarelle*: Oui, cela était autrefois ainsi, mais nous avons changé tout cela, et nous faison maintenant la médecine d'une méthode toute nouvelle.

nouvelle cuisine A modern style of (originally French) cooking, in which rich, heavy foods are avoided, and freshness of ingredients and elegance of presentation are emphasized.

> 'These three-star chefs have between them changed French cooking radically. The new style ... which they have developed together over the years is called Nouvelle Cuisine, and its principles are that food should have a 'lyrical lightness': M. Guérard, *Cuisine Gourmande* 9, tr C. Conran & C. Hobhouse (1978).

nouvelle vague 'A new movement or trend, esp. in the arts; *spec.* (now *hist.*)': *OED.*

> 'In terms of chronology the celebrated *nouvelle vague* of the late Fifties must by now be reckoned the old guard': *The Times*, 26th April 16/3, 1974.

nouveau pauvre In contradistinction to *nouveau riche*, *q.v*, one who, formerly rich, is now poor, though retaining the polite manners and tastes of an earlier age.

nouveau riche 'A person who has recently acquired wealth, *esp.* one who displays this in an ostentatious or vulgar fashion. Also with *pl.* concord (usu. with *the*): such people as a class': *OED. C. f. nouveau pauvre.*

> 'When an oligarch wants to reach for a gun, he heads for Holland and Holland, purveyors of shotguns and tweed plus-fours to the gentry and the nouveaux riches, and [Roman] Abramovich has been spotted there': Dominic Midgley, 'Oiling up the

Oligarchs', *The Spectator*, 8th October 2005, p 15.

nuance/nuancé Literally, the noun means 'a shade of colour, language or music'. The adjective *nuancé* means 'Possessing or exhibiting delicate gradations in tone, expression or meaning'.

'O quel cul t'as! ('Oh Calcutta!'). 'Oh Calcutta!' is known to English-speakers chiefly as the title of a 1970 stage production by Kenneth Tynan, a show noted for the nudity of the caste. The title was taken from a painting, *'Oh! Calcutta! Calcutta!'*, (1946) by Camille Clovis Trouille (1889-1975) of a nude woman shown from the rear. Trouille's title *Oh! Calcutta! Calcutta*! is a play on the words 'O quel cul t'as!', /okɛlkyta/, 'Oh, what a bottom you have!' Trouille was a weekend painter. His full-time job was in a factory making wax shop-window dummies. In 1919 Marcel Duchamps (1887-1968), a Dada painter, had drawn in a black moustache and small Vandyke beard on a reproduction of the *La Joconde* (*La Gioconda* or the *Mona Lisa)* and had entitled it L. H. O. O. Q. The letters when read out in French make 'Elle a chaud au cul': 'She has a hot bottom', /ɛl-aʃo-o-ky/.

'The Surrealist painting in question is Clovis Trouille's *Oh! Calcutta! Calcutta!* of 1946, No. 78 in his *catalogue raisonné'*: Patrick Hughes, London EC2. 'Letters to the Editor', *London Review of Books,* Vol 24, No 3; 7th February 2002.

'O liberté! O liberté! Que de crimes on commet en ton nom! ' 'O liberty, O liberty, what crimes are committed in thy name!': Madame Roland (1754-1793), in Lamartine, *Histoire des Girondins* (1847), livre li, ch 8.

obéissance 'Obedience to someone; a literal or figurative gesture of respectful submission'. Strictly, a fully anglicized word, having come to us in Norman French. If we regard it as such, it ought to be spelt *obeisance* and pronounced /ə'beɪsəns/. However, since the notion is hardly an everyday one in these days, people tend to regard the word as an import from French and pronounce it /ɔbeiɑ̃s/. A note of caution needs to be sounded here. The International Phonetic Alphabet (the IPA), being a creation originally of French philologist and linguistics professionals, can represent the sounds of French with relatively simple *single* alphabetic and special symbols, whereas the representation of English vowel-sounds requires *combinations* of letters and symbols to convey the highly diphthongal nature of the language. In consequence of this, there is sometimes a conflict between phonetic renderings. The complications can be resolved only by a more complex reliance on the IPA. If one sticks to a simple application of the IPA, there will occur some confusion, but very rarely. In the rendering of the French pronunciation, above, of *obéissance*, the *separate* signs /ei/ are used. They are intended to be pronounced individually, not as the diphthong /ei/ as it is used when rendering English words – that is, to represent the vowel-sound in *rain* and *pain*. Thus, the French word *obéissance* has four syllables: the English word 'obeisance' has only three.

objet d'art 'A decorative or artistic object, typically when regarded as a collectable item': *OED*. Pronounced /ɔbʒɛdɑʁ/.

odalisque 'A female slave or concubine in a harem, esp. in the seraglio of the Sultan of Turkey (now *hist.*). In extended use: an exotic, sexually attractive woman; a representation of a sexually attractive figure in art': *OED*. The word is derived through French from the Turkish *odalik*, with the same meaning. It has picked up an epenthetic intrusive letter *s* on the way. Pronounced /ɔdalisk/.

-on and -oon With exceptions only from a very few non-French roots, every word in English ending *-oon* derives from a French word, native to France or imported into France, ending *-on*. They are: balloon, barracoon, bassoon, batoon, blatteroon, bridoon, buccoon, buffoon, caisson†, canton†, cantoonment, cardoon, carroon, cartoon, ceroon, cocoon, doubloon, dragoon, ducatoon, espontoon, festoon, flocoon, frigatoon, gaboon, gadroon, galloon, gambroon, godroon, gooderoon, gossoon, gorsoon, harpoon, jargoon, lagoon, lampoon, cardoon, macaroon, mallagatoon, mantoon, maroon (*n, adj* and *v*), melocotoon, monsoon, musketoon, octoon, octoroon, pantaloon, patacoon, patroon, picaroon, platoon, poltroon, pompoon, pontoon, pulpatoon, quadroon, quintroon, ramoon, ratoon, rigadoon, saccoon, secoon, santoon, sashoon, segond v†, segonde n†, saloon, shabaroon, shabroon, shaffroon, shalloon, shapperoon, sherdoon, simoon, spadroon, tenoroon, terceroon, testoon, tierceroon, terceroon, tycoon, typhoon and Walloon (*n* and *adj*). Words marked with a dagger have changed pronunciation, and now imitate the original French spelling.

It is difficult intuitively to understand how, on being imported into English, the French nasalized *-on* uniformly acquired the sound /uːn/, (except in the very few instances where spelling has intervened). Our instinct tells us that a simple /on/ in English comes much closer to today's French /-õ/ than /uːn/. After all, though we have 'cartoon', we also have 'carton' – and no-one ever feels impelled to call Georges-Jacques Danton *Dantoon*.

We recall that characters from Shakespeare, and from as recently as W. S. Gilbert, use the word 'mounseer' for the French 'mister'. The note that appeared in the *Online OED* in December 2002, dealing with the word *monsieur* (reproduced below in this entry), concentrates on the second syllable, but unfortunately creates a misleading impression about the first.

Most of us would probably instinctively pronounce the word 'mounseer' with the first vowel as we pronounce it in 'mouse'. *That is a sound that simply does not occur in French.* On the other hand, if the word is pronounced with the first vowel sounding as in *mousse*, we should probably arrive at the traditional pronunciation of 'mounseer'. It is easy to accept that the first syllable of *monsieur* might, years ago, have been pronounced /mun/ or, if nasalized, /mũ/, which, either way, would assuredly have carried over into English as /muː/. And what might have been true of the first syllable of *monsieur* might equally well have been true of all syllables *-on*. If, on the contrary, the French syllable *mon-* and other syllables *-on* were *not* pronounced /mun/ or, if nasalized, /mũ/, but were pronounced as they are today, we are left with the 74 inexplicable problem of the *-oon* words.

The note below, from the *OED*, though not helping to elucidate the *-oon* problem, does explain the ways in which the pronunciation of both French and English perceptibly alters over the generations.

> The pronunciation of this word [monsieur] varied considerably before 1900. The stress seems to have been placed on the first syllable by at least some speakers: it is so marked by Johnson and as late as the *Imperial Dict.* (1850); the occasional spelling of the second syllable as *-er* in the 16th and 17th cent. perhaps corroborates this. However, J. Walker *Dict. Eng. Lang.* (1775) already indicates stress on the second syllable. The frequent early spelling of the first syllable as *moun-* seems to indicate the diphthong of *mount*, which is borne out by the by-form MOUNSEER

> *n.*; this may have been obsolete in 'polite' use by the 18th cent., since dictionaries do not record it. A few sources before the mid 19th cent. imply the presence of a short vowel (present-day British English /ɒ/ or /ʌ/), followed by *n*, in the first syllable; from the mid 19th cent. onwards, dictionaries tend to recommend the non-pronunciation of the *n* together with some variety of *o* or schwa, evidently in imitation of the French pronunciation.

It is, surely, quite astonishing that *every single instance of* -on *words imported, eighty-six of them, should uniformly be pronounced so as to rhyme with 'moon'.* The normally pellucid John Walker (1732-1807) consistently fudges the issue. In his *A Critical Pronouncing Dictionary and Expositor of the English Language*, 1791. He notes, in his preface 'Principles of English Pronunciation',§ 164, that *poltron, ponton* and *sponton* 'ought rather to be written with *oo* in the last syllable', and in the body of the dictionary, *sub voce* 'poltron', he takes his own medicine and pronounces it, as we do, /pɔl'tɹuːn/. He adds, 'This is one of those half French half English words that shows at once our desire to imitate the nasal vowel and our incapacity to do it properly': Walker was no doubt writing before the radical change in the pronunciation of French that occurred with the Revolution (*cf connoisseur, above,*) though his dictionary was in the press during the convulsions in society that occurred between 1798 and 1792 and was thus technically still malleable and ductile.

Of course, it might well have been the case that, by 1791, the pronunciation of the syllable *-on* had already changed, in France itself, so that there was no longer an audible /u/ sound there, whether nasalized or not. The radical change in the pronunciation of the diphthong *-oi* at the time of the Revolution in France is reasonable well documented. Other Revolutionary changes are not so well documented, but is it not quite likely that many other changes took place, too? Perhaps one was in the actual sound of the syllable *-on*. It is tempting to conclude, intuitively, that in earlier days, the syllable was indeed pronounced /ũ/? In Provençal the vowel *o* often sounds as /u/; and nasalization is also often present in Provençal, though it sometimes appears to be an infiltration from *Francien* French:

> 'Aro, moun bèl enfant, iéu, ai fa moun devé … Es à tu de t'entrina : te laisse libre.': Frédéric Mistral (1830-1914): *Mirèio* (1848):
>
> 'Maintenant, mon beau gars, moi j'ai fait mon devoir… C'est à toi de choisir la voie qui te convient: je te laisse libre'.
>
> 'Now, my fine young man, I've done my duty … .It's up to you to choose the course that suits you: I leave you free.'

Moreover, one sees written, from F. W. Maitland's Anglo-Norman pupil to present-day *phonetic* Creole, the words *moun* and *toun* for *mon* and *ton*. (Maitland reminds us that the little boy in Walter of Bibelesworth, *fl* 1270, was taught his personal pronouns: 'moun et ma, toun et ta, soun et sa'. See Thomas Wright, *Vocabularies,* 1. 144, (1857).

Alas, for the while the problem posed by the *-oon* words in English remains unresolved. But *eighty-three* English words derived from French and ending *-oon* will not remain silent for ever!

On dit 'One says'. Used to attribute an opinion, etc., to people in general rather than to the speaker: 'it is said', 'they say'.

opéra bouffe A species of comic opera, essentially lighthearted, with dialogue in recitative in the French language and with characters drawn from everyday life. A *calque* (*q.v.*) of the Italian *opera buffa (q.v.* in the Italian Lexicon).

ormolu Not a French word but a word derived from *or*, 'gold', and *moulu* (Old French *molu*) 'ground', past participle of 'to grind'. Originally: gold or gold leaf ground and prepared for gilding brass, bronze, or other metal. In later use: gilded bronze or a gold-coloured alloy of copper, zinc, and tin used to decorate furniture, make ornaments, etc.; (also) articles made of or decorated with this. Always to be pronounced /ˈɔːməljuː/.

'Où sont les neiges d'antan?' See 'Mais où sont les neiges d'antan?', *above*.

outrance, à See *à l'outrance, above.*

outré An adjectival use of the past participle of *outrer*, 'to push to the limit, to go beyond limits, to push to excess'. 'Beyond the bounds of what is usual or considered correct and proper; unusual, peculiar; eccentric, unorthodox; extreme': *OED*.

outremer From *outre-mer* 'overseas' (*c*1100 as *ultre mer*; 13th cent. in the sense 'Holy Land'). The shorthand word used to refer to the Latin kingdoms created as a result of the Crusades. *Cf* Anglo-Norman and Old French, Middle French and French *outre mer*, 'overseas, abroad' and, with ellipsis of *mer*, Anglo-Norman *de la outre* 'from overseas, from abroad'. The plea of *Outremer* was one of essoins or excuses for non-attendance in court.

> 'They had been sent by the noble Barons of France, who had taken the Cross, to beg Venice to have pity on the 'Land of Outremer', and to provide ships of war and transport': H. F. Brown, *Venice*, (edn 2), vii, 117 (1895). 'Outremer... consisted of Armenia, the principality of Antioch and the county of Edessa on the north, the long strip of the principality of Tripoli in the centre, and on the south the kingdom of Jerusalem.': H. Lamb, *The Crusades*, I, xl, 262 (1930).

Pages roses, Les A section in *Larousse* dictionaries entitled *Locutions Latines et Étrangères*, printed on pink paper and providing a remarkably informative and impressive conspectus of the extent to which other languages, despite the disastrous inhibiting influence of *l'Académie française*, have penetrated the French language. Latin sayings inevitably predominate. They afford a powerful insight into the breadth of Classical learning in French society. One of the Latin locutions, from Horace's Epistles (I, 10, 24) is particularly relevant to the attitude of the Academy, and that is his sagacious *Naturam expelles furca, tamen usque recurret,* 'You may expel Nature with a pitchfork, but she will always find her way back', a lesson *l'Académie* might one day learn.

paillasse A purely French word for a mattress made from sacking or other stout material and filled with straw, hay or other stuffing. The ancestors (there were many) of this word came into the English language through Norman French *but not directly*. Before the eighteenth century the word is found only in Scotch sources. The word used nowadays among English-speakers is 'palliasse', a completely naturalized word. We see in that word a classic example of metathesis (shifting of sounds within a word) so as to approximate to sounds already familiar to the speaker. Hence, this word, 'palliasse', pronounced /ˈpælıæs/–the homely 'pally-ass'.

pair/impair 'Even/odd'. Terms from roulette.

'This [*sc.* roulette] is played on a table with 37 numbers from zero to 36, the so-called 'even chance' bets being *pair* and *impair, passe* and *manque, rouge* and *noir*': J. Binstock, *Casino Administration,* vi. 72 (1969).

palette A thin flat board on which an artist lays and mixes colours. Typically oval in shape and having a thumb hole so that it can be carried with one hand while the artist paints with the other. Also used figuratively in other spheres where choice is offered.

panache Originally, a tuft or plume of feathers, especially for a headdress or as a showy decoration for a helmet, hat, or cap. So, by degrees, an epithet for bravado, self confidence, showiness, and swagger themselves. There are signs that the word is losing its slightly pejorative tone: it is increasing becoming desirable to possess and manifest *panache*.

'Ralliez-vous à mon panache blanc!': battle-cry attributed to Henri IV.

Pangloss[e], le docteur The tutor and philosopher in Voltaire's *Candide,* ch 30 (1759). His directing principle was distilled into the proposition: 'Tout est pour le mieux dans le meilleur des mondes possible': 'All is for the best in the best of possible worlds'. This *dicton* summarized the boundless and mindless optimism Voltaire professed to see in the philosophy of Gottfried Wilhelm von Leibniz (1646-1716). The *ODQ* (1992) has 'Dans ce meilleur des mondes possible...tout est au mieux', 'In this best of possible worlds ...all is for the best', *ibid,* ch 1.

papier mâché Literally, 'chewed paper'. 'A malleable mixture of paper and glue, or paper, flour, and water, which becomes hard when dry, used to make boxes, ornaments, etc. For more delicate work, papier mâché may also be formed from sheets of paper pasted together': *OED*.

par excellence 'By virtue of special excellence or manifest superiority; pre-eminently; supremely, above all': *OED*. After Classical Latin *per excellentiam.*

paramour From the Old French phrase *par amur, 'for love'.* The Old French phrase was written as one word from an early date, and came to be treated in English as a noun, both in the sense of 'love' and in the sense of 'one's beloved, a lover'. This might have come about partly through a mistaken analysis of the early colloquial phrase 'to love paramour', a mixture of the English 'to love' and the French (adverb) *paramour*, the hybrid phrase meaning 'to be in love with'. That is, *paramour* might have been taken for a noun. At all events, it is certainly a noun today. It cannot properly be pronounced as French and so should be accepted among the words from Norman French that have become denizens and thus pronounced in a roundly English fashion, /ˈpærəmʊəːɹ/.

pari mutuel In horse racing, a form of betting in which those backing the first three horses divide the total of the losers' stakes (less the operator's commission). A totalizator system. Also in extended use and in other sports.The earliest system of *pari-mutuel* betting was set up and managed by the French government.

'A board is exhibited, containing the names of the horses starting. A person who wishes to back a horse pays in a pound, or as many pounds as he likes, to the officer in charge of the totalisator. When the race is over, all the money staked is divided between the backers of the winning horse, less ten per cent, which is the profit of the management': *Quarterly Review*, October 455 (1885).

'Paris vaut bien une messe' 'Paris is well worth a mass'. Attributed to Henry of Navarre (1553-1610), who converted to Catholicism in order to secure the throne of France. It has been suggested that, if the remark was not made by Henry himself, it was made to Henry by his intimate companion, Maximilien de Béthune, Baron de Rosny, later Duc de Sully (1559-1641). No contemporary evidence of the remark is extent, though the *Caquets de l'accouchée*, a satirical collection published in 1622, speaks of Rosny's saying to Henry IV, 'Sire, Sire, la couronne vaut bien une messe'.

Despite his superb skill at managing the French economy in his heyday as minister of Henry IV, Sully spent much of his old age promoting a scheme for perpetual peace he ascribed, on very slender grounds, to Henry. It was, in essence, a scheme for a perpetual coalition against the Holy Roman Empire. His credibility as a witness to contemporaneous events is gravely weakened by his practice, in old age, as is now well known, of forging documents.

parole Literally, 'word'. Related to 'word of honour'. Used specifically in regard to the release of prisoners of war; *cf* French *prisonnier sur sa parole*, *prisonnier sur parole*, 1694 or earlier; also Middle French *prisonniers pour la parole* (1560). Nowadays, used, particularly in the USA, to denote the conditional release of a prisoner, especially before the expiry of a custodial sentence, and either temporarily for a special purpose or permanently, on the promise of good behaviour; 'On probation' is the comparable term in the UK.

In linguistics, it has become the practice to refer to the actual linguistic behaviour or performance of individuals on specific occasions – the practice of *using* a language; spoken or written – as *parole*, the French word, in contrast to language viewed as an abstract system, which is referred to as *langue*. The distinction between *parole* and *langue* was made in these terms by the Swiss linguist Ferdinand de Saussure (1857-1913) in lectures delivered at Geneva from 1907 to 1911; these lectures were later compiled from students' notes into the *Cours de Linguistique Générale* (1916). This was not translated into English until 1959 (in which 'speaking' and 'language' respectively were used). By that time, F. de Saussure's French terms had been widely adopted. They have remained in use to the present time.

parterre In general, a level space in a garden occupied by an ornamental arrangement of flower beds. The part of the ground floor of a theatre in front of the orchestra; the stalls. In the USA, the part of an auditorium beneath the galleries; also, the occupants of this area.

parti pris Literally, 'part taken'. 'Prejudice', in which sense it dates, in French, from 1810 or a little before. Earlier (1734 or earlier), it meant 'a decision, a position taken or adopted'. It nowadays implies 'having taken someone's part, having a preconceived view; a bias or prejudice', and, adjectivally, 'biased, prejudiced; favouring one particular side, faction, or party'. The quotations below will show the wide range of constructions possible in English.

> 'Those who may consider this statement an exaggeration can easily satisfy themselves (provided they go without any *parti pris*, either on one side or the other)': *Once a Week* 18th August, p 215/1 (1860). 'That fatal spirit of *parti-pris* which has led to the rooting of so much injustice, disorder, immobility and darkness in English intelligence': John Morley, *Carlyle* in *Crit. Misc.* (1878) p 189 (1871). 'In his letter his parti pris emotionalism was too evident to

convince his readers properly': H. Crane, *Let* 18 Feb 1923. 'Personally I think we both have made a mess of it, and I have no *partipris* in the matter': Lawrence Durrell, *Mountolive,* v 103 1977 (1958). 'With none of the characters in Lawrence's life is he *parti-pris*': 125 1973 *The Times Literary Supplement,* p 660/3, 15th June 1965. 'The ideological *parti-pris* of these last two sources does not invalidate their generally rigorous and sound historical documentation': N.Y. Review of Books, p 12/2, 9th June 1977. 'Any reader without a parti pris would see the play that emerged after O'Malley's fifth draft as one slanted to the Palestinian side': 2003 *Weekly Standard* (Nexis) 17 Feb 2003. 'A growing conservative historiography that seems to proceed from the belief that for too long *parti pris* liberals have shaped our understanding of the recent past.': *N.Y. Review of Books,* p 22/2 30 November 2000.

pas de deux 'Dance, especially ballet. A dance for two people. In extended use: a partnership or liaison between two people, countries, etc, especially one which is difficult to initiate or requires careful handling': *OED.*

'Venus and Adonis form a *pas-de-deux*, or duet-dance': G. A. Gallini, *Treatise on the Art of Dancing, p 282* (1762).

pas devant les enfants/les domestiques/les valets: 'Not before or in the presence of the children, the domestic servants, the waiting servants or waiters'. A caution in French used in English households to advise discretion. The use of French is an instance of what the Preface to the *Book of Common Prayer* (1551 and 1662) calls 'a language not understanded of the people'.

'Pas trop de zèle' A counsel generally attributed to Charles-Maurice de Talleyrand-Périgord (1754-1838). Sainte-Beuve, in *Portraits des femmes, Madame de Staël,* p 131 (1858) attributes to him 'N'ayez pas de zèle'. Philarète Chasles (1798-1873), the son of a *Conventionel,* has Talleyrand saying, 'Surtout, Messieurs, point de zèle': *Voyages d'un critique à travers la vie et les livres,* vol 2, p 407 (1868).

passé The *OED* says, 'Past one's prime; especially (of a woman) past the period of greatest beauty; no longer young'. Without tipping one's hat in the direction of political correctness, one is bound to say that the association between the word *passé* and a woman's age is not one that would strike the average English-speaker as being by any means inevitable. Fashions, opinions and ideologies are nowadays often branded as *passé,* but not women.

passe partout Strictly, a document or other item that permits its possessor to go wherever he pleases. 'A kind of adhesive paper or tape used for framing pictures': *OED.*

parvenu 'A person from a humble background who has rapidly gained wealth or an influential social position; a *nouveau riche*; an upstart, a social climber. Generally used with the implication that the person concerned is unsuited to the new social position, esp. through lacking the necessary manners or accomplishments': *OED.* The OED explains the progression of the past participle of the Latin *pervenire,* 'to arrive at, to reach (a place)', through the past participle of the French verb *parvenir* (late 10th century) with the same meaning as the Latin, and then, next, to *parvenu,* 'having arrived at a desired outcome' (*circa* 1165), and ultimately to a meaning of 'having risen to an influential social position' (1559). *Cf arriviste* and *nouveau riche, above,* and the phrase, 'He has arrived'.

pastiche A novel, poem, painting, piece of music, etc, incorporating several different styles or characteristic mannerisms; sometimes, an item, particularly a piece of music, made up of parts, often reorchestrated, drawn from a variety of sources. In music, sometimes applied to a medley of elements intended to resemble the style of a given composer, where the Italian *pasticcio,* /pɑstitʃo/ is also used. *Pasticcio* is a dish containing a mixture of pasta and meat. The French *pastiche* is a *calque (q.v.)* of *pastichio.* Both words, *pastiche* and *pasticcio,* are nowadays used in a dismissive sense. (See also *pot pourri.*)

pastille Of many meanings, only one effectively remains: 'a small, flat, usually round, sweet, often coated with sugar and sometimes medicated; a lozenge. Any sweet of a similar shape': *OED.* In practice, the word very rarely relates to the shape of a lozenge as strictly defined by the *OED* itself: 'A plane rectilineal figure, having four equal sides and two acute and two obtuse angles; a rhomb, "diamond"': *OED. Lozenge* in the pharmaceutical and confectionary senses has drifted inseparably apart from the geometric (and heraldic) meaning of *lozenge.* A further characteristic of many pastilles is that they are of a gummy consistency.

pâté A rich paste or spread made from finely minced and seasoned meat, commonly the liver of poultry, but sometimes comprising, as an alternative, fish or vegetables. All forms of *pâté* are usually cooked in a *terrine* (*q.v.*) and served cold, often with toast. (See next.) For the pronunciation of the first vowel in *pâté,* see *Circumflex Accent, above.*

pâté de foie gras A variety of *pâté* made from the livers of geese and ducks that have been reared so as to develop a condition that causes the liver to grow to an excessive degree. The object is to increase the saleable product. A speciality of Strasbourg.

> 'Most prized ... are the ducks and geese whose livers are turned into *pâté de foie gras*': S. Fallon & M. Rothschild , *World Food: France,* p 168 (2000).

patois A word of doubtful etymology. The *OED* has a careful explanatory note: 'A dialect spoken by the people of a particular region (especially of France or French-speaking Switzerland), and differing substantially from the standard written language of the country. Also generally (frequently depreciative): a regional dialect; a variety of language specific to a particular area, nationality, etc., which is considered to differ from the standard or orthodox version. Some French scholars formerly distinguished dialects, as regional varieties of a language prior to the formation of a written standard, from *patois,* as regional varieties after the formation of a written standard of that language. The term *patois* is now no longer used in linguistics, although it is still very common in non-technical usage, where it is usually depreciative.'

pavé A paved road or path constructed of small paving blocks or cobbles; a cut of meat served as a slab.

paysage The countryside seen as picturesque and often idealized, as frequently depicted in painting; the country as a subject for contemplation or description.

> 'So have I known some beauteous Paisage rise/ In suddain flowres and arbours to my Eies': Henry Vaughan the Silurist, *Silex Scintillans,* 104 (1650).

peignoir A woman's light dressing-gown; a *negligée.* The word occurs in the 15th cent. as *peignouer* in the sense 'an undergarment put on the shoulders while combing one's hair', from *peigner*, 'to comb' (second half of the 12th century in Old French as *peignier)*. The necessary connection with combing has been lost over the years. Pronounced /peɲwɑ/.

> 'Swathed in a brilliant white peignoir, the perfect foil for her mane of dark tresses, she shows no embarrassment at being depicted in a pre-coiffed state': *The Times*, II. 14/2, 5th December 2001.

penchant A leaning or an inclination towards something; a strong or habitual inclination; a tendency to do something; a taste or liking for a person or thing. Pronounced /pɑ̃ʃɑ̃/.

persiflage A word derived from *sifler*, 'to whistle'. During the Enlightenment in France, the word came to denote a special kind of small-talk that disparaged in particular the most cherished 'old-fashioned' virtues and beliefs, religion being the most obvious target for the mocking railleries of those who adopted this stance.

> 'The cold compound of irony, irreligion, selfishness, and sneer, which make up what the French … so well express by the term *persiflage*': Hannah More, *Strictures on the Modern System of Female Education* (ed. 4), I, p 15 (1799). 'They felt that if *persiflage* be the great thing, there never was such a *persifleur* [as Voltaire]': Thomas Carlyle, *Heroes*, i (1840).

pétanque *Pétanque* is a Provençal variant of the French game of *boule[s] (q.v.)*. *Le Petit Robert* explains the derivation of the word as follows: 'Provençale *pèd tanco*, 'pied fixé' (au sol), d'oû *jouer à pétanque*, puis *jouer à la pétanque*. See *boule[s]*.

petit bourgeois Literally, 'little citizen'. Used in its primary sense, a term to denote a member of the middle or commercial classes in a society, the 'shopkeepers'. It has two secondary senses: the first is the Communist one that entirely discounts the utility of the class and would readily extirpate it; the second is the more generalized use of the term among the modern *intelligentsia*, a highly derogatory and rancorous one that discounts and dismisses the class as having irremediably conventional or conservative political and social attitudes.

petit mal, le 'The milder or imperfectly developed form of epilepsy, when the fits are abortive or incomplete: there is only momentary confusion or unconsciousness without general convulsions or other major manifestations': *OED*. *Cf grand mal, le*.

petit-point A stitch in needlework; also used in tapestry.

> 'Tent Stitch, this stitch is also known as 'petit point' and 'perlenstich'': Caulfeild, Sophia F. A. & Saward, Blanche C., *The Dictionary of Needlework, 32/1 (*1882).

petits pois Green peas either of the Sugar Pea variety or of any variety of pea harvested early.

> 'Peas vary in size from the small 'petit pois' to large ones': Good Housekeeping Home Encyclopedia, 591/1 (1951).

petits soins Attention to the small details associated with caring for oneself or others; attention to one's appearance, to one's sartorial details. Also, towards others, to afford particular assistance, to dance attendance on.

Philosophes, les *Les Philosophes* was a name given in the 18th century to a school of French writers and thinkers whose defining characteristic was sympathy with the

Enlightenment. In the *Encyclopédie (q.v.)*, which was their most potent sounding-board, the word *philosophe* was defined not only as a scrupulous observer and rational thinker but also as 'un honnête homme qui veut plaire et se rendre utile': 'a decent man who wishes to please and to make himself useful'. The *Philosophes* established themselves solidly in society and exerted a profound influence on the *Académie française*. Their *encomia* abound: reproaches are scarcer: history is written by the victors. Pronounced /filozof/.

> 'Madame du Deffand hates *les philosophes*': Horace Walpole, *Letters*, 28th September 1774, (edn 1904), IX, p59. 'The *philosophes*, except Buffon, are solemn, arrogant, dictatorial coxcombs': *ibid*, 7th July 1779, X, p 441. 'All the *philosophes*, all the Encyclopedists, shared the Baconian belief that science could save mankind': *The Listener*, p 37/2, 9th January 1969. 'Despite his genuine and profound erudition, Gibbon was a *philosophe* far more than a philosopher, though he hankered after being a philosopher of history': *New York Review of Books*, p 8/3. 13th October 1977.

picaresque Belonging or relating to rogues or knaves: applied especially to a style of literary fiction, chiefly of Spanish origin, narrating the adventures of rogues. See *Picaresco* in the Spanish Lexicon.

> 'A type of fiction termed by the Spaniards as of '*Gusto Picaresco*': *Life of Defoe* in *Defoe's Works*; J Ballantyne (1810). 'This [the Lazarillo de Tormes by Mendoza] is the first known specimen in Spain of the picaresque, or rogue style': Hallam, *Hist. Lit.* I. viii. §48 (1837-9).

pièce de résistance Originally, the most substantial dish in a repast; nowadays, rarely used in that sense but rather for the chief item in a collection, group, or series.

pied-à-terre A small town house, an apartment, flat, or room used for short periods of residence, as distinct from one's principal residence.

pied de la lettre, au See *au pied de la lettre.*

pied noir 'Black foot'. A term originally applied to Algerian stokers, who worked barefoot. They were proud of their name. Eventually the word was applied to all nationals of Algeria, even to those of Metropolitan French origin. With the transfer of power in Algeria in 1962, many *colons* returned to Metropolitan France, to be widely dubbed *pieds noirs*. Today the expression is sometimes used also in a general sense for Algerians of all description, and, loosely, to the repatriated colonialists from other former French possessions. This is a loaded term and is perhaps better avoided.

pierrot A familiar diminutive of *Pierre*, a typical peasant name applied to a character in French pantomime: now, in English, applied in somewhat literary contexts to a buffoon or itinerant minstrel having, like the stage *Pierrot*, a whitened face, and loose white fancy dress. Two clowns in contemporary English circuses have whitened faces: *Pierrot*, who wears a predominantly white costume, often with a layered ruffled collar, and a conical hat with a pom-pom; and *Harlequin*, whose costume sometimes includes colourful tights and a mask, and occasionally a jester's cap and bells. The typical Pierrot acts as a 'dignified' clown.

Concert-parties performing on the piers of English holiday resorts were often punningly referred to, and publicized themselves as, 'pierrots'.

pince-nez Spectacles that do not depend on sidepieces that rest on the ears but, instead, have a spring mechanism that grips the bridge of the nose.

piquant 'Agreeably pungent or sharp of taste; sharp, stinging, biting; stimulating or whetting to the appetite; appetizing... figuratively, that acts upon the mind as a piquant sauce, or the like, upon the palate; that stimulates or excites keen interest or curiosity; pleasantly stimulating or disquieting': *OED*. The pronunciation is nowadays always a close approximation to the original French pronunciation, /pikɑ̃/.

There has been a discernible tendency in English writing to use the feminine form, even in the works of such an accomplished writer as Sir Walter Scott. In English usage, there is no need for this, even when the English substantive being qualified is of the feminine gender.

> 'The monkey has a turn for satire, too, by all that is piquante': Sir Walter Scott, *Peveril of the Peak*, xxix, (1823). 'The face of a rather piquante and pretty girl': Rider Haggard, *Doctor Therne*, I 15 (1898).

pique 'A feeling of anger, resentment, or ill-will, resulting from some slight or injury, esp. such as wounds one's pride or vanity; offence taken': *OED*.

piqué From *piquer*, 'to prick, pierce, backstitch as in quilting'. A type of cotton fabric woven so as to give the impression of having been quilted in parallel rows, as with marcella. Between the two world wars, it was introduced, owing to its relative stiffness, into the manufacture of shirts with attached collars for wearing with the less formal double-breasted dinner-jacket (tuxedo), then growing in popularity. *Piqué* was much less constricting that the stiffly starched shirts and collars worn with the full-dress dinner suit and the older, single-breasted dinner-jacket. (*Piqué* is also French slang for 'batty, potty, dotty'.)

pis aller Literally, 'worse go' or 'worst go'. 'The worst that can be, or can happen; what one would do, take, choose, etc., in the event of things coming to the worst; what one accepts when one can do no better; a do-no-better, a last resource'. Increasingly, the sense of 'an enforced choice that is better than nothing' is gaining acceptance.

plaque A flat tablet or plate bearing some decoration or lettering intended to be hung or set in a wall, etc. Another meaning has been popularized by tooth-paste advertising: a coating or layer formed on the teeth in which bacteria can breed.

plain-chant The form of music that has been in use in the Christian church from very early times. It is unisonal and modal in character. Though the form *plain-chant* is in use in English, the form *plainsong* is better, as helping to preserve the distinction between plainsong properly so called and the chanting of versicles and responsories in Divine Service, which is most often not akin to plainsong.

plat du jour The dish of the day; one of a restaurant's specialities on any particular occasion.

plateau 'An elevated tract of comparatively flat or level land; a table-land': *OED*. Often used figuratively, as in 'a plateau of learning'. The pronunciation is the French pronunciation except in the plural, when English-speakers must signify the plural in an audible fashion: hence, /platoz/.

plus ça change In full, 'Plus ça change, plus c'est la même chose'; 'The more it changes, the more it's the same thing': Alphonse Karr (1808-90), *Les Guêpes*, January 1849, (sixth series 1859) p 305. The saying either was or has become proverbial in France in the form 'Plus ça change, plus c'est pareil'.

poêle, une This word, meaning 'a frying pan' *(une poêle à frire),* is, unlike most French words, decidedly unphonetic in its pronunciation. It is pronounced /pwal/, exactly as the word for 'hair' or 'bristle', *poile,* is pronounced. See next.

poêle or **poële, un** 'An oven'. Like *la poêle, le poêle* or *poële* is pronounced /pwal/, spelt either way. This word and the previous word are included solely to underline that, once given its fundamental pronunciation system, the French language is overwhelmingly phonetic. Unpredictable pronunciations are rare in French. Some instances of completely unexpected pronunciations occur with common words, such as *oignon,* not /waɲõ/ but /ɔjõ/, and some with words not quite so common, as *ciguë* and *exiguë*, where the diaereses are placed on what seem to be the wrong letters. In fact, as to words of this description (*ciguë, ambiguë, ambiguïté,* etc), the Conseil Supérieur de la Langue Française proposed in 1990 a regularization of such words so that the *tréma*, the diaeresis, should fall on the actual vowel to be sounded. Thus the words would be spelt *aigüe, ambigüe*, etc.. (The pronunciation of the place-name and family-name *Vogüé* is perfectly rendered by the written form.)

poilu 'The hairy one', implying, also, virility. A name bestowed by the Press on French soldiers, particularly those who fought in the First World War.

point d'appui A point of support; a fulcrum. This is the strict meaning of the phrase. It may, of course, be used literally, as in the first quotation below, and figuratively, as in the second quotation below. It ought not, however, to be used for forced figurative purposes. *Point d'appui* does not mean 'pressurepoint', the alternative to a *tourniquet (q.v.).*

> 'The boatman, with his spoon-shaped paddle fixed against a jutting rock, for a point d'appui': Lady Morgan, *Florence Macarthy, an Irish Tale*, I, iv, 141 (1819).
> 'Gibraltar...furnished a perfect example of the value of sea power, combined with that ability to retain physical possession of a *point d'appui*': R. Hargreaves, *Enemy at the Gate*, p 103 (1945).

point faible One's Achilles Heel.

poubelle A dustbin (garbage can), named after a *Prefet* of the Seine who in 1884 ordered that every household should provide a receptacle to facilitate the carrying away of refuse.

pouffe This seems to be a mis-spelling of the French word *pouf*, which *le Petit Robert* defines as, 'Siège bas, gros coussin capitonné, généralement cylindrique, posé à même le sol': 'Low seat, large upholstered cushion, generally cylindrical, directly in contact with the floor'.

poujadiste An adherent of the mainly reactionary and conservative political philosophy advocated by Pierre Poujade (1920-2003), French publisher and bookseller, who in 1954 founded a movement for the protection of artisans and small shopkeepers (*l'Union de Défense des Commerçants et Artisans*), protesting chiefly against the French tax system then in force. The words *poujadiste* and *poujadisme* are sometimes used to denote similar movements acting in the interests of small-scale commercial enterprises.

Port-Royal The name of a Cistercian convent in the Vallée de Chevreuse to the

South-West of Paris, later known as *Port-Royal des Champs* when the community moved to Paris *(Port-Royal de Paris)*. In the 17th century the convent became the focal point for Jansenism. The Jansenists were a puritanical faction of largely celebrated personages who adopted the teachings of the eponymous Cornelius Jansen (1585-1638), Bishop of Ypres, as mediated to them by Jean du Vergier de Hauranne, (1581-1643), l'Abbé de Saint-Cyran. A number of these celebrated lay personalities took up occupation of the conventual buildings at Port-Royal-les-Champs and led a communal life under the title *Solitaires*. They established a number of schools for boys in the vicinity and produced some excellent textbooks for use in their schools, among which the best known was *La Logique, ou l'Art de Penser* (1661), the celebrated 'Port Royal Logic'. A dispassionate history of Port-Royal is hard to find. Racine, a former pupil at Port-Royal-des-Champs, wrote an elegant *Abrégé de l'Histoire de Port-Royal,* and Sainte-Beuve wrote *Port-Royal,* a six-part (in nine volumes) rhapsodic account of this era of ferment.

portmanteau Spelt in this way, the word is not French. The French word resembling this entry is *portemanteau.* In practice the French word means, nowadays, only 'a coat-hanger'. A suitcase is *une valise* or *une mallette.* A trunk is *une malle.* Since there is no difference in English between the meanings of 'portmanteau' and 'suitcase', 'portmanteau' has virtually disappeared as a name for a suitcase. Where it is used, it is pronounced in a completely anglicized way, /pɔːɹt'mæntəʊ/. To try to pronounce the English word spelt 'portmanteau' as a French word produces the completely unrecognizable /pɔʁmɑ̃to/.

There is, however, an important surviving use of the word 'portmanteau' that warrants a comprehensive mention. In *Alice through the Looking-Glass,* Lewis Carroll has Humpty-Dumpty explain to Alice some of his special words: ' Well, 'slithy' means 'lithe and slimy' ...You see it's like a portmanteau – there are two meanings packed up into one word... 'Mimsy' is 'flimsy and miserable' (there's another portmanteau for you)': 'Lewis Carroll', *Alice through the Looking-Glass,* vi, p 127 (1872). The words 'brunch'and 'motel' are modern instance. Curiously, the science of linguistics has taken up Carroll's idea and consistently uses such expression as 'portmanteau morph', a morph that represents two morphemes simultaneously.

> 'A more interesting blend, called a portmanteau word by Lewis Carroll, combines two words with similar meanings into one: 'instantaneous' and 'momentary' into 'momentaneous', 'splinters' and 'blisters' into 'splisters', 'shifting' and 'switching' into 'swifting' and 'edited' and 'annotated' into 'editated'': *Scientific American,* p 116/2, December 1973. 'If we find it more convenient to regard these forms as single morphs, we must at least take them to be portmanteaus, and not completely arbitrary ones': *Language* XXVI. 84. 'Portmanteau morph, a single morph which stands for two morphemes. The best known example is French *au* |o| 'to the' which represents *à* + *le*': Hartman & Stork, *Dictionary of Language & Linguistics,* 180/1 (1972).

poseur One who poses or attitudinizes.

poste, en A diplomatist is said to be *en poste* when he is officially 'posted' to a foreign state.

> 'He ... since being *en poste* in Cairo, has interested himself mainly in Egyptology': Nancy Mitford, *Christmas Pudding,* ix, p 137 (1932). 'While he was *en poste* in Paris

he gathered much of the material': *John o' London's Weekly*, 31st May 1962.

poste restante 'A direction written upon a letter which is to remain at the post office till called for; in English use, transferred to the department in a post office in which letters for travellers or visitors are kept till applied for': *OED*.

'Do write to me, and direct your letters 'poste restante, Dresden'': Washington Irving, *Life & Letters*, II, p 131 (1822). "There is a Poste Restante both at the General Post Office St. Martin's-le-Grand, and at the Charing Cross Post Office, where letters 'to be called for' can be obtained between the hours of 9 A.M. and 5 P.M': *British Postal Guide*, 92 (1880).

postiche A hair-piece; a patch of false hair or small wig to cover a bald place. The word is a *calque* (*q.v.*) of the Italian *posticchio*, the fundamental meaning of which is something 'counterfeit' or 'feigned'. See *toupée*, *below*.

potage Soup. This word, in the form 'pottage', has been in use for many centuries, but nowadays it is confined to the phrase 'mess of pottage', as in the story (Gen 25:29-34) of how Jacob induces his brother Esau to forgo his birthright 'for a mess of potage'. Curiously, the phrase 'mess of pottage' does not occur in the Authorized Version, or in the actual text of any Bible in English. The phrase crept into the language from the headings of Chapter 25 in the Bibles of 1537 ('Matthews' Bible') and 1539 (the 'Great Bible'), and from that in the Geneva Bible of 1560. In the form *potage*, however, it is a conscious import from modern French, and is much used, normally for a somewhat thick soup. Pronounced /pɔtaʒ/.

pot-pourri One of the curiosities of etymology. Literally, 'rotten pot', from *pot*, 'pot', and *pourri*, the past participle of *pourrir*, from the Latin *puté.re*, 'to rot, to be rotten'. The expression is a *calque* (*q.v.*) of the equally inexplicable Spanish expression *olla podrida* (see the Spanish Lexicon), which, literally, means exactly the same, 'rotten pot'. The Spanish expression was a figurative one signifying a dish of different kinds of meat stewed together. It was what we should nowadays call a stew. The dish was formerly known in England as a 'hotch-pot' (see in the Law French Appendix, *below*) or 'hotchpotch'. 'Hot-pot' as in, for example, Lancashire hot-pot, is a quite different dish – a dish comprising mutton or beef with potatoes, or potatoes and onions, cooked in an oven in an earthenware pot having a tightly fitting cover. Perhaps the *olla podrida* is most closely resembled, nowadays, by a *ragoût*. The word *podrida* perhaps became associated with the dish in that scraps, leftovers and off-cuts were cast into the pot as they were said, perhaps jocosely, to be on the verge of mouldering. (The etymologists are curiously silent on the derivation of the word *podrida* in *olla podrida*. The *OED* hazards a guess: 'It is not known why *olla podrida* was so called in Spanish; perhaps from the resemblance of the bubbling and swelling appearance of the slow-cooking stew to festering putrefaction': Draft Revision, March 2004.)

The survival of this odd expression has been guaranteed by a secondary meaning that has grown up over the years. The expression *pot pourri* came to be applied to a ceramic or other vase or bowl, often with a lid, containing fragrant dried fruits, herbs and spices, and hence the word was also applied to its contents. The vessel was left, lid off, in reception and other rooms to sweeten the air.

Gradually, the expression *pot pourri* became applied, figuratively, to mixtures of various sorts, in particular to medleys of music. Countless programmes in the early days of broadcasting – in the early days of 'the wireless' – were announced as 'pot pourris', pronounced /popuˈɹiz/. An early dumbing-down policy in certain 'light-music' *échelons* in the BBC dictated a short-term change of vocabulary, so that a *pot pourri* became for a while a 'musical switch'. The expression 'musical switch' died the death very rapidly.

poulbot The name of a type of cartoon character created by the eponymous Francisque Poulbot (1879-1946) and emblemizing in an affectionate way the street-urchins of, particularly, Montmartre.

'Pour encourager les autres'. 'Dans ce pay-ci il est bon de tuer de temps en temps un amiral pout encourager les autres': Voltaire, *Candide*, ch 23 (1759). 'In this country [England] it is good from time to time to kill an admiral to encourage the others'. Voltaire alludes to the execution of Admiral John Byng in 1757. Sent in 1756 to prevent the French from taking Minorca, Byng arrived when the island was already under siege. After an indecisive naval engagement, he withdrew without relieving the siege. He was court-martialled and executed for 'failure to do his utmost'.

pourboire A tip left so that the waiter might buy himself a drink. Often used figuratively. See *douceur*.

pourparler(s) Preliminary talks held in preparation for more formal discussions and conferences.

pourriture noble A grey mould, *Botrytis cinerea*, affecting grapes. It is deliberately cultivated to perfect certain French and German wines, and, in Hungary, Tokay. The mechanism by which this improvement is effected is touched on in the entry *Eiswein* in the German Lexicon. See, also, *die Edelfäule* in the German Lexicon.

'A full and scented wine, the product of the *pourriture noble*': Raymond Postgate, *The Plain Man's Guide to Wine*, vi, p 98 (1951). 'The *vin jaune* grapes are not harvested until November, by which time they have been withered by the pourriture noble ... that affects Sauternes and the great sweet wines of Germany': *Country Life*, 1658/3, 14th December 1972.

'Pourvu que ça dure' On being congratulated on her son's success, Bonaparte's mother, *Madame Mère*, cautiously agreed, saying 'Pourvu que ça dure' – 'Provided it lasts'.

précis 'A concise or abridged statement; a summary; an abstract': *OED*. The verb in English, 'to précis', is pronounced in the same way, and is inflected throughout the tenses exactly as an English verb would be. It is easy to *say* the past participle of the English verb – to rhyme with 'hayseed' – but it is extremely difficult to *write* it to the satisfaction of everyone. *Résumé* (*q.v. below*) does not present similar problems, since it is never conjugated. Written use of the verb *précis* in English, except in the infinitive, is perhaps best avoided if that is possible. Verbatim reporters have our commiserations: perhaps the diplomatic replacement of 'epitomized' in place of this unspellable past participle would be the best way out. (Similar problems arise with the Anglicized verb 'to début': *cf above*.)

'Premier pas qui coûte'. On hearing Cardinal de Polignac's saying that the decapitated St Denis had walked two leagues with his head in his hands, Madame du Deffand said, 'La distance n'y fait rien; il n'y a que le premier pas qui coûte': 'The distance is nothing; it's only the first step that's difficult': reported in a letter to Jean Le Rond d'Alembert, 17th July 1763 (Gaston

Maugras, *Trois mois à la cour de Frédéric* (1886), p 28).

première Short for *première représentation:* the first night of a stage or other production. In England, used as a noun and a verb. In England, the pronunciation either follows (but less and less) the precedent of 'premier' for Prime Minister, and is thus pronounced /'pɹɛmːjə/, or else it is pronounced as it would be in French, /pʁəmjɛʁ(ə)/. In the USA, normally pronounced /prə'mir/. Conjugating throughout the tenses does not in practice present problems with any of these pronunciations.

prêt-à-manger See next.

prêt-à-porter Literally, 'ready to carry or wear'; ready-made, ready-to-wear (of clothing); not bespoke (made to measure) but 'off the shelf'. 'Le prêt-à-porter', used substantivally, means 'readymade clothing'. The phrase *prêt-à-manger* is not a French idiom but the name of a chain of sandwich-shops in England that has with great astuteness coined a phrase that has caught on.

prestige Originally, the word was connected with conjuring tricks, with sleight of hand (*cf legerdemain, above*), but, in modern French, the meaning has moved to 'Blinding or dazzling influence; 'magic', glamour; influence or reputation derived from previous character, achievements, or associations, or, especially, from past success': *OED.*

prie-Dieu Literally, 'pray God'. An item of furniture that is more easily recognized than described. The *OED* defines the word thus: 'A desk made to support a book or books, and having a foot-piece on which to kneel; a praying-desk, kneeling-desk. A chair with tall sloping back, for the same purpose; also, a chair of this form for ordinary use'. The plural is *des prie-Dieu*: see *Le Grevisse (1993)*, § 517, p 811, which also confirms the capitalization of *Dieu*. For a succinct account of how conundrums of this type –how to form the plurals of *noms composés*– are solved in France, see *Le Grevisse*, 'Marques du Pluriel', § 514-520. We can be quite sure that, when Laurence Sterne was uttering the celebrated opening words of his *A Sentimental Journey* (1768), 'They order ... this matter better in France', he was not referring to the simplification of language.

prix fixe A fixed-price *table-d'hôte* menu. Pronounced /prifiks/.

profile An almost completely naturalized word, meaning the outline of the face seen from the side. Also much used by journalists to mean a brief outline (of a life, a career, etc). By far the most prevalent pronunciation in England is /'prouːfɑil/, though /'prouːfɪl/ is often heard in academic circles. The French /pʁɔfil/ is rarely heard in the context of ordinary English speech. *Fowler 1926* gives only /'profil/.

Pronunciation of Latin by the French The pronunciation of a third language within a second language by a speaker whose mother tongue is the first language can be a veritable nightmare.

With the increasing importance that has been placed since the 1960s on authenticity in the performance of Early Music, it was inevitable that musicologists and performers would come to examine the *pronunciation* of the words they were studying and singing. Much Early Music was of course written to be sung to Latin words. Until the last quarter of the 19th century, very few scholars attempted to pronounce Latin as it was pronounced in the Classical period: each country had its own mode of articulating the language, though, except in England, there was a core pronunciation not unlike the pronunciation the Italians have always used for Latin. The Germans did not follow the Italian pronunciation of the letter *c* before the vowels *e* and *i*, which the Italians pronounce /tʃ/, as in *coelum*, 'the sky, heaven', /tʃeːluːm/, but used the sound /ts/, /tseːlum/. There was a good deal of national sentiment at work, particularly during the Enlightenment. In Germany Febronianism, in France Gallicanism and in other European states forms of ecclesiastical nationalism (Josephism, 'Pombalism', 'Richerisme', and so on) promoted a national pronunciation that lasted, effectively, until those brought up before the French Revolution and their influence had died out. Dr Johnson's comments on the national pronunciations of Latin, which he discloses in his *Life of Milton*, is characteristic of the general acceptance of national pronunciations of Latin:

> 'There is little reason for preferring the Italian pronunciation to our own, except that it is more general; and to teach it to an Englishman is only to make him a foreigner at home. He who travels, if he speaks Latin, may so soon learn the sounds which every native gives it, that he need make no provision before his journey; and if strangers visit us, it is their business to practise such conformity to our modes as they expect from us in their own countries'.

The 'Roman' pronunciation – essentially what Dr Johnson called the 'Italian' pronunciation – asserted itself from more or less the First Vatican Council (1869) until about 1960, at which time the quest for authenticity in the performance of ancient music impelled scholars and executants to examine how exactly choirs had pronounced Latin under, say, *le Roi Soleil*. By the time Marc-Antoine Charpentier's *Prélude du Te Deum* became the signature tune (theme song) of the European Broadcasting Union in 1954, almost all performers of French Baroque music had become convinced that they should pronounce Latin as Rameau, Mondonville, and the family Couperin would have heard it pronounced. Thus, the pronunciation of the opening words of the *Te Deum*, which for a good half-century or more had at all times consistently and without fail been heard as /te'deːum'laʊdɑːmus\ te'dɒmin͵um͵confit'eːmuːr/ (that is, in the 'Roman' pronunciation), would from about 1960 have been heard as /tɛdɛœmlodɑmys\ tɛdominœmcõfitɛmyr/.

That came as a profound shock to many French ears. In essence, the Gallican pronunciation of Latin required the speaker to pronounced Latin as though it was French. Since French is a Romance language, the difference was not great – certainly not great in comparison with the pronunciation of Latin developed in England after the Reformation, which requires the words *vice versa* to be pronounced as /'vʌɪsɪ 'vəːɹsə/, or, even more colloquially, /'vʌɪsɪ' vœsə/.

With the decline in the teaching of Latin in France, the Classical pronunciation – /juljuskaisɑr/ – is little heard in ordinary conversation. The occasional Latin tag that crops up is instinctively pronounced as French. *Asinus asinum fricat* ('One donkey scratches another') would be heard as /azinysazinœmfʁikat/. That, then, is the lesson: in French, pronounce Latin as though it were French.

propos, à Often anglicized to 'apropos'. 'With regard *to*, in respect *of*, as suggested by. (Fr. *à propos de*.) *Absol.* (as introductory to an incidental observation or question): By the way': *OED*. The phrase 'apropos of nothing' is a *calque* (*q.v.*) of *à propos de rien*.

'Propriété c'est le vol': 'Property is theft'. In 1840, Pierre-Joseph Proudhon (1809-65) wrote a book entitled *Qu'est-ce que la Propriété?*, answering the question in the first paragraph of his first chapter. His answer is, 'Propriété c'est le vol'. In four words he succeeds in encapsulating both the battle-cry and the death-knell of Socialism.

protegé Literally, ' a protected one'. 'One who is under the protection or care of another, esp. of a person of superior position or influence': *OED*.

quenelle A small seasoned ball, of which the chief ingredient, commonly meat or fish, has been reduced to a paste.

> '*Richelieu garnish*, quenelles of chicken, cockscombs and slices of fat livers in brown onion sauce': J Whitehead, *Steward's Handbook*, IV, 420/1 (1889). 'Decorate the tops of each *paupiette* with small fillets of anchovy and the *quenelles* with strips of anchovy': Lucas & Hume, *Au Petit Cordon Bleu*, 53 (1936).

provenance From *provenant*, the present participle of the verb *provenir*, 'to come forth, to arise', from the Latin *prōven re*. The word means the source or origin of an artefact, or the route by which an artefact came to notice.

purée A much used word of surprisingly obscure etymology. In use, it is clearly felt to be the adjective formed from the past participle of some verb, and the feminine adjective, too, but *which* verb is open to discussion. In principle, the word is used as a name for soups, but in practice it seems that the word is reserved for such things as mashed potato (*pommes de terre purées*), with an absolute use as in 'a *purée* of mixed fruits'.

> '*Purée*, fruit, vegetable, meat or fish pounded or sieved into a finely divided pulp. The thickness of the purée depends on the amount of liquid present before sieving: a purée of cooked green peas and potatoes ... is very stiff and can be piped for decoration': *Good Housekeeping Home Encyclopedia*, p 623/1 (1951).

'Que diable allait-il faire dans cette galère?'; 'What the devil is he doing in this galley?':

Molière, *Les Fourberies de Scapin*, II vii. The word *galère* means 'galley' as in the ship propelled in part by oars wielded by galley-slaves. It means, in Moliere's play, a place where no-one would wish to be or where none of his well-wishers would wish him to be. It does not mean 'gallery' in any sense, and it does not, except remotely, refer to the galley in a ship, the place where food is prepared.

queue 'A tail'. Fully anglicized to mean a line of people standing and waiting to be served in a shop, at a booking-office, etc. In the US, 'a line'.

'Qui mange du pape en meurt'; 'Who eats the pope dies of it'. A proverbial French saying implying that whoever tangles with the Papacy will rue the day. Said by Mussolini, apropos Charles Maurras, 'Qui mange du pape en crève', ascribing the sentiment to a Roman proverb. The saying has also been attributed to Joseph de Maistre (1755-1821). It epitomizes the practical side of his closely reasoned Ultramontanism but antedates him by many years. The sentiment appears to be proverbial in both French and Italian.

'Qu'ils mangent de la brioche': 'Let them eat cake'. On her hearing that the people had no bread, Marie-Antoinette is said by her relentless and rancorous enemies to have responded, 'Qu'ils mangent de la brioche'. In fact, the remark ante-dated her by perhaps a full century. Jean-Jacques Rousseau (1712-1778) in his *Confessions*, bk 6 (1740) says, 'Enfin je me rappelai le pis-aller d'une grande full century. Jean-Jacques Rousseau (1712-1778) in his *Confessions,* bk 6 (1740) says, 'Enfin je me rappelai le pis-aller d'une grande Princesse à qui l'on disoit que les paysans n'avoient pas de pain & qui répondit, qu'ils mangent de la brioche': 'Anyhow, I recall the get-out of a great princess to whom someone said that the peasants hadn't any bread and who replied that they should eat cake'.

Qui vive Strictly, a question. 'Who lives?' To be on the *qui vive* is to be on the alert, on the lookout. The origin of the phrase is to be found in the asking for a pass-word. The sentinel asked , '[Long] live who?' The party of whom the question was asked then declared his loyalty by responding, '[Vive] le roi!', '[Vive] la France!'.

Quiproquo A Latin expression used by the French to mean 'a misunderstanding', 'getting hold of the wrong end of the stick', not a 'tit-for-tat'.

Rabelaisian The adjective from the name of the French author François *Rabelais* (*c* 1490-1553), whose works are distinguished by exuberance of imagination and language, combined with an extravagance and coarseness of humour and satire.

raconteur A 'recounter'. 'One skilled in relating anecdotes or stories': *OED*.

rafle A round-up. According to *Hatzfeld-Darmesteter*, of indeterminate etymology. The word is remembered principally for *la Grande Rafle du Vélodrome d'Hiver*, the 'great round-up' of 16-17 July 1942, in which more than 13,000 Jews were rounded up by the Vichy authorities and transported to a cycle-stadium, 'le Vél d'Hiv', where they were detained in appalling conditions for days until they were ultimately deported to various death-camps in the East.

ragoût 'A dish usually consisting of meat cut in small pieces, stewed with vegetables and highly seasoned' : *OED*.

raison d'être 'Reason for being'; the objective, rational basis for existence.

> 'There were a few trees and fields, and even a small colony of expensive privately-built houses, which was rare for a place for which the *raison d'être* now was Rimelby Main [colliery]': John Braine, *Vodi*, vii, p 102 (1959). 'A possible *raison d'être* for these sites was the chert [a form of flint], a desirable raw material': J. G. Evans, *Early Man in the British Isles*, v, p 104 (1975).

râle An abnormal sound from the lungs, not one of the normal sounds detected on ausculation.

> '"For want" says he [Laennec] "of a better or more generic term, I use the word râle, rattle, or rhoncus, to express all the sounds, besides those of health, which the act of respiration occasions"': *Good's Study Med.* (ed. 3) I, p 537 (1829)

ramequin Nowadays, a small fire-proof, normally ceramic, pot, in which savoury dishes, often cheese-based, are cooked in the oven. Sometimes desserts such as *crème brulée* are cooked in the same way. *Ramequins* are normally of a size to contain an individual portion per person. There is an obsolescent English word 'ramekin' (/ˈræməkɪn/), that denotes the pot but also denote a variety of the dishes prepared in the ramequin, some resembling a pot of Welsh Rabbit.

> '*Ramequin* [*s.v.* 'Cookery'] toasted Cheese and Bread, a Toast and Cheese. Ramequins are also small slices of Bread-crum cover'd with a Farce made of pounded Cheese, Eggs and other Ingredients bak'd in a Pie-pan': Edward Phillips, *The New World of*

English Words: or, a General Dictionary 1658 (1662, 1678, 1696; ed. 6 by J. Kersey 1706).

rapport 'Reference, relationship; connexion, correspondence, conformity. Also, harmonious accord, co-ordination': *OED*. Pronounced /ʁapoʁ/. The word is not directly related to the present-day English word 'report'.

rapporteur A functionary who provides an account of, *e.g.*, the proceedings of deliberative bodies, committees, conferences, etc for the information of superior bodies. (See *rédaction, below*.) The term is not used in England of secretaries, minute-takers, minute-keepers and so on, and certainly never of newspaper reporters. However, our increasing implication in the European Community means that we increasingly see the word in our reading matter. (The word *rapporteur* is also the French schoolchildren's equivalent to the English 'telltale'.)

rapprochement A coming or bringing together; an establishment of harmonious relations. Note that the *re-* in this word does not imply the *re*-establishment of cordial relations. It applies equally to the initial establishment of good relations.

rebours, à See *à rebours, above.*

Received Pronunciation, The *OED* defines this contentious term in an admirably dispassionate way:

> Of language or pronunciation: received pronun ciation, the pronunciation of that variety of British English widely considered to be least regional, being originally that used by educated speakers in southern England; also, the accepted standard pronunciation of any specified area. Received Standard; Received Standard English, the spoken language of a linguistic area (usu. Britain) in its traditionally most correct and acceptable form. Hence in other derived uses.

It is necessary to refer to Received Pronunciation (known for short as RP) in a *French* lexicon since one of the characteristic features of French culture is to pronounce French in an acceptable manner. 'Nous avons pris comme norme la conversation soignée du Parisien cultivé': A. Lucot & J. Rey-Debove, 'Principes Généraux de la Transcription Phonétique' *Le Petit Robert*, pXXIV (1970). It would, thus, be anomalous in the extreme to neglect what is, after all, the reciprocal of that principle – the acceptable pronunciation of *English*. However, in the early years of this present century, the waters of controversy have been poisoned by social considerations – by class considerations – that, again anomalously, find no place in the egalitarian system enjoined on France by its republican ideals. In England at the moment, the official policy of the Department of Education and the BBC is to encourage the use of 'regional accents', but experience teaches that these 'regional accents' are inextricably mixed with the ignorant misuse of words and phrases, gross and nonsensical grammar, and all the solecisms that humanity has been taught over the centuries to avoid. The public has begun to suspect that what we are being offered in place of RP is nothing better than the *argot* of the gutter.

The case of the BBC is particularly deplorable. For years the expression 'BBC English' was, for the plain man, a synonym for 'the King's English' or 'Oxford English'. 'The BBC employs an entire pronunciation unit, a small group of dedicated orthoepists (professional pronouncers) who spend their working lives getting to grips with the illogical pronunciations': Bill Bryson, *Mother*

Tongue, xiii, p 197 (1990). It must surely be recognized that there is something radically wrong with a system that professes to say how, for example, the name of the capital of Lower Slobovia is pronounced and yet is prohibited from saying how the words 'double U' are to be pronounced. It is a strange combination of absurdities that has those who most deride President George W. Bush as 'Dubbya' are themselves mostly incapable of pronouncing 'double U'. (The pronunciation of 'double U' among those who speak in 'regional dialects' is normally 'dubbuh you', as one hears with mind-numbing frequency when e-mail addresses are quoted. The sound of the letter *l* is conspicuously missing from the formulaic 'dubbuh you, dubbuh you, dubbuh you, dot BBC, dot Co, dot UK'. The full horror of the actual pronunciation is masked in 'imitated pronunciation', which cannot capture the estuarine – the Thames Estuary – sound of the vowel *u* in e-mail addresses. In the International Phonetic Alphabet it sounds /ˈdʌbəˌyː/, /ˈdʌbəˌyː/,/ˈdʌbəˌyː/. (See *déjà vu, above.*)

réchauffé Re-heated; warmed up.

recherché 'Carefully sought out'. Nowadays in England the word has come to mean 'out-of-the-way, out-of-the-ordinary, perhaps far-fetched, certainly not commonplace'.

réclame A word that, among literary people in England, seems to mean a commendable acclaim, glory, fame. However, the use of the word in France conjures up a somewhat different shade of meaning, closer, at worst, to notoriety, and, at best, to attention-seeking. The way in which French-speakers would translate our slightly old-fashioned expression, 'to puff a product', meaning to praise it in advertisements, would be *Faire de la réclame*. Items on sale are publicized as *en réclame*.

reconnaissance Originally a purely military term, but a term of such utility that it has become almost an imperative in business, politics and, in short, all human activities. Strictly, it means an examination or survey of a tract of country, carried out, before making a move, with a view to ascertaining the position or strength of an enemy, or to discovering the nature of the terrain or of the resources of the region. The difference between the French pronunciation and the anglicized one is not very noticeable. (For a discussion of the spelling and pronunciation of the word, see next.)

> 'When I went to Setuval [Setubal], it was a dark and foggy day, and the reconnaissance which I was able to make of the place was very imperfect': Wellington in Gurwood, John, ed, *The Dispatches of… the Duke of Wellington 1799–1818* (1834–38) VI, p 93 (1810).'

reconnoitre To engage in a reconnaissance, literally or figuratively. The verb came into English at a time when the spelling *oi* of the sound *ai*, /ɛ/, was common. By constant use the word became anglicized in speech, and later the pronunciation followed the spelling. That contrasts with the case of *reconnaissance*, which was brought into line with present-day French spelling. The explanation for this anomaly is to be found in the fact that the diphthong *oi* in *reconnoitre,* pronounced /ɔɪ/, carries the tonic accent and is thus the most prominent sound in the word. The diphthongs *oi* or *ai* in *reconnoissance, reconnaissance,* on the other hand, carry virtually no accent at all, being pronounced indifferently as a schwa, /ə/. The change in spelling of *reconnoissance, reconnaissance* was imperceptibly accomplished by the end of the Revolutionary Wars (1815), but the spelling and the pronunciation of the verb remained unassailably anglicized.

rédaction The word means 'sub-editing or copy preparation, the action or process of preparing matter for publication; the reduction of rough notes and drafts into literary form; revision; rearrangement'. Spelt without the acute accent and pronounced /rə'dæk:ʃn/, the word is fully anglicized but is extremely rarely used. However, the accommodating nature of the English language will no doubt find room for *rédaction* to describe what the *rapporteurs* (*q.v.*) and *rédacteurs* (including the *rédacteurs-en-chef*) will increasingly provide in this *communautaire* (*q.v.*) age. The language has already digested, as a *calque*, the expression 'margin of appreciation' for 'degree of discretion'. In *the case of Goodwin* v *UK* the courts held that the United Kingdom could 'no longer claim' that the matter fell within its 'margin of appreciation' and that the fair balance in the convention 'now' tilted in favour of the applicant: Re *Spectrum Plus Ltd. National Westminster Bank plc* v *Spectrum Plus Ltd & Ors* [2005] 4 *All ER* 209 at 222-25. When a matter that comes before the courts involves the application of 'Strasbourg legislation', one hears phrases employed such as 'Article 1 of the First Protocol was engaged in the instant case': *Beaulane Properties Ltd* v *Palmer* [2005] 4 All ER 461 at *h*. As young people eschew engagement, lawyers seem correspondingly anxious to embrace it. At all events, *rédacteur* and *rédacteur-en-chef* are terms much used in France. It is important that English-speakers should recognized them at sight, but it is not necessary to *translate* them each time they occur. For instance, *rédacteur-en-chef* does not necessarily mean 'chief sub-editor'. It might very well mean 'editor-in-chief'. The terms are best left untranslated.

redingote Though an approximation to the English word 'riding-coat', this word, pronounced /rədɛ̃gɔt/, is a proper French word, having been admitted by *l'Académie française* to the French language in 1789.

régime A particular system of rule or government, a word sometimes applied outside the sphere of politics. *Cf*, also, *ancien Régime, above.*

renaissance The enlargement of learning, art and literature, inspired by Classical models, that began in Italy in the 14th century and continued through the next two centuries. Pronounced either (anglicized) /rɪn'eɪsɑːns/ or (French) /rənɛss/ . There is of course also the spelling (and pronunciation) 'Renascence', but, despite its merits, this form has never been popular.

rendez-vous 'An appointed place of meeting or gathering; a place of common resort': *OED*. In most instances, the English pronunciation approximates closely to the French. The English plural is made merely by pronouncing the final letter *s*. Sometimes spelt without the hyphen, as one word.

rentier One who lives off *les rentes* ('government stock'), and, by enlargement, other stocks and property; one whose income derives from investment, particularly in shares and in property. Sometimes a term of disparagement (see the quotation from 1921); sometimes a neutral description of those living on fixed incomes in times of inflation (see the quotation from 1969).

> 'If it [*sc.* a society] is to ... avoid the creation of a class of *rentier*, it must not use for current consumption the whole of the wealth annually produced': R. H. Tawney *The Acquisitive Society* v. 68 (1921).
> 'Maria's uncle...is a rentier, living on an unelastic income': Aldous Huxley, *Letters*, 25 January 1969, p 579.

repartee The word *repartee* is not a French word. The French for 'A ready, witty, or smart reply; a quick and clever retort' is *une repartie*. Though, on its adoption into

English, the word *repartie* was first spelt correctly almost uniformly, the erroneous form has by now completely ousted the correct form, despite the fact that the incorrect form is an impossible form, the infinitive, *repartir*, being of the conjugation that makes its past participles in *-i* and *-ie*, not in *-é* or *-ée*. There is no doubt about the usefulness of the word–a single word for sharpness of wit in sudden reply is very valuable–but it is not a word on everyone's lips. It is surprising that a relatively sophisticated word should be universally mis-spelt, but that is the fact. At least the sound is reasonably accurate. We should probably accept the word, now, as a completely English word, not a mis-spelt French one. (The *OED*, 2nd edn, 1989, gives two pronunciations, /rɛpə'tiː/ and /rɛpɑːˈtiː/. The latter is the current pronunciation in England.)

> 'The foolish alternation of repartees in a series of single lines will never be found in Racine': Hallam, *Hist. Lit.* IV. vi. §17 (1839). 'The smiling glances of pretty barmaids, and the repartees of jocose ostlers': George Eliot, *F Holt* I (1866).

repêcher Literally, 'to re-fish'. Used in educational circles to designate having a second chance to sit an examination.

repertoire The collection of pieces, etc, that a dramatic company or an orchestra is practised in and offers to perform; of individuals, 'party-pieces'.

répondez, s'il vous plaît On invitations, 'Reply, if you please'.

repoussé Of metalwork, hammered or beaten out towards the viewer. 'Raised or beaten into relief, ornamented in relief, by means of hammering from the back or reverse side': *OED*.

restaurant Literally, a place where one restores oneself, one's energies, one's flagging spirits; a place where one eats relatively formal and often elaborate meals.

> 'The use of F. *restaurant* in this sense is stated to have originated in Paris in 1765': *OED*, 2nd edn (1989). 'The first restaurant proprietor is believed to have been one A. Boulanger, a soup vendor, who opened his business in Paris in 1765': *Encyclopaedia Britannica. Macropaedia* XV. 778/1.

On the whole, the pronunciation of the word in English is not too distant from the French. The earlier pronunciation, /'rɛstrɔŋ/, seems to have yielded, on the whole, to /'rɛstəɔ̃/.

restaurateur One who keeps or owns or manages a *restaurant*. The word merits a separate mention only by reason of the appalling prevalence of a mis-pronunciation of the word. It is commonplace to hear people say /'rɛstərɔntøɹ/ – that is, putting the letter *n* into the word where it has never existed. In this case, we cannot blame a too-religious attachment to spelling, which impels people to pronounce the letter *t* in 'soften', since spelling argues against the inclusion of the letter *n*. Nor can we blame what is sometimes called 'hyper-correction' – the influence that persuades people to say (in imitated pronunciation) 'Sweeden' rather than 'Sweed'n', and 'curtin' or 'curtayne' rather than 'curt'n'. H. W. Fowler, in *Modern English Usage* (1926) castigates the 'academic speakers who affect a more precise enunciation than their neighbours and insist on dĕ´vĭl and pĭ´ktūr instead of dĕ´vl and pĭ´kcher'. There never was a letter *n* in *restaurateur*. There is absolutely no excuse for putting one in.

résumé A *précis* (*q.v.*), a summary, an epitome. *Résumé*, most often without the accents, is frequently used in the USA for a *curriculum vitae* or C. V.

retroussé Of the nose, 'turned up'.

reveille In many ways, a difficult word. Its derivation is from *réveillez*, imperative plural of *réveiller*, 'to wake someone up, to rouse someone'. In English it means a military wake-up call, given by bugle or trumpet, or sometimes by drum. However, the French military term for this call is not *reveille* but *le reveil*, as in *Sonnez le reveil.* A poetic alternative, but actually used, is *Sonnez la diane. Le reveil* is simply 'the awaking' and is used in all circumstances, not merely military circumstances. In the British armed services the word is generally pronounced /rə'væl:ɪ/, the power of the known English word 'valley' attracting the word into that sound, but those with some knowledge of French pronounce the word /rə'vɛl:ɪ/, to rhyme with 'Kelly'. Since those with some knowledge of French were in former times normally commissioned officers, it was noticeable that the officers said /rə'vɛl:ɪ/ and the other ranks said /rə'væl:ɪ/. The pronunciation of the word in the US armed services is /'rɛv:əlɪ/, that is, with the tonic accent on the first syllable. (The *OED* says that the pronunciation in the US armed services is /rɛvə'li:/, that is, with the tonic accent on the last syllable, but that seems to be an error.)

> 'After the houre of nyne of the clock at night, ... untill the Revelly hath beaten the next morninge': in T. C. Hine *Nottingham* (1876) App. (1644). 'Soon after hearing the Drums beat the Revallie, all began to rouse their Spirits': *Memoirs of Captain P. Drake*, I. xii. 87 (1755).

revoir, au See *au revoir, above.*

revue A theatrical entertainment presenting a review (usually satirical) of current events, etc.; hence also an elaborate musical show consisting of numerous unrelated scenes or sketches. The French for 'a review', meaning 'a survey or reconsideration of some subject, perhaps with a view to a revision', is spelt *revue* but in English the spelling differential is essential: 'revue' means a stage show; 'review' means a re-consideration (or a formal inspection of troops).

ricochet Originally, the skipping of a shot, or of a flat stone on the water. In English, the word applies, in technical contexts (for example, in ballistics), to projectiles that intentionally skim or skip. Loosely, a bullet is said to *ricochet* if it bounces off something other than the target. The English pronunciation is /'rikəʃei/, which is close to the French. The English verb is pronounced as the noun, and is conjugated through the moods and tenses exactly as an English verb would be. (The final *t* is never sounded.)

'Rien ne va plus!' See *'Les jeux sont faits', above.*

riposte 'A response'. In earlier use, and still in fencing, a quick thrust given after parrying a lunge; a return thrust. In figurative use, a witty, sharp, prompt verbal response. *Cf repartee, above.*

risqué 'Bordering upon, suggestive of, what is morally objectionable or offensive': *OED*.

rissole A dish comprising seasoned meat or fish finely chopped, mixed with herbs and bread-crumbs, and then with egg to bind the ingredients, patted into small cakes and fried. The word is really a completely anglicized word, having been in the language since at least 1340. Moreover, the modern French for the dish is *croquette*.

robe de chambre A dressing-gown. The first vowel is short.

Robert, le A contemporary dictionary, *Dictionnaire alphabétique et analogique de la langue française*, compiled by Paul Robert and published from 1953 to 1964, and in 1970. A second edition was published in 1985. Almost every entry is supported by examples of usage, and usages are derived from the 16th to the 20th centuries. Synonyms and antonyms are generously provided. The dictionary is a splendid example of lexicography, modern enough to meet contemporary needs and yet scholarly enough to serve even the most demanding linguist or academic.

Rois Fainéants, les The last of the Merovingians kings of France, who were rendered powerless by their Mayors of the Palace. A *fainéant* is someone who would prefer to do nothing, an idle person, a lazybones. See *fainéant, above.*

role The part an actor takes; by extension, the part any person or thing performs in a given operation. In its own textual comments, the *OED* prints the word without its circumflex accent, and, indeed, most of the examples the *OED* quotes (the earliest being from 1606) are without the accent. It is of course open to users to recall the French origin of the word by including the accent, or to accept that the word is thoroughly naturalized and exclude the accent. The pronunciation would not be at risk either way, since those who keep the accent and those who do not still pronounced the word in the same way, which is, in any event, a pronunciation sufficiently close to the French to pass muster in almost all circumstances.

roman à clé or **roman à clef** Literally 'a novel with a key', both spellings pronounced *clé.* A novel describing real-life events behind a *façade* of fiction. The 'key', not present in the text, is the correspondence between events and characters in the novel and events and characters in real life. *Romans à clé* are often satirical and are generally written to report inside information on scandals without giving rise to charges of libel. They also give the author the opportunity to turn the tale the way he would like it to have gone. (The French tend to spell the key of a door *clé* and the musical term *clef,* though pronouncing both words identically.)

rosbif A French adaptation of 'roast beef'. First recorded from 1698 in the form *ros de bif* and in its present form from 1798. It means a slice of beef, generally cut from the sirloin, and roasted or intended for roasting. Also, sometimes, an Englishman.

rôtisserie '*Rôtisserie*, with the accent omitted, seems to be an Americanism. It signifies an eating-house wherein chickens and butcher's meat are roasted at a charcoal-grill, usually in the show-window of the establishment': H. L. Mencken, *The American Language* edn 4, p 215 (1936). Now, frequently used for the automatic, rotating spit-roasting machines found in supermarkets.

route, en On the way; in the course of a journey.

roué A reprobate; one who lives only for profligate pleasure and sensuality; a debauchee, a rake. The adjective is the past participle of *rouer*, 'to break on the wheel'. The name was first given to the profligate companions of the Duke of Orléans (*c* 1720), to suggest that they deserved that punishment.

roulade A quick succession of musical notes, in principle sung to one syllable. Also used to denote savoury and sweet dishes made with, as a stage in preparation, the rolling up of the constituents, as in a Swiss Roll.

roulette 'A game of chance played on a table with a revolving centre, on which a ball is set in motion, and finally drops into one of a set of numbered compartments': *OED*.

russe, à la See *à la russe, above*. It is perhaps worth mentioning that the word *russe* is so spelt and so pronounced. It is not *rousse*, as is so often heard. *Rousse* is a feminine adjective meaning reddish-brown, whence our 'russet'. *Russe* is pronounced /ʏys/.

ruché An adjective applied to fabrics that have been goffered, permanently, as, for example, garments with frills, or temporarily, as with lace curtains when they are hung, so that they hang 'fluted' rather than taut and flat. The goffering so produced is a *ruche*.

rusé An adjective applied to one who employs ruses; to one who is sly, shifty, cunning or deceitful.

'Sa poule au pot' Henry IV of France and Navarre is reputed to have said, 'Je veux qu'il n'y ait si pauvre paysan en mon royaume qu'il n'ait tous les dimanches sa poule au pot'; 'I wish that there might be no peasant in my kingdom so poor that he does not have a chicken in his pot every Sunday': in Hardouin de Péréfixe, *Histoire de Henry le Grand* (1681).

sabordage/sabotage Two words resembling each other in appearance and, to some extent, in meaning. *Sabordage* is the scuttling of a ship. For *sabotage*, see quotations.

> 'We have lately been busy in deploring the *sabotage* of the French railway strikers': *Church Times*, p 631/2, 11th November 1910. 'Sabotage, wanton destruction of property to embarrass or injure an enemy; such as the smashing of machinery, flooding of mines, burning of wheat and grain, destroying fruit and provisions, dynamiting reservoirs and aqueducts, tying up railroads, etc': E. S. Farrow *Dictionary of Military Terms*, p 528 (1918).

sabot A clog. A wooden shoe made of a single piece of wood shaped and hollowed out to fit the foot, as with Dutch clogs; a kind of shoe having a thick wooden sole and uppers of coarse leather, as with Lancashire clogs.

sabretache 'A leather satchel suspended on the left side by long straps from the sword-belt of a cavalry officer': *OED*. The derivation into French is from German *Säbeltasche*, from *Säbel*, 'sabre' and *Tasche*, 'pocket'. When this item is spoken of by English-speaking people, the pronunciation is /ˈsæbəɹtɑʃ/. The *OED* makes a rare correction of pronunciation by commenting that the pronunciation /ˈseɪbəɹtɑʃ/ is incorrect.

sachet Now usually a small sealed bag-like container, of flexible plastic, for holding a liquid, a powder, or scented air. Formerly much used to denote small fabric pouches or packets containing, for example, fragrant dried flowers, for placing in linen presses, drawers, cupboards and suitcases.

salmi[s] 'A *ragoût* of partly roasted game, stewed with sauce, wine, bread, and condiments': Garrett's *Encyclopaedia of Cookery* 1892). Most often served with *une sauce salmis*. The word in England is normally spelt 'salmi', though sometimes the final (silent) *s* appears. It almost always appears in writing with the letter *s*, though the word is recorded as *salmi* as early as 1718.

salon There are four meanings for this hard-worked word. It originally meant, and still means, a large reception room in, for example, a palace, mansion or other great house; also, the reception room of a Parisian lady of fashion, and those who frequent it; also *Le Salon*, the annual exhibition in Paris of painting, sculpture, etc. by living artists (and *cf le Salon des Refusés,* an exhibition ordered by Louis Napoleon in 1863 to display pictures rejected by the official Salon); and also, the most frequently encounted use today, the place of work of a hairdresser or beauty consultant.

sang-froid The character of being dispassionate, of not betraying the emotions; coolness in adversity. It ought to be remembered that the phrase is not in any way to be taken as meaning 'in cold blood' in the English sense, as in 'to kill in cold blood', or 'a cold-blooded murderer'. Pronounced /sɑ̃fʁwa/ or /sɑ̃fʁwɑ/.

sans-culotte One without breeches. The name given to the mob in Revolutionary Paris because, (it is said) unlike the better-off, they wore trousers rather than knee-breeches. The derivation is disputed.

> 'A desperate set of obscure adventurers, who led to every mischief, a blind and bloody band of Sans-Culottes': Edmund Burke, *On the Policy of the Allies*, Works, 1802, IV. P 104 (1793).

sans-gêne A useful adjectival phrase described in *le Petit Robert* thus: 'Qui agit avec une liberté, une familiarity excessive'. No word in English seems completely to capture the incisiveness of *sans-gêne.* It combines 'forwardness', 'cheek', 'insolence' and 'pushiness'.

sans peur et sans reproche See *Chevalier sans peur et sans reproche, above.*

sans serif 'Without serif'. The serif is a typographical term for the 'brackets' at the terminations of strokes in the letters known as Roman.

These characters have serifs

These characters do not have serifs

> 'The fine lines, and the cross strokes at the tops and bottoms of letters, are termed by the letter founders ceriphs': Savage *Dictionary of Printing,* p 163 (1841).

The expression 'sans serif' is almost certainly not a French expression. Its origin is lost in the mist of typographical antiquity. The etymology of the very word 'serif' is clouded in mystery. The French for 'a serif' is *un empattement,* no doubt because serifs at the end of the shanks of letter such as capital *I* have the appearance of being like the webbed feet (*les pattes*) at the end of the duck's leg. *Le Petit Robert (q.v.)* defines *un empattement* as 'Trait horizontale plus ou moins épais au pied et à la tête d'un jambage': 'A horizontal stroke more or less slender at the foot of and at the head of a down-stroke'.

The enigma of the word 'serif' is compounded by the fact that the first recorded instance in print of the use of 'sans-serif' antedates by eleven years the first noted appearance of the word 'serif' itself in print. (The absence of earlier references to serifs is easily explained: until about 1830 all typefaces had serifs. In about 1830 typefaces without serifs appeared in the typefounders' catalogues, under the generic name of 'Grotesques' or, in the USA, also 'Gothics'.)

The probability is that the word 'sans' as added to 'serif' was no more a conscious importation from modern French than Shakespeare's:

Last scene of all,
That ends this strange, eventful history,
Is second childishness, and mere oblivion,
Sans teeth, sans eyes, sans taste, sans everything.

As You Like It (1599), Act II, sc vii, 139

sans-souci Literally, 'without care'. The name Frederick the Great gave to his palace at Potsdam.

sauté 'Tossed'. Used to describe meat and vegetables that have been fried with frequent tossing.

sauve-qui-peut Literally, '[let him] save [himself] who can'. A nominal (that is, a nounal) use of the phrase, used to mean 'a general rout or fleeing, as of an army in disorderly retreat, in disarray'.

> '*Sauve qui peut!* Fr. Let those escape that can. This expression is familiar to the French in moments of defeat, and great disorder': C. James, *Military Dictionary, s.v. Sauve* (1802). 'La garde impériale entendit le sauve-qui-peut! qui avait remplacé le vive l'empereur'; Victor Hugo, in *le Petit Robert, s.v. sauve-qui-peut.*

savant 'A man of learning or science; esp. one professionally engaged in learned or scientific research.': *OED.*

savate A type of armed shoe such as was worn by those in armour to protect the foot. The word is cognate with Spanish *zapata*, 'a boot'. Now, a style of French boxing in which kicking is permitted.

savoir-faire 'To know to do'. An instinctive or acquired knowledge of what is correct or appropriate in a wide range of activities.

séance 'A sitting', from Old French *soir, to sit,* from Latin *sedére*. Nowadays, used in English only for sittings to experience spiritualist phenomena.

secateurs Pruning shears (pruners or clippers) with crossed blades. Rare in the singular. The word is an irregular formation, nominally from Latin *sector*, 'one who cuts'. The regular formation would have been *secteur*, but that word is already in use.

> 'For pruning purposes a variety of instruments have been invented, under the names of sécateurs, pruning-shears, pruning-scissors, etc': *Encyclopaedia Britannica*, XII, p 234/1 (1881). 'In certain positions it is difficult to sever a shoot with the knife without steadying it with the other hand; the sécateurs steady and cut at the same time': *The Gardener,* p 1052/2, 12th January 1901.

second (vb) Only one sense is dealt with here: 'Temporarily to transfer an officer from his regiment or corps for employment elsewhere (on the staff, or in some other extra-regimental appointment)'. The verb was adapted from the French terms *Capitaine en Second, Lieutenant en Second*, etc, to mean 'officers whose companies have been reduced, but who do duty in others, and are destined to fill up the first vacancies'. See quotation for 1802. The pronunciation of *second,* as in those ranks, is /səgɔ̃/. With characteristic opportunism, we adopted the word as a *verb,* with its authentic pronunciation of *c* as *g*, and, in order to facilitate the conjugation of this new verb, we took and pronounced the letter *d.* Moreover, we interpreted the *-on nasalized* syllable as *-oon* (see, *above, -on* and *-oon*). Thus there grew up an entire vocabulary: 'to segoond an officer', 'an officer was segoonded', 'in segoonding an officer', etc, always placing the tonic accent on the second syllable.

As to the verb 'to second', it is worth noting that within living memory the infinitive 'to second' has been pronounced /sə'gu:nd/ by elderly officers (and by one old officer still serving in 1950). The verb was fully inflected: the past participle, /səgu:ndɪd/, perfectly rhymed with 'wounded': see the quotation below for 1833.

> '*Capitaine en Second...Lieutenant en Second...*are officers whose companies have been reduced, but who do duty in others, and are destined to fill up the first vacancies. We have borrowed the expression and say, *To be seconded.* When an officer is *seconded,* he remains upon full pay, his rank goes on, and he may purchase the next vacant step, without being obliged to memorial in a manner that a half-pay officer must': C. James, *Military Dictionary, s.v. Second* (1802). 'How to cut down an army of 300,000 men to one of 100,000, with the least subsequent expense of half-pay, is a problem that ought to be solved ...; and the solution would be found in the obsolete practice of *second*-ing (or as the proper pronunciation in a mess-room is, *segoond*-ing)': *Westminster Review*, p 308, April 1833.

secondes noces, en 'In or by a second marriage'. Pronounced /ɔ̃ səgɔ̃d nɒs/.

serviette A table-napkin; a hand-towel; a (flexible) attach*é*-case. No social stigma attaches to the use of *serviette* in French.

'Si Dieu n'existait pas, il faudrait l'inventer'. 'If God was not in existence, it would be necessary to invent Him': Voltaire, *Épîtres*, no 96, *À l'Auteur du Livre des Trois Imposteurs: Œuvres complètes de Voltaire*, ed. Louis Moland, Paris: Garnier, 1877-1885, tome 10, pp 402-405. Voltaire's sentiments were not atheistic but deistic or theistic: he was a professed believer in a Supreme Being. He characterized the work he was refuting in this way: 'Ce livre des *Trois Imposteurs* est un très-mauvais ouvrage, plein d'un athéisme grossier, sans esprit, et sans philosophie': 'This book, *The Three Conspirators,* is a very bad work, full of gross atheism, without wit and without philosophy'.

'Si jeunesse savoit; si viellesse pouvoit' ; 'If youth knew; if age could': Henri Estienne (1531-98) printer, *Les Prémices,* bk 4, epigram 4 (1594). For a note on the pronunciation of the combination *-oi-* in earlier French, see *connoisseur, above.*

silhouette A portrait in profile, the area bounded by the outline painted solid. The *OED* has another of its extremely scholarly notes in the second edition, 1989, this one dealing with the derivation of this word:

> According to the usual account, which is that given by Mercier *Tableau de Paris* 147, the name was intended to ridicule the petty economies introduced by [Étienne de] Silhouette [1709-67] while holding the office of Controller-general in 1759, but *Hatzfeld & Darmesteter* take it to refer to his brief tenure of that office. *Littré,* however, also quotes a statement that Silhouette himself made outline portraits with which he decorated the walls of his château at Bry-sur-Marne.

sobriquet/soubriquet A nickname, not so much 'Buster' or 'Ginger' as 'The Bard of Avon' for Shakespeare or 'Le Petit Caporal' for Bonaparte. The modern French spelling is the former; the English spelling has tended to be the latter: the word was incorporated into English at a time when the French spelling was either, and, in consequence, the word has been used almost indiscriminately in either spelling. It thus seems that either spelling and their resultant pronunciations will co-exist for the foreseeable future.

> 'The soubriquet of *gapers* appears to have been attached to the citizens of Athens': Thomas Mitchell *tr*, *The Comedies of Aristophanes*, 1820-22; *The Acharnians*, p 121 n.

soi-disant 'Self-named' or 'self-styled'. A useful distinction is facilitated by the use of this expression: not so much 'so-called' as 'named by himself or itself', with the implication 'but not by others'. A suggestion of vain-glory is often implied.

Soigné/soignée The past participles masculine and feminine of *soigner*, 'to care for, to take care of; to 'look after'. Dressed, adorned, tended, or prepared with great care and attention to detail; well-groomed. More often seen in the feminine form, *soignée*.

> 'William Powell is of course William Powell – suave and *soigné* and perfectly poised': *Punch*, p 710/2, 24th June 1936. 'That being the case, why didn't he marry a well-bred, wide-hipped German girl who could fill up a nursery bim-bam? Certainly a clever *soigné* [*sic*] beauty like Kate would hardly seem the ideal choice for a man of Herr Jaeger's constrained austerity': Truman Capote, *Kate McCleod*, edn 1987, p 133 (1965). 'Nous avons pris comme norme la conversation soignée du Parisien cultivé': A. Lucot & J. Rey-Debove, 'Principes Généraux de la Transcription Phonétique' *Le Petit Robert*, p XXIV (1970). 'The *soignée* women and immaculate men…who could afford places like the Hilton': J Gardner, *Dancing Dodo*, xxxv, p 276 (1978).

soirée An evening party, gathering, or social event.

'Soldats, songez que, de hauts de ces pyramides, quarante siècles vous contemplent'; 'Soldiers, think! From the summit of these pyramids, forty centuries look down upon you'. Speech by Bonaparte to the Army of Egypt before the Battle of the Pyramids, in Gaspard Gouraud, *Mémoires*, vol 2, 'Egypt – Bataille des Pyramides' (1832).

sommelier Originally, the person charged by his lord (or his religious superior) with supervising the provisioning of the table in all its aspects, including, with a feudal lord, the requirements of the table during travel. The *sommelier* was responsible for superintending *la somme*, 'the pack'(that is, the baggage, including all cooking utensils and all foodstuffs, not forgetting what was to drink. The importance of that last item is reflected in the contemporary meaning of *sommelier*: the wine-waiter in a restaurant.

(As an indication of the durability of the Auld Alliance, there was a Scotch word 'somler' , meaning 'butler', in use until, more or less, the Act of Union of 1707, though the word hung on for some years after among the gentry who persevered in the speaking of Lallans.)

sortie Literally, 'a going-out'. 'A dash or sally by a besieged garrison upon an investing force' (*OED*) – their 'going out' of their fortress. Used more loosely for other military forays. Used, as well, for non-military 'goings-out', as with yachtsmen and amateur longshoremen.

soubrette This is a word for which there is absolutely no English word. It derives from the feminine adjective in Provençal that means 'coy'. In its international acceptation, it means 'A maid-servant or lady's maid as a character in a play or opera, usually one of a pert, coquettish, or intriguing character; an actress or singer taking such a part. In extended use, a woman playing a role or roles in light entertainment, e.g. on television or at a seaside variety show, with implications of pertness, coquetry, intrigue, etc': *OED*.

soufflé 'A light dish, either sweet or savoury, made by mixing materials with white of egg beaten up to a froth, and heating the mixture in an oven until it puffs up': *OED*. The over-use of the feminine form *soufflée* is no doubt due to its occurrence in one of the most popular earlier manifestations of the *soufflé*, the *omelette soufflée*.

soupçon 'A suspicion'.

soutane 'A clergyman's cassock'.

souvenir In English as spoken, the word 'souvenir', completely naturalized, tends to mean an object acquired to help its possessor to remember the occasion of its purchase. In French, the word tends to mean the *recollection* of the occasion itself, rather than anything else. *Cf* Edith Piaf's 'avec mes souvenirs': she did not mean *articles* that reminded her of the past but her actual *memories* of the past.

'Style est l'homme, le' 'Ces chose sont hors de l'homme, le style est l'homme'; 'These things [the subject matter] are external to the man; style is the man': Georges-Louis Leclerc, Comte de Buffon (1707-88), naturalist: *Discours sur le style* (an address given to the *Académie française*, 25th August 1753).

succès d'estime Yet another instance of an expression for which there is simply no English equivalent. It means a success by virtue of the reputation of the author, composer, etc, though in fact the piece might well *objectively* lack merit. (In the modern English usage of the expression, there is a hint that the audience feels that the piece *must* be good because of the reputation of the author or composer.)

succès fou Literally, a 'mad success'. A run-away success. Pronounced /syksɛfu/.

suède Literally, 'Swedish'. First introduced in 'suede gloves', gloves once extremely fashionable, made from undressed kid-skin originally imported from Sweden. The word was increasingly used, as a substantive, to mean the pelt itself. The word *suède* became for a while a colour in its own right, to describe the grey that characterized the undyed skin. Now also applied to other kinds of leather finished to resemble undressed kid-skin. The anglicized pronunciation, which is predominant, is /sweɪdː/; the French pronunciation is /sɥɛd/.

surveillance 'Watch or guard kept over a person, etc, especially over a suspected person, a prisoner, or the like; often, spying, supervision; less commonly, supervision for the purpose of direction or control, superintendence': *OED*. The generally accepted pronunciation in England is /sɛɹ'veɪːləns/, though actors in police dramas on television seem to wish to confuse 'surveillance' with 'surveyance' and create a new pronunciation, /sɛɹ' veɪːjəns/ for the practice of surveying the activities of criminals.

svelte A delicate word that almost defies definition. It means 'slim, slight, slender, supple, willowy, sylph-like', always in a fragile sense. Oddly, one could not use the adjective to describe a willow-tree: in practice, it applies only to persons – that is, men also. Its supposed etymology seems to stem from the past participle of a post-Classical unattested verb *exvellére*, meaning 'to pluck out', thus 'to select'. There does not, however, seem to be an apparent link between being selected and being *svelte* in its modern sense, except perhaps that people select for admiration others who are so formed. However, if its use is limited to slim, slender, supple, willowy persons who appear fragile rather than lithe and coiled for action, the user will not be far wrong.

table d'hôte *Dîner à la table d'hôte*: 'to dine from a fixed or set menu'.

tableau vivant Literally, 'living picture'. An obsolete form of entertainment resembling a *charade (q.v.)* in which one or more persons represent, in dumb-show and motionless, a personage, a scene, an incident, or a well known painting or sculpture, often with elaborate constumes and sometimes properties.

tache/tâche There are two very similar words in French that are sometimes, though rarely, used in English. The first is *tache*, 'a stain', which also survives in dialectal form as a verb. There is a useful Scotch verb, 'to tash', which means 'to blemish, deface; to tarnish or spoil slightly by handling or use; to make the worse for wear': *OED*. The other word is *tâche*, 'a task'. That word made a hesitant and perhaps virtually unnoticed entry into Lallans as 'tach', which did not survive. The word is cognate with the word 'tax', which certainly *did* survive. The presence of the circumflex accent in the second of these two words ought to preserve their distinction in speech, but (*cf. Circumflex Accent, above*) that is an increasingly unlikely contingency in practice.

tant pis 'So much the worse'. This phrase and its congener *tant mieux*, 'so much the better', are perfectly current French expressions, but they are not used together, as English people use them, as a 'saying': 'Tant pis, tant mieux'. If English people expect a smile from the French when they utter that 'saying', they will be disappointed. The probability is that English people have been marked by the schoolboy joke, '*Tant pis, tant mieux*: 'Auntie leaves the room, Auntie feels much better'.

> 'Madeleine convertie, tant pis : Madeleine pécheresse, tant mieux : ou plutôt, Madeleine débauchée, tans pis : Madeleine convertie, tant mieux. Tant pis, tant mieux, ce sont les deux membres de mon second point': R. P. Esprit de Tinchebray OFM Cap, *Sermon prononcé dans l'Eglise des Dames Religieuses de Haute Bruyère, 22 July 1694*; S. Pestel, pour la collection électronique de la Bibliothèque Municipale de Lisieux, 1996 (1694). '*Tant pis* and *tant mieux* being two of the great hinges in French conversation, a stranger would do well to set himself right in the use of them': Laurence Sterne, *A Sentimental Journey*, I, p 92 (1768).

Tartuffe The name of the principal character, a religious hypocrite, in a comedy, *Le Tartuffe*, by Molière (Jean-Baptiste Poquelin, 1622-73), performed in 1664 and published in 1669. Hence, a *sobriquet* for any religious hypocrite.

terrasse 'In France, etc.: a flat, paved area outside a building, especially a café, where people sit to take refreshments': *OED*. By contrast, the *OED* defines the naturalized English word 'terrace' thus: 'A raised level place for walking, with a vertical or sloping front or sides faced with masonry, turf, or the like, and sometimes having a balustrade; *especially* a raised walk in a garden, or a level surface formed in front of a house on naturally sloping ground, or on the bank of a river, as 'The Terrace' at the Palace of Westminster'. The distinction in pronunciation is no doubt worth preserving.

The *OED* also mentions 'the terraces', the tiers of seats in sports arena, the stands or even 'grandstands', ('bleachers' in the USA), and 'terraced houses'. To translate 'the terraces' into French one would say, 'la tribune' or 'les tribunes'. To translate 'terraced houses' ('row houses') into French, one would probably be obliged to employ a periphrasis, *une range de maisons de style uniforme*.

terrain Fundamentally, a tract of country considered from the point of view of its natural features, configuration, etc. The word was principally in military use, with emphasis on the tactical advantages of the land, its fitness for manœuvring, etc., but is now widely used in planning, civil engineering, touristic descriptions etc. The word is so much a part of English that it is best pronounced /tər'eɪːn/.

terrine An stoneware or similar fireproof cooking vessel, normally oval, especially one in which the comestible dish called *une terrine* is cooked. The comestible dish (that is, not the earthenware dish), is a form of *pâté*, the numerous recipes for which are of varying complexity. The word is best pronounced as uncompromisingly French, /tɛʁin/. There is a poetic and scientific English word 'terrene', meaning 'Belonging to the earth or to this world; earthly; worldly, secular, temporal, material, human (as opposed to heavenly, eternal, spiritual, divine': *OED*. It is pronounced /'tɛriːn/. The *Vulgate* translates I *Cor* 15:47: 'Primus homo de terra terrenus'; the *AV* translates it: 'The first man is of the earth, earthy'.

There is also an English word 'tureen', meaning a deep earthenware or silver-plated vessel, normally oval, with a shallow dome-shaped lid, soup being ladled from the tureen to the diner's plate. Sometimes the word is applied to a smaller vessel of similar shape used for the serving of sauce or gravy, though that smaller vessel is usually called a 'sauce-boat' or 'gravy-boat'.

> Beautiful Soup, so rich and green
> Waiting in a hot tureen!
> Who for such dainties would not stoop?
> Soup of the evening, beautiful Soup!
>
> 'Lewis Carroll', Charles Lutwidge Dodgson,(1832–1898), 'The Mock Turtle's Song', *Alice's Adventures in Wonderland*, ch. X, (1865).

The word 'tureen' derives directly from the French word *terrine*. The vowel *u* seems to have appeared because of a supposed connection with the city Turin. Though the pronunciation /tjə'riːn/ is widespread, the spelling is still patient of the older and better /tə'riːn/.

terroir A locality and its land seen from the point of view of its agricultural aptitudes, particularly as regards the cultivation of grapes for wine-production. Used also in constructions such as *Un vin qui a un goût de terroir*, to imply 'A wine that has particular characteristics associated with the nature of the soil and the climate where the vines grow'.

tête-à-tête 'Head to head'. Intimately.

timbale A dish made of finely minced meat, fish, or vegetables, cooked under a pastry-crust, often in a mould. It is so called from its appearance, which, when the pastry crust behaves itself, resembles a drum-head.

timbre Another word for which there is simply no native English alternative. The *OED* definition is exhaustive and exemplary: 'The character or quality of a musical or vocal sound (distinct from its pitch and intensity) depending upon the particular voice or instrument producing it, and distinguishing it from sounds proceeding from other sources; caused by the proportion in which the fundamental tone is combined with the harmonics or overtones (= Ger. *klangfarbe*)': *OED* 2nd edn (1989).

'Tirez le rideau, la farce est jouée': 'Ring down the curtain, the farce is over'. Words attributed to François Rabelais (1494?-1553) on his deathbed. See Jean Fleury, *Rabelais et* *ses Œuvres* (1877) vil 1, ch 3, pt 15, where it is said that none of his contemporaries authenticated the remarks. The words have nevertheless become part of the 'Rabelaisian legend'.

toilette Originally a drape or cover (*toilette* is the diminutive of *toile*, 'linen cloth'), for the dressing-table at which a lady and her maid-servant performed her grooming. Later, the action or process of dressing, itself, or, more recently, of washing and grooming in general. The progression from 'dressing-table' to 'action or process' came about, it seems, from the expression, 'the lady is at her *toilette*'. Pronounced as still fully French: /twalet/.

By a euphemism, the term *les toilettes* is substituted for such antiquated expressions as *cabinet d'aisances*. The letters *W.C.*, for 'water closet', are also much used and pronounced /dubləve se/. They seem to have no social stigma attached to them, and, moreover, appear to be destined for a lengthy future.

toque A kind of small closely fitting ladies' hat without a projecting brim, or with a very small or closely turned-up brim. Also, a chef's tall white hat. Pronounced /tɔk/.

'Touché!' In fencing and in general, an exclamation to acknowledge 'a hit, a very palpable hit'.

toupée A hair-piece; a small wig; 'a patch of false hair or small wig to cover a bald place': *OED*. Like 'repartee', and despite its acute accent, this word is not in fact French, though it no doubt derives from the French *toupet*, 'a forelock or tuft of hair'. *Un faux toupet* would be a way of expressing in French the meaning of the English word 'toupée'; see, also, *postiche, below*. There is no prospect of returning to the former anglicized pronunciation /'tupiː/. It seems likely, therefore, that we shall continue to use this 'faux-French' word written with an acute accent, and to pronounce it tolerably as a Frenchman would pronounce it.

> 'My hair hung on my head as if it were a cut-price toupée': Martin Amis, *Rachel Papers*, p 81 (1973). 'He is having his toupee fixed and his hair dyed': V. S. Pritchett, *Tale Bearers*, p 20 (1980).

tour de force A feat of strength, power, or skill.

> 'The execution of the best Artists is always a splendid tour-de-force': John Ruskin, *Lectures on Art*, I (1875) p 15 (1870).

tour d'horizon 'An extensive tour. Usu. *fig.*, a broad, general survey': *OED*.

tourniquet From *tourner*, 'to turn'. 'A surgical instrument, consisting of a bandage, a pad, and a screw, for stopping or checking the flow of blood through an artery by compression; also, a bandage tightened by twisting a rigid bar put through it': *OED*.

'Tous les jours, à tous points de vue, je vais de mieux en mieux' ; 'Each day, from all points of view, I get better and better': Émile Coué (1857-1926), psychologist, to be said morning and evening ten to twenty times. The surname of the psychologist is pronounced as a single long syllable, /kweː/.

tout, le A term for a specially successful result in certain games such as backgammon and solo.

'Tout comprendre, c'est tout pardoner': 'To understand everything is to pardon everything': Anne-Louise Germaine Necker, Madame de Staël (1766-1817).

tout court 'In short; simply; without qualification'. Pronounced /tu kur/.

tout ensemble See *ensemble, above.*

'Tout est perdu fors honneur'. Adapted from a letter written by Francois I of France to his mother after his defeat at the battle of Pavia in 1525. He had written, 'De toutes choses ne m'est demeuré que l'honneur et la vie qui est saulvé ...'; 'Of all the things I had, only honour and my life were spared'. The letter is in Dulaure, *Histoire Civile, Physique et Morale de Paris,* 1821-1825).

'Tout est pour le mieux dans le meilleur des mondes possible': 'All is for the best in the best of possible worlds'. The *dicton* summarizes the boundless optimism of Dr. *Pangloss,* philosopher and tutor in Voltaire's *Candide,* ch 30 (1759), in which characterization Voltaire satirizes one aspect of the chaotic philosophy of G. W. von Leibniz (1646-1716), his sanguine compacency. The *ODQ* (1992) has 'Dans ce meilleur des mondes possible...tout est au mieux', 'In this best of possible worlds...all is for the best', *ibid,* ch 1.

trait 'A particular feature of mind or character; a distinguishing quality; a characteristic; specifically of a culture or social group': *OED*. The pronunciation, after modern French, /tʁɛ/, was in the 19th century considered in England the correct one but has since become much less often heard; in the USA the pronunciation /treɪt/ is the established one. That pronunciation, /treɪt/, appears to be most likely to displace the pronunciation /tʁɛ/ in England. This trend is in stark contrast to the trend noted in *niche, above,* where it was suggested that foreign travel biased our language in favour of the original pronunciations of foreign words. However, there is no arguing with usage. Horace summarized matters thus:

> *Multa renascentur quae iam cicedere, cadentque*
> *Quae nunc sunt in honore vocabula, si volet usus,*
> *Quem penes arbitrium est et ius et norma loquendi.*
>
> *Ars Poetica,* 1 70.

> Many terms shall be reborn that are now dead, and others shall fall that are now held in high esteem if usage so wills it –usage, to which belongs the final judgement as to what is right and proper speech.

traiteur In France, a shopkeeper who prepares food to be purchased at retail, to be consumed off his premises, and who will also, normally, send out meals to order. 'In later use: a caterer; (one who runs) a delicatessen selling prepared meals': *OED*. This newer definition implies a much higher degree of refinement than is implicit in the expression 'takeaway'.

> 'On some evenings Flavia walked down to the village with a napkin and bowl and brought back a *plat à emporter* from the *traiteur*': Sybille Bedford, *Favourite of the Gods,* III ii, p 279 (1963). 'Our new Harrods Traiteur Department offers a delectable range of professionally prepared gourmet dishes': *Harrods Magazine,* p 34, Christmas 1985.

tranche Literally, 'a slice', as off a joint of meat. Much used in recent years in business circles as a name for instalments on, for example, a loan; a portion of an amount agreed to be borrowed and lent. 'Especially in Economics: specifically, an instalment of a loan, a quota, a block of bonds or (especially government) stock': *OED*.

> 'The first business of the bank will be the arrangement of a loan to raise $300 million ... The first *tranche* of the combined loan is expected to be offered about the end of May': *The Economist,* p 10/1, 10 May

(Suppl.) 1930. 'On 9 May a further tranche, amounting to £300 million, of 5 per cent Treasury Stock 1986-89 was issued at £84½ per cent': *Annual Register 1962*, p 477 (1963).

travesti, en This phrase is only one of many enigmas associated with cross dressing. The phrase in question, *en travesti*, though comprising French words, is not used by the French themselves. It represents a misinterpretation of the French past participle as a noun. Nevertheless, it is used widely in the English-speaking world. In theatrical circles, it is used in its original etymological sense to mean an alteration of dress or appearance; a disguise, specifically, dressing in the attire of the opposite sex. When sopranos and contraltos are cast to sing parts written for young males, or male parts originally written for *castrati*, they are said to perform 'trouser *rôles*', sometimes 'trousers *rôles*'. So also in the theatre when actresses are required to adopt male costumes. (The term does not work in reverse: a theatrical knight dressed up as the Widow Twanky is not said to be *en travesti*.)

tréma *Un tréma*, the French for the dieresis. The function of the two dots over the letters *e, i* and *u* is to signify that they and the vowels that precede them are pronounced not as diphthongs but as separate sounds, as, for example, in *celluloïde*. The *tréma* has several other highly specific function for which the reader is advised to consult *Le Grevisse (q.v.)* 1993, § 104, p 129.

triage A term adopted by hospitals beginning about the middle of the last century to denote the process of assorting and grading admissions according to the nature and severity of the wounds or sicknesses. The term had been in use for centuries in such activities as wool-production and coffee-bean cultivation. Traditionally, it was seen as the natural joining of 'try' and '-age' (as in 'carriage', 'leafage' and 'luggage') and was accordingly pronounced /ˈtraiːɪdʒ/.

The fundamental French verb is *trier*, 'to sort', which is used in such expressions as *bureau de tri* ('postal sorting office'), *triage à la main* ('handsorting') and *manœuvres de triage* ('railway shunting operations'). The verb has greatly influenced our language since Norman times, and in ways hardly suspected by users. 'To try a case in a Court of Law', for example, is one of many applications of the fundamental verb. This legal use appears to be either a Norman-French or an Anglo-French usage, since it is unknown in French itself. 'To try a person's patience' is another use. 'To try a door or window to see if it is locked' is yet another.

It seems that the French pronunciation of *triage* that is standard in hospitals is owing to the mistaken belief that this stage in the hospital-admissions procedure is a French innovation. Though that belief probably rests solely on the appearance of the word *triage*, we must accept that the French pronunciation has come to stay: it seems we must all say /tʁɪɑːʒ/ or run the risk of being thought ignorant of French.

'A special triage officer at once surveys the patients to determine the urgency of their injuries': F A Pottle, *Stretchers*, p 22 (1930). 'The word 'triage', literally 'assessment according to quality', has recently been adopted to describe the process': *Journal of the Royal Army Medical Corps*, 84 p 125 (1945). 'Chicago's Michael Reese Hospital…has instituted a 'triage', or selection system, whereby incoming patients are evaluated by an RN [Registered Nurse] as to their degree of urgency, and sent to the appropriate area': *Parade*, 18th February 8/1 (1973).

tribune A gallery, almost always in a church, reserved for notables; often, in a church, for members of the family that endowed the church. Typically, tribunes are found on the right-hand side of the nave, near the chancel, often projecting somewhat and curtained so that occupants might have a view of the chancel without being observed by the congregation. *Les tribunes* means also the stands at a race-course: see *terrasse, above*.

trompe-l'œil Literally, 'deception of the eye'. A term used for describing a genre (*q.v.*) of painting, normally of still-life subjects, in which the artist's control of perspective and his ability to paint with consummate realism are combined to produce a result that, when framed and exhibited, gives a vivid impression of being a window looking onto a real three-dimensional scene. Also used of painted surfaces in architectural settings, where, for instance, flat walls are painted to resemble marble pilasters or book-lined shelves. Pronounced /tʁɔ̃plœj/.

trottoir 'The footpath, pavement or sidewalk', used where the French word is intended to convey some special connotation of the part of a metalled road where French pedestrians walk. Often introduced into English prose to establish *couleur locale* (*q.v.*).

trou normand A renewal of appetite after having drunk, typically, a small measure of Calvados between courses in a meal. Calvados (apple brandy) is a prime product of Normandy. Calvados is one of the departments in the former province of Normandy.

> 'In his late work Caulfield [a painter] could move easily from the spare to the involved. *Trou Normand* (literally meaning 'Normandy hole', and slang for the resurgence of appetite following a glass of Calvados) is almost a riot of interlocking colours': Obituary of the artist Patrick Caulfield, *The Daily Telegraph*, 30th September 2005.

troubadour/trouvères Of the first: 'One of a class of lyric poets, living in southern France, eastern Spain, and northern Italy, from the 11th to the 13th centuries, who sang in Provençal (*langue d'oc*), chiefly of chivalry and gallantry, sometimes including wandering minstrels and jongleurs': *OED*. As to the second: The counterparts of the troubadours: Those poets and minstrels who lived in the more Northerly parts of France, where the language was *la langue d'oil*. The traditional etymology for the two words derives them from a Latin root meaning 'to find' or 'to discover', but there are problems with this derivation. The words themselves, however, are well established and precise.

trouvaille 'A find, a happy or lucky find'. Sometimes, 'a windfall'. In a general sense, anything we are glad to find for ourselves, sometimes in the plural, 'nos trouvailles'.

tulle 'A fine silk bobbin-net used for women's dresses, veils, hats, etc': *OED*. According to *Littré*, the word derives from the place-name *Tulle*, chief town of the department of Corrèze, where the fabric was first manufactured. That is far from unlikely: a number of fabrics have derived their names from the places from which they originated. Instances are 'denim' ('de Nîmes'), 'lisle' (the older spelling of Lille), and 'lawn' as in 'the lawn sleeves of bishops' (from Laon). The pronunciation in England is /tjuːl/.

turquoise Literally, 'Turkish [stone]'. A precious stone found in Persia, much prized as a gem, of a sky-blue to apple-green colour, frequently opaque but sometimes translucent, consisting of hydrous phosphate of aluminium. Hence, the name of the artist's and dyer's, etc, colour. The pronunciation has altered dramatically over the years. Nowadays, it is most often heard as /'tɛɹkwoiz/, sometimes as /'tɛɹkwɑːz/ and, rarely, as French /tyʁkwɑz/. Both in French and in English, the diphthong *-oi* has undergone the variation in pronunciation discussed under *connoisseur, above.* An edition of Walker's *Critical Pronouncing Dictionary* as late as 1857 gives as the sole, unique pronunciation /tɛɹ'kiːz/.

Ubu Roi The name of a play by Alfred Jarry (1873-1907), first performed as a puppet-show for his school friends in 1888 and, later, given its stage première in 1896. It prefigures the Theatre of the Absurd. It has the distinction of commencing with *le Mot de Cambronne* (*q.v.*).

United States of America There are several place-names in the USA that recall French influence in earlier times. There are, for example: *Baton Rouge,* 'Red Stick', in Louisiana; *Boise*, from *boisé,* 'wooded'; in Idaho; *Concord*, in New Hampshire; *Detroit*, 'of the narrows', in Michigan; *Des Moines*, 'of the monks', in Iowa; *Juneau* (probably a proper name) in Alaska; *Montgomery*, certainly a surname, in Alabama; *Montpelier*, the place-name (in the USA with a single *l*) in Vermont; *Pierre (*'Peter' or 'stone', in South Dakota; *Providence* in Rhode Island, and *Saint Paul* in Minnesota.

vaudeville 'A play or stage performance of a light and amusing character interspersed with songs; also, without article, this species of play or comedy. Now in frequent use in the US to designate variety theatre or music hall': *OED*. In the USA, the word 'vaudeville' a light, often comic, type of theatrical production frequently combining pantomime, dialogue, dancing, and song, sometimes comprising animals, acrobats, comedians, dancers and singers. The pronunciation is completely anglicized: /'voudəvɪl/.

> 'There are vaudeville theatres in America and variety theatres in England': G. B. Shaw, *Daily Graphic*, 4/3, 2nd December 1911. 'You would find them in tank town vaudeville acts...in the cheap burlesque houses': Raymond Chandler, *Farewell, my Lovely*, v, p 30 (1940).

vaut le détour 'Worth the detour', a phrase occurring in *le Guide Michelin* (*q.v.*) to draw the reader's attention to some place of interest that, although off the most direct route from place to place, is nevertheless 'worth the detour'. The comment is often (unjustly) thought to be a somewhat diluted recommendation.

vedette Originally, *un soldat en vedette* was a soldierplaced in front of his lines so as to observe the enemy and report his observations. The term was adopted by printers for a short text at the head of a chapter, printed somewhat larger and/or bolder than the body-matter. Hence, by extension, it came to mean, also, the names of 'stars' printed in large characters on theatrical bill-boards and programmes. By a further extension, the word came to be applied to the 'stars' themselves.

velours 'Velvet'.

vent, dans le Literally, 'in the wind'. A phrase used to convey the notion that an idea, etc, is in fashion.

'Ventre affamé n'a point d'oreilles' : 'A hungry belly has no ears'. Jean de La Fontaine, Fables IX, fable 17 (1678-1679).

venue The place where something will happen.

'A steeple-chase in which both Universities were to take part ... The venue was fixed at B': George A. Lawrence, *Guy Livingstone; or, Thorough* iv, (1857). 'It showed a great want of judgement ... to select the former town as the venue for the semi-final tie': *Truth*, p. 362/2 13th March 1884. 'The question of the venue of the annual meeting: at present this was held on one of four greens': *The Scotsman,* p 5/4, 12th March 1901.

vespasienne A cylindrical cast-iron public urinal. A shortening of *colonne vespasienne* 'Vespasian column', from the name of Vespasian (Titus Flavius Vespasianus), Roman Emperor, AD 69-79, who introduced a tax on public lavatories. An adaptation of a passage in Suetonius's *Lives of the Caesars* tells us that, on his being rebuked by his son and successor, Titus, for making money out of urine, Vespasian replied, holding a coin to Titus's nose, 'Pecuniam non olet!': 'Money doesn't stink'.

Vichy The name of an elegant spa-town in the department of Allier in Central France, used attributively and elliptically to designate a mineral water obtained from springs there. The puppet French government operated from Vichy from 1940 to 1944.

'Victor Hugo, hélas!' In 1902, the review *L'Ermitage* asked the following question of two hundred poets: 'Quel est votre poète?' André Gide's response was, 'Victor Hugo, hélas!'

vide-grenier A clear-out of the attic.

vieillesse est l'enfer des femmes, la 'Old age is women's hell'. Attributed to Ninon de L'Enclos (1620-1705).

vieux jeu Literally, 'old game': the equivalent to 'old hat'.

vignette Originally, a design in a manuscript or book comprising vine leaves, tendrils and stems. Now, in the graphic arts: 'An ornamental or decorative design on a blank space in a book or among printed matter, esp. at the beginning or end of a chapter or other division, usually one of small size or occupying a small proportion of the space; specifically, any embellishment, illustration, or picture unenclosed in a border, or having the edges shading off into the surrounding paper; a head-piece or tail-piece...A photographic portrait, showing only the head or the head and shoulders, with the edges of the print [image] shading off into the background': *OED.*

vin de pays 'Wine of the country'; a wine from a specified region of production. The *terroir* (*q.v.*) of a region having a significant effect on the characteristics of the wine, it is important to know where the wine comes from.

vin ordinaire Simply, 'ordinary wine, table wine, wine for drinking when one is not celebrating'. The term is not a derogatory one.

vinaigrette A sauce made from oil and vinegar, often with herbs added, and used for dressing salads and cold vegetables.

vingt-et-un A card game the object of which is to achieve a score of up to twenty one but not more, counting the pips on the cards, court cards counting as ten and the ace counting as one or eleven, as the holder chooses. The game was popularly known as 'Van John' in the nineteenth century, and is nowadays much more commonly known as 'pontoon'. Both 'Van John and 'pontoon' are approximations to the French term *vingt-et-un.*

Violin d'Ingres A hobby of which one is prouder than of one's real skills. Strictly speaking, there is no overt suggestion that the executant fails to achieve an acceptable standard in his hobby. *Le Petit Robert* says, 'Le fait, pour un artiste, de practiquer un art qui n'est pas le sien (comme le peintre [Dominique]Ingres [1780-1867] pratiquant le violon). Activité artistique exercée en dehors d'une profession. 'L'aquarelle est son violin d'Ingres'': 'The fact, for an artist, of practising an art that is not his own (as the painter Ingres playing the violin). An artistic activity undertaken outside a profession. 'Water-colour is his violon d'Ingres''. Pronounced /viɔlɔ̃dɛ̃gʁ/.

vis-à-vis Over against, in comparison with, in relation to; also, literally, facing, face to face with.

visé The word *visa* as used in connection with a passport is the Latin feminine plural adjective meaning 'things *seen*'. When an entry, note or stamp has been made on a passport, it is said to be 'visaed' or 'visa'd', both of which forms are easy to say but difficult or ungainly to write. Hence, some use the French word, as in 'My passport was *visé* this afternoon'.

vivandière A *vivandier* was, literally, an authorized victualler who followed in the wake of armies so as to be able to supply them with food and other necessaries. For reasons not at all clear, the feminine form predominates in 19th-century works about Continental wars. A generic name for those not in military service but who provided support services to armies was 'camp follower', but this name, too, has attracted opprobrious connotations. No doubt many camp followers were women of questionable morals, but the general present-day acceptation of the words 'vivandier /vivandière' and 'camp follower' as being immoral hangers-on is unhistorical; see the quotation below from 1876.

> 'Operations so near to the enemy, as that the *vivandiers* and other attendants on the troops cannot with safety remain near them': Wellington in Gurwood, John, ed, *The Dispatches of … the Duke of Wellington 1799–1818* (1834–38) X 321 (1813). 'Those unfortunates who are known under the euphemistic appellation of 'camp followers'': *The Daily News,* 5/4, 3rd November 1876.

'Vive le Québec libre!'; 'Long live Free Quebec!': From a speech Général de Gaulle made in Quebec on 24th July 1967: *Discours et messages*, p 192 (1970).

voie sans issue A one-way street. See *cul-de-sac* and *impasse.*

voilà Literally, 'See there'; *voi[s],* the second-person singular imperative of the verb *voir*, 'to see', and *là*, 'there'. An exclamation approximating to 'There you are!'

voix céleste 'Celestial voice'; a stop on an organ.

voix humaine 'Human voice'; a stop on an organ.

vol-au-vent Literally, 'flight in the wind'; a puff-pastry case filled with prepared meat, fish, or vegetable matter.

volte-face A *calque (q.v.)* of the Italian expression *volta faccia*, from *volta* turn and *faccia* face, meaning, literally, the act of turning so as to face in the opposite direction, but used only figuratively to mean a complete change of attitude or opinion.

> 'He is getting to believe in evolution and has to make some curious *voltes-face* in order to retain at the same time his belief in theism': *The Atheneum*, 493/2, 20th October 1883. 'The sudden *volte-face*

> which Mr. Gladstone and Sir William Harcourt performed in 1886': *The Spectator*, 627/1, 9th November 1889.

Voudriez-vous que je m'échorchasse?' Jules-Amédée Barbey d'Aurevilly (1808-1889). 'Cela se passes rue Royale. Il est très tard. Plus personne dans les rues; Aurevilly qui, ce soir-là, a bu beaucoup de petit vin blanc en compagnie de son ami X, se soulage. Passe un sergent de ville. 'Tout de même, Monsieur, vous pourriez au moins vous rapprocher du mur'. Car Barbey garde le sentiment des distances. Alors il se retourne et 'Voudriez-vous que je m'écorchasse?". 'This happens in rue Royale. It's very late. Nobody still in the streets. Aurevilly, who, that night, had drunk plenty of white wine with his friend X, relieves himself. A policeman passes. 'All the same, Sir, you could at least get a bit closer to the wall'. Barbey, who was always careful to respect distances, [social and other], considers the matter. He then turns back and asks, 'Would you have me *skin* myself?'' (André Gide, *Journal 1889-1939*, 25th October 1929; Gallimard 1940; Bibliothèque de la Pléiade, no 54, p 948). Barbey d'Aurevilly never lost his sense of style, as is shown by his perfectly correct use of the literary imperfect subjunctive, something that cannot really be conveyed by the translation 'Would you have me *skin* myself?'

> 'Modern authors have focussed on the [French] imperfect subjunctive as a hypercorrect grammatical form and have used it to characterize or satirize the pedantic and the pretentious': *Archivum Linguisticum*, III, 4 (1972).

'Vous l'avez voulu, Georges Dandin, vous l'avez voulu'; 'You asked for it, Georges Dandin, you asked for it': Moliere, *Georges Dandin*, I, ix. George Dandin deliberately marries above his station and his life thereafter is made miserable by his in-laws. The moral of the story is, 'Vous l'avez voulu, Georges Dandin, vous l'avez voulu!'

voyeur Literally, 'a looker'; a 'peeping Tom', particularly one whose motives are sexual.

wagon-lit A railway sleeping-carriage.

Zèle See *Pas trop de zèle, above.*

Zizanie, semer la Literally, to sow tares, darnell, cockle, among the wheat. Figuratively, to foment dissension among members of the family, etc.

> Cum autem dormirent homines venit inimicus eius et superseminavit zizania in medio tritici et obit: Matt 13:25 *Vg*. 'But while men slept, his enemy came and sowed tares among the wheat, and went his way': *Matt* 13:25 *AV*.

APPENDIX

Law French

> 'Je sais que chaque science et chaque art a ses termes propres, inconnu au commun des hommes': *Fleury*
> Quotation of the title page of John Bouvier, *A Law Dictionary*, 6th edn, 1856.

Anglo-Norman and Law French

> That the Norman Conquest profoundly affected the vocabulary of English is no new discovery, but the precise nature of that transformation has so far been only imperfectly examined and its implications for the study of English etymology only partially understood: W. Rothwell, 'The Missing Link in English Etymology: Anglo-French', *Medium Aevum*, Vol 60 1991, p 173.

Professor Rothwell's comments, though pessimistic, are realistic too. However, another face of things is seen if one refers to, for example, Professor J. H. Baker's paper 'The Three Languages of the Common Law', (1998) 43 *McGill Law Journal* 5. A considerable amount of work is being done at the moment on a variety of aspects of Anglo-French as a literary and spoken language, and some of that effort inevitably elucidates some of the many obscure corners of that sub-set of Anglo-French called Law French. It is salutary to recall that 120 years ago F. W. Maitland (1850-1906) had to invest a considerable part of his energies in what was in truth *fundamental research* into Anglo-French. The field was almost completely bare of anything of a scholarly nature on the language. Robert Kelham's well-meaning *A Dictionary of the Norman or Old French Language* of 1779 was ludicrously inadequate, and, in any event, did not profess to assay the subjects of grammar and syntax. Maitland virtually started from scratch: he virtually rediscovered Anglo-French and Law French.

We have come a long way since Maitland published his account of the detective work he indulged in so gleefully and so successfully, but there are still many aspects of Law French that are shrouded in obscurity.

What is not shrouded in obscurity is the indebtedness of English-speakers to the French language as it was spoken and written in England during some five centuries. Our debt to the French of France over the subsequent centuries cannot, of course, be ignored. In fact, there is little danger of that. What can easily be ignored, on the other hand, is the salient debt we owe to our own French, Anglo-French.

An astonishing number of *French* words came into the *English* language and stayed in the language simply because they were essential words in the vocabulary of the last users of French as a vernacular in England, the lawyers. F. W. Maitland assembles a small fraction of those words: they comprise, of course, words that are essential to legal exposition, such as 'ancestor', 'heir,' 'descend,' 'revert,' and 'remain,', but he cites, also, words of a much more general application:

> 'to allege, to aver, to assert, to affirm, to avow, to suppose, to surmise (*surmettre*), to certify, to maintain, to doubt, to deny, to except (*excepciuner*), to demur, to determine, to reply, to traverse, to join issue, to try, to examine, to prove. We see a debate, a reason, a premiss, a conclusion, a distinction, an affirmative, a negative, a maxim, a suggestion. We see repugnant, contrariant, discordant. We see impertinent and inconvenient in their good old senses. We even see *sophistry*'.

See Maitland's Introduction to *The Year Books of Edward II* in the Selden Society *Rolls Series*, edited by Maitland himself. A crucial extract from Maitland's Introduction can be found at this URL (in one line):

> http://www.orbilat.com/Influences_of_Rom ance/English/RIFL-English-French-The_Anglo-French_Law_ Language.html

The great debt the English language owes to Law French has never been properly recognized by English-speakers. On the contrary, Law French has been the object of a sustained process of denigration and even execration for almost six centuries. We might perhaps attribute this sustained vilification to the innate desire of us all to emulate Dick, in *Henry VI* pt 2, act 4, sc2, lines 83-84: 'The first thing we do, let's kill all the lawyers'.

From very shortly after the advent of William the Conqueror until about AD 1400 the language of English lawyers, like that of the Royal Court, Parliament and the governing classes, was French, the French of Normandy but nonetheless French. Over the years following the Conquest, the Norman variety of French developed into a clearly recognizable dialect of French, comparable in acceptability with, for example, Picard or Poitevin. Gradually, the characteristics that identified the language as the language used in England, rather than in Normandy, came to predominate, and for that reason the dialect ought progressively, though the centuries, to acquire the name *Anglo-French,* in place of *Anglo-Norman* or *Norman French.*

It is crucially important to recognize that this language was not a mongrelized language. In the early days of the Norman dynasty, '[I]t was, in an emphatic sense,...the best form of the language spoken in Normandy': (*Black's Legal Dictionary*, 5th edn, p.1029 (1979). Later, it was 'the Frensshe of Stratford-atte-Bowe' of Chaucer's well-bred Prioress, of whom the much-travelled, cosmopolitan Chaucer simply remarks, 'for Frensshe of Paris was to her unknowe'. We sometimes forget that he had already said, immediately before, 'And Frensshe she spak full faire and fetisely'.

Indeed, Chaucer himself, as a diplomatist, must have been aware that much Anglo-French output and the products of, say, the Paris Chancery were *indistinguishable* in point of vocabulary and syntax. There were instances in both *genres* of, for example, what nowadays are immediately seen as glaring false concords. The writers of both French of the Île-de-France and of Anglo-Norman seem to have been easygoing in respects such as that. (The absence of diacritical accents in all species of early French creates a sinking feeling in modern stomachs. Fainter spirits insert them, and perhaps they are right to do so.)

It is tempting to make use, in this context, of a construct of the philologists, namely, the 'language' they have christened *Francien* for the dialect of French spoken in the Île-de-France – the dialect that has become *French* without any distinguishing adjective. No-one ever consciously spoke *Francien.* It is not merely Monsieur Jourdain's not being aware that he spoke prose: it is that *literally* no-one ever knew that he spoke *Francien* because the word for his *langue* and *parole* had not been invented at the time he was speaking it. The same applies to another linguistic construct, *Occitan.*

That which we call French is no less a dialect than Anglo-French, and the champions of 'the Frensshe of Paris' would do well to recall that fact from time to time. But this is not a point-scoring exercise: the *main* point is that the word *dialect* does not imply disparagement.

As English gradually became the language of all *strata* in English society, the fortunes of French in England deteriorated rapidly. As early as 1362 a bill was brought into Parliament that had as its objective to substitute, as the oral language in the law-courts, *la lange du paiis* in place of *la lange francais, qest trope desconue.*

In commenting on the desire of rebels in Devon to have their old Latin Mass restored, Cranmer (1489-1556) likened the use of Latin in liturgy to the use of Law French in litigation.

> In 1549 Archbishop Cranmer, contending with the rebels of Devonshire over the propriety of using English speech in the services of the Church, said, 'I have heard suitors murmur at the bar because their

attornies pleaded their causes in the French tongue which they understood not': Cranmer, *Remains*, Parker Society, p. 170

Dr Johnson tells us, in his *Life* of Milton:

> About this time, Elwood the Quaker, being recommended to him [the by-now-blind Milton] as one who would read Latin to him for the advantage of his conversation, attended him every afternoon except on Sundays. Milton, who, in his letter to Hartlib, had declared, that 'to read Latin with an English mouth is as ill a hearing as Law French', required that Elwood should learn and practise the Italian pronunciation, which, he said, was necessary, if he would talk with foreigners'.

Though he was an inveterate conservative, Sir William Blackstone (1723-80), the first Vinerian Professor, waxes indignant about the use in the courts of an alien language:

> The *record* [pronounced, in the Law, with the tonic accent on the *second* syllable, as with the verb] is a history of the most material proceedings in the cause, entered on a parchment roll, and continued down to the present time; in which must be stated the original writ and summons, all the pleadings, the declaration, view or oyer prayed, the imparlances, plea, replication, rejoinder, continuances, and whatever farther proceedings have been had; all entered verbatim on the roll, and also the issue or demurrer, and joinder therein. These were formerly all written, as indeed all public proceedings were, in Norman or law French, and even the arguments of the counsel and decisions of the court were in the same barbarous dialect.

But Blackstone's impartiality is immediately impugned by his next comment:

> An evident and shameful badge, it must be owned, of tyranny and foreign servitude; being introduced under the auspices of William the Norman, and his sons: whereby the observation of the Roman satirist was once more verified, that *Gallia causidicos docuit facunda Britannos*: Juv. XV. III.

Blackstone's invocation of Juvenal's blissfully peremptory 'Gaul has taught the British pleaders eloquence' betrays his staunchly schoolboy, 'Robin Hood', acceptance of the *Saxon 'good', Norman 'bad'* equation. He reminds us of Kipling's Norman baron and his death-bed advice to his son:

> The Saxon is not like us Normans,
> His manners are not so polite.
> But he never means anything serious
> till he talks about justice and right.
> When he stands like an ox in the furrow
> with his sullen set eyes on your own,
> And grumbles, 'This isn't fair dealings,'
> my son, leave the Saxon alone.

But, more absorbing, what did *Juvenal* mean? Sir Matthew Hale, unwittingly, gives us one explanation:

> Mr Camden and some others have thought, there was ever some Congruity between the ancient Customs of this Island and those of the Country of France, both in Matters Religious and Civil; and tells us of the ancient Druids, who were the common Instructors of both Countries. *Gallia Causidicos docuit facunda Britannos: The History of the Common Law of England* (1713)

However the lay public might have disliked and mistrusted the use of a language well and truly *desconue*, the Law adamantly adhered to it. The Law was the last stronghold of French as a living language in England.

The use of French in the courts was discontinued in 1650, under the Commonwealth, but restored to use at the Restoration. However, by 1733 its use had become indefensibly anachronistic, and in that year its use was abolished by statute – *371 years* after a bill had been introduced in Parliament to legislate its abolition.

Perhaps that counts as the longest rearguard action in history.

How did Law French remain in favour among lawyers for so many years after it had ceased to be a vernacular in England? Inevitably, it had drifted further and further from the French spoken day-by-day by the French themselves. No-one learnt it from the cradle. It was of no use in diplomacy or in international commerce. It did not facilitate Continental travel. It had no recreational literature. How, then, did it survive for so long? The answer is a two-fold one.

In the first place, there was an immensely powerful incentive for young students-at-law to become proficient in the use of Law French. Owing to the immense influence of the Year Books (the predecessors of the Law Reports) and the copious extracts from them in the legal text-books, the manner in which Law French was formally written remained in general correct over the centuries, though of course it was increasingly fossilized, if it was viewed as a living language. Nevertheless, as a technical jargon, if one can use that word without also importing its pejorative meaning, Law French was a superbly efficient means of communication. Proficiency in its use was encouraged: the rewards of success were great, particularly for the Serjeants: they practised in the Court of Common Pleas, in which they represented landed proprietors in Real Actions (actions concerning real property). Law French was heard in Real Actions until 1733. Lawyers had constant recourse to the Year Books: the text-books were replete with extracts from the Year Books. The moots of the Inns of Court and Chancery, their traditional debates-cum-mock-trials, were conducted in Law French, and in these moots the precedents of past ages were quoted in the very language they had been originally written in – no risk of *tradutore, traditore*!

The second reason for the persistence of Law French, despite its increasing corruption and degeneration into Blackstone's 'barbarous dialect', was that is was very *convenient* to use. The vast and utterly precise technical vocabulary of Law French is, even today, the object of admiration and even veneration by those who have had the privilege and pleasure of studying it.

In our own day we are accustomed to seeing official shorthand-writers in court, and are implicitly reliant on sophisticated means of publishing law reports. In addition, we have a multiplicity of means of copying matter, however lengthy and however complex. Picture the busy lawyer without any of these aids! Little wonder that his note-taking had to be terse to the point of incomprehensibility to the layman, and little wonder he had no time for the niceties of style.

Law French had many of the characteristics of the sort of speed-writing used today by those who do not profess to be verbatim shorthand-writers.

> The law Norman useth to contract many words … and the Poictevin will mince the word': J. Howell, *Instructions for Forreine Travel*, x, 127 (1642).

Abbreviation has always been the hallmark of legal note-taking, as indeed it is to this day, with Junior Counsel producing what seem to be endless reams of abbreviated longhand. The correspondence of lawyers has always been marked by the same characteristic: in *Bleak House*, when Messrs Kenge & Carboy write to Esther Summerson, the first sentence of their letter runs: 'Our clt Mr Jarndyce being abt to rece into his house, under an Order of the Ct of Chy in this cause, for whom he wishes to secure an elgble compn'.

That usage – rapid note-taking – was fatal to faultless expression. Coupled with the fact that Law French ceased to be a truly spoken language by about the middle of the fourteenth century, the increasing artificiality of the Law French exposed it to infiltration from the vernacular. It has to be remembered that a language such as Law French has no means of making new words. Once it ceases to be spoken from the cradle, any language becomes an *ossified*, a *fossilized* language. It will inevitably import words from the living language surrounding it, in the case of Law French, the language practitioners themselves used for every other form of expression. Maitland draws our attention to a case in one of the last Year Books, of the reign of Henry VIII, in which a host of English words are incorporated into the Law French: 'deer, hound, otters, foxes, fowl, tame, thrush, keeper, hunting': Y. B. 12 Hen. VIII, f. 3 (Trin. pl. 3); Pollock, *First Book of Jurisprudence,* 281. Assuredly, those words were available in Law French, but the 'legal folk-memory' was fading. Rapid note-taking and note-making do not go hand-in-hand with the consulting of dictionaries, and, in any event, there was no specifically Law-French dictionary available.

The reign of Henry VIII saw the end of the Year Books. Perhaps the admission of 'deer, hound, otters, foxes, fowl, tame, thrush, keeper, hunting' into a Year Book rang the death-knell of Law French.

A frequently quoted – quoted, perhaps, *ad nauseam* – example of the resulting mixed English-French language comes from a manuscript marginal note in *Dyer's Reports*, King's Bench 1513-81, *Anon*, 188b (1631):

> Richardson ch. Just. de C. Banc al assises at Salisbury in Summer 1631, fuit assault per prisoner la condemne pur felony que puis son condemnation ject un Brickbat a le dit Justice que narrowly mist, & pur ceo immediately fuit Indictment drawn per Noy envers le prisoner, & son dexter manus ampute & fix al Gibbet sur que luy mesme immediatement hange in presence de Court.

A recent writer comments:

> This [account] parallels the report of an affray towards the end of Elizabeth I's reign, in the trial of which, in the Star Chamber, Sir Edward Coke prosecuted. A Lancashire mayor had refused to give the accused lodging whereupon one Johnson '*done luy blowe del eare*'. Even in its last phase, the language of the courts had lost nothing of its old vigour, even though its elegance had long since vanished: Keeton, *The Norman Conquest and The Common Law* (1966), p 169.

Before we laugh too riotously at these mish-mashes of languages, we ought to recall that much of it was written for the writer's own use. In the first case above, it appeared in one of the broad margins that were characteristic of text-book production in those days – intentionally so, in order to permit diligent practitioners to keep up-to-date by doing precisely what that writer was doing, making marginal manuscript notes. But who *was* that writer? It seems he was none other than Sir George Treby (1644-1700), ultimately Lord Chief Justice of the Court of Common Pleas

(1692), a learned lawyer, a sound judge – and no fool.

Perhaps, one day, we shall experience a surfeit of this quotation about 'jecting un brickbat'. 'Enough, no more!/ T'is not so sweet now as it was before'.

Even someone of the stature of F. W. Maitland, the most dedicated of the researchers into the history of the language of the Law, was a little sardonic about the latter days of Law French:

> We know 'law French' in its last days, in the age that lies between the Restoration and the ['Glorious'] Revolution [of 1688], as a debased jargon. Lawyers still wrote it; lawyers still pronounced or pretended to pronounce it. Not only was it the language in which the moots were holden at the Inns of Court until those ancient exercises ceased, but it might sometimes be heard in the courts of law, more especially if some belated real action made its way thither. The pleadings, which had been put into Latin for the record, were also put into French in order that they might be 'mumbled' by a serjeant to the judges, who, however, were not bound to listen to his mumblings, since they could see what was written in 'the paper books.' What is more, there still were men living who thought about law in this queer slang – for a slang it had become. Roger North [1653-1734] has told us that such was the case of his brother Francis [the Lord Keeper 1682-85]. If the Lord Keeper was writing hurriedly or only for himself, he wrote in French. 'Really,' said Roger, 'the Law is scarcely expressible properly in English.' A legal proposition couched in the vulgar language looked to his eyes 'very uncouth.' So young gentlemen were adjured to despise translations and read Littleton's *Tenures* in the original.
>
> Roger North was no pedant; but he was a Tory, and not only was the admission of English to the sacred plea rolls one of those exploits of the sour faction that had been undone by a joyous monarchy, but there was a not unreasonable belief current in royalist circles that the old French law books enshrined many a goodly prerogative, and that the specious learning of the parliamentarians might be encountered by deeper and honester research. Nevertheless, that is a remarkable sentence coming from one who lived on until 1734: 'Really the Law is scarcely expressible properly in English.': from F. W. Maitland's introduction to the Selden Society's editions of the Year Books of Edward II, excerpted from *The Cambridge History of English & American Literature*, 1907-21, vol 1, §1, 'Retention of French in the Courts'. Maitland is citing Roger North, *Lives of the Norths*, I, p 33, edn 1826, (1735); R. North, *A Discourse on the Study of the Laws*, p. 13 (1824).

Roger North tells us that his brother was fluent in contemporary French. This much enhanced his fluency in Law French. For the generality of the legal profession, however, the two languages were poles apart.

And they have stayed poles apart. How, then, is Law French pronounced today, in the few instances in which it is used?

The few, isolated Law French terms that we hear used today sound almost as though they were modern English. They look like misspelt French on paper, but they certainly don't sound at all like French, misspelt or not, when they are spoken.

In truth, the pronunciation of law French has been lost.

Let us take and examine the first two Law-French terms in this Appendix, *autrefois acquit* and *autrefois convict*, and see what Professor Glanville Williams, a former Rouse Ball Professor of English Law at Cambridge, has to say of them:

> Law French words are pronounced much as they were in the Middle Ages; it is a solecism to pronounce them as if they were modern French. The pronunciation is, indeed, much nearer to modern English that it is to French. The town crier quite correctly said, 'Oy-ez,' not 'Oy-ay': Granville Williams, *Learning the Law*, p 62 (1973).

Granted, *Learning the Law* is an inexpensive paperback written for law-students. It is not intended to be a work of any profundity. Nevertheless, it purports to offer authentic, factual information to its readers. In his own imitated pronunciation, Professor Granville Williams pronounces the two terms we are examining in this way: 'oterfoyz acquit' and 'otefoyz convict', with, as he says, 'acquit' and 'convict' pronounced as usual in English', and he is perfectly correct in saying that that is exactly how the two phrases are pronounced today. However, it is extremely difficult to accept his further comment, which is a classic instance of ambiguity: 'The pronunciation is, indeed, much nearer to modern English than it is to French'. If that is intended to mean that lawyers today pronounce Law French in much the same way that their mediaeval predecessors did, then one cannot possibly agree. On the other hand, it is very easy to agree that modern Law French 'is much nearer to modern English than it is to French', though that is plainly not what Professor Williams *intended* to say.

The town crier quite correctly said, 'Oy-ez,' not 'Oy-ay'. That is perfectly true. In earlier times the final letter *z* was clearly pronounced, both in the French of France and in Anglo-French. But what is not nearly so clear is that the town crier nowadays says 'Oy-ez' because that is the way people pronounced the word in mediaeval times. It is very much more likely that the town crier says 'Oy-ez' because his script reads 'Oyez', and he reads it as English. The variability in how modern town criers (and employees of Oyez Stationers, a prominent English firm of law stationers) pronounce 'Oyez' is no doubt owing to the uncertainty of English spelling. In any event, how *exactly* does one pronounce 'Oyez'? The Anglo-Norman and Law French verb 'to hear' is *oir, oyr, oier, oyer*, in modern French *ouïr*. The town crier is using the second person plural imperative –but the *OED* gives no fewer than *five pronunciations* of that word.

In the spelling of Law-French words and phrases that have appeared in the books over the centuries there are numerous indications that anglicization of pronunciation has proceeded relentlessly. 'Pour autre vie' appears as '*pur* autre vie', which is within the tolerance we must allow to mediaeval scribes. '*Per* autre vie' no doubt shows the influence of Latin. The spelling 'pour *auter* vie', however, clearly echoes the spoken rendering. It plainly indicates a further departure from the spoken French of mediaeval times and a reciprocal further approximation to the spoken English of today, as spoken English has developed over the centuries. The trend that turns *autre* into *auter* is precisely the trend that, in spite of the spelling (in England), turns *louvre* from /luvʁ/ into /ˈluvəɹ/. Similarly, we read *in venter sa mere*, rather than *en ventre sa mere*. (The suppression of the particle *de* is common in the French of those days.)

But it seems that we have seen the turning of the tide. So few people now need to use Law French, and thus so few people hear it pronounced, that the French we learn at school is inevitably going to take its toll on Law French. We shall hear, but *de*creasingly, *feme sole* /fem səʊːl/ and feme covert /fem cʌvət/. We shall hear, but *in*creasingly, /fam sɔl/ and /fam kuvɛʁt/.

At best one really cannot say much more than this: the pronunciation of the few remnants of Law French that remain in currency is by common consent fixed by convention. Lawyers echo what their seniors have said. That is, as to the spoken Law French, what Maitland found to be true of the written Law French when he commenced his labours. For those not privy to the pronunciation used by those learned in the Law, the only guide to the pronunciation of the occasional Law French term one comes across is to pronounce it as a English person would pronounce School-French. It is not uncommon to hear the phrase we have discussed above, *in venter sa mere,* pronounced as good French in the courts nowadays, including, *de bene esse*, the genitive particle *de*.

How do English-speakers pronounce the title of Sir Thomas Malory's *Le Morte Darthur*? Each man to his choice, no doubt. In a review of Christina Hardyment's *Malory* in *The Times Literary Supplement.* (p 11, 13th January 2006), Carolyne Larrington says, 'Malory is absent from the legal records in England at this time [the 1410s to 1920s], either because he is not yet born, or because he is learning the French of France (rather than English French, as spoken by Chaucer's Prioress), the geography of the Continent and general savoir-faire'. Note, though, the masculine definite article, *le*, with the feminine form *morte*. Either Malory was not an attentive, diligent pupil or Maitland's observation was well made about the *insouciance* of our ancestors, both English and French, as to the genders of things.

Once in a while, the judges quote the Year Books *viva voce*. They appear to use the same pronunciation as Englishmen do when they say, 'La plume de ma tante' – that is, as they recall hearing it at school, not as they reconstruct it from their readings of the Year Books. The days are gone for ever during which Law French was the language of vigorous dispute in the court-room – the days in which Counsel might aver that 'La ley est raisoun', to be promptly rebutted by a vigorous denial from the Bench: 'Nenny! Nenny! La ley est la volonté des justices!'

In conclusion, it ought to be said that there is still a flourishing activity that makes day-to-day use of Anglo-French: that is, the art of blazonry in heraldry. The concision and accuracy that characterizes Law French also characterizes the art of blazonry – an entire continent in its own right *apart*!

Law French Lexicon

autrefois acquit/convict 'Previously acquitted or convicted'. It is a fundamental principle of English Common-Law jurisprudence that a man shall not be put into danger in respect of a given charge if he has already been either acquitted or convicted of that or a similar offence. 'Double jeopardy' will not be countenanced. The principle is interpreted liberally in favour of the accused person so as to discourage a practice sometimes encountered by means of which the prosecuting authorities bring a number of discrete but similar charges. The pronunciation heard in the Courts today, every day, is /'əʊteɹfɔiːz\ɔək'wict/ and /'əʊteɹfɔiːz\cən'vict/.

baron In Law French, *baron* means 'husband' and *feme* means 'wife'.

> 'Husband and wife, or, as most of our elder law books call them, *baron* and *feme*': H. J.

> Stephen, *New Commentaries on the Laws of England, 1841-45, II,* 238 (1874). '*Baron* and *feme* we call husband and wife, and *coverture* we term marriage': J. H. Burton, *The Book Hunter*, II, 132 (1862).

cestui que trust A person for whom another is trustee; a beneficiary. *Cestui,* /sɛt'wi/, sometimes /'sɛti/ was in Old French and Anglo-Norman the demonstrative pronoun 'that person'. It was originally only the accusative form, the nominative form being *cest. Cestui* represents the Late Latin *ecce istum*. The grammar of the phrase *cestui que trust* is irregular. In defining the comparable phrase, *cestui que vie (q.v.),* Thomas Blount (1618-79), in his *A Law Dictionary* 1670 (1691) says, '*Cestui qui vie* (in true French, *Cestui a vie de qui*), is he for whose life any Land or Tenement is granted'. Jeremy Bentham (1748-1832) was unhappy with the syntax of these '*cestui*' phrases, *cestui que trust, cestui que use* and *cestui que vie*, and, concentrating of the predominant one, elucidated it as follows: 'The phrase in full length would run in some such manner as this, *cestuy al use de qui le trust est créé:* 'he to whose use the trust or benefit is created'': *Principles of Legislation*, xviii, §25 *note* (1789). It was particularly important to demonstrate the real – the correct syntax – that underlies the phrases, since some practitioners had been imagining a verb to exist, *truster*, and had invented, in furtherance of their notion, a completely illusory plural form of the primary phrase, as, for example, in 'the obligations due from trustees to their *cestui que trustent*'. The New Jersey Foreclosure Statute 1937 at 2A:50–15 speaks of 'cestuis que trustent', which secures agreement in number, though, of course, the verb *truster,* even so, does not exist. (At 2A:50–13, the statute introduces an odd combination of singular and plural when it speaks of 'any cestui que trustent'.) It is perhaps small wonder that the term 'beneficiary' is the favoured term these days. However, in the next two entries we see these venerable phrases in use in a way that technical terms in all professions have a way of being used – rather well.

cestui que use A person to whose use or benefit lands or other hereditaments are held by another person. The Law interprets the word 'use' as the act or fact of using, holding, or possessing land or other property so as to derive revenue, profit, or other benefit from such using, holding, etc. 'They conveyed their full estates of their lands in their good health, to friends in trust...and this trust was called, the use of the land': Bacon, *The Elements of the Common Lawes; Maxims and Use,* II (1635) 57.

cestui que vie 'Where a person is entitled to an estate or interest in property during the life of another, the latter is called the *cestui que vie*': *Osborn's Concise Law Dictionary* (1976).

conge d'eslire (often *congé* with *d'elire* or *d'élire*). Literally, 'permission to elect'. By 25 Hen, 8, cap 20, the Crown, on the vacancy of an archbishopric or bishopric, issues Letter Patent giving permission to and requiring the dean and chapter of the see in question to elect the Crown's nominee, named in an accompanying Letter Missive.

> 'A gentleman having said that a *congé d'élire* has not, perhaps, the force of a command, but may be considered only as a strong recommendation; 'Sir, (replied Johnson, who overheard him), it is such a recommendation, as if I should throw you out of a two-pair of stairs window, and recommend to you to fall soft'': Boswell, *Life of Johnson*, June 1784.

culprit This word is one of the most astonishing words in the English language. That it *is* part of the English language no-one will doubt who has moved in all ranks in English society. The 'culprit' is the one who 'did it'. Everyone from the uppermost point of society down to the very pit of Hell knows the word 'culprit' and uses it – and yet the word ought not, in truth, to exists *at all.*

Its existence is owing entirely to the practice of law clerks of using abbreviations as a matter of course. The most concise account of how this utterly confected word came into currency is probably that given by Thomas Blount in *A Law Dictionary,* 1670 (1691):

> Culprit is compounded of two words, *i.e. Cul* and *Prit, viz. Cul,* which is the Abbreviation of *Culpabilis,* and is a Reply of a proper Officer in the behalf of the King, affirming the Party to be guilty after he hath pleaded Not Guilty, without which the Issue is not joined: The other word *Prit* is derived from the French word *Prest, i.e.* ready; and 'tis as much as to say, That he is ready to prove the Party guilty.

Blount means, there, that an old past participle of *prendre,* is involved, *prist,* which we should nowadays read as *prêt.*

The second edition of the *OED* (1989) supplies an informative note to the definition as in *Blount*: This explanation is in accordance with the fact that the formula *prest* (*prist*) is of constant occurrence in mediæval procedure, to signify that the parties are ready to go to judgement on a point of law, or to trial on an issue of fact: see the old Year-books *passim*; e.g. *Year-book 35 Edw. I* (Rolls) 451 '*Herle.* La pasture de Strepham tut une e nent severe; prest. *Passeley.* Issi severe qe vous ne devez comuner outre les boundes, etc. prest. *Bereford* [Justice]. Vous estes a issue', etc. The force of *prest* further appears in *Year-bk. Michaelmas 12 Edw. III,* Plea 15 'Le defendant dit..qe les blees furent sciez et emporte[z]; prest, etc.', where another MS. for 'prest, etc.' reads 'et demanda jugement'. Moreover *non cul prist* actually appears as an abbreviated form. In the *Liber Assisarum,* anno 22° Edw. I., placitum 41, we find in the report (*Livre des Assises,* 1679, p. 94) '*Bank.* Il semble que vous luy fistes tresp'..Pur que r[espo]nd[ez]. *Richm.* [for *Defendant*] De rien culpable, prest daverrer nostre bill', etc. This, in Brooke's *Abridgement* (1568) fol. 7, Section *Accion sur le case,* Plea 78, is thus cited: '*Banke Justic.* Vous luy fist tort..p' q' rñd'. *Richm.* non cul prist, etc.'.

detinue The feminine past participle of the verb *retenir.* The unlawful detaining of goods belonging to another. Nowadays a more common expression is 'detention of goods'. The modern sense of 'to detain' is to delay the departure of someone, as in, 'Don't let me detain you'. 'Detaining' in the legal sense may be seen as delaying the return to someone of his lawful possessions. An action of *detinue* lies where a person is unlawfully denied return or release of his goods. By the action of detinue, he claims the specific return of goods wrongfully detained from him, or their value, with or without a claim for hire or for damages for detention. (Nowadays, rights of this nature are enforced by means of a Writ of Delivery.)

> '[Detinue is an action] that lies against him who having goods or chattels delivered to him to keep [*scil,* to keep safe], refuses to re-deliver them': *Termes de la Ley,* 1641.

distress The act or fact of distraining, which is the legal seizure and detention of a chattel, originally for the purpose of constraining the owner to pay money owed by him or to make satisfaction for some wrong done by him, or to do some other act (*e.g.*, to appear in court). In modern times, the term means the seizure of goods, either the actual physical seizure of the goods or a legal equivalent (*e.g.*, 'walking possession'), in order that they might be sold if they are not redeemed within a fixed period. If they are sold, the creditor is reimbursed from the proceeds of the sale. Distress is most frequently employed these days for the recovery of rent unpaid. The active verb is 'to distrain [upon]', or 'to levy a distress [upon]' the goods or chattels seized.

distress damage feasant 'Distress doing damage'. Originally an adjectival phrase but also used as a noun. An ancient common-law remedy, a species of self-help. If one found the livestock of another on one's land one was entitled to detain the animals until satisfaction had been made for any damage done: 'the cow's in the meadow, the sheep's in the corn'. 'Feasant' is the present participle of the verb *faire*; in Modern French, *faisant*. The Animals Act 1971 sec 7 replaced the common-law remedy with a statutory right to detain and sell trespassing livestock.

emblements 'The profits of sown land'. Pronounced /ɛmbləmənts/, not /ɛmbəlmənts/. The word derives from the old infinitive *emblaier*, 'to sow with corn (*blé*)'. In Modern French, *emblayer* or, with an epenthetic *v*, *emblaver*. At common law, a tenant for life or a lessee whose estate was of uncertain duration had the right, if the contingency on which the determination of his estate depended occurred between his sowing and reaping crops, to re-enter to harvest those crops, provided the determination of his estate was not due to his own act.

Where there exists a tenancy of uncertain duration, as above, the common-law right to re-enter to reap the emblements has been replaced by a right to stay in possession until a notice to quit of 12 months has been given and has expired.

en ventre sa mere 'In the womb of its mother'. Said of a child not yet born.

> 'A child *en ventre sa mère* is ... a life in being': Wharton, *Law Lexicon*, 9/12 (1848). 'Beyond all question, for many purposes, a child *en ventre sa mere* is considered as being alive': *Law Times*, XC 461/2 (1891).

Modern legislation favouring abortion calls into question these two unequivocal statements. The missing particle *de*, denoting the possessive case, is extremely common in Anglo-French. F. W. Maitland found innumerable examples of the construction (not by any mans limited to the present instance of *en ventre sa mere*) throughout the Year Books from their inception to their demise so that we might confidently say that *en ventre de sa mère* is in truth a perfectly acceptable *idiom* of Law French.

By metonymy, the noun *ventre* or *venter* is used to denote one or other of two or more wives who are (successively or otherwise) sources of offspring to the same person. Usually in phrases such as *per autre venter,* indicating that there is other issue than the issue of the matrimonial union under review).

estoppel A rule of evidence and, to some, a doctrine of law that precludes a person from denying the truth of some statement formerly made by him or denying the existence of some state of affairs that he has directly or by implication proffered as the truth, so that others alter their position to their detriment. See next. The verb is 'to estop'; it is fully inflected and is normally used in the passive: 'The defendant is estopped from denying the recitals to his own deed'.

estoppel in pais In Modern French, *en pays,* 'in the country'. The phrase *in pais* implies that some 'out in the open' conduct of a party has given legitimate rise to a belief on which other parties have acted. So, for example, a tenant, having taken a lease, cannot then dispute his lessor's title.

estovers In full, 'commons of estovers'. One of the valuable rights that existed under feudal common law. It implied the right to take from the woods or waste lands of another person with whom the claimant was in some relevant legal relationship a reasonable portion of timber or underwood for use in the tenement of the claimant. The uses to which estovers, sub-divided into housebote, haibote, and plowbote (and more), might be put ranged from fire-wood through to using offcuts from coppicing and pollarding for fence-making and fence repair, to felling timber needed to keep his dwelling in good repair, and even timber needed to build from scratch a completely new tenement. Pronoun ced /ɪ'stəʊːverz/.

estrays Valuable animals without an owner found straying in any manor or lordship. After proclamation and the lapse of a year and a day, they belong to the Crown, or, by special grant, to the lord of the manor.

feme Literally, 'a woman'.

feme couverte Much more frequently, *feme covert.* Literally, 'a covered woman', the perfectly natural and neutral word for a married woman in Law French. *Couverte* has the simple technical meaning of 'protected'.

feme sole An unmarried woman.

formedon A writ of right formerly used for claiming entailed property. The word is a Law-French creation of the law clerks. The Latin phrase was *per formam doni,* 'in the form of a gift'. The language of the actual pleading (that is, in modern French, *la plaidoirie* or *le plaidoyer*, the oral presentation of a case), as distinct from the reduction into writing of the judgement, was Law French, not Latin. The clerks thus assimilated *per formam doni* into Law French as *formedon.* Pronounced /'fɔːmɪdɒn/.

> 'There be three kinde of Writs of Formedon, viz. The first in the Discender to be brought by the issue in taile, which claime by discent *Per formam doni.* The second is in the Reuerter, which lieth for him in the reuersion or his heires or Assignes after the state taile be spent. The third is [in] the Remainder, which the Law giueth to him in the remainder, his Heires or Assignes after the determination of the estate taile': *Coke on Littleton*, 326b (1628).

feoffment Originally, the overt (*scil,* 'open') or public delivery of the possession of land by the owner, the *feoffor*, to the grantee or purchaser, the *feoffee*, comprising the ceremony called 'livery of seisin'. In the ages before literacy was prevalent, such ceremonies embodied the physical delivery of property into the corporeal possession of a person; in the case of a house, by ceremoniously giving him, for example, the ring, latch, or key of the door; in the case of land, by delivering to him a twig, a piece of turf, or the like. Such ceremonies were of crucial importance in marking dates, grants, boundaries, exceptions, inclusions and so on, which were thereafter a part of the folk heritage of the community. The origin of the jury was in part owing to the constant recourse to a body of persons who 'remembered' this and that event.

Later, as the written word gained the upper hand, the grant of seisin was reduced into writing and was known as the charter or deed of enfeoffment. The tonic accent always falls on the syllable *-feoff* except when the speaker intends to differentiate between *feoffor* and *feoffee,* in which case the tonic accent falls on the last syllable. The pronunciation of the core syllable always rhymes with 'deaf'.

'Haro, mon prince!' There is in Jersey an ancient means of seeking the assistance of the courts. It is known as the *Clameur de Haro* and is available to those whose property interests are being threatened. The *Clameur* is raised by the aggrieved party, known as the *criant*, going down on one knee on the threatened property and, bareheaded, hands clasped, and in the presence of two witnesses, saying in the hearing of the alleged wrongdoer: 'Haro! Haro! Haro! A l'aide mon Prince, on me fait tort': 'Haro! Haro! Haro! Come to my aid, my Prince, someone does me wrong'.

hotch-pot From *hocher*, 'to shake up' and *pot* 'pot'. The blending or gathering together of properties for the purpose of securing equality of division, as, for example, in the distribution of the property of an intestate parent. Some beneficiaries might already by, for example, advancement (anticipation), have received benefits, in which case they will be required to add their special share (only for the purpose of computing the share of each beneficiary) to the fund before it is distributed. They are said to bring their special share *into hotch-pot.* The procedure is in general analogous to the *collatio bonorum* of the Civil Law.

jeofail In Law French, a noun made by the law clerks from *Jeo faill*, 'I am at fault, I mistake'. The noun was the term of art for 'mistake' or 'oversight' in pleadings or other legal proceedings, and was also used to denote an acknowledgment of such error. (*Jeo* is Law French for *Je*. Despite the spelling, it is pronounced /ʤə/.)

A series of statutes attempted to remedy the frequent recourse of advocates to purely technical slips in the drafting of pleadings. These statutes are conveniently grouped under the heading of *Statutes of Jeofails.* In view of the frequently heard charge that the Law itself connives at arid technicalities, it is salutary to note that there were no fewer than *thirteen* Statutes of Jeofails between 14 Edw. 3 (1340) and 5 Geo. 1 (1718).

> 'Mistakes are also effectually helped by the statutes of amendment and *jeofails*: so called, because when a pleader perceives any slip in the form of his proceedings, and acknowledges such error (*jeo faile*) he is at liberty by those statutes to amend it': Sir Wm Blackstone, *Commentaries*, III, xxv, 407 (1768).

laches Anglo-French, 'laxity'. Pronounced /ˈlætʃɪs/. The pronunciation /ˈleitʃiz/ is sometimes heard, but that is solely owing to a mistaken belief that the word is Latin. If that were the case, the English pronunciation of the word would certainly be /ˈleitʃiz/. The prestigious textbook, *Snell on Equity*, 6th edn (1982) perpetuates this erroneous pronunciation, which is corroborated in Glanville Williams, *Learning the Law*, p 62 (1973). The word denoted negligence in the performance of any legal duty; nowadays, it denotes a delay in asserting a right, claiming a privilege, or making application for redress, by reason of which delay a litigant might forfeit his rights. The word crystallizes the equitable doctrine that delay defeats equities, or that equity aids the vigilant and not the indolent: *Leges vigilantibus, non dormientibus, subveniunt:* 'The laws come to the assistance of the vigilant, not the sleepers'.

> 'A court of equity has always refused its aid to stale demands, where a party has slept on his rights and acquiesced for a great length of time. Nothing can call forth this court into activity but conscience, good faith and reasonable diligence; when these are wanting the court is passive and does nothing. Laches and neglect are always discountenanced, and therefore, from the beginning of this jurisdiction, there was always a limitation to suits in this court': *Smith* v. *Clay*, 2 Amb. 645,(1767); 3 Bro. C.C. 639 n, per Lord Camden LC.

lese majesty 'Lèse majesté': 'treason'. Strictly, not an English common-law term but a term from the Civil Law: its presence in English jurisprudence is owing to its use in Scotch jurisprudence.

lien 'A tie', from *lier*, to tie (up). A right to retain physical possession of property (whether land, goods, or money) until a debt due in respect of it to the person detaining it is satisfied. Pronounced /'li:ən/ in England and, normally, /li:n/ in the USA.

mesne Pronounced /mi:n/ and at the root of the expression 'in the meantime': 'the middle part'. Current uses are in practice restricted to *mesne process*, the process employed in a lawsuit and authorized by the court to ensure the initial appearance of a defendant: *mesne landlord,* one who grants an underlease; and *mesne profits,* the profits of an estate received by a tenant whose possession is declared to be wrongful, most often the computation of the rent a tenant in unlawful possession would have been obliged to pay if he had been in lawful possession.

misfeasance/malfeasance/nonfeasance Three terms of art that, by themselves, seem to justify the retention of Law-French terms in our Law. They means, simply, 'wrong-doing', 'bad-doing' and 'non-doing', but smack less of the nursery than 'wrong-doing', 'bad-doing' and 'non-doing.

naif/nief Fundamentally, this word, variously spelt, is cognate with 'native' and implies 'born in a specific relationship to a feudal lordship' (perhaps a serf, *adcriptus glebae*; thus, one of the 'country folk'; hence, 'simple, uncultivated'; hence, in modern usage, 'naïve'.

Oyer and terminer Anglo-Norman *oyer et terminer*, 'to hear and determine'. In full, *commission of oyer and terminer*, or *writ of oyer and terminer*. A commission authorizing a judge on circuit to hold courts (formerly only for the hearing of certain specified offences, such as treasons, felonies, etc.). Effectively abolished by the Courts Act 1971. See *Pronunciation of Law French, below.*

parol An adjective meaning 'oral'. Said of agreements and contracts not reduced into writing or under seal. The pronunciation in this acceptation is /'pæɫəl/, rhyming precisely with 'barrel'. The acceptation relating to a released prisoner's word of honour or the conditions on which he is released before his full time is served is pronounced /pəɫ'o:l/

peine fort et dure A form of torture used on a prisoner who refused to plead, in which the prisoner's body was pressed with heavy weights until submission or death. *Peine forte et dure* was abolished by the Felony and Piracy Act 1772, in which refusal to plead to a charge was made equivalent to pleading guilty. One of the curiosities of the Common Law was that death owing to *peine fort et dure* ensured that only the deceased's goods but not his land were forfeited, which consideration persuaded many a husband and father to persevere to the end.

> 'He shall haue peyn forte & dure (that is to saye) he shall be pressyd to dethe and he shall

there forfeyte his goodes and not his landes': C. St. German, *Dyaloge Doctoure & Student* (rev.edn.) II, xli, f cv 1 (1531).

puisne Literally, 'born later, junior, inferior'. In Modern French, *puîné*. See *aîné* in the main Lexicon, *above.*

pur autre vie 'For another life'. Leases and other interests were formerly frequently granted to endure for the duration of the natural life of other nominated persons rather than for a fixed term of years certain. Tenants thus seised were said to be *tenants pur autre vie.*

replevin The restoration to, or recovery by, a person of goods or chattels distrained or taken from him, upon his giving security to have the matter tried in a court of justice and to return the goods if the case is decided against him. See *distress, above.*

rescous Cognate with 'rescue'. A species of self-help condoned within limits by the Law, entailing the forcible taking of a person or goods out of legal custody; forcible recovery (by the owner) of goods distrained.

seisin See *feoffment, above.*

semble 'It seems', an interjection in pleadings and in judgements whereby the speaker draws an inference that might not necessarily prove to be correct.

tail Literally, *taillé*, 'cut', that is, 'limited'). The Anglo-French past participle *tailé* of *tailier*, 'to cut'. (The accented last syllable was dropped in Anglo-French.) An 'entailed estate' is an estate limited in some way, as, for example, one limited to the heirs of the body of the testator.

tort This is fundamentally the simple French word for 'wrong'. Every schoolboy know 'Vous avez tort', but the genius of Law French was and is to give to that word a precise and determinate meaning that everyone can rely on as being *immutable.* In contract law and in so many other aspects of living, certainty is crucial. The Law gives to the word *tort* a fixed and determinate meaning that will withstand all the assaults of all the Philadelphia lawyers till Kingdom Come.

> An act which causes harm to a determinate person, whether intentionally or not, not being a breach of a duty arising out of a personal relation[ship] or contract, and which is either contrary to law, or an omission of a specific legal duty, or a violation of an absolute right [citing Sir Frederick Pollard]; A civil wrong for which the remedy is a common law action for unliquidated damages, and which is not exclusively the breach of a contract, or the breach of a trust or other merely equitable obligation [citing Salmond]: Osborn's *Concise Law Dictionary*, 6th edn (1976).

treasure trove Literally, *trésor trouvé*, 'treasure found'. This phrase is a clear instance of a Law French term's finding its way into the common stock of English. It would be ludicrous to pronounce 'treasure trove' as *trésor trouvé.*

trustee de son tort Said of a person who, because of his own fault, is deemed to assume the role of trustee on behalf of the beneficiary whose interest might otherwise be injured by reason of the *trustee de son tort's* acts.

venue The past participle of *venir*, to come. Pronounced /'vEnju:/. The county, district, or locality where an action is laid; the place where a jury is summoned to come for the trial of a case. Frequently in phrases such as *to lay, fix, place* or *change the venue.*

villein One of the class of serfs in the feudal system; specifically a peasant occupier or cultivator entirely subject to a lord; a tenant in villeinage; also applied to a person regarded as holding a similar position in other communities, a bondsman. The spelling *villein* is preferred nowadays so as to distinguish the word in its feudal sense from the pejorative alternative *villain* derived from the same root, though both spellings have traditionally been used for the feudal sense. The ultimate derivation is from the Latin *villa*, a country house and estate with farm buildings and land appurtenant and, hence, with bondsmen to perform the *role* of farm labourers.

> 'Time out of mind the services of the villains had been commutable for money payments': Rogers, *Agriculture and Prices*, I, iii p 62 (1866). 'The villain was not a slave, but a freeman minus the very important rights of his lord. As against all men but his lord, he was free': Freeman, *The Norman Conquest*, V, p 478 (1876).

Voir dire Sometimes *voire dire*. 'To speak the truth'. Not related to the verb *voir*, 'to see', but translating the Latin *veritatem dicere*. A preliminary examination of a witness by the judge in which he is required 'to speak the truth' with respect to the questions put to him. If his incompetency appears, because, for example, he is not of sound mind, or, if purporting to qualify as an expert, he is found to lack the requisite skill or experience, he is rejected. Often referred to as 'a trial within a trial'.

> 'Police testimony was called and a voir-dire – a trial within a trial – was held to determine whether a statement from one of the accused was admissible evidence': *Daily Colonist* (Victoria, B. C.) 13th September 42/3, 1968. 'The voire dire examination as to the qualifications of this witness…revealed that he lacked the background which would qualify him as an expert': *New York Law Journal,* 19th July 12/3, 1973. 'His Lordship was prepared to assume that the voire dire (trial within a trial) and the verdict taken together did constitute a final judgement on the same issues': *The Times*, 18th January 10/4 1980.

ACKNOWLEDGEMENTS

I am extremely grateful to my collaborators for their valued help in compiling this Lexicon. Thanks are due, in alphabetical order, to:

Sandy Atkinson, Dr Michael H Carl, Rosemary and Roy Croft, Caroline Hamilton, Hélène Hartley, Mark Hartley, Stephen Haskell, William Hosking, Trevor Martin, Neil Munro, and Dr Günther Schmigalle.

I believe I need hardly add that the expressions of deeply held, perhaps *perverse*, convictions that are scattered throughly this French Lexicon ought not to be attributed to any of my contributors. They are the compiler's own.

I must make a special mention of my indebtedness to Stephen Haskell in the compilation of this French Lexicon. His knowledge of the French language and his appreciation of French literature in its widest acceptation have been of immense help to me, something for which I shall always be most profoundly grateful.

GERMAN

The first impetus to the compiling of this Lexicon was a casual conversation among friends. I mentioned to them that a friend of mine, an autodidact coming from South Africa, had remarked, many years ago, how strange it was that only two German words had been incorporated into English, 'sobeit' and 'albeit'. He pronounced the two words exactly as if they had truly been German words, /zobaɪt/ and /albaɪt/.

We friends speculated idly about the actual number of German words and phrases that had been adopted into English and, before many minutes had passed, we were astonished at the number a few friends could conjure up relying only on memory. We decided, therefore, to go into the matter more deeply and perhaps circulate a word-list. From that simple word-list has developed this present Lexicon, and, inferentially, the other Lexicons in this book.

We gradually built up a cadre of correspondents, on whom we gratefully depended for submissions and for comments. I acknowledge by name their extremely valuable help at the end of this German Lexicon. In particular, I acknowledge our debt to our German friends, who have unstintingly given us their reaction to our forays into their mother-tongue.

None of us mentioned in this German Lexicon is a professional in linguistics, though we speak or read a variety of languages. We are alive to current usage in English, and are perhaps somewhat hypersensitized (because of our common interest in this Lexicon) to the subtle introduction of German words, phrases and ideas into our language.

In order to establish that the German words and phrases in this Lexicon are in fact used or understood by English-speakers, we have taken the presence of those words and phrases in the *Oxford English Dictionary*, the *OED*, including its current online version, as adequate proof of their use among English-speakers. In those cases, we quote the operative part of the *OED* entry. Where the text in this Lexicon is not attributed to the *OED*, it has been supplied by the compiler.

When we had reached the twentieth revision of the Lexicon, we were obliged to notice the number of words and phrases showing Germanic roots that have come into the vocabularies of English-speakers, particularly Americans, through the Yiddish language. We have therefore added a separate, self-contained appendix devoted to this aspect of our national borrowing.

We believe that the debt we owe to German life and letters is only vaguely appreciated by many English-speakers. We should like to correct that, and, in particular, we hope that, in a small way, we might do something further to heal the wounds inflicted on our societies by two World Wars in a single generation. We fervently believe that Anglo-German understanding must inevitably be immensely assisted by the recognition of the extent to which our language has benefitted from our voracious absorption of the words and phrases that follow.

The Lexicon

Abitur (abbrev. of *Abiturium*, 1881, from mod. L *abiturire*, desiderative of *abire*, 'to go away'). '[A]n examination in a wide range of subjects taken in the final year of [German] secondary school. Successful candidates were formerly entitled to a university place; the examination now forms part of the selection process for universities and other centres of higher education': *OED*.

Ablaut Literally, *ab* 'off' and *laut* 'sound'. 'Vowel permutation; systematic passage of the root vowel into others in derivation, as in *sing, sang, song, sung,* apart from the phonetic influence of a succeeding vowel as in umlaut': *OED*.

Abseil (an English adaptation of *abseilen*, literally, 'to rope down'). 'A technique in mountaineering. The technique of descent of a steep face by means of a doubled rope fixed above the climber. So, as verb intransitive, to use the *abseil* or 'rope down' technique in descent. Hence *abseiling,* [an English] verbal noun': *OED*. In colloquial German, *sich abseilen* can mean 'to disappear when trouble lies ahead'.

Abwehr The German Counter-Intelligence Service.

Achtung! Literally, 'Attention!'.

Afrika Korps (**Das Deutsche Afrika Korps** or **DAK**). The corps-level headquarters controlling the German Panzer divisions in Libya and the Western Desert, Egypt, in 1941 and 1942. The name is commonly used for both the corps headquarters and the combat units themselves. The Afrika Korps comprised four armoured divisions, four light divisions and two infantry divisions, together with Luftwaffe and Kriegsmarine support.

Aktiengesellschaft Literally, 'share-company'. A company or corporation, the liability of which is limited by shares; a joint-stock company. Approximately equivalent to a British public limited company (PLC); a company, the shares in which are in principle publicly traded. The letters *AG* are appended to the name of the company. See *Gesellschaft, GmbH* and *KG*.

Almanach de Gotha, also known as *Der Gotha*. 'From 1763 until the Russians stopped the presses when they swept into eastern Germany towards the end of the second world war [1944], the Almanach de Gotha published elaborate lists and potted genealogies of Europe's royal, semi-royal and leading ducal families. It was relaunched in 1998 ...': *The Economist*, 24 January 2002. 'Successively suppressed by Hitler, Stalin and Adenauer': Brewer's *Dictionary of Phrase & Fable*, 14th edn (1989). From 1763 to 1944 the language of the *Almanach* was French. The re-launched *Almanach* is in English.

Alpenhorn Literally, 'alpine horn'. The German-speaking nations call this musical instrument the *Alphorn*. The probable explanation of the English aberration, *Alpenhorn*, is that the shorter and more correct form gives the impression that the letters *ph* might be sounded as they are in *telephone*.

Alpenstock Literally, 'alpine stick'. 'A long staff pointed with iron, used in climbing the Alps, whence it has passed into general use in mountain climbing': *OED*.

> 'The *Alpenstock* is the name of the long iron-spiked pole, in common use on the Alps, in the hands of the chamois-hunter and the pedestrian traveller': C. Latrobe, *The Alpenstock; or Sketches of Swiss Scenery,* Advt. 5 (1829).

'Alte Jude, Der!' From an exclamation attributed to Prince Bismarck in reference to Disraeli's success on behalf of Great Britain at the Congress of Berlin (1878). The entire quotation is, 'Der alte Jude! Das ist der Mann!' ('The old Jew! *That* is the man!').

Alzheimer's Disease ('From the name of Alois *Alzheimer,* 1864-1915, German neurologist.) A grave disorder of the brain which manifests itself in premature senility': *OED.*

An die Freude Literally, 'To Joy', the title of Schiller's poem that, to music by Beethoven, has become the anthem of the European Union.

An sich Literally, 'in itself'. 'Originally taken from German philosophy': *OED.* Applied to a concept intended to be considered *in itself,* in the abstract, not in relation to anything else. See *Ding an sich.*

Angst 'anxiety, anguish, neurotic fear; guilt, remorse': *OED.*

Anschluss Literally, 'addition, annexation, union', from *anschliessen,* to join, annex. 'Annexation or union, specifically of Austria to Germany (either the actual union in 1938 or as proposed before that date)': *OED.*

Arbeit macht frei Literally, 'Work makes [you] free'. A sign above the gates of many concentration camps in Nazi Germany and the occupied countries.

Auf Wiedersehen Literally, 'to seeing again!'. A form of farewell corresponding to the English 'Goodbye'.

Aufklärung Literally, 'enlightenment'. 'The name given to a European intellectual movement in the 18th century laying claim to extraordinary intellectual illumination and enlightenment': *OED. Die Aufklärung* is the German equivalent of *The Enlightenment: cf* the French *l'Âge* or *Siècle des Lumières.* The tonic accent or stress in the word *Aufklärung* is on the first syllable.)

Aufsichtsrat Literally, 'the Inspection Board'. The supervisory board of a German company, comprising directors, managers and employees. See *Vorstand.*

Augenblick Literally, 'eye-glance'. A moment, the time taken by a glance; an instant, the twinkling of an eye.

Ausländer Literally, 'a foreigner'.

Auslese Literally, 'choice, selection', from *aus* 'out' and *Lese* 'picking, vintage'. '(Medium-)sweet wine, usually white, made (especially in Germany) from selected late-picked bunches of grapes (an official category of German wine); a wine of this category': *OED.* (*Kabinett* and *Spätlese* below.)

Autobahn A German motorway or freeway.

Baedeker Any of the series of guide-books issued by Karl *Baedeker* (1801-59) at Coblenz, or by his successors; also applied loosely to any guide-book. Also figurative.

> 'We followed the advice of our faithful Baedeker': *Miss Jemima's Swiss Jrnl.,* 29 June 1863, ii, 23 (1963). 'In the 20th century 'Baedeker' had become a synonym for guidebook and there are Baedekers not merely for the principal

European countries, but for Palestine and Syria [&c.]': *Chambers's Encycl.* I. 659/2 (1935). '*Balzac et son Monde* is an indispensable Baedeker to the *Comédie Humaine*': *Listener* 30 Apr 1959, 767/1.

Hence *Baedeker raid*, one of a series of raids by the German Air Force in April and May of 1942 upon places of cultural and historical importance in Britain.

'The 'Baedeker' raids have put the Luftwaffe in a grave dilemma': *Daily Mail* 1 May 1942, 4/7 .

(Caption) 'York's Guildhall as it appeared on the night of April 28 after it had been struck by incendiaries in one of Hitler's 'Baedeker raids' on Britain's cultural heritage. After the legitimate R.A.F. raids on Rostock, where the Heinkel factory and other munition works were destroyed, German officials frankly stated that the Luftwaffe would go out for every building in Britain which is marked with three stars in Baedeker's guide-books': *War Illustrated,* 29 May 1942, 705.

Battenberg The name of a town in Germany, in Hesse; or, alternatively, the name of the Schloss Battenberg, near Darmstadt. Used attributively to designate a kind of oblong cake, usually of two colours (with square cross-section showing alternating blocks of colour) and covered with almond paste. The name might derive from the coat of arms of the Battenbergs, though that comprised only vertical 'stripes'. (The British branch of the Battenbergs naturalized their name *Battenberg* by a direct translation to *Mountbatten.*)

Bauhaus Literally, 'architecture house', from *Bau* 'building' (*bauen* 'to build') and *Haus* 'house'. 'The name of a school of design founded in Weimar, Germany, in 1919 by Walter Gropius (1883–1969); used for the principles or traditions characteristic of the Bauhaus': *OED.*

Bayreuth 'The name of a Bavarian town in which festivals of the music of Richard Wagner have been held since 1876 in a theatre specially built for the production of his operas. Also *attrib.* and *ellipt.*' *OED***.**

Beerenauslese: See *Trockenbeerenauslese below***.**

Biedermaier An adjective derived from the name of a fictitious, naive and unintentionally comic poet, Gottlieb *Biedermaier*, lampooned in the Munich humorous weekly *Fliegende Blätter*. The name embodies *bieder*, 'worthy' and the common surname *Maier (Mayer, Maier, Mayer)*. It is applied attributively to the period between 1815 and 1848 in Germany and to styles, furnishings, etc., characteristic of that period, *esp* to a type of furniture derived from the French Empire style. Also, transferred, with the derogatory implication: conventional, bourgeois. Often mis-spelt *Biedermeier* or *Biedermayer*, though in fact the mis-spelling *Biedermeier* is nowadays virtually universal.

'The Biedermeier style ... is characterized by chairs with curved legs and sofas with rolled arms and generous upholstery': *Encycl. Brit.* IX. 948E/2 (1957).

Biergarten Literally, 'beer garden'.

Bierkeller Literally, 'beer-cellar'.

Bildungsroman Literally, *Bildung* 'education' and *Roman* 'novel'. 'A novel that has as its main theme the formative years or spiritual education of one person (a type of novel traditional in German literature). Hence *Bildungs(roman)-hero*, the main character in such a novel': *OED*.

Blaue Reiter, der Literally, 'The Blue Rider'. An art movement started in Europe just after the turn of the 20th century. The participants were considered to be the pioneers of abstract art, and their work was characterized by exuberant colour and profoundly felt emotionalism. The first exhibitions of *der blaue Reiter* included works by Wassily Kandinsky, Franz Marc, Pablo Picasso, Paul Klee, Henri Rousseau, Robert Delaunay, and Arnold Schönberg. The name of the group derived from a drawing by Wassily Kandinsky that appeared on the cover of *The Almanac*. It depicted a blue horseman. Blue was Franz Marc's favourite colour and, for both Kandinsky and Marc, the horse was a particularly favoured subject.

Blitz Short for *Blitzkrieg*, literally, *Blitz* 'lightning' and *Krieg* 'war'. 'An attack or offensive launched suddenly with great violence with the object of reducing the defences immediately …':*OED*; used by the Germans to denote the rapid and successful invasions of the early days of the Second World War. Later applied by the British to 'an air-raid or a series of them conducted in this way, especially the series of air-raids made on London in 1940': *OED*. Used colloquially in Britain as in, 'Let's have a blitz on cleaning the house!'

Blonde Bestie, die Literally, 'the blond beast'. 'A man of the Nordic type': *OED*. In English-speaking circles this phrase is habitually taken to be a description Friedrich Wilhelm Nietzsche (1844-1900) applied to what is often referred to as the typical 'Aryan' racial type. The phrase has thus found a place in the 20th century's anthology of rancour and recrimination. Nietzsche actually wrote: 'Auf dem Grunde aller dieser vornehmen Rassen ist das Raubthier, die prachtvolle nach Beute und Sieg lüstern schweifende blonde Bestie nicht zu verkennen': *Zur Genealogie der Moral,* I. 11 (1887). In discussing what might today be termed 'leadership qualities' in mankind, he had immediately before referred to the beasts of the jungle, and specifically to the lion. He then refers to the leaders of nations and to leading nations. A translation of Nietzsche's words might be: 'Clearly to be seen as common to all these lordly races is the predator, the magnificent blond beast constantly roving in search of booty and victory.' He immediately equates the leaders of different races ('Arabs and Japanese' included) with this blond beast. Though Nietzsche might not have intended to continue his reference to the lion in this passage, but to have transferred his attention to the *human* predator, it is nevertheless difficult to discern a *racial* intention in the passage: Arabs and Japanese are clearly not blonds.

> 'Nietzsche … is the victim in England of a single much quoted … phrase 'big blonde beast': G. B. Shaw, *Major Barbara*, Preface, 151 (1907). 'The man … was a magnificent creature … In structure he was the blonde beast of Nietzsche': G. K. Chesterton, *The Innocence of Father Brown*x, 266 (1911). 'My auburn hair was never really Highland red like my sister Agnes's. But I was a 'blonde beast' of Danish type unmistakably': G. B. Shaw, *Sixteen Self Sketches*, xiv, 105 (1949).

Blücher A strong leather half-boot or high shoe, the actual pattern varying with the fashion, named, on the analogy of the Wellington boot, after his co-victor the celebrated Prussian commander Field

Marshal Gebhard von *Blücher* (see *'Was für plündern!', below*). Having now made *une amende honorable* in the direction of Marschall Vorwärts ('Marshal Forwards'), we might be permitted a degree of facetiousness. There was also another meaning for the word *Blücher*, once popular in England. In addition to the private carriages they allowed into railway stations, 'The railway companies recognize two other classes of cabs, called *the privileged* and *the Bluchers*'. The latter were the 'snappers-up of unconsidered trifles'. They were 'named after the Prussian Field Marshal who arrived on the field of Waterloo only to do the work that chanced to be undone': *Athenæum* 5 Mar 1870, 328. (The German conception of the *role* Marschall Vorwärts played at Waterloo is understandably quite different from the English view. There is a colloquial expression in contemporary German, *Er geht ran wie Blücher*, 'He doesn't hang about'.)

Strictly, the name of the family is pronounced /blʏçər/ but in the context of the boots and the cabs it is very commonly mispronounced (blʊtʃə(r)) or (bluːkə). Even English-speakers who are careful of their pronunciation of German frequently ignore the existence of the sound in German represented in the International Phonetic Alphabet as /ç/, pronouncing, for example, Blücher as though it contained the sounds /χ/ or /ʃ/. The letters *ch* in the name ought to be pronounced as the letter *g* in *sagen*, /zaːˌən/, is pronounced in North Germany.

Blut und Boden Literally, 'blood and soil'. 'A Nazi catch-phrase, used *attrib.* to denote Nazi members or ideology': *OED*. In fact, the phrase significantly antedates the Nazi *régime*. It became a catch-phrase of the *Heimatkunst* ('Homeland-art') movement from the end of the 19th century, and was used to epitomize and typify the aims of that movement, which were to promote anti-urban and anti-metropolitan sentiments among fiction-writers, who were encouraged to write about the regions they grew up in and knew intimately. The subjective, *völkisch*, *heimisch*, aspects of the movement, as epitomized by the slogan *Blut und Boden*, led easily to virulent nationalism. It was this factor that attracted the Nazis to the slogan. Significantly, the local Munich newspaper *Der Münchner Beobachter*, founded in 1887 and imbued with *Heimatkunst* principles, was bought by the Nazi Party in 1920, was re-named *Der Völkische Beobachter*, and was the official organ of the party until the newspaper's closure in 1945. Paradoxically, the principles underlying the slogan *Blut und Boden* have to some extent imbued Zionism. (The slogan as translated, 'Blood and Soil', has been much used by English-speakers, in the context, among others, of 'Green' politics. The original German, however, still retains the slogan's sinister associations with German imperialism and Nazi expansionism.)

> 'The success of Fascist blood-and-soil ideology': W.H. Auden, *I Believe,* 22 (1940). 'In a small farcical form, such a charter has been refabricated in the *Blut und Boden* doctrine of modern Naziism': B. Malinowski, *Sci. Theory of Culture,* 16 (1942). 'There was a pile of stuff ... put out by some kind of East-Prussian patriotic blood-and-soil gang': M. K. Joseph, *I'll Soldier no More,* xii, 223 (1958).

Blut und Eisen Literally, 'blood and iron'. '[M]ilitary force as distinguished from diplomacy, especially in *the man of blood and iron*, Prince Bismarck, who advocated the use of this as his policy': *OED.*

> 'You will find him [Bismarck] indeed a man of "blood and iron"': *New Dominion Monthly* Oct 195/1 (1872).

'"There," they are saying, "nothing succeeds like blood-and-iron policy"': H. P. Hughes, *Social Chr.* v, 74 (1889).

Bock In full, *bock beer*, from *Bockbier*, earlier shortened from *Eimbockbier*, now *Einbecker Bier*, from *Einbeck*, *Eimbeck*, a town south of Hanover. A strong, dark-coloured variety of German beer. Also, a glass of this or any other beer. The use of the simple word 'bock' to mean, in non-German-speaking countries, the contents of a glass of any beer or the glass itself has spread considerably since the end of the First World War.

'There is a Bavarian lager beer which is called *bock*': *Illinois State Register*, 26 June 4/3 (1856). '*Bock-beer*, a favourite Bavarian double strong malt beverage, of the best lager description': Simmonds, *Dict. Trade Suppl.* (1867). 'A bock, or glass of light and frothy beer': G. A. Sala, *Paris Herself Again,* I. 183 (1879). 'Allsopp at fifty centimes the bock': *ibid.*186. 'I go there on foot daily and have a *bock*': Oscar Wilde, *Lett* (1962) 784 (1899). 'Let us ... sit for half an hour and drink our bocks': T. S. Eliot, *Prufrock,* 19 (1917).

Bocksbeutel Literally, 'buck's bag', from a perceived resemblance to a buck's or he-goat's testicle or scrotum. The name given to a flattened spherical bottle, called in the English-speaking wine trade 'a flagon', traditionally containing certain Franconian wines. Franconia (Franken) is a region of Germany bordering the river Main. In mediaeval times it was a duchy. By extension, the word *Bocksbeutel* now means, in German-speaking countries, all bottles of that shape.

Buhl from *Boulle,* the name of André-Charles *Boulle* (1642-1732), a celebrated wood-carver in France in the reign of Louis XIV. (*Buhl* appears to be a modern Germanized spelling.) 'Brass, tortoise-shell, or other material, worked into ornamental patterns for inlaying; work inlaid with buhl. Also *attrib.*': *OED.*

'Buhl-work consists of inlaid veneers; and differs from marquetry in being confined to decorative scroll-work': Ure, *Dictionary of the Arts* (1875), *s.v. Buhl.*

Bühnendeutsch See *Hochdeutsch.*

Bummel *n* and *v* (from *Bummel* 'a stroll', *bummeln* 'to stroll'). *N*: 'A leisurely stroll or journey'. *V intr*: 'To stroll or wander in a leisurely fashion'. Hence 'bummelling', *English vbl n*, 'wandering, sauntering'. *Bummeln* is also used to denote 'going slow at work', from which *Bummelstreik.*

'The verb to 'bummeln', apparently an equivalent of the French 'flâner'': *Pall Mall Gaz.,* 29 Aug 3/2 (1891). 'We do not 'bummeln' so much or so thoroughly as the Germans': *ibid. Three Men on the Bummel,* the title of a work by Jerome K.Jerome (1900). 'I should describe [a bummel] as a journey, long or short, without an end': *ibid.* xiv, 327. 'He lays out his time bummelling, beer drinking, and fighting': *ibid.* xiii, 284. 'I had already been 'bummeling' about Nepal for five months': H. W. Tilman, *Nepal Himalaya* ii. xviii, 212, (1952).

Bund (related to English usage as in 'this band of brothers', 'banded together', and 'to bind'). 'A league, confederacy, or association: specifically, (*a*) the confederation of German states; (*b*) a Jewish Social Democratic workers' organization in Eastern Europe, founded in 1897; (*c*) *US*, an American pro-Nazi organization founded in 1936. Hence *Bundist*': *OED.*

[For *(a)*:] 'The Governments of Prussia, Saxony, and Hanover have therefore agreed, according to the 11th Article of the Act of Confederation, to enter into a union (*bund*) that has for its object the mutual protection of its members': *Annual Register, 1849* 363/2 (1850). [For *(b)*:] 'After the massacre at Kischineff, after the bloodshed at Homel, the idea of self-defence took root ... and the 'Bund' was organised': *Westminster Gazette,* 4 July 4/1 1907. 'Our *Bund* is the soul of the Russian revolution; our self-defence bands are bringing back the days of Judas Maccabæus': Israel Zangwill, *Ghetto Comedies* 357 1907, and 'A Bundist!' ... From the bravest revolutionary party in Russia he could surely cull a recruit or two': *ibid.* 398. [For *(c)*]: 'But I don't think he'd dare approach any of the Bundists he once used': F. Castle, *Violent Hours,* 1956 (1966). 'Did you ever do any work on the German-American Bund?' *ibid.* vii, 72.

Bundesrat (formerly *-rath*: from genitive of *bund*, as above, and *rat(h)* council). 'A federal council; specifically, (*a*) the upper house of the German or Austrian parliament; (*b*) the federal council of Switzerland': *OED.*

[For (*a*)]: 'This Bill was adopted by the Reichstag; but the *Bundesrath*, or Federal Council, refused to pass it': *Annual Register, 1871* I 239 (1872). 'Delegates of the various confederated Governments form the Bundesrath': *Encyclopaedia Britannica,* IX. 62/1 (1879). 'The emperor has power, with the consent of the Bundesrath, to declare war in name of the empire': *ibid.* 62/2. [For (*b*)]: 'The [Swiss] federal council or executive (Bundesrath) consisted of seven members elected by the federal assembly': *ibid.* XXII. 795/2 (1887). [For Germany post-1949]: 'The ... Constitution for the 'Federal Republic of Germany'... provided for ... two Chambers, the *Bundestag* (or Lower House), elected for 4 years according to a mixed electoral system, and the *Bundesrat* (or Upper House), representing the constituent confederate *Länder* and consisting of members of their Governments appointed by them': *Annual Register, 1949* 233 (1950).

Bundesrepublik Deutschland, die Literally, 'German Federal Republic'. After the cessation of hostilities in 1945, Germany was divided by the Allies into four regions administered respectively by the American, British, French and Russian Military Governments. The civil administrations of the regions controlled by the US, Britain and France evolved into eleven *Länder* (Regions) of the *Bundesrepublik.* In September 1948 a Parliamentary Council of 65 met to discuss a constitution for a Germany returned to independence. The members of the Council were chosen by the parliaments of the eleven *Länder*, Bayern (Bavaria), Bremen, Hamburg, Hessen (Hesse), Niedersachsen (Lower Saxony), Nordrhein-Westfalen (North Rhine-Westphalia), Rheinland-Pfalz (Rhineland-Palatinate), and Schleswig-Holstein. Three original *Länder* – that is, Baden, Württemberg-Baden, and Württemberg-Hohenzollern – were merged in 1952 to form Baden-Württemberg, and in 1957 the Saarland became the 10th *Land.* The Council completed its work in the early spring of 1949, and the Federal Republic of Germany, *die Bundesrepublik Deutschland,* came into being in May 1949. Berlin also became a *Land* in that year.

In 1990 the German Federal Republic and the German Democratic Republic (DDR) were merged to form a re-unified Germany. The DDR had been a unitary state and did not have *Länder*. The territory of the former DDR was sub-divided along traditional lines and became the *Länder* of Brandenburg, Mecklenburg-Vorpommern (Mecklenburg-Pomerania), Sachsen (Saxony), Sachsen-Anhalt (Saxony-Anhalt) and Thüringen (Thuringia). *Bundestag* (as *Bund* and *-tag*, probably from *tagen* 'to meet, sit daily in conference', from *Tag* 'day', from which derives the international word *diet*). 'An assembly of representatives of a league, confederacy, etc.; specifically (from 1949) the lower house of parliament of the Federal Republic of Germany' (*OED*.), and, since the reunification of Germany in 1990, the lower house of the Republic of Germany.

Bunsen Burner 'Attributive use of the name of Professor R. W. E. *Bunsen* of Heidelberg (1811-1899), denoting appliances invented by him: *Bunsen('s) burner, lamp*, a kind of gas-burner used for heating and for blowpipe work, in which gas is burnt along with air. *Bunsen(s) battery*, a voltaic battery in which the elements are carbon and zinc, and in which nitric and sulphuric acids, or solution of bichromate of potash and sulphuric acid, are employed. *Bunsen cell*, one of the cells of which a Bunsen battery is composed': *OED*. The Bunsen Burner was in fact Bunsen's development, in 1885, of a burner invented by Michael Faraday (1791-1867). Professor Robert Wilhelm Eberhard von Bunsen should be distinguished from the Prussian diplomatist Christian Karl Josias Freiherr von Bunsen (1791–1860), widely known in European society as *Baron Bunsen*.

Bürgermeister Literally, 'Citizen-Master'. The Mayor of a German town.

Choral(e) (From *choral*, in *choral-gesang*, translating mediaeval Latin *cantus choralis*, choral singing). 'A sacred choral song characteristic of the reformed church of Germany; a metrical hymn set to a tune of simple devotional character, and usually sung in unison. Also used of the tune without reference to the words': *OED*. Apparently the *e* has been added by English-speakers to indicate stress on the second syllable of the German word (*cf* the equivalent English-speaking practice with the spelling of the French words *local* and *moral*, which are spelt in English *locale* and *morale*). The final *e* in *chorale* is sometimes mistakenly pronounced as a separate syllable.

> 'Well known examples are Luther's *Ein' feste Burg* and Crüger's *Nun danket alle Gott*. *Choral-gesang* was originally the Plain-song of the Latin church, which Luther wished to retain. It was only when German metrical hymns gradually superseded in common use the other parts of the service, that the name *choral* in course of time became restricted to the melodies of these hymns': J. R. M[ilne] in Grove, *Dictionary of Music*, 4th edn *Appendix*. After Frederick the Great's victory at Leuthen on 5 December 1757 against the Austrians under Field-Marshal Charles of Lorraine, the Emperor Francis I's brother, 20,000 Prussian soldiers sang the chorale *Nun danket alle Gott*, 'Now thank we all our God', which from that time has been known as *The Leuthen Chorale*. The chorale *O Haupt voll Blut und Wunden*, translated, among others, by Robert Bridges ('O Sacred Head sore wounded, defiled and put to scorn') is known as *The Passion Chorale*.

Creutzfeldt-Jakob Disease 'The names of Hans G. *Creutzfeldt* (1885-1964) and Alfons M. *Jakob* (1882-1927), German neurologists. *Cf.* earlier German *Creutzfeldt-Jakobsche Krankheit*': *OED*.

Used attributively and in the possessive, usually in *Creutzfeldt-Jakob disease*, to designate a communicable progressive disease of the human brain, caused by a prion, in which the degeneration and loss of neurones result in dementia and loss of mobility, and which is accompanied by histological changes characteristic of other spongiform encephalopathies.

Dachshund Literally, 'badger-dog'. German-speakers nowadays use the word *Dackel.*

Delikatessen (formerly spelt *Delicatessen*, and still in English-speaking contexts so spelt: German *Delikatessen*, Dutch *delicatessen*, from French *délicatesse*. Literally, 'delicate food'.) Delicacies or relishes for the table; especially attributively, in *delicatessen shop*, *store*. And elliptically for the shop itself.

> 'A house which abounds in foreign dainties of all sorts: Lingner's Delicatessen Handlung, 46, Old Compton Street, Soho': E. S. Dallas, *Kettner's Book of the Table,* 399 (1877).

Deutsche Mark, die Literally, 'the German mark'. The monetary unit of the German Federal Republic, instituted in June 1948; also, a coin representing one Deutsche mark. Abbreviated *DM* or *Dmark*. More recently the abbreviation *DEM* has become common in financial circles. Incorrectly, *Deutschmark*.

Deutschland über Alles! (Literally, 'Germany above everything!'). From the first line of a German national song, *das Deutschlandlied.*

Deutschland, Deutschland über alles,
Über alles in der Welt,
Wenn es stets zu Schutz und Trutze
Brüderlich zusammenhält.
Von der Maas bis an die Memel,
Von der Etsch bis an den Belt,
Deutschland, Deutschland über alles,
Über alles in der Welt.

Germany, Germany above everything
Above everything in the world
When it always, for protection and defence,
Fraternally stands together.
From the Meuse to the Niemen
From the Adige to the Belt,
Germany, Germany above everything
Above everything in the world!

The words were written by August Heinrich Hoffmann (1798-1874) in 1841 not as a national anthem but as a patriotic song intended to promote the concept of a united Germany, as distinct from the fragmented complex of independent and quasi-independent territories that characterized the German-speaking lands at that time. (Hoffmann added to his name 'von Fallersleben', the place of his birth, as an ironic anti-aristocratic gesture.)

The German empire that came into being in 1870 never formally adopted a national anthem. The anthem commencing *Heil Dir im Siegerkranz* ('Hail to you in the Victor's Wreath'), commonly also called *Die Kaiserhymne* ('The Emperor Anthem'), was generally used on occasions when the Kaiser was directly or indirectly involved. It used a text written in 1790 by Heinrich Harries (1762-1802) and a melody attributed to Henry Carey (1687-1743). The music is best known as the melody to Great Britain's *God Save the Queen*, and serves also as Liechtenstein's anthem and as the melody of the American patriotic anthem *My Country, 'tis of Thee.* The melody that was adopted during the Wilhelmine *régime* for *das Deutschlandlied* was the melody composed by Haydn or adapted from his works for the text written in 1797 by L. L. Haschka (1749-1827) and dedicated to the Holy Roman Emperor, the words of which persisted more or less unchanged until 1918: *Gott erhalte, Gott beschütze / Unsern Kaiser, unser Land!*

Carl Ebert (1871-1925), the first President of the Weimar Republic, formally adopted the first three stanzas of Hoffmann's words, and the melody by Haydn, as the German National Anthem. After the end of the War in 1945, the first two verses of the Anthem, above, were proscribed. They are no longer officially proscribed but are rarely sung except at *revanchiste* rallies and assemblies. The German National Anthem now starts with the words *Einigkeit und Recht und Freiheit.*

In the propaganda wars of the 20th century, non-German-speakers have interpreted, and have been encouraged to interpret, the phrase *Deutschland über Alles!* as meaning 'Germany above all other *nations*!', whereas the true grammatical meaning is 'above all *else*'. However, the lines

> *Von der Maas bis an die Memel,*
> *Von der Etsch bis an den Belt*

present problems. The River Meuse is in Belgium (only 1 per cent, or about 70,000, Belgian citizens speak German); the Memel is the (German) name for the lower course of the Polish River Niemen; the Etsch is otherwise the Italian River Adige; and the Belt is otherwise the two shallow straits connecting the Kattegat with the Baltic Sea. The *Store Bælt* (Great Belt) separates Sjælland (Zealand) and Fyn (Funen) islands. The *Lille Bælt* (Little Belt) separates Fyn and Jylland (Jutland).

It might perhaps be said that the historical events of 1914-18 and 1938-45 add their own commentary on Hoffmann's cryptic words.

Present-day Germans tend to accept that List, Sylt, in Schleswig-Holstein, is the most northerly point of the German Republic, with Obersdorf, in Bavaria, as its southernmost point, Millen, North Rhine-Westphalia, as it westernmost point, and Deschka, Saxony, as its easternmost point.

An Australian Internet website:
http://alexander.nu/deutschlandlied/#LdDTT

provides a great deal of information on this topic.

Diesel 'The name of Rudolf *Diesel* (1858-1913), German engineer, used *attrib.* to designate a type of internal-combustion engine invented by him, in which air alone is drawn into the cylinder, this air being so highly compressed that the heat generated ignites the fuel-oil when it enters [*scil*, when it is injected into] the combustion space. Also *ellipt.*, a diesel engine; a locomotive, motor diesel etc., driven by a diesel engine (also *attrib.*)': *OED.*

Diktat Literally, ' a dictate', as a noun. 'A severe settlement or decision, especially one imposed by a victorious nation upon a defeated nation, a dictated peace; used specifically with reference to the Treaty of Versailles of 1919. Also, a dictate, decree, or command; a categorical assertion': *OED***.**

Ding an sich Literally, 'thing as such'. See *An sich above.*

> 'An existence may be viewed in relation to itself, or in relation to the things around it; it may be existence *an sich* or existence *für andere*': J. D. Morell, *An Historical View of Speculative Philosophy* II. v, 142 (1846). 'Others, as Kant for example, have denied intellectualism's pretension to define reality *an sich* or in its absolute

capacity': William James, *Pluralistic Universe,* v, 215 (1909). 'Not the matter *an sich*, which is unknowable, but the matter as we know it': T. S. Eliot in Ezra Pound, *Selected Poems*, p. xvii (1928).

Dirndl (dialect, diminutive of *Dirne* girl). 'A style of woman's dress imitating Alpine peasant costume with bodice and full skirt; also *dirndl skirt,* a full skirt with a tight waistband': *OED.* (*Dirne* is nowadays used only as a synonym for *prostitute.*)

Dobermann Pinscher (Name of Ludwig *Dobermann,* a 19th century German dogbreeder of Thuringia, and *Pinscher*, a short-coated, often dark-coloured terrier of the breed so called, usually having pricked ears and a docked tail). 'A kind of German hound with a smooth coat and docked tail': *OED.*

Dom (from Latin *domus (Dei)*, 'house (of God)'). A cathedral church. So *Domkirche* in the same sense.

Donner und Blitzen! correctly *Donner und Blitz!* Literally 'Thunder and lightning!'. A mild and dated expletive.

Doppelgänger Literally, 'the apparition of a living person; a double; a wraith'.

Doppler (Effect, etc.) 'The name of C. J. *Doppler* (1803-53), Austrian mathematician and physicist, used attributively or in the possessive to designate an effect first explained by him in 1842 (in *Abh. d. k. böhm. Ges. d. Wiss.* (1843) 5th ser. II. 465.82) and other phenomena related to it or caused by it, as *Doppler broadening* (of spectral lines), *Doppler('s) principle*; *Doppler effect,* the effect on sound, light, or other waves of relative motion between the source of the waves and the observer: the observed frequency of the waves is higher or lower than the emitted frequency according as the source (or the observer) is moving towards or away from the observer (or the source); *Doppler shift*, the change of the frequency resulting from the Doppler effect. Also in equipment or procedures utilizing the Doppler effect, as *Doppler navigation, radar*': *OED.*

Drang nach Osten Literally, 'pressure to the east', a name given to the German expansionist policy towards the east: see, *below*, *Lebensraum.*

'The *Drang nach Osten* or the Pan-German Peril': heading in V. Yovanovitch, *Near-Eastern Problem,* iii.,21 (1909). 'The economic interests of the hour are paramount, and the real peril against which the Europe of the twentieth century must fight is the *Drang nach Osten* – in other words, the tendency of the Germans towards universal economic supremacy': *ibid.* 22. 'Crusading, for Wallenstein, was merely an excuse for the *Drang nach Osten*': Aldous Huxley, *Grey Eminence,* viii, 171 (1941).

Dresden 'The name of a town in Saxony, used *attrib.* or *absol.* to designate a variety of white porcelain made at Meißen near Dresden, or an object made of this, characterized by elaborate decoration and figure-pieces in delicate colourings. Hence (often *attrib.*) used to designate anything of a delicate or frail prettiness': *OED.* The clay (the 'paste') and the porcelain *objets d'art* themselves, when genuine, are often referred to as *Meißen.* Porcelain production was established in Meißen in 1710 by August der Starke, (Augustus the Strong), 1670-1733, Elector of Saxony and King of Poland, whose obsession with the fragile material – or his 'maladie de porcelaine', as he called it – drove him to acquire more than 14,500 Chinese and Japanese pieces by the year 1721. Augustus relaunched porcelain production in Europe, which had not succeeded under the Medici family. Augustus founded what was to become the world-renowned Meißen manufacturing company in 1710 under the alchemist Johann Friedrich Böttger, who had fled the service of Frederick the Great, having failed to transmute base metals into gold. But Augustus feared war, fire and espionage in Dresden. He therefore moved Böttger to the Albrechtsburg, in nearby Meißen, where Böttger succeeded in manufacturing excellent hard porcelain. The Albrechtsburg in Meißen thus became the first German *Porzellan Manufaktur*. Later manufactures were to follow in Berlin, Höchst, Copenhagen, Ludwigsburg and Nymphenburg.

> 'Phebe, the Dresden-china shepherdess': G. K. Hunter, *John Lyly,* iv, 233 (1962). 'How bored she was with that face! Fair hair, big blue eyes, little pouting mouth, pink and white complexion. Like a doll. Yet Chris approved. 'A Dresden Shepherdess,' he'd called her': D. Devine, *Illegal Tender,* I. 5 (1970).

Since the end of the Second World War, the name *Dresden* has also come to be associated with the firebomb raids the Allies carried out in early 1945 on what was universally recognized as a city possessing prime examples of Baroque architecture, an expedient variously seen by the Allies as a continuing *riposte* to the Baedeker Raids (*q.v.*), of earlier in the Second World War, and as a corollary of the doctrine of total war as espoused by the German nation itself after 1938. The human tragedy was incomparably greater than the historic and aesthetic one, since the number of civilian casualties was greatly swollen by the presence of thousands of refugees, for whom there was no possibility of escape or even of sheltering from the fire-storms that ensued.

Dummkopf Literally, 'dumbhead'.

Echt Literally, 'real, true, genuine'. Authentic, genuine, typical.

> 'Many Englishmen who know Germany, and whose social opinions are *echt* Junker opinions, hail this war as a means of forcing England to adopt the Prussian system': G. B. Shaw, *New Age,* 25 May 1916. 'England has never produced an artist so '*echt*-English' as Mussorgsky is '*echt*-Russian', or Renoir '*echt*-French'': Constant Lambert, *Music Ho!* iii, 173 (1934). 'The opening is echt Joice [*sic*]': Ezra Pound, *Lett. J. Joyce* (1917) II 414 (1966).

> '"Are you married?" he asked. "I see your ring, but is that camouflage or *echt*?"': Nicholas Freeling, *Love in Amsterdam*, ii. 70 (1962).

Edelfäule, die The name given to a common grey mould, *Botrytis cinerea,* affecting grapes, which is deliberately cultivated to perfect certain white wines; also applied to the condition of being affected by this mould. The technique is much used in France, to perfect, for example, certain strains of *Sauterne*, and in Hungary to perfect *Tokay.* The mechanism of the improvement is touched on in *Eiswein, below.* See also *la pourriture noble* in the French Lexicon.

Edelweiss Literally, *edel* 'noble' and *weiss* 'white'. 'An Alpine plant, *Gnaphalium Leontopodium* or *Leontopodium alpinum*, remarkable for its white flower, growing in rocky places, often scarcely accessible, on the Swiss mountains': *OED.*

Ein Volk, ein Reich, ein Führer ('One People, One Empire, One Leader'). A slogan of the Nazi Party. On 23 February 1895, in a speech from the throne in the Reichstag, the Kaiser, seizing a flag of the First Guards Regiment, renewed his vow to the German people and the German lands in these words: 'Ein Reich, Ein Volk, Ein Gott!'. The sentiment finds echoes in the strangest places. For example, we find in Hugo von Hofmannsthal's *Ariadne*, 'ein Reich, wo alles rein ist', and, again, 'Es hat auch einen Namen: Totenreichs'.

Einfühlung Literally, 'one touch' or 'one feeling'. The first word used for the psychological state now more commonly known as *empathy*.

Einsatzgruppen/Einsatzkommando Immediately after the invasion of Poland in 1939, Heinrich Himmler was appointed by Hitler to take measures to strengthen German ethnicity in the occupied territories and to create *Lebensraum (q. v., below)* for German citizens. Himmler thus created special task forces within the SS, the *Einsatzgruppen,* and placed them under the command of Reinhard Heydrich. On 21 September 1939, Heydrich instructed those under his command to observe a distinction between the 'final solution', which would take some time, and 'the steps necessary for reaching it which can be applied more or less at once'. The *Einsatzgruppen* became 'mobile killing units' charged with liquidating all political enemies of the Reich. The *Einsatzkommando* were special units designed to 'lead the struggle against enemies of the Reich and support the fighting troops'. They reported directly to the Head Office of the Reich Security Police (the *RSHA, Reichssicherheitshauptamt*). which in turn was answerable to the *Reichsministerium des Innern,* Heinrich Himmler's Interior Ministry.

Eisbock ('ice-beer'). Beer that has been frozen, the end-product of a process of isotopic fractionation whereby the beer is first frozen, and then the ice cover (of pure water) is discarded. The alcohol content of the remaining liquid is thus higher than that of the original volume. The hazard present in this extremely simple method of distillation is that the toxic *fusel* elements are retained in the volume of increased alcohol content, whereas, in conventional condensation fractionation, they do not condense at the temperature at which the desired alcohol condenses, and are thus discarded. (The word *Fusel* is a colloquial word for bad brandy or other spirits, formerly applied in Low-German dialects also to bad tobacco: *cf fuseln* 'to bungle'. *Fusel oil* is a trade and technical term for a mixture of several homologous alcohols, chiefly amylic alcohol, and especially applied to this mixture when in its crude form (*Syd. Soc. Lex.*1885).

Eiswein Literally, 'ice-wine'. 'Wine made from ripe grapes picked while the frost is on them, and still frozen when they go into the press': *OED. Eiswein* is an extreme rarity these days. The quality secured by harvesting in the conditions described seems to have nothing to do with increasing the alcohol content of the wine produced. In that respect, *Eiswein* and *Eisbock* (*q. v.*) are not really comparable. The subtle increase in quality resulting from this technique appears to be much closer to the increase in quality secured by harvesting grapes that have been allowed to become infected by *die Edelfäule* (*la pourriture noble* in the French Lexicon), a grey mould, *Botrytis cinerea,* affecting grapes, which is deliberately cultivated to perfect certain French and German wines, and, in Hungary, Tokay.

> 'It seems proper to mention Eiswein, which has received some publicity recently': *Times* 8 Feb 12/6 1963. 'The proper degree of frost at the right moment for making Eiswein has occurred only 10 times during the last

> 100 years': *Daily Tel.* 17 May 16/6 1967. 'Wines of *eiswein* quality': *Times* 27 Nov (Wines & Spirits Suppl.) p. iii/5 (1972). 'Intensely sweet wines also include that curiosity known as Eiswein or ice wine, originally made by chance but now suddenly fashionable ... Confusion exists about Eiswein, but it is essentially a wine made from fully ripe grapes picked very early in the morning while they are lightly frozen': P. V. Price, *Taste of Wine*, v, 75/2 (1975). '*Eiswein* is seldom made nowaday': *Listener* 20 Feb 13/3 s, 1986.

Empfindsamkeit Literally, 'sensibility, sentimentality'. A characteristic of German music and literature at the beginning of the Romantic Era, a period known as *Das Zeitalter der Empfindsamkeit*, 'the Age of Sentimentalism'.

Ersatz Literally, 'compensation, replacement', and as adjective ersatz. 'A substitute or imitation (usually, an inferior article instead of the real thing)': *OED.*

> 'Those who are exempted are passed into the *Ersatz* reserve': *Encyclopaedia Britannica,* II. 594/2 ('German Army'), (1875). 'Another word not seldom met with is 'ersatz'. It is the German 'substitute'': 'War Terms' in *The Athenæum* 1 Aug 695/1 (1919). 'The coffee ... will be ... tempered with a judicious mixture of 'ersatz'': *The Observer*, 9 Mar 1930.

Eszett Literally, 'Ess Zed', the letters *S* and *Z*. The name of the ligature or combined character (in roman type ß and in italic type *ß*) used in conventional German typography to represent double *s* when double *s* is part of a single syllable (as in **Löß** in this Lexicon), but not when the two letters *s* are of different syllables. It is confined to lower-case typesetting; it never appears as a capital. It is sometimes called 'scharfes *s*' ('sharp *s*'). The *Eszett* is still used extensively in Germany, less often in Austria and rarely in Switzerland. The ligature presents several problems. Its name is in fact a misnomer, since the ligature nowadays represents two letters *s* and not the letters *s* and *z*. The ligature misleadingly resembles the letter *B* in appearance. Its treatment in words that are broken at the ends of lines of type is subject to complex rules. Recent activities under the name *Rechtschreibreform* ('spelling reform'), particularly the recommendations of the *Internationaler Arbeitskreis für Orthographie* ('the International Working-Party for Correct Spelling'), and specifically its *Sonderfall ss/ß (Neuregelung)* ('Special Case ss/ß (New Rules)') are widely believed to have compounded the problems.

Fahrenheit 'The name of a Prussian physicist [Gabriel Daniel *Fahrenheit*] (1686–1736), inventor of the mercurial thermometer. Used attributively and elliptically to denote the thermometric scale introduced by him and still in common use in England and the U.S., according to which the freezing point of water is 32° and the boiling point 212°': *OED.*

Fasching (unique word).

> 'In Munich we are in the middle of Fasching, which is the South German word for what the Rhineland calls carnival. It began on Epiphany (January 6) and lasts until Shrove Tuesday': *The Guardian* 21 February 1963, 9/5.

Fest, ein Literally, 'a festival, a party, a feast, a celebration, etc.' So, *Festschrift*, literally, 'festival-writing'. 'A collection of writings forming a volume presented to a scholar or savant on the occasion of his attaining a certain age or period in his career': *OED*. From this usage, popularized in the USA, have stemmed many nonce-uses, mostly jocular.

> 'Hallowe'en-fest at the London Dungeon': advertisement on London Underground, 8 November 2004. 'A First Glimpse of frightfest': article on 'Horror-Poster Art', *The Independent*, 9 November 2004. 'A Festschrift is awarded to someone on their birthday, ... a memorial publication for the dead ... is a Gedenkschrift ...': letter from René Lavanchy, *Private Eye*, 11-24 November, 2005, p 16.

Flak An acronym originally derived from the initials of the elements of Fl*ug*A*bwehr*K*anone*. *Flugabwehr*, abbreviated to *Fla*, stands for all anti-aircraft fire from surface-based artillery. Widely used idiomatically in English to denote criticism or opposition, as in, 'I got a lot of flak over that decision'.

Flak Jacket A protective jacket of heavy fabric containing metal strips or plates.

Flammenwerfer (*Flamme* 'flame' and *Werfer* 'thrower, mortar', from *werfen* 'to throw'). A weapon comprising a reservoir from which a long spray of flame can be ejected against the enemy.

> ' 'Flammenwerfer' (flame-projector) in action': *War Illustrated,* 4 Sept 1917). 'It was against the Sussex men that the Germans used their 'flammenwerfer' or flame-jets': P. Gibbs, *Battles of Somme,* 178 (1917).

Also **Minenwerfer**, from *Minen* 'a mine'. 'A kind of trench mortar first used by German forces in the First World War ... (also, occas.) the projectile fired by this mortar': *OED*. The projectiles from these mortars were called *Moaning Minnies,* from the sound they made in flight. Also *Nebelwerfer*, named after its inventor, Rudolf Nebel 1894-1978, 'A six-barrelled rocket mortar used by the German forces in the Second World War': *OED*. Though the mortar was sometimes used for laying smoke-screens, its use was predominantly for projecting explosive mortar shells, six at a time with an extremely high rate of repetition. The name *Nebelwerfer,* by implication derived from *Nebel* 'mist, fog, haze', was deliberately applied during the development of the weapon as a means of disguising its primary purpose, which was to establish a rocket-based artillery for the *Wehrmacht*, see *below*.

Föhn 'A warm dry south wind which blows down the valleys on the north side of the Alps': *OED*.

> 'Föhn, the name given in Switzerland to the hot southerly winds of summer (the sirocco)': Page, *Geol. Terms*, (1865).

'Also **Foehn**. A warm dry katabatic wind developing on the lee side of a mountain range in response to air moving across the range. Also *föhn wind*': *OED*.

> 'Temporary foehns are produced whenever there is a cyclone so situated as to draw a current of air over a high mountain range': W. Ferrel, *Pop. Treat. Winds*, vi, 333 (1889). 'Greenland föhn winds ... blow down warm and dry, raising the temperature even 30E or 40E above the winter mean, and melting the snow': *Encycl. Brit.* VI, 523/2 (1910). 'In North America the foehn, known as the chinook, has a climatic influence on a very wide belt east of the Rocky Mountains': F. Defant in T. F. Malone, *Compend. Meteorol.* 667/1 (1951).

Fraktur Traditionally, German was printed in a Gothic style known generally as *die deutsche Schrift*. It comprised *Fraktur*, a general text alphabet, and *Schwabacher*, used for variety and for headlines.

The use of *die deutsche Schrift* had initially been seen by the National Socialists as essentially German – essentially *Aryan* – but on 3 January 1941 Martin Bormann announced that the use of the Gothic scripts would cease, on the newly discovered conviction that Schwabacher was of Jewish origin. It seems that the real reason for the abandonment of *die deutsche Schrift* was that it was proving an obstacle to communication in the occupied territories, and especially in its handwritten form, called *Sütterlin* after its designer, Ludwig Sütterlin (1865-1917).

Sütterlin was introduced into Prussia in 1915, and in Germany as a whole in 1920. From 1945 the Roman and Italic faces used universally for the Latin alphabet were adopted in Germany, where they are called, generically, *Antiqua*.

The use of italics for emphasis or differentiation, as employed in non-German printing, was not available to printers using the type-faces based on Fraktur and Schwabacher, which are solely upright, not sloping, type-faces. Compositors thus followed the practice already established in the setting of Classical Greek, whereby letter-spacing was employed between the individual letters of words or phrases intended to be emphasized or differentiated.

It is a German idiom to say, when one wishes to be outspoken with someone, 'Fraktur reden'.

Frankfurter (*Frankfurter Wurst*, 'Frankfurt sausage'). A highly seasoned smoked beef and pork sausage, originally made at Frankfurt am Main. Nowadays the word *Frankfurter* often refers to the newspaper the *Frankfurter Allgemeine Zeitung*.

Frankreich Literally, 'France'. Used also to denote a land of luxury and plenty, as in the phrase 'Er lebt wie Gott in Frankreich', 'He lived like God in France'. *Cf* English *Land of Cockaigne* or *Cockayne*.

> 'There is a Jewish freethinker's saying about Paris – *wie Gott in Frankreich*. Meaning that even God took his holidays in France. Why? Because the French are atheists and among them God himself could be carefree, a *flâneur*, like any tourist': Saul Bellow, *Ravelstein*, p 171 (2000).

Frauendienst Literally, 'women-service'. Courtly love as expressed by the mediaeval poets and minstrels of the German-speaking lands.

Fremde(r) Literally, 'a stranger'. Also Yiddish.

Froebel See *Kindergarten, below.*

Führer Literally, 'leader'. 'Part of the title (*Führer und Reichskanzler*) assumed by Adolf Hitler in 1934 as head of the Third Reich': *OED.*

Führerprinzip Literally, 'leader-principle'. Hitler's fundamental policy, whereby 'ultimate authority rested with him and extended downward. At each level, the superior was to give the orders, the subordinates to follow them to the letter. In practice the command relationships were more subtle and complex, especially at the lower levels, but Hitler did have the final say on any subject in which he took a direct interest, including the details of military operations, that is, the actual direction of armies in the field': Geoffrey Megargee, on BBC website:

> http://www.bbc.co.uk/history/worldwars/wwtwo/hitler_commander_01.shtml

The term has also been applied more generally to the delegation of authority in other spheres than warfare.

Fusel See *Eisbock above.*

Gastarbeiter Literally, 'guest-worker', f. *Gast* 'guest' and *Arbeiter* 'worker'. Plural unchanged or denoted with -s. 'A person with temporary permission to work in another country, an immigrant worker. Applied esp. to those encouraged into Germany after 1945 to assist in the post-war economic revival': *OED.*

> 'It is all part of the service for the 1,200,000 or so *Gastarbeiter*, the 'guest workers' who help to keep the economy growing': *The Economist,* 2 July 27/1 1966. 'The Portuguese contingents of Gastarbeiter in Europe are swelling the unemployment figures towards 20 per cent': *The Listener* 13 Nov. 631/2, 1975. 'Affluent German workers prefer to draw unemployment benefit rather than compete for jobs with *Gastarbeiters*': *New Society* 3 June 544/3 1976. 'They accused the Turkish gastarbeiter of driving the tenants from their flats': *The Financial Times* 17 June 3/2, 1982. 'I ask a Turkish Gastarbeiter what he thinks of it [*sc.* the Berlin wall]': *The Daily Telegraph* (Colour Suppl.) 3 June 31/1, 1989.

Gasthaus Literally, 'guesthouse'.

> *'Oberprechtal-in-the-Black-Forest*: We came slipping and sliding down the steep, rocky trail through the shadowed light of the pine trees and out into a glaring clearing where a sawmill and a white plastered Gasthaus baked in the sun': Ernest Hemingway, *By-Line*, 'German Innkeepers', p 51 (1933).

Gauleiter Literally, 'district leader'. 'A political official controlling a district under Nazi rule': *OED.*

Gauss (named after K. F. *Gauss*, 1777-1855**).** 'The electromagnetic unit of magnetic induction (flux density) in the C.G.S. [centimetre-gramme-second] system, defined as the induction that exerts a force of one dyne on each centimetre of a straight wire carrying one e.m.u. [electromagnetic unit] (10 amp) of current, when the induction is perpendicular to the wire. (In the International System of Units the gauss is replaced by the tesla, or weber per square metre, equal to 10,000 gauss.)': *OED.*

> 'The name has been suggested for various magnetic units. The original sense was the C.G.S. unit of magnetic field strength (later called an *oersted*), and, because in the C.G.S. system the electromagnetic units of field strength and of induction have the same dimensions and *in vacuo* are numerically the same, the word has freq. been used for both indiscriminately': *OED.*

So, **Degauss**, or **De-Gauss,** verb transitive, 'To protect (a ship) against magnetic mines by encircling it with an electrically charged cable (called the *degaussing belt* or *girdle*), so as to demagnetize it. Also in extended use, to remove unwanted magnetism from, to demagnetize': *OED.*

Geborgenheit see *Habseligkeiten below.*

Gedankenexperiment (from *Gedanke* 'thought' and *Experiment* 'experiment'). 'An experiment carried out only in imagination or thought; an appeal to imagined experience; a thought-experiment': *OED.*

> 'The first presentation involves a *gedankenexperiment*; it supposes a super-microscope more powerful than any electronic microscope': N. R. Hanson, *Patterns of Discovery* vi. 137 (1958). 'The child in his [*sc.* Ayer's] *Gedankenexperiment* is taught the use of psychological concepts by a recorded voice': *Amer. Philos. Q.* III. 306/2 (1966).

Geiger (from the name of Hans *Geiger* (1882-1945), German physicist). In *Geiger counter*, an instrument for detecting and counting ionizing radiation, used especially for measuring radioactivity. Also *Geiger-Müller counter.*

Gemütlichkeit 'Comfortableness; friendliness; informality; cosiness, snugness': The adjective: *gemütlich. Collins German-English English-German Dictionary* 1980.

> '"Dear Miss Self, I was well pleased with the amiable fellow you arranged to meet me at the Yale Club this past September 11th. So much so that I would like to get to know him better in a more gemütlich atmosphere"': Truman Capote, *Kate McCloud*, p 129 (1965).

Gesellschaft 'A social relationship between individuals based on duty to society or an organization; contrasted with *Gemeinschaft*, ... a social relationship between individuals based on affection, kinship, or membership of a community, as within a family or group of friends': *OED.* (See *Aktiengesellschaft.*)

Gestalt Literally, 'form, shape'. 'A 'shape', 'configuration', or 'structure' which as an object of perception forms a specific whole or unity incapable of expression simply in terms of its parts (*e.g.* a melody in distinction from the notes that make it up) ... *Gestalt* psychology, a school of psychology which holds that perceptions, reactions, etc., are Gestalts [*sic*, for *Gestalten*]': *OED.*

Gestapo (acronym from the initial letters of Ge*heime* Sta*ats*-Po*lizei*, literally, 'Secret State-Police'). The non-uniformed Secret State-Police, set up by Hermann Göring in Prussia in 1933 and extended to the whole of Germany in January 1934.

Gesundheit Literally, 'health'. 'An exclamation used to wish good health to a person, especially to someone who sneezes': *OED.* Also Yiddish.

Glockenspiel Literally, 'bell-play'. 'A musical instrument consisting of a series of small bells or metal bars which are struck with a hammer, or by levers acted upon by a keyboard': *OED.*

> 'The glockenspiel proper consists of a set of eight or more clock bells, mounted on a central spindle, which is inserted in a wooden handle': *Work,* 2 July 253/3 (1892).

Glühwein Mulled wine.

GmbH (Gesellschaft mit beschränkter Haftung) ('Company with Limited Liability'). Equivalent to a private limited company or corporation. (See *Aktiengesellschaft, Gesellschaft* and *KG,* herein.)

Gotha '1919. A town in Germany. A large German aeroplane': *Shorter OED*. The first *Grossflugzeug* ('large aeroplane/airplane') built by the Gothaer Waggonfabrik AG was developed by the German Army from a prototype flown for the first time in January 1915. A few of these flying machines, built by Gotha under licencse, were intended for ground-attack and general tactical duties and were employed on the Western and Eastern Fronts. The design was further developed and became the largest bomber in German service. The first daylight raid on London was carried out by 14 Gothas on 13 June 1917. On 7 July, 22 Gothas raided London. Night raids began in August of 1917, and continued until May 1918, when they were abandoned because of the increasingly heavy losses. At the peak of their employment, in April 1918, 36 Gothas were in service. Their name is associated with the commencement of the policy of bombing civilian targets, which became a feature of 20th-century warfare.

Gott im Himmel! 'God in Heaven!'

Gott mit Uns! Literally, 'God with us!'. A motto that appeared on German soldiers' belt-buckles and on certain cap-badges in the uniforms made familiar by the wars beginning in 1870, 1914 and 1939.

Götterdämmerung Literally, 'twilight of the gods'. 'Used figuratively to denote the complete downfall of a régime, institution, etc. Popularized by Wagner's use of it as the title of the last opera of the Ring cycle': *OED.*

> 'Which brings us to Kate McCloud. Kate! McCloud! My love, my anguish, my Götterdämmerung, my very own *Death in Venice*: inevitable, perilous as the asp at Cleopatra's breast': Truman Capote, *Unspoiled Monsters*, edn 1987, p 73 (1965).

Graf The German equivalent of Count and Earl.

Habseligkeiten (approximately, one's most treasured possessions, often of sentimental value only). *Habseligkeiten* was chosen as the most beautiful German word in October 2004 in a competition initiated by the Goethe Institut and the Council for the German Language. Over 22,000 respondents co-operated. The nomination of the word *Habseligkeiten* suggests that the word combines two completely opposite areas of life: worldly belongings, *hab-* from *haben*, 'to have', and the eternal search for happiness, *Seligkeit*, that is, 'a state of bliss of being blest'. That is certainly the popular etymology, but the Council for the German Language was severely criticized for its choice, since the nomination is manifestly etymologically wrong. The word does not consist of the parts *hab* and *Seligkeiten*, but instead of *Habsel* and the common suffix-*eit*, where *Habsel* is a material possession of small value.

The word that came second was *Geborgenheit*, 'the feeling of being safe'. The third was *lieben*, 'to love', in part because, with the change of one letter, it became *Leben*, 'life'. The winner in the Junior Survey was *Libelle*, 'dragonfly'.

Hamburger (in full *Hamburger steak,* from the town from which the dish is said to have originated). 'Chopped beef, spiced and flavoured, formed into a cake and fried, often served between two halves of a toasted bun. So *hamburger bar*, etc: orig US': *OED.* The initial syllable of the word has led to the supposition that the dish contains ham; hence the formation *beef-burger* for a hamburger that does not comprise ham.

There is an amiable belief that the word gained currency in America owing to the presence of hamburger steaks at every meal on the Hamburg-Amerika Line. There are very many inhabitants of Hamburg who, on behalf of their city, strongly disavow the credit or blame for having devised this fast-food item. (The name of the town Hamburg is also used in England to denote a species of grape and a small variety of domestic fowl, both known as *the Black Hamburg* or *Hamburgh.*)

Hamster Literally, 'the hoarder'. 'A species of rodent (*Cricetus frumentarius*) allied to the mouse and rat, found in parts of Europe and Asia; it has cheek-pouches in which it carries the grain with which it stores its burrows; ... it hibernates during the winter. Also applied to other pouched rodents allied to or resembling this': *OED.* The species is not indigenous to the British Isles. (The verb *hamstern* is used in exactly the same sense as the English verb 'to hoard', meaning to build up stocks in good times, even to the detriment of others.)

> 'The skins of Hamsters are very durable': Topsell, *Four-Footed Beasts* 413 (1658). 'The *Cricetus*, or German rat, which Mr. Buffon calls the hamster': O Goldsmith, *Natural History* (1862) I, VI, i. 454 (1744). 'Dormice and hamsters are found in the stony region South of Judea': *Edinburgh Review* 350 April 350 1886. '[Roman] Abramovich once told *Le Monde* that the difference between a rat and a hamster was PR [Public Relations] ...': Dominic Midgley, 'Oiling up the Oligarchs', *The Spectator*, 8 October 2005, pp14-15.

Hände hoch! Literally, 'Hands high!'. 'Hands up!', the military command to prisoners and as used in gangster and cowboy stories.

Hanse Literally, in English usage, 'A company or guild of merchants in former times; an association of merchants trading with foreign parts; the merchant guild of a town; also, the privileges and monopolies possessed by it; sometimes, apparently, the guildhall or 'hanse-house'': *OED*. The *OED* continues: 'The *Old Hanse* was the Fellowship of the London Merchants which had a monopoly of the foreign trade of London since Norman times; the *New Hanse* was the company of Merchant Adventurers first incorporated in 1497, which received charters from Henry VII in 1505 and Elizabeth in 1566'. In application to Germany, the *OED* adds: 'The name of a famous political and commercial league of Germanic towns, which had also a house in London'. The proper noun is much used in the plural: 'The Hanse towns or their citizens'. The phrase *The Hanseatic League* is also much used in English history books. The last diet of the League was held in 1669 but the League has never been formally dissolved. Lübeck, Hamburg, and Bremen are still known as Hanseatic cities.

Hausfrau Literally, 'housewife', often one *exclusively* engaged in domestic matters.

> 'My sister Bertha was charming: now she is a house-frau': R. Wilson *Martin Schüler* xi. 120 (1918). 'Her Majesty Queen Charlotte, the prim German hausfrau': E. Barrington, *Divine Lady* ii. xv. 213 (1925). 'The big German newspapers, cognisant of the power of the hausfrau': *Observer* 20 Apr 8/4 (1930). 'Women in West Germany appear to have taken a tremendous leap forward from *hausfrau* to high executive positions': *Punch* 9 May 706/2 (1962). 'She looked like

> Marianne Moore; a stouter, Teutonized Miss Moore. Grey hausfrau braids pinioned her narrow skull; she wore no makeup, and her suit, one might say uniform, was of prison-matron blue serge ...': Truman Capote, *Unspoiled Monsters*, edn 1987, p 53 (1965).

Heil Literally, 'prosperity, salvation', and, by extension, 'Hail!'. 'Used in the expression *Heil Hitler!* by the Germans during the Nazi régime. Also '*Ski-heil!*', 'Good skiing!': *OED.*

Heimat Literally, 'home, home-country'. The word conveys an aura of home-loving, childhood memories, nostalgia, and, sometimes, a patriotism that can resemble chauvinism. So, *Heimweh,* 'homesickness'; *Heimatkunst*: see *Blut und Boden, below*.

Heimisch Literally, 'homely, unpretentious: *OED*'. In German the word conveys a benevolent meaning, with all the connotations of the English word *home*. In American English – quite anomalously – the adjective *homely* applied to women conveys the notion of plainness.

Heldentenor Literally, 'hero-tenor'. 'A powerful tenor voice suited to the singing of heroic roles in opera; a person with such a voice': *OED.*

Herrenvolk Literally, 'master-race'. 'The Nazi conception of the German people as born to mastery': *OED.*

> 'A *Herrenvolk* to dominate other peoples': D. Wilson, *Germany's 'New Order'*, 22 (1943). 'Forms of warfare which, according to the German view, should be the strict monopoly of the *Herrenvolk*': W. S. Churchill, *The End of the Beginning,* 103 (1943). 'Nations each of which regards itself as The Chosen Race or *Herrenvolk* appointed by God to own and rule all the others': G. B. Shaw, *Everybody's Political What's What*, X, 82 (144).

Hertz A unit of measurement used to denote rotational speed, equal to one cycle per second. Names after H. R. *Hertz* (1857-1894), a German physicist.

Hinterland (from *hinter-* 'behind' and *Land* 'land').

> 'The district behind that lying along the coast (or along the shore of a river); the 'back country'. Also applied specifically to the area lying behind a port, and to the fringe areas of a town or city': *OED.*

Hitlerjugend Literally, 'Hitler Youth', an organization set up by Adolf Hitler in 1933 for educating and training male youth in Nazi principles. Under the leadership of Baldur von Schirach, head of all German youth programmes, the Hitler Youth included by 1935 almost 60 per cent of German boys. On 1 July 1936, it became a state agency that all young 'Aryan' Germans were expected to join.

Hochdeutsch Literally, 'High German'. 'The variety of Teutonic speech, originally confined to 'High' or southern Germany [the territories characterized by high altitudes], but now accepted as the literary language throughout the whole of Germany; its chief characteristic is that certain consonants have been altered by what is called the 'second sound-shifting' from their original Teutonic sounds, which the other dialects in the main preserve. *'Plattdeutsch'* [is] the general name for the dialects of Germany which are not High German; but [is] also applied by philologists to all the West Germanic dialects except High German (including, *e.g.* English,

Dutch, Frisian); and formerly in a still wider sense including also Gothic and Scandinavian': *OED*. Anomalously, the *OED* employs *Plattdeutsch* as its catch-word or head-word but not *Hochdeutsch,* for which it employs the catch-word *High German*. The term *Hochdeutsch* is much more widely used by English-speakers than *High German* as the name for the spoken and written language of contemporary Germany.

> 'The High German is indeed a *lingua communis* ... the choice and fragrancy of all the dialects': S. T. Coleridge, *Biog Lit* 100 (1817). 'The German or Teutonic language may be divided into two great branches ... the High German, or the language of Southern Germany; and the Low German, or Saxon': *Penny Cycl.* XI. 192 (1838). 'Luther ... made the High German the literary language of all German-speaking people'; Morris, *Hist. Outl. Eng. Accid.* i. 5 (1872). 'The West Teutonic branch includes ... Saxon or Low German': W. W. Skeat, *Princ. Eng. Etym.* Ser. I. vi. §55 (1887). '*Franconian*, a group of medieval West Germanic dialects, combining the characteristics of Low and High German, and subdivided into Lower Franconian ... and Middle and Upper Franconian': Pei & Gaynor, *Dict. Linguistics* 76 (1954).

Standard German is known today simply as 'Hochdeutsch'. It is used almost always for written German. Books and newspapers, for example, are almost exclusively printed in standard German. 'Hochdeutsch' is also *spoken* by educated speakers in all the German-speaking lands, including the German-speaking cantons in Switzerland. However, owing largely to some residual influence of the old dialects, and also to some residual local patriotism, regional variants of *spoken* Hochdeutsch persist. Spoken Hochdeutsch that has been purged of this residual regionalism can be heard on the classical stage, in which case it is known as *Bühnendeutsch* (literally, 'Stage German').

Hock Shortened from *Hockamore*, see below. 'The wine called in German *Hochheimer*, produced at Hochheim on the Main; hence, commercially extended to other white German wines': *OED*. Attrib., as in *hock-bottle, hock-glass*, a bottle, or wineglass, made of coloured glass, used for hock or other white wine; also *hock-cup*.

> '*John*. What wine is it? *Fred*. Hock': Fletcher, *Chances,* V iii (1625). 'It would be curious to trace the progress of the perversion whereby the wines which in the fifteenth century used to be correctly designated 'wines of Rhin' have come to be called Hocks. Hocheim [*sic*]... lies on the Main and not on the Rhein [*sic*]': I. Taylor *Words & Places* 282 (1864). 'Hock bottles from their deep red or orange colour, are useful for various parts of the work': Burton, *Modern Photography*, (ed 10) 1892.

Earlier, *Hockamore*, [Anglicized form of *Hochheimer*, from *Hochheim* on the Main.]

> 'I am very well, and drink much Hockamore': Shadwell, *Epsom Wells* III. 40 (Stanf.) (1673). 'Suppose, by keeping cyder-royal too long, it should become unpleasant, and as unfit to bottle as old hockamore': *Gentleman's Magazine*, 28 (1747).

The *English* practice of extending the *English* term *hock* to all Rhenish Wine is of long standing. Matthew Maty (1718-1786), Secretary of the Royal Society, in his translation of Riesbeck's *Travels*, alludes to

'The little village of Hocheim [*sic*], from whence the English give all kinds of Rhenish wine the name of Hock': *Riesbeck's Travels through Germany*, III. 189 (1787). Queen Victoria's supposed *penchant* for hock has little to do with either the use of the name *hock* or the popularity of hock itself in Britain, both of which antedate her reign by at least two centuries.

Homburg 'The name of a town near Wiesbaden, Germany. In full *Homburg hat*. A soft felt hat with a curled brim and a dented crown, first worn at Homburg, once a fashionable health-resort': *OED*.

> ' "The Homburg Hat", as worn by H. R. H. Prince of Wales, 10s 6d': *Country Gentlemen's Catalogue,* 155/1 (1894). 'At one time any man who wore a 'Homburg' was popularly supposed to be either an actor or an artist': *To-Day*, 29 June 1904. 'He ... put his Homburg hat on the table': Edgar Wallace, *Valley of Ghosts*, xv, 142 (1922). 'Anthony Eden, the Foreign Secretary, had reintroduced the black Homburg hat, known as the 'Eden' in Savile Row': Graves & Hodges, *Long-Week-End*, xxi, 376 (1940). 'Dark suit and Anthony Eden hat during the week, tweed jacket and flannels at the week-end': D. Davin, *Sullen Bell*, II, iv, 128 (1956). 'How did the soft black Homburg, with a bound, turned-up edge, come to be called an 'Anthony Eden'?': *The Spectator*, 130/1, 31 Jan 1958. 'Characters ... who kept getting locked up in cellars under the river by sinister men in Homburg hats and raincoats': P. G. Wodehouse, *Pearls, Girls & Monty Bodkin*, v, 68 (1972).

Horst Wessel Lied, Das *Horst Wessel* (1907-1930) was the author of the words of what became the official anthem of the German Nazi Party. Wessel was murdered, reputedly by political opponents of the Nazi Party, and was thereafter venerated as a martyr by the Party. The opening words are *Die Fahne hoch!* ('The Flag high!'). It appears that Wessel adapted to his words the tune of the marine reservist song *Vorbei, vorbei, sind all die schönen Stunden*, a melody that was widely known at that time and was evidently a popular tune played on hurdygurdies and barrel-organs.

> 'Hundreds of arms went out in the Hitler salute, hundreds of voices yelled the Horst Wessel Lied': Vernon Bartlett, *This is my Life,* x. 165 (1937). 'The Horst Wessel song was one of the greatest hymns of hate that had ever been composed': J. Blackburn, *Young Man from Lima,* xvii, (1968).

Howitzer 'A short piece of ordnance, usually of light weight, specially designed for the horizontal firing of shells with small charges, and adapted for use in a mountainous country': *OED*. The word 'horizontal' in this definition, which is taken from the Oxford English Dictionary, is clearly wrong: 'vertical' (or, rather, for obvious reasons, *nearly* vertical) would be more appropriate. The howitzer differs from such pieces as the field-gun or the gun of position primarily in that its trajectory is high; it tends to 'lob' its projectile upwards in a distinct parabola, rather than in the ideal 'flat' trajectory of the other ordnance. The word *Howitzer* is not in fact a German word, though it is widely thought to be so in English-speaking countries. The word originated in Bohemia in the 15th century, during the Hussite Wars. It appears in a recognizable form in 1663 as Dutch *houvietser*, later *houwitser*. The modern German word is *Haubitze*, *s f*; the French is *obusier s m* (an older form, *obus s m*, is still sometimes used); the Italian is *obice, s m.*

> 'The signal ... was given by four hawbitzers fired in the air': *Hist. Europe* in *Ann. Reg.* 14/1, 1760.

Hun See *Soldaten! below.*

'Hunde! Wollt Ihr [denn] ewig leben?' Literally, 'Dogs! Would you [then] live for ever?'. The battle of Kolin (18th June 1757) against the Austrians under Marschall Daun ended in a crushing defeat for the Prussians. Of 16,000 Prussian infantry there remained only 4,000. Towards the end of the battle Frederick the Great leapt among his fleeing battalions and in the greatest frustration cried, *'Ihr Racker, wollt Ihr denn ewig leben?' Racker* derives from the same root as *rascal* but is considerably stronger. It is doubtful that Frederick used either the pejorative *Hunde*, which is the most popularly quoted epithet, or *Racker*. He is alternatively reported as having said, '*Kerle!*' (a word from the same root as 'churl', but completely without the overtone 'churlish'). This was a much more likely choice, since his father's extremely tall bodyguards were called *die langen Kerls*. David Fraser (*Frederick the Great*, Allen Lane, 2000), favours *Kerle!*, and he adds, 'The story goes that an old grenadier called out, 'Listen, Fritz, I thought for thirteen pfennigs pay we'd done enough!'' (See also 'Kinder, Ihr habt heute einen schlimmen Tag gehabt', below.)

Hundler (*cf* German *Händler* 'trader, dealer'). A 'wheeler-dealer'.

'Ich bin ein Berliner' Literally, 'I am a Berliner'. Announced by President Kennedy in West Berlin on 26 June 1963 (*New York Times*, 27 June 1963, p 12), echoing Cicero's '*Civis Romanus sum*' ('I am a Roman citizen': *In Verrem*, 5, ch 147) and Lord Palmerston's implied but not uttered '*Civis Britannicus sum*': (in the Don Pacifico debate, *Hansard*, 25 June 1850, col 444). According to the *Oxford Dictionary of Quotations*, *'Ein Berliner* being the name given in Germany to a doughnut' Kennedy's slip was 'the occasion, therefore, of much hilarity'. It appears that Kennedy ought to have said, '*Ich bin Berliner*'.

Ich Dien Literally, 'I serve'. The motto of the Prince of Wales. The blind John of Luxemburg, King of Bohemia, was killed on the battle-field of Crécy (26 August 1346). Edward the Black Prince, Prince of Wales, assumed the dead king's crest, the three feathers, and his motto, *Ich Dien.*

'Ich kann nicht anders' Martin Luther's reputed expression of resolution after having, in 1517, affixed his Ninety-Five Theses to the door of a church in Wittenberg: 'Hier stehe ich. Ich kann nicht anders. Gott helfe mir! Amen': 'Here I stand. I can do no other. God help me! Amen'. Luther certainly said these words at the Reichstag of Worms on 18April 1521, *die Reichstag zu Worms*, an event always chronicled in English history-books (much to the amusement of English schoolboys) as 'the Diet of Worms' (literally, *Diät der Würmer*).

Im Westen nichts Neues ('All Quiet on the Western Front'). The title of the novel by 'Erich Maria Remarque' (Eric Paul Remark, 1898-1970), published in 1929 and subsequently filmed.

Infobahn (modelled on *Autobahn*, *q. v.*). The 'information superhighway'. In English-speaking usage, the word *Infobahn* tends to denote the Internet with specific reference to its information-retrieval capabilities rather than its inter-communication capabilities.

'Italien ist [nur] ein geographischer Begriff' ('Italy is [only] a geographical expression'). Attributed to Prince Metternich (1773-1859).

'"Italy is [only] a geographical expression", in discussing the Italian question with Palmerston in 1847'; in *Memoires, Documents, etc, de Metternich publiés par son fils* (1883), vol 7, p 413: *ODQ*.

Jawohl Literally, 'Yes, indeed!', but popularly associated in the minds of English-speakers with a ready acknowledgment and acceptance of military orders.

Judenhetze Literally, 'Jew-baiting'. 'Systematic persecution of the Jews': *OED*.

'Those forces which Europe has confessed are too powerful for it to deal with, and which have led to persecution in Russia and to *Judenhetze* in Germany': *19th Century*, Aug 1882, 254.

Judenrat Literally, 'Jewish council'. A council comprising Nazi-appointed Jews set up for controlling the local Jewish population.

Judenrein Literally, 'free of Jews'. 'Of a society or organization: without Jewish members, out of which Jews have been expelled': *OED*.

'It is not merely central and eastern Europe which are being 'purged', or rendered 'Judenrein', as the Nazis like to say': *New Republic*, 21 December 1942, 817. 'When Hitler came to power, the German banks were already almost *judenrein*': Hannah Arendt, *Origins of Totalitarianism*, i, 4 (1960). 'The survivors ... were rounded up and sent to the death camps, Warsaw being now *judenrein*': C. Roth, *Short Hist. Jewish People* (rev. ed.) VI. xxxi. 444 (1969).

Jugendstil *Jugend* 'youth' (the name of a German magazine started in 1896) and *Stil* 'style'. The German equivalent of *art nouveau* (see the French Lexicon). Also *attrib.* (occas. with lower-case initial).

Junker (from earlier *Junkher*, *-herr(e)*, from Middle High German *junc*, modern German *jung* 'young', and *herre*, 'sir'). 'A young German noble; as a term of reproach, a narrow-minded, overbearing (younger) member of the aristocracy of Prussia, etc.; specifically, a member of the reactionary party of the aristocracy whose aim it is to maintain the exclusive social and political privileges of their class': *OED*. Also used adjectivally.

'Bismarck is by instinct a Junker': *Blackwoods Mag*, Oct. 462, 1891.

K und K In 1867 a formula, *Der Ausgleich* ('The Compromise'), was achieved whereby the polity of the former Holy Roman Empire and, then, the Austrian Empire could in principle be re-modelled to take account of the nationalist aspirations of the Hungarians, the most numerous linguistic group in the Empire after the German-speakers. Thus came into being *Die kaiserliche und königliche Doppelmonarchie*, 'the Imperial and Royal Dual Monarchy' in which an Austrian and a Hungarian entity existed in an equal partnership. The letters *K und K* were prefixed to organs of the State that affected both parts of the Dual Monarch. Elaborate permutations on the letters and their Hungarian equivalents were employed to denominate organs of the State that affected one or other of the parts of the Dual Monarchy but not both.

From Nov. 14, 1868, the Emperor's style for treaties and in diplomatic acts became *Kaiser von Österreich, König von Böhmen, u. s. w. und Apostolischer König von Ungarn* (or, in abbreviated form, *Kaiser von Österreich und Apostolischer König von Ungarn*) and the empire became the *Österreichisch-Ungarisches Reich*, or 'the Austro-Hungarian Empire'.

Kabinett One of the degrees of quality used to classify German and Austrian wines. In ascending order of merit, the degrees of quality are: *Qualitätswein, Kabinett, Spätlese, Auslese, Beerenauslese/Eiswein,* and *Trockenbeerenauslese.*

Kaffeeklatsch Literally, 'coffee-gossip'. 'Gossip over coffee cups; a coffee party': *OED.*

Kaiser Literally, 'Caesar'. The title was formerly accorded only to the Holy Roman Emperor. Subsequently, from 1806 to 1919, the Emperors of Austria used the title. From 1870 to 1919, the Kings of Prussia, as *de facto* Emperors of Germany, also used the title. To English-speakers, the term 'the Kaiser' means, simply, Wilhelm II (1859-1941), who was Emperor of Germany from 1888 until 1918.

Kapelle, Kapellmeister 'In Germany, a musical establishment consisting of a band or orchestra, with or without a choir, such as used to be maintained at most of the German courts. Hence *Kapellmeister*, the leader or conductor of a *kapelle,* chapel choir, or orchestra': *OED.* (The tonic accent falls on the second syllable of *Kapelle* and *Kapellmeister.*) *Die Rote Kapelle* ('the Red Orchestra'). A Soviet spy-ring run by Leopold Trepper from Berlin from 1938 to 1943. It comprised Soviet sympathizers in France, the Low Countries and eventually in Germany itself. In 1943, the Orchestra's transmitters were traced and monitored, and the organization was destroyed. Trepper, once captured, collaborated with the Gestapo, then made an escape. Most of those who had trusted him were executed. Trepper made his way back to Moscow, where, because of his brief collaboration with the Nazis, he was imprisoned until 1954. In 1957, he returned to his birthplace, Poland; in 1974, he emigrated to Israel. He died in 1983.

Kapo A concentration-camp guard chosen from among the inmates.

Kaput or kaputt 'German *kaputt,* from French *(être) capot* (to be) without tricks in the card-game of piquet ... Finished, worn out; dead or destroyed; rendered useless or unable to function': *OED.*

> 'When Prussian military despotism is 'Kaputt', to use the Germans' favourite word about their foe, meaning *done*': Duchess of Sutherland, *Six Weeks at the War,* p. xiv (1914).

Kartell 'An agreement or association between two or more business houses for regulating output, fixing prices, etc.; also, the businesses thus combined; a trust or syndicate': *OED.* German and Austro-Hungarian domestic law traditionally permitted degrees of price-fixing and other monopolistic practices that elsewhere were considered to distort competition. European Union legislation has moved against such practices.

> 'The new cartel includes practically every important iron and steel interest in the Dual Monarchy': *The Westminster Gazette,* 24 November 1902, 10/1.

So, **Kartellamt**, the German governmental office broadly similar to the British Monopolies & Mergers Commission.

Katzenjammer The American strip-cartoon 'The Katzenjammer Kids' made the word *Katzenjammer* familiar to all English-speakers. Most English-speakers would link the word, as a common noun, to the English word 'caterwauling' in its primary sense: 'The cry of cats at rutting time; their rutting or heat': *OED.* In fact, that primary sense is obsolete in Modern German. 'Ich habe einen Katzenjammer' means 'I have a hangover'.

'Kennst du das Land, wo die Zitronen blühn?' 'Know you the land where the lemon-trees bloom?' J. W. Von Goethe, *Wilhelm Meisters Lehrjahre,* (1795-6) bk 3, ch 1.

KG (Kommanditgesellschaft). A limited partnership. A company to which persons advance capital without assuming the functions of partner, or incurring any responsibility beyond their investment. The letters *KG* are added to the name of the partnership. (See *Aktiengesellschaft, Gesellschaft* and *GmbH.*)

'Kinder, Ihr habt heute einen schlimmen Tag gehabt' ('Children, you have had a bad day today'). During the evening of 18 June 1757, after the disastrous battle of Kolin, Frederick the Great encountered the survivors of his First Guards Battalion and called out to them the words above. ('*Kinder*' was his usual method of addressing his troops. See *'Hunde! Wollt Ihr denn ewig leben?' above.*) The grenadiers murmured that they had been badly led. The mood was wretched. See Wolfgang Venohr, *Der grosse König; Friedrich der Grosse im Siebenjährigen Krieg,* p 101, and, by the same author, *Fridericus Rex – Porträt einer Doppelnatur,* pp 252-253.

Kinder, Küche, Kirche ('Children, Kitchen, Church'). In an opinion attributed to Bismarck, these are the proper spheres of a woman's interests.

Kindergarten Literally, 'children's garden'. 'A school for the instruction of young children according to a method devised by Friedrich Froebel (1782-1852), for developing the intelligence of children by interesting object-lessons, exercises with toys, games, singing, etc': *OED*. The word was coined by Froebel in 1840: 'Entwurf ... eines Kinder-Gartens', 1 May 1840 in *Kindergarten-Briefe* 132 (1887). See *Montessori* in the Italian Lexicon.

Kindertransport One of the charitable efforts organized to transport Jewish children to safe haven in the years immediately preceding the Second World War.

Kirsch, Kirchwasser (*Kirsch(en)wasser*, from *Kirsche* 'cherry' and *Wasser* 'water'). 'An alcoholic spirit distilled in Germany and Switzerland from a fermented liquor obtained by crushing wild cherries': *OED.*

Kitsch Literally, 'trash'. 'Art or *objets d'art* characterized by worthless pretentiousness; the qualities associated with such art or artifacts': *OED.*

Kohl-rabi or **Kohlrabi** Also *erron.* **khol-**. From Italian *cavoli* (or *cauli*) *rape*, plural of *cavolo rapa* (F. *chou-rave*) 'cole-rape'; the first element being assimilated to G. *kohl* (earlier from Latin *caulis,* 'stalk, cabbage'. 'A cabbage with a turnip-shaped stem, varieties of which are cultivated as food for cattle in England, and as a vegetable in India and Germany; the turnip-cabbage': *OED*. Towards the close of the 20th century in England, the respectable vegetable the kohl-rabi found its way back onto the tables of the middle class.

> 'The khol rabi, or above ground turnip cabbage': Vancouver, *Agriculture in Devon* 191 (1807). 'The ground was

> cropped with ... one [acre] of kohlrabi': J C Curwen, *Hints on Economic Feeding* 50 (1808). 'Two varieties of Kohl rabi are cultivated – the green and the purple': Stephens, *The Book of the Farm* (ed 2) II 88/2 (1851). 'A large breadth of kohlrabi, which was a fair plant': *The Times* (weekly ed.) 9 September 17/1, 1887.

Konditorei, plural **Konditoreien** (*Konditor*, 'confectioner'). Confectionery; a confectioner's shop, a shop where pastries are sold.

Konzern Literally, 'a concern', nominally as in, for example, 'a family concern', but with overtones. The word *Konzern* is used by both German-speakers and English-speakers to denote a typical, specifically German, form of conglomerate. This type of conglomerate was frequently set up in the 1920s to circumvent the anti-monopoly peace terms imposed by the Allies. A classic example was I. G. Farben, *Interessengemeinschaft Farben*. Today the word connotes commercial organizations comprising a large number of enterprises with links to each other not only through affiliation but also through common directors and common shareholders, and, very typical of German business, considerable lending to and investment in the component parts of the *Konzern* by the same major bank, which is often the primary link and sometimes the only link.

Konzertmeister Literally, 'concert-master'. The first violinist in an orchestra, called in England 'the leader of the orchestra' and in the USA 'the concert-master'.

Kraft durch Freude Literally, 'Health through Joy', with, as an overtone, 'Health' meaning what 'Health and Strength' meant in an Anglo-Saxon context. The motto of the Nazi Party's *Gemeinschaft Kraft durch Freude* (Health through Joy Organization), a section of the *Deutsche Arbeitsfront*, the German National Labour Organization. The head of the KdF was Dr Robert Ley. It was essentially designed for the purpose of providing organized leisure for the German work-force as a means of maximizing production.

Kraut Literally, 'herb, vegetable, cabbage'. Among English-speakers, a widely used derogatory term for a German, probably owing to the popularity among the Germans of the dish **Sauerkraut** (*q.v.*).

> 'She said; 'You know all about me but I know quite a bit about you. How you married that Kraut bastard and how he kicked you out and kept the kid": Truman Capote, *Answered Prayers: The Unfinished Novel*, edn 1987, p 118 (1987).

Kreutzer A small German and Austrian coin of varying values, so called from its having been originally marked with a cross.

'Krieg ist nichts als eine Fortsetzung des politischen Verkehrs mit Einmischung anderer Mittel, Der' 'War is nothing else than the extension of politics with the admixture of other means': Carl von Clausewitz (1780-1831), *Vom Kriege*, bk 8, ch 6, s B.

Kriegsmarine Literally, 'war-navy'. The German Navy from 1936 to 1945.

Kristallnacht Literally, 'Crystal-Night', 9November 1938, also known as 'the Night of Broken Glass'. It was so called because the windows of shops and other premises throughout Germany that were owned by Jews were smashed during that night. The ostensible reason for these 'popular expressions of opinion' was the assassination on 7 November 1938 of the Third Secretary at the German Embassy in Paris, Ernst vom

Rath, by a 17-year-old Jewish youth, Herschel Grynszpan.

Kultur Literally, 'culture'. 'Civilization as conceived by the Germans; especially used in a derogatory sense during the 1914-18 and 1939-45 wars, as involving notions of racial and cultural arrogance, militarism, and imperialism': *OED*. In spite of the undoubted annexation by the *Großdeutsch* tendency of the word *Kultur* (see, for example, *Kulturkampf, below*) many Germans persisted in using the word *Kultur* in a sense accurately translated as 'civilization', and it is that sense that has prevailed. It is in this liberal sense that the word *Kultur* ought to be interpreted when one analyses Hermann Göring's reputed outburst, 'Whenever I hear the word *culture*, I reach for my revolver'. He might well have been quoting words from Hanns Johst's play *Schlageter* (1933): 'Wenn ich *Kultur* höre ... entsichere ich meinen Browning' ('When I hear the word *culture* I slip back the safety catch of my Browning [revolver]'): Act 1, Scene 1.

> 'It is the peculiar essence of German Kultur, which is the German religion, that it is Germany's moral duty to break every tie, every restriction that binds man to fellow-man, if she thinks it will pay': Rudyard Kipling, *Kipling's Message* (1918).

Kulturkampf Literally, 'culture-struggle'. The conflict from 1872 to 1887 between the German government under Bismarck and the Catholic Church in Germany, largely concerned with the control of schools, the appointment of persons to ecclesiastical office and the general subordination of the Church to the State.

Kümmel 'From *Kümmel*. MHG. *kümel*, OHG. *kumil*, variant. *kumîn*: Cumin. A liqueur, flavoured with cumin, manufactured in North Germany': *OED*.

Kurhaus Literally, 'cure-house'). The buildings comprising a German or Austro-Hungarian spa.

Kursaal Literally, 'cure-room'. The reception room(s) of a German or Austro-Hungarian spa.

Lager (*lager-bier*, beer brewed for keeping rather than immediate drinking, from *lager* 'a store' and *bier* 'beer'). 'A light beer, consumed largely in Germany and America, and to some [increasing] extent in England': *OED*.

Lammergeyer Also *Lammergeier*. Correctly, *Lämmergeier*, f. *Lämmer*, pl. of *Lamm* 'lamb', and *Geier* 'vulture'. 'The Bearded Vulture, *Gypaetus barbatus*; it is the largest European bird of prey, and inhabits lofty mountains in Southern Europe, Asia, and Northern Africa': *OED*.

> 'An inaccessible shelf of rock ... upon which a lammergeyer ... once alighted with an infant it had carried away': L. Simond, *Switzerland* I, 239 (1822).
> 'The Lammergeyer is easily distinguished from the other vultures by its pointed wings and wedge-shaped tail': A. L. Adams, *Wand. Nat. India* 78 (1867).

Land ohne Musik, Das Literally, 'The Land without Music'. A description of England by Hans von Bülow (1830-94), pianist and conductor.

Landauer 'A Landau'. 'A four-wheeled carriage, the top of which, being made in two parts, may be closed or thrown open. When open, the rear part is folded back, and the front part entirely removed': *OED*. The name derives from the name of the town in which the vehicle was first made. The German name for the carriage is *Landauer*, short for *landauer Wagen*.

> 'The body of a landau carriage differs nothing in shape from a Coach. The landau is the Coach form, the landaulet the Chariot form': W. Felton, *Carriages*, I, p 22 (1794). 'The landau ... combines more than the advantages of three distinct vehicles: a close carriage; a barouche or half-headed carriage; and one entirely open': *Cassell's Technical Educator*, IV, 306/1 (1879).

Landsknecht Literally, 'rural servant'. One of a class of mercenary soldiers in Germany and other continental countries in the 16th and 17th centuries.

Landsturm Literally, 'landstorm'. 'In Germany, Switzerland, etc. a general levy in time of war; the forces so called out; the militia force consisting of those men not serving in the army or navy or in the *landwehr*': *OED*.

Landwehr Literally, 'landforce'. 'In Germany and some other countries, that part of the organized land forces (corresponding to the militia of Great Britain) of which continuous service is required only in time of war': *OED*. In the United Kingdom, the modern equivalent of the Landwehr would no doubt be the Territorial Army.

Langlauf 'Cross-country skiing; a cross-country skiing race. Hence**, Langläufer**, a competitor in such a race': *OED*.

Leben 'to live'. See *Habseligkeiten above.*

Lebensborn Literally, 'life's fountain'. The name given to a Nazi programme aimed at promoting the 'Aryan' race by eugenic means. Initially, its objectives were secured by the provision of ante-natal and maternity facilities for unmarried mothers of 'Aryan' stock, but subsequently the programme also encompassed such extremes as the forcible sterilization or even killing of 'the unfit', and, in another equally extreme manifestation, the kidnapping of 'Aryan'-looking children in the Occupied Territories and the placing of them in homes so that they might be brought up as Nazis.

Lebensraum (genitive of *Leben* 'life' and *Raum* 'space'). 'Territory which the Germans believed was needed for their natural development': *OED*. The concept of *Lebensraum* is akin to the graphic and widespread concept of 'land-hunger'. *Lebensraum* was one of the motive forces behind the Wilhelmine government's desire to establish colonies in Africa and elsewhere. (See *'Unser Platz an der Sonne' below.*) Among the most significant emotional influences towards a positive, expansionist embodiment of *Lebensraum* was Hans Grimm's novel *Volk ohne Raum,* 'People without Space', published in 1926. In 1944, the *Todt Organisation* placed an order for an astonishingly large number of copies – no fewer than *half a million copies*!

> 'Moravia and Bohemia had been overrun by the Nazi armies and declared German Protectorates – part of the German people's 'lebensraum'': *War Illustrated,* 9 Dec 393/1 1939. 'Kurt Vohwinkel (1939) ... distinguishes three kinds of German *Lebensraum*. The first kind is the real area occupied solidly by Germans; the second the area where besides Germans there are other people but the German cultural influence prevails; and the third is the one in which Germans are outnumbered by others but still because of their racial and cultural superiority have a right to

dominate': S. van Valkenburg in G. Taylor, *Geography in the Twentieth Century* iv, 109 (1951). 'Hitler worked on the premiss provided by the geographer, Friedrich Ratzel (1844-1904), and developed by the geopolitician, [General] Karl Haushofer [1869-1946], that nations need 'living space' (Lebensraum) if they are not to decline, a notion that had become part of the pre-1914 Pan German agenda, and also on the assumption that France represented an irreconcilable opponent of German expansion. In *Mein Kampf* he had argued that, before 1914, Germany was confronted by two alternatives: either a policy of world trade, colonies and a large fleet or, and this was Hitler's preferred option, the acquisition of territory in Europe at the expense of Russia': Jeremy Noakes, review of *Hitler's Second Book*, *The Times Literary Supplement,* 5 December 2003.

Lederhosen 'Leather shorts, as worn in Alpine regions': *OED*.

Leitmotiv Literally, 'leading motive'. 'In the musical drama of Wagner and his imitators, a theme associated throughout the work with a particular person, situation, or sentiment. Also in extended use': *OED*.

'Ninety-nine music graduates out of a hundred will say that the Leitmotiv (or Leitmotif, or leading motive) … was invented by Wagner. Wrong … The correct answer is: Friedrich Wilhelm Jähns, and even he applied it not to Wagner but to Weber': *Composer & Conductor,* Aug. 1/1 1972.

Libelle ('dragonfly'). See *Habseligkeiten* above.

Lieben 'to love'. See *Habseligkeiten* above.

Liebesoboe The *oboe d'amore*. See the Italian Lexicon.

Liebestod Literally, 'love's death'. 'An aria or a duet proclaiming the suicide of lovers …; hence, such a suicide': *OED.*

'*Liebestod*, the title used today for Isolde's death scene in Wagner's *Tristan und Isolde*, but used by Wagner of the mystic love duet in Act 2': *Concise Oxford Dictionary of Opera* 223/2 (1964).

Liebfraumilch Literally, 'Milk of Our Lady'. 'A white wine originally produced at Worms; also loosely applied to German white wines': *OED.* In Britain, the appellation seems to have lost much of its prestige over the years, as indicated by the last quotation below. In Germany and elsewhere, however, the appellation *Liebfrauenmilch* (that is, with the extra syllable) is reserved for the few thousand bottles produced every year from the original vineyard, continues to enjoy esteem. See also *Hock, above.*

'The Liebfrauenmilch … is a well-bodied wine, grown at Worms': C. Redding, *The History of Modern Wines* vii. 204 (1833). ' The best Hock, which is sold under a number of well-known names, e.g. Johannisberger, … Liebfraumilch': *Good Housekeeping Home Encyclopaedia* 508/2. 1951. 'Rheinhessen wines, distinctive in their own right, are so named; the remainder call themselves Liebfraumilch': A. Lichine, *Encyclopaedia of Wines,* 323/1 (1967). 'Liebfraumilch is an invented name for almost any ordinary German white wine not worthy of its own district label': *The Guardian* 28 June 1973, 11/6.

Lied, *plural* **Lieder** 'A song, especially one characteristic of the German Romantic Era': *OED.*

Lippizan 'Of or pertaining to Lipizza or Lippiza, the home of the former Austrian Imperial Stud, esp. designating a strain of horse originally bred there. So *Lippizaner*, a horse of this breed; also *attrib.*': *OED.* A variety of spellings is accepted.

> '"Muestoso-Moschina", a Lipizza stallion, one of the eight famous stallions at the ... Spanish Court Riding-School in Vienna': M. C. Grimsgaard, *Orig. Handbk. Riders* Suppl S20 (caption) 1911. 'Twelve of the famous Lippizaner horses ... The Lippizana is a perfectly separate and peculiar breed of horse, in appearance much like an Arab, but ... more massive': *The Observer* 17 June 27/3 1928. 'General Patton ... fulfilled the request made to him that the Lipizzan stud ... be brought back to Austria': A. Podhajsky, *Spanish Riding School* (ed. 2) 4/1 (1954). 'Those beautiful leaps and dancing steps made by the white Lipizzan stallions of the Spanish Riding School': *The Islander* (Victoria, B.C.) 30 May 2/4 1971. 'The 58 photogenic white Lippizaner stallions of the Spanish Riding School which has just celebrated its four hundredth anniversary': *The Guardian* 4 Oct. 4/6 1972.

Loess, Löss, Löß (German dialect *lösz*). 'A deposit of fine yellowish-grey loam which occurs extensively from north-central Europe to eastern China, in the American mid-west, and elsewhere, esp. in the basins of large rivers, and which is usually considered to be composed of material transported by the wind during and after the Glacial Period': *OED.*

Lorelei or **Loreley** '[Name of a rock on the Rhine near Coblenz.]. In German legend, a beautiful woman with long blonde hair who sat on the Lorelei rock and with her fine singing distracted boatmen, so that they drowned when their ships foundered on the rock': *OED.* The Lorelei is the subject of poems by Clemens Brentano (1778-1842), Heinrich Heine (1797-1856) and Joseph von Eichendorff (1788-1857).

Luftwaffe Literally, 'air-weapon'. The German Air-Force.

Luger 'Also (erron.) *Lueger, Lüger*. The name of G. *Luger*, German firearms expert, used *attrib.* or *absol.* to designate a German type of automatic pistol': *OED.*

> 'The Borchardt Leuger or 'Parabellum' automatic pistol belongs to Class I': W. B. Wallace *Text Bk. Small Arms* 178 (1904).

Lumpenproletariat (from Karl Marx, 1850, in *Die Klassenkämpfe in Frankreich* and, 1852, in *Der achtzehnte Brumaire des Louis Bonaparte*, from *lumpen*, 'rag', *Lump* 'ragamuffin' and *Proletariat*). 'A term applied, originally by Karl Marx, to the lowest and most degraded section of the proletariat; the 'down and outs' who make no contribution to the workers' cause. So *lumpenproletarian a.* and *n.* Also *lumpen a.*, boorish, stupid, unenlightened, used derisively to describe persons, attitudes, etc., supposed to be characteristic of the *lumpenproletariat*; also *ellipt.* or as *n*': *OED.*

Lustiges Wien Literally, 'Merry Vienna'.

Mach (from the name of Ernst *Mach* (1838-1916), Austrian physicist and philosopher of Moravian origin). *Mach('s) number*, a number to denominate speed in, for example, aviation; the ratio of the speed of a body and a fluid to the speed of sound at the same point; so *Mach One*, *Two* (or *1*, *2*), etc., a speed corresponding to a Mach number of one, two, etc. A draft revision of the 1969 edition of the *OED* on which the above definition is based was proposed in the online edition of the *OED* in March 2000. It should be consulted if complete accuracy is required.

Märchen Literally, 'fairy-tale'. 'A folk-tale or story. Usually construed as a plural': *OED*.

> 'There is no doubt ... that the story of the shadowy Anglian king Offa, blended with *märchen* elements, was well known in England in the time of Cynewulf': *Modern Philology* V 402 1908. 'Study of *märchen*, both for their own sake and for the light that they throw upon sophisticated literature.': W. W. Lawrence,*Beowulf & Epic Tradition* 166 (1928).

Mauser (from the names of the inventors, P. P. and W. *Mauser*). A military rifle adopted by the German military experts in 1871, and perfected in 1884. The proprietary name for 'any of a family of bolt-action rifles designed by the Mausers, formerly the basic infantry weapon of the German army': *OED*.

> 'In the original Mauser ... the soldier had to give the stock a smart stroke so as to throw out the used cartridge': *Pall Mall Gazette,* 25 January 3/1 (1887).

Meerschaum Literally, 'sea-foam'. 'A soft white, grey, or yellowish mineral resembling a hardened clay, which consists of orthorhombic hydrated magnesium trisilicate. Also called *sepiolite*. Specifically, by transference, a tobacco-pipe having a bowl made of meerschaum': *OED*.

> 'A German word designating a soft white mineral sometimes found floating on the Black Sea, and rather suggestive of sea-foam': *Encycl. Brit.* XVIII. 72 (1911). 'A pipe of a particular kind, that has been smoked for a year or so, will sell here [*i.e.* at Ratzeburg] for twenty Guineas': S. T. Coleridge, *Let.* 14 Jan 1799. I. 463 (1956). 'A *meerschaum* pipe nearly *black* with smoking is considered a treasure': J. Nott in T. Dekker, *Guls Horne-bk.* 176 (1812). 'One Stradivarius, I confess, Two Meerschaums, I would fain possess': O. W. Holmes, *Autocrat of Breakfast-table* xi (1858).

'Mehr Licht!' ('More light!'). Goethe's last words, understood by some to urge an increasing extension of *die Aufklärung*. In fact, his words were 'Macht doch den zweiten Fensterladen in der Stube auch auf, damit mehr Licht hereinkomme': Karl Wilhelm Müller, *Letzte literarische Thätigkeit, Verhältniss zum Ausland und Scheiden*, Jena 1832; 29: ('Open the second shutter in the room, so that more light can come in',) Our collaborator Dr Günther Schmigalle has added the following: 'Goethe, in his pronunciation, had a definite dialectal tinge, *i.e.* the influence of the dialect of Hessen, where he was born, or of Saxony, where he spent the greater part of his life, or of both, were clearly audible when he spoke. So, this story goes, what he was going to say on his deathbed was: 'Mer liecht hier so schlächt' [= *Man liegt hier so schlecht*], *i.e.* he was going to complain that he felt uncomfortable in his bed. But, after pronouncing the first two words, his breath failed; and posterity interpreted 'Mer liecht' as 'Mehr Licht'.

Mein Kampf ('My Struggle'). Adolf Hitler's most influential publication. He was imprisoned in the fortress at Landsberg am

Lech as a consequence of his failed 'Beerhall Putsch' of 11 November 1923. While in prison, he dictated the book to his fellow inmate, Rudolf Hess. It was published in 1925. During the period of the Third Reich (1933-1945), every German family was required to possess a copy. From 1936 on, it was handed out to couples getting married in the registrar's office, and by 1943 nearly 10 million copies of it had been distributed in Germany.

Meistersinger (Middle High German *Meistersinger*, from *Meister* 'master' and *Singer* 'singer'. In modern German *-singer* is restricted to use in compounds with mediaeval reference, as in *Meistersinger* and *Minnesinger*; the usual word for 'singer' is *Sänger*. The singular and plural forms of *Meistersinger* are identical.) A member of any of the German guilds for lyric poets and musicians that flourished in the 14th to 16th centuries, known for their elaborate technique.

> 'The Meistersinger were either preoccupied with the observance of rules or were rarely visited with inspiration': *Grove's Dict. Music* (ed. 5) VII. 912/2 (1954). 'The *Meistersinger* were not popular figures, as Wagner's opera *Die Meistersinger* suggests; they were largely ignored by professional men': *Encycl. Brit.* XV. 118/2 (1968).

Also **Minnesinger** (singular and plural). Any of the German-speaking poets and performers of the 12th to the 14th century whose works were chiefly concerned with courtly love, **Frauendienst**, see above. The *Minnesinger* were the Germanic equivalent of the *troubadours* and *trouvères*.

Mischling 'A person of mixed race, *esp.* one of partly Jewish descent': *OED*. *Cf mischen* 'to mix'. From the 17th century *Mischling* has meant a person with parents of different racial descent. The plural *Mischlinge* follows the German usage.

> '*Mischlinge*, or persons of 25% or 50% Jewish blood, may marry *with consent of the authorities* an 'Aryan' or a 25% *Mischling*': *Biometrika* 28 33 (1936). 'In the Mannheim Elementary schools there are now 79 *Mischlings* (i.e. children whose fathers are Negroes and whose mothers are white Germans)': *Journal of Negro Education,* 23 180 (1954). 'Had not Eva married ... a gentile? And here I was the fruit of a forbidden union, a *mischling*': D. Hopkinson, *Incense Tree* i. 9 (1968). 'Fürstner had been a *Mischling*': D. Hart-Davis, *Hitler's Games* xvii. 236 (1968). 'She was Catholic ... But two of her four grandparents were Jewish, so she was classified as a *mischling*, first degree': M. Atwood, *Robber Bride* xlvi. 357 (1993).

Mitteleuropa Literally, 'Central Europe'. Central Europe but with overtones of the former Habsburg dominions.

> 'By the mid-19th century, the handiest language for a traveller through *Mitteleuropa* was the German spoken by the Habsburg monarchs who reined over Hungarians, Czechs and many others': *The Economist*, 33, 7 August 2004.

Mittelstand Literally, 'the middle ground'. The middle classes (or the German equivalent of 'Middle England'). Now increasingly used as a technical term to mean small and medium-sized companies in Germany. They are considered to be the backbone of the German economy, producing considerably more GDP than the large corporations. These enterprises are mostly family owned, they operate with very little borrowing and they are extremely flexible in adapting to changes in technology and in the market place. They often have a patriarchal structure, look after their employees and run their own distribution networks throughout the world.

> '[Mittelstand is] a term covering perhaps 3.4m companies employing 26m people': *The Economist*, 20 November 2004, p 91.

Munchausen 'The name of Baron Munchausen (in Ger. form *Münchhausen*), the hero of a pseudo-autobiographical narrative of impossible adventures, written in English by the German Rudolf Eric Raspe (1785): used to denote an extravagantly mendacious story of marvellous adventure': *OED*. The phrase *Munchausen syndrome by proxy* has been widely applied in recent years to denote a complex psychological disorder.

> 'The terms 'Munchausen syndrome by proxy' or 'Polle syndrome' have been used to describe children who are victims of parentally induced or fabricated illness': *Pediatrics* 71 715 (1983). 'Child Welfare officials took the child, alleging the mother suffered from Munchausen Syndrome by Proxy, a rare disorder in which parents will take their children from doctor to doctor complaining of fabricated or induced illness': *Calgary Herald*, 7 May 1994. 'The Department of Health and the Royal College of Paediatrics and Child Health ... both now refer to the problem as 'fabricated or induced illness in children by carers': *Brit. Med. Jrnl*, 11 Aug. 2001. 'Relabelled last month by the Royal College of Paediatricians and Child Health as *fabricated or induced illness by carers (FII)*, the syndrome recasts traditional role': *Observer*, 21 Apr. 2002.

München 'The German name of the capital of Bavaria used with reference to a meeting of representatives of Germany, Great Britain, France, and Italy on 29 September 1938, when (by the Munich Agreement) the Sudetenland of N. Czechoslovakia was ceded to Germany; also *transf.* as a typical example of dishonourable appeasement': *OED*. The English name for *München* is *Munich*, pronounced \ˈmjuːnɪk\. It was transmitted through French. To pronounce it as though it were a German word, \ˈmyːnɪx\, is absurd.

'Muss es sein? Es muss sein!' Beethoven published his String Quartet in F Maj, Op 135, shortly after he had learnt that he was becoming irremediably deaf. He added an epigraph to this quartet, '*Muss es sein? Es muss sein*!': 'Must it be? It must be!'

Narrenschiff Literally, 'the Ship of Fools'. The title of Sebastian Brant's satirical work *Das Narrenschiff* (1494), translated into English by Alexander Barclay as *The shyp of folys of the worlde* (1509), a ship whose passengers represent various types of vice or folly.

> '"A ship of fools" he shriek'd in spite': Tennyson *Voyage* x, in *Enoch Arden* 149 (1864). 'He Who launched our Ship of Fools many anchors gave us': R. Kipling, *Debits & Credits* (1926) 358 (1919). 'The Apocalypse as depicted by Bosch, the upside-down world of Goya, the Ship of Fools having landed its cargo': *Times Literary Supplement* 7 Feb. 126/4, 1975.

Nazi (abbreviation of *Nationalsozialist,* reproducing the pronunciation of the first two syllables of the word in German). 'A member of the National Socialist German

Workers' Party (NSDAP), led by Adolf Hitler from 1920 and in power from 1933-45': *OED.* Also an adjective.

Neanderthaler or, now, **Neandertaler** Also with lower-case initial. (From the name of a valley east of Düsseldorf in North Rhine-Westphalia, western Germany, where, in 1856, the bones of the hominid named after the location were first discovered.) 'Designating, relating to, or characteristic of a Middle Palaeolithic fossil hominid with a receding forehead and prominent brow ridges, known from Europe, Africa, and Asia. Neanderthal 'man' was originally regarded as a separate species, *Homo neanderthalensis* (so named by W. King in *Q. Jrnl. Sci.* (1864) 1 88-97; and later as a subspecies of *H. sapiens, H. sapiens neanderthalensis*; it is now once again and increasingly viewed as a separate species, probably at the end of a different evolutionary line from *H. sapiens.* Used also, figuratively (humorously or pejoratively), to denote primitive, uncivilized, loutish persons or behaviour; often specifically directed at politically or socially reactionary opinions': *OED.*

Neue Sachlichkeit Literally, 'new objectivity'. 'A movement in the fine arts, music, and literature, which developed in Germany during the 1920s and was characterized by realism and a deliberate rejection of romantic attitudes': *OED.* See also *Sachlichkeit below.*

> 'The new group ... wanted super-concrete precision; after the elimination of objects, journalistic reporting of time and place. This was the starting-point for German *vérisme,* the 'Neue Sachlichkeit', and the art of such men as Max Beckmann, Otto Dix, George Grosz and their like': (C. Fullman *tr*) Thoene, *Modern German Art* 87 (1938). 'There appeared a movement since classified as *Neue Sachlichkeit,* or 'New Objectivity', begun in 1920 by Otto Dix and George Grosz': B. S. Myers *Modern Art in Making* xix. 351 (1950). '*Neue Sachlichkeit,* a term that came into fashion in Germany between the two world wars. It describes a tendency in some composers of that time to write music entirely detached from sentiment and free from any pictorial suggestion': *Grove's Dict. Mus.* VI. 53/1 (1954). 'A deliberately impersonal quality marks much of the art of that time [*sc* the late 1920s], as the words 'Neue Sachlichkeit' themselves imply': J. Willett, *Theatre of Bertolt Brecht,* vii. 194. (1959). 'After its first performance in 1923 [Hindemith's] *Marienleben* was hailed as a shining example of *Neue Sachlichkeit,* a new matter-of-fact contrapuntal style then emerging, which represented a conscious reaction against the hyper-romantic attitude prevalent earlier this century': *Listener* 17 Sept. 445/1 (1964). '*Neue Sachlichkeit,* a movement in German art and literature that arose in the mid 1920s. It represented a sharp reaction against experimental and idealistic art of any sort. Artists strove for an 'honest objectivity' (*Sachlichkeit*), depicting with matter-of-fact literalness their everyday experience': *Oxf. Compan. Art* 772/2 (1970).

Nibelungenlied 'A 13th-cent. Middle High German epic telling the story of Siegfried and the curse of the Nibelungs' treasure. Also in extended use. There have been many adaptations of the story, including Wagner's epic music drama *Der Ring des Nibelungen* (libretto published Zürich, 1853)': *OED.*

Nuremberg The English name for the city in Southern Germany, *Nürnberg*. 'The adjective *Nuremberg* is used *attrib.* to designate a connection with the German National Socialist Party with which the city was associated, as *Nuremberg Laws*, laws promulgated in 1935 barring Jews from German citizenship and forbidding intermarriage between 'Aryans' and Jews; **Nuremberg Rally**, one of the mass meetings of the German National Socialist Party which were held annually at Nuremberg from 1933 to 1938; **Nuremberg Trials**, a series of trials of former Nazi leaders for alleged war crimes and crimes against humanity presided over by an International Military Tribunal formed from the victorious Allied Powers and held in Nuremberg in 1945–6': *OED*.

Nürnberg see **Nuremberg**, immediately above.

Nymphenburg 'The name of a former village in Bavaria, now a suburb of Munich, used *attrib.* to designate pottery manufactured there from 1761': *OED*.

> 'A collection of Nymphenburg equestrian statuettes': *House & Garden* Oct. 112/1, 1960.

Oberammergau A village in the Bavarian Alps, the location of the celebrated Passion Play. Oberammergau's Passion Play was brought into being as a result of the bubonic plague of 1633, which ravaged Bavaria after the Thirty Years War. More than a tenth of the population of the village had already died when the survivors made a solemn vow: if God spared them, they would re-enact the Passion every decade for ever more. The death-rate immediately fell, and the Passion Play has been performed at ten-year intervals from that time, barring some dislocations to timing owing to international events.

Oflag (abbreviation for *Offizier(s)lager* 'officers' camp'). 'In Nazi Germany: a prison-camp for captured enemy officers': *OED*. See *Stalag, below.*

Oktoberfest An annual celebration originated in Bavaria in 1810. The Munich *Oktoberfest*, known by the locals as the 'Wiesn', is the biggest public festival in the world. Each year, it is attended by about 6 million visitors, who drink about 5 million litres of beer and consume over 200,000 pairs of pork sausages, primarily in the 'beer tents' put up by the traditional Munich breweries. Anomalously, the *Oktoberfest* is celebrated during the last two weeks in September.

Ostalgie Nostalgia for the former German Democratic Republic.

Ostpolitik (from *Ost* 'east' and *Politik* 'policy'). 'German policy towards Eastern Europe, associated mainly with the Federal Republic of Germany's cultivation of good relations with the Communist block during the 1960s, but applied also, by extension, to the policies of other western countries regarding the East as a whole': *OED*. English-speaking critics have sometimes seen Ostpolitik as being a recrudescence of *Der Drang nach Osten, above.*

> 'They will scarcely overlook Hitler's statement … "The goal of *Ostpolitik* is to open up an area of settlement for one hundred million Germans": T. Prittie, *Germany Divided* vi. 155 (1961). 'The politicians of Bonn are rather unhappy at the widespread use of the term. 'Ostpolitik.' by their Western allies. In the history of twentieth-century Germany, this term has signified a whole range of activities, from Hindenburg's humiliation of Russia at Brest-Litovsk to the East-West balancing act of

Rapallo, and back to the domination of the East by Schacht's financial diplomacy and Hitler's armies': *The Times Literary Supplement,* 15 October 1971 1246/2.

Otto 'The name of Nikolaus August *Otto* (1832-1891), German engineer, used *attrib.* to designate (*a*) the four-stroke cycle employed in most petrol, diesel and gas engines; idealized as adiabatic compression followed by heat addition at constant volume, adiabatic expansion, and heat rejection at constant volume; and *(b)* an engine employing this cycle. The cycle was orig. proposed by A. Beau de Rochas in 1862, but Otto was the first to build an engine employing it (in 1876) after conceiving the idea independently': *OED.*

Panzer Literally, 'mail, a coat of mail'. 'Used attributively of or pertaining to a German armoured unit; also in *Panzerdivision.* As a noun, a panzer unit or a member of such a unit': *OED.* So, *Panzerfaust* ('mailed fist'), an anti-tank grenade. Used also to denote armour for men and horses.

Pfennig 'A small copper coin of Germany, formerly of varying value, now the hundredth part of a mark': *OED.* (See *Deutsche Mark, above*)

Pickelhaube Literally, 'spiked bonnet'. The characteristic spiked stiff-leather helmet worn by German soldiers before and for the first part of the First World War.

Pilates [Exercises] Also with lower-case initial. From the name of Joseph Hubertus *Pilates* (1880-1967), a German-born physical-fitness specialist, who developed the exercises and apparatus. Used attributively to denote a system of exercises designed to improve physical strength, flexibility, and posture, and to enhance mental awareness and control of body movement, originally (but now not always) using specialized apparatus. Also: designating techniques and equipment used in performing such exercises. Pilates' own name for the system was *contrology.*

Pilsner (from *Pilsen* (Czech *Plzeò*), a province and city in West Bohemia, the Czech Republic. In full *Pils(e)nerbeer.* A pale-coloured lager beer with a strong hop flavour. The name now designates the type of beer rather than the origin of the beer and trade-mark attorneys are much in demand. The authentic beer from Plzeò itself is nowadays known as *Pils(e)ner Urquell* ('original source'). See *Ur below.*

Plattdeutsch See *Hochdeutsch above.*

Poltergeist Literally, a 'noisy ghost', from *Polter,* 'noise, uproar', and *Geist,* 'ghost'. A supposed phenomenon whereby a ghostly presence, often thought to be mischievous, manifests itself by means of noise.

Pommersche Grenadier, der In 1876 Austria was on the point of going to war against Russia over Bulgaria. Bismarck warned Austria that Germany would not support Austria: 'Der Balkan ist nicht einmal die Knochen eines einzigen pommerschen Grenadiers wert!': 'The Balkans are not worth the bones of a single Pomeranian Grenadier'. The expression *Der Balkan* is also applied figuratively to countries and regions considered to be less than ideally civilized or less advanced politically and socially than the speaker's own country.

Pretzel from **Brezel, Bretzel** 'A crisp biscuit baked in the form of a knot and flavoured with salt; used esp. by Germans as a relish with beer. Also *fig.* and *attrib.*': *OED.* Derived from German *brezel, pretzel, bretzel,* in OHG *brizzilla* = It. *bracciello* (Florio) a cracknel; usually taken as from mediaeval

Latin *bracellus* a bracelet; also a kind of cake or biscuit (Du Cange, *Glossarium ad Scriptores mediae et infimae Latinitatis* (1678)). For a fuller etymology of this word, see Kluge, *Etymologisches Wörterbuch der Deutschen Sprache* 21st edn (1975) *s.v. Brezel.* The initial letter *P*, as used in the United States to the virtual exclusion of the initial *B*. is no doubt owing to the influence of the numerous immigrants from the Southern regions of Germany who flocked to the US in the 19th century.

Privatdocent, Privatdozent (from *privat* 'private' and *Docent* or *Dozent*, from Latin *docēre*, to teach). 'In German and some other universities: A private teacher or lecturer recognized by the university but not on the salaried staff': *OED.*

Pumpernickel (origin uncertain: *cf Pumpernickel* 'lout, booby, yokel'). 'Bread made (in Germany) from coarsely ground unbolted rye; wholemeal rye bread: associated especially with Westphalia': *OED.*

> 'Their bread is of the very coarsest kind, ill baked, and as black as a coal, for they never sift their flour. The people of the country call it *Pompernickel*': Nugent, *Grand Tour: Germany,* II. 80 (1756).

Putsch (Swiss German: 'knock, thrust, blow'). 'A revolutionary attempt': *OED.*

Qualitätswein Literally, 'wine of quality'.

> 'There will be three categories of wine: *tafelweine* for all the *vins ordinaires*; *qualitätswein* for the middle quality wines ...; and *qualitätswein mit prädikat*': *The Times,* 27 November 1972. (Wines & Spirits Supplement) p. iii/5. *Mit Prädikat* means 'with commendation'.

Realpolitik 'Practical politics; policy determined by practical, rather than moral or ideological, considerations': *OED.*

Reich Literally, 'kingdom, realm, state'. 'Chiefly during the period 1871–1945, the German state or commonwealth; also, one of a sequence of empires or *régimes* in Germany, especially the Third Reich. Apart from *Third Reich*, collocations with an ordinal are rare and do not constitute recognized English historical terminology': *OED.* The Germans themselves did not generally use *das zweite Reich*, preferring to use *das deutsche Reich* from 1871 to 1918.

Reichsmark, die The monetary unit of the German Reich, replaced in 1948 by the *Deutsche Mark* (*q.v.*).

Reichstag (from the genitive singular of *Reich* and *Tag,* as in *tagen* 'to meet, sit daily in conference', from *Tag* 'day'). The diet or parliament of the German Empire (1871-1918). Before that, the diet of the North German Confederation, and, after that, the diet of post-Imperial Germany until 1945. Also, the name of the building in Berlin in which these diets met. (The word *diet*, meaning the deliberative organ of a state, itself derives from the Latin *dies*, meaning 'day'.)

Reichswehr (*Wehr* 'defence'). The German Regular Army from 1919 to 1935.

Rentenmark, die (from *Renten,* 'securities'). A unit of currency introduced in Germany in November 1923 and tied to the nation's industrial and agricultural resources; in 1924 it was replaced by the *Reichsmark*': *OED.*

> 'The Rentenmark note was not itself land, nor was there any method by which the holder of a Rentenmark note could possess himself of the land that was supposed to be behind his

note': Geoffrey Crowther, *Outline of Money*, I, 19 (1940). 'The Rentenmark was a new unit of currency supposedly backed by the land of the Reich': *The Spectator*, 21 December 1974, 803/1.

Rollmops A rolled fillet of herring, flavoured with sliced onions, spices, etc., and pickled in brine. Sometimes erroneously treated as a plural.

Rottweiler (also **Rottweiller**), from *Rottweil*, the name of a town in Württemberg, South West Germany. 'A large black-and-tan dog belonging to the breed so called, having a short, coarse coat, docked tail, and a broad head with pendent ears. Also *attrib.*': *OED.*

> 'The Rottweil Dog, usually called the *Rottweiler Metzgerhund*, or butcher's dog of the town of Rottweil in South Germany': R. Leighton, *New Bk. Dog* 521/2 (1907).

Rotwelsch (formerly *Rothwelsch*) from MHG. *Rot* 'beggar' and *Welsch* 'stranger's language': see *Welsch, below*. A form of slang or cant used by vagrants and criminals in Germany and Austria.

> 'The lowest type of speech is the thieves' and beggars' cant known in German as *Rotwelsch* or *Gaunersprache*': Priebsch & Collinson *German Lang.* 260 (1934). 'The *argot* of the French underworld, the *Rotwelsch* of Germany, is paralleled by the *Cant* of English rogues and vagabonds': *John o' London's* 30 Nov. 610, 1961. ' 'Please, put away that firecracker,' said the Major, lapsing into Rotwelsch, the slang of Vienna's underworld': *Reader's Digest* Feb 122/2 1973.

Rucksack Literally, 'backpack'.

SA (abbreviation for *Sturmabteilung*, 'Storm-Section'). The Stormtroopers or Brownshirts of the early days of Nazism. Many had been members of the *Freikorps*, private armies that recruited disillusioned ex-service-men. The association with the colour brown arose from the wearing by the early members of the SA of army-surplus uniforms originally intended for German troops in the former German colonies in Africa. The SA was effectively dissolved on 13 July 1934. Hitler himself gave this purge its name, *The Night of the Long Knives* (a phrase from a popular Nazi song).

Sachertorte (named after *Sacher*, proprietor of an hotel in Vienna, or the hotel itself, and *torte*, cake). 'A rich chocolate cake of a kind originally made in Vienna': *OED.*

Sachlichkeit Literally, 'objectivity'. 'Objectivism, realism; specifically in the fine arts': *OED.*

> 'The general characteristics to be found in contemporary German painting ... belong to the spiritual categories of a post-war world: Despair and its concomitants – satire and irony; realism, matter-of-factness': Fullman tr. P. Thoene, *Mod. German Art,* 9 (1938). 'A generation of excellent artist-designers, such as Bruno Paul, Hans Poelzig and the brothers Taut, all worked in the spirit which was already associated with the word *Sachlichkeit,* which – taken literally – means 'thingness'; it is usually translated as 'matter-of-fact', 'realistic', 'sober', 'objective', and gained currency in matters of art and design early in this century': *Listener,* 3 Oct 436/1 (1968). See *Neue Sachlichkeit above.*

Sauerkraut Literally, 'sour vegetable' or, specifically, 'sour cabbage'. A popular dish in Germany comprising cabbage that has undergone acid fermentation. It is traditionally eaten with smoked sausages, pork, bacon and lightly smoked pork loin. It is popular also in Alsace, and in the rest of France under the name *choucroute*. In the quotation, a metaphor for 'Germanism'.

> 'The canned sauerkraut of Spengler's "Prussian Socialism", the commonplaces of the Wasteland, the cheap mental stimulants of Alienation, the cant and rant of pipsqueaks about inauthenticity and Forlornness': Saul Bellow, *Herzog*, p 81 (1977).

Schadenfreude Literally, *Schaden* 'harm' and *Freude* 'joy'. 'Malicious enjoyment of the misfortunes of others': *OED*.

> 'What a fearful thing is it that any language should have a word expressive of the pleasure which men feel at the calamities of others; for the existence of the word bears testimony to the existence of the thing. And yet in more than one [language] such a word is found. In the Greek *επιχαιρεκακια*, in the German, *Schadenfreude*': R. C. Trench, *Study of Words* (ed. 3) ii. 29 (1852).

Schlamperei 'Indolent slovenliness, muddleheadedness; especially designating a supposed south German and Austrian characteristic': *OED*. The word is cognate with *Schlampe*, 'a woman having low standards of cleanliness, given to gossiping and of loose morals'. *Schlamperei* is also used to characterize poor standards of performance by the State and the Civil Service, and is also applied to unsatisfactory projects in, for example, architecture and military and industrial hardware.

Schlieffen 'The name of Alfred, Graf von *Schlieffen* (1833-1913), German general, used *attrib.* of a plan for the invasion and defeat of France that was formulated by him before 1905 and applied, with modifications, in 1914': *OED*.

> 'The Schlieffen plan of attacking France through Belgium was intended to stave off from Germany the first vital danger': A. P. F. von Tirpitz, *My Memoirs* II xvii 289 (1919). 'He drew up the celebrated 'Schlieffen Plan' in which the whole strength of Germany was to be directed from the outset with the utmost rapidity upon France by means of a wheeling movement through Belgium': W. S. Churchill, *World Crisis* VI vi 89 (1931). 'In the Schlieffen plan, the railways ... took troops to Belgium and northern France': *The Listener*, 4 August 140/2 1977.

Schloss 'A (German) castle': *OED*. Also, 'a lock'.

Schmalz Literally, 'cooking fat, dripping. Excessive sentimentality'. Influenced by usage among Jews of the cognate Yiddish word *shmalts* (*q.v.*).

Schnaps 'An ardent spirit resembling Hollands Gin': *OED*. Also sometimes spelt *Schnapps* in English.

Schnauzer (from *die Schnauze*, 'the snout'). 'A black or pepper-and-salt wire-haired terrier belonging to the breed so called, which includes large, standard, and miniature dogs distinguished by a stocky, robust build, docked tail, blunt, bearded muzzle, and ears that droop forwards; formerly called the wirehaired pinscher': *OED*. Also, an older name for the type of moustache as worn by Hitler.

Schnitzel 'A veal cutlet, esp. in *Wiener Schnitzel*, one coated with egg and breadcrumbs, fried and often garnished with lemon, capers, anchovies, etc., in the Viennese style': *OED*. *Cf Wiener*. The term *Schnitzel* is also applied to wood shavings and chips, and to shredded paper, etc.

Schnorkel Also *Schnorchel* and *snorkel* (from *Schnorchel*, the name given to the device, related to *schnarchen*, 'to snore'). By origin, and usually *schnorkel*, *Schnorkel*: an airshaft, invented in the Netherlands and developed in Germany, that was fitted to diesel-engined submarines so that air could reach the engines, allowing them to function and their exhaust gases to be expelled, while the vessel was submerged to periscope level; also a submarine fitted with such an airshaft. In sporting use, and normally *snorkel*: a short breathing-tube used by underwater swimmers. In firefighting, usually as *Snorkel*: a proprietary name for a piece of apparatus used in fighting fires in tall buildings, consisting of a platform that may be elevated and extended.

Schottische (*der*) *schottische* (*Tanz*), 'the Scottish dance'. 'A dance of foreign origin resembling the polka, first introduced in England in 1848. Also the music for such a dance': *OED*. The quasi-French pronunciation used in Britain, \ʃo:ˋtɪʃ\, has no justification; the spelling used in French is *scottish*: it is regarded as an English word and is pronounced \skɔtiʃ\; *Littré* gives in addition the semi-German spellings *schottish*, *schotisch*, but with the same pronunciation. In German the pronunciation is \ˋʃotɪʃə\.

Schrecklichkeit Literally, 'frightfulness'. A term used during the autumn of 1914 to denote what the Allies considered to be a deliberate policy of the German Great High Command, of terrorizing noncombatants as a legitimate means of waging war. Though this usage was and is widely recognized in Britain and the Allied countries, it is unclear to what extent, or in what form, it may have been employed by the Germans themselves.

> 'Belgium is the country where three civilians have been killed to every one soldier. That damnable policy of 'frightfulness' succeeded for a time': Rupert Brooke, *Letters*. 11 Nov 1914.(1968) 632. 'It was only when special orders for "frightfulness" had been issued ... that the rank and file of the enemy's army committed its brutalities': P. Gibbs *Soul of War* 155 (1915). 'As to the deliberate *Schrecklichkeit* of the Germans in Belgium no man should judge unless he knows the military history of all invasions, and of that very British institution, the punitive expedition': G. B. Shaw in *New Republic* 6 Jan. 274/1, 1917.

Schuss Literally, 'shot'. '[In skiing] A straight, down-hill run; the slope on which such a run is executed': *OED*. It is also used to mean a sprig or sprout on a bush or tree. The phrase 'Ein Schuss Wein' means 'a dash of wine'.

Schwabacher See *Fraktur, above.*

Schwärmerei (from *schwärmen*, 'to swarm, to display enthusiasm, to rave'). 'Religious zeal, fanaticism, extravagant enthusiasm for a cause or a person; an erotic attachment, especially of one woman or adolescent girl for another; a "crush"': *OED*.

Schweinehund (from *Schwein* 'swine' and *Hund* 'dog'). 'A German term of abuse: "filthy dog"; "swine", "bastard"': *OED*.

Schwerpunkt ('centre of gravity, focal point', f. *schwer* 'heavy, weighty' and *Punkt* 'point'). 'Focus, emphasis; strong point; esp. Mil., the point of main effort': *OED*. So, *Schwerpunktindustrie* 'key industry', *Schwerpunktprogramm* 'main points of emphasis', *Schwerpunktverlagerung* 'change of emphasis', etc.

'He [*sc.* Hitler] had insisted on placing the Schwerpunkt of the offensive in the Ardennes': Chester Wilmot, *Struggle for Europe*, I 19 (1952). 'Hanover would be the diplomatic schwerpunkt of Europe, where Southern as well as Northern problems would have to be solved': J. H. Plumb, *Sir Robert Walpole* II ii 51 (1961). 'The Liberals worked up a very creditable schwerpunkt in many areas during the local elections': *The Spectator*, 615/1, 11 May 1962. 'During the day Bragg realized that the Schwerpunkt of Grant's attack was directed on the right flank at Tunnel Hill': J. Marshall-Cornwall, *Grant as Military Commander*, xvi 125 (1970). 'Once a suitable gap [in NATO's defences] has been found, it becomes the schwerpunkt ... through which the Soviets pour available operational maneuver groups and reinforcements': *Foreign Affairs* Spring 728 1988.

Sehnsucht A yearning, wistful longing.

'It is no blame to them that after marriage this *Sehnsucht nach der Liebe* subsides': W M Thackeray, *Vanity Fair* iv. 28 (1848). 'An excellent old German Lady used to describe to me her *Sehnsucht* that she might yet visit 'Philadelphia', whose wondrous name had always haunted her imagination': William James, *Varieties of Religious Experience,* xvi. 383 (1902).

Sekt A sparkling white wine. *Sekt* was frequently colloquially called, in England, 'German champagne', though its quality very rarely approached that of the authentic champagne, produced in the region of Rheims from Pinot Noir and Chardonnay grapes and by the *Méthode Champenoise.* A *Sekt* made from Riesling grapes by the *Méthode Champenoise* has recently acquired some authenticity.

Seltzer (alteration of *Selterser*, from *Selters*, the name of a village in Hesse-Nassau). 'An effervescent mineral water obtained near Nieder-Selters, containing sodium chloride and small quantities of sodium, calcium, and magnesium carbonates. Also an artificial mineral water of similar composition': *OED*.

Sicherheitsdienst, SD Literally, 'Security Service'. The Security Service of the *SS* (*q.v.*).

Sieg Heil! Literally, 'Hail Victory!' A patriotic exclamation, much used in Nazi Germany. It was also the chorus of a song popular among the Hitler Youth, *Ade, mein liebes Schätzelein/ Ade, ade, ade/ Es muß, es muß geschieden sein/ Ade, ade, ade/ Es geht um Deutschlands Gloria/ Gloria, Gloria/ Sieg Heil! Sieg Heil! Viktoria! Sieg Heil! Viktoria!*

Singspiel (from *singen* 'to sing' and *Spiel* 'a play'). 'A semi-dramatic performance in which song and dialogue alternate, popular in Germany in the latter part of the eighteenth century': *OED*.

'The 'Singspiel' or 'operette' as constructed by Hiller, makes use of the spoken dialogue, as does the French comic opera': F. L. Ritter, *History of Music* 266 (1876). 'That best and truest form of German Opera, the 'Singspiel'': *Grove's Dictionary of Music* II. 519/1 1880. 'English ballad opera crept into Germany by the back door and served as the direct model for the German Singspiel': Eric Blom, *Music in England*, ii 24 1942. 'Cherubini evolved a style of *opéra comique* not unlike the *singspiel* of Mozart ('Seraglio')': *Guardian* 7 Feb 9/1 1962.

'Soldaten! Seid wie die Hunnen!' Literally, 'Soldiers! Be as the Huns!' One of several journalistic condensations of a speech made at Bremerhaven in 1900 by Wilhelm II, Emperor of Germany. The speech was largely responsible for the subsequent widespread use of the opprobrious word Hun in application to German troops. The Kaiser's speech was made to German troops about to depart for China to assist in putting down the Boxer Uprising, in which the German Ambassador to the Chinese Empire had been murdered. The Kaiser's words, as taken down in shorthand by a journalist at the ceremony, were as follows – the official version as released later omits all reference to Attila and the Huns:

> 'Kommt ihr vor den Feind, so wird derselbe geschlagen! Pardon wird nicht gegeben! Gefangene werden nicht gemacht! Wer euch in die Hände fällt, sei euch verfallen! Wie vor tausend Jahren die Hunnen, unter ihren König Etzel [Attila] sich einen Namen gemacht, der sie noch jetzt in Überlieferung und Märchen gewaltig erscheinen läßt, so möge der Name Deutscher in China auf 1000 Jahre durch euch in einer Weise bestätigt werden, daß es niemals wieder ein Chinese wagt, einen Deutschen scheel anzusehen!': Kaiser Wilhelm II, *Rede* (*Hunnenrede*) in der inoffiziellen, nicht korrigierten, Variante der entscheidenden Passage.

> 'When you meet the enemy, he will be defeated! Neither shall quarter be given, nor prisoners taken! Whoever falls into your hands is in your power! Just as a thousand years ago the Huns, under their king, Attila, achieved such fame, that even today their name resounds with their might in story and fable, so let your conduct impress the German name for a thousand years in China, that no Chinese will ever again dare to look disrespectfully at a German!' Emperor Wilhelm II, *Speech (Hun Speech)*, as in the unofficial, uncorrected variant of the definitive version.

Sonderweg Literally, 'special way'. See quotation below. The concept of *Sonderweg* is sometimes invoked, consciously or unconsciously, by former Chancellor Gerhard Schröder's *Deutscher Weg*.

> 'From the early nineteenth century, the positive denotation of a *Sonderweg* stressed a German superiority to the tenets of the French Revolution; a belief that a strong monarchy, army, and authoritarian structure destined Germany for world power status; and a belief in the importance of placing spiritual over material values *Kultur* over *Zivilisation*': review of Blackbourne & Eley *The Peculiarities of German History*; Matthew Andrews on http://userwww.sfsu.edu/~epf/1998/andrews.html

Spandau (a district in Berlin, the location of an armaments concern). A German machine-gun made at Spandau and widely used during the war of 1914-18. Also applied to other machine-guns of German design, especially the MG34 and MG42 of the war of 1939-45. After the Nuremberg Trials, Rudolf Hess was detained in a prison in Spandau.

Spätlese (from *spät* 'late' and *Lese* 'picking, vintage'). A white wine made (especially in

Germany) from grapes normally gathered later than the general harvest, though Spätlese grapes need not be gathered later than the rest of the crop. It is sufficient that the *Öchsle Grad,* the measure of alcoholic content of the wine according to its relative density (specific gravity) is above the legal minimum. (See *Auslese, Beerenauslese, Kabinett, Spätlese, Qualitätswein* and *Trockenbeerenauslese* for indications of quality-levels.)

Spitz (also *Spitzhund*) Noun use of adjective *spitz* 'pointed, peaked'. A dog belonging to one of a group of northern breeds distinguished by thick fur, a pointed muzzle, pricked ears, and a tail curled over the back. Also *attrib.*, as *Spitz dog*. Often, in English, 'Pomeranian'.

Spritzer A chiefly North American adaptation of the German word for a mixture of wine and soda water. The correct German forms for wine to which mineral water has been added are *der Gespritzte* and *ein Gespritzter*. The mixture is also known as *eine Schorle.*

> 1961 in *Webster*. 'Drink *Spritzer* (dry white wine and soda)': 1964 *Vogue* Apr. 71/1, 1972.

SS (abbreviation for *Schutzstaffel*, 'Protective Échelon'). The SS began as a special guard for Adolf Hitler and other Nazi party leaders. The black-shirted SS members formed a small, elite group whose members also served as auxiliary policemen and, later, as concentration-camp guards. Eventually overshadowing the Storm Troopers (*SA, q.v.*) in importance, the SS became, after 1934, the private army of the Nazi party.

Stahlhelm Literally, 'steel helmet'. 'The Steel Helmet organization. Also *attrib. Stahlhelmer*, a member of this organization': *OED.*

> 'It is the Stahlhelmers' boast that they embody the traditions of the old Army': *The Times* 4 June 13/2 1928. 'The *Stahlhelm*, the Steel Helmets, is a voluntary organization of khaki-uniformed veterans tending ... to be brought into semi-official relationship with the Nazi party': *New Republic* 18 July 249/2, 1934. '*Stahlhelm*, association of ex-servicemen founded on 29 Dec. 1918 ... The Stahlhelm was anti-republican and from the late twenties it became militant in its demand for an authoritarian government ... In 1934 it was converted into a 'National Socialist front-line fighters' union', but dissensions with the new Nazi members led to its dissolution in 1935': W. Fest, *Dictionary of German History*, 150 (1978).

Stalag (abbreviation of *stammlager* 'main camp'). 'In Nazi Germany: a prison-camp primarily for captured enemy private soldiers and non-commissioned officers. *Stalag Luft, Stalagluft* (German, *Luft* 'air'), such a camp for Air Force personnel': *OED.* See also *Oflag.*

> 'There are three types of camps for British prisoners known officially as Oflag, Stalag, and Dulag (contractions for Offizierslager, Stammlager, and Durchgangslager)': *The Times* 30 July 1940 7/3.

Also **Marlag** and **Milag**, internment camps for, respectively, Naval and Mercantile Marine personnel.

Standpunkt 'Standpoint'. The English word was fashioned after the German in the 19th century, under the influence of what H. W. Fowler dubbed 'Saxonism'. See *Vorwort, below*. Friedrich Kluge (1856-1926) noted in Germany a similar tendency to favour ostensibly *völkische* roots in preference to Latinate roots: '*Tageblatt* n. Ersatzwort für *Journal*': *Etymologisches Wörterbuch des Deutschen Sprache* (1975).

Stasi (abbreviated from *Staatssicherheits-polizei* or *Staatssicherheitsdienst*, 'State security police or service', *Staat* 'State' and *Sicherheit* 'security, safety'). The internal security force or secret police of the former German Democratic Republic (East Germany).

Stein (from *Stein* 'stone'). An older word for a large (earthenware) mug used especially for beer; the quantity of beer that a *Stein* holds.

Stiftung A donation, trust or foundation established under German and Austrian law, normally on a not-for-profit basis and often for charitable purposes.

Stimmung Literally, 'Mood, spirit, atmosphere, feeling': *OED*.

> 'We may cite certain impressionistic or symbolic styles where the general mood or *Stimmung* is almost palpable': W. M. Urban, *Valuation* v. 123 (1909). 'Words as you use them ... give me more of what the Germans call stimmung ... than painting can ever do': R. Fry, *Letters* 13 May 123, II. 534 (1972). 'He [*sc.* Eliot] cannot keep the poetic *stimmung* up as long as Bridges can': E. H. W. Meyerstein, *Letters* 4 April 1939, 222 (1959). 'I could not help imbibing from my very American father much Stimmung, a certain sentiment, and a lot about the Civil War': Wyndham Lewis, *Letters* 18 Oct. 1948, 463. 'The Riffelalp had its own stimmung': *The Guardian* 12 August 1972, 8. 'The 'Kaiserwalzer'..is..[an] emanation of the Viennese spirit, Stimmung': *The Times*, 23 March 1961, 16/6 . 'In memory the whole *Stimmung* changes and our recollections become like a story we have read before': R. Adams, *Girl in Swing* iv. 59 (1980).

Stollen 'A rich fruit loaf, often made with nuts added': *OED*.

Strafe (from the phrase *Gott strafe England*, 'God punish England', in *Schwert und Myrte* by Alfred Funke (1809–?). It was a common salutation in Germany in 1914 and the following years). **To strafe**: 'Used (originally by British soldiers in the war[s] against Germany) in various senses suggested by its origin: To punish; to do damage to; to attack fiercely; to heap imprecations on; also *absolute*. In later military usage, to attack from low-flying aircraft with bombs or machine-gun fire, etc.; also *transf.* and *fig.*': *OED*.

> '[Strafe] is becoming a comic English word': *The Times Literary Supplement*, 10 February 62/1 1916. 'The word *strafe* is now almost universally used. Not only is an effective bombardment of the enemy's lines or a successful trench raid described by Tommy as 'strafing the Fritzes,' but there are occasions when certain 'brass hats'... are strafed by imprecation. And quite recently the present writer heard a working-class woman ... shout to one of her offspring 'Wait till I git 'old of yer, I'll strarfe yer, I will!'': *Daily Mail*, 1 November 1916. 'Most of the fighter escort of the 1,600 bombers ... dropped to telephone-pole level to strafe trucks and trains heading from Frankfurt to the Saarbrucken battle

zone': *The Baltimore Sun*, 12 December 1944 20/1.

Strudel Literally, 'eddy, whirlpool'. A baked sweet of Austrian origin, made of very thin layers of pastry with a filling, usually of fruit. Also used attributively to denote the kind of dough or pastry used in such confections. *Apfelstrudel,* 'apple strudel'.

Struwwelpeter 'The name of a character in a children's book of the same name by Heinrich Hoffmann (1809-94), formerly used attributively to designate (a person with) long, thick, and unkempt hair. So, *Struwwelpeter-haired.* Hence *Struwwelpeterdom*, (pertaining to the dominance of long hair), an English nonce-word for the condition of being thick-haired and untidy. So, 'shockheaded Peter'. Erroneously, *Struwelpeter.*

Stuka Abbreviation of *Sturzkampfflugzeug,* 'dive-bomber'. 'A dive-bomber of the German air force [the Junkers JU87], especially as used in the war of 1939-45': *OED.*

Sturm und Drang Literally, 'storm and stress'. 'A phrase used to designate the movement in German literature about 1770-82, due to a school of young writers characterized by extravagance in the representation of violent passion, and by energetic repudiation of the 'rules' of the French critics ... *Sturm und Drang*, the title of a play by F. M. Klinger (1776), was seized upon by the historians of literature as aptly expressing the spirit of the school to which the author belonged': *OED.*

'This period, so styled by Goethe, after the title of one of the dramas of Klinger, *Sturm und Drang*': F. L. J. Thimm, *Literature of Germany* 85 (1844). 'The period known as the Storm and Stress period was then about to astonish Germany, and to startle all conventions, by works such as Gerstenberg's *Ugolino,* Goethe's *Götz von Berlichingen*, Klinger's *Sturm und Drang* (from whence the name), and Schiller's *Robbers*': G. H. Lewes, *Goethe* I. iii. I. 140 [1771] (1855). 'That group of men whom collectively we take to illustrate the early Storm and Stress': F. H. Stoddard, *The Evolution of the English Novel* iv. 144 (1900). 'In that wild period, which was called at the time *Genieperiode*, but has since acquired the name of *Sturm und Drang*, the great watchwords *Genius, Originality*, and *Creative* acquired a resonance ... which they had certainly never possessed in England': L. P. Smith, *Words & Idioms* iii. 105 (1925).

Stürmer, Der Literally, 'The Stormer'. A virulently anti-Semitic publication edited by Julius Streicher from 1923 to 1945. He made the infamous words of Heinrich von Treitschke (in *Ein Wort über unser Judentum*, Berlin 1880) into a household expression, including them on the front page of almost every issue: *'D ie Juden sind unser Unglück!'* ('The Jews are our Misfortune'). Streicher was tried at Nuremberg and hanged in 1946.

Sudeten *adj.* Of, pertaining to or designating the predominantly German-speaking areas of Czechoslovakia in the vicinity of the Sudeten mountains (the Sudetenland), which was annexed by Germany from 1938 to 1945. Frequently as merely *Sudeten, n.,* an inhabitant of the Sudetenland; a Sudeten German.

'Czechoslovakia and the Sudeten Germans': *The Times,* 20 Oct 1937, 13/2 (headline) 'Dissensions within the Sudetendeutsch Party': *ibid.* 'At the time of the annexation by Germany of the Sudeten areas of Czechoslovakia there were in the country some 5,000 refugees from the old Reich and from Austria': *Encycl. Brit. Bk. of Year* 526 (1939). 'Henlein, Sudeten-German leader, committed suicide': W. S. Churchill, *Victory* 131 (1946). 'Sudeten Germans with Bavarian dialect adapt themselves slowly to Swabian': W. F. Leopold in J. A. Fishman, *Readings Sociol. of Lang.*, 355 (1968). 'The Sudeten 'problem' was being manipulated both by appeasers here and ... by Hitler': *The Listener,* 25 Apr 1974, 530/2. 'Gradually, up to 1933, the Sudeten Germans had become reconciled to the [Czechoslovak] Republic': S. G. Duff *Parting of Ways* xv. 135(1982). 'The Sudetens could not approve of a pro-Russian and anti-German policy': Harold Nicolson, *Diary,* 13 May 1938, 341 (1966). 'The term *Sudetens*, extremely frequent in the news columns of 1938, did not exist before that year': *American Speech* XVIII 1943, 200. 'The Sudetens had some real grievances, even though they were the best-treated minority in Europe ... The Czech government knew that their real problem had nothing to do with Sudeten grievances': Kingsley Martin, *Editor* xii. 252 (1968).

Tafelmusik Literally, 'table music'. Originally, music so printed that parts can be read from the same page by two or more persons seated on opposite sides of a table. Now, 'Music intended to be performed at a banquet or a convivial meal, especially popular in the eighteenth century': *OED.*

> '(1) Music intended to be sung or played at meal times. (2) Music so arranged that two persons seated at opposite sides of a table can sing from the same page': T. S. Wotton, *Dictionary of Foreign Musical Terms* 193 (1907). 'Much of this [18th-century] music was, in fact, conceived as *Tafelmusik* and aural tapestry around the busy room': George Steiner, *In Bluebeard's Castle* iv. 92 (1971). 'One of Telemann's many pieces of *tafelmusik*': *The Times*, 19 August 1980.

Tafelwein Literally, 'table wine'. 'Wine of less than middle quality, suitable for drinking with an ordinary meal': *OED.* Increasingly, wine-makers are adopting the term *Tafelwein* for their better quality products as a means of circumventing the irksome and oppressive European wine legislation.

> 'There will be three categories of wine: *tafelweine* for all the *vins ordinaires*; *qualitätswein* for the middle quality wines; and *qualitätswein mit prädikat: The Times* 27 November 1972 (Wines & Spirits Suppl.) p. iii/5.

Tag, Der Literally, 'the Day': 'a day on which an important event is expected to occur; especially a day of military conflict or victory': *OED.* Though this usage was and is widely recognized in Britain and the Allied countries, it is unclear to what extent, or in what form, it may have been employed by the Germans themselves.

> 'It was in Stockholm in those days that I first heard from Swedish Naval officers, who in common waters were in constant and intimate touch with the German Navy, of a mysterious ward-room toast '*Der Tag,*' which was drunk in the warships of the latter. My naval friends had never any doubt as to which navy and which nation was contemplated as the eventual antagonist. That such a toast was pledged in the German Navy was, in the early days of the war, denied in

Germany. But it was well known in Sweden before 1908': Sir J. R. Rodd, *Social and Diplomatic Memories*, 3 vols (1922-5): Chapter IV: Stockholm 1906-08. 'About 1895 (in Germany) the dream of World Domination solidified into something more than a dream. Officials of the Army, Navy, and State Departments began to formulate the steps required to attain it. France and Russia – the competing land powers – could easily be smashed; but England, whose empire stretched around the earth, could be reached and overcome only on the sea. So Germany started to build a great navy, and the naval officers at their mess drank regularly their toast *Auf den Tag,* 'To the Day' when they should be strong enough to meet the hated English': Arthur L. Frothingham, *A Handbook of War Facts and Peace Problems*, National Security League, New York (1919), citing Wm. R. Thayer in 'Out of their Own Mouths', Introduction. 'Just as the lieutenants of the German and British navies … looked forward to 'der Tag' when the preparations would be brought to the test of warfare, the lieutenants of the United States navy are already looking forward … to 'The Day' when the British and American fleets shall fight for that power to blockade [&c.]': G. B. Shaw, *What I really Wrote*, ii, 30 (1930).

Tannenbaum, O Literally, 'O Pine-Tree!'. A song based on existing folk-songs, adapted in 1819 by J. A. Zarnack as a song of forlorn love, and then, in 1824, further adapted by E. Arnschütz for use as a carol. In Britain the melody is used for a Socialist anthem, *The Red Flag,* the first lines of which are 'The people's flag is deepest red/ Dyed with the blood of our glorious dead'. A satirical parody of the anthem exists, commencing: 'The working class can kiss my arse/ I've got the foreman's job at last'.

Thalweg (also, following the reformed German spelling, *Talweg*: literally, 'bottom path of a valley', from *Thal* 'valley' and *Weg* 'way'). 'The line in the bottom of a valley in which the slopes of the two sides meet, and which forms a natural watercourse; also the line following the deepest part of the bed or channel of a river or lake': *OED*.

Traité de Paris (Littré) 1815. 'Thalweg … is a German geographical term, employed in the records of the Congress of Berlin, which designates the line of lowest level formed by the two opposite slopes of a valley': *Harper's Mag.* LXIV. 275 (1881). 'Thence it [the boundary] shall follow the 'thalweg' of the Nile southwards to Lake Albert': *Agreement between Great Britain & Congo State* in *Parl. Papers Eng.* XCVI. 26, 12 May 1894. 'The opposite of the talweg itself is a divide, *i.e.*, the lines joining all high points in topography': R. W. Fairbridge, *Encycl. Geomorphol.* 1149/1 (1968).

Trockenbeerenauslese Literally, 'dry grape selection'. The word derives from *trocken* 'dry', *Beeren* plural of *Beere* 'berry (grape)', and *Auslese* 'selection or choice'. German white wine of superior quality, normally somewhat sweet, made from individually selected grapes affected by noble rot. *Trockenbeerenauslese* wines need not be sweet, though a higher *Restzucker* (residual sugar) content is tolerated.

'*Beerenauslesen* and *Trockenbeerenauslesen*. These latter terms mean, respectively, wines made from selected over-ripe single grapes and those made from over-ripe single grapes which are in effect sun-dried raisins, in a state of *pourriture noble*': *The Times,* 8 February 1963, 12/5.

U-boot, for **Unterseeboot** Literally, 'undersea boat'. The name for the German submarine, the U-Boat.

Über In recent years there has appeared a tendency to insert *über* in front of English nouns as a means of indicating much the same qualities as the insertion of *super-* has had in cases such as *superman* and *superpower.*

> 'The Ulster-born ex-*Financial Times* journalist [Gay Firth] cheerily offered her services as überproofreader in the early chaotic days when we often worked through the night to meet deadlines': *Prospect* magazine, January 2005. 'Following his fall from power in 1982, [Helmut] Schmidt has become a sort of *über*-chancellor to his fellow countrymen, an elder statesman who overshadows his successors': *The Times Literary Supplement,* 11 February 2005, p 31. 'None of this would interest anyone in Ray Mears's *Bushcraft* ... where the nation's über Boy Scout was building a birch bark canoe helped by some gnarled wilderness lovers, who did not use a tape measure but 'listened to what the wood was telling them'':*Daily Telegraph,* 23 April 2005, Arts Section, page 20/4. 'Add to this the 'hyperinflation' of our language, as just detected by the Oxford English Dictionary. Prefixes such as 'ova-' and 'uber-' and 'mega-' are diluting the power of our words. One of its experts said this week that, 'to be called a hero used to be the highest honour. Now you have to be a superhero to make an impact': Quentin Letts, 'Opinion', *The Daily Telegraph,* 8 October 2005.

Übermensch Literally, 'superman', from *über* 'over' and *Mensch* 'man', coined by F. W. Nietzsche, 1844-1900. See *Untermensch, below.*

> 'Where Bismarck exerted the full ... strength of the *Übermensch,* Bülow always remains the polite orator': *Pall Mall Gazette* XXVI. 405/1 (1902). 'It is assumed, on the strength of the single word Superman (Übermensch) borrowed by me from Nietzsche, that I look for the salvation of society to the despotism of a single Napoleonic Superman': G. B. Shaw, *Major Barbara,* Preface 152 (1902). 'I should like to know whether the Irish would be reckoned by him among the Übermenschen or the Untermenschen': *The Times* 2 September 11/4 1977.

Uhlan (from F. *uhlan, hulan, houlan,* G. *ulan,* Da. and Sw. *ulan,* It. *ulano,* Polish *u≤an, hu≤an,* Czech *ulan, hulan,* Serb. *ulan,* Russ. *ulan;* ultimately from Turk. *oghlQn* (pop. *ZlQn*), *n* 'son, youth, servant'). 'A special type of cavalryman or lancer in various European armies (originally in Slavonic countries, especially Poland; subsequently specifically in the German Empire)': *OED.*

Umlaut (from *um-* 'about' and *Laut* 'sound'). 'A change in the sound of a vowel produced by partial assimilation to an adjacent sound (usually that of a vowel or semivowel in the following syllable); ...The diacritical sign (¨) placed over a vowel to indicate that such a change has taken place': *OED.* The diacritical sign itself is called in English the *diaeresis.* In English it has a completely different function from its function in German. In English it signifies the division of one syllable into two, especially by the separation of a diphthong into two simple vowels (*e.g., coöperation* in

American English). Its function in English, of differentiating two contiguous vowels, is the same in French (in which language it is known as *le tréma*) and in other Romance languages. In practical use in German the word signifies the change from *a, o* and *u* to *ä, ö* and *ü,* often required to mark the change from singular to plural: *der Wald, die Wälder; der Kloß, die Klöße; das Buch, die Bücher.*

'Unser Platz an der Sonne'. 'Mit einem Worte: wir wollen niemand in der Schatten stellen, aber wir verlangen auch unseren Platz an der Sonne': Prince von Bülow, to the Reichstag, 6 December 1897. ('In a word: we do not wish to put anybody in the shade but to demand our own place in the sun.')

Untermensch Literally, 'under-man'. See *Übermensch above.* Used by the Nazi Party to characterize Jews, Gipsies, Slavs and other races considered inferior to the 'Aryan' race, and also to refer to those with mental or physical defects.

Ur- (reproducing the German *ur-*, denoting 'primitive, original, earliest,' as in *Ur-Hamlet, Ur-origin, Ur-stock*, etc., and in such words as *Urheimat, Urschleim, Ursprache, Urtext*). '*Ursprache*, meaning *primitive language*, has been frequently used in recent English philological works': *OED. Urquelle* (*Ur-* and *Quelle*, 'spring, source, fountain') has been frequently used in Biblical criticism to mean the original source for given texts and readings. *Die Ursache* 'the original thing' is used to convey the notion of *reason*, in the sense of Aristotle's Primary Cause. In English, the use of the particle is spreading to all types of writing in addition to scholarly writing.

> 'At one point Defoe provides an Ur-Beaufort scale of wind force': *The Times Literary Supplement*, 4 July 2003, 15.

Vaterland Literally, 'fatherland'. 'A German's fatherland': *OED.* In British and American usage, the word *Vaterland* emphasizes the masculine aspects of dedication to one's country's interests at the expense of the more feminine, maternal, connotations of *motherland* and *mother country.*

> 'Germans whose every act and thought was directed … toward the enhancement of the *Vaterland*': *New Yorker* 26 August 1950 70/2.

Verboten 'Forbidden; not allowed'.

> 'Meads towards Haslingfield and Coton/ Where *das Betreten*'s not *verboten*' [i.e., where there are no 'Keep off the Grass' signs] : Rupert Brooke, *Old Vicarage, Grantchester* 8 (1912). 'I got very bored, for I had no-thing to read and my pipe was *verboten*': John Buchan, *Greenmantle*, v. 63 (1916). 'The unfortunate German, bred and trained from childhood to understand that everything is *verboten* unless specifically permitted': E. Benn, *Happier Days* xviii. 217 (1949). 'The obviously important but almost verboten subject of the implicit structure of rewards': Finch & Cain in J. Marmor *Mod. Psychoanal.* xvii. 446 (1968). 'She was *verboten*, strictly off limits': R. Mutch, *Gemstone* viii. 94 (1879).

Völkisch Literally, 'of the people'. 'Popular, nationalistic, racialist': *OED*. Though the *OED*'s definition is true of the Nazis' use of the word, and of a more limited use of the adjective before 1933, *volkisch* can legitimately be translated by the popular and benign American usage *folksy,* which derives from an acceptation of the word that antedates the racial use of the word by several centuries.

Volkswagen Literally, 'people's car'. The small, inexpensive car first produced in 1938 and in continuous production in Germany until 1978. It remained in production in other locations, for instance in Mexico until 30 July 2003, when the last unit of the first generation was manufactured. The car is affectionately known as 'the Beetle'. It was first named, by Adolf Hitler in 1938, as the KdF-Wagen. See *Kraft durch Freude above.* It was officially renamed the *Volkswagen* by the British Military Government in December 1945. (A new generation of Volkswagen 'Beetle' was announced and launched in 2003.)

Vorsprung durch Technik Literally, 'Progress through Engineering'. A slogan used in a series of highly successful advertisements for Audi cars.

Vorstand The directorate or management of a German company not comprising representatives of the workers or the independent nominees. See **Aufsichtsrat**, above.

Vorwort Literally, 'before-word'. The word in English dictionaries, *foreword*, a *calque* of *Vorwort*, is a creation of the 19th century. The normal word is *preface*. H. W. Fowler (1858-1933) condemned the tendency exemplified in the works of E. A. Freeman(1823-1892) to employ as many words as possible of purely English extraction and termed it 'Saxonism'. The *DNB* says of Freeman's foible: '[H]is desire to use so far as possible only words which are purely English limited his vocabulary and was some drawback to his sentences'. See **Standpunkt**, above.

Wacht am Rhein, Die Literally, 'The Watch on the Rhine'. A patriotic poem written by M. Schneckenburger in 1840 when the French were threatening to annexe a part of the Rhineland. It was set to music by Karl Wilhelm in 1854. Its widespread popularity in Germany dates from the Franco-Prussian War (1870). In the sequence in Rick's Café in the film *Casablanca* in which the French National Anthem, *la Marseillaise*, eventually drowns out a German national air, the German national air was *Die Wacht am Rhein*.

Waffen SS 'Waffen-Schutzstaffel', 'Armed Defence Échelon'; from *Waffen*, literally, 'weapons'. And see *SS*. 'In Nazi Germany during the war of 1939–45: the combat units of the S.S.': *OED*.

Walpurgisnacht ('Walpurgis-night', from the name Walpurga or Walburga, an 8th-c AngloSaxon saint and missionary in Heidenheim, Germany). 'In German folklore, and especially in Goethe's *Faust*, a feast of the powers of darkness or witches' sabbath celebrated on the Brocken, a peak in the Harz mountains, on 30 April. Also *transf.*, an orgiastic celebration or party': *OED*.

Walther 'The name of a German firm of firearm manufacturers, used *attrib.* and *absol.* to designate pistols and rifles made by them': *OED*.

> 'As a point of historical interest, this is the first time that the Walther pistol, a shoulder-holstered gun introduced into the Royal Ulster Constabulary last year, has been fired in action': *The Guardian*, 28 Sept 1971.

Waltz (*Walzer*, from *walzen* 'to roll, revolve, dance the waltz'. The letter *t* is an English addition.) 'A dance performed to music in triple time by couples who, almost embracing each other, swing round and round in the same direction with smooth and even steps, moving on as they gyrate ... A piece of music to accompany this dance, in the same time and rhythm': *OED. Die Walz* is also used to connote the time a craftsman spends on the road after his apprenticeship (in English, a *journeyman)* without returning to his home town, traditionally three years and a day. The principle was to encourage insights into different practices and production methods. A man is still said to be 'auf der Walz' if he has not yet settled in.

Wanderlust 'An eager desire or fondness for wandering or travelling': *OED.*

Wandervogel Literally, 'bird of passage'. 'A member of the German youth organization founded by H. Hoffmann at the end of the 19th century for the promotion of out-of-door activities, *esp.* hiking, and folk culture, as a reaction against the materialistic values of middle-class city life. Also *transf.*, a rambler or hiker': *OED.* Also, in English, as a verbal noun, 'to wandervogel'.

> 'If it's going to be Youth, then let it be Youth on the warpath, not wandervogeling and piping imitation nature tunes to the taste of milk and chocolate': D. H. Lawrence *Let.* 9 Aug. 1924, 606 (1932). 'Around 1930, alienated and disaffected youth was being manufactured mainly in Germany, where the First War had produced the biggest earthquake. Some of them called themselves the *Wandervögel,* and wandered around Europe with their guitars and their interchangeable girlfriends, living on what they could get wherever sympathisers would accept them': *The Listener* 30 Nov. 705/3, 1967.

'Was für plündern!' Literally, 'What [a city] to plunder!' An ungrammatical exclamation attributed to Gebhard Lebrecht von Blücher, (1742-1819), Prussian Field Marshal, on a visit to London. The exclamation is given as above in the second edition of the *Oxford Dictionary of Quotations* (1953). However in the fourth edition (1992) the following entry appears:

> Gebhard Lebrecht Blücher 1742–1819
> *Prussian Field Marshall*
> *Was für Plunder!*
> What rubbish!
>
> Of London, as seen from the Monument in June 1814; in Evelyn Princess Blücher *Memoirs of Prince Blücher* (1932) p. 33 (often misquoted 'Was für plündern!' [What a place to plunder!'])

Princess Blücher's edition of the *Memoirs* of her husband, the fourth Prince, gives this account of the incident: 'It is said that during his [Blücher's] first visit [to London, in 1814] after Napoleon's exile to Elb ... he was received everywhere as a conquering hero ... It was during this visit that while he was being shown the sights he climbed the Monument and looked over London from its top. An Englishman accompanying him was expatiating on the magnificence of the vista when Blücher the outspoken, who could hardly see the muddy Thames a few dozen yards away, impatiently muttered '*Was für plunder*', the literal translation of which is 'What rubbish' and referred to the Englishman's vapourings about the roofs, smoke and fog which were all that was visible! People standing by partly overheard the remark and, as people will about famous persons, distorted it into a statement that Blücher had said 'What a place to plunder'; thus is history so often made': Evelyn Princess Blücher, *Memoirs of Prince Blücher*, John Murray (1932), pp 32–33.

Wehrmacht Literally, 'Defence Force'. The name for the German defence forces between 1935 and 1945. Between 1921 and 1935 they were the Reichwehr.

Weimar 'The name of a city in Thuringia, Germany, where the democratic constitution under which Germany was governed from 1919 until the start of the Third Reich in 1933 was drawn up. Used *attrib.* and *absol.* with reference to the political, social, and cultural aspects of Germany during this period, esp. in phr. *Weimar Republic* [*Weimarer Republik*]': *OED.*

'Many of the important buildings of Weimar are associated with the German writers Goethe and Schiller, who lived there for many years and who died there. During this period, the late 18th and early 19th century, Weimar was the intellectual centre of Germany': *Encyclopedia Britannica*, 1968 edition, vol. 23, p. 381.

> 'Alexander von Humboldt and his brother Wilhelm belonged to the most talented intellectual circle in Europe, centered on Goethe's Weimar': *Times Literary Supplement*, 22 July, 2005, p. 3.

Weimaraner 'A (breed of) grey, short-coated, drop-eared pointer, which was originally bred as a hunting dog in the Weimar region': *OED.*

> 'The upper middles have recently taken to foreign breeds, weimaraners and rotweilers [*sic*]': *Daily Mail* 26 Oct. 25/2 1979.

Welsch Fundamentally, *Welsch n* and *welsch adj* traditionally meant 'not speaking German'. It was thus used by the Germanic tribes for their non-German-speaking neighbours, for example, the Gauls and the Romanized Celts in general, and by the Angles and Saxons for the Britons, whence our present-day English word *Welsh*. Such a usage persists in Switzerland, where *Welschland* means 'French-speaking Switzerland' (compare *la Suisse Romande*) and *Welschschweizer* means 'Swiss French'. In older uses, the word often means 'Romance-speaking', and so can include, for example, the Italians. In Austrian slang, *die Welschen* means 'the Italians'. There are German turns of phrase in which *welsch* implies moral or commercial laxity, tricky practices, and so on, as in *welsche Sitten und Gebräuche*, 'dubious morals and practices'. (See *Rotwelsch, above.*) Sometimes intended to mean 'hotblooded', in reference to, for instance, the people of the Mediterranean nations.

Weltanschauung (from *Welt* 'world' and *Anschauung* 'perception'). 'A particular philosophy or view of life; a concept of the world held by an individual or a group': *OED.*

> 'The impact of the Christian *Weltanschauung* upon the Jewish mind': J. Jocz, *The Theology of Election* I. 11 (1958). 'The main reason why evolutionism made such slow progress is that it was the replacement of one entire *Weltanschauung* by a different one': *Science* 2 June 1972 988/1. 'Speakers of different cultures, having different *Weltanschauungen*, ideologies, interests, paradigms, etc': N. Jardine in Hookway & Pettit, *Action & Interpretation* 124 (1878).

Weltschmerz Literally, 'world' and 'pain'. 'A weary or pessimistic feeling about life; an apathetic or vaguely yearning attitude': *OED.* Also used ironically of one who ostentatiously 'suffers'.

> 'I have also been having a … jaundice lying on my liver, which reduced me to a fearful state of weltschmerz and incapacity to do anything': Aldous Huxley *Let.* 2 Sept. (1969) 218 (1923)

Wiener Schnitzel and **Wienerschnitzel** Literally, a *Schnitzel* made in the Viennese fashion. See *Schnitzel.*

Wir fahren gegen Engeland, ('We sail against England') also known as *Das Engelandslied.* A patriotic song written by Hermann Löns (1864-1914) and adopted by the Kriegsmarine as their anthem.

Wirtschaftswunder (*erron. Wirtschaftwunder*). 'The 'economic miracle' of West Germany, the substantial and lasting recovery in its economic state and standard of living following the war of 1939-45': *OED.*

Wunderbar! Literally, 'Wonderful!'.

Wunderkind Literally, 'wonder child'. 'A highly talented child, a child prodigy, especially in music. A talented or successful young man, a 'whizz-kid'': *OED.*

Wurst Literally, 'sausage'. Used especially to denote a sausage of the German type; a 'German sausage'. So, *Blutwurst, Bockwurst, Bratwurst, Knackwurst, Leberwurst* and *Mettwurst,* all varieties of sausage.

Yodel Also spelt **yodle**, **jodel**, *erron.* **jödel**. Anglicized from *jodeln* (Bavarian dialect *jodln, jolen*), properly, to utter the syllable *jo.* 'To sing or warble with interchange of the ordinary and falsetto voice, in the manner of Swiss and Tyrolese mountaineers': *OED.*

Zeitgeist Literally, *Zeit* 'time' and *Geist* 'spirit'. 'The spirit or genius which marks the thought or feeling of a period or age': *OED.*

> 'It is what we call the *Time-Spirit* that is sapping the proof from miracles –it is the 'Zeist-Geist' itself': Matthew Arnold, *Letters,* November 1848, 95 [1932]. 'A clear mark of the Zeitgeist of the late 1960's and the 1970's is the increased demand for participation in decision-making by those affected by it': *Science* 2 June 991/3 1972.

Zeppelin Literally, the name of the German Count Ferdinand von *Zeppelin,* 1838-1917. In full, *Zeppelin airship,* a dirigible airship; properly one of a type designed and constructed by Count Zeppelin from 1900 but used generically for all dirigible airships in use during the First World War except those under the control of the German Navy, which were called *Luftschiffe.*

> 'The Zeppelin Air-ship, now [1899] in construction on an island of the Boden See, is a cylindrical frame of aluminium in partitions, each holding a gas-bag': *Whitaker's Almanach,* 665/2 1990. 'A Zeppelin has dropped bombs on Antwerp': F. T. Jane in *Land & Water* 12 September 1914, 15/1.

Zimbelstern Literally, 'cymbal-star'. An organ-stop comprising, instead of pipes, a metal or wooden star or wheel mounted high on the organ case to which several small bells are affixed. When the stop is engaged, the star rotates, producing a continuous tinkling sound. It was common in northern Europe, Germany in particular, throughout the 16th, 17th and 18th centuries. After *ca* 1700 the bells were sometimes tuned to particular notes.

Zollverein Literally, *Zoll,* 'customs duties' and *Verein* 'union'. 'A union, originally between certain states of the German empire, after 1833 including all the states, for the maintenance of a uniform rate of customs duties from other countries and of free trade among themselves; hence generally of other countries': *OED*. Also the name of one of the coal-mines in the Ruhr area, now closed for mining but in increasing use as a centre for cultural events.

Zugzwang (from *Zug* 'move' and *Zwang* 'compulsion, obligation'). A term used in chess; 'a position in which a player is obliged to move but cannot do so without disadvantage; the disagreeable obligation to make such a move': *OED*. As a phrase: 'in Zugzwang'. As a verb: 'to manœuvre an opponent into such a position'. Sometimes used in connection with other games than chess. Also used figuratively in business and politics. Incorrectly, *Zugwang* and *Zugswang*.

Yiddish

The Oxford English Dictionary defines Yiddish as follows:

> Anglicization of G. *jüdisch* 'Jewish'; the full German name is *jüdisch deutsch* 'Jewish-German'. The English word has been adopted in German as *Jiddisch.* The language used by Jews in Europe and America, consisting mainly of [mediaeval] German (orig. from the Middle Rhine area) with admixture (according to local or individual usage) of Balto-Slavic or Hebrew words, and printed in Hebrew characters.

Yiddish has been the traditional language of the *Ashkenazim,* the Jews of middle and northern Europe, as distinguished from the *Sephardim,* or Jews of the mediaeval Iberian Peninsula, whose traditional language is *Ladino,* a language derived from mediaeval Spanish. Ladino is commonly called *Judezmo* in Yiddish.

The need, for practical purposes, to transliterate from Hebrew characters into a Romanized system led to the introduction by the Institute for Jewish Research *(Yiddisher Visenshaftlicher Institut, YIVO)* of a phonetic system known as the YIVO Romanization and developed in Vilnius, Lithuania, between the two World Wars. It is used here. However, traditional usage is so influential that it is difficult to employ the YIVO Romanization consistently. Even the word Yiddish is universally so spelt in English-speaking countries, though the YIVO system rationally excludes doubled consonants. (The YIVO form is thus *YIDISH.)*

There are several additional problems. The resemblance between Yiddish and its second-cousin, modern German, has led writers into the widespread use of German spelling practices such as the use of *sch* when transliterating Yiddish words rather than the YIVO *sh,* and the use of *qu-* rather than *kv-*. There are many others.

Moreover, the desire to imitate in Latin characters the sounds of Yiddish have led many writers into adopting phonetic practices idiosyncratically their own. Hence, for instance, the form *shtoom* for YIVO *shtum,* 'silent, mute'. *Shtoom* is an unreliable phonetic form: it works only with Anglo-Saxon speakers. It is hoped that readers of this Lexicon will be able to reconcile such variant readings as *stumm, shtum, shtumm,* and *shtoom.*

In addition, there is a further problem arising from the different dialects of Yiddish. The two predominant ones, *Litvak* (the pronunciation of Lithuanian Jews) and Galitsianer (the pronunciation of Galician or Polish Jews) are sufficiently different to warrant different YIVO Romanizations, as also are the other minor dialectal versions of Yiddish. Nevertheless, there are recognizable family resemblances between these variants that should permit the reader to make an intelligent guess.

Unlike German nouns, Yiddish common nouns are not capitalized unless they begin sentences.

The presence of words and phrases in this Appendix does not mean that the words are exclusively Yiddish: many are current German words too.

Lastly, many Yiddish words appear to derive from Germanic roots but are in fact from other linguistic groups. *Shmate, for 'clothing'* (often written *schmatte* or *shmutter),* is from the Polish *szmata,* 'a rag'. *Nebish,* is a

Ukrainian word. The exclamation *Nu* is Russian and Polish. *Shlmiel* (often written *schlemiel* or *schlemihl)* probably comes from the Hebrew proper name *Shelumiel,* the name of a person in *Num.* i. 6, said by the Talmud to have met with an unhappy end. The taboo word *Shmok* or *Schmock* and its euphemism *shmo* are not related to the German noun *Schmuck,* 'decoration or adornment'.

The Lexicon

Babkes Literally, 'beans'. Figuratively, 'nothing'.

> 'What did he give me? Babkes he gives me': Michael Bywater, 'Madonna wishes she was 'zaftig'': *The Independent*, 17th January 2006.

Bagel or Beigel (in Yiddish *beygel)*, apparently, according to *Webster*, from Middle High German **böugel*, whence German dialectal form *beugel*, *bäugl*, diminutive of MHG *boug-*, *bouc-* ring, bracelet. A hard ring-shaped salty roll of bread.

> 'Bagels are like large wooden curtain-rings to look at... She cut them and buttered them': Louis Golding, *Magnolia Street* x. 165 1932. 'I got lox and bagels. You hungry, Baruch?': Lucille Stern, *Midas Touch* III. xxiii. 174 1957.

Bissel Literally, 'a bit', but the implication is often 'a large bit'.

Drek Also **dreck**. Yiddish *drek* (*cf* German *Dreck*) filth, dregs, dung. 'Rubbish, trash, worthless debris': *OED*.

> 'The anonymous countryside littered with hetero geneous *dreck': Horizon,* February 90 (1947). *'Drek* your dolls are! I wouldn't stick my customers with such junk!': E Lacy, *Double Trouble*, v 58 (1965). ' 'You *are* dreck,' she said. 'I hope you are killed.': O. Hesky, *Time for Treason* v. (1967); 'Meat better than the usual *drek* we get': E West, *Night is the Time for Listening* i 13 38 (1966). 'You'll come out of all this dreck smelling like a roast': Saul Bellow, *Herzog*, p 88, (1977).

Fin or **finif** (*finif* 'five': *cf* German *fünf*) A five-dollar bill.

> 'When Rex Stout's fictional detective, Archie Goodwin, bribed an informer in the 1930s, he usually didn't have to part with more than a finif or sawbuck –five or ten dollars': Rosemarie Ostler, 'Words that Skiddooed', *Saturday Evening Post Society*, May 2000.

Fremde(r) Literally, 'a stranger'. Also German.

Frum (cf German *fromm* 'pious'). Adjective to define an observant Jew. See *Link below*.

> '"What! Aren't you *froom*?" she said. "No, I'm a regular wrong 'un", he replied. "As for phylacteries, I almost forget how to lay them"': I Zangwill, *Children of the Ghetto,* xi 243 (1892). '"Dolly", who was a Jewess, but one who was links rather than froom, was about forty years old': *The Referee*, 3 February 2/3 1892.

Gefilte fish (*cf* German *gefüllt* 'filled, stuffed', from *füllen* 'to fill'). 'A Jewish dish of stewed or baked stuffed fish or fish-cakes, boiled in a fish or vegetable broth': *OED*.

> 'There is even *gefüllte Fisch*, which is stuffed fish without bones': I Zangwill, *Children of the Ghetto* II iv 114 (1892).

'That crowd of tired *hoi-polloi* fighting for a spot to stand to get their corned beef and cabbage, or *gefuellte* fish': J Lait, *Beef, Iron & Wine* 15 (1917). 'I am sitting in Mindy's restaurant putting on the gefillte fish': Damon Runyon, *Guys & Dolls* iv 71 (1931). 'Don't your Old Lady make gefüllte fish any more for Shabbath dinner?' L G Blochmann, *See You at the Morgue* ix 61 (1941). 'The nicest piece of gefilte fish you could wish to find on a plate': Harold Pinter, *Birthday Party* II 26 (1959).

Gelt (cf German *geld* 'money'**)**. Money.

'Fourteen *Shtibbur's* a lot of *Gelt'*: I. Zangwill, *Children of the Ghetto* II xxii 165(1892). 'Had I ever heard the underworld saying: No grass ever grasses for gelt alone?': *The Observer* 24 January 7/1 1960. ' 'The gelt?' said Reed… 'Four thousand dollars,' said Miss Pocket': C. Drummond, *Death & Leaping Ladies* iv 80 (1968).

Genug! 'Enough! Often, *Genug schon!*, 'Enough, already!'

'Father Herzog, silent and wry, laughed under his breath. 'Jonah – I beg you. *Genug schon.*': Saul Bellow, *Herzog*, p 142 (1977)

Gevalt! or **Gevald**! (Cf German *Gewalt*, 'power, force)'. 'A cry of fear, astonishment, amazement: 'Gevalt! What happened?' A cry for help. 'Gevalt! Help! Burglars!'. A desperate expression of protest: *'Gevalt!*, Lord, enough already!' : adapted from Leo Rosten's *Joys of Yiddish* (1968). Often prefixed by 'Oy!'

Glat Kosher (*cf* German *glatt* 'smooth, slippery'). Applied to meat prepared in conformity with the strictest Jewish dietary laws, according to which the lungs of the animal must be completely smooth and free from any blemish. *Kosher* derives from the Hebrew *k̄ashēr* 'Right, good; applied to meat and other food prepared according to the Jewish law': *OED*.

Glitzy (*cf* German *glitzern* 'to glitter'; *glitzerig* 'glittering'. 'Characterized by glitter or extravagant show; ostentatious, glamorous; hence, tawdry, gaudy; glitteringly spectacular, but in poor taste': *OED*. Also **Glitz** *n* and other derived parts of speech.

-ishkait Literally, '-ishness'. A useful Yiddish enclitic, founded on Germanic roots, that permits non-Germanic words to be grafted onto Yiddish, as, for example, *Goyishkait* ('Gentile-ness'), from Hebrew *goy*, 'a Gentile'.

'These activities will bring about increased Divine blessing, particularly in Eretz Yisroel [the State of Israel], by having a government that promises to be strong and to prevent *goyim* and *goyishkeit* from entering Eretz Yisroel. This will hasten the coming of the Messianic Redemption, when we will ascend to Yerushalayim and to the *Beis HaMikdash* ['the Holy Temple']. May it be in the immediate future!' See the web-site: http://beismoshiach.org/dvar%20Malchus/sie283.htm.

Kibitz (*cf* German *kiebitzen* to look on at cards, from *Kiebitz* 'lapwing, pewit'; an interfering onlooker at cards.) '*Intr.* To look on at cards, or some other activity, esp. in an interfering manner (*e.g.* by standing close to the shoulders of the players); to offer gratuitous advice to a player; to act as a *kibitzer*. Also *trans.*, to watch (a game, person, etc.), esp. in an officious or meddling way. Hence *kibitzing*, English verbal noun and participial adjective': *OED*. See also *croupier* in the French Lexicon.

Kluts, klutz, klotz (*cf* German *Klotz*, literally 'a block of wood, a log'. 'A clumsy, awkward person, esp. one considered socially inept; a fool. Also as *v.* So *klutzy a.*, awkward, foolish': *OED*.

Kvetshn (Yiddish, literally, 'to complain, to whine': *cf* German *quatschen*, either 'to talk rubbish' or 'to squelch', and German *quetschen* 'to squash, to crush, to mash'). 'Yiddish *kvetsh*, ad. G. *Quetsche* 'crusher, presser': *OED*. To complain in a persistent and nagging fashion. In the UK, 'to moan'. So, *kvetshe*(*r*), one who complains.

> 'She's got a disgusting father and a kvetsch of a mother': S. Bellow, *Herzog* 61(1965). 'There was Ozzie Waldman, Ozzie the kvetch. For his favor you could die. He gave away nothing': W. Markfield, *To an Early Grave* (1965) xi. 187 (1964). 'The idiom of the New Yorker, Gentile or Jew … has a lot of Yiddish words, like *schlepp* … *shiksa* and *kvetsch*': *New Society*, 12 May 9/2 1996. 'What a congenital kvetcher! *Ibid*. 'It will take forever, he's such a kvetch' : Leo Rosten, *The Joys of Yiddish* 200 (1968).

In North Germany, the word *Quetschkommode* ('squash chest–of-drawers') is used to denote the accordion; *cf.* the English usage 'squeeze-box'.

Landtsman A fellow-countryman; a compatriot.

> 'Was Ravitch actually your uncle, or only a landtsman? I was never certain': Saul Bellow, *Herzog*, 141, (1977). 'It amused the boys to hear how their father coaxed drunken Ravitch to get to his feet. It was family theatre. '*Nu, landtsman*? Can you walk? It's freezing": *ibid*, pp 142-3.

Lig in drerd As used in the phrase, 'Lig in drerd!', an exclamation not intended to imply that the object of the remark should die (should 'lie in the earth'), but precisely (almost) the opposite: 'May the object of the remark *not* lie in the earth!'. Often intuitively, and correctly, translated 'G-d forbid!'.

Link (*cf* German adjective *linke(r, s)* 'left, left-handed, clumsy'). In Yiddish use: 'Not pious, not orthodox (in religion)': *OED*. See *Frum above*. Perhaps the origin of the English expression, 'A left-handed compliment', to denote a disparaging personal observation.

> '"Dolly", who was a Jewess, but one who was link rather than froom, was about forty years old': *The Referee*, 3 Feb 2/3 1889. '"Suppose," she said slowly, "I wanted to marry a Christian? If I was to marry a very *link* Jew, you'd think it almost as bad": Israel Zangwill, *Children of the Ghetto* II 90 (1892). 'But I am so link (irreligious)?': – , *Ghetto Comedies* ii 380 (1892).

Lox (plural **lox**, **loxes)** from Yiddish *laks*, *cf* G. *lachs* 'salmon'. A kind of brine-cured smoked salmon, often eaten with bagels (*cf above*). (If the word *lox* is pronounced as Americans tend to pronounce it, its relationship to *Lachs* becomes obvious.)

Magen David The Star of David. Literally, Yiddish, 'The Shield of David', pronounced /mɑgən 'dɑːvɪd/. The six-pointed figure consisting of two superimposed equilateral triangles, used for centuries as a Jewish emblem. The present Israeli flag.

Mensh, mensch (from Middle High German *Mensch*, *Mensche*, 'a person'). In

Jewish usage: a person of integrity or rectitude; a person who is morally just, honest, or honourable.

> 'I want you to be a *mensch*': Saul Bellow, *The Adventures of Augie March* 43 (1953). 'The key to being 'a real *mensh*' is nothing less than character: rectitude, dignity, a sense of what is right, responsible, decorous. Many a poor man, many an ignorant man, is a *mensh*': Leo Rosten, *The Joys of Yiddish*, 234 (1968). '"You're not like those other university phonies. You're a *mensch*. What good are those effing eggheads? It takes an ignorant bastard like me to fight liberal causes"': Saul Bellow, *Herzog*, p 87 (1977).

Meshuggener A crazy person.

Nisht gut! 'Not good!'

Nosh (Yiddish *nashn,* from Middle High German *naschen*, *neschen,* 'to eat dainty food or delicacies'. Old High German *nascn*; German *naschen* 'to nibble, eat on the sly, to eat dainty food or delicacies'), cognate with Middle Low German *naschen*, Swedish regional *naska*, Danish *naske*, all in sense 'to eat dainty food or delicacies'; further etymology uncertain.) Originally: to nibble a snack, delicacy, etc, often between meals. Later more generally: to eat, have a meal. The original sense of snacking persists to some extent in the USA: in Britain the sense, at least among gentiles, is nowadays of a main meal, and often a large one (as in 'a [right] nosh-up').

Nu? An interrogative interjection that speaks oceans. With a shrugging of the shoulders, *Nu?* means, 'So?', 'So what?', 'And ... ?' 'What do you expect me to do about it?', and so on.

Oi vei! or **Oy vey**! Literally 'Oh! Woe!' *Cf* German *Weh*, 'woe'. An expression of dismay or hurt. Often as *Oi, vei is mir* 'O, woe is me!'

Schnorrer, **shnorrer**. [Yiddish var. of G. *schnurrer*, f. *schnurren* (slang) to go begging.] A Jewish beggar. Now in extended *US* use, a beggar, layabout, scrounger, good-for-nothing: *OED*.

Shlep from *shlepn*, to drag (cf German *schleppen*). 'To haul, carry, drag. Also *transf.* and *fig:* to toil, to 'slave'; to go or travel with effort, to traipse': *OED*.

> 'Oh, give him time. Why should I *schlepp* out my guts?': Saul Bellow, *Herzog*, p 142 (1977).

Shnorer Yiddish variant of G. *Schnorrer*, f. *schnorren,* 'to cadge or scrounge'. A Jewish beggar. A beggar, layabout, scrounger, good-for-nothing.

shmalts Used in two senses: Melted chicken fat; (and also in the kitchen, *schmaltz herring*, a form of pickled herring); and, figuratively, sentimentality, emotionalism; excessively sentimental music, writing, etc.

> 'Isn't it touching? They drugged you with schmaltz.' Saul Bellow, Herzog, p194 (1977).

Shpiel or **Spiel** (perhaps not introduced through Yiddish but through German immigrant influence in the USA: from *spielen*, to play, gamble, sing.)

> 'Talk, a story; a speech intended to persuade or advertise, patter. A swindle, a dishonest line of business. To gamble, to play music, to talk, esp. volubly or glibly; to patter. To tell, to reel *off*; to announce; to perform': *OED*.

Shtik (*cf* German *Stück* 'piece, play'). 'An act or stage routine; a joke, a 'gag'. Hence *transf.*(freq. slightly *derog.*), a patter, a 'line'; a gimmick or characteristic style, originally Theatrical. A particular area of activity or interest, a sphere or 'scene' ': *OED*

Shtum (*cf* German *stumm* 'silent, mute'). 'Silent, speechless, dumb. Esp. in phr. to keep (or stay) shtoom. Occas. also as *n.*': *OED.*

Trepverter Retorts that come too late; latter-wit; *l'esprit d'escalier*. See quotation.

'At first there was no pattern to the notes he made. They were fragments – nonsense syllables, exclamations, twisted proverbs and quotations or, in the Yiddish of his long-dead mother, *Trepverter* – retorts that came too late, when you were already on your way down the stairs'; Saul Bellow, *Herzog,* p 9 (1977).

Acknowledgements

I am extremely grateful to my collaborators for their valued help in compiling this Lexicon. Thanks are due, in alphabetical order, to:

Sandy Atkinson, Elke and Frank Beckmann, Frederike Beckmann, Dr Michael H Carl, Rosemary and Roy Croft, George Fleischhack, Hélène Hartley, Mark Hartley, Stephen Haskell, William Hosking, Matt Huber, Trevor Martin, Sir Alan Munro, Neil Munro, Dr Günther Schmigalle and the late Eric Zinnow.

Without their valued help (and forbearance), this Lexicon could not have been completed.

Neil Munro, Stephen Haskell, Trevor Martin, Michael Carl, the late Eric Zinnow, George Fleischhack and Günther Schmigalle have been particularly productive and particularly patient. There is abundant evidence of their influence throughout the entire Lexicon. Neil Munro's intimate familiarity with the German language has been an inestimable boon. He has steered me away from many a pitfall, and on an almost daily basis, too.

ITALIAN

This Lexicon is the third in a series of relatively concise lists of words and phrases from foreign languages that have been adopted by reasonably well educated English-speakers.

The second Lexicon comprised German words and phrases. It was generally believed among our collaborators that there would not be many German terms in use by English-speakers, or, at least, that few would be recognized by reasonably educated English-speakers. However, that belief turned out to be far from the truth. On the contrary, we found no fewer than 375 German items that merited inclusion in our German Lexicon.

We began the compilation of a French Lexicon in the knowledge that there would be many more French words and phrases known to English-speakers and used by them than German words and phrases, owing to a number of strong influences, the primary one being the profound impression that French culture made on English-speakers during the Enlightenment. The 'metrics' are as follows: the German Lexicon ran to 40 pages; the French Lexicon ran to 86 pages.

The Italian Lexicon has proved to be reasonably fecund, in the light of the immense debt civilization owes to the Italian peninsula. There is a Latin Lexicon in this series, but, even subtracting the Roman element from what the world owes to Italy, there remains a stupendous obligation that every English-speaker must readily acknowledge to those who spoke and speak what is now effectively the unified language Italian.

It is virtually impossible to carry on a rational conversation about the fine arts without adopting, unconsciously, a vocabulary studded with Italian words and phrases. In the spheres of painting and sculpture we should be lost without our liberal borrowing from Italian. In music our debt is stupendous. In literature we owe more than we shall ever know. In such applied arts and sciences as architecture, our debt is colossal. Even in our discourse about modern technology, we find that, if we talk of helicopters, we talk of Leonardo da Vinci; and if we talk of the planets and the Universe, we talk of Galileo. Even if we conclude, as sophisticated adults, that Galileo probably didn't say, *Eppur se muove*, we still know that phrase and shall never forget it. We murmur, *Se non è vero, è molto ben trovato*. And shall we ever forget Dante's *Lasciate ogni speranza, voi ch' entrate*?

This Lexicon would be very much longer if it were not for the fact that virtually incalculable vocabulary has been created in English by the mere adaptation to our tongue of purely Italian words. We easily adapt and adopt them. We are grateful for that.

As to the pronunciation of Italian, the tongues of English-speakers do not find it so hard as they find French. Italian is an almost completely phonetic language: its spelling is a good guide to its pronunciation. In this respect, it is like German and unlike French and English. The use made of the International Phonetic Alphabet in the German Lexicon in this series is extremely light. Its use in the French Lexicon is, conversely, extremely heavy. In this Italian Lexicon use of the International Phonetic alphabet is also extremely light.

The vowels of Italian are simple sounds, not diphthongs, unlike most vowel-sounds in English, which are profoundly diphthongal; some are even triphthongal. Thus, there are five long sounds for the vowels in Italian and five short sounds. In ways only slightly over-simplified, they equate to the sound in the

English exclamation 'Ah!' and to the sound in 'hat'; to the sound in the exclamation 'Eh?' and to the sound in 'pet'; to the sound in 'teeth' and the sound in 'pit'; to the sound in the exclamation 'Oh!' and the sound in 'top'; and to the sound in 'doom' and the sound in 'put' (as in 'put up with'). The last sound is the sound as in 'He is a marvellous putter-in-place of bumptious people'. The second to the last sound is as in 'Mr Pooter' – as in 'Lupin Pooter'.

In principle, the consonants in Italian, apart from *s* and *z*, have only one value each but their sound is often modified by the presence, immediately before or immediately after, of another consonant, as follows.

The consonant *s* has two values, equivalent to the English consonants *s* and z: the choice between sounds is arbitrary in concept but consistent in practice – requiring merely a good memory. The combination *zz* is sometimes pronounced as *tz* and sometimes as *dz*. Only memory can help in these *zz* combinations, though Italian dictionaries offer their rare but always helpful phonetic interventions with words containing *s* and *zz*.

The letter *c* is pronounced as the first sound in 'chick' or, if hardened by a following *h*, it has the last sound in 'chick'. The letter *g* is alway soft, as in 'geometry' except when hardened by a following *h*. Double consonants (two of the same consonant) are really single sounds: perhaps some future orthographic reform will completely abolish them, as has happened in Spanish and Portuguese. Double consonants (a pair of different consonants) have a marked aural effect. As mentioned, *ch* sounds as *k* and *gh* sounds as *g* in 'giggle'. For example, without the letter *h* in *ghetto*, the initial sound would be the initial sound of the English word 'judge'. In the combination *gl*, the letter *g* palatizes the sound of the letter *l*: the surname of the celebrated tenor, Beniamino Gigli, was pronounced not 'Jeelly' but 'Jeelyee'. The combination *gu* as in *guado*, 'a ford', gives the sound gw. Tho two sounds 'lyee' and 'gw' do not exist in native English (though the Welsh place-name Gwent has the second sound) but neither sound presents any difficulty to English-speakers. The combination *gn* gives the palatized sound as in English 'onion'. The combination *sc* gives the English sound as in 'shut'. The combination *sch* gives the initial sound as in 'Scotch'.

The letter *h* by itself (that is, not hardening *c* or g) is obsolete in modern Italian, as are the letter *j* and the combinations *ph* and *th*.

There are few references to cookery in the Italian Lexicon. The reason can perhaps be best extracted from the fact that the *OED* had 166 references to *pasta* alone.

The Lexicon

abbate Literally, 'abbot', but nowadays almost always a courtesy title for a priest lacking a more specific mode of address. Compare the French *Abbé.*

abbellimenti 'Embellishments'. From the verb *abbellire,* 'to adorn, to embellish'. A generic name for the many graces and ornaments (also called *gruppetti*) employed in the performance of music, some of which are referred to in the 1994 quotation below and in their alphabetical places in this Lexicon.

> 'These terms ... are rather indefinitely employed in music to denote, in general, every species of musical ornament which consists of several small notes': J. F. Warner, *Universal Dictionary of Musical Terms,* p xliv/2, s.v. *Groppo, Gruppo, gruppetto* (1842). 'These numerous recordings ... serve to display his ... command of many now forgotten vocal graces such as the morendo or diminuendo, accacciatura [*sic*], messa di voce, fermata and gruppetto': *The Guardian,* G2, 9/4, 3rd January 1994.

acca The letter *h* in the Italian alphabet. Apart from its function of hardening the letters *c* and *g* when placed after that letter, it has no purpose. Perhaps for that reason there exist Italian sayings employing the letter *as a letter*: for example, *non capire un' acca,* 'not to understand anything', and *questo libro non vale un' acca,* 'this book isn't worth a dime'.

acciaccatura An ornament or grace-note in music, consisting of a small note (or two at a distance of not more than a minor third from each other) performed as quickly as possible before an essential note of a melody, the single small note (or first of the two) being a semitone below the substantive note; a 'crush-note'. From *acciaccare,* 'to crush'. This is the only word used by English-speakers for this phenomenon. See, *below, appoggiatura.*

aggio or agio Literally, 'ease'. An old fashioned word that denoted the percentage charge on the exchange of paper-money into cash, or for the exchange of a less valuable metallic or paper currency into a more valuable one; hence, the excess value of one currency over another. Though the word clearly indicates the origin of such balancing practices, originating in the trading states such as Venice and Genoa, the principle of the *aggio* was fundamental to the stability of the world's finances during the dominance of the pound sterling.

aggiornamento The process of modernization or of bringing up to date; specifically applied to the revision of doctrines, policies, etc., in the Catholic Church, initiated by Pope John XXIII at the Second Vatican Council (1962-65). From aggiornare, 'to bring up to date'.

al dente Foodstuffs that are cooked so as to be tender but still to be firm when they are bitten are said to be cooked *al dente.*

> 'In Italy it [*sc.* pasta] is cooked 'al dente', as they call it – sufficiently firm to be felt 'under the tooth'': M. Morphy, *Recipes of All Nations,* p 133 (1935). 'Macaroni must be cooked in plenty of boiling salt water 'al dente', i.e. done but not soft': W. Bickel tr *Hering's Dictionary of Cookery* p 600 (1958). 'For dessert, we ordered apple strudel. Served hot, the strudel had a generous supply of *al dente* apples, and the leaves, though not especially crisp, were enjoyable': *Chicago,* 210/2 June 1978. 'Our vegetables are

> cooked *al dente*. Should you require your vegetables well done, please advise on lacing your order': *The Listener*, 5th 10/2 April 1984.

albergo An inn; a place of rest and refreshment for travellers. The word derives from a Germanic root, MHG *herberge*, OHG. *heri-berga*, literally, 'army shelter', progressing from 'tent' to 'camp' to 'inn': cf. G. *herberge*, Fr *auberge*, and English 'harbour'. The word was much used for the quarters of Crusaders, especially of the quarters the Knights Hospitaller and Knights Templar established for their troops in transit to Outremer (*q.v.* in French Lexicon).

Alberti Bass A style of bass accompaniment consisting of broken chords or arpeggios: the notes of the chord are played in the order *lowest, highest, middle, highest.* This pattern is then repeated. It was named after Domenico Alberti (1710-1740), who used it extensively, although he was not the first to use it.

allegro 'Brisk, lively'. One of the five grades of musical pace and character, being the quickest except for *presto*. The five grades are: *grave, largo, andante, allegro* and *presto.*

Allegro, L' See *Il Penseroso, below.*

alt, in The musical expression *in alt* denotes the bracket of notes in the first octave above the treble stave, beginning with G (*nota bene*, *not* with Middle C). See next.

altissimo, in The musical expression *in altissimo* denotes the bracket of notes in the second octave above the treble stave, beginning with G (*nota bene*, *not* with Middle C). See preceding.

andante 'Going-ly'. One of the five grades of musical pace and character, being the middle grade. The five grades are *grave, largo, andante, allegro* and *presto.*

appoggiatura A grace-note or passing-note played or sung before the substantive note, from the Italian 'to support or buttress'. The only word used by English-speakers for this phenomenon. See *acciaccatura, above.*

arpeggio A technique in music whereby the notes of a chord are individually played or sung in rapid succession instead of simultaneously, the result being similar to the technique of harp-playing, hence the name. The strumming of a stringed instrument with the thumb or fingers is a species of arpeggiation. See *rasgado, rasgueado* in the Spanish-Portuguese Lexicon.

aria 'Air, melody'. Conventionally used to denote a solo in opera.

arietta 'Little aria'. A short *aria. Cf cavatina, below.*

> 'An arietta of her own composing': Smollett, *Humphrey Clinker* (1771). 'A short air, generally of sprightly character, and having no second part': Hullah in Grove, *Dictionary of Music* (1880).

assai 'Enough'. One of a number of words used somewhat imprecisely to modify musical directions. *Moderato assai* means approximately 'moderately enough'. Directions of this description are frequently simply broad *hints* to the executant. See also, e.g., *più, below.*

bagno This word has been partly anglicized as *bagnio.* From Latin *balineeum,* 'a bath' or 'bathing'. A bath-house, particularly one provided with hot baths, vapour-baths and steamrooms. The word was widely used to denote what is now called in English a 'turkish bath', primarily with reference to establishments in the Near East, though comparable establishments in Europe were called by this name or a naturalized variant of it. Nowadays the word *bagno* or *bagnio* tends to be used of oriental bath-houses for purposes of lending local colour to writing. There is another Continental use of *bagno* and its national variants, to mean a prison, *uno bagno penale*, but there is no equivalent usage in English. How the word acquired this secondary meaning is obscure.

barcaruola A barcarole. From *barcaruolo*, a *gondoliere* (*cf gondola, below*). A song as typically sung by the Venetian gondoliers.

basilica From the Greek *βασιλική οίκια* or *στοα*. 'Literally and originally, a royal palace; thence, a large rectangular building or hall, with double colonnades and a semicircular apse at the end, used for a court of justice and place of public assembly. A building of the preceding type, used for Christian worship. A hall of justice handed over by Roman emperors and consecrated for religious use; thence applied to other early churches built on the same plan, and improperly to churches generally. In Rome applied specifically to the seven principal churches founded by Constantine.

basso-rilievo 'Low relief'. Sculpture or carved work in which the figures project less than one half of their true proportions from the surface on which they are carved. See *mezzo-rilievo, below.*

bel canto 'Good singing'. A slightly ambiguous, slightly partisan term of art. In the first place, it does not mean, simply, 'good singing'. In principle, it denotes a school of singing and its style characterized by the use of the voice as a 'gymnastic' musical instrument rather than as a means of conveying emotion, dramatic significance or pathos. Its heyday drew to a close as far as composition was concerned (but not as regards performance) with the death of Vincenzo Bellini (1801-35). The concept of *bel canto* is bound up with the concept of *coloratura* singing, a style of singing extensively employing 'Divisions, runs, trills, cadenzas, and other florid passages in vocal music': (Stainer & Barrett, *A Dictionary of Musical Terms,* 1876). In general terms, the expression *bel canto* denotes singing in which the expertise of the performer, coupled with the innate quality of performer's voice, is of paramount importance. It is unhelpful to limit the expression to a set epoch, though there is a tendency to look on Bellini's *Norma* and comparable works as being the last flourishing of the school of composition that catered for the public's desire for *bel canto.* Nevertheless, some arias by, for example, Rossini, would certainly qualify as *belcanto* arias.

> 'This comprehensive term covers the vocal qualities of the great singers of the seventeenth and eighteenth centuries – the palmy days of Italian singing': *The Oxford Companion to Music* (1938).

belladonna Literally, 'beautiful lady'. The name given in Italy and thence to medicine for the plant now called *Atropa belladonna*, in English 'Deadly Nightshade'. The reason for the name 'beautiful lady' is disputed. See the quotations below.

> 'Bella-donna is the name, which the Italians, and particularly the Venetians, apply to this plant; and Mr. Ray observes, that it is so called because the Italian ladies make a cosmetic from the juice': Pultney in *Philosophical Transactions* L, 62 (1851). 'Belladonna, because it was employed by Leucota, a famous poisoner of Italy, to destroy the

beautiful women': E. Hamilton, *Flora Homœopathica,* Opera iii 64 (1851).

Botteghe Oscure A multilingual literary magazine founded, funded and produced by the American-born Princess Marguerite Caetano twice a year from 1948 to 1960. She chose the name *Botteghe Oscure* because her husband's Roman palace was in the Via delle Botteghe Oscure, 'the street of dark shops'. No fewer than 650 writers of 30 nationalities had passed through the review's pages in its 12 years of existence. In its issue No IX, Spring 1952, it included a piece by Dylan Thomas entitled 'Llareggub: A Piece of Broadcasting Perhaps'. Those keen to explore to the full the significance of everything modern and creative searched their gazetteers in vain for an occurrence of this Welsh place-name. Someone, no doubt an assiduous toiler in the field of crossword-puzzles, tumbled to the key to the mystery – by spelling the word backwards.

bozzetto A small rough model for a larger sculpture; also, a sketch for a larger painting. See *modello* and *pensiero, below*.

braggadoccio Not an Italian word but a name devised by Edmund Spenser for a vainglorious character Bragg in his *Faery Queen* (formed from *bragg-* and the common Italian augmentative *-occio* or *-occhio)*.

'Vaine Braggadocchio, getting Guyons horse, is made the scorne of knighthood trew'. Spenser, *Faery Queen,* II, iii Argument (1590).

Bucentoro, il Anglicized as 'the Bucentaur'. The state barge in which the Doge of Venice sailed out once a year to throw a ring in the Adriatic, to signify Venice's being wedded to that sea.

cadenza A passage of optional form given to a solo voice or instrument to permit the virtuosity of the performer to be shown off to best effect. Some composers have written out whatever *cadenze* they wish to be performed, but conventional practice is for the performer to create the *cadenza*. Sometimes (less frequently than in earlier times) the cadenza is improvised. The correct Italian pronunciation is /ka'denːtʃa/ but an anglicized pronunciation, /kə'dɛnːzə/, is much more often heard among English-speakers.

caffè macchiato Literally, 'stained coffee'. Coffee (usually espresso) served with a very small amount of hot or foamed milk. Pronounced /kaf'eː mak'jɑto/.

cammeo Anglicized as 'cameo'. The Italian word has the tonic accent on the second syllable. This is a word with a prodigious ancestry, its earliest antecedents being completely unknown. It appears in mediaeval Latin literature as *cammaeus*. Nowadays it denotes a precious stone having two layers of different colours, in the upper of which a figure is carved in relief, while the lower serves as a ground. For this purpose the ancients used onyx and agate, and especially sardonyx, 'a variety of chalcedony, consisting of alternate parallel layers of white and red chalcedony' (*OED*), which was carved so as to leave a white figure in relief on a red ground. Thence extended to all lapidary's work of the same kind; and in modern times ('by abuse', *Littré* says) to similar carving in shells of molluscs, of which the inner stratum is differently coloured from the outer. Jewelry with the opposite characteristics to *cameo* – with incised images rather than relief images – is known as *intaglio* (work), the word being pronounced /in'taːʎo/. Modern languages have created new words from *cameo,* (for instance, French *camaïeu*, 'a monochrome'), and new senses (for instance, in English, a 'cameo part' in a play or film, in which a celebrated actor has a small but prestigious *role).*

Camorra A (former) secret society resembling the Mafia (*q.v.*) that flourished in Naples and Neapolitan cities.

campanile A bell-tower; especially applied to the lofty detached bell-towers of Italy. The plural is *campanili.* Pronounced /kampan'iːle/ and /kampan'iːli/.

cantabile A musical direction indicating that the performer should execute the item in a 'singing' manner, that is, as one would *normally* sing a song, without *staccato* (*q.v.*), without pauses, without *crescendo* and without *diminuendo* (*qq.v.*).

cantata 'Sung'. Originally, a narrative, very often in verse, set to recitative, or alternating recitative and air, almost always for a single voice and accompanied by one or more instruments. Nowadays the word always denotes a sacred choral work resembling an oratorio (*q.v.*) but shorter. Sometimes, though rarely, the word is applied to a secular subject, as, for example, to a lyric drama set to music. No cantata is intended to be acted.

canto One of the divisions of a long poem; such a part as the minstrel might sing at one 'fit' or strain of music. (Used in Italian by Dante, and in English by, for instance, Spenser, Byron and Pound.)

capisce? 'Do you understand?'. This is the third person singular, present indicative, of *capire*, 'to understand'. Its use as an interrogative interjection dates back to at least 1294. The use of the third person singular with individuals is a formal, courteous form of address, which would make the expression 'Capisce?' ('Capeesh') as used in Mafia-orientated fiction rather surprising. The familiar, second person singular, form would be *'Capisci?'*, /kaːpiʃi/.

capo mafioso A Mafia chief. *Capo di tutti capi*: a person who runs every branch of the Mafia in a region.

carbonara, alla Descriptive of dishes, usually *pasta*, served with a creamy sauce, typically made from eggs, bacon or ham, and cheese. The reason for the presence of this term in a Lexicon that otherwise is obliged to exclude the thousands of Italian words and expressions relating to the kitchen is that its etymology is well worth noting. In the first place, the word *carbonaro* means 'charcoal-burner', but there is no plausible link between this sauce and frugal diet of the traditional charcoal-burner or with the secret political organization, *I Carbonari* (see next). The second thing worth noting is the extreme newness of the expression. The conundrum over this expression has been to some extent elucidated as follows:

> *Spaghetti alla carbonara* ... It has been suggested that this is a traditional dish of the *carbonari*, or charcoal burners, but that is implausible. A more credible explanation is that it was invented in 1944 as a result of the American occupation troops having their lavish rations of eggs and bacon prepared by local cooks. The name would then be from a Rome restaurant, the 'Carbonara', which makes a speciality of the dish: A. Davidson, *Oxford Companion to Food*, 740/3 (1999).

When the jesting Byron asked, 'Have Carbonaro cooks not carbonadoed/ Each course enough?': *Age of Bronze*, xii (1823), his verb referred to a method of cooking in which pieces of meat are cross-scored and grilled (broiled) directly on the open fire. The connection with charcoal is purely the self-evident one: charcoal produces the best glowing embers. The Belgian dish *le carbonnade* (so spelt, and comprising beef, onions and beer stewed slowly) owes its anomalous name – not being in any way connected with charcoal – to its orginal method of cooking, which did involve char-grilling, or, at least. to a gradual transference from cooking on an open fire to slow stewing in a covered pot.

Carbonari, I The members of a secret political association formed in the Bonapartist Kingdom of Naples (1806-1815), which was a puppet *régime* set up during the French occupation of Southern Italy under Joachim Murat (1767-1815). The political association had as its objective the introduction of a republican government.

> 'In 1799 ... when driven to the forest of the Abruzzi they [republicans] are believed to have disguised themselves as charcoal-burners. In the course of twenty years the name *Carbonari* was borne by a society, or confederate societies, ranging all over Italy': W. Cory, *Modern English History*, I, p 128 *n* (1880).

castrato A male singer castrated in boyhood so as to retain a treble or alto voice.

cavatina A short song of simple character, properly one without a second strain and repeat – in other words, not a *da capo aria* (*q.v., below*); 'frequently applied to a smooth melodious air, forming part of a grand scena or movement": (Grove, *Dictionary of Music (*1954). The word derives from *cavare,* 'to dig, to excavate, to extract'. *Cf arietta, above.*

chi va piano, va sano 'Who goes gently goes safely'. The saying is commonly concluded: 'Chi va sano, va lontano': 'Who goes safely goes far'.

Chianti A dry red wine, less often also a white wine, produced in a specified area of Tuscany; loosely applied to various inferior Italian wines. Characteristically sold in flasks covered with woven straw.

> 'Chianti wine ... is an agreeable thin red wine ... of the claret type, usually rather dry ... Chianti is usually bottled in straw-covered flasks': *Chambers's Encyclopaedia*, III, 394/2 (1959).

chiar' oscuro A noun denoting the treatment of light and shade in a picture. See quotations.

> 'Explication of Terms, *Chiaro-Scuro* ... Secondly, taken for the disposing of the Lights and Shadows Skilfully; as when we say, A Painter understands well the Chiaro-Scuro': W. Aglionby, *Painting Illustrated* (1686). ' Letter 19 May, His management of the *chiaro oscuro*, or light and shadow ... is altogether wonderful': Tobias Smollett, *Humphrey Clinker* (1771). '"Chiaroscuro" includes not only light and shadow as it affects each separate part, but the proper division and distribution of the whole surface of a picture into bright or dark masses, whether the darkness be produced by shadow, or by the proper colour of ... the objects represented': John Opie, *Lectures on Art*, iii, 'Chiaroscuro', (1848) p 295 (1807).

ciao A familiar form of saying 'Hello' or 'Goodbye'. Though the word is so frequently met with and used, it deserves a place in this Lexicon for its bizarre lineage. It derives from a Venetian-dialect salutation, *s-ciàvo*, or, if the letter *v* is vocalized (as in Classical Latin), *sciào,* which meant '[I am your] slave', *schiavo* in Italian. The word *schiavo* derives from mediaeval Latin *sclavus,* which in turn derives from the name *Slav*. The *OED* explains the transference of the notion of servitude from 'Slav' and 'slave' as follows: 'the Slavonic population in parts of central Europe having been reduced to a servile condition by conquest ... the transferred sense is clearly evidenced in documents of the 9th century'. The exclamation *ciao!* was originally a form of salutation used from servant to master, but it became a formal salutation even among the Venetian aristocracy before gradually assuming its present degree of affable informality.

cicerone A puzzling word. It means a guide who shows and explains the antiquities or curiosities of a place to strangers, particularly in Rome. The word is the Italian form of Cicero, Marcus Tullius Cicero (106-43 BC), the Roman writer and advocate, but why the name should have attached to the guides at Rome is inexplicable. Indeed, the practice of calling the guides to Rome *ciceroni* does not appear to be of Italian origin, in that the first recorded uses of the term are in English works, not Italian works.

> 'Apparently originally given to learned Italian antiquarians, whose services were sought by visitors seeking information about the antiquities of a place; subsequently usurped by the ordinary professional 'guide'': *OED*, 2nd edn (1989).

cicisbeo The name formerly given in Italy to the recognized gallant, escort or *cavalier servente* of a married woman. Three things are worthy of note. The first is that the word is stressed on the second to the last syllable. The second is that the letter *s* is pronounced as a *z*. The third is that the form *cavalier*, not *cavaliere* (the normal form of the word), is correct in this usage. In the International Phonetic Alphabet, the pronunciation is rendered /tʃitʃizb'eo/.

The etymology of the word is complex. According to the authoritative *Vocabolario della Crusca*, perhaps an inversion of *bel cece*, 'beautiful chick (pea)', a colloquial expression conveying the same sense. Pasqualino, cited by Diez, hazards that the word come from the (obsolete) French *chiche beau*, 'beautiful chick-pea'.The modern French expressions are *sigisbée* and *cavalier servant*.

> 'The word was formerly a 'Cicisbeo', But that is now grown vulgar and indecent. But 'Cavalier Servente' is the phrase': Byron, *Beppo*, xxvii (1817)

cinquecento A term applied in Italy to the 16th century, and to the style of art and architecture of that period, characterized by a reversion to classical forms. The phenomenon arose about 1500. (When a century is being named, Italian usage is to ignore the first thousand years, and to use the next numeral together with *cento*. So, *e.g.*, *seicento*, for what we call 'the seventeenth century'.

clarino Formerly the name of a trumpet with a narrow bore capable of producing notes of considerable brilliance, it is upper register. Now used as an adjective for the method or style of playing the trumpet in its upper register, in which, without the use of keys or valves, it is capable of producing a full diatonic scale. So, 'passages of clarino playing' and, loosely, 'clarino trumpets'.

coda 'A tail'. 'A passage of more or less independent character introduced after the completion of the essential parts of a movement, so as to form a more definite and satisfactory conclusion': *OED*.

cognoscente 'One who knows'. Plural: *cognoscenti*. An expert; one who knows a subject thoroughly; *cf.* *connoisseur* in the French Lexicon. The words *dilettante*, and *virtuoso, qq.v*, are closely related to *cognoscente*, though they are more often used in reference to the fine arts than *cognoscente*, which tends to be applied to knowledge in general. The word *cognoscenti* is increasingly used to denote, without rancour, 'those in the know'. The pronunciations are /koɲo'ʃeːnte/ and koɲo'ʃeːnti/.

coloratura See *bel canto, above.*

come del morire From Giovanni Boccaccio (1313-1375), *Il Filostrato*, canto 4, stanza 140. Translated 'As sure as death' by Ben Jonson, *Every Man in his Humour*, act 2, sc 1, (1598).

Commedia dell' Arte Semi-improvised popular comedy as played in Italian theatres and across Europe by professional touring companies from the sixteenth to the early eighteenth centuries. The performers took highly conventionalized parts and worked from a skeletal scenario, the *canovaccio* or *soggetto*. The best-known of the caste of characters appearing in the Commedia dell' Arte are *Arlecchino* (Harlequin) and *Colombina* (Columbine), but other characters, too, gripped the popular fancy: the greedy Venetian mechant *Pantalone* (Pantaloon), the Bolognese attorney Dr Graziano, the Neapolitan *Scaramuccia* (Scaramouche) and the clowns (the *zanni*, from which word we derive our word 'zany'). The principal characters wore readily recognizable costumes that persist to some extent in today's circus dress. *Arlecchino* wore particoloured bespangled tights and a visor, and carried a light 'bat' or lath as a magic wand. See *pierrot* in the French Lexicon.

> 'Today the commedia dell'arte continues to live in the Harlequins and Columbines of carnival masks and children's puppet shows': *The Macmillan Dictionary of Italian Literature*, eds Bondanella & Bondanella, p 127 (1979).

confetti 'Bon-bons, or plaster or paper imitations of these, thrown during carnival in Italy; in UK, US, etc., *esp.* little discs, etc., of coloured paper thrown at the bride and bridegroom at weddings': *OED*.

concertino See *ripieno, below.*

concerto A composition for one, or sometimes more, solo instruments accompanied by orchestra; nowadays almost always in three movements. Formerly applied more widely to various compositions for a number of instruments.

consigliere A counsellor; an adviser. In modern English usage, the name of a Mafia post. See quotation. The plural is *consiglieri* and the pronunciations are /konsiːʎ'ɛre/ and /konsiːʎ'ɛri/.

> 'In the Mafia … directly under the boss is an underboss and a consigliere or counselor, and under them are captains and 'soldiers'': *The New York Times*, 14th April 1969, p 30.

continuo A term used in music, particularly in Baroque music, to denote the crucial part played by one or more performers as a species of accompaniment or background to recitatives and arias. Characteristically, continuo players were, for example, keyboard players, bass viol players or theorbo players. Continuo players were commonly extremely experienced executants who improvised in sympathy with the soloists and who gave performances a solid framework whereby the isolation that soloists sometimes experienced could be obviated.

contra-tenore See *falsetto, below.*

conversazione A word of immense importance that has virtually died the death in English usage. Its fundamental meaning is, of course, 'conversation', but it has no fewer than four other meanings noted in the *OED* sufficiently distinct from 'conversation' and from each other to warrant attention. The first is of historical importance: 'In Italy, the name for an evening assembly for conversation, social recreation, and amusement (often described by travellers in the 18th century). The second is: 'Introduced into England [as the Italian word itself], and applied to the private assembly now known as an 'At Home'. (Occasionally anglicized as 'Conversation' [though, it must said, *rarely*])'. The third is: ' From about the close of the 18th century, chiefly applied to assemblies of an intellectual character, in connexion with literature, art, or science'. The practice, in this particular context, still exists, but under other names, such as the lectures organized by independent agencies, at which questions are solicited from the audience, many of which lead to something resembling the *converzationi* of earlier years. The fourth, from the 2nd edition of the *OED* (of 1989) is: 'Now chiefly used for a *soirée* given by a learned body or society of arts, at which the society's work is illustrated by the exhibition of specimens, experiments, and demonstrations'. It is perhaps in this last respect that one most regrets the growing irrelevance of the word in the light of the procedures of our learned bodies. *Conversazioni* under that name are nowadays simply not held, which is a great pity. The open-endedness of the *conversazione* is perhaps most closely approached, nowadays, by Melvyn Bragg's programme on the BBC, *Start the Week.*

credenza 'A credence-table'. An item of church furniture; a small table positioned to the right of the altar on which are placed the materials and vessels to be used during a Communion service. Also loosely applied to secular items of furniture such as bed-side cupboards, buffets and side-boards. The connection with the verb *credere,* 'to believe', is no doubt through the notion of 'trust'. The tasting or 'assaying' of meats formerly practised in a royal or noble household as a precaution against poisoning was known as *la credenza* or, in English, 'the credence'.

crescendo 'An increasing, an augmentation'. A musical direction requiring a (gradual) increase in volume (or, as some definitions prefer) in 'intensity of tone'. The termination *-endo* indicates the present participle, importing the notion of gradualness. *Cf diminuendo, below.*

culturati Probably a factitious word calqued on *literati (q.v.)* and used to mean cultured people considered as a class; the members of a cultural elite. The word is not Classical Latin. If the word had been truly an Italian word, it would have taken the form *colturati.* The precedent of *literati* and the emergence of this word *culturati* has led to the introduction into the English language of the word 'glitterati', *q.v.*

> 'So say the formerly beautiful people, once the jet set, now called the glitterati, which appears to be a combination of literati, or illuminati, with a glittering generality': *The New York Times Magazine*, p 23/2, 23rd July 1978. 'The yuppies and the culturati get fashionable shows that suck up to them while members of America's underclass are largely served by atrocious crap': *Esquire,* 35/1 January 2000.

dilettante Literally, 'a delighter'. 'A lover of the fine arts; originally, one who cultivates them for the love of them rather than professionally, and so *amateur* as opposed to *professional*; but in later use generally applied more or less depreciatively to one who interests himself in an art or science merely as a pastime and without serious aim or study ('a mere dilettante')': *OED*. *Cf cognoscente, above*, and *virtuoso, below*.

> 'Sir Patrick O'Prism, a dilettante painter of high renown': T. L. Peacock, *Headlong Hall*, iii (1821). 'The dilettante believer is indeed not a strong spirit, but the weakest': J. Morley, *Voltaire*, edn 1886, p 57 (1871).

diminuendo 'A lessening; a diminishing'. A musical direction requiring a (gradual) diminution in volume (or, as some definitions prefer) in 'intensity of tone'. The termination *-endo* indicates the present participle, importing the notion of gradualness. *Cf crescendo, above.* The word *decrescendo* is also used, though its use ought to be restricted to a direction coming after a sustained *crescendo.*

ditto Not generally thought of as an Italian word but in fact a variant of *detto*, 'said', used as in English formal and legal parlance (*il detto libro*, 'the said book') and also to avoid repeating a word or phrase, as in 'Breakfast served in the Morning Room. Morning coffee, ditto. Afternoon tea, ditto'. Also in 'ditto marks', denoting the two inverted commas or the double prime, used to indicate 'the same', in lists, etc.

diva A distinguished female singer; a *prima donna, q.v.;* a 'divine one', 'a goddess'.

dolce far niente 'Sweet to do nothing'. 'Delightful idleness': *OED*.

> 'It is there … that the dolce far niente of a summer evening is most heavenly': Longfellow, in *Life* I, p 187 1891. 'That form of the *dolce far niente* which is termed meditation': W. H. Russell, in *The Nineteenth Century*, p 490, September 1893.

dolce stil nuovo, il Literally, 'the sweet new style'. A much-discussed phrase occurring in 'Il Purgatorio' canto 24 of *La Divina Commedia*. A minor poet, Bonagiunta Orbicciani da Lucca, addressing Dante, asks indirectly whether he is not seeing before him the originator of *il dolce stil nuovo.* The actual implications of the conversation are open to many interpretations. In what is probably an inadmissibly loose interpretation of the phrase *il dolce stil nuovo,* many *belle lettristes* have adopted it as a laudatory synonym for the emergent literary language, Italian, which had such a profound effect on the way Italian unification was to proceed. Cardinal Pietro Bembo (1470-1547), furthering Dante's historical work *De Vulgari Eloquentia,* actually employed Italian rather than Latin in his *Prose della Volgar Lingua.* Bembo, following Dante (1265-1321), Petrarch (1304-1375) and Boccaccio (1313-1375), adumbrates the 'ideal language', the Tuscan as written and spoken by Petrarch and Boccaccio, a language purged of all barbarisms and provincialisms, orderly, dignified, expressive and suffused with classical beauty – 'the beautiful language that is modern Italian', as Linda Proud concludes her review of Carol Kidwell, *Pietro Bembo,* in *History Today*, pp 63-4, January 2006.

dolce vita, la 'The sweet life'. 'A life of luxury, pleasure, and self-indulgence': *OED.*

> 'L'esperienza di questa dolce vita': Dante, *La Divina Commedia,* 'Il Paradiso', canto 20, line 47. '*La Dolce Vita* is a film … 'making up an apocalyptic fresco of seven nightmarish nights and seven sobering dawns'': *The Times*, p 15/3, 7th December 1960.

Duce, Il 'The Leader'. The title Mussolini chose for himself as head of the Fascist Party and Dictator of Italy.

'E 'n la sua volontate è nostra pace': 'In His will is our peace': Dante Alighieri (1265-1321), *La Divina Commedia*, 'Il Paradiso', canto 3, line 85.

'Eppur si muove' 'But it does move'. Attributed to Galileo Galilei (1564-1642) after his recantation in 1632 of his hypothesis that the earth moves round the sun. There is no contemporaneous evidence for the attribution. It seems that the first appearance in print of the phrase is in *The Italian Library; containing an Account of the Lives and Works of the most valuable Authors of Italy; with preface*, London, 1757, 8vo. 15, by Giuseppe Baretti (1719-1789). Despite Dr Johnson's general approval of Baretti, the long delay between the supposed uttering of the phrase and its first appearance in print – 125 years – tends to call into question its authenticity. Its anti-Papal potential, however, will guarantee its popularity for many years to come.

It is important, from the point of view of historical accuracy, to point out that Galileo is celebrated in history for his promoting the heliocentric theories of Nicholas Copernicus (1473-1543), a Canon of Frauenburg Cathedral, on the Baltic., a cleric of whom there was never even a scintilla of ecclesiastical disapproval. Galileo was prohibited from promoting his beliefs as *fact* rather than (as they undoubtedly were at that time) *theory*. The prime mover in the promulgation of the decree restricting Galileo's liberty to promoting his ideas, Cardinal Robert Bellarmine (1542-1621), wrote a closely reasoned letter on 12th April 1615 to Paolo Antonio Foscarini (1565-1616), the Carmelite Provincial for Calabria, a man who had consistently championed Galileo's position. In this letter Bellarmine conceded:

> 'Third. I say that if there were a true demonstration that the sun was in the center of the universe and the earth in the third sphere, and that the sun did not travel around the earth but the earth circled the sun, then it would be necessary to proceed with great caution in explaining the passages of Scripture which seemed contrary, and we would rather have to say that we did not understand them than to say that something was false which has been demonstrated.'

However, it is fair to say that Bellarmine concluded that he himself did not believe that Galileo had made out his case. Indeed, the majority of those equipped to decide these matters in that entire period were solidly Ptolomaeans.

An English translation of Foscarini's tract on the Copernican system can be found in Richard J. Blackwell, *Galileo, Bellarmine, and the Bible*, Notre Dame: University of Notre Dame Press, 1991, pp. 217-251. See also Maurice Finocchiaro, *The Galileo Affair: A Documentary History*, Berkeley: University of California Press, 1989, and Thomas Campanella, *Defense of Galileo,* tr. Richard J. Blackwell, Notre Dame, 1994. Note, also, Irving A. Kelter's 'Paolo Foscarini's Letter to Galileo: The search for proofs of the earth's motion': *The Modern Schoolman* 70, pp 31-44, November 1992.

> 'Although the Ptolemæan system was a wrong one, yet even from its eccentric point of view, laws were discovered determining the true movements of the heavenly bodies': Max Müller, *Scientific Language*, i, p 17 (1861).

espresso, caffè espresso Literally, 'expressed coffee', coffee made by the use of steam pressure.

falsetto A register of the male voice above that for which the male vocal chords are normally considered suited. It is a register that is brought into play when a male, often naturally a bass, employs the 'head voice'. The *tessitura* (*q.v.*) of the *falsetto* register centres about *b* below *c* in alt. See *mezzo-soprano, below*. Singers who habitually employ the *falsetto* register are known as 'male altos', the usage familiar in church music, or as 'counter-tenors', a usage applied in both the opera-house and in other secular applications, though the term is gaining ground at the expense of 'male alto'. The Italian word for one who sings in the *falsetto* register is *sopranisto*. On the Continent the French term *sopraniste* is widely used in all languages as a catch-all expression for all adult male trebles and altos. See, in general, *castrato, above.*

fascia In architecture and archaeology, any long, flat surface of wood, stone or marble, especially in the Doric Order; the band that divides the architrave, and in the Ionic and Corinthian orders, each of the three surfaces into which the architrave is divided. In present-day usage, the anglicized form *facia* is predominant, especially when denoting the only two live usages, namely, the flat space above a shop window on which the name of the proprietor or the trading name of the business is displayed, and the facia or facia-board or facia-panel on which are displayed the range of instruments facing the car-driver (known colloquially as 'the dash-board').

Fascism The principles and practices of the Fascist Parties. The name *Fascist* derives ultimately from the name for the bundle of rods or sticks, the *fasces* (in Italian, *fasci*), surrounding the axes that the Lictors carried in attendance on the Magistrates. A *Dictator* had twenty-four Lictors, a *Consul* twelve. The symbolism, both ancient and modern, behind the bundles of sticks was doubtless that 'Unity is strength'. The attendance of the Lictors in numbers no doubt further reinforced the notion of strength. In pre-modern and modern Italy, the *fasci* were groups of men organized for political purposes. Their leaders tended to employ the imagery of the Lictors: the *Fasci dei Lavoratori* in Sicily in the last years of the 19th century are an example of that trend. There was in those years widespread discontent, 'a discontent of which Socialist agitators took advantage to organize the workmen of the towns and the peasants of the country into groups known as *fasci*': *Encyclopaedia Britannica*, XXIX, 649/1 (1902). The Marxist historian Eric Hobsbawm recognizes the Socialist origins of Fascism: 'The great peasant rising of the Fasci saw it [*sc.* the Mafia] on the side of reaction, or at best neutral': E.J. Hobsbawm, *Primitive Rebels* iii. 42 (1959). In 1915 Socialist groups known as *Fasci interventisti* became active, favouring Italy's entry in the First World War as a means of securing the liberation of those territories still *irredenti* ('unredeemed') such as Trieste, and, at the same time, of securing the establishment of a Socialist polity. Until 1914, Benito Mussolini (1883-1945) was the organizer of the Milanese *fascio*. The return home of soldiers to Italy had the same effect as the return of soldiers in the other European countries, a sense of discontent that was aggravated, for the Italians, by the recognition that, despite the loss of no fewer than 600,000 Italian lives, no significant advantages had been gained for the Italian people. Among ex-Servicemen, four factions predominated, named from the colour of the item of *adhoc* uniform they adopted: the Red Guards (the Socialists), the Blue Shirts (the Nationalists), the Grey Shirts (the Liberals), and the Black Shirts (the grouping that became the Fascist Party).

In other countries, Fascist principles spread with some rapidity. In France, for example, Fascism flourished as though it was a natural efflorescence of something native to the French character. After all, the coat of arms of the French Republic ('le symbole de la République française') was and is the Lictor's axe and *fasces* in a *cartouche*. The *fasces* figure prominently on the Arc de Triomphe. The Israeli historian Zev Sternhell considers that there is nothing 'un-French' about Fascism: Fascism, he argues, had its roots in the revolutionary left. It owed as much to Pierre-Joseph Proudhon and Albert Sorel as to Charles Maurras and Maurice Barrès. In 1840, Pierre-Joseph Proudhon (1809-65) wrote *Qu'est-ce que la Propriété?,* answering the question in the first paragraph of his first chapter. His answer was, 'Propriété c'est le vol': 'Property is theft'.

In France Jacques Doriot (1898-1945) joined the newly formed French Communist Party in 1920 and rose quickly through the ranks to become a member of the presidium of the executive committee of the Communist Internationale 1922, to become Secretary of the French Federation of Young Communists in 1923, to be elected member of the Chamber of Deputies for the Seine in 1924, and in 1931 to become Mayor of Saint Denis. After factional differences in 1934, he founded his Parti Populaire Français, a profoundly Fascist party, though, to Doriot and to those who were led by him, the transition seemed a stepless one.

In England a party, eventually called the British Union of Fascists and National Socialists, was formed in 1931 by the former Labour MP for Smethwick, Oswald Mosley (1896-1980). Though it never achieved any discernible success in political or social terms, it at least demonstrated that no nation is completely immune from the seductive attraction of totalitarianism.

The word *Fasci*st, in whatever language, has become a stick with which the Left beats the Right. It has become a term of abuse. The Soviet Union consistently encouraged its citizens and its many 'useful idiots' to employ the term *fascist* as a portmanteau word to denote all the elements of society that were anti-Communist, and, to a large extent, that campaign was successful. To this day, Left-Wing propagandists, in flagrant defiance of idiom, will refer to such *grotesqueries* as 'the Great Anti-Fascist War of 1939 to 1945', conveniently forgetting that, as far as the Soviet Union was concerned, the commencement of warfare was deferred *until June 1941*, when Joseph Stalin's ally, Adolf Hitler, turned on his ally and invaded the Soviet Union.

Inevitably, the inquiring mind asks to know what were the *fundamental principles* of Fascism. It was repressive and totalitarian, but so was and is Marxism in all its manifestations. So also was and is Communism: in government, it has never been anything but autocratic. Fascism was nationalistic, but then so were and are Communist China and Socialist Myanmar.

What were the essential ingredients that defined Fascism and made it recognizably different from the other forms of authoritarian *régime* that flourished between the Wars? The major characteristic that distinguished Fascism from the other inter-War dictatorial régimes was the principle of *the Corporative State.* The concept of *il Stato Corporativo* is enshrined in the Fascist Party's *Carta del Lavoro,* section 7, of 12th April 1927. The Corporative State was frequently described as being divided 'vertically' rather than 'horizontally': in other words, the different industries and trades – and professions, too – that comprise Society were organized by the State into 'Corporations'. Those 'Corporations' comprised all those engaged in each of the different, separate, 'vertical' divisions of Society, (or 'market sectors', as we might nowadays say). Bosses, managers and workers engaged in, say, steel manufacture were grouped together, 'vertically', by the State, rather than, as in other polities, 'horizontally'. The Fascists saw the horizontal divisions in Society as being divisive and disruptive. If bosses formed their *cabals* at one end of the social spectrum and workers formed their anarchic *jacqueries* at the other end – all bosses pulling together one way, all workers pulling together the other way – then, as the Fascists said, the result must inevitably be to divide and disrupt. Other interests would say, of course, that the non-Corporatist approach, with organizations representing only employers or only workers, was more responsive to the dictates of democracy than the Fascist model. The Fascists responded by pointing out that in other *régimes* trades unions existed but were subordinated to the all-powerful State, and, in cases where trades unions were not dominated by the State, they were themselves all-powerful and thus autocratic.

A characteristic peculiar to Italian Fascism was a desire to re-live the Roman Empire. Mussolini's ambitions could be clearly read in one single element of his flamboyant rhetoric – his adoption of the Ancient Roman practice of referring to the Mediterranean as *Mare nostrum* – 'our sea'. The imagery of Fascism abounded with she-wolves suckling baby boys. The letters *SPQR* (Senatus Populusque Romanns) appeared everywhere. His avid promotion of the Italian colonies in North and East Africa and his disastrous war – disastrous in public-relations terms – in Abyssinia were further tokens of his imperialistic aspirations, which were widely shared by the members of his Fascist Party.

In almost every other respect, Fascism was identical with the other totalitarian *régimes* that sprang up in the era immediately following the First World War. The era had specifically Italian resonances. In consequence, the Italians had a special name for the era, *il Dopoguerra.* 'the after-War', but the Italians did not in any way reject the common adulation of Big Brother. In might truly be said that, apart from Corporatism or Corporativism (both terms, and other variants of the root 'corporate', were in use), the only thing that distinguished Italian Fascism from the rest of totalitarianism *dopo guerra* was its musical-comedy element: it was difficult to take Mussolini seriously. As the years roll by, it is increasingly easy to see him as 'one whose name was writ in water'. Agreed, it is utterly impossible to recall without revulsion the tactics of the brutal *squadisti*, with their rubber truncheons and the doses of castor oil they administered to those under interrogation, but, compared with the *millions* killed under the Soviets in the Gulags or allowed to die in the famines arising from collectivization, the evils of Fascism assume their true and relatively minor proportions against the ludicrous background painted by International Socialism, with Fascism at one end of the good-and-evil spectrum and Communism at the other.

There is in truth no possible extenuation of the still-current practice of labelling Nazism as Fascist. The Nazis themselves never adopted the label: on the contrary, they adopted the name *Socialist.* The Nazis had no use for the Corporative State. The Nazis professed to be anti-Communist. The Fascists *were* anti-Communist – they never entered into any sort of pact with the Soviet Union. There are no *facts* that might lead anyone to the conclusion that Nazism was Fascist. The converse is equally and forcibly true. There are no facts that make Fascism Nazi. In fact, credit must be given to the contemporary world: it makes no attempt to label Fascism a Nazi polity. The inference from that must be that the converse must also be true, and, thus, that thinking persons would conscientiously refrain from using Fascism as a synonym for Nazism.

This entry is as long as it is only because the word *Fascist* is *still* quite improperly used as the antithesis of that *failed God* Communism. The word *Fascism* has its own meaning and its own load of guilt: there is absolutely no justification for making it a general-purpose synonym for anti-Communism.

fermata 'A pause of unspecified length; the sign indicating such a pause': *OED*. *Sed quaere*. Eric Blom, in Grove's *Dictionary of Music*, 5th edn (1954), is terse: 'Usually understood to be the current Italian term for a pause on a note or chord, which, however, is not *fermata* but *corona* or, more rarely, *punto coronato*. *Fermata*, frequently used in the wrong sense, means 'pedal point': Vol III, p 64/2. 'Pedal point' is often called *point d'orgue* in English contexts, though in fact there is no distinction intended between the two terms. Unfortunately, German has adopted *Fermate* for 'pause'. See *abbellimenti*, *above*, for further references to the embellishments.

fiasco Literally, 'a flask or bottle'. The word is much used in European languages in a figurative sense of 'to be responsible for or be involved in a notable failure, orginally a theatrical failure (in the production or in individual acting)'. The Italian idiom is *far fiasco*, meaning 'to break a bottle'. A number of theatrical incidents have been postulated as the origin of the expression, but none is convincing.

folio 'A leaf'. A word having many meanings, most of them obsolete or obsolescent. A usage that is still current in the printing trade is to refer to a *leaf of paper* (in a book, for example) as 'a folio'. Each folio has a front face, which appears on the right-hand side of an open book and is hence called 'the recto', or, simply, 'recto', and a reverse side, which is on the left after the leaf is turned. That side of the leaf is called 'the verso'.

forte A musical direction indicate a strong, loud volume in performance. For a use denoting one's strong-point, see the French Lexicon *s.v. forte*.

forte-piano A musical direction indicatingthat the piece or passage should be sung or played midway between softly and loudly. The word *forte-piano* is also the name of an instrument that was the immediate precursor of the pianoforte we know today. The instrument has enjoyed a re-birth of popularity as a result of the emphasis in the Baroque revival on 'authentic' instruments, a trend that has extended to the slightly later music sometimes classed as *le style galant*.

'Galeotto fu il libro e chi lo scrisse' A verse from Dante's 'L' Inferno', *La Divina Commedia*, canto 5, line 137:

Galeotto fu il libro e chi lo scrisse:
Quel giorno più non vi leggemmo avant.

A pander was the book and he who wrote it
That day we did not read any more.

The word *galeotto* originally meant a galley-slave, but, by extension, came to mean someone of little worth and, specifically, as in these verses, a pander, a pimp, a procurer.

Gesù Literally, 'Jesus'. The full name of the first Jesuit Church in the Via deli Astalli, Rome, is *il Santissimo Nome di Gesù*, 'the Most Holy Name of Jesus'.

ghetto In its primary sense, and still the sense in which the word is normally employed, it connotes the quarter in a city, chiefly in Italy, to which the Jews were restricted. The etymology traditionally ascribed to the word seems to have withstood the test of academic scrutiny. The first well documented instance of the employment of the word *getto,* so spelt (which means, simply, 'a jet' or, by extension, 'a foundry'), dates from the foundation of the first ghetto in Venice in 1516, which was on the site of a gun-foundry that, conveniently, had a curtain-wall round it that lent itself to the choice of a place of confinement. Phonologically, the intrusion of the letter *h*, which serves to harden the pronunciation of the letter *g*, is inexplicable. That there had been earlier places for the confinement of Jews is, of course, indisputable, as in Old Jewry, in the city of London, and in Les Juiveries in countless towns in France. It is not easy to see why the name of the Jewish Quarter of Venice should give its name to Jewish Quarters in general. The further development, in more recent times, of applying the word figuratively to any delimited area populated by a definable and under-privileged ethnic or social group is a further proof of the eagerness with which the language seizes on convenient turns of phrase – greatly underscored by the term 'ghetto-blaster'.

gigolo Not a native Italian word but a French one. See *gigolo* in the French Lexicon. The Italian for *gigolo* is *ganzo* or *mantenuto*. The word *mantenuto* means 'a maintained or kept man'. The word *mantenuta* means a mistress. A hoary Italian charade plays punningly on this latter word: the performer merely holds his hand in his belt. The meaning is *mantenuta incinta*, 'a hand held in a belt' or 'a pregnant mistress'.

Gioconda, la The name of a painting by Leonardo da Vinci (1452-1519),also known in English-speaking circles as the *Mona Lisa*, 'Mona' for *Monna*, short for *Madonna*. See *la Joconde* in the French Lexicon.

giovinezza Literally, 'youth'. The title of the anthem of the Italian Fascist Party, and, after 1943, the national anthem of Mussolini's puppet republic of Salò. It has been justly dismissed as *una barcaruola* (q.v.).

glitterati 'A punning name for the celebrities or 'glittering' stars of fashionable society, or of the literary and show-business world': *OED*. The word is calqued on *literati* and *culturati*, *qq.v.* The word gained some prominence in the wake of Frederic Raphael's *The Glittering Prizes* (1976).

gondola A word of unknown origin. 'A light flat-bottomed boat or skiff in use on the Venetian canals, having a cabin amidships and rising to a sharp point at either end; it is usually propelled by one man [*il gondoliere*] at the stern with a single oar': *OED*. See *barcarola, above*. The tonic accent in *gondola* falls on the first syllable.

graffito From *graffiare*, 'to scratch'; sometimes *sgraffiare*. Originally used to denote scratched inscriptions on the walls of ancient buildings, as at Rome and Pompeii, or on [shards of] pottery; later, used to denote a type of decoration of ceramic ware in which a layer of contrasting coloured material is applied to an unfired pot and then has a design 'scratched' through it, so as to expose the underlying tone. More recently denoting, particularly in the plural *graffiti*, images scrawled on the walls of buildings, most frequently with aerosol-propelled paint, and with fibre-pad pens on other surfaces such as vehicle bodies.

grave Pronounced /'graːve/, that is, in two syllables. One of the five grades of musical pace and character, being the slowest. The five grades are *grave, largo, andante, allegro* and *presto.*

grotto A cave or cavern, sometimes artificially created; in particular, one that is picturesque, or that forms an agreeable, cool retreat. It is sometimes wondered at that English speakers should have changed the gender of the word, which in Italian is undoubtedly feminine – though Dante himself has, also, *grotto*. The word is a remarkable instance of the almost infinite adaptability of language to suit mankind's needs. The word derives, ultimately, from the Greek κρύπτη, 'a vault', from the verb κρύπτειν, 'to hide'. Literary Latin took the words in as *crypta*, from which we can discern yet another contemporary English meaning, and Low Latin altered the word somewhat further, to *crupta* and *grupta*, whence Provençal *crota*, Spanish and Portuguese *gruta* and French *crote* or *croute*. The French *croûte, 'a crust',* is from a completely different root. The modern French *grotte* is from the Italian.

Guelfo A member of one of the two great parties in mediaeval Italian politics, characterized chiefly by supporting the popes against the emperors. The word derives from the Germanic *Welf*, the name (and perhaps the war-cry) of a clan that is now identified with the House of Brunswick. The opposing party, which supported the Emperors, originally the Hohenstauffen Emperors, against the Pope were the Ghibellines. During the period immediately before the House of Windsor adopted that name, there was some discussion about whether the name of the Royal Family was Saxe-Coburg Gotha, which was seen by most people as a territorial title, not a name. Many believed that the family name was *Welf*.

gusto Literally, 'taste', in all the senses in which the word 'taste' is used in English. The Italian word itself, *gusto*, is used in modern English only to mean 'with enthusiasm'.

> '[He] seems to have thrown himself with special gusto into the character': Leslie Stephen, *Hours in the Library*, I, ii p 88, edn 1892 (1874)

I lunga 'Long *I*'. The letter *j*. The letter *j* is obsolete in Italian, occurring only historically and in, for example, the name of the princely family, the Doria Pamphilij. (The combination *ph* is also obsolete except historically and in that family's name.)

'Il maestro di color che sanno': 'The master of those who know', Dante's acknowledgment of Aristotle: *La Divina Commedia*, 'Il Paradiso', canto 4, line 131.

Illuminati, gli See *Secolo dei lumi, below.*

'Il più bel fior ne coglie': 'It collects only the finest flowers'. The motto of l' Accademia della Crusca, the Academy established at Florence in 1582, mainly with the object of sifting and purifying the Italian language *(crusca* means 'bran'); whence both its name and its emblem, a sieve. The first edition of its Dictionary, the *Vocabolario degli Accademici della Crusca*, appeared in 1612. The fourth edition, 1729-38, has long been considered as the standard authority for the Italian language. A new edition on more historical lines was begun in 1881.

'Il treno arriva all' orario' 'Voglio partire in perfetto orario ... D'ora innanzi ogni cosa deve camminare alla perfezione': Benito Mussolini (18831945): 'We must leave exactly on time ... From now on, everything must function to perfection'. Said to a station-master: see Giorgio Pini, *Mussolini* (1939), vol 2, ch 6 p 251.

> 'The first benefit of Benito Mussolini's direction in Italy begins to be felt when one crosses the Italian frontier and hears 'Il treno arriva all' orario'': H. R. H. Infanta Eulalia of Spain, *Courts and Countries after the War* (1925) ch 13.

in petto 'In the breast. See Blunt's definition below. The phrase among English-speakers is nowadays virtually restricted to references to the Pope's intention to bestow the Cardinal's

Hat on un-named prelates. He keeps his intention secret, 'within his breast'. Owing, no doubt, to a confusion with the word 'petty', the phrase *in petto* is sometimes misused to convey the notion of 'in miniature'.

> '*In Petto* (Ital.), in design, in the breast or thought, and not yet put in execution': Thomas Blount, *Glossographia, or a dictionary interpreting Such Hard Words ... as are now used,* 4th edn, 1674. 'In small (or, as people now cheerfully and wrongly say, *in petto*)': *Country Life*, 7/4, 29th March 1994.

impresario One who organizes public entertainments; especially the manager of an operatic or concert company. Latterly, the *entrepreneur* who arranges concerts, etc, dealing with artistes' agents, concert-hall proprietors and the media. The term *impresario* was the word for the function in the second half of the 18th century, giving way to the word *entrepreneur* itself at the beginning of the 19th century. In the 20th century the word *impresario* regained its monopoly, owing no doubt to the growing use of the word *entrepreneur* in a wider sense, meaning a thrusting, innovative businessman willing to take risks. The Italian pronunciation of *impresario* has the English *z* sound for the letter *s.* The anglicized pronunciation pronounces the letter *s* as the *s* in 'sound'.

influenza The common malady. The word was adopted into English with a slight alteration in pronunciation. The Italian word means, primarily, 'influence'. Epidemics and pandemics were attributed for many years to the influence of the planets and stars. The word was applied in 1743 specifically to an epidemic (called also *la grippe*) that then raged in Italy, and spread over Europe generally, and for which the Italian word (anglicized in pronunciation) became the English specific name, commonly abbreviated to 'the flu' or, sometimes, 'the 'flu'.

intaglio See *cammeo, above.*

intermezzo 'A short dramatic, musical, or other performance, of a light and pleasing character, introduced between the acts of a drama or opera (or, subsequently, in the latter half of the 18th century, performed independently, and merging in the Opera Buffa)': *OED*. Nowadays, more often a short movement serving as a connecting link between the main divisions of a large musical work, instrumental or vocal; sometimes used for an independent piece of similar character.

'I pensieri stretti ed il viso sciolto'. The context that has given this saying wide currency is "I pensieri stretti ed il viso sciolto" [secret thoughts and an open countenance] will go safely over the whole world'. From Scipione Alberti (?), quoted by Sir Henry Wotton (1568-1639) in a letter of 13th April 1638 to John Milton (1608-74) (advice on how behave at Rome). Milton was an insufferable prig and needed guidance on how to behave. In the event, he behaved with a commendable combination of dignity and courtesy in Rome, though exercising a degree of freedom of speech he was not prepared, in his *Areopagitica*, to concede to those who differed from him in matters of religion. (The compiler has failed to ascertain who exactly this 'Scipione Alberti' was. Any information readers might be able to give about this elusive personage would be much appreciated. If information is sent to me care of the publishers of this book, acknowledgment will be prompt, and recognition will be given in subsequent editions.

> 'At my departure toward Rome … I had won confidence enough to beg his advice [Alberto Scipione's] how I might carry myself securely there without offence of others, or of mine own conscience. '*Signor Arrigo mio*', says he, '*I pensieri stretti ed il viso sciolto* will go safely over the whole world': quoted in the Preface to *Comus*, 1645 edn.

irridentista An irridentist. In Italian politics after 1878, an adherent of the party that advocated the recovery and union to Italy of all Italian-speaking regions occupied by other nations. From the past participle of *redimere*, 'to redeem'.

> 'Capponi … was not an out-and-out Irredentist clamouring for Trieste and Istria, the Canton Ticino, Nice, Corsica, and Malta': *The Edinburgh Review*, p 405 1, April 1887.

Italia farà da sè, l' 'Italy will manage by herself'. A saying expressing Italian self-confidence, much used during the Unification of Italy.

'L' amor che muove il sole e l' altre stelle': 'The love that moves the sun and the other stars': Dante Alighieri (1265-1321), *La Divina Commedia*, 'Il Paradiso', canto 33, line 145.

largo One of the five grades of musical pace and character, being the second to the slowest. The five grades are *grave, largo, andante, allegro* and *presto.* (The *aria* 'Ombra mai fù', from Handel's *Serse* (*Xerxes*), often called 'Handel's *Largo*' is in fact marked *grave.*)

'Lasciate ogni speranza …' The inscription over the gates of Hell in Dante's 'Inferno':

PER ME SI VA NELLA CITTÀ DOLENTE,
PER ME SI VA NELL' ETERNO DOLORE,
PER ME SI VA TRA LA PERDUTA GENTE …
LASCIATE OGNI SPERANZA VOI CH'ENTRATE!

Dante Alighieri (1265-1321), *Divina Commedia*, 'L'Inferno', canto 3, line 1.

Through me to the sorrowful city,
Through me to eternal suffering,
Through me to the lost people …
All hope abandon, ye who enter!

latte, caffè latte 'Coffee made with more or less equal amounts of water and steamed milk': *OED*. A 'skinny *latte*' is a *latte* made with skimmed or semi-skimmed milk.

libera Chiesa in libero Stato 'A free Church in a free State'. The fundamental principle on which Count Cavour (Camillo Benso di Cavour, 1810-1861) wished to pacify the clerical elements in Italian society. In March and April 1861 Cavour made much of the expression 'libera Chiesa in libero Stato', which became a powerful slogan. In a speech to the Parliament in Turin in 1861 he addressed the Pope thus, 'Santo Padre … noi siamo pronti a proclamare nell'Italia questo gran principio: libera Chiesa in libero Stato'. In the same year he proclaimed the Kingdom of Italy under Victor Emmanuel of Savoy and legislated the new Italian Constitution into law. Article 7 of the Constitution precisely guaranteed a free Church in a free State. Cavour died before the proclamation of Rome as the capital of the Kingdom of Italy, which was not in fact achieved without the military occupation and annexation of the rump of the Papal States. The *rapprochement* between the Italian State and the Holy See was not finally accomplished until 1929, in which year the Lateran Treaty was signed.

libretto 'Little book', from *libro*, 'book'. 'The text or 'words' to which an opera or other extended musical composition is set': *OED*. With musical comedies and lighter productions, the word 'book' is preferred.

> 'If the Libretto, as they call it, is not approved, the Opera ... will be condemned': Richardson, *Pamela*, IV, p. 113 (1845). 'The libretto of *Jean de Nivelle* is very beautiful, and ought to have new music written to it': Ruskin, *Arrows of the Chace* [*sic*], *being a Collection of Scattered Letters 1840–80*, II, p 281 (1880).

lingua Franca Literally, 'Frankish tongue'. A mixed language formerly very widely used in the Levant, comprising a vocabulary of largely Italian words but stripped of their inflexions. Thus, the infinitive form of verbs predominates; indeed, it often excludes all other forms. To this *sub-stratum* were added words from all the other languages in use in the Mediterranean, the incidence of national words depending on the portion of the Mediterranean in which the trade was conducted. Thus, there was much use of Spanish, Portuguese and Maghribi Arabic words at the Western end of the Mediterranean, of Levantine Arabic, Turkish, and Persian words at the Eastern end, and a blend of all these national words across the entire extent of the Mediterranean.

Many French and Provençal words were adopted during the Crusades, French being, with Latin, the '*lingua Franca*' of the Crusades and the Latin kingdoms that comprised *Outremer* (*q.v.* in the French Lexicon), hence, of course, the name *lingua Franca*. The use of *lingua Franca* long outlived the hegemony of the Latin Kingdoms and was, in fact, an indispensable ingredient of the highly successful trading history of the Mediterranean until the turn of the 18th century.

It appears anomalous at first sight that there should be so many *Spanish* words in use in *Lingua Franca* at the *Levantine* end of the Mediterranean basin, but that phenomenon is perfectly accounted for by the profound importance in the Levant of Ladino-speaking Sephardic Jewish merchants. For *Ladino*, see the Spanish & Portuguese Lexicon.

Molière's *Le Bourgeois Gentilhomme* has a 'Turkish Ceremony' in which *Lingua Franca* is used to great effect by the actors playing the part of Turks ennobling Monsieur Jourdain.

Since the use of *lingua Franca* lapsed before the advent of recording machines, and since the 'jargon' has not been the subject of much academic research, it might be interesting to the readers of this Lexicon to see in print a little of this tantalizing 'lingo' – the word 'lingo' being in all probability itself an adoption from *lingua Franca*.

> Bon giorno Signor. *Good day, sir.*
> Come ti star? *How are you?*
> Mi star bonu, e ti? *I am well, and you.*
> Mi star contento mirar per ti. *I am happy to see you.*
> Grazia. *Thank you.*
> Mi pudir servir per ti per qualche cosa? *Can I serve you something?*
> Muchu grazia. [*No,*] *thank you very much.*
> Ti dar una cadiera al Signor. *Give a chair to the gentleman.*
> Non bisogna. *It is not necessary.*
> Mi star bene ecus. *I am fine like this.*
> Come star il fratello di ti? *How is your brother?*
> Star muchu bonu. *He is very well.*
> Star in casa? *Is he at home?*
> No, star forà. *No, he is away.*
> E il padre de ti come star? *And how is your father?*
> Non star buona. *He is not well.*

> Cosa tenir? *What is the matter?*
> Tenir febra. *He has a fever.*
> Dispiacer muchu per mi. *That upsets me very much.*
> Molto tempo ti non mirato Signor M? *It is a long time since you saw Mr M?*
> Mi mirato ieri. *I saw him yesterday.*
> Star buona genti. *He is a good person.*
> Quando ti mirar per ellu, salutar mucho per la parte dimi. *When you see him, give him warm greetings from me.*
> Adios, amigo! *Goodbye!, friend!*

The dialogue above is taken from *Un Dictionnaire de la Langue Franque ou Petit Mauresque, suivi de quelques dialogues familiers* (Marseilles, 1830), as given by Alan D. Corré, *A Glossary of Lingua Franca*, 5th edn (2005): *cf*

http://www.uwm.edu/~corre/franca/go.html

literati 'The lettered'. Probably this word ought to be classed as a Latin word, though it certainly appears in Italian usage as the plural of *literato* (now anomalously written *litterato* by virtue of recent orthographic reforms in Italian). In the many instances of 17th- and 18th century English usage, there is some confusion evident as to the actual 'nationality' of this word: the singulars *literatus* and *literato* exist side-by-side. The pronunciation of the word *literati* used by English-speakers today argues fairly strongly in favour of an acknowledgment of its Italian extraction. Though the pronunciation of *literati* in the Classical pronunciation of Latin, /liter'aːti/, is very close to the present-day Italian, the English pronunciation of Latin, which prevailed until largely displaced by the Classical Association's scheme about the last decade of the 19th century, would have established a practice of pronouncing the word /litər'eɪːtaɪ/, which was in fact rarely heard. Nevertheless, Dr Walker (1732-1807) gives only the English-Latin pronunciation /litər'e ɪːtaɪ/ in every edition of his *Critical Pronouncing Dictionary*, from the first, in 1791, to the edition of 1857, edited by Edward Smith. (See also *culturati* and *glitterati, above*.)

'Lo spirito è pronto, ma la carne è debole': 'The spirit is willing but the flesh is weak': Francesco Petrarch, in 'Rapido fiume, che d' alpestra vena': A. Lejeune (ed), *The Concise Dictionary of Foreign Quotations*, 1998. See *Mt* 26:41: *Spiritus quidem promptus est caro autem infirma*; 'The spirit is willing but the flesh is indeed weak'.

locanda A boarding-house.

> 'To make ends meet, she decided to run her house as a locanda (a humble lodging house), taking in paying guests': Obituary of Daphne Phelps, *The Daily Telegraph*, 18th December 2005.

lollo rosso 'A variety of lettuce having pale green leaves with ruffled red edges': *OED*. It has been necessary in this Lexicon to curtail the number of terms and expressions deriving from *la cucina*, for fear their very number might force out every other term and expression. But it is imperative to include a mention of this species of lettuce, which has become widely available in English-speaking countries since about 1950.

The etymology of the name is astounding! It must have perplexed many people that they could not find in their orthodox Italian dictionaries the word *lollo*. The following might allay their perplexity. The name *lollo rossa* (1980 or earlier; also in the form *lollo rosso*) was, it seems, devised uniquely for this species of curly-leafed lettuce. It derives from *La Lollo*, nickname of Gina *Lollobrigida* (born 1927 as Luigina Lollobrigida), Italian film actress, with reference to the distinctive short, tousled hairstyle she wore in the 1950s and 1960s), to which was added *rossa*, feminine of *rosso* red, from classical Latin *russus*, 'red'. The compiler admits that it has so far proved impossible to learn what this species of lettuce was called before the days of Gina Lollobrigida. Better informed readers might be able to supply this deficiency. Perhaps, also, better informed readers might be able to say whether this lettuce has yet acquired a Linnaean name.

macaroni A variety of pasta made in short tubes, slightly or noticeably curved. The word is a curiosity: the Italian word is *maccheroni*. The version of the word used in England, *macaroni*, which has been used consistently since the dish was first offered in England (as recently as the mid 18th century) is in fact an obsolete or at least a regional variant of the standard *maccheroni*, a form that has been in use in Italy since the 15th century. As with *spaghetti*, the word is used in the plural in Italian, but usage in England dictates a singular construction.

The etymology of the word *maccheroni* is one of the most unexpected, comparable to the etymology of the word *canapé* noticed in the French Lexicon, from which we see that that species of 'finger-food' has a name that derives from the Ancient Egyptians' bed with integral, 'fitted' mosquito-net. As to *macaroni, The Oxford English Dictionary Online* in March 2003 published a scholarly draft revision that takes to a completely new and unexpected stage our knowledge of the course this word *macaroni* has taken since its first appearance in, plausibly, the archaic period of Greek history. The probability is that the word was first used as a name for barley broth served either as a religious offering or as a charitable gift to the needy. The word *μακάριος* strikes a dramatically resonant note to those who followed the career of the first President of the Greek Republic of Cyprus, Archbishop Makarios. (Readers are recommended to use the English spelling 'macaroni' in English and not to criticize the printer when they see *maccheroni* on a menu in an Italian restaurant.)

maestoso A direction in music: 'masterly', *i.e.*, to be performed in a masterly fashion.

Maestrale, il A north-westerly wind that blows in the Adriatic, especially in summer. The name applies also to any of several north-westerly winds blowing in other parts of the Mediterranean. See quotation. The name derives from *maestro*, 'the master [wind]' and is cognate with *le mistral*.

> 'The *maestro* (or *maestrale*), although bearing the same name as the mistral of the Rhône valley, is not to be confused with it. The name is given to NW winds in the Adriatic, and NW, N., and NE winds in Liguria and Tuscany. In the west the maestrale is a winter wind (Genoa), but is less cold and dry than the mistral proper. In the Adriatic it is a summer wind': *Italy*, Geographic Handbook Series B.R. 517, Admiralty, Naval Intelligence Division, I, v, p 415.

maestro Literally, 'master'. A title formerly given by public acclaim to someone, especially an Italian, who has mastered some discipline or *métier*. Nowadays, the title is tacitly accorded to one who has achieved eminence in a skill or profession, especially (in recent years) a musician or (nowadays) a conductor – literally, a vocative form of address and admiration.

> 'Il maestro di color che sanno': 'The master of those who know', Dante's acknowledgement of Aristotle: *La Divina Commedia*, 'Il Paradiso', canto 4, line 131. 'Toscanini was

conducting, but I could not afford the cost of a seat to hear the maestro': Edward Heath, *Travels*, I, p 20 (1977).

maestro di capella In Italy, the chief musician of a church or chapel; a choirmaster. Unlike the German word *Kapellmeister* (see the German Lexicon), the Italian word is restricted to a church application.

Mafia or **Maffia** An organized secret society of criminals, thought to have originated in Sicily but now operating internationally, especially in the United States. The etymology of the word is obscure and disputed. See *Camorro, above*, and *'Ndrangheta, below.*

magenta Magenta, the name of a town in Northern Italy near which the French and Sardinians under Napoleon III defeated the Austrians in 1859. The place-name was applied to a dyestuff discovered shortly after the battle and is now applied to the colour itself, which is pink with a minor touch of purple. It is one of the trichromatic colours that, with cyan (blue-green) and yellow, permit full-colour reproduction. Magenta, otherwise 'minus-green', represents a third of the spectrum; cyan ('minus red') and green ('minus magenta') represent the other two thirds.

Magnifico An honorary title enjoyed by the magnates of the Republic of Venice. Nowadays confined, in Italy, to the Rector of an Italian University. The Rector of the University of Malta is also so addressed.

maiolica 'A fine kind of Renaissance Italian earthenware with coloured decoration on an opaque white tin-glaze; (more generally) any tin-glazed earthenware in the same stylistic tradition, especially Hispano-Moresque lustreware. Also: any of various other kinds of glazed and ornamented Italian ware (also called *faience* and *Raffaelle* ware)': *OED*. There appears to be considerable dispute about the adoption of the term *faience* for *maiolica*, and there appears also to be some attempt to distinguish between what is denoted by the spellings *maiolica* and the frequently met with obsolete spelling *majolica*. The words are derived from the mediaeval name for Mallorca, from where the ceramic articles originated.

For a discussion of the complex etymology of the word, see the lengthy note in the *OED On-line*, *s.v. Majolica*, Draft Revision 2001.

'The pieces … which, in the fifteenth century, were curtly termed by the Italians 'Majorca' or 'Majorica', and thence by corruption 'Majolica', a term which ultimately obtained a place in the language, and was applied indiscriminately to all kinds of glazed earthenware': *Catalogue of the Soulages Collection*, p 50. (1856). 'The general term 'Maiolica', also spelt 'Majolica', has long been and is still erroneously applied to all varieties of glazed earthenware of Italian origin. We have seen that it was not so originally, but that the term was restricted to the lustred wares': C D E Fortnum, *Descriptive Catalogue of Majolica*, pxxxv (1873).

malaria Literally, 'bad air'. 'The name given to any of a group of diseases of humans and other vertebrates caused by protozoans of the genus *Plasmodium* (phylum Apicomplexa) transmitted by mosquitoes. They parasitize red blood cells, resulting in haemolysis, periodic fever, and various other symptoms': *OED*. The word *malaria* was originally applied to what was considered to be the unhealthy atmosphere of the marshlands of Italy and other hot countries, which was considered to be, itself, the cause of the signs and symptoms that were so well known to inhabitants and travellers alike.

Malebolge The name given by Dante (*Inferno* XVIII) to the eighth circle of Hell, comprising ten rockbound concentric circular valleys. From *male-*, 'bad' and *bolge*, the plural of *bolgia*, 'a sack or, figuratively, a concave valley'.

malvasia A variety of grape, and the wines (dry and sweet) produced from it, grown widely in Iberia and Italy. From this variety of grape stem the Madeiras (Malmsey, Sercial, Bual) and several Greek wines in addition to the Italian wines of this name. The variety of grape was called, in Byzantine Greek, *Μονεμβασια*, after the town of that name, Monemvasia, and its environs in the Peloponnese. (Monemvasia is spelt Μο*νεμβασία* in Modern Greek; the town is still sometimes known as Napoli di Malvasia, the name given to the rock during its periods of Venetian occupation.)

malocchio The Evil Eye.

mandolino 'Mandolin'. A musical instrument of the lute family typically having a rounded back and from eight to twelve metal strings set in pairs, usually played with a plectrum. The modern mandolin has four courses of paired strings, and is tuned like the violin. The pairing of strings (the placement of a second or 'sympathetic' string behind each played string) gives the mandolin its characteristic and attractive 'buzz', particularly when the instrument is played in its traditional style, with much *vibrato (q.v.)* and arpeggiation. See *rasgado, rasgueado* in the Spanish-Portuguese Lexicon.

maniera The characteristic style of an artist or school of artists, the sum of the characteristics that permits the ready identification of an artist, especially the exaggerated style of a Mannerist artist.

> 'The word *maniera*, from which Mannerism is derived, was used by Vasari ... to describe the schematic quality of much of the work produced, based on intellectual preconceptions rather than direct visual perceptions': P. & L. Murray, *Dictionary of Art & Artists*, p 192 (1959). 'The Maniera of the first Mannerist generation, and its development in high Maniera more so, is a phenomenon that exhibits both the admirable and morbid characteristics of a cultural *fin de race*': S. J. Freedberg, *Painting in Italy*, vii, p 287 (1971). 'What was transferred from painter to painter was a *maniera*, a style, normally understood as a distinctive way of representing figures': *The New York Review of Books*, 18/3, 19th July 1990.

manifesto A public declaration or pronouncement, typically giving details of the author's stance on given issues – by which his stance is 'made manifest'. Much used nowadays to denote the policy statement on which a political party goes to the polls. See Spanish & Portuguese Lexicon *s.v. manifiesto*.

maraschino A strong sweet liqueur distilled from the marasca cherry, a small black Dalmatian cherry, *Prunus cerasus*, variety *marasca***.** The Italian pronunciation is perfectly regular, /marask'iːno/, not /mara'ʃiːno/. Some modern dictionaries anomalously give the second pronunciation, bowing to the will of users who believe their conception of spelling and pronunciation is the supreme legislator. Some dictionaries have treated the Spanish word *machismo* in much the same way, treating is though it were an Italian word. See *machismo* in the Spanish & Portuguese Lexicon.

marina A recent import, *via* the US. A dock, harbour, or basin in which yachts and other small craft are moored, usually a complex specially designed for the purpose, with facilities for connection to an electricity supply, a water supply and a means of disposing of sewage; occasionally, a leisure complex centred on such a mooring area.

marrano See *Marano* in the Spanish & Portuguese Lexicon.

martello Shortened from Martello Tower. A small circular fort with thick stone walls, especially any of those erected in the British Isles as a coastal defence during the Napoleonic Wars. For an exhaustive review of the disputed etymology of this term, see the *OED On-line* Draft Revision for December 2000.

mascara A cosmetic preparation for darkening, lengthening, and thickening the eyelashes and, sometimes, to emphasizing the eyebrows, usually applied with a small brush. The etymology of this word would indicate a spelling *maschera,* from the Italian root for 'to mask', but the unetymological English spelling *mascara* has taken possession of the word and has been imported into the Romance languages that could otherwise have been expected to import a form such as *maschera*. In the spelling *mascara*, the accent is nowadays always on the second syllable. For a note on an alternative etymology for the word *mascara*, see the Spanish & Portuguese Lexicon, *s.v. mascara*.

mascarpone In defiance of the policy in this Lexicon to exclude terms to do with gastronomy, because of their great number, this word must be included, since there is no native English alternative. The word denotes a very mild cow's milk cheese with a soft, creamy consistency, originating from the Lombardy region of Italy. It is often served with fruit and other desserts.

medico 'A physician, a 'medical man''. Used in English parlance with a slightly jocose substratum of meaning, sometimes suggesting a resistance on the part of the public to according the title 'doctor' to those who are in the main merely *bachelors* of medicine.

melodrama From the Greek *μέλος* 'music' and *δρᾶμα* 'deed, action, a play, especially a tragedy'. The word has been through many transitions before arriving at the only surviving contemporary (and hardly commendatory) use, 'A dramatic piece characterized by exaggerated characters and a sensational plot intended to appeal to the emotions'.

merenda A light meal or snack. Sometimes used for 'lunch'; sometimes for 'afternoon tea' – and even (see quotation) for a mid-morning snack.

> 'Do as the Romans do and get a slab of hot pizza *bianca* (without tomato sauce) fresh out of the oven for your *merenda* (midmorning snack)': *Food & Wine*, 102/1, October 1994.

messa di voce A swelling of the voice during the singing of a single note; a *crescendo* (*q.v.*) followed by a *diminuendo* (*q.v.*) in a sustained note. Used also with reference to a similar instrumental technique.

> '*Messa di voce*, an expression applied by the Italians to a swell of the voice upon a holding note': T. Busby, *A Complete Dictionary of Music, s.v.* 'Messa di voce' (1786). 'A messa di voce, a swelling and diminishing of volume within a single note, produced by a finger flattement on the nearest open hole': N. Toff, *A Flute Book*, p 109 (1985).

messer An obsolete courteous form of address and reference, as in *Messer Philippo Minutulo*. Derived from Old French *mes sire*, the subjective case singular of which the objective case singular is *mon sire*. Our business word 'Messrs' is not derived from the old Italian *messer*, but ultimately and fairly remotely from the same root, *mes sire*.

mesto A musical direction indicating performance in a sad or mournful fashion.

> '*Mesto*, 'sadly'; a term used three times by Beethoven, in the pianoforte sonatas, op. 10, no. 3, and op. 59, and in the slow movement of Quartet op. 18, no. 7. The slow movement of the first of these is called Largo e mesto, and of the second and third Adagio molto e mesto. It is also used by Chopin in the Mazurkas, op. 33, nos. 1 and 4': G. Grove, *Dictionary of Music*, II, 315/2 (1880).

mezzaluna 'Half moon'. A word that enjoys a typically felicitous *OED* definition: 'A crescent-shaped cutting utensil comprising a semi-circular blade with a handle on top or at either end, used with a rocking motion for chopping ingredients. The utensil is frequently used with a chopping board having a concave surface'. To be distinguished from the Spanish *media luna*: see the Spanish & Portuguese Lexicon.

mezzanine See *mezzanine* in the French Lexicon.

mezzo Literally, 'half'. This particle occurs frequently in words we have borrowed from Italian. Examples are *mezzo-soprano, mezzanine,* and *mezzalune* (*qq.v.*). The pronuciation is one of the very few Italian pronunciations that seem difficult to English-speakers. In fact, the issue resolves itself into nothing more than a minor feat of memory. There are in Italian two sounds that reproduce the spelling *-zz*. Most words having in them *-zz* are pronounced /ts/: for example, *pizza* and *pizzicato*. The second is /ʤ/: in English, as in the *-ds* in 'heads you win'. The moral is to listen attentively and remember assiduously.

mezzogiorno This word presents the same latent problems as the French word *midi*. It can mean either 'midday' or the part of the Italian peninsula corresponding roughly to Abruzzi, Molise, Campania, Puglia, Basilicata, and Calabria, and the islands of Sicily and Sardinia – that is, no doubt, those parts of Italy where the sun shines more brightly and fiercely at mid-day than in other parts of the country at mid-day.

mezzo-rilievo Relief carvings in which the figures project to half their true depth from the surface. *Cf basso-rilievo, above.*

mezzo-soprano Originally, the name for a vocal register between the treble (soprano) and the alto (contralto). Nowadays, the female voice having a register mid-way between the soprano and the alto (or contralto), and the name of those who sing in that register. Much of the repertoire that has been conventionally given to mezzo-contraltos is now, owing to the Baroque Revival, restored to the male alto (and, though more rarely, to the male treble). The countertenor register, a *falsetto* (*q.v.*) register, approximates to the mezzo-soprano. There is also a register much favoured by the French, called *haut-contre*, a high tenor *not* falsetto, that occupies the conventional mezzo-soprano register.

> '*Haut*, high or shrill … *Haut Contre* (in Musick Books) signifies Counter Tenor. *Haut Dessus*, first Treble' N. Bailey, *Dictionary* (1731). '*Mezzo*, signifies half, and is often found in

composition with some other word; as, mezzo *soprano*, is the haut centre [read, *contre*], or high tenor, which has the cleff C *sol ut* on the second line': J. Grassineau, *De Brossard's Musical Dictionary* s.v. *mezzo* (1740). '*Mezzo Soprano*, in the Italian music, is the high tenor, which has the cleff C on the second line': E. Chambers, *Cyclopaedia* Supplement (1753). 'He took particular delight in the beautiful mezzo-soprano of his daughter, Magda, inherited from her mother': Y. W. Vance, *Anton Dvorak*, tr P. Stefan, iv, p 275 (1941).

millefiori 'Thousand flowers'. 'A kind of ornamental glass in which a number of glass rods of different sizes and colours are fused together and cut into sections which form various patterns or figures, usually embedded in colourless transparent glass to make paperweights, etc': *OED*.

mille miglia 'Thousand miles'. A sports-car racing event comprising a race over public roads run from 1927 to 1941, originally from Breccia to Rome, but over different routes from time to time. It was revived from 1946 to 1957 but was limited to cars made during the years of the orginal series. Sometimes used figuratively.

> 'The event was revived a dozen years ago as the Historic Mille Miglia, a sort of extended time trial run on roads still open to the public, with entries limited to cars made during the years the race was run': *The Times* (Car 95 Supplement.1/2 27th May 1995.

minestrone Any of various *thick* vegetable soups containing pasta or rice, made throughout Italy, and elsewhere. In Italy, the variety of vegetables used varies from region to region. In England minestrone tends to be thin, not thick, and to contain small strands of spaghetti.

> 'There are ... dozens of versions of Minestrone, which is a really solid soup thick with vegetables and cheese and rice or pasta and intended, with bread and wine, to constitute the entire midday meal of hungry working people. *The Sunday Times*, 21/6 29th March 1959.

mondo cane Literally, 'dog world'. The use of the expression by English-speakers dates from the release in 1962 of a documentary film *Mondo Cane* (in England, 'A Dog's Life') jointly directed by several hands and with Rossano Brazzi as himself on which many bizarre aspects of life are depicted. The film led to a short-lived spate of copycat motion pictures, sometimes referred to as 'shockumentaries'.

monsignore Adapted from the French *monseigneur*, 'my lord'. 'An honorific title of, or form of address to, a Roman Catholic of ecclesiastical rank, as a prelate, archbishop, etc., indicating a distinction bestowed by the Pope, sometimes in conjunction with an office': *OED*. When the title precedes a surname, it is usually spelt *Monsignor*. Abbreviated to *Mgr* or, sometimes, *Msgr*.

monte di pietà Literally, 'mount (otherwise *fund*) of money'. A charitable pawn-shop established in, for example, Perugia in 1462 in order to provide loans on small security and at very low rates of interest. The institutions spread rapidly and are still to be found in Italy today, either managed by the Church or by the State.

> 'The *Monte di Pietà* was established first at Florence, in the year 1496, to restrain the usury of the Jews': P. Beckford, *Familiar Letters from Italy*, I, xxiv 231 (1805).

Montessori Denoting or relating to the child-centred educational system devised by Maria Montessori (1870-1972), that emphasizes the individual development of young children through free but guided play with apparatus designed to encourage curiosity and sense perception. In a wider, more general sense, denoting any non-traditional teaching method, system, etc., that seeks to develop natural interests and abilities in young children, especially through experiential learning.

> 'What is the fundamental principle of the Montessori system? It is the development of the child's individuality, unrestricted by the traditional nursery discipline': E. Wharton, *French Ways*, VI, I, p101 (1919).

morbidezza A quality in painting in which the flesh-tones of subjects are delicately depicted. This is a word with an extremely problematical derivation. The ultimate root has to do with death and disease. Compare our word 'morbid' as used by the medical profession, and 'morbid' as used to mean an excessive interest in death, disease and other disturbing subjects. The earlier imprecision in the use of the terms can be gauged from the *OED*'s listing of usages: 'Italian *morbidezza:* softness, delicacy, nonchalant grace, (of women and children) delicacy of complexion (14th cent.), softness of tonality or harmony of light and shade in a painting, harmony of proportions in a statue or relief (16th cent.) From *morbido* MORBID *a.* + -*ezza* -ESS… Cf. Middle French *morbidezza* nonchalant grace (1588), French *morbidezza*, used of works of art (1666), French *morbidesse* softness, delicacy (1801)'. The probability is that the word arrived at its present stage of development because paleness (but not pallor) is seen as attractive – 'alone and palely loitering': Keats, *La Belle Dame sans Merci*. Writers are inclined to see characters as 'interestingly pale': they do not see them as 'interestingly rubicund'.

morendo 'Dying', the present participle and gerund of *morire*, 'to die'. A musical direction signifying that the sound should gradually die away; in English language usage, an adjective describing a style characterized by use of that effect. *Cf abbellimenti, above.*

> 'These numerous recordings … serve to display his … command of many now forgotten vocal graces such as the morendo or diminuendo, accacciatura [*sic*], messa di voce, fermata and gruppetto': *The Guardian*, II, 9/4 3rd January 1994.

morisco See *morisco* in the Spanish & Portuguese Lexicon.

mosso 'Moved'. The past participle of *muovere*. As an indication of *tempo* (*q.v.*) in music: animated, fast. Usually modified (*e.g., più mosso* or *meno mosso*).

moto perpetuo 'A rapidly and constantly moving instrumental composition consisting mainly of notes of equal and very short length in an unbroken sequence': *OED*. This expression is not strictly a term of art in music; it is really a shorthand way of defining pieces conforming to the definition just given. The term has been explicitly adopted by individual composers as the name of specific pieces (e.g., Paganini's *Opus 11*, Saint-Säens's *Opus 135 No. 3*, MacDowell's *Opus 46, No. 2*) and might properly be used to classify such pieces as N. A. Rimsky-Korsakov's *Flight of the Bumble Bee* and the *Hora Staccato* by Grigoras Dinicu.

motto A word with an extremely complex etymology. In its simplest use among English-speakers, it means one of the current Italian acceptations, 'a pithy expression of a state of mind' – of aspiration, or resolution, or dedication – that is perhaps most simply summed up by reference to the Scouts' motto, 'Be Prepared!'. The Italian is normally *motto*, but with a variant *mutto*. Both Italian words mean, depending on context, 'a short sententious phrase' (*a*1294); 'a clever, witty saying' (*a*1321); and 'a poetic composition' (14th century)'. A link with contemporary English can be found in both the root in post-classical Latin, *muttum* 'an uttered sound' (which has resonances in Germanic roots) and, in an anomalous opposition, the English word 'mute'. There are two other uses worth noting. The first is the use of the word to mean a air or snatch of melody occurring throughout a larger work: (*cf Leitmotiv* in the German Lexicon) and a short printed verse or a printed joke, riddle, etc, found inside a cracker (Christmas-party favor) or wrapped round a sweet (a candy).

muta The imperative of *mutare*, 'to change'.A direction on a musical score indicating that a performer (a horn-player and a trombonist, for example) needs to change the tuning of his instrument so as to permit him to play in a different key.

'Natura il face, e poi roppe la stampa': 'Nature made him and then broke the mould': Ludovico Arioso (1474-1533): *Orlando Furioso* (1532) canto 10, stanza 84.

'Ndrangheta A Mafia-type organization active in Calabria. The anomalous apostrophe at the beginning of the word is said to sound like a grunt. The derivation of the word is obscure: some scholars derive the word from a Calabrian-dialect word for a fool (or, alternatively, a thief); other derive it from Greek. In Antiquity, Greek influence in Calabria was strong, enduring for centuries. There survives into Modern Greek the word *ἀνδραθία*, 'courage, manly virtue, integrity'. When one considers the possible derivation of *omertà* (*q.v.*) and, indeed, the general cult of *machismo* in Southern-European society, one tends to favour this derivation. For *machismo*, see the Spanish & Portuguese Lexicon.

'Nel mezzo del cammin di nostra vita' The opening verse of Dante's *Divina Commedia*: 'L'Inferno', canto 1, line 1: 'In the midst of the path of our life'.

' ... non lo conoco' 'Qui giace l'Aretin poeta tosco, che disse mal d' ognun fuor che di Dio, scusandosi col dir non lo conoco': 'Here lies the Tuscan poet Aretino, who slandered everyone except God, excusing himself by saying he did not know God'. The epitaph of Pietro Aretino (1492-1556), reputedly written by Paolo Giovi (1483-1552).

novella Originally: a short fictitious narrative. Now (usually): a short novel, a long short story.

> 'The brief Novella has ever been a prodigious favorite with the nation [Italy] since the days of Boccaccio': *North American Review*, 25, p 186 (1827). 'H. E. Bates has made the *novella*, which is more generally referred to as the 'long-short story', a form of fiction which is very much his own': *John o' London' Weekly*, p 350/1 17th December.

The *OED* includes among the quotations under *novella* the following:

> 'If the commentator had studied the whole Novella, and compared it with other passages, even his moderate knowledge of the Civil Law would have enabled him to see the true meaning of the passage he quotes': *North American Review*, 36 401 1 (1833).

However, from the mention of the Civil Law – that is, Roman Law – the 1833 quotation evidently refers not to the work of fiction 'the novel' but to the Latin word *novella*, the informal name for any of the *Leges Novellae*, 'new [*i.e.*, supplementary] laws', enacted by Justinian after the publication of his (second) Code, the *Codex Repetitae Praelectionis* in AD 534.

numero uno 'Number One'. The best or most important example of a person or thing (1884 or earlier in this sense). Also, 'Number One', as in 'Look after Numero Uno,' – oneself.

nuncio 'A messenger', now spelt *nunzio* in Italian. A papal ambassador to a foreign court or government. The Italian pronunciation is /'nunːtzio/. The spelling *nuncio* represents an alternative older Italian spelling: *cf.* French *nonce*. The anglicized word 'nuncio' was formerly pronounced /nʌnʃɪəʊ/ but is now pronounced /nʌnsɪəʊ/.

obbligato A portion of a piece of music that, though subordinate to the work as a whole, is nevertheless an essential or *obligatory* part of the work and is not to be omitted. Often an obbligato takes the form of a prominent, virtuosic instrumental part. Loosely, a solo passage performed as part of the entire work.

oboe da caccia 'Oboe of the chase', *i.e.*, 'hunting oboe'. A curved, tenor oboe, a fifth lower in pitch than the ordinary instrument, in use from about 1720 to 1760, and, until the Baroque Revival, superseded by the *corno inglese,* the *cor anglais* (*q.v.* in the French Lexicon).

oboe d'amore A mezzo-soprano oboe with a pear-shaped bell and a pitch a minor third below that of the ordinary oboe. It produces a soft and sweet tone. Though the term is translated as 'oboe of love', it seems more likely that it should be termed and translated *oboe moresco*, 'Moorish oboe'.

ocarina 'A small keyless wind instrument in the form of a hollow egg-shaped (usually terracotta) body with finger-holes and a simple mouthpiece': *OED*.

> 'A musical wind instrument ... preferably formed of clay, and then baked or burnt; it is to be called the "Ocarina"': T. Zach, British Patent 1020 (1877).

omertà The name for the Mafia (*q.v.*) code of honour. The word probably derives from the Sicilian *omu* (from Latin *homo*, 'man') and can best be understood as implying that two of the most significant characteristics of the Mafia *régime,* respect for one's chiefs and silence when being questioned by the authorities, are of the essence of 'manliness'. *Cf Camorra* and *'Ndrangheta, above*.

opera In Latin the word *opera* is the nominative, vocative and accusative plural of *ŏpus*, 'activity, effort, labour, work'. During the Renaissance period the word *opera* acquired, in Italian, the singular number and in that form has passed into other languages to mean a dramatic musical work in which singing with orchestral accompaniment forms an essential part. The singing consists chiefly of recitatives, arias, and choruses. Two anglicized pronunciations are heard today: /'ɒpərə/, a trisyllable, and /ɒprə/, a disyllable. A pronunciation akin to the Italian pronunciation is sometimes heard on the lips of conscientious speakers: /'oːpera/.

opera buffa and **opera seria** *Opera buffa*: comic opera, with dialogue in recitative and characters drawn from everyday life. *Opera seria*: Serious or tragic opera; specifically, a type of opera with elaborate arias, prevalent in the 18th century and usually based on a classical or mythological subject.

> 'A week after our arrive at Sienna, was an Opera represented ... with severall changes of Scenes ... and other Machines, at which the Italians are spoke to be excellent': J. Raymond, *Itinerary of a Voyage to Italy*, p 174 (1648) .'*Opera*; the Signification of this Word is so well known that it needs no Explanation: I shall only observe, That it properly signifies Work, and is thus often used. *Opera Prima*, First Work [etc.].': – , *A Short Explication of such Foreign Words as are made use of in Musick Books* (1724).

operetta A short (originally one-act) opera, usually on a light or humorous theme. Now, also, the genre of music that is characteristic of such works. Instances of the genre are *The Student Prince* (1924) by Sigmund Romberg (1887-1951), and *Im weißen Rößl* (stageplay1897, musical 1930; English title, *The White Horse Inn*), the music for which was produced by a team of composers.

> '*Operetta*, a coinage which was first introduced at the Lyceum, or English Opera House': *Once a Week*, 12, p 235, 1865.

oratorio A large-scale, usually narrative, musical work for orchestra and voices, typically on a sacred theme and performed with little or no costume, scenery, or action. Among English-speaking people, Handel's *Messiah* is the most outstanding oratorio. The term *oratorio* is derived from the name of the principal church of the order of priests founded by St Philip Neri, the Congregation of the Oratory, recognized by Pope Gregory XIII in 1575. Gregory gave the congregation the church of Santa Maria in Vallicella; they rebuilt the old church in 1577 and in that year transferred themselves to the new building in the Baroque style, the *Oratorio* or *Chiesa Nuova.* The church lent itself particularly well to the musical services the Oratorians celebrated, which tended to resemble theatrical performances but with sacred subjects and devoid of scenery, effects, and so on. This style of representation spread rapidly through Europe. Two other pre-eminent oratorios are Bach's *Christmas Oratorio* and Haydn's *Die Schöpfung* ('The Creation').

orchestra Originally, a large semicircular area in front of the stage in ancient Greek and Roman theatres. In Greek theatres the chorus danced and sang in the orchestra; in the Roman theatre, the area was reserved for the seats of senators and other notables. In more recent times, the word *orchestra* denotes the part of a theatre, opera house, or other public building where the musicians perform (often called 'the orchestra pit' or 'the pit', though 'the pit' also means the part of the lowest level of the theatre behind the stalls). The seats in the front section of the stalls in an English theatre are called 'the orchestra stalls'; in the US, simply 'the orchestra', a practice once common in England. The predominant meaning of *orchestra* is nowadays 'a group of instrumentalists performing concert music, especially one combining string, woodwind, brass and percussion sections. Now also more generally: a (usually large) group of musicians of any kind': *OED*.

ossobuco Formerly two separate words. A veal stew made from shin steak, vegetables, wine and, critically, a marrowbone. The word is included in this Lexicon though so many other Italian culinary terms have been omitted because there is some misapprehension about the meaning of the second half of the word. *Osso* plainly means 'bone'. However, the second part, *buco* sometimes give rise to confusion, particularly to those with some knowledge of Latin. There is a Latin word *bucca* (or *bŭca*) meaning 'the mouth' (and also 'the cheek'), and also a word *bucco*, meaning 'a babbler, a 'mouthy' person'. These words have given rise to the Italian words *bocca*, meaning 'the mouth' (sometimes called in English medical parlance 'the buccal cavity'), and also to *buco* (more rarely, *buca*), meaning, broadly, 'a hole'. Though the mouth itself is 'the cavity' that links all three Italian words, the *buco* in *ossobuco* it is not in fact 'the mouth', as, for example, in the French idiom *une bonne bouche* . The hole is in fact the hole or hollow in the bone, the hollow that contains *il midolo* ('the marrow') that gives the dish its particular appeal.

osteria A hostelry; an inn; an establishment generally and ostensibly offering accommodation. Nowadays, sometimes a restaurant. *Cf albergo, above*, and *trattoria, below*.

ostinato Of a melodic or rhythmical figure or phrase: continuously repeated. So called because the repeated item 'obstinately' remains.

ottava rima 'Eighth rhyme' or 'octave verse'. The stanza devised by Boccaccio and adopted by Tasso and Ariosto, so that it became the normal Italian heroic metre. The eight-line rhyming scheme is *abababcc*. The metre was used by Byron for *Don Juan*. See *terza rima, below.*

padre 'Father'. In English-language usage, a name for and form of address to a priest or clergyman of any denomination, in particular in military circles. In the US the usage stems from close proximity to Spanish-speaking neighbours. In England the word was greatly influenced by the Italian word, but in trade and exploration the identical word in Spanish and Portuguese reinforced the usage of the word in reference to Catholic priests. With the appointment of Catholic chaplains to the British Army, the usage spread to all chaplains.

paesano Literally, 'a countryman', and, by extension, 'a fellow-countryman'. In the US, a fellow Italian-American, sometimes implying a *mafioso*. See *paisano* in the Spanish and Portuguese Lexicon.

palio Any of various traditional horse races held in particular Italian towns; especially one held every July and August in the city of Siena.The word *palio* is also the name of the cloth or banner of velvet, silk, etc., awarded to the winner of such a race.

> 'Over the weekend the historic Tuscan town was enlivened with ... the Palio horse race in Renaissance costumes': *The Times*, 19/1, 18th September 1972. 'For many, Siena is known for the Palio, a twice-yearly horse race in the main piazza, in which riders compete for a prestigious banner honouring the Virgin': *Building Design*, 24/1, 18th February 2000.

paliotto A painting on the frontal of an altarpiece.

pandora A musical instrument similar to a lute, with metal strings set in pairs and a scalloped body.

papabile 'Pope-worthy'; a prelate likely or worthy to be elected Pope. Loosely, persons electable in any sense.

paparazzo 'A freelance photographer who pursues celebrities to take photographs of them, usually for sale to popular newspapers and magazines. Chiefly in *pl.*': *OED*. This word owes its immense popularity to its appearance as the surname of a society photographer in Federico Fellini's film *La Dolce Vita* (1960 (*q.v., above*). The elaborate conjectures about how the name came to be chosen are neatly summarized in the *OED* revision of March 2005.

parlando A musical direction indicating that the singer should perform the marked item in a speaking rather than a singing manner. Sometimes the word *parlante* is used. Before the turn of the 18th century, *parlando* and *parlante* often meant 'in a striking, declamatory, 'speech-making' style'. Also used, perhaps unfairly, of the wooden manner in which singers not versed in speech-diction read out the content of letters in opera. See *cantabile, above.*

> 'Sometimes the singer will begin a song in a speaking tone, and after a few words glide into song. Often a parlando verse will be contrasted with a cantabile refrain': Van der Merwe, *Origins of the Popular Style,* xvii, p 146.

parroco A parish priest.

partita A suite of several movements. Also: (in baroque music) a set of variations.

> 'He [*sc.* Bach] also wrote three Partitas (in the Suite-form) for the lute. The name has very seldom been used since Bach ... But in the modern rage for revivals it may possibly reappear': G, Grove, *Dictionary of Music*, II, p 656/1 (1880). 'Bach clearly distinguishes the forms in his six sonatas for violin alone by calling those in church style 'sonatas' and those in chamber style 'partitas'': I. Spink, *A Historic Approach to Musical Form*, iii, 67 1 (1967).

passacaglia A slow musical composition written in triple time, usually consisting of continuous variations over a ground bass. There existed an early Spanish dance called *una pasacalle* that was danced in the street, *pasa calle.* It is conjectured that *passacaglia* derives from this Spanish word. The word *passacaglia* is now extremely familiar, thanks to the Baroque revival, and is thus pronounced well among English-speakers – in other words, the combination *-gli* is given its correct liquescent value, *not* the sound of *g* in 'drag'. Nevertheless, cosmopolitan diners-out who patronize Quaglino's Restaurant, in London, persistently pronounce the name of that restaurant with that sound in it, the sound of *-ag* as in 'drag'. The correct pronunciation of the name is /kwa'ʎiːno/, with the permissible z-sound as a mark of the English possessive case, /kwa'ʎiːnoz/.

pasticcio Pronounced /pas'tiːtʃio/. By origin, *pasticcio* is a dish containing a mixture of pasta and meat. By extension, it is widely used to mean a novel, poem, painting, piece of music, etc, incorporating several different styles or characteristic mannerisms; sometimes, an item, particularly a piece of music, made up of parts, often re-orchestrated, drawn from a variety of sources. In music, sometimes applied to a medley of elements intended to resemble the style of a given composer. The French *pastiche* is also used in this sense. Both words, *pastiche* and *pasticcio,* are nowadays used in a dismissive sense. See also *pot pourri.*)

pastorale An instrumental or vocal composition, generally in a six-in-a-measure or twelve-in-a-measure time, intended to evoke scenes of (Italian) shepherds' playing on their bagpipes. A notable characteristic of the *pastorale* is the presence of bass notes emulating the drone of the shepherds' pipes.

> '*Pastorale*, is an Air composed after a very sweet, easy, gentle Manner, in

Imitation of those Airs which Shepherds are supposed to play': –, *A Short Explication of such Foreign Words as are made use of in Musick Books* (1724). 'In Christmas time, all quarters of Naples resound with *Pastorali* or *Siciliane*, a kind of simple rural music, executed by … shepherds, upon a species of bagpipes': *Char.* in *Annual Register*, p 11/2 1782. 'The theme of the Pastorale in Handel's 'Messiah' has been derived from the Pifferari, Italian peasants': G. Engel, *Introduction to the Study of National Music*, I, p 9 (1866).

patina A thin coating or layer on the surface of metal or stone, usually as a result of an extended period of weathering or burial; a green or bluish-green film of corrosion produced naturally or artificially by oxidation on the surface of bronze and copper, consisting mainly of basic copper sulphate. Compare 'verdigris'. Also generally applied to the natural sheen acquired by old furniture and, to some extent, old paintings.

peccadillo A little sin; a trivial, excusable fault.

pellagra A vitamin-deficiency condition characterized by dermatitis, diarrhoea and mental disturbance, and often linked to and attributed to an over-dependence on maize in the diet. Once common in Northern Italy.

Penseroso, Il 'The thinker'. The word has been accommodated into English largely as a result of Milton's having chosen this expression as the title of one of his poems. In the sense that Milton, the Latin Secretary to the Commonwealth, uses the term, it ought probably to be translated as 'the pensive one', 'the thoughtful one','the gloomy one', not 'the thinker'. That a Puritan element creeps into Milton's use of the word is strongly corroborated by his choice of title for the opposite side of his poem, *L'Allegro*.

pensiero Literally, 'a thought'. In fine-art circles, a sketch, *esquisse*, rough design. *Cf bozzetto* and *modello, above.*

'Most of the drawings are *pensieri': The Times, p* 5/6, 2nd October 1959. 'Each artist was supplied with a design, or *pensiero*, which laid down the pose, proportions and drapery pattern of the statue': *The Times Literary Supplement*, p 378/4, 4th April 1975.

pensione A lodging-house; a small hotel.

pentimento Physical evidence of over-painting in oil-painting, indicating a change of mind of the painter. Nowadays. most evidence of *pentimenti* derives from advanced photographic techniques such as employ below-red energy, but earlier evidence was revealed by destructively peeling away the later layers of paint. The word is cognate with our word 'repentance', though the Italian word is much closer in true signification to our 'second thoughts'.

pentito One who has repented. 'Originally and chiefly in Italy: a person formerly involved in criminal activity (esp. as a member of the Mafia) who collaborates with law-enforcement authorities in return for a lenient sentence or immunity from prosecution; an informer': *OED*. The word in the plural, *i pentiti*, has gained considerable currency as the generic name for prosecution witnesses in Mafia-related trials in Italy and the US.

piano 'Soft'. The instrument we know as the 'piano' or 'pianoforte' was in a slightly earlier manifestation called the 'fortepiano', *forte* being Italian for 'strong' or 'loud' and 'piano' meaning, for this purpose, 'softly' or 'quietly'.

The chief characteristic that differentiated these instruments from the harpsichord and the other comparable older keyboard instruments, and also that gave the newer instruments their names, was that, in simple terms and within reason, the harder the executant hit the keys, the louder would be the sound produced, and *vice versa*. With the earlier keyboard instruments, the mechanism that connected the keys with the strings nullified the effect of varying impacts on the keys. With the harpsichord (Italian, *il cembalo*) and its congeners (*e.g.*, the spinet, the virginals, etc), the effective mechanism is plucking, and, with the clavichord, percussion, but the percussion in that case is limited to the invariable force related to the weight of the tangents falling on the strings, which is the means of making sound with the clavichord. It owes nothing directly to the force applied to the keys themselves.

A expedient in the design of some of the last production harpsichords in the eighteenth century was similar to the swell mechanism of the organ. In one configuration, a screen similar to a Venetian blind was built above the strings that could be opened and shut by pedal to increase or decrease the sound emitted.

With the advent of the fortepiano and the pianoforte there was another innovation that profoundly affected keyboard music and that was the introduction of pedals to control *volume*. This innovation meant that the performer could achieve additional levels of sound by the use of two pedals. With neither pedal applied, the strings are inherently partly 'damped' (they are under slightly pressure from pads at all times when neither pedal is depressed). With one pedal, the loud or sustaining pedal, applied, the inherent partial damping of the instrument is suspended and the volume is resultantly increased. When the other pedal, the soft pedal, is applied, an increased pressure is exerted on the strings, further reducing the inherent, already partly damped, volume of their output. The degrees of 'expression' that the executant can thus achieve by virtue of the characteristics of the fortepiano and the pianoforte transformed the performance of music and led to a widespread increase in the use of dynamics markings on music scores – the familiar *forte, fortissimo, piano, pianissimo*, and so on. For the meanings of such exotic indications of expression as *sforzando* and *sforzato*, the reader should consult a musical dictionary.

pietà 'Piety'. A representation, in painting or sculpture, of the Virgin Mary holding the dead body of Christ on her lap.

più 'More'. Much used in musical directions: for example, *più piano*, 'more quietly'.

pizza Literally, 'a pie'. A savoury dish of Italian origin, consisting of a base of dough, spread with a selection of such ingredients as olives, tomatoes, cheese, anchovies, etc., and baked in a very hot oven; dough so prepared and baked.

> 'In its most primitive form *pizza* is a round of yeast dough spread with tomatoes and mozzarella cheese and baked in a hot oven. The most famous of the many *pizze* is the Neapolitan pizza … The Roman pizza … has plenty of onions but no tomatoes; the Ligurian *pizza* has onions, black olives and anchovies': Simon & How, *Dictionary of Gastronomy*, 303/1 (1970).

pizzicato Said of a note or passage played on a violin or other stringed instrument by plucking the string with the finger instead of using the bow. The direction indicating a return to bowing is *arco*, 'the bow', or *col arco*, 'with the bow'.

presto 'Quick, in quick time'. One of the five grades of musical pace and character, being the fastest. The five grades are *grave, largo, andante, allegro* and *presto.*

prima donna The first or principal female singer in an opera. Also *prima donna assoluta,* meaning, literally, 'an absolute *prima donna*', a prima donna of outstanding excellence. *Cf diva, above.*

> 'The term *Prima Donna Assoluta* ('absolute first lady') is sometimes used to make perfectly clear the position of the *very* most important woman member of an opera company': *The Oxford Companion to Music, p* 749/2 (1938). '[title] *Callas: Prima Donna Assoluta*, S. Galatopoulos (1976).

putto In fine art, a representation of a child, nude or in swaddling bands, a cherub, from *putto*, 'boy, lad, stripling. More frequently encountered in the plural, *i putti.*

Quarant' Ore Literally, 'forty hours'.

> '*Forty hours' devotion* (also known as the *Quarant' Ore* or *Quarantore*), a modern Catholic devotion in which the Blessed Sacrament is exposed ... for a period of *c.* forty hours, and the faithful pray before it by turns throughout this time': F. L. Cross, *The Oxford Dictionary of the Christian Church* (edn 2) p 524/2.

rallentando A musical direction to the performer to slow down. From *rallentare*, 'to relent'.

ricercar, ricercare The rather imprecise designation given to a wide variety of musical forms composed in the 16th, 17th and 18th centuries, characterized by a strongly fugal structure. From *ricercare*, 'to search out'.

ripieno A musical term that has in recent years assumed is former importance. See quotation.

> 'In the Concerto Grosso ... the idea is ... that *two bodies* of instruments are ... responding to one another antiphonally ... The larger body is called *Ripieno* ... and the smaller one '*Concertino*'': Percy Scholes, *Radio Times Music Handbook*, p 18 (1935).

ristorante A restaurant. Generally an eating-house serving set meals to be eaten on the premises; that is, not a takeaway (food to go). In that respect a *ristorante* is unlike most *trattorie* (*cf, below*).A *ristorante* would not normally offer accommodation: cf *albergo* and *osteria above.*

ritornello 'A little return'. 'An instrumental refrain, interlude, or prelude in a vocal work': *OED*. The implication of a return to an earlier strain has been lost over the years.

riviera Literally, 'coast' or 'shore'. Strictly, the Italian sea-board around Genoa (Genova), but generally applied also to the Mediterranean coast from Marseilles in France to La Spezia in Italy. This coastline became a fashionable winter resort in the 19th century and more recently has become popular for summer holidays too. The definite article is always used with *riviera.* In recent years, the French part of the *riviera* has tended, among English-speakers, to monopolize the word, rendering the earlier expression, the *French Riviera*, a little dated.

scherzo A movement of a lively character, occupying the second or third place in a symphony or sonata. From a Teutonic root: *cf* Modern German, *Scherz*, 'a joke, a jest, a sport'. Though the German is pronounced

/ʃɛːrtʃ/, the Italian derivative is pronounced /'skɛːrtso/.

> 'Scherzo: a piece of jocular and cheerful character': E. Pauer in *Programme*, 8th March 1862.

sciolto See *I pensieri stretti ... above.*

scordatura A style of string-playing that requires individual strings to be tuned differently from ordinary tuning, so as the create a strange, unusual effect. From *scordare,* 'to be out of tune', short for *discordare.* The technique was demonstrated with superb skill in the works of the composer H. I. F. von Biber (1644-1704).

'Se non è vero, è [molto] ben trovato': Literally, 'If it is not true, it is [very] well found'. That is, 'Even if it's not true, still, it's a happy invention'. Proverbial since at least the 16th century.

'Secolo dei Lumi, il' Literally, 'The Age of Lights', an unhappy *calque* of *L'Age des Lumières.* An alternative phrase to denote the Enlightenment, *L' Illuminismo,* is scarcely more felicitous, in that it suggests the anti-rationalism of the *Illuminati,* the fundamental principle of which movement, a special endowment of insight, is clearly antagonistic to the fundamental principle of the Enlightenment, which is rationalism.

> 'Wilhelm is deemed worthy of admission to the society of the *Illuminati,* that is, those who have pierced the secret of life, and know what it is to be and to do': Margaret Fuller, *Life Without and Life Within,* 1860, p 41 (1850).

***Sei personaggi in cerca d'autore*:** 'Six characters in search of an author'. The title of a play (1921) by Luigi Pirandello (1867-1936).

serenata Originally, a musical work suitable for performance out of doors in the serenity of, for example, a calm evening. Later, a piece of instrumental music, developed from the orchestral suite, and usually composed of a march and a minuet interposed between two movements of another kind.

Serenissima, La The Republic of Venice.

> 'Though continually at war with some other power, the Venetian Republic was known as *la Serenissima,* 'the most Serene": D. Vare, *Ghosts of the Rialto,* ii (1956).

sol-fa The root of this and other closely similar words lies in Mediaeval plainsong, and is of profound significance to the entire concept of musical notation, and thus to the entire concept of music itself.

When the Benedictine monk Guido d'Arezzo (995-1050) faced the problem of singing the Offices, he was met with the problem he shared in common with the whole of humanity. Apart from the highly dubious aid afforded by the monochord, Antiquity had given the world absolutely nothing in the way of recording in writing the way music sounded. It is difficult for us, nowadays, to comprehend such a state of affairs, but a moment's thought will suffice to establish how underprivileged our ancestors were in comparison with ourselves.

Guido d'Arezzo devised an astonishingly simple means of recording music in writing. The present-day means of capturing music on paper, though it looks a little different from the Plainsong notation that Guido directly facilitated, nevertheless undoubtedly owes its existence to Guido. In order to solve the problem of getting down in writing not only what was *said* but what was *sung,* he pitched on the idea of naming certain sounds by means of using the syllables to which, it so happened, those sounds were applied in the first verse of a certain office hymn:

As a matter of interest, the verse in question chosen by Guido d'Arezzo is assigned in the Roman Breviary to Vespers for the feast of St John Baptist. With the relevant syllables in bold italics, it runs:

> ***UT*** queant laxis ***RE***sonare fibris
> ***MI***ra gestorum
> ***FA***muli tuorum,
> ***SOL***ve polluti ***LA***bii reatum, ***S***ancte
> ***I***oannes.

The syllables in question are printed above in bold italics. (More of the verse in question in a moment.)

The notes to be sung to the syllables above were notes of music on what is now our major scale. It seems Guido discerned that this scale, known in his time as the Ionian Mode, was destined to be the predominant one in Western Music, and that in fact defines the characteristic 'flavour' of Western Music.

It seems that Guido jotted these notes down on a sort of ladder, from which developed, through the four lines and three spaces notation of Plainsong, to the conventional five lines and four spaces we know nowadays as the stave, or, loosely, the clef. There are in fact, more strictly using the language, three clefs in use, symbols affixed to the left-hand side of staves of music. They are the *C*, which is the tenor or alto clef, the *G*, or treble clef, and the *F*, or bass clef, which denote respectively the middle *C* on a piano, the *G* above, and the *F* below. Plainsong notation has equivalent clefs.

Early music had many 'scales', known as 'modes', but Guido concentrated, as we have seen, on what he recognized as (for reasons we need not discuss) the predominant mode, the mode that is now known as the diatonic scale of C and, in consequence, those syllables have, with minor modification, become the names of those actual notes of music they denote. The notes in question thus received the names *ut* (later changed to the more singable *do* –among English-speakers, *doh*), *re, mi, fa, sol, la,* and *si* (this last changed in English-speaking circles to *tee*, to avoid the sometimes troublesome sibilant *s).* Quite apart from a recollection from early school days of 'the tonic sol-fa', English-speakers will recognize the Continental way of naming musical compositions: what to an English-speaker is Bach's Suite No 3 in D Major is, or course, to a Frenchman Bach's Suite Numéro 3 en Ré Mineur.

At the risk of over-simplification, it might be said that sight-reading and the sol-fa, particularly the development of the *tonic* sol-fa introduced by Rev John Curwen (1816-1880), and, with even more particularity, the fundamental concept of 'the moveable *doh*', have transformed choral singing, for, since all that one needs to do is to say to choristers that their *doh* is a certain note produced by, say, a tuning-fork, and the choristers have no longer any need to worry about 'the key of E Sharp Major' and so on – given a little further knowledge, about the minor scale. Thus, for unison singing, a given melody can start on virtually any note and can then be sung by any register from soprano down to basso profundo. Voices in those registers will not, of course, be able to start on the same *absolute* note, but they will be able to start on the same *relative* note – based on their own *doh*.

One of the derivative words from *sol-fa* is *solfeggio*, meaning, strictly, 'An exercise for the voice, in which the sol-fa syllables are employed; also *transf.*, an exercise for a musical instrument': *OED*. Sometimes, and excusably, the word *solfeggio* is used to denote the complete system of *sol-fa*, which is not a bad development.

'... soltanto la buona parte'. When Bonaparte was campaigning in Liguria, and riding at the head of a column of his troops, he encountered a felled tree, clearly an obstacle placed by the inhabitants. An old *paesano* was sitting on the felled tree. The First Consul shook his fist at the *paesano* and shouted, 'Tutti voialtri Italiani siete briganti!': 'All you Italians are brigands!' The elderly *paesano* calmly and punningly replied, 'Nossignore. Non 'tutti'. Soltanto la buona parte': 'No, sir. Not 'all'. Only the better part'.

> 'Sir, Legend has it that when marching across Lombardy the Grande Armée was held up yet again by an improvised road-block. Napoleon shouted angrily at an old Italian peasant standing nearby, 'Voialtri Italiani siete tutti briganti!' To which the old man, bowing deeply, replied, 'Tutti no, signore, ma buona parte, si ...'': Francis Rentoul, Letters to the Editor, *The Spectator*, 24th February 1996, p 28.

soprano The highest vocal register in women and boys (boys are normally called *trebles*), having a compass from about middle C to two octaves above it.

sordino, con 'With mute'. A direction that a means of damping appropriate to the instrument should be used, to reduce the volume or alter in some respect the tone of the instrument.

sotto voce Literally, 'below the voice', meaning, in speech and singing, quietly, with low volume. Much used figuratively.

SpA 'Società per Azioni': A company limited by shares; *SpA* is a formula by law obliged to be affixed to a trading name if the enterprise is of limited liability.

spaghetti Literally, 'strings', from *spaghetti*, 'thin string or twine'. It is hardly relevant to mention that the word is technically a *plural*, since no-one suggests that, in the context of spoken English, we should treat is as such.

The word has come into our language a second time, in 'Spaghetti Junction', the colloquial name for a specific convoluted multi-lane motorway junction, the Gravelly Hill Interchange on the 1966 M6 Motorway, Birmingham, a veritable three-dimensional maze. Other similar interchanges on UK motorways (highways, freeways, turnpikes) have also qualified for the name.)

staccato A musical direction that the note or passage marked should be sung or played in a detached, disconnected manner, that is, with breaks between successive notes. Individual notes intended to be sung or played staccato are marked with a dot placed over them.

stanza In the vocabulary of versification, a crucially important word, as the *OED* definitions testifies: 'A group of lines of verse (usually not less than four), arranged according to a definite scheme which regulates the number of lines, the metre, and (in rhymed poetry) the sequence of rhymes; normally forming a division of a song or poem consisting of a series of such groups constructed according to the same scheme. Also, any of the particular types of structure according to which stanzas are framed'. If it is desired to refer to a single line of verse, the word is 'verse'.

stretto Literally, 'narrow, strict, tight, strait'. A musical direction indicating, rather imprecisely, that a repetition or restatement of, for example, a fugue, and appearing at the end of a musical work, should be performed in a more pronounced and emphatic a manner, which commonly means quicker.

tempo 'Time'. Plural, *tempi*. Relative speed or rate of movement in music; pace; time; specifically, the proper or characteristic speed and rhythm of a dance or other tune (for example, in the phrases *tempo di gavotta, tempo di marcia, tempo di minuetto*, etc). The expression *tempo giusto*, 'strict time', sometimes *tempo ordinario*, indicates the proper speed that a style of music demands; it is normally taken for granted but is explicitly indicated if a *tempo* other than *tempo giusto* has previously been indicated (sometimes *tempo giusto* appears simply as *tempo*). Two other time-directions are: *tempo primo*, the first or previous time; a direction to resume the original speed after an alteration of speed; *tempo rubato*, robbed or stolen time, by which is meant a practice in which time is occasionally slackened or hastened for the purposes of expression, which is achieved by robbing one note of a part of its time-value and giving that portion to another note, the general, overall *tempo* not being affected.

> 'Verbal directions as to tempo are generally written in Italian': F. Taylor in Grove, *Dictionary of Music*, IV, p 82 (1884).

terra cotta 'Cooked earth'. 'A hard unglazed pottery of a fine quality, of which decorative tiles and bricks, architectural decorations, statuary, vases, and the like are made': *OED*.

terza rima An Italian form of iambic verse employed by Dante in *La Divina Commedia,* comprising sets of three lines, the middle line of each set rhyming with the first and last of the succeeding (*a b a*, *b c b*, *c d c*, etc.). For a more thorough explanation of this metre, see H. W. Fowler, *Modern English Usage* (1926) s.v. 'Technical Terms: terza rima'. See *ottava rima, above.*

tessitura An invaluable import from Italian: there is simply no English word that could do service for *tessitura*. The difference referred to in the 1884 quotation below between 'range' and *tessitura* is characteristic of the difference between home-grown words and imported words: almost without a single exception, these importations have given us completely new words without the least risk that we shall sacrifice a single word of our own. It is reflections such as that that impel English-speakers to view with incredulity the dog-in-the-manger attitude of *l'Académie Française.*

This crucial term of art originally denoted the part of the total compass of a voice-part (rather than of a given singer) in which most of its tones lie. Less strictly, the word usefully denotes the part of the register of a given singer that most suits a given piece of music. Vocalists look on the *tessitura* of their own voices as the notes in which their own particular voices are most 'at home'.

> 'A term … used by the Italians to indicate how the music of a piece 'lies'; … what is the prevailing or average position of its notes in relation to the compass of the voice or instrument for which it is written … 'Range' does not at all give the idea, as the range may be extended, and the general *tessitura* limited; while the range may be high and the *tessitura* low or medium': Grove, Dictionary of Music, IV, p 94/1 (1884).

tutti possono sbagliare A proverb: 'We can all make mistakes'.

tosto 'Rather', as in time-directions such as *tosto allegro*, 'rather quickly'.

traddutore, traditore 'Translator, traitor'. A pessimistic aphorism that has been proverbial in Italian for centuries, the meaning of which is that however faithful a translation might be to the orginal, it is still a traitor to the original.

trattoria An eating house, a takeaway (food to go). In principle, an establishment having fewer pretensions than *uno ristorante (q.v, above),* and not having the residential accommodation offered by most *alberghi (cf albergo, above).* Nevertheless, the translation 'takeaway' ('food to go') would often be a bad one: many *trattorie* offer a superb off-premises service, and will efficiently cater off-the-premises for wedding receptions and prestigious functions of all descriptions. The word is derived from *trattare*, 'to treat', *trattore*, 'a host'. *Trattore* is a close approximation to the French *traiteur*, 'a caterer'.

tremolo 'A tremulous or vibrating effect produced on certain musical instruments or in the human voice in singing, especially to express intensity of emotion': *OED. Tremolo* is closely akin to another musical phenomenon, *vibrato*, also employed to express intensity of emotion. Historically, there has been some conflict between the authorities as to the distinction between *tremolo* and *vibrato*, with a tendency to use either term for either phenomenon. It would certainly be very helpful if these two terms could be narrowly defined, since it is clear that they are two similar but distinct phenomena. It has recently seemed that there was a developing consensus that *tremolo* ought to mean a variation in the *volume* of the note sung or played, whereas *vibrato* ought to mean a variation in the *pitch* of the note sung or played. However, there is still much regrettable ambiguity attendant on the use of these two words.
There is a notable revulsion from the use of *vibrato* – the 'wobble '– in present-day performance. Performers are increasingly confining *vibrato* to the Romantic *repertoire*; its use in the Baroque *repertoire* is extremely restricted. *Tremolo*, when it means a variation in pitch, is not so frowned on, Indeed, there is an effect available on some organs, known as the *tremulant*, that produces, especially on organs having low wind-pressures (for example, organs with Baroque voicing), an attractive and highly characteristic result.

> 'A Tremulant is a contrivance that gives to the tone of any department of an Organ to which it may be applied, a waving, or undulating effect': John Hiles, *Catechism of the Organ*, iii edn 1878, p 20 (1876). 'The instrumental tremolo is more nearly allied to the vocal vibrato. Indeed, what is called 'vibrato' on bowed instruments is what would be 'tremolo' in vocal music': H. C. Deacon, in *Grove's Dictionary of Music*, IV, 166/2 (1884). 'Fender's Stratocaster electric guitar with tremolo (for a vibrato effect) and case': *Money*, April 1984, p 34/3.

Uffizi, gli '[The Gallery of] The Offices'. The Uffizi Gallery, Florence, occupies the top floor of the large building erected by Giorgio Vasari between 1560 and 1580 to house the administrative offices of the Duchy of Tuscany, hence the name. The French boldly translate the name of the Gallery as *Les Offices*.

'Vedi Napoli e muori!' 'See Naples and die!' An enthusiastic slogan by which the Italians express their admiration for Naples and its magnificent gulf. It seems inherently unlikely that the saying depends on a exhortation to travellers to see both Naples and the adjacent (unremarkable) village called *Mori*. Similarly, one can forget the tale that a Thomas Cook poster urged traveller to see Naples and the adjacent place called *Die*.

vendetta 'Revenge'. A blood-feud between families usually persisting from generation to generation in Corsica and certain parts of Italy.

vibrato See *tremolo, above*.

viola d'amore A bowed instrument not unlike the treble viol in structure, with six or seven gut strings and with a secondary or sympathetic set of strings made of fine brass or steel wire, lying close to the belly.

viola da gamba 'Leg viol'. The bass viol, the only member of the viol family to co-exist to the present day with the dominant violin family. The entire viol family, has, however, been revived in the last half century or so.

virtù Sometimes (incorrectly) *vertù*. Nowadays, after a chequered career, a word meaning, among English-speakers, articles, specifically *objets d'art* (*q.v.* in the French Lexicon), in which virtuosos (see immediately below) are interested. The word includes curios, antiques and other products of the fine arts. The construction is 'an article, object or piece of *virtù*'. The written grave accent indicates the tonic accent.

virtuoso A word that can mean many things. Of the definitions given in the Second Edition (1989) of the *OED*, the dictionary itself is frank to admit that '[I]t is frequently difficult in particular instances to decide which of the senses is intended'. The first of two definitions of contemporary relevance is: 'One who has a special interest in, or taste for, the fine arts; a student or collector of antiquities, natural curiosities or rarities, etc.; a connoisseur; freq., one who carries on such pursuits in a dilettante or trifling manner'. The second relevant definition reads: 'One who has special knowledge or skill in music; *spec.*, in modern use, one who excels in, or devotes special attention to, technique in playing or singing'. The pejorative implication referred to in the first *OED* definition, 'a connoisseur; freq., one who carries on such pursuits in a dilettante or trifling manner', is perhaps nowadays attached more to *dilettante* (q.v.) than to *virtuoso*. The pronunciation of the word is always anglicized. The plural is almost always 'virtuosos', though *Fowler* (1926) gives only *virtuosi*.

zingaro A gypsy. In English usage, and in the plural, *I Zingari*, an amateur cricket club founded in 1845.

zuppa inglese 'English soup'. The Italian name for the English 'trifle'.

ACKNOWLEDGEMENTS

'My favourite culinary term, *zuppa inglese*, the Italian's idea of a sickly English trifle': Fenton Bresler, *You and the Law*, p 77 (1975). 'One way and another, [the book is] a *zuppa inglese*, heavy with leftovers and alcoholic seasonings': *The Listener*, p 189/2, 10th February 1977. 'We'd decided on *Zuppa inglese* for pud... Who can resist trifle in hooch?': J. Gash, *Vatican Rip*, xii, p 101 (1981)I acknowledge with thanks the encouragement I have had from my many Italophile friends. They will know who they are.

Spanish & Portuguese

One of the chief problems in compiling a Lexicon of Spanish and Portuguese words that have been adopted into the English language is that most of them have been slightly *adapted* – but, by that slight adaptation, they have ceased to be strictly Spanish or Portuguese words. It has been very easy, over the centuries, for English-speakers to knock off the last syllable of a Spanish or Portuguese word and make a word that has, by that simple means, become completely acclimatized to the English-speaking environment. Take the word 'contraband' as an instance. We took the Spanish word *contrabando*, 'smuggling', knocked the final *o* off the word and gave ourselves a perfectly English word, 'contraband'. Other examples are 'cigar' from *cigarro*; 'manifest' (the shipping document) from *manifesto*; 'marinade' from *marinado* (the form with the letter *t* coming through French); 'marmalade' from Portuguese *marmelada*, 'quince conserve'; and 'renegade', from *renegado*. It is often difficult to determine precisely the route by which words have arrived in the language, since French, too, adopted Iberian words that we, in turn, adopted from the French. The following list will indicate how fruitful the termination *-ado* has been:

accolade, ambassade, ambuscade, arcade, balustrade, bastonnade, brigade, cannonade, cascade, cavalcade, comrade, crusade, enfilade, escalade, esplanade, fanfaronnade, lemonade, marmalade, masquerade, palisade, parade, rodomontade, serenade, tirade.

Other slight adaptations have effectively changed the nationality of words: Portuguese *mandarim* loses its final nasalization and changes *m* to *n*, to give 'mandarin'. Sometimes a word appears in a purely Spanish or Portuguese form, though it has come to us by indirect means: a classic case is the word *paladin*, one of the twelve peers of Charlemagne, the word deriving ultimately from the Latin *palatinus*, a adjective stemming by origin from the Palatine Hill in Rome, and thus acquiring the meaning 'Imperial', or 'associated with an emperor'.

English-speakers are not on the whole well versed in the literature of Spain and Portugal. That is plain from the low incidence of quotations in this Lexicon, compared with the quotations in, say, the French Lexicon. That is to be regretted, but it is, alas!, a recognition of reality.

A point worth mentioning is that, since Brazil, with 172,000,000 inhabitants, has about 51 per cent of South America's population, Portuguese is the most widely spoken language in South America.

The Lexicon

adios 'To God!' The Spanish salutation on parting, equivalent to *Adieu* and *Addio*. The equivalent in Portuguese is *Adeus*.

adobe In its primary sense, the word is a substantive denoting an unburnt brick dried in the sun. It has been widely adopted in the US, from Mexico, as an adjective denoting the method of building dwellings, as in 'adobe houses'. Of recent years, the word has become a registered trade-mark denoting the products of a leading company in the world of desktop publishing and word processing.

adelantado 'One who has been advanced'. A Spanish grandee; one appointed to the governing of a province.

aficionado A fan of a pursuit, sport or pastime, especially of bullfighting.

aguardiente 'Ardent water', *scil*, brandy.

aia Portuguese: a nurse, not a wet-nurse but a nurse for older children; sometimes 'a governess'; *cf.* Spanish *ayo* and Italian *aio* (formerly *ajo*), 'a tutor'. Introduced by the Portuguese into India, where the word was adopted into Anglo-Indian parlance, spelt *ayah*, to denote a native nurse or maidservant. See *ama, below*.

al- The Arabic definitive article, retained as an essential part of a great number of Spanish and Portuguese words. Many words of Arabic origin that have been adopted into English have been mediated *via* Spanish and Portuguese, *e.g.*, *alcohol*, *alcove*, *alcoran*, *algebra*, *alkali*, *almagest*, *almanac*, and many, many others.

alameda 'A public walk or promenade with a row of trees on each side': *OED*. From *álamo*, the poplar tree: see next.

Álamo, the 'The poplar tree'. This is an interesting instance of the use of a single Spanish word that produces an effect that resonates throughout the US. Until the word *chauvinism* (*q.v.* in the French Lexicon) was hijacked by the Feminist Movement, we might have found it useful to quote the *Encylcopaedia Britannica* to exemplify American chauvinism: 'An old mission-fort, the Alamo, in San Antonio, has been called the 'cradle of Texas liberty'. Its defense and the deaths of the more than 180 men who defended it inspired the cry, 'Remember the Alamo!' Texas soldiers shouted this at the battle of San Jacinto, which brought Texas its independence from Mexico'. *Sed quaere*. Independence from whom? Despite the doctrine of the independence of each State of the Union, there must be many thousands of American Democrats who question, under a Texan president, that Texas has in fact been independent since the Alamo – not to mention the submerged under-class of Hispanic Texans.

Another emotive instance of the use of this word, but in its plural, *los Álamos*, relates to the location of the atomic-physics laboratory at Los Alamos, Texas, where the Manhattan Project was developed, concluding in the first and second atomic bombs, on Hiroshima and Nagasaki respectively in 1945.

albino A human or animal distinguished by the congenital absence (partial or total) of pigmentation in the skin and hair, which are abnormally white, and in the eyes, which are of a pink colour and unable to bear the ordinary light. The word is a Portuguese word: the better pronunciation is thus /ælbinəʊ/, not /ælbaɪnəʊ/ – that is, *not* to rhyme with 'wino', which would suggest that the word is Latin (pronounced in the English fashion: see the Latin Lexicon *s.v. Pronunciation*).

alcaïd 'The governor or commander of a fortress; the warden of a prison; (in Spain, Portugal, Barbary, etc.)': *OED*. The *OED* comments, 'Sometimes confounded with *alcalde*'. See next.

alcalde The *OED* says, 'A magistrate of a town, a sheriff or justice, in Spain and Portugal'. This word, and the comparable word *alcaïd* (more general in Portugal for the civil, judicial acceptation) derive from the Arabic etymons meaning 'to lead' and 'to judge'. The form *alcalde* tends to be used in reference, both historically and at the present time, to the civil, judicial acceptation,the form *alcaïd* being reserved for the military or governmental *role* of the holder of the title. However, there is some ambiguity in English over the distinction to be drawn between the two forms.

alcazar A fortress or a castle, from the Arabic *alqaçr' al* the + *qaçr* in the plural, a castle. Specifically, the Alcazar, an architectural masterpiece at Segovia, near Madrid, built in the eleventh century and rebuilt in the early fifteenth.

alfaceiro An eater of lettuce, the colloquial name for the inhabitants of Lisbon, said to be owing to their gentle nature.

alfalfa The Spanish name for a variety of the fodder crop Lucerne, *Medicago sativa*, in use also in parts of the United States.

algebra There is a meaning of the word *algebra* that survives in Spanish, retaining intact one of the earliest meanings of the word, *bone-setting*, from the Arabic *al-jebr*, the redintegration or reunion of broken parts, from *jabara* to reunite, redintegrate, consolidate, restore; *hence*, the surgical treatment of fractures, bone-setting.

almanac 'An annual table, or (more usually) a book of tables, containing a calendar of months and days, with astronomical data and calculations, ecclesiastical and other anniversaries, besides other useful information, and, in former days, astrological and astrometeorological forecasts': *OED*. The word has on its face the clear hallmarks of a borrowing from Arabic, in particular the appararent definite article *al-*, which is a characteristic of many Spanish and Portuguese words developed from Arabic. The word *almanac(h)* begins to appear in Mediaeval Latin towards the end of the 13th century; later, we have in Pedro de Alcalá, in his Arabic-Castilian *Vocabulista arábigo en lingua castellana* (1505), the gloss '*manākh*, almanaque, calendario'; and also '*mana;* ', (probably meant to be the same word), meaning *relox del sol*, 'sundial'. But the word occurs nowhere else in Arabic literature, and there is no plausible etymology for the word.

Old Moore's Almanac was first published in 1697 by Francis Moore under the title *Vox Stellarum*, 'Voice of the Stars', and was for many years an immense publishing success. It is still published today. It relies for its continuing success on astrological prediction.

> 'A book or table, containing a calendar of days, and months, to which astronomical data and various statistics are often added, such as the times of the rising and setting of the sun and moon, eclipses, hours of full tide, stated festivals of churches, terms of courts, etc': *Webster's Dictionary*, 1913. 'Nautical almanac, an almanac, or year book, containing astronomical calculations (lunar, stellar, etc.), and other information useful to mariners': *Webster's Dictionary*, 1913.

alpaca A Peruvian quadruped, *Lama pacos*, a species of llama, bred by reason of its long fine woolly hair.

alumbrado A member of the *Illuminati* or Perfectionists, a sect that arose about 1575. It was suppressed by the Inquisition; the word is sometimes applied to any one claiming special spiritual illumination.

ama Portuguese: ' A (wet) nurse'. A word, normally spelt 'amah' by English-speakers, formerly much used in South India among Europeans and thought by many to be a word native to the Indian subcontinent. See *aya, below*.

ambuscade One of a number of pseudo-Spanish words that anomalously crept into English literature during a period of its development, a procedure well identified by the *OED*: 'An affected refashioning of *ambuscade* after Spanish. Here Englishmen may have confused the Spanish past participle. *emboscado*, 'ambushed', in *estar emboscado* to lie in ambush, with the feminine noun *emboscada*, 'ambuscade'. The prime object of these affected refashionings seems to have been the creation of local colour, encouraged by the romantic aura of such notions as *El Dorado*, 'the golden', 'the gilded'. A certain swashbuckling, piratical note was achieved by the use of genuine Iberian words, such as *desperado* and *renegado*, and further verisimilitude was sought by the pure invention of words such as *tornado, q.v., below*. This 'affected refashioning' is roundly condemned by the *OED* as 'An ignorant sonorous refashioning of nouns in *-ade*, from the French *-ade* … Spanish *-ada*, Italian *-ata*) probably after the assumed analogy of *renegade = renegado*; *e.g. ambuscado, bastinado, bravado, barricado, carbonado, camisado, crusado, grenade, gambado, palisado, panado, scalado, stoccado, strappado*, all of which in Spanish have (or would have) *-ada*. So *armada*, an obsolete variant of *armada*'.

Amontillado Formerly, a wine of the sherry type produced in Montilla; now, a matured sherry in which the *flor* has developed. In the last hundred years or so there has been a shift of meaning in the technical terms employed in the production of sherry: see the quotations below. See, also, *oloroso below.*

> 'The driest species of Sherry is the Amontillado': Alexander Henderson, *The Quarterly Journal of Science and the Arts*, XVIII, p 130 (1825). 'There are three main types of sherry: *finos*, which are dry, light, and pale; *amontillados*, which are softer, fuller, and less dry; and *olorosos*, which are sweet, rich dessert wines': *The Times*, p 13/5, 16th January 1961.

Apache A tribe of Athapascan Indians indigenous to New Mexico and Arizona. Their name has been in use since the first European colonists landed in the New World: see the 1907 quotation below. The French adopted the word to mean a ruffian of a type infesting Paris about the turn of the 19th century–at the height of *la Belle Époque* (*q. v.* in the French Lexicon). The pronunciations are, respectively, /a'patʃe/ for the original use and /apaʃ/ for the French use.

> '*Apache* (probably from *ápachu*, 'enemy', the Zuni name for the Navaho, who were designated 'Apaches de Nabaju' by the early Spaniards in New Mexico). They were first mentioned as Apaches by Oñate in 1598': F. W. Hodge, *American Indians*, I, p 63

armada Strictly, 'army', used in precisely the same sense as the English word 'army', the French *armée*, the Italian *armata*. All the Romance languages have taken the Latin past participle of the verb *armāre*, *armata*, as a feminine singular to mean 'armed force, army, navy, fleet'. The historical term 'the Spanish Armada' is a specific, not exclusive, use of the word.

armadillo 'Little armed [creature]' One of the burrowing order *Edenta*, peculiar to South America, having a strong scaly or bony body-armour, the survival of which species is largely due to its practice of curling itself up into a ball that is virtually impregnable to what would otherwise be the armadillo's natural predators.

arraez The captain of a vessel. Portuguese: *arraes*, *arrais*. From the Arabic *ras*, a head.

asiento 'An assent, contract or agreement'. Formerly spelt *assiento*. Historically, the agreement made between Great Britain and Spain at the peace of Utrecht in 1713. See the quotations.

> 'The Assiento, or Contract for allowing the Subjects of Great Britain the Liberty of Importing Negroes into the Spanish America [*sic*]': *The London Gazette*, No 5213/3 (1714). 'The English slave-trade began to attain its great activity after the assiento treat': Bancroft, *History of the United States*, II, xlii, p 555 (1876).

assimilado The past participle of *assimilar*, 'to assimilate', used as an adjectival noun to designate inhabitants of Angola, Mozambique and the other former Portuguese colonies in Africa who had applied for and had been granted full Portuguese citizenship. Conditions such as fluency in Portuguese and literacy were prerequisites. The policy of the Portuguese administration was intended to be enlightened but was widely seen as discriminatory, In comparison with the overtly racial colonial *régimes* in other parts of Africa, particularly in the Republic of South Africa, it might be thought, with hindsight, that the timely and voluntary creation by the Portuguese administration in 1950 of an entire, discrete grouping of emancipated indigenes, *os Assimilados*, was indeed an enlightened step. It might, moreover, be a moot point whether the Afro-American troops Colonel Castro later sent to former Portuguese Africa were in any way freer than the *Assimilados* had been under their former colonial masters.

> 'It's even possible for a Mozambique native to become a full Portuguese citizen. About 4,000 Africans have reached this 'assimilado' status': *The Wall Street Journal*, p 4/5, 24th July 1953. 'Out of a black population of 4 million, Angola has 30,000 *assimilados* who enjoy the basic rights denied to their fellows': *The Economist*, p 550/1, 6th May 1961.

auto-da-fé Portuguese for 'act of the faith'. The Spanish term is *auto-de-fé*, 'act of faith'. The term denoted the formal step in the judicial process followed by the Inquisition in Portugal and Spain whereby invincible heretics were relaxed to tβhe secular arm and repentant heretics were absolved and reconciled.

> '*Act of Faith, Auto da fe* ... a solemn day held by the inquisition, for the punishment of heretics, and the absolution of the innocent accused': *Chambers Cyclopaedia*, 1727-41.

avanía Portuguese and Italian for an imposition by the Ottoman government, a compulsory tax or arbitrary exaction. The French is *avarie*; the modern Greek is *aβanía* This word is thought to be a euphemism borrowed from Christian kings, in that the word seems to be a plural form of Arabic usages implying 'aid', 'benevolence', terms frequently met with in the fiscal history of Christendom as a softened alternative to 'tax'.

The second edition of the *OED*, of 1989, includes an extensive note on this word. It demonstrates to perfection the myriad permutations and combinations through which ideas and the words that express them can undergo, making even the permutations and combinations of computing annuities seem child's-play. This impeccably scholarly note merits quotation in its entirety.

> The etymology of *avania* has been variously sought in Arabic, Persian, Turkish: see Devic, in Littré's *Suppt.*, and G[eorge] P. Marsh, *Notes and Additions* to Wedgewood [Hensleigh Wedgwood, *A Dictionary of English Etymology, 1859-65*]. The variant Arabic form *awārl* (whence Eng. *avaria, uvaria* ...) as well as original correspondence of meaning, suggests a connexion with It. *avaría*–see AVERAGE n.: in fact, Mr. Marsh proposed the derivation of the latter from this word. But, on the other hand, the various and uncertain form of the word in Arabic may be merely adaptations of Fr. *avarie* or It. *avaría,* assimilated to native words or roots (e.g. *awār* oppression, injustice, *hawān* contempt, etc.) 'The plur. *aavaniet* is now in popular use in Syria, to express government exactions, the singular signifying *aid, help*, just as *benevolence* in Europe sometimes meant a compulsory tax' (Marsh). The word has been adopted in It. and Pg. in the transferred sense: It. *avanía* 'an undeserved wrong, a secret grudge, an insulting injury' (Florio); Pg. *avanía* 'wrong, injury', ([Anthony] Vieyra), *Dictionary of the Portuguese and English Languages*, (1827).

aviso A term of art from earlier diplomacy: intelligence, information; a notification, dispatch, or formal advice.

avocado 'Advocate', substituted by popular etymology for the Aztec *ahuacatl.* The fruit of a West Indian tree (*Persea gratissima*); a large pear-shaped fruit, called also, in English, 'the Avocado Pear'.

> 'The Avogato Pear-tree is as big as most Pear-trees ... the Fruit as big as a large Lemon': W. Dampier, *Voyages*, I, p 203 (1697).

ayah See *aia, above.*

azimuth, zenith and nadir Three astronomical terms that, as to *azimuth* and *zenith*, have been mediated to English in the same spelling as in Portuguese, and, as to *nadir*, that has been mediated to us in the common Romance of Italian, Spanish and Portuguese. The word *azimuth* denotes an arc of the heavens extending from the zenith to the horizon, which it cuts at right angles. The word derives from the Arabic *as-sumūt*, the plural of *samūt,* 'way', 'direction', 'a direction or point of the compass or horizon, and the arc extending from it to the zenith'. *Cf. samt-al-rā's,* 'the direction or point over head', whence the second term, *zenith*, derives obscurely from Arabic *samt*, in *samt ar-rās*, literally, 'the way or path over the head' (*samt*, 'way', *al* 'the', and *rās*, 'head'. The third term, *nadir*, denotes a point on the celestial sphere diametrically opposite to some other point, especially the sun. The word derives from the Arabic *nazīr al samt*, 'opposite to the zenith. For better explanations of these three technical terms, the reader is advised to consult an illustrated dictionary. Nevertheless, the two random quotations below show how effective words alone can be, and how indestructible they can be once they have demonstrated their efficacy and have established their normative forms.

> 'The centre þat standeth a-Middes the narwest cercle is cleped the senyth ... this forseide cenyth is ymagened to ben the

verrey point ouer the crowne of thyn heued, & also this senyth is the verrey pool of the orisonte in euery region': Geoffrey Chaucer. *Treatise on the Astrolabe*, I, §18 (1391). 'The point that is rycht abufe our hede is callit zenyth,..ande as oft as ve change fra place to place, as oft ve sal hef ane vthir zenytht': *The Complete Scot*, vi, p 50(1549).

bandillera A little dart, ornamented with a banderole or small banner that skilful bull-fighters stick into the neck and shoulders of the bull during the *corrida*: *q.v.*

barocco In the light of the development of the Baroque Revival in music, this obscure Portuguese word, meaning an imperfect or mis-shapen pearl, deserves a few lines of comment. To start with, the word was unambiguously pejorative. *Barocco* and the Italian term *rococo,* 'rock-work', were sometimes used without distinction, especially in architectural parlance, for styles of ornament characterized by profusion, oddity of combinations, or abnormal features generally. Nowadays, in English-speaking circles, the word *baroque*, taken to be French, is used to describe a more severe style of architecture that preceded what is now called *rococo*. Much of the best baroque architecture is understandable to be found in Italy, particularly in Rome, but the fundamental, essential, baroque style in architecture is perhaps well captured in the cathedral of St-Louis in Versailles, originally designed by François Mansart (1598-1666). A good modern exemplar of the style is Brompton Oratory, in London. The rococo style is perfectly exemplified in the works of Balthasar Neumann (1687-1753) and Johann Bernhard Fischer von Erlach (1656-1723).

bacalao 'Cod-fish'. In Portuguese, *bacalhau*.

bando 'A decree or proclamation'.

barranca A deep ravine with precipitous sides, a word used in the US as well as in Spanish-speaking regions.

barrio A district; a suburb. 'A ward or quarter of a city or town in Spain or a Spanish-speaking country; in some Spanish-speaking countries, a rural settlement': *OED*.

batata, papa dulce or **boniato** The sweet potato *Batatas edulis*, family *Convolvulaceæ*, having an edible tuberous root, called also 'Spanish Potato', a native of the West Indies, whence it was introduced into Spain (and to Portugal, as *batata doce*) early in the 16th century. Also, simply *batata*, the very common tuber vegetable *Solanum tuberosum*, a native of the Pacific slopes of South America, introduced into Europe late in the 16th century, and now extremely widely cultivated for its farinaceous tubers.

batatas bravas 'Fierce potatoes'. A Spanish dish of sautéed potatoes in or with a spicy tomato sauce, frequently served as a *tapa* *(q.v.)*.

bizarro This word is a false friend, in that it means 'brave, courageous', and, by extension, 'of a soldierly bearing'.There is no hint in Spanish and Portuguese of oddness, except as an overt, conscious adoption of the French implication. See *bizarre* in the French Lexicon.

bodega A fashionable word. It was originally used in English circles to denote a Spanish wine-cellar for the sampling and sale of wine, though the modern English implication, of a subterranean location, is absent from the Spanish. By no means all wine-cellars are below ground. Nowadays the word can variously mean a dispense or pantry (*despensa*), the hold of a ship, a granary, a tavern or bar and a warehouse.

'The bodega ... unlike the English idea of a wine cellar, is a large building above ground': *Vineyard to Decanter*, p 18 (1876).

bolas 'Balls'. A plural noun denoting the species of sling used in South America comprising two or more balls of stone or metal inter-connected by thongs. The *bolas* are thrown at animals and birds and wrap round and entangle them.

bolero A Spanish dance in 3/4 time characterized by sharp turns, stamping of the feet and sudden pauses with one arm curved over the head. Pronounced in English /bəˈlɛrəʊ/. Also, a loose waist-length jacket open at the front, worn by Spanish men and also featuring in women's *couture*. In this second sense, sometimes pronounced /ˈbəlɛrəʊ/ in English.

bonanza Literally, 'fair weather, prosperity', used in Mexican and other Latin-American mining communities to denote a mine that has proved extremely productive. By extension, an additional bonus to any enterprise, a 'turn-up for the book'.

bongós Plural noun. The pair of small drums held between the knees and played with the fingers, characteristic of, typically, Cuban music. In Latin America, the tonic accent falls on the second syllable, as the written accentuation indicates. Elsewhere, the accent seems to fall on the first syllable.

bravada In English the spelling has been altered to 'bravado'. The meaning remains the same: 'vain bragging'. More fully, 'Boastful or threatening behaviour; ostentatious display of courage or boldness; bold or daring action intended to intimidate or to express defiance; often, an assumption of courage or hardihood to conceal felt timidity, or to carry one out of a doubtful or difficult position': *OED*. The *OED* adds a useful note on usage: 'Now usually in the singular, without *a*: less commonly *a bravado* or in plural'.

bronco An untamed or partly tamed horse; a cross between a domesticated horse and a mustang (a wild horse); a native horse of California or New Mexico. Also, generically, any horse, especially in the phrase 'a bucking bronco'.

Bual See *Madeira*, below.

Buen Retiro 'Good retreat', the name of a royal palace near Madrid. Used attributively to denote a soft-paste porcelain made there during the reign of Don Carlos III.

búfalo 'The buffalo'. A word denoting several species of oxen, especially *Bos bubalus*, originally a native of India but mansuete in most of Asia and Southern Europe. Inaccurately applied to the bison of North America, *Bison Americanus*.

burro An ass or donkey. *Burrito*: a young donkey or ass.

cabana A cabin; especially nowadays in the US, a hut or shelter at a beach or swimming-pool.

caballero A (Spanish) gentleman.

cacique A prince or chief of the aboriginal inhabitants of the West Indies and adjacent parts of the former Spanish possession in America.

caldera Literally, 'a cauldron'. The word is used in geological and topographic contexts to denote a deep cauldron-like cavity or basin on the summit of an extinct volcano.

Calderón Pedro Calderón de la Barca (1600-1681), a dramatist of great distinction, following historically but not greatly influenced by the work of Lope de Vega (1562-1635) and Tirso de Molina (1571-1648), *qq.v.* Calderón is primarily but not exclusively valued as a dramatist: his non-dramatic prose works (except for a meritorious treatise on painting) are not rated highly. His dramatic works are studded with much lyric poetry of high quality, which has only sporadically and patchily been anthologized. In later life Calderón took Holy Orders and was an exemplary clergyman, like Tirso de Molina but unlike Lope de Vega, *qq.v.* Calderón's lyricism had a marked influence on the Romanticism that blossomed and flourished in all European countries during the two centuries following his own.

camarero Spanish for 'waiter'. In Portugal, either *criado* or *empregador* is used. In Spain, *criado* means a household servant.

camisado A night attack; originally one in which the attacking party wore shirts over their armour as a means of mutual recognition. (A very common word in 16th and 17th centuries.) The word conjures up the much later expression *Los Descamisados*, 'the shirtless ones', the phrase used by Eva Perón (1919-1952) in her wooing of the economically oppressed in Argentina. The term *Los Descamisados* has a history in the Peninsula too: it was a nickname given to the ultra-liberals in the Spanish revolutionary war of 1820-23, and is still sometimes used in an analogous sense.

Camões Luís Vaz de Camões (c 1524-1580) is recognized as Portugal's greatest poet. In English-speaking and other circles, his name is frequently spelt *Camoens*. In its Portuguese form it is pronounced /lu'iʃvaʃdə'kəmõjʃ/. His mastery of verse is often favourably compared to that of Homer, Virgil, Dante and Shakespeare. In his earlier life, as with his Spanish fellow-poets Cervantes, Lope de Vega and Tirso de Molina, he had considerable experience of warfare and travel. He wrote a considerable amount of lyrical poetry and drama, published posthumously, but is best remembered for his epic work of 1572, *Os Lusíadas* ('The Lusiads'). In Roman times, Portugal was known as Lusitania: Camões's poem is a magnificently patriotic glorification of Portugal's heritage from Imperial Rome and of her contemporary role in world affairs. Among other salient events, it tells the story of the explorer Vasco da Gama and, with great narrative skill, incorporates much Portuguese history. It was immediately acclaimed and has become the country's national epic. Its strongly patriotic note struck a chord with his fellow-countrymen. In the year of his death, his country was occupied by the world's most powerful empire, Spain, yet within 60 years Portugal seceded from Spain and regained her independence.

It is far from easy for someone who is not Portuguese to appreciate to the full the flavour of *Os Lusíadas*. Perhaps the following short extract will convey the burning sense of indebtedness of Portugal – of *Lusitania* – to Imperial Rome and to her civilization, including that boon of all boons, the Latin language. (Regrettably, the present editor's literal translation completely fails to capture the easy flow of the orginal.)

> Sustentava contra ele Vénus bela,
> Afeiçoada à gente Lusitania,
> Por quantas qualidades via nela
> Da antiga tão amada sua Romana;
> Nos fortes corações, na grande estrela,
> Que mostraram na terra Tingitana,
> E na língua, na qual quando imagina
> Com pouca corrupção crê que é a Latina.
> *Sustained against him the beautiful Venus,*
> *Devoted to the Lusitanian people,*
> *For the many qualities she saw in them*
> *Of her ancient so-beloved* Romanitas;
> *In the strong hearts, in the great star,*

> *That they had shown in the land of Tangier,*
> *And in the language, when she reflects on which,*
> *She believes is, with little corruption,* Latin.

It is not for nothing that Portuguese is often called *A língua de Camões*, 'the language of Camões'. In the first line of a sonnet, the Brazilian poet Olavo Bilac (1865-1918) apostrophizes Portuguese as *Ultima flor do Lácio, inculta e bela,* 'Last flower of Latium, wild and beautiful'.

campesino A peasant farmer.

cañada In the Western States of North America, a narrow valley or glen; a ravine or small *cañon*.

canasta A basket. Known in English-speaking contexts as the name of a game of cards originating in Uruguay. The word *canasta* also means a combination of seven cards.

cañon A deep gorge or ravine at the bottom of which a river or stream flows (or has flown) between high and often vertical sides; a physical feature characteristic of the Rocky Mountains, the Sierra Nevada, and the western plateaus of North America.

The spelling common in the US, 'canyon', is accounted for by the absence of the character *ñ* in most North American type-faces. For a note on the function of the diacritical sign here employed, the *tilde*, see *below s.v. tilde/til.*

cantar See the quotation for 1959 under *cantiga*.

cantiga A Spanish or Portuguese poem or folksong.

> 'Written in the Galician-Portuguese language there is not a page of the *Cantigas* which does not throw some curious light on the life of the thirteenth [century] ... Some of these poems express beautiful and widely-extended legends': A. F. G. Bell, *Modern Languages Review*, X, p 338 (1915). '*Cantiga* or *cantar* was the designation of all forms of poetry ... *cantiga de amor* ... *cantiga de amigo* ... *cantiga de escárneo* (satirical). The religious songs are represented by the *Cantigas de Santa Maria*': *Chambers's Encyclopaedia*, II, p 56/2 (1959). 'The single-voiced *cantigas* of Alfonso the Wise (1221-1284), who turned the art of the *trobadors* to spiritual ends': *The Times*, p 11/3, 18th May 1963.

cantina As far as concerns this Lexicon, the word denotes a bar-room, a saloon (in Central and South America and south-west U.S.)': *OED*. The English word 'canteen' covers a highly surprising range of meanings, well worth exploring in another context.

canto hondo, or **jondo** A popular type of Spanish song, often mournful.

> 'The gypsy style is supposed to have originated in the early 19th century from the *cante hondo* or *jondo* ... of Andalusia, a highly emotional and tragic type of song probably influenced by the Sephardic Jews': W. Apel, *The Havard Dictionary of Music*, p 268/1 (1944).

carbonado A dark, opaque variety of diamond, found near Bahia in Brazil, used in rock-drilling and stone-polishing.

> 'Black or dark-coloured ... diamonds, carbonado and bort (or boart), of no value as gems, are used for rock-drills': J. R. Parrington, *General and Inorganic Chemistry*, (2nd edn), xvii, p 439 (1951).

Carioca A colloquial name for an inhabitant of Rio de Janeiro. Also a cartoon character,

José (or Zé) Carioca, known to English-speaking film-goers as 'Joe Carioca', an Amazon parrot.

> 'The term Carioca is applied to a citizen of Rio in the same sense as cockney to a citizen of London': E. Walsh, *Notices of Brazil*, I, p 499 (1830).

carnauba The Brazilian wax-palm, *Copernicia cerifera*; 'carnauba wax', a wax exuded from the leaves of the carnauba and used in the manufacture of high quality polishes, candles, etc.

> '*Wax, Carnauba* ... From the leaves of a palm in Brazil; soluble in hot alcohol and ether': R. D. Thompson, *Dictionary of Chemistry*, p 521/1 (1854). 'It is a question whether there is a more wonderful or more useful tree to man than the carnauba (or carnahuba) tree of Brazil': *Chambers's Journal*, p 271/1 April 1919.

Cáscara 'Bark'. A laxative remedy known as *Cascara sagrada* ('sacred bark') made from the bark of a Californian buckthorn, *Rhamnus purshiana,* was formerly much prescribed. In the popular diction, the tonic accent always fell, incorrectly, on the middle syllable, a mispronunciation that was irreversibly reinforced by a humorous monologue by Billy Bennett (1887-1942), *The Foreign Legion*:

> I've served in the French Foreign Legion
> It's Hell! The life couldn't be harder,
> For it's war to the knife as you run for
> your life
> On the plains of Cascara Sagrada.

cassava The Portuguese word (Spanish *cassabe*, English 'cassava') for the *manioc, Manihot utilissima* (family *Euphorbiaceæ*), two varieties (or species) of which are extensively cultivated in the West Indies and tropical America, as also in Africa, for their fleshy tuberous roots, a staple of the indigenous diet, certainly of tropical America. The root of the Sweet Cassava (*M. Aipi*) is wholesome and is commonly prepared as a vegetable. The root of the Bitter Cassava contains a most virulent poisonous juice, which is however highly volatile, and is expelled by heat, the residual farinaceous matter being highly comestible. Both varieties provide a nutritious starch or flour from which a bread is made. One of the prepared forms of manioc flour is our *tapioca.*

castañeta Normally anglicized as 'castanet'. 'An instrument consisting of a small concave shell of ivory or hard wood, used by the Spaniards, Moors, and others, to produce a rattling sound as an accompaniment to dancing; a pair of them, fastened to the thumb, are held in the palm of the hand, and struck with the middle finger': *OED.*

castellan A governor or constable of a castle.

castellano The masculine adjective from *Castella*, 'Castile', the province of Spain so called from the numerous castles Alfonso I built for its defence. Owing to the political importance and ultimate dominance of the province, its dialect, *Castellano*, (in English, 'Castilian') assumed the ascendancy and is now considered to be standard Spanish, as distinct from any provincial dialect. There is much dissatisfaction about this situation among speakers of minority dialects of Spanish, particularly since Castellano is a somewhat idiosyncratic dialect, not by any means central to the range of dialects of the Iberian peninsula. A marked characteristic of *Castellano* is the pronunciation of the letters *z* and *c* before *e* and *i* as the breathed spirant /θ/. The occurrence of common phonemes in Provence to the East and Portugal and Galicia to the West – for example, the sound as in Portuguese *céu*, 'sky' and *chapéu*, 'hat' –

and their conspicuous absence in *Castellano* is striking and unmistakable. It serves to indicate the great, one might almost say *seismic*, linguistic obtrusion of *Castellano* into the otherwise normal, orderly, *expected* linguistic graduations in the varieties of Romance spoken from Rumania in the East to the Iberian Peninsula in the West. Nevertheless, Castilian is now the undoubted *de-facto* norm in the Peninsula, and, purged of its more extreme idiosyncrasies – the 'lisp', in particular – is also the *lingua franca* for the Spanish-speaking world. The differences that undoubtedly mark out the various local varieties of Spanish shrink into insignificance when they are compared with the monumental *heterogeneity* of International Spanish.

'The Castilian is driving all the provincial idioms of Spain from the field': *All Year Round*, No 68, p 419 (1860). 'Whose pure Castilian accent made his Spanish perfectly intelligible'; M. E. Herbert, *Impressions of Spain*, p 122 (1867).

Caudillo, el A title assumed by the head or chief of state of a Spanish-speaking country; specifically, the title (*el Caudillo*) assumed by General Francisco Franco in 1938 as head of the Spanish state, in imitation of *Duce* and *Führer*. Englishmen with some pretensions to a knowledge of Latin found it hard to take seriously a man who adopted a title that seemed to mean 'Little Tail'.

In England, in the years following the end of the Second World War, it was salutary to see that the 'anti-Fascist' elements in society, who had so effectively derided and vilified the 'cult of personality' that characterized the *régimes* of Hitler and Mussolini, with their lick-spittling *Duce* and *Führer*, should themselves drop the time-honored local-government titles 'Mayor' and 'Lord Mayor' and adopt, in their place, the title – *'Leader'*.

cedilla Originally, 'little *z*'. The mark used in French, Portuguese and Turkish under the letter *c* to show that it has the soft sound of s in positions in which, otherwise, the *c* would be pronounced hard, as before the vowels *a*, *o* and *u*.

Cervantes Miguel de Cervantes Saavedra (1547-1616), the author of a celebrated novel in two parts: *El Ingenioso Hidalgo Don Quixote de la Mancha* (1605) and *Segundo Parte del Ingenioso Caballero Don Quixote de la Mancha* (1615). The 'plot' can be gleaned from any number of epitomes in encyclopaedias and textbooks. The first volume is more amusing than the second, but the second volume is more plausible as to the action and characterization.

The work has been of perennial attraction to readers of every description ever since its publication. In essence, the story gently ridicules its principal character's infatuation with the mediaeval romances of chivalry that had anomalously maintained their popularity in Spain after they had completely lost their charm elsewhere. Interest in the entire *Matière de Bretagne* had evaporated. Of Sir Thomas Malory's *Morte d'Arthur*, Roger Ascham (1515-1568) tartly remarked, 'The whole pleasure of this book standeth in two special poyntes, in open manslaughter and bold bawdrye'. The Spanish government banned the exportation of chivalrous romances to their newly established colonies in the New World and even contemplated banning their sale in Spain itself. In the event, *Don Quixote* completely obviated the need for such measures: *Don Quixote* indeed *annihilated* the entire genre of chivalric romances.

Owing to the orthographic reforms that the Spanish language has undergone, the spelling *Quixote* is obsolete: the spelling *Quijote* is now the recognized spelling in Spanish. The pronunciation in Cervantes's time was very close to the present-day French pronunciation, as realized by the French spelling *Don Quichotte*, a spelling that was adopted by Telemann for his celebrated orchestral suite *Burlesque Don Quichotte*. The contemporary pronunciation in Spain is /kiχ'ote/. The pronunciation in English-speaking circles is normally /'kwɪksət/, though foreign travel has increased the frequency with which a passable attempt at the contemporary Spanish pronunciation has been made. In addition, the play and film *The Man of La Mancha* have greatly influenced the pronunciation of the name. (The pronunciations of derivatives in English, such as 'quixotic', are completely English in sound.)

Memorable phrases from the work include 'The Knight of the Sorrowful Countenance' (*El Caballero de la Triste Figura*); 'Hunger is the best sauce in the world' (*La mejor salsa del mundo es el hambre*); 'He's a muddle-headed fool, with frequent lucid intervals' (*Es un entreverado loco, lleno de lúcidos intervalos*); 'There are only two families in the world, as a grandmother of mine used to say: the haves and the have-nots' (*Dos linajes solos hay en el mundo, como decía una abuela mia, que son el tener y el no tener*); and 'What I say is, patience, and shuffle the cards' (*Digo, paciencia y barajar*). In addition, the image of 'tilting at windmills' has become an inseparable part of English idiom. In the same way, 'Sancho Panza' became the embodiment of the faithful though unimpressionable feudal retainer. So, also, the Christian name 'Dulcinea' (*q.v.*) became for some time a *sobriquet* for the object of a chivalrous man's amorous attentions. The utterly engaging tone-of-voice of Cervantes's narrative is such that even the name of the Don's jade or nag, *Rozinante* (*Rocinante*), became, in English, a recognizable epithet for a clapped-out but faithful hack – and that with people *who had never read two consecutive words of Cervantes!*

chaparral From *chaparra, -arro,* the evergreen oak and *-al,* a common ending for a grove, plantation, or collection of trees, as in *almendral, cafetal,* etc. The word properly means a thicket of low evergreen oak. By extension it has come to mean, in Mexico and the American States neighbouring Mexico, dense, entangled brushwood, composed of low, thorny shrubs and bushes, brambles, briars, etc., such as flourishes on the poor soils of Mexico and Texas. The word came into use in the US during the Mexican War of 1846, and has been widely disseminated by the popular television series *The High Chaparral.*

Chicano, chicano 'A person of Mexican birth or descent resident in the US (particularly in those areas annexed in 1848), esp. one who is proud of his Mexican origins and concerned to improve the position of Mexicans in the U.S.; a Mexican-American': *OED.* The word *chicano* comes from an abbreviation of *Mejicano.*

> 'In California and Texas, [the terms] Mexican- American and Chicano are most widely used. But as you travel farther south in both states, ... Mexicano is more common. In New Mexico ... many Latinos ... refer to themselves as Spanish-Americans or Hispano': *Willoughby* (Ohio) *News-Herald*, 12th May 1981.

chinchilla The *Chinchilla laniger*, an indigenous species of small rodent in Peru and Chile noted for the soft greyish chinchilla fur much prized in commerce. Also, a variety of rabbit bred for its fur; also, the fur obtained from this animal.

chorizo A sausage of which the chief ingredient is pork. Pronounced /tʃori:θo/ or /tʃori:so/, not /kori:θo/ or /kori:so/.

'The rich red sausage, the *chorizo*': R. Ford, *Gatherings from Spain*, xi, p 129 (1846). 'The red *chorizos* and *pimentisco* from Estremadura': *Chambers's Journal*, p 33 (1918). '*Chorizo*, a small Spanish sausage … heavily flavoured with garlic and paprika': *The Sunday Times*, Colour Supplement, p 27, 27th June 1971.

Cid, el Rodrigo (or Ruy) Diáz de Vivar (1040-1099), a commander under Don Alfonso VI of Castile in the eleventh century. He is the central figure in *el Poema del Cid* or *Cantar del Mio Cid*), the great epic of mediaeval Spain. It chronicles the life of Diáz de Vivar, a soldier of fortune rather than a Spanish patriot; he fought for Don Alfonso against the Moors and later fought for the Moors against Don Alfonso. He is perhaps best considered as an independent ruling prince, able in honour to make alliances as suited his *realpolitik*. For example, he conquered the Kingdom of Valencia for himself; he ruled there until his death. His honorific title itself,, *El Cid Campeador*, emblematizes his (to modern eyes) equivocal status: it comprises the Moorish Arabic *al Saïd*, 'lord, chief, commander', and the Spanish *Campeador*, 'champion'.

El Poema del Cid is the oldest monument of Spanish literature. It is a truly epic poem of a little over 3700 lines (as it has reached us – several hundred lines being missing). It is written with Homeric simplicity in an emerging, *recognizable* Spanish. The versification is often erratic, no doubt in part from careless copying, but the overall effect is quintessentially poetic.

The legend of *El Cid* has furnished material for many dramatic writers, notably Pierre Corneille (1606-84) for his acclaimed tragedy, 'Le Cid', which was profoundly influential in propagating the legend. It is probably true to say that, in our own time, the film *El Cid* (1961), starring Charlton Heston and Sophia Loren, which won three Academy Awards, was equally influential. At least, it did much to establish the fact that there exists a legend about El Cid. The actual *Poema* itself remains a closed book to most English-speakers.

Pronunciation: Spanish, /el θið/, anglicized, /el sɪd/.

cimarrón Properly, an adjective meaning 'untamed'. In use as the name of the Rocky Mountain sheep or bighorn (*el carnero cimarrón)*.

cobra de capella 'Cobra with hood' .The Hooded or Spectacle Snake (*Naja tripudians*), a very venomous serpent found in India and adjacent countries, remarkable for its power of dilating the neck and sides of the head when irritated, so as to produce the resemblance of a hood. The marking on the hood when it is distended somewhat resembles the shape of a pair of spectacles.

Cocoa For a learned discussion of this word and the word coco-nut, see *OED*, 2nd edn (1989). The discussion is particularly interesting in that it indicates that the anomalous, unphonetic letter *a* at the end of the (English) word *cocoa* came into existence by virtue of a typographical error in Dr Johnson's Dictionary.

colibri A sort of humming-bird. In England, a registered trademark for a prestigious make of cigarette-lighter.

compadre Literally, 'godfather'. By extension, a benefactor; a friend. Used also as a form of address.

commando This word, from the Portuguese verb *commandar*, 'to command', has three meanings in English usage, two historical, the third contemporary. The first denoted a body of colonial settlers in Southern Africa raised by official command (hence the word) with the object of carrying out a quasi-military punitive expedition against natives, in order, for example, to repossess land. The word originated on the borders between what is now the Republic of South Africa and Angola and Mozambique. The second meaning is an adaptation of the first: it denoted a unit of the Boers' armed forces raised in the South African War (1899-1902) from the male population of an electoral district. The third meaning is 'A member of a body of picked men trained originally (in 1940) as shock troops for the repelling of the threatened German invasion of England, later for the carrying out of raids on the Continent and elsewhere. Also applied to similar troops of other countries': *OED*.

comprador Portuguese for 'buyer', from *comprar*, 'to buy'. The title of the functionary in foreign businesses and households in China, responsible for handling most of the transactions of the house with the local suppliers. Formerly, a name in India for a servant of Europeans responsible for local purchasing.

cóndor or **condór** 'A very large South American bird of the vulture kind (*Sarcorhamphus gryphus*), inhabiting chiefly the high regions of the Andes, having blackish plumage, mixed with white in the wings, and remarkable for the caruncle [fleshy excrescence] that falls over the bill. *California Condor*: the great vulture of California (*Cathartes californianus*), resembling the South American Condor in size and other characteristics': *OED*.

conga A dance performed in 'snake' fashion, characterized by three steps forward and a kick.

conquistador Literally, 'conqueror. Used of the early Spanish conquerors of Mexico and Peru.

conta Portuguese. The bill or check in, *e.g.*, a restaurant. The masculine word, *o conto*, means a thousand; by implication, a thousand of whatever currency is relevant.

contrabando 'Contraband; smuggling; that which is smuggled'. From *contra*, 'against', and *bando*, 'proclamation or statute' (from Late Latin *bandum* or *bannum*). The word was first used unnaturalized in relation to illegal trade with the Spanish possessions towards the end of the sixteenth century.

copita Literally, 'a small cup'. A tulip-shaped glass traditionally used in Spain for drinking sherry, the configuration of which is considered important for savouring the quality of the wine; also used to mean (the contents of) a glass of sherry.

copra 'The dried kernel of the coco-nut, prepared and exported for the expression of coco-nut oil': *OED*. The quotation below is perhaps the most vivid possible instance of how our verbal usages change. When one considers that the stanzas below were written in 1914, the quotation indicates, also, at what *rate* our verbal usages change. A recitation entitled *The Whitest Man I Know* would alone take the breath away in 2006, but the next two stanzas would positively annihilate audiences of thousands.

The Whitest Man I Know

by J. Milton Hayes & R. Fenton Gower (1914)

He's a'-cruisin' in a pearler with a dirty
nigger crew, A' buyin' pearls and copra for
a stingy Spanish Jew.

cordillera 'A mountain chain or ridge, one of a series of parallel ridges; in *pl* applied originally by the Spaniards to the parallel chains of the Andes in South America (*las Cordilleras de los Andes*), subsequently extended to the continuation of the same system through Central America and Mexico': *OED*.

corposant Portuguese, from *corpo santo*, 'holy body'. A globe of luminous matter or energy that is sometimes seen on a sailing-ship or other rigged vessel, particularly round the mast or yard-arms during a storm. Also known as 'St Elmo's Fire'. The derivation of the expression is from Latin, *corpus sanctum*, 'holy body', or *corpus sancti*, 'saint's body'.

Scientific explanations are not abundant, but the following, extracted from a fuller explanation, gives the bare bones of the phenomenon.

> The phenomenon is scientifically known as a corona or point discharge. It occurs on objects, especially pointed ones, when the electrical field potential strength reaches about one thousand volts per centimetre. (When the electrical potential field is great enough to overcome the resistance of the medium across which it occurs, a current of electrons will result (Ohm's Law).) During fair weather, the electrical field strength of the atmosphere is about 1 volt per centimetre. In the initial stages of cumulonimbus (thunderstorm) formation, however, the field increases to 5 volts per centimetre, and just before a lightning flash, reaches ten thousand volts per centimetre. Thus, the atmospheric electrical field is only strong enough, under normal circumstances, to produce St. Elmo's Fire during thundery weather. When the storm is particularly heavily charged, leaves, blades of grass and even the horns of cattle may glow at their tips. In fact, the glow of St. Elmo's Fire has often been observed on sharp objects in the vicinity of tornadoes.

For a fuller account, see the entire contribution:

http://www.astrologix.de/forum/ForumID56/23.html

> 'After four a clock the Thunder and the Rain abated, and then we saw a *Corpus Sant* at our Main-topmast head ... This sight rejoic'd our Men ... for the height of the Storm is commonly over when the *Corpus Sant* is seen aloft': W. Dampier, *Voyages*, edn 1698, I, xv p 414 (1697).'A Vapor ... by Marriners call'd a Corpo Zanto': *The British Apollo*, III, No 94, p 2/1 (1710). 'Those luminous bodies which at sea skip about the masts and yards of ships, and are called *corpusanse* by the mariners': T. Shaw, *Travels in the Levant*, p 363 (1738). 'Captain Watson states that during the night the mastheads and yard-arms of his ship were 'studded with corposants'': Judkin, *Krakatoa*, p 20 (1888).

corral 'An enclosure or pen for horses, cattle, etc.; a fold; a stockade. (Chiefly in Spanish America and U.S.)': *OED*. Also as a verb, 'to corral'. The word has been imported into Afrikaans via Mozambique and Angola as *kraal*, whence into all languages to denote a small hamlet of native Africans.

corregidor The principal magistrate of a place, meaning, literally, 'the corrector'.

corrida In full, *corrida de toros*, 'course of bulls'. A bull-fight; bull-fighting. See *matador, below*.

Cortes, las The two 'Courts' or Houses of Parliament in Spain. Portuguese, *as Cortes*.

Cuba Libre Nowadays, a long drink containing rum and lime-juice. See the 1898 quotation for an earlier meaning. For a modern recipe, see the 1964 quotation.

> 'We … rode through the swamp, sometimes drinking a little 'Cuba libre' (water and brown sugar)': *Harper's Weekly*, p 813/1, 20th August, 1898. '*Cuba Libre.* Shake one measure of Bacardi rum with the juice of half a lime or lemon. Pour into a tall glass with ice and top up with iced Coca-Cola': *House & Garden*, p 106/2, November 1964.

Curaçao A liqueur consisting of spirits flavoured with the peel of bitter oranges, and sweetened. So called either because first received from the island of Curaçao, or because Curaçao oranges were used in its preparation. Curaçao is a dependency in the Netherlands Antilles, in the Caribbean near the coast of Venezuela. *Curaçao* is the Spanish (and so Dutch and French) spelling; the English spelling *curaçoa* is clearly a mis-spelling but its use in English is so widespread that it must be considered inveterate. The English pronunciation (of the mis-spelling, understood) is /kʊəɫə'səʊ/ or /'kʊəɫəsəʊ/.

cucaracha 'Cockroach'. The indigenous American species of black beetle, *Blatta occidentalis,* of a somewhat lighter coloration than the European species, *B. Orientalis.* Tens of thousands of English-speakers have listened enraptured by the popular Latin-American folk melody *La Cucaracha* without for a moment realizing that they were listening to a tune dedicated to the cockroach.

Cursillo 'A short, evangelizing course of intensive religious study and exercise, organized mainly by lay people and orig. developed in Spain in 1949 to counteract an apparent decline in popular religious commitment': *OED. Cf. ultreya, below.*

> 'A Cursillo (from *Cursillos de Cristiandad*, Little Courses in Christianity) is a three-day program of intensive prayer, study, discussion and community living': *Ave Maria*, p 5/2, February 1964. 'Cursillo, unlike a retreat, is not silent': *Oxford Diocesan Magazine*, p 11/1, November 1987. 'The Cursillo goal of Christianizing one's environment': *Washington Diocese*, p 4/1, November 1987.

cuspidor Portuguese. 'A spittoon'. Literally, 'a spitter; one who spits', from *cuspir*, 'to spit' and Latin *conspuĕre*.

desaparecido Literally, 'one who had disappeared', used, normally in the plural, to denote the many people in Argentina who disappeared during the military regime between 1976 and 1983, presumed killed by members of the armed services or by the police.

Descamisados, los See *camisado, above.*

desperado The past participle of the Old Spanish verb *desperar*, 'to despair'. The word is used in English to denote a desperate or reckless man; one who has lost hope, who has nothing to lose, who is ready for any deed of lawlessness or violence. There are difficulties with this word. In modern Spanish the comparable past participle would be *desesperado*, from *desesperar*, but there is no record of the use of either *desperado* or *desesperado* in Spanish as a substantive, as *desperado* is used in English. There was at one period a fashionable trend in English literature to add *-ado* to words to give them a touch of drama: perhaps *desperado* is such a word.

Diego The Christian name 'James', popular in Spain as the name of the patron saint of Spain, St James of Compostella. It is said to have given rise to the word 'dago', an opprobrious name for Latinos. The *OED* comments: 'A name originally given in the south-western section of the United States to a man of Spanish parentage; now extended to include Spaniards, Portuguese, and Italians in general, or as a disparaging term for any foreigner'.

dinero The name of various coins over the years: from Latin, *denarius*, a penny. Now, colloquial US for 'money'.

> '"Here's a little bunch of the *dinero* that I drawed out of the bank this morning," says he, and shows a roll of twenties and fifties': 'O. Henry', *Heart of the West,* vi, p 84 (1907).

dodo Portuguese: 'a simpleton, a fool'; also used adjectivally: 'foolish, stupid'. An extinct bird, *Didus ineptus*, belonging to the family *Columbidae*, formerly inhabiting the island of Mauritius; it had a massive clumsy body, and small wings of no use for flight; applied figuratively in English to a old-fashioned, stupid, inactive, or unenlightened person, and in the expression, 'As dead as the [or a] dodo'.

Dom A title affixed to the Christian names of Portuguese kings (*e.g.,* Dom Alfonso III), cardinals, bishops and persons on whom the title has been confirmed by royal authority.

Don A title of respect in Spanish. Formerly accorded to noblemen but today purely a courtesy title and mode of address. In English, a familiar word for a university dignitary.

Doña and **Dona** The Spanish and Portuguese equivalents, respectively, of *Don* and *Dom.* In Portugal, the polite form by which to refer to a lady is 'Senhora Dona [Christian name] [surname]: in Brazil, often simply 'Dona [Christian name]. The word *dona* is also used in such expressions as *dona de casa* and *dona de iate*, 'housewife' (or 'lady of the house') and 'yachtswoman'. See also *senhor, below.*

The words 'dona', 'donah' and 'doner'occur in English and American slang, meaning 'woman'. There are four possible routes by which this slang word arrived in English. The first is direct from Spanish and/or Portuguese, the first of which is the favoured route for the word in American slang. The second is through Ladino (*q.v.*), the language of Sephardic Jews. The third is through Polari, the cant language of showmen, circus people, actors and homosexuals in Britain (though in those *milieux*, 'polone' is more common). The fourth is, via seamen and traders, through *Lingua Franca (q..v.* in the Italian Lexicon). The quotations below amplify these comments on provenance.

> '*Dona and feeles,* a woman and children': *A Dictionary of Slang* (1873). 'A circus man almost always speaks of a circus woman, not as a woman, but a dona': *The Athenaeum,* p 545, 24th April 1875. 'Blokes and donahs ... of the foulest slums': J. Farrell, *How He Died,* p 62 (1887). 'The little donah': *The Yellow Book,* I, p 79 (1894).

Dorado, El Literally 'the gilded one'. 'The name of a fictitious country (according to others a city) abounding in gold, believed by the Spaniards and by Sir W. Raleigh to exist upon the Amazon within the jurisdiction of the governor of Guiana': *OED.*

Douro, O The province of Portugal from which Port wine comes. It is also the name of the river, *o Douro* (literally, river 'of wine', since in Classical times the rocks were seen to shine with gold). Contrary to the general English supposition, the word is pronounced /doru/ not /duro/: the vowel sounds are transposed from what the average English eye and ear would suppose. The chief port of shipment for Port is *o Porto* ('the Port'), anglicized as 'Oporto'.

dragoman Strictly, an interpreter in regions where Arabic, Turkish or Persian is spoken. From Old Arabic *targum*, now *tarjum* (*tarjam, tarjum*), through late Greek *δραγούμανος* to modern European languages. English has adopted the Spanish form.

Dueña Formerly, in English usage, *duenna* (hence the title of R. B. Sheridan's play *The Duenna*). The feminine of *dueño*, 'master'. *La Dueña* was the chief lady in waiting on the Queen of Spain. In general, the term was applied to an elderly, respectable woman having charge over the girls of a Spanish family and, depending on circumstances, occupying a position somewhere between a governess, a *chaperon* and a companion.

Dulcinea The name given by Don Quixote to his mistress in the romance of that name by Cervantes (*q.v.*); hence, a mistress, a sweetheart, an object of one's devotion. *Cf Cervantes.*

elíxir Spanish: In alchemy, a preparation by means of which it was attempted to transmute base metals into gold. Sometimes identified with 'the Philosopher's Stone'. Often used loosely to refer to mixtures of materials with supposed extraordinary properties. Also, as *elixir vitae*, 'elixir of life', a supposed drug or essence with the property of indefinitely extending life. By extension, used by quacks as an name for their nostrums. Portuguese: *elexir*. From the Arabic *al-iksīr*, 'the mixture', 'the preparation' or some such connotation, perhaps from late Greek *ξήριον*, a drying powder for the treatment of open wounds.

embarcadero A wharf or quay.

embargo from *embargar*, 'to arrest or impede'. 'A prohibitory order, forbidding the ships of a foreign power to enter or leave the ports of a country, or native ships to proceed thither, generally issued in anticipation of war. An embargo may also be laid on particular branches of commerce, for fiscal purpose. A suspension of commerce, either general or of some particular branch, imposed by municipal law. Also in phrases: to be under, to lay (on), to take off an embargo': *OED*. To a large extent the modern but ambiguous word 'sanctions' has usurped the function of the word *embargo* in its traditional sense, but 'embargo', as a purely English word, has taken on a new lease of life in the field of Public Relations, in which it denotes a condition imposed (in trust rather than contractually) that the recipient of a Press Release will not disclose the contents of the Press Release until a certain and stated time has elapsed.

enchilada The feminine adjective from the verb 'to season with chile'. The present predominant use is as a noun, denoting a *tortilla* (*q.v.*) served with a sauce seasoned with chile. There is a US idiom that has gained popularity in recent years, 'the whole *enchilada*', meaning 'the whole subject or matter'. It seems to be a (quasi)-Latin-American calque on the Yiddish-based 'the whole *shtik*'. For mass-entertainment purposes, it is fashionable among 'rootless cosmopolitan' circles in the US to dress characteristic *shtetl* situations up in the trappings of Sicilian extended families, as with Bea's mother in *The Golden Girls*, who purports to come from Sicily but the essence of her humour is that it is pure Byalistok. Much the same transferred-insider approach characterizes TV comedy shows purporting to depict Latino situations. The practice applies to other situations too, as, for example, to the scene in *Blazing Saddles* in which the Indian Chief speaks Yiddish.

escudo Literally, 'shield'. A denomination of Portuguese currency; also at various times the name of coins, gold or silver, in Spain, Portugal and Latin America. The name of the coin derives from the presence of a shield on the coin. The pronunciation of the unit of currency in the Peninsula, /əʃ'ku:du/, links us easily to the *scudo*, the former unit of currency of many of the Italian states, and, less directly, to the *écu*.

esparto A kind of rush (*Macrochloa* or *Stipa tenacissima*), called by some 'Spanish Grass', imported into England from Spain and the north coast of Africa for the manufacture of a superior quality of paper. In ancient times it was, and in Spain is still, made into cordage, shoes, and other articles. Also called 'esparto grass'. See *espadrille* in the French Lexicon: the French word derives from the same root as *esparto*.

estancia A cattle-ranch in Latin America. (*Rancho* means a mess, a company of persons who eat together; in Spanish America the word denotes the huts occupied by herdsmen or labourers.)

fado Portuguese, 'fate'. The name given to a highly popular Portuguese folk-song of melancholy type, probably the word after *saudade* (*q.v., below*) that most characterizes Portugal. The *fado* is an art form in its own right. It must be said, it is an acquired taste – and not everyone acquires it. To some extent the traditional *fado* has been commandeered by the social 'protest-song' movement, but its essential core character remains discernible almost all the time, especially in the performances of the most celebrated *fado* singer, Amália Rodriguez, *a Raina do Fado*, 'the Queen of the Fado' (1920-1999).

> 'The nearest we can get to the original significance of the word is to call the '*fado*' the laborer's song of fate; which is more than we can do with the present form, for the Portuguese indiscriminately call '*fados*' what we designate as serenades, ballads, jigs, and sailor's hornpipes': *Journal of American Folklore*, p 165, July-September 1902. 'The *fado*, that remarkable modern product of Portuguese popular genius': *Discovery*, p 396/2, December 1936. 'A brilliant run-through of Portuguese poetry and prose, the inevitable chapter on the *fado*': *The Times Literary Supplement*, p 736/3 1957. 'The most typical way to spend an evening in Lisbon is to listen to *fados*, the traditional song of the Portuguese town worker; but make sure that you go to a genuine *fado* restaurant': *The Times*, p viii/5, 1st November 1969.

faena Literally, 'task'. The last part of a bullfight. A trisyllable, /fa'ena/.

> '[The] ... *faena* (the part when the matador plays the bull alone with the red cloth)': *The Times*, p 7/7, 12th October 1957.

faja A sash or girdle.

falange Literally, 'a phalanx'. The word *Falange* assumed importance with the birth of *la Falange Española*, a Spanish political party, founded in 1933 as a Fascist movement by José Antonio Primo de Rivera (1903-1975). (*Cf Fascism* in the Italian Lexicon.) It was merged in 1937 with traditional right-wing elements, such as the Carlists, to form the ruling party, the *Falange Española Tradicionalista*, under General Francisco Franco Bahamonde (1892-1975), though Franco himself had never been either a Carlist or a Falangist. The Falange was in fact so much of an amalgam of widely disparate interests that was not in any modern sense a political party. Franco governed as an autocrat. The Fascist elements with which Primo de Rivera's party were freighted were, under Franco, attenuated in practice, except in the eyes of International Communism, though there were elements of classical Fascism in the Franquist polity, such as, for instance, the Corporativist State (*q.v.* in the Italian Lexicon), with its concomitant blemishes of subservient Market Sectors and ineffectual trades unions.

fandango A lively dance in ¾ time, very popular in Spain and Spanish America.

farinha Often an alternative name for *cassava (q.v., above)* but more correctly the flour made by mixing the pure extract with some of the woody, fibrous part of the plant.

favela Brazilian Portuguese. A shack, an improvised shelter, normally in the plural, *favelas*, to denote the shanty-towns that exist in Rio de Janeiro, São Paulo. And other Brazilian towns. Hence, *favelado*, one who lives in a *favela*.

> 'In the midst of all this beauty and elegance, you discover the favelas ... The *favela* is a wretched, ramshackle, filthy hut run up out of sticks, rotting planks, dirty rags and cardboard, as a rule in less than twenty-four hours ... The *favelas* have no electricity (unless, as frequently happens, an enterprising favelado manages to tap an electric cable)': George Mikes, *Tango*, p 18 (1961).

fazenda See *hacienda***.** The Portuguese *fazer*, 'to do or to make' is the analogue of the Spanish *hacer*.

fidalgo The analogue in Portuguese of the Spanish *hidalgo (q.v., below.)*. From *filho de algo*, 'son of something'.

Fidelismo The methods and policies of Colonel Fidel Castro's autocratic *régime* in Cuba; *Castroismo*. Hence *Fidelista*, an adherent of Fidel Castro.

fiesta A (Spanish and Latino) religious festival; also, any festivity or holiday. Portuguese: *festa*.

Filipino[a] An inhabitant of the Phillippines *(las Islas Filipinos*), especially one of mixed Spanish and indigenous blood.

finca A landed property; a (country) estate; a ranch. Portuguese: *fazenda, granja, propriedade*.

fino The driest of the sherries.

> 'Those [sherries] only which exhibit great delicacy, body, and flavour are called *finos* or fine': E. Ford, *Gatherings from Spain*, xiv, p 155 (1846). 'The Amontillado class may be ... subdivided into Fino and Oloroso': *Encyclopaedia Britannica*, XXIV, p 607/1 (1888). 'The finos which the Spaniards æ drink are considerably drier than those which they export': W. James, *The Word-Book of Wine*, p 78 (1959).

flamenco A Spanish gipsy style of singing or dancing; a song or dance in this style. The word means, literally, 'Flemish' in Spanish. The Portuguese analogue is *flamengo*. Since there is no plausible connection between Flanders and gipsies, the derivation of the name of the dance must be from the bird 'the flamingo', in that the gestures of the dancers in the *flamenco* resemble to some extent the gait of the flamingo, *Phoenicopterus*, which has extremely long and slender legs and neck.

flor A whitish film of yeast, usually of the genus *Mycoderma*, that grows on the surface of various sherries, especially dry sherries, during fermentation, giving them a distinctive and highly prized flavour. (See, in general, *pourriture noble* in the French Lexicon and *Eiswein* in the German Lexicon.)

flotilla A word meaning a small fleet, the diminutive of *flota*, 'a fleet'. The word is nowadays used in English only to denote a small detachment of warships of unspecified number and description.

folia Literally, 'folly'. The word denote a type of dance similar to a *fandango* (q.v.). The melody generally known as *La Folia di Spagna*, by origin Portuguese, captivated generations of composers and has given rise to scores of variations, perhaps even hundreds.

fonda An hôtel, inn or roadhouse in Spain and North Africa; this word derives from the Arabic *funduq*, 'an inn', which itself derives from the Greek *πανδοκος, πανδοκευς* 'an innkeeper', and whence *πάνδοκεîον*, 'an inn'.

Frente Popular The Spanish manifestation in 1936 of an international movement instigated by the Comintern, the Communist International, the international organization of the Communist Party, founded in 1919 and dissolved in 1943. The strategy of the Comintern was to work towards the unification of all the parties of the Left. The watchword of International Communism was *Pas d'ennemi à gauche.* In Spain the *Frente Popular* achieved a parliamentary majority in 1936 with 34.3 per cent of the electorate of 13,553,710 (9.864,401 voted), as against 33.2 per cent of the votes cast in favour of the Right and Centre bloc: Tusell Gómes *et al, Las Elecciones del Frente Popular en Espana,* ii, p 13 (1971).

friagem Portuguese: 'a cold spell'. For a specific usage, see quotations.

'On the middle Amazon there is usually a cool spell of 5 or 6 days in May or June, brought by a south wind called 'friagem": W. G. Kendrew, *Climate Control*, xl, p 327 (1922). 'Cold waves known as 'friagems": A. A. Miller, *Climatology*, vi, p 130 (1931). 'Throughout the world, invasions of markedly cold air into equatorial regions are usually rare, and consequently the *friagem* is a very interesting meteorological phenomenon': Haurwitz & Austin, *Climatology*, x, p 225 (1944). 'Occasional outbursts of unusually cold, relatively dry air ..., originating over the expanded frozen surfaces around Antarctica, make their way much farther north than is normal and sometimes actually cross the equator ... Such weather in Brazil is called a *friagem*': G. R. Rumney, *Climatology*, xiv, 288 (1968).

fronton A building in which *pelote* (*q.v.*) is played.

gaita A musical instrument resembling the Scotch bagpipes. So, *gaitero*, 'a piper'.

'The *gaita* ... is a bagpipe, green in color, which is the same as the better-known bagpipes of Scotland and Ireland': 'La Meri', *Spanish Dancing* (2nd edn) ii, p 32 (1967).

Gallejo, Gallego A Galician: traditionally pronounced /ga"ʎego/.

garrocha A picador's spear or goad.

garrote A method of executing capital punishment. A cord is wound round the neck of the convicted person and is then tightened by the use of a stick inserted in the loop of the cord. The stick is then turned progressively until the convicted person is strangled to death. The word is also used for a method of criminal murder employing the same technique. The spelling *garrotte* is owing to French influence.

> 'I have no hesitation in pronouncing death by the garrot, at once the most manly, and the least offensive to the eye': John Richardson, *Movements of the British Legion; with Strictures on the Course of Conduct pursued by Lieut.-General Evans*, viii (2nd edn) p 210 (1837).

gazpacho A cold soup. See quotations.

> 'Gazpacho … .is a cold vegetable soup, and is composed of onions, garlic, cucumbers, *pepinos*, pimientas, all chopped up very small and mixed with crumbs of bread, and then put into a bowl of oil, vinegar, and fresh water': Richard Ford, *Hand-Book for Travellers in Spain* I, I, p 59 (1845). '*Gazpacho* is traditionally served accompanied by individual small bowls of raw vegetables and garlic *croûtons*': Robert Carrier, *Great Dishes of the World*, p 56/2 (1963). 'Gazpacho should rest and 'marry' for a time before being eaten': *The New Yorker*, p 164/2, 20th September 1969.

gaucho Loosely, a Latin-American cowboy. More accurately, as described in the following quotation.

> 'The Gauchos of the South American Pampas, [are] a mixed European and Indian race of equestrian herdsmen': Edward B. Tyler, *Primitive Culture*, I, p 41 (1871).

gitano A (male) gipsy. Pronounced /χit'aːno/. Hence, *gitana*, a female gipsy.

granadilla The diminutive of *granada*, 'pomegranate. Sometimes spelt *granedilla or grenadilla* in English. The generic name *granadilla* is used to denote various tropical species of the Passion-flower; especially the *Passiflora quadrangularis* and its fruit, which is highly esteemed as a dessert fruit.

grifo 'Marijuana'. The word *grifo* is possibly the origin of the English-language word 'reefer' for a marihuana cigarette.

gringo A Mexican-Spanish opprobrious word for a citizen of the United States; used also of Englishmen. The origin of the word is so obscure as to be virtually unknown. Suggestions have been made linking the word with a Mexican slang word *gringo* meaning 'gibberish', but that word seems to be a back-formation from the substantive *Gringo*. A suggestion has been made that the word is a corruption of *griego*, 'Greek', alluding to the ability of Anglo-Saxons to speak any language provided it is English: 'it's all Greek to me'. Francophone etymologists have speculated that the word might be cognate with the French word *grigou*, 'a wretch'.

guacamole A Mexican dish made from avocado pears mixed with onions, tomatoes, chili peppers, and seasoning.

> 'A frequently-told urban legend in Labour Party circles has it that [Peter] Mandelson, visiting a fish-and-chip shop in his new constituency, saw the mushy peas and asked the proprietor about the 'guacamole dip': see *Wikipedia*:

http://en.wikipedia.org/wiki/Peter_Mandels on

Guanche An aboriginal inhabitant of the Canary Islands. The race, of Berber stock, was absorbed by the Spanish on their conquest of the islands in the fifteenth century. Also, the language of the Guanches.

guano 'A natural manure found in great abundance on some sea-coasts, esp. on the Chincha and other islands about Peru, consisting of the excrement of sea-fowl': *OED*.

Guardia Civil 'A force formed in Spain in 1844 to take over police duties from the military, and chiefly responsible for public order and safety': *OED*.

guava A tree of the myrtaceous genus *Psidium* of tropical America, esp. *P. Guayava* (now naturalized in many tropical countries). It produces a fruit that has a strong acid flavour somewhat like that of a quince, and inedible unless preserved or made into a jelly.

guerrilla Properly, 'a small war'. From the time of the Peninsular Wars, there has been a tendency among English-speakers (see quotation, below, for 1809) to use this word in application to those who wage the small wars rather than restricting it to the small wars themselves. There has always been a serviceable Spanish word, *guerrillero*, for one who participates in such small wars, but it has never caught on among English-speakers. It is now much too late to hope to restore the proper meanings to these words, since the word *guerrilla* has been so widely used in the Second World War, to the utter exclusion of *guerrilleros*. (The form with the single letter *r* is due to the French word *guèrilla*.)

> 'I have recommended to the Junta to set … the Guerrillas to work towards Madrid': Wellington in John Gurwood, ed, *The Dispatches of … the Duke of Wellington 1799–1818* (1835,) V, p 9 (1810).

Habanero A (male) inhabitant of Havana, Cuba. Also, a Cuban cigar. Georges Bizet gave the eponymous Carmen an aria called *La Habanera* in his opera *Carmen*, a piece in feeling reminiscent of the *contradanza* in 2/4 time that was and is very popular in Havana. In fact, the dance is not known as *La Habanera* in Havana itself but merely as *la contradanza*. As its popularity spread, the dance became universally known as *La Habanera*.

hacienda A multi-functional concept. The *OED* definition is as follows: ' In Spain, and existing or former Sp. colonies: An estate or 'plantation' with a dwelling-house upon it; a farming, stock-raising, mining, or manufacturing establishment in the country; sometimes, a country-house'. The proprietor of a *hacienda* is a *hacendado (haciendado)*. The close analogue to *hacienda* in Portuguese is *fazenda*.

'¡Hasta la vista!' 'To the [re-]seeing!' 'Au revoir!'

horchata A popular soft drink flavoured with *chuva*, ground almond (*Cyperus esculentus*) and served chilled.

huerta Literally, 'a garden', from Latin, *hortus*.

> 'From the Ebro delta to Cape de la Nao in Valencia, the irrigated districts ('huertas', from Lat. *hortus* = a garden) are practically continuous along the coast': M. R. Shackleton, *Europe*, vii, p 89 (1934).
> 'Originally developed by the Moslems, the 'huertas' are small, highly cultivated plots which depend on irrigation water brought by an intricate system of channels, aqueducts and lifts': Fisher & Bowen-Jones, *Spain*, iv, p 52 (1958).

hidalgo From *hijo de algo*, 'son of something'. A gentleman by birth; one of the gentry or lower nobility. No-one who was not a hidalgo was formerly entitle to the appellation *Don*. *Cf fidalgo, above.*

incomunicado So spelt in present-day Spanish. Literally, 'out of communication', formally (by process of law) cut of from the outside world; deprived of the right to communicate with others.

> 'The prisoners will be ... detained again under the Terrorism Act by the Special Branch, permitted to hold any person *incommunicado* for any length of time': *The Observer*, p 4/7, 13th September 1970.

indulto A duty levied by the Kings of Spain and Portugal on imports, trade and other activities.

Infante 'A son of the king and queen of Spain or Portugal other than the heir to the throne (who is called *principe*); *spec.* the second son. Sometimes erroneously applied to the heir to the throne': *OED.* So, *infanta*, the eldest daughter who is not heir to the throne.

intrado A formal entry, *scil*, of a personage; a piece of music composed to accompany a formal entry. Also, formerly, an item of income, from its being an 'entry' in book-keeping terms.

ipecacuanha 'The root of *Cephaëlis Ipecacuanha*, N.O. *Cinchonaceæ*, a South American small shrubby plant, which possesses emetic, diaphoretic, and purgative properties': *OED.*

Jerez de la Frontera The centre of production of the slightly fortified white wine known in English-speaking circles as 'sherry'. The pronunciation is /'χereθ/. The older spelling of the place-name was *Xerez*, which was pronounced /'ʃeres/, whence the earlier English name 'sherris'. Over the years, 'sherris' was taken to be a plural and the imagined singular, 'sherry', became the name for the drink.

jornada Formerly, an act of a play; a book or canto of a poem. In Mexico, a march or journey performed in a day; specifically, a journey across a tract where there is no water and consequently no place to halt; also, the waterless district thus traversed.

jota A popular Spanish folk-dance in 3/4 or 3/8 time.

> 'The Spanish dance is intensely national. The snapping of the castanets, the short and insolent skirt, the exciting rhythm of the music, do not alone suffice for the performance of the *jota* or *fandango*, as some foreign artists would appear to suppose': J. E. C. Flitch, *Modern Dancing and Dancers*, xiii, p 195 (1912). 'It is said that the Jota, 'the fastest dance in the world', is less a dance than an endurance contest': 'La Meri', *Spanish Dancing* (ed. 2) ii, p 36 (1967).

junta In a neutral sense, a deliberative or administrative council or committee. In modern English history, the term *junta* is applied to the local councils set up to resist Bonaparte's invasion of Spain in the Summer of 1808. In a more partisan sense, the word *junta* – in particular, '*military junta*' – is applied to groupings of (right-wing) army officers who, by means of a *coup d'ètat*, have gained power by force of arms. In some way, neither Colonel Castro's *coup d'ètat* in Cuba in 1959 or General Antonio dos Santos Ramalha Eanes's in Portugal in 1974 have attracted the opprobrious epithet *junta*, or, indeed, other similarly charged words such as *putsch*. Even the unambiguously totalitarian military regime in Myanmar (Burma) has not earned anything like the opprobrium the Colonel's Ruritanian fiasco earned in Greece during their reign there from 1967 to 1974.

Ladino The language of the Spanish and Portuguese Jews expelled from, respectively, Spain in 1492 and Portugal in 1497, still spoken in Mediterranean regions. It is fundamentally mediaeval Spanish with many

Hebrew words incorporated, and with further admixtures of the local languages in the regions in which it is or was spoken. It is written, primarily, in Hebrew characters (*Rashi* script) but is nowadays often helpfully transliterated into the Latin alphabet. It is also known *as Judeo-Spanish, Judeo-español, Djudezmo, Spanyolit, Spaniol de mosotros*, and *Sephardí;* in Morocco it was called *Haketía*, and in Yugoslavia, *Djidó*. *Cf. Tudesco, below.*

lagniappe Not strictly a Spanish word but a popular gallicization originating in Louisiana of the Spanish *la ñapa*. It originally signified something given in addition to what was purchased, as a mean whereby the retailer could express his gratitude for the patronage of the customer. The word ultimately derives from the phrase *de ñapa*, meaning 'into the bargain'.

lambada A fast, rhythmical, and erotic dance originating in Brazil in which couples dance in close physical contact. The word derives from the Portuguese *lambar* meaning 'to beat' or 'to whip'. It is tempting to infer that the English colloquial word 'lambast', 'to beat', 'to thrash', might derive from *lambar*. The English word is more often encountered as 'lambast' than in the spelling favoured by the *OED*, 'lambaste', and it is clearly observable that the word and its cognates are normally pronounced /'læmbæst/, not /'læmbeɪst/, and so on. The route by which *lambar* might well have passed into colloquial English is the under-explored one involving Ladino, Polary, *Lingua Franca* and thieves'-cant.

lariat Not a Spanish word but an anglicization of *la reata*, (or, sometimes, *riata*), 'the halter'. The Portuguese is *reate, arreata, arriata*), from *reatar,* 'to tie again'. The word 'lariat' denotes a rope used for picketing horses or mules; a cord or rope with a noose used in catching wild cattle; the lasso of Mexico and South America. *Cf lasso, below.*

larga In bull-fighting, a pass making full use of the cape.

lascar An East-Indian seaman. Frequently spelt with a capital initial, as though the word were the proper name of a tribe or race. In fact, the word seems to be a Portuguese approximate use of the Urdu word, of Persian provenance, *lashkarī*, from *lashkar*, 'an army' or 'an army camp'. The word has also been used for 'foot-soldier', and sometimes for 'a horseman'. There is sometimes a supposed difference made between *luscar*, 'a soldier' and *lascar*, 'a sailor'. The word has also been applied to native constables in colonial police-forces.

lasso Strictly, not a Spanish word in that spelling. The word *lazo*, pronounced /'laso/ in the Americas, denotes a long rope of untanned hide, from 10 to 30 metres in length, having at the end a noose to catch cattle and wild horses; the word is used chiefly in Spanish America. There is a particularly nice instance of inadvertent disingenuousness in the entry for *lasso* in the Second Edition of the *OED* (1989). The *OED* quite rightly points out that H. W. Fowler was (uncharacteristically) wrong when he said, in *Modern English Usage* (1928), 'Lasso is pronounced l*a*sōō' by those who use it; but the English pronunciation is lă'sō'. The Second Edition of the *OED* comments, 'In ed. 2 (1965)[of Modern English Usage], Sir E. Gowers changed this to '*lasso* is pronounced l*a*sōō' by those who use it, and by most English people too". What the *OED* fails to mention is that H. W. Fowler's original sentence in its entirety read: 'Lasso is pronounced l*a*sōō' by those who use it; but the English pronunciation is lă'sō, & the *OED* gives that only'.

latifundista One possessed of large estates, from Latin *latifundium*, 'a broad estate'.

Latino A (male) person of Latin-American origin, appearance or affiliations. The increasing immigration, legal or illegal, of Spanish-speaking persons into the United States, and the increasing political awareness of that grouping, has led to a rapid increase in the use of the word *Latino*, which is almost unique in the sphere of racial and ethnic matters in being used completely without rancour by every section of the community, though in areas where an ethnic imbalance is apprehended by 'the indigenes', opprobrious terms such as 'spik' are in use. (The derivation of 'spik', meaning a Latino, is that he will no doubt, when addressed, respond, 'I no spik English'. Opprobrious epithets have a habit of settling down into the mainstream – or of disappearing completely. Few Canadians nowadays would object to being called 'Canucks', and few Poles would object to being called 'Polacks'. Even fewer Welshmen would object to being called 'Taffies', even with the immense over-burden of implication – Taffy was a Welshman, Taffy was a thief./ Taffy came to my house and stole a leg of beef'.

Leveche An extremely hot, dry wind that affects South-Eastern Spain. Pronounced /le'betʃe/.

> 'The eastern part of this [southern] zone is the part of Spain which is liable to be visited from time to time by the scorching and blasting *Leveche*, the name given in Spain to the sirocco': *Encyclopaedia Britannica*, XXII, p 296/2 (1887). 'The Mediterranean area also is the home of a hot, searing, dust-laden wind off the Sahara, known in various localities as *sirocco, khamsin, leveche*, or *samiel*': J. E. Van Riper, *Man's Physical World*, vii, p 222/2 (1962).

lidia Literally, 'fight'. Applied particularly to the earlier stages of a bullfight, during which the *quadrilla* or *cuadrilla* (the troupe of a matador) prepare the bull for the *faena* (*q.v.*)

lingoa Portuguese for 'tongue, language', the etymon of the English 'lingo'. *Lingoa geral*: 'general language': an amalgam of Tupi, a local language in Brazil, and Portuguese promoted by the Jesuits with considerable success, to the extent that it became a *lingua franca* in Brazil. It eventually yielded to Portuguese.

llama A South-American ruminant quadruped, *Auchenia llama*, akin to the camel but humpless, used as a beast of burden in the Andes.

llano A level, treeless plain or steppe in the Northern parts of South America.

lobo The large grey wolf *Canis lupus occidentalis* indigenous to the South-Western United States.

loco Insane. Formerly applied colloquially to marihuana in the form 'loco-weed'.

Lope de Vega Felix Lope de Vega y Carpio (1562-1635). An extremely prolific playwright, the author of over 1800 *comedias* and several hundred shorter dramatic pieces. In the pantheon of Spanish writing, he stands second only to Cervantes. He has not made a significant impact on English-speaking life and letters, as witness the rough-and-ready evidence from the dictionaries of quotations. *Bartlett's Familiar Quotations*, 15th edn (1980), for example, has two quotations (see below). *The Oxford Dictionary of Quotations*, 4th edn (1992), has none. (*Cf Calderón, above*, and *Tirso de Molina, below*.)

> 'Harmony is pure love, for love is complete agreement': Lope de Vega,

Fuenteovejuna, act 1, ln 381 (c 1613), *tr* Flores & Kittel in *Spanish Drama* (1962). 'Except for God, the King's our only lord': *ibid*, ln 1701.

machete 'A broad, heavy knife or cutlass used as an implement or as a weapon, originating in Central America and the Caribbean': *OED*. In conformity with the *OED*'s present policy (Draft Revision March 2003), the Spanish pronunciation of the word is not given. Perhaps that is forgivable in the light of the extremely complex history of this word in the English language, for which see the current entry for the word in the *OED Online*. An acceptable pronunciation would be /matʃ'ɛti/.

macho, machismo *Macho* may be either a substantive or an adjective: it signifies as a substantive 'a male' or, in the abstract, 'maleness'. It has come in recent years to mean 'a notably or ostentatiously masculine, tough, or vigorous man; one who is aggressively proud of his masculinity': *OED*. The exact use of the word *macho* and its preferred abstract form *machismo* in the US is coloured by the proximity of that country to Mexico: a Mexican *nuance* of meaning, largely favourable, is present in the US usage, though increasingly there appears to be a undercurrent of scepticism about the desirability of *machismo*. In other Latin-American countries the exact meaning of *macho* and *machismo* can vary considerably. A search on the Internet against *machismo* will reveal the extent of this variation. Users of the word in South America are advised to look into these regional variations.

The *OED* suggests that the erroneous pronunciation /ma'kizmo/ is due to the belief that the word has the combination *-ch-* as sounded in words from Greek roots. If we examine that protean word 'machine', we shall find that there is no uniformity, nowadays, in the pronunciations of words derived from Greek and containing the letters 'ch'. A straw poll among English users of the word indicates that this mistaken pronunciation is owing to the belief that the word should be pronounced as an *Italian* word. The pronunciation should be firmly /'matʃo/ and /ma'tʃismo/.

Madeira The name of the island in the Atlantic Ocean about 440 miles (719 km) west of Morocco, so called because it was thickly wooded when discovered (*madeira* being the Portuguese for 'timber'). The word 'Madeira' in English connotes a range of four fortified wines produced in Madeira with a Gay-Lussac reading of about 20 per cent, comprising dry, medium and sweet varieties. The driest, *Sercial*, /sɛrs'jal/, is pale in coloration, and is said to be produced from varieties of the grape that, in more Northerly parts of Europe, produces hock. Less dry is *Verdelho*, /vɛr'dɛʎu/. *Bual* (in Portuguese, *Boal*, pronounced /bwal/) is sweeter, and there is a still sweeter one, the celebrated *Malmsey*, *Malvasia*, named from the place Napoli di Malvasia in the Peloponnese, (*Μονεμβασία*) where the Malmsey variety of grape originated and 'held the gorgeous East in fee' for generations.

There is nowadays an unfortified wine, a Madeiran table wine, produced in great quantity, considering the small size of the island of Madeira, from the anomalously named Pino Verde ('green pine') grape, which is in fact a black grape. This recent development reminds is that, before fortification with grape brandy became mandatory with the Madeiras (to permit long voyages to the New World) unfortified Madeiran wines were very highly esteemed.

Madrileno An inhabitant of Madrid.

Maja Desnuda, la 'The Nude Maja'. One of two paintings, the other *La Maja Vestida* ('The Clothed Maja'), painted by Francisco de Goya (1746-1828) at some time between 1797 and 1800. *Maja* means 'a woman who dresses gaily; a pretty young woman, originally one of the lower classes': *OED.*

majolica See *majolica* in the Italian Lexicon.

mañana 'Tomorrow'.

> 'The elaborate etiquette and principle of mañana (leave everything until tomorrow, in the absolute confidence that tomorrow will never arrive), which dominates all dealings in South America': C. Bonington, *Next Horizon*, xiv, p 201 (1973).

mandarin An early Portuguese adaptation of the Malay word *menteri,* from Sanskrit *mantrin,* 'a counsellor, and applied by Europeans to officials of the Chinese Empire. The Chinese word was *guān* or *kuān*, signifying 'Imperial'. The language of the mandarins was called Mandarin, a term still used for what has become, under somewhat different names, the official standard language of China. The adjective and substantive 'Mandarin' has become attached in England to the style of writing and speaking of highly placed civil servants and to those civil servants themselves.

The entries in the *OED* dealing with the word *mandarin* and its etymology and widespread application are well worth a consultation.

manifesto A public declaration or pronouncement, typically giving details of the author's stance on given issues – by which his stance is 'made manifest'. Much used nowadays to denote the policy statement on which a political party goes to the polls. The spelling *manifesto* is Portuguese (and Italian): the Spanish spelling is *maniefesto*. The word *manifesto* in a general sense is part of the common stock of European diplomatic and legal parlance, but its application to the Iberian peninsula has been influenced by the unstable political situation there and in Latin America, in both of which spheres of influence politicians have been given to issuing manifestos with some frequency. (Trade with Spanish- and Portuguese-speaking regions has perhaps tended to mingle *manifesto* with *manifest*, the list of a ship's cargo, signed by the master, for the information and use of Customs officers.)

Malvasia In English, 'Malmsey'. See *Madeira*, above.

mano a mano 'Hand-to-hand', or 'one to one'. Said of a contest, either literally or figuratively.

> '*Mano a mano* ... a corrida in which two matadors alternate in fighting two of three bulls each': *Random House Dictionary of the English Language*, 2nd edn, 1987. 'Everyone in the jammed courtroom sucked in a little air as it became clear that a real courtroom mano a mano had begun': *Vanity Fair*, p 147/21, May 1990.

mantilla Nowadays used in English-speaking circles only for a headdress comprising a comb and a veil as used for formal audiences with the Pope.

Manzanilla A kind of pale dry sherry produced in Sanlúcar de Barrameda, near Jerez de la Frontera. Pronounced /manθa'niʎa/. In spite of its appearance, the word is masculine.

> 'Pale dry Sherries, such as Manzanilla, Fino ... and Montilla, are ideal appetizers': H. J. Grossman, *Guide to Wines, Spirits and Beers*, ix, p 114/1 (1940).

margarita A cocktail usually made with tequila, orange liqueur, and citrus fruit juice. The origin of the name is unknown: it is not native to any variety of Spanish.

> 'She's from Mexico … and her name is the Margarita Cocktail … 1 ounce tequila. Dash of Triple Sec. Juice of ½ lime or lemon [etc.]': *Esquire*, p 76/3 December 1956. '*Margarita*, mixed drink made from tequila and citrus juice, drunk from vessel whose rim has been dipped in salt': O. A. Mendelsohn, *A Dictionary of Drink*, p 212 (1965).

marianismo 'A pattern of behaviour that is regarded as conforming to a traditional or archetypal female role; female submissiveness. Freq. opposed to *machismo*. Chiefly used with reference to Latin American women': *OED*.

> 'Cubans have always been able to assimilate dualities such as the sacred and profane (Roman Catholicism and *santeria*), *machismo* and *marianismo*, and equality and separatencss': K. L. Stoner, *From House to Street*, p 5 (1991). 'The femininity scale acts as a measure of marianismo (female virtue, gentleness, and willingness to sacrifice), the Colombian cultural norm for women': *Journal of the American Academy of Child & Adolescent Psychiatry* (Nexis), p 485 1st April 2003.

maricón An effeminate but, by origin, not necessarily a homosexual man. Also used as a term of abuse or contempt. In Castilian, *maricón* is nowadays used to mean, specifically, a homosexual; the masculine noun *marica* tends to mean only 'effeminate'. Both words derive from the Christian name *M aría. Cf. Menina, below*.

marijuana The cannabis plant *Cannabis sativa*, subspecies *indica*, used as an intoxicating and hallucinogenic drug, especially in the form of a crude cigarette made of the dried leaves, flowering tops, and stem of the plant. Still known in the Old World as *(Indian) hemp* and *cannabis*. The Mexican Spanish word is *mariguana* or *marihuana*, of uncertain origin: the letter *j* seems to have been introduced to preserve an aspirate deriving from the letter *h* in *marihuana* – an aspirate that does not in fact exist in the Spanish. (There are some indications that *marijuana* is a spelling being increasingly adopted by native Spanish-speakers.)

marimba A deep-toned wooden xylophone apparently indigenous to Angola but now much used in modern music. Portuguese appears to have been the language of entry of this word into modern languages.

mariposa Literally, 'butterfly'. A highly characteristic movement in which the bull-fighter draws the bull by flapping the cape behind his own back.

marmelada 'Marmalade'. The close trading associations between Portugal and England account for the virtually intact adoption of this Portuguese word into English. It originally denoted a preserve based on boiling quince with sugar, to which mixture were added any of a wide range of flavours. Nowadays limited to confections based on citrus fruits, especially bitter oranges, of which the Seville orange, *Citrus Bigaradia*, is most prized.

Marrano A word dating from the 13th century to denote a Jew or Muslim who had converted to Christianity. The etymology of the word is much disputed: for an overview of the complex emergence of the word, see the *OED Online*'s Draft Revision of December 2000. Modern scholarship has tended to stress that the identicity between this word *Marrano* and the Spanish word for a hog, *marrano*, is purely coincidental, though, as with all coincidences, this coincidence grips the popular imagination.

mascara A cosmetic preparation for darkening, lengthening, and thickening the eyelashes and (occasionally) the eyebrows, usually applied with a small brush. See the Italian Lexicon for a note on a possible etymology, from the Italian *maschera*, or Spanish *máscara*, 'mask'. There is an alternative derivation, which perhaps has more credibility: it postulates Catalan *mascara* or Portuguese (16th century) *mascarra*, which mean respectively 'soot and black smear' and 'stain or smut'. Contemporary Portuguese has *mascarrar*, ' to daub, to smear', attested from 1813.

This alternative derivation leaves undisturbed the tonic accent in the modern cosmetic word, which is always, in all languages where a tonic accent is present, on the middle syllable. Moreover, it preserves the meaning, more or less intact, of darkening the eyebrows and eyelashes, something that the analogy to a mask does not subserve. The idea of 'a smudge or stain' is met with in other Romance languages and dialects: for example, there appears in Middle French (Gascon) *mascaret*, 'spotted cow', from *mascar*, an adjective, 'black spotted'. In Old Occitan, *mascarar* appears *circa* 1240, in Old French of *circa* 1200 *mascurer* appears, and in Early Modern French, (Randle Cotgrave 1611) *mâchurer* appears, all denoting 'to daub, to black the face'.

matador A term from *la corrida*, 'bull-fighting'. The name given to the bull-fighter who strives to kill the bull by a sword-thrust between the shoulder-blades. A *toreador* is one who engages in a (Spanish) bull-fight, especially on horse-back; the popularity of the word *toreador* for the *matador* in bull-fighting no doubt arises from the popularity of Bizet's *Carmen*. The *picador* is the mounted man who opens the contest by provoking the bull with a lance. The *banderilleros* are the team of bull-fighters who thrust *banderillas* into the neck and shoulders of the bull. The *banderilla* is a little dart, ornamented with a banderole, that the *banderilleros* aim at the neck and shoulders of the bull to goad and enrage it.

maté A bitter infusion made from the leaves of a South American shrub, *Ilex paraguariensis*, of the holly family, drunk as a stimulant for its high caffeine content. Also called *Paraguay tea* and *Yerba-maté.*

media luna 'Half moon'. An instrument consisting of a crescent-shaped blade attached to a long wooden pole, formerly used in bullfighting to hamstring a bull that could not be overcome by other means. Contrast with *mezza luna* in the Italian Lexicon.

media vuelta 'Half turn'. A movement in which the bull is approached from behind and stabbed as it turns.

membrillo A sweet conserve made of quinces.

menina 'In Spanish and Portuguese contexts: a young girl; (sometimes) *spec.* a young lady-in-waiting': *OED*. There are many differences in the precise meaning of certain words in Spanish and Portuguese: the specific country in which the two are spoken can have a marked influence on the meanings of those words – generally, on the *shades* of meaning implicit in those words. Not infrequently words have an ostensibly unremarkable meaning in dictionaries but when spoken can shock and insult. Differences in this respect between Peninsular Portuguese and Brazilian

Portuguese can frequently lead to serious misunderstandings. In Portugal, the word *rapariga*, the analogue of the masculine *rapaz*, means simply 'a girl'. In Brazil it can mean 'a mistress' or 'a prostitute': *moça* is the ordinary Brazilian word for 'girl'. The word *biche* means, in Portugal, 'a line or queue', in Brazil 'a male homosexual', *fila* being the Brazilian word for 'a line or queue'. (The probability is that the Brazilian implication of *biche* has been influenced by the criminal argot of American prisons, in which a macho prisoner's catamite is known as his 'bitch'.) In Portugal, the linear descendant of the Latin *putus*, a boy-child, namely *puto* (*cf. putto* in the Italian Lexicon), would not cause eyebrows to be raised. In some circles in Brazil, the word would convey the notion of a homosexual youth.

Sometimes the inquiring mind has to *infer* that there is a clash between Peninsular Portuguese and the Portuguese of Brazil. Readers who recall the exotic singer and dancer Carmen Miranda (1909-1955) will remember her Carnival song:

Mamãe eu quero, mamãe eu quero
Mamãe eu quero mamár;
Dá a chupeta, dá a chupeta
Dá a chupeta pro bebê não chorár.

In Portugal the song went:

Mamãe eu quero, mamãe eu quero
Mamãe eu quero mamár;
Dá-me a chupeta, dá-me a chupeta
Dá-me a chupeta para o menino não
chorár.

One has to ask, 'Does the word *bebê* have a connotation in the Peninsula that's absent in Brazil?'

There is a further curiosity about this word *menina*. The *OED* says of this word: 'The corresponding Portuguese masculine form, *menino* boy, also occurs as a loanword in the text cited in quot. 1787'. But the text cited for 1787, (a new one, for the Draft Entry 2001), refers the reader to '1787 W. Beckford, *Portuguese Jrnl.* 10 June (1954) 72' and reads; 'I passed half an hour not disagreeably in talking of music, gardens, roses and devotions with the menina' – in the feminine form, not the masculine form as indicated by the text'. In fact, knowing the proclivities of William Beckford (1760-1844), we may be sure it was *um menino* he passed half an hour with. See, in general, *mozo, below*.

mercado 'A market or market-place'.

merienda An afternoon snack. In Portuguese, 'uma merenda'. It is frequently the case that manual workers, starting their day very early, have their *merienda* mid-morning. *Cf. merenda* in the Italian Lexicon.

merino A sheep of a breed prized for the fineness of its wool, originating in Spain and introduced to England for breeding purposes towards the end of the 18th century.

mesa From Latin *mensa*, 'a table'. 'A high rocky tableland or plateau; specifically, a flat-topped hill or plateau of rock with one or more steep sides, usually rising abruptly from a surrounding plain and common in the arid and semi-arid areas of the United States': *OED*. Chiefly a Latin-American expression.

mescal 'Any of various plants of the genus *Agave*, of Mexico and the south-western United States; *esp.* any of several large agaves with paniculate inflorescences, including those grown for ornament and hedging (e.g. the American aloe, *A. americana*), those whose bud, root, etc., is cooked as a vegetable (e.g. *A. palmeri* and *A. parryi*), and those whose fermented sap is distilled to produce an alcoholic spirit (the plant in this context being more commonly called *maguey*)': *OED*. In the sphere of cactus-plants and what may be derived from them, there is very considerable confusion, among lay-people at least, arising out of, first, the wide variety of trivial names by which cactus-plants are known in Latin America and the States of the US bordering on Mexico, and, secondly, a certain ambiguity about what name should be adopted for the 'finished products'. See *pulque, tequila* and *mescaline* in this Lexicon.

The principal source of the hallucinogenic alkaloid *Mescaline* is the button-like top, the *peyote*, of any of several small desert cacti of the genus *Lophophora,* particularly *L. williamsii*, of northern Mexico and southern Texas, a plant unconnected with the cactus from which *mescal* is distilled. The *OED* definition of *mescal* is: 'A strong intoxicating spirit distilled from the fermented sap of an agave. *Cf.* TEQUILA *n.*, PULQUE *n*.' Thus, the dried preparation from these button-like excrescences on the top of *Lophophora williamsii* is unconnected with the alcoholic beverage of virtually the same name. *Lucus a non lucendo.*

mestizo A man of mixed European, especially Spanish or Portuguese, and non-European parentage. The Portuguese word is *mestiço*. Also used to denote the wool of Latin-American sheep of mixed breeds.

mirador 'A turret or belvedere on top of a house, commanding an extensive view; a balcony with a panoramic view': *OED*.

mojo A Cuban dressing comprising olive oil, crushed garlic and sour citrus fruits.

mordida From *morder*, 'to bite'. A Central-American, Mexican, and Chilean colloquialism for a bribe or payment to, in particular, an official to facilitate the performance of his duty or to avoid the issue of a fine or to avoid prosecution.

Morisco In general, a Moor. The word is used in a specific sense in European history to denote any of the Moors in Spain who were converted to Christianity, or their descendants, who remained in Spain until their expulsion in 1609-14. *Cf. Marrano, above* and *Mudéjar, below*.

Mozárabe One who continued to practice Christianity after the occupation of the Iberian Peninsula by the Muslim invaders (from the 8th to the 15th century). The Mozárabes adopted many aspects of Islamic culture, including the language of the invaders. Large Muslim cities such as Toledo, Córdoba, and Seville contained separate enclaves of Mozárabes, who formed wealthy communities ruled by their own officials and subject to their own (Visigothic) legal system. They also maintained their own churches, bishoprics, and monasteries, and developed their own liturgy, which, even today, is still used on fixed occasions.

mozo Originally, simply 'a boy'. Differentiation has occurred between Peninsular and Latin-American Spanish. In Latin American Spanish *mozo* tends to mean a male servant, an attendant, a groom, a labourer. In Peninsular Spanish a more restricted acceptation prevails: see the quotation below. See also, in general *menina, above.*

> 'Every matador has got a valet, his *mozo de estoques*, whose important days are those on which there is a fight, not only in the dressing of his master but the duties of attendance ... at the ring-side, preparing the *muletas* and handing to his master the swords as he requires them': H. Baerlein, *Belmonte the Matador*, iii, p 37 (1934). '*Mozo(s)*, the badly paid and often brave

ring-attendants who clean up the mess, accompany the picador on foot, [etc.]': J. McCormick & M. S. Mascareñas, *The Complete Aficionado*, iv, p 146 (1967).

muchacho[a] A boy, a young man, a male servant. A girl, a young woman; a female servant.

mudéjar A Muslim (Moorish) inhabitant of the Iberian Peninsula after the reconquest by Christian monarchs of the territories formerly occupied by the Muslim invaders. The *Mudéjares* were allowed to retain Islamic laws, customs, and religion and to live in their own quarters in return for owing allegiance and paying tribute to a Christian monarch. The *Mudéjares* are the analogue after the *Reconquista* of the *Mozárabes (q.v.)* before the *Reconquista.* (The *Moriscos (q.v.)* were former Muslims, converted to Christianity: the *Mudéjares* were Muslims who remained Muslims.)

'Recent studies of ... Mudéjar communities indicate that their conversion to Christianity was unforced, and the result of having lived in close contact with their Christian neighbours for a number of centuries': Trevor Dadson, reviewing L. P. Harvey, *Muslims in Spain, 1500 to 1614* in *The Times Literary Supplement*, p 28, 10th February 2006.

mulatto[a] A word nowadays considered offensive, denoting a person of mixed blood.

muleta The matador's red cape, nowadays a square of red fabric attached to a stick.

'They present the *moleta*, or little scarlet banner, always carried in their left hand ... When he [*sc.* the bull] turns quick upon them, they ... let fall their moleta': J. Townsend, *Journey in Spain*, I, p 345 (1791). 'The matador ... prepares to give him his last blow ... The right hand, holding a sword, is raised to the height of his head; the left, extended, holds the *muleta*': *New England Magazine*, p 259, October 1835.

nacho 'A tortilla chip, typically topped with melted cheese, chilli sauce, etc. Usu. in *pl.* A Texan or Mexican dish consisting of these, freq. served as a snack or appetizer with savoury dips': *OED*.

'Nacho Specials. This simple yet delicious snack originated some years ago in Old Victory Club in Piedras Negras, Mexico, when a group of Eagle Pass women asked the chef, Nacho [Ignacio 'Nacho' Anaya], to make something for them to eat with their cocktails': *For Goodness Sake!*, Church of the Redeemer, Eagle Pass, Texas, 89 (1970).

Negrillo and Negrito Two technical terms from anthropology, deriving ultimately from Spanish and now used nowadays to denote two species of small black persons distributed in parts of Africa and Asia.

negro Fundamentally, merely the Spanish and Portuguese adjective 'black'. It has at various times been applied to non-Europeans of dark complexion, (to the Moors, for example) but it early became the specific substantive in English to denote the inhabitants of sub-Saharan Africa and those descended from them. During the 19th century the word was much used, replacing the colloquial 'nigger', and in the process manifesting a growing sensitivity towards those to whom it was applied. In official contexts, it ultimately acquired a capital initial letter and the status of the formal appellation of those inhabitants and their descendants. In the latter half of the 20th century, many Americans of African origin reacted unfavorably to the term 'Negro' and advocated and used the term 'black', and it is now clear that the preferred appellation 'black' as both noun and adjective is predominant, probably with a capital initial letter. Nevertheless, there are signs of an increasing dissatisfaction among Blacks with the term. 'Person of color' is much canvassed at the moment as an acceptable alternative to 'Black'.

Niño, El Shortened form of *El Niño de Navidad* ('The Christmas Child'): originally, a term denoting simply a natural phenomenon involving the warming of the water off the coast of northern Peru that occurs each year between Christmas and March as a southward current of warm equatorial water displaces the northward Peru or Humboldt Current. *El Niño* is also used as the name the warm current itself. Much the most important application of this term is to the more extreme version of the phenomenon, known more fully as the *El-Niño-Southern Oscillation*, which occurs at irregular intervals and extends westwards across the equatorial Pacific Ocean. It is associated with widespread changes in weather and severe ecological damage.

olé 'An exclamation of praise or encouragement, usually associated with Spanish music and dance and with bullfighting; "bravo", "well done"' *OED*. Of uncertain derivation.

olla A cooking pot for stewing. And a meat and vegetable stew generally cooked in an olla. Portuguese: *olha. Cf. puchero, below.*

olla podrida A highly spiced stew made from various kinds of meat and vegetables. The dish was formerly known in England as a 'hotch-pot' (see in the Law French Appendix to the French Lexicon) or 'hotchpotch'. 'Hot-pot' as in, for example, Lancashire hot-pot, is a quite different dish –a dish comprising mutton or beef with potatoes, or potatoes and onions, cooked in an oven in an earthenware pot having a tightly fitting cover. An alternative name for an *olla podrida* in England was the curious 'gallimaufry'.

Perhaps the *olla podrida* is most closely resembled, nowadays, by a *ragoût*. The word *podrida* perhaps became associated with the dish in that scraps, leftovers and off-cuts were cast into the pot as they were said, perhaps jocosely, to be on the verge of mouldering. (The etymologists are curiously silent on the derivation of the word *podrida* in *olla podrida*. The *OED* hazards a guess: 'It is not known why *olla podrida* was so called in Spanish; perhaps from the resemblance of the bubbling and swelling appearance of the slow-cooking stew to festering putrefaction': *Draft Revision, March 2004.* (See *pot pourri* in the French Section.)

Oloroso A medium-dry wine produced in the region of Jerez de la Frontera that does not develop a covering of '*flor*' during production. This wine is drunk by producers and connoisseurs in its natural state, but the bulk of production is used as a basis for *Oloroso* sherries and cream sherries. The principal ultimate product, intermediate in sweetness between *Amontillado* (*q.v., above*) and the cream sherries, is a heavy, dark, fragrant, medium-sweet sherry comprising *Oloroso*, a colorant and sweetening varieties of other wines. The resulting blend has tended to usurp the name *Oloroso*.

padre 'Father' in Spanish, Portugese and Italian. In English-language usage, a name for and form of address to a priest or clergyman of any denomination, in particular in military circles. In the US the usage stems from close proximity to Spanish-speaking neighbours. In England the word was greatly influenced by the Italian word, but in trade and exploration the identical word in Spanish and Portuguese reinforced the usage of the word in reference to Catholic priests. With the appointment of Catholic chaplains to the British Army, the usage spread to all chaplains.

paella A dish comprising saffron-flavoured rice and a very wide and varied range of other ingredients (see quotations), cooked in large a shallow pan, a *paella*, from which the dish derives its name.

> 'Paella with all the right things in it, squids and octopuses and chicken and lobster-tails and paprika and sherry and peas and onion and pimento and pork, all done with saffron rice': 'D. Halliday', *Dollie and the Cookie Bird*, VIII, p 99 (1970). 'A paella contains short grain rice, garlic, parsley, olive oil and saffron. The popular image of paella is a pan of saffron-coloured rice bursting with shellfish, known as *paella de mariscos*': R. Sterling, *World Food: Spain*, p 59/1 (2000).

pagoda 'In South and South-East Asia: a Hindu or (in later use esp.) Buddhist temple or sacred building, typically having the form of a many-tiered tower with storeys of diminishing size, each with an ornamented projecting roof': *OED*. The origins of the word are much disputed. English has taken the Spanish spelling and the Portuguese pronunciation. (The Portuguese word is *pagode*, pronounced /pa'ɡodə/.)

paisano Originally, and still in Peninsular Spanish, 'a fellow-countryman'. In Latin America nowadays, 'a peasant'. Cognate with the French *paysan*. Also the local name for the bird, the Roadrunner (genus *Geococcyx Mexiçanus*), probably from a popular connection with *faysán*, 'pheasant'.

palanquin In modern Portuguese, *palaquim*. A litter; a covered conveyance, usually for one person, consisting of a large box carried on two horizontal poles by four or six (rarely two) bearers, used especially in South, South-East, and East Asia.

palaver An anglicization of the Portuguese *palavra*, meaning 'word, speech, talk'. A term picked up by English sailors and traders from usages in Coastal Africa, in which the word meant discussions with local chiefs. In its extended sense in modern English the word means 'wordy, prolix discussion'.

palomino The word has two meanings in contemporary English. The first is the name of a variety of grape, otherwise known as *Listán Blanca*, much used in the production of the drier sherries. The second meaning is predominant in the US: it denotes 'a light golden-brown or tan-coloured horse with a white or pale mane and tail, originally bred in the south-western U.S': *OED*.

pampas An extensive treeless plain in South America south of the Amazon; such plains collectively; terrain resembling the steppes of South-East Europe and Siberia. Other technical terms closely associated with *pampas* are *llano* and *savannah*.

panatela A long, thin cigar, particularly one that tapers at the mouth end, Variously spelt: *panatella*, *panetella*, etc. Also used of a biscuit of similar characteristics, and of a long, thin cigarette made of marijuana.

parador Originally, an inn, specifically a hostel supplying residential facilities for travellers. Later, a comfortable, well managed inn. More recently, a luxurious hôtel managed by the Spanish government. There is a close approximation to the Spanish idea in Portugal, going by the name *pousada*.

Pasionaria, La 'The Passionflower', the nickname of Dolores Ibárruri Gómez (1895-1989), Basque Communist leader renowned for her emotional oratory and colourful personality. After the death of Franco, Ibárruri returned to Spain and in 1977 was elected deputy to the Cortes.

paso doble 'Double pace'. A dance in double time, thought to resemble the quick march in Latin-American military drill.

patata Older form of *batata*, 'potato'.

pelota A word traditionally denoting any of a variety of games not unlike tennis played in an enclosed court (a *fronton*) using a small, hard ball, which is itself also called *la pelota*. The naked hand may be used to catch and return the ball, or a cane or wicker raquet fixed to the hand may be used. The game is also called *jai alai*, Basque for 'festival' and 'merry'. In Portuguese, *pelota basca*.

picador 'The pricker'. A mounted member of the matador's retinue whose function is to goad the bull with his lance.

picaresco 'Roguish, knavish'. More commonly met with in English in its French form, *picaresque*. Nevertheless, this is a fundamentally Spanish word, denoting a species of literary composition of a fictional nature, dealing with the adventures of rogues and knaves.

> 'This [the Lazarillo de Tormes by Mendoza] is the first known specimen in Spain of the picaresque, or rogue style': Hallam, *The History of Literature*, I, viii, §48 (1837-9).

pimenta Sometimes, in English, *pimento*: the dried aromatic berries of the tree *Pimenta dioica*; also called *Jamaica pepper* or *allspice* (Portuguese: *pimenta da Jamaica*). For the trivial name, 'allspice', see the quotation below.

> 'Pimento combines the flavour and properties of many of the oriental spices': *Vegetable Substances used for the Food of Man*, p 364 (1832)

pintada Sometimes *pintado* in English usage. The Guinea-fowl: a gallinaceous bird of the genus *Numida*, especially *N. Meleagris*, which is a common domestic fowl in Europe. It has slate-coloured plumage with white spots formed as though modelled on a chequer-board, hence, no doubt, the name 'painted one'.

> 'A kind of Pheasants, which are called Pintadoes, because they are as it were painted in colours': J. Davies, *History of the Caribby Isles*, p 89 (1666). 'The Pintada [*ed.* 1862 pintado] or Guinea-Hen: in some measure unites the characteristics of the pheasant and the turkey': Oliver Goldsmith, *Natural History*, V, p 192 (1774).

piranha A carnivorous freshwater fish of the genus *Serrasalmus*, belonging to the family *Characidae* and native to South America. Pronounced /pi'raɲə/.

pistachio A nut, or, rather, the kernel, of the *Pistacia vera* (family *Anacardiaceæ*), a native of Western Asia, having a greenish hue and a highly characteristic flavour, much cultivated in the south of Europe and in Turkey. The word is used in English as either a Spanish word or an Italian word. The distinction lies in the pronunciation: if the Spanish derivation is favoured, the pronunciation is /pis'tatʃo/; if the Italian derivation is favoured, the pronunciation is /pis'takjo/ (three syllables) or /pis'takio/ (four syllables). The former pronunciation is recommended. The influence of the Spanish element in trade (in the Mediterranean as much so as in the Atlantic) seems to predispose the word to the Spanish pronunciation.

plaza Literally, 'place'. In a Spanish-speaking country, a market-place, square or public place. (Portuguese: *praça*.) Also, in the US, a public square or open space; in extended uses (originally and chiefly North American), a large paved area surrounded by or adjacent to buildings, especially as a feature of a shopping complex. In US usage, the pronunciation is /'plaːzə /; in Spain, /'plaθa/; in Latin America, /'plaza/. In Portuguese, /'prasə/.

Also in *Plaza de Toros*: see quotation below.

> 'I remember clearly the first bullfight I ever saw, in Barcelona ... The *plaza de toros* was packed': *The Saturday Review*, p 29/1, 25th September 1973.

poblador 'In Spanish America, a settler, a colonist; *spec.* a country person who moves to settle or squat in a town': *OED*.

pousada. See *parador, above*.

pochismo 'A form of slang used by speakers of Mexican Spanish and others along the border with the U.S., consisting of English words given a Spanish form or pronunciation; a word of this sort': *OED*. See *pocho, below*.

> 'The Mexican Academy has appointed a committee to eradicate 'pochismos – that is English words and phrases used in speaking Spanish': *The New York Herald Tribune*, p 10/3, 5th August 1944. '*Pochismo*, derived from *pocho*, an adjective which originally meant discolored, has now come to mean a type of popular slang in Mexico': *Modern Languages Journal*, p 345, October 1946. 'They [*sc.* Kickapoos] have incorporated many Spanish words into their speech and many *pochismos* ... such as *lonche* ('lunch')': F. A. & D. L. Latorre, *Mexican Kickapoo Indians*, I, .p 29 (1976).

pocho A mildly derogatory term for a citizen of the United States of Mexican origin; a culturally Americanized Mexican. See *pochismo, above*.

> 'A pocho in good standing will drag his fititoes (feet) up the estrita (street)': *Newsweek*, p 76/3, 14th August 76/3 1944. 'Slapstick actors like Tin Tan ... who gets comic effects with pocho patter': *ibid*.

politico A politician; a political agent; a political activist.

poncho A Latin-American garment formed by a rectangle of cloth, sometimes waterproofed, with an aperture cut in it through which the head passes.

porgar Ladino (Judaeo-Spanish), 'to porge'. Spanish *purgar*, 'to purge', 'to cleanse'. In Jewish practice, to render ritually clean an animal slaughtered in accordance with Jewish custom. Porging comprises drawing out and removing the sinews and veins, with particular attention paid to the sinews and veins of the hinder quarters. Genesis 32 recounts Jacob's wrestling with 'a man' who 'touched the hollow of his [Jacob's] thigh', and, from Genesis 32.32 we learn: 'Therefore the children of Israel eat not the sinew of the hip which is upon the hollow of the thigh, unto this day: because he touched the hollow of Jacob's thigh in the sinew of the hip'. The man who performs the operation of porging is called, in Ladino, the *porgador*; in English, the 'porger'.

porrón A wine-flask with a long spout from which the contents are drunk directly.

> 'Francisco tilted the teapot-shaped *porrón* and ejected a stream of wine from the spout. It curved through the air ... into his open mouth': K. Bird, *Smash Glass Image*, iv, p 50 (1968).

praia Portuguese. 'A beach', 'a sea-shore', 'a water-front'.

presidio 'In Spain and in parts of America originally settled by Spaniards, e.g. the southwestern United States: A fort, a fortified settlement, a military station, a garrison town. Also, a Spanish penal settlement in a foreign country': *OED*.

prest 'Priest' in Spanish and Portuguese. Whence 'Prester John'.

pronunciamiento Literally, 'a pronouncement'. A proclamation or manifesto; often applied to one issued by insurrectionists, especially in the Spanish-speaking Latin-American republics. The word is by now thoroughly naturalized, especially when it is used in political contexts not related to Spanish-speaking *régimes*. In ordinary English use, it is pronounced /prəˈnɨnsɪə, mɪɛntəʊ/ (and, frequently and slackly, /prəˈnʌnsɪəˌ mɛntəʊ/). The Spanish pronunciation is /proˈnunθjaˌmjento/.

> 'Marshal da Fonseca … made a pronunciamiento, in Spanish fashion, against the Ministry': *The Spectator*, p 835, 14th December 1889. 'Then came Zhdanov's pronunciamento in Russia condemning jazz as degenerate and unfit for proletarian amusement': E. Paul, *Springtime in Paris*, xi, p 202 (1951).

puchero A glazed earthenware cooking pot; *cf., olla, above.* A stew composed of beef or lamb, ham or bacon, and vegetables, originally or primarily cooked in a *puchero*.

pueblo Literally, 'people'. A town or village, particularly of Indians in Mexico and the Spanish-influenced regions in the US. So, 'pueblo Indians', not the name of a tribe but Indians grouped and living in their own towns and villages.

pulque A fermented drink made in Mexico and some parts of Central America from the sap of the agave or maguey (*Agave americana*). *Pulqueria*: a shop of bar selling *pulque*.

> 'Pulque is slightly intoxicating, but by [further] distillation a very strong liquor is made from it, called mescal': G. W. Kendal, *Narrative of the Texan Santa Fé Expedition*, II, p 126 (1844).

puntillo 'A nice point of behaviour, social or other', normally anglicized as 'punctilio', the presence of the letter *c* being due to the misguided archaizing of spelling at the Renaissance and the termination *-ilio* being due to a desire to capture the Spanish pronunciation phonetically. The notion underlying the word is well expressed by its adjective, 'punctilious'.

> 'The noble Lord talks of Spanish punctilios': *Anecdotes of William Pitt*, III, xxviii, p 281 (1792).

pundonor Abbreviation of *punto de honore*, 'point of honour'.

> 'The Spaniards do so much stand upon their pundonores': Lord Herbert of Cherbury, *Life*, 1886 edn, p 205 (1648).

puta 'A whore'. A vivid commentary on modern life is provided by a feature of the *OED*, the date-chart. The date-chart for *puta* shows the first recorded instance of the use in print of this word in an English-speaking context as having occurred in 1967, yet we all know that the word was on countless lips in the US, let alone in Europe, decades before that date. It or its analogues are irrepressible. The word comes from late popular Latin *putida*, 'Stinking, rotten, disgusting', which clearly indicates that those who coined the word were out of sympathy with the oldest profession.

quebrada A mountain stream (in Latin America), from *quebrar*, 'to break, to break out'.

quien sabe? 'Who knows?'

> 'To all our other questions with regard to this ancient town, we received the usual Mexican reply of 'quien sabe?'': J. W. Abert, *Journal*, 17th October in *Rep. Exam. Of New Mexico*, 51 1 (1846). 'Do you think I am kind and unpossessive? Quien sabe?': Aldous Huxley, *Letters*, 13th August, 1969 edn, p 372 (1933).

quinoa An annual plant, *Chenopodium Quinoa*, N.O. *Chenopodiaceae*, found on the Pacific slopes of the Andes and cultivated in Chile and Peru for its edible farinaceous seeds. Pronounced /'kinwa/.

quina The bark of several species of *Cinchona* that yield quinine

quinquina A reduplication of *quina, above*. 'In Quichua [Peru], when the name of a plant is reduplicated, it almost invariably implies that it possesses some medicinal qualities'. C. R. Markham *Peruvian Bark*, p 5 (1880). Peruvian or Jesuits' bark; the bark of several species of cinchona, yielding quinine – *Cinchona pubescens* Vahl (*Rubiaceae*) – m and other febrifugal alkaloids.

The Natural History Museum, London, has a website http://internt.nhm.ac.uk/jdsml/nature-online/ from which one gathers the following:

'By 1650 the production of quinquina as it was known at the time had been identified with the Jesuits and it became known as Jesuit's bark. Protestants in Europe had fought shy of using it because of Jesuit (and thus Catholic) control of the drug. By refusing to take what he called 'the powder of the devil', Oliver Cromwell succumbed to malaria and died'.

> 'I haue made known ... in these partes, a barke of a tree that infallibly cureth all intermittent feauours. It cometh from Peru; and is the barke of a tree called by the Spaniardes Kinkina': Sir Kenelm Digby, Letters in *The Winthrop Papers*, p 15, 1849 edn, p 15 (1656). *Bellon's New Mystery in Physick discovered by curing of Fevers and Agues by Quinquina or Jesuites' Powder* (tr of title) (1681).

quinta By origin, this word meant, in both Spanish and Portuguese, an agricultural property let at a rent of one fifth (*quinta parte*) of its net annual worth – at one fifth of the value of its produce. The word has developed slightly different shades of meaning in the linguistic regions in which Spanish and Portuguese are spoken. It is used to denote a country-house or villa in Spain or Portugal. It can also mean a country estate. In Portugal, it is widely used to denote a wine-growing estate. In South America, it frequently denotes a house or estate on the outskirts of a town.

Quinta Columna 'Fifth column'. In its strict historical meaning, the 'column' of supporters in Madrid in 1936 on which General Emilio Mola's four columns of Nationalist troops believed they could depend for support in their advance on the capital. By extension, those who aid the enemies of their own countries from within their own countries.

> 'Police last night began a house-to-house search for Rebels in Madrid ... Orders for these raids ... apparently were instigated by a recent broadcast over the Rebel radio station by General Emilio Mola. He stated he was counting on four columns of troops outside Madrid and another column of

persons hiding within the city who would join the invaders as soon as they entered the capital': *The New York Times*, p 2/2, 16th October 1936. 'Parliament has given us the powers to put down Fifth Column activities with a strong hand': W. S. Churchill, *Into Battle*, p 222 (1941).

ramada 'A porch'. 'In the Western US: an (orig. temporary) arbor or similar structure': *OED*.

rancho A word, as 'ranch', that has moved a long way from its origins. It originally meant, and still retains this connotation, a mess or company of persons who eat together. In Spanish-speaking America it is applied to huts occupied by herdsmen or labourers. The word often denotes a roughly-built house, a hut or hovel; it is also applied to a collection of these forming a small village. By extension, it can mean a rough-and-ready inn or roadhouse. In Mexico the word is in some respects assuming a meaning far divorced from its originally meaning, and in the US its meaning is, of course, a 'spread' for cattle-rearing.

rasgado, rasgueado From *rasgar* or *rasguear*, 'to tear' or 'to strum'. *Le mot juste* for the action of striking the strings of an instrument such as a guitar so as to produce arpeggiated chords.

> '*Rasgado* ... , to sweep the strings of a guitar with the thumb, for the purpose of producing a full chord, *arpeggio*': Stainer & Barrett, *A Dictionary of Musical Terms*, p 374/2 (1876). '*Rasgado*, ... in guitar playing, sweeping the strings with the thumb to produce an arpeggio': W. Apel, *The Havard Dictionary of Music*, p 628/1 (1944). 'Guitar arrangements in the popular *rasgado* or strumming style': *Early Music*, p 185/2, July 1974.

rebozo A log scarf used by Latin-American women as a shawl and head-covering.

recibiendo 'Receiving'. An action in bull-fighting whereby the bullfighter 'receives' the bull head on, on the point of his sword.

reja A wrought-iron screen or grille used to protect windows; to prevent access to such things as tom bs in churches and chapels; to prevent access to houses via balconies, etc.

> 'Renaissance Architecture in Spain could not be fully appreciated without examining the towering wrought-iron grilles, or *Rejas*, of the period': Byne & Stapley, *Rejeria of the Spanish Renaissance*, p vii (1924). 'One remembers Spanish cathedrals very notably on account of their *rejas* or wrought iron screens which are a feature peculiar to Spain': Sacheverell Sitwell, *Gothic Europe*, p 139 (1969).

rejón A wooden-handled short lance, usually thrust into the bull from horse-back. See quotations below.

> 'The rider plays the bull with the horse itself, placing long banderillas, darts known as *rejones*, and killing with a long lance, also called a *rejón*': McCormick & Mascareñas, *The Complete Aficionado*, i, p 19 (1967). 'They attempt to finish him [*sc.* the bull] off with a *rejon*, a long-bladed, wooden-handled spear': *The Times*, p 15/1, 5th December 1973.

rejoneador A mounted bull-fighter who places *rejones*. *Rejoneo*: the art of bull-fighting on horse-back and using *rejones*.

renegado 'A renegade'. See the quotation for 1599. By extension, the word denotes someone who abandons a previously professed cause.

'He was a Renegado, which is one that first was a Christian, and afterwards becommeth a Turke': Hakluyt, *Voyages*, II,i, p 186 (1599). 'A dignified informer, a French refugee, and a renegado to the Church of England': J. Shebbeare, *Lydia*, II, p 190 (1769).

requeté A member of a Carlist militia, *el Requeté*, which took the Nationalist side during the Spanish Civil War of 1936-39.

'The troops engaged on the insurgent side have consisted of *requetés*, Navarrese volunteers almost to a man': *The Times*, p 12/4, 26th August 1936. 'The Requeté movement drew its main strength from the Basque provinces, especially from Navarre': Peter Kemp, *Mine were of Trouble*, ii, p 21 (1957). 'The requeté ... were a sort of Basque militia ... Fought for Franco': D. Robinson, *Eldorado Network*, xvii, p 129 (1979).

revolera An action on the part of the matador in which he flutters his cape above his head.

'At times, good matadors prefer to finish off their series of passes in a gentler way with a *larga*, ... in the form the *revolera* in which the cape swirls above the man's head ... The term *revolera* is often loosely used for *serpentina* and *vice versa*': A. MacNab, *Bulls of Iberia*, vi, p 60 (1957).

Rioja The name of a district of northern Spain and of a wine produced there. See quotations.

'Other light Spanish wines of this class (of the Riojas, etc., we may speak separately) are excellent': George Saintsbury, *Notes on a Cellar-Book*, ii, p 18 *(1920)*. 'White Rioja (a capital beverage liquor)': *ibid*, vi, p 89. 'Of table wines which a foreigner may be offered, Rioja ('J' pronounced as 'H') is ... a full, strong wine produced in the north, mostly red and with a heavy plush-like flavour': Raymond Postgate, *The Plain Man's Guide to Wine*, vii, p 108 (1951). 'Rioja ... comes from the north of the country, about 100 miles south of the western Pyrenees': *Country Life*, p 1162/1, 26th April 1973. 'There is both red and white Rioja ... and the red is certainly the more distinguished': *ibid*, p 1162/3.

rodeo In English-speaking usage, especially in the US, a public exhibition of skill, often in the form of a competition, in the riding of unbroken horses ('bucking broncos'), the roping of calves and the bringing down of fully grown steers, and including demonstrations of efficiency with the lariat, wrestling with steers, and so on.

rondeña A variety of song and dance native to Ronda, in Andalusia.

'Most forms [of Andalusian song] ... have four lines of eight syllables, and these include forms such as *granadinas, rondeñas* ... descended directly or indirectly from the *fandango*': *Groves' Dictionary of Music,* 5th edn, III, p 372 (1954). 'The Rondeñas originated as a lover's serenade under the window of his sweetheart, as did the Tarantos of the Levant': 'La Meri', *Spanish Dancing*, 2nd edn, vi, p 82 (1954).

rumba 'An Afro-Cuban dance; a ballroom dance imitative of this, danced on the spot with a pronounced movement of the hips. Also, the dance rhythm of the rum ba; a musical composition with this rhythm. Also *transf.*': *OED*.

saeta Literally, 'an arrow'. An unaccompanied Andalusian folk-song, of a haunting, plaintive nature, sung during religious processions, particularly in Seville during Holy Week and at Easter.

> 'Somewhere in the crowd a woman is singing a *saeta*, sad and undulating, like no other music on earth': *Chambers's Journal*, p 213/1, March 1923. 'Clusters of microtones which resemble nothing so much as the ululations of the *saeta* singers in the Easter Day procession in Seville': *New Statesman*, p 297/1, 26th August 1966.

salsifi Portuguese *sersifim*. There are two varieties of this esculent vegetable, both worthy of much greater recognition. The first is a biennial composite plant, traditionally called in England 'the Purple Goat's-beard', *Tragopogon porrifolius*, indigenous to Great Britain and the Continent of Europe, and the American variety, 'Meadow salsify' (the Yellow Goat's-beard, *Tragopogon pratensis)*, both having a tuber-like root of a light coloration. The second variety has a completely different appearance: it is the Black or Spanish Salsify, *Scorzonera hispanica*, having long, thin, black finger-like roots. *S. Hispanic* was at one time called *Viper's grass*, in that it was thought to be a specific against the bite of the viper.

> 'Salsafay is estimable both for its roots..and for the young shoots rising in the spring': John Abercrombie, *Every Man His Own Gardener*, 1803 edn, p 85 (1767). 'Scorzonera hispanica ... is a native of Spain, but is cultivated in this country; and its root is sold in the markets as *Scorzonera*': John Lindley, *The Treasury of Botany* 1866. 'The Salsafy (or Salsify) ... is a hardy biennial, with long cylindrical fleshy esculent roots': *Encyclopaedia Britannica*, XII, p 287/2 (1881). 'Salsify ... when boiled in milk ... has a peculiar resemblance to oysters': *Garden*, p 425/3, 11th November 1882. 'Scorzonera, French, *Scorzonera picroides* (*Picridium vulgare*). Scorzonera, Garden, *Scorzonera hispanica*' W. Miller, Plant-Names, p 122 (1884).

'¡Salud!' 'Health!'. Portuguese, 'Saude!'

samba A dance of African origin, now a ballroom dance.

sancocho Literally, the adjective 'parboiled' or 'half cooked'. In South America and the West Indies, a soup made of meat, plantain, yucca, etc.

> '*Sancocho*, a truly native dish with its tropical ingredients, takes the place in the Dominican Republic of the pucheros encochidos in cooler Latin-American countries': C. Brown, *South American Cookbook*, p 361 (1939). 'The wonderful soup-stew of Latin countries, *sancocho*, is undoubtedly the [Dominican Republic] people's choice for a national dish': M. Waldo, *Complete Round-the-World Cookbook*, p 361 (1954). '*sancocho*, ... Latin-American souplike stew containing fish, fowl, meat, seafood, vegetables, and spices': R. & D. De Sola, *Dictionary of Cooking*, p 199/2 (1969).

Sandinista A follower of the revolutionary Nicaraguan organization founded in 1963 and taking its name from the Nicaraguan nationalist leader Augusto Cesar Sandino (1893-1934).

sangre azul 'Blue blood'; the blood of old or aristocratic families.

Sangria A drink made from red wine, slices of fruit, ice and water.

sardana A Catalan dance to pipe and drum accompaniment.

saudade Generally reckoned to be the most difficult Portuguese word to translate. It means a wistful, grave yearning for something (often undefinable) that is not in existence and yet might possibly not be welcome if it were in existence. It is often manifest in nostalgia, home-sickness and similar states of mind. The quotations below are an excellent review of the complexities of this intriguing word.

Though *saudade* is commonly assumed to be wholly melancholy, that is by no means necessarily so. In 1955 Rio de Janeiro commemorated the fiftieth anniversary of the death of their darling, Carmen Miranda (1909-1955) (see *menina, above*), and employed for publicity purposes a logotype featuring a cartoon illustration of Carmen Miranda wearing one of her most characteristic hall-marks, her tropical-fruit head-dress. Surrounding the logotype were the words *50 anos de saudade*.

> 'The famous *saudade* of the Portuguese is a vague and constant desire for something that does not and probably cannot exist, for something other than the present, a turning towards the past or towards the future; not an active discontent or poignant sadness but an indolent dreaming wistfulness': A. F. G. Bell, *In Portugal*, I, p 7 (1912). 'In a word saudade is yearning: yearning for something so indefinite as to be indefinable: an unrestrained indulgence in yearning': R. Gallop, *Portugal*, xi, p 262 (1936). 'It [scil. Portugal] is an intensely poetic country, and it is the country of saudade, that mysterious melancholy which sighs at the back of every joy': R. Campbell, *Portugal*, p ix (1957).

saya A type of dress worn in Spanish-speaking countries. See quotation.

> 'This female Gypsy fashion ... is more properly the fashion of Andalusia, the principal characteristic of which is the saya, which is extremely short, with many rows of flounces': George Borrow, *Zincali*, I, ii, v (1841).

seguidilla A dance in 3/4 or 3/8 time.

seguiriyas In full, *seguiriyas gitana*, 'gipsy seguiriyas'): a regional variety of flamenco music; the song or dance that accompanies this.

> 'Rhythm-forms of flamenco dances are: Alegrias, Soleares, Bulerias, Farruca, Zapateado, Tango, Zambra, and seguiriyas': Chujoy & Manchester, *Dance Encyclopaedia* (revised edn) p 856/1 (1967).

Sendero Luminoso The name of a neo-Maoist revolutionary movement in Peru, founded in 1970 as the Communist Party of Peru, but subsequently becoming a clandestine guerrilla organization. It engaged in terrorist activities throughout the 1980s.

> 'In 1970, he [*sc.* Abimael Guzmán] and his followers ... founded the Communist Party of Peru, the organization that would become known as Sendero Luminoso. The term is taken from an earlier Peruvian ideologist, José Carlos Mariátegui: 'Marxism-Leninism will open the shining path to revolution'': *The New York Times Magazine*, p 22/2, 31st July 1983. 'The treasury is so empty that the government ... certainly cannot pay all the soldiers needed to protect candidates around the country from the fanatical Sendero Luminoso guerrillas': *The Observer*, p 17/3, 1st April 1990.

senhor 'In Portuguese use, or with reference to Portuguese: A term of respect placed before the name of a man in addressing him or speaking of him, equivalent to the English 'Mr.' Also used without the name as a form of address, equivalent to 'sir' in English. Hence, a Portuguese gentleman': *OED*. The feminine is *senhora* if the lady is known to be married, or *senorita* (sometimes *senhorinha*) if the lady is known to be unmarried. In Portugal, *senhora* predominates. Sometimes the word *senhorinho,* the masculine, is used to signify a young gentleman, but the usage has declined in recent years. Nowadays, a somewhat pejorative sense is implied by the use of the word *senhorinho*. (In general, see *don* and *dona, above.*)

It might be helpful to recall that the Spanish realize the palatized sound of *n mouillé* as *ñ*. The exactly equivalent sound is achieved in written Portuguese by placing the letter *h* after the letter *n*. Similarly, the letter *h* has the effect of palatizing the letter *l*: that is, the exactly similar sound to the Spanish *ll* is achieved in written Portuguese by writing *lh*. Thus, Spanish *cedilla* is Portuguese *cedilha*.

Sercial See *Madeira*, above.

Sertão The name of an arid, barren region in the interior of Pernambuco and neighbouring states in North East Brazil; applied also to other areas in Brazil of similar character. Also, more widely, the remote interior or outback of Brazil.

> 'A particular vegetation type of these drier lands is the *caatinga* of the north-east, the *sertão*. This region of semi-desert has a vegetation cover made up of sparse thorn forest ... *Sertão* in this sense means a particular place – the dry interior of north-east Brazil; in a more general usage *Sertão* means the sparsely inhabited backlands of the interior of Brazil. It is the equivalent of the Australian "outback"': K. Webb tr Pohl & Zepp's *Latin America*, ii, p 43 (1966).

sherry See *Jerez de la Frontera, above*. In 1967, an attempt was made in England by a body of (Spanish) producers of sherry to protect the name 'sherry', on the precedent that the English courts had earlier protected the name 'champagne' in the interests of the producers of that wine in the Rheims region of France. See the quotation below.

> '"Sherry" means a wine coming from the Jerez district of Spain. The Court, giving judgement, ... decided that it would be unjust now to restrain Vine Products Ltd ... from using the expressions "British sherry", "English sherry", "Cyprus sherry", "South African sherry", and "Australian sherry", used for certain wines in England': *The Times*, p 6/5, 1st August 1967.

sierra Literally, 'a saw'. A word and name applied to ranges of mountains with a profile suggesting the cutting edge of a saw.

siesta 'The sixth [hour]'. In Portuguese, *sesta*. The afternoon rest or nap, taken during the hottest part of the day.

sindicato In Spain, Portugal and Latin America, a trades union.

Siroco The Sirocco, so normally spelt in English, is an intensely hot, dry, dusty wind originating in the Sahara and blowing from the North coast of Africa over the Mediterranean, during is passage over which it picks up moisture to become humid and debilitating. It is also found in the spelling *Xaloque*; the Portuguese is *Xarouco*: all are from the Arabic *šarq*, from *šaraqa* '[the sun] rose'.

solera By origin, a blend of sherries, but nowadays a crucially important term of art in the production of sherry. See the quotation, below, from 1965.

> 'The solera system is … a … method of refreshing delicately flavoured old wines still in cask with small quantities of slightly younger wine of the same character in order to keep a continuous stock of mature wine of one type and character always available': A. Michel, *The Penguin Book of Wines*, III, p 227 (1965).

sombrero 'A broad-brimmed hat, usually of felt or some soft material, of a type common in Spain and Spanish America': *OED*. Portuguese: *sombreiro*.

suerte 'An action or pass performed in bull-fighting; one of the three stages of a bull-fight': *OED*. *Cf. tercia, below.* In the original sense (*scil*, 'chance, luck, a hazard') the Portuguese is *sorte*.

taco A Mexican dish comprising a fried pancake made of unleavened corn-meal (a *tortilla*) filled with seasoned mincemeat, chicken, cheese, beans, etc.

tamal Plural *tamales*. A Mexican delicacy made of crushed maize, flavoured with pieces of meat or chicken and red pepper, etc., wrapped in maize-husks and baked.

tapa[s] 'Lid[s], cover[s]'. Small snacks of sausage or cured meat served with wine or sherry in Spanish bars and *cafés*. The slices of sausage, meat, etc, were formerly placed on the glass as lids, hence the name.

> 'I should like to draw attention to … the admirable habit of the 'tapa'. In Spain, when you order a drink in a bar … you will always be given … something to eat': C. Salter, *Introducing Spain*, iv, p 36 (1953). '*Tapas*, small dishes served gratis in boat-shaped saucers with every glass of wine ordered … in a Spanish bodega or café': W. James, *Word-book of Wine*, p 186 (1959).

tapioca See *cassava, above.*

Tempranillo A diminutive of *temprano*, 'early'. The grape is probably so-named because of its tendency to ripen early. A Spanish variety of black grape, used esp. in making Rioja. Also, the specific name of a Red Rioja wine made from such grapes.

tequila A spirit distilled in Mexico from the fermented sap of the *Agave tequilana*, a giant, fleshy-leaved prickly cactus-plant indigenous to Mexico and the south-western United States, a sub-species of the American aloe, *Agave americana*. See also *mescal* and *pulque, above*.

tercio One of the three parts or stages of a bullfight: see. Also, each of the three concentric circles into which a bull-ring is technically divided.

terra roxa Portuguese; 'purple-red soil'. 'A deep, humus-rich soil of a dark reddish-purple colour on the Paraná Plateau in southern Brazil.

> 'The terra roxa of Campinas Paulo is … the continuation of the drift-paste of the higher lands and seaward slope of the serra': C. F. Hartt, *The Thayer Expedition: Scientific Results*, xvii, p 514 (1870). 'Areas with larger concentrations of *terra roxas*, the soil of exceptional fertility for coffee, are usually associated with higher levels of production.' *Economic Geography*, LIII, 78/2 (1977).

Tia Maria 'Aunt Mary'. The proprietary name for a liqueur made from rum and coffee.

tinto 'Tinted', but in practice used as a synonym for 'red'. The single word *tinto* often means *vino tinto* or, in Portuguese, *vinho tinto*.

Tio Pepe 'Uncle Joe'. The proprietary name, owned by Gonzales Byass & Co, for a fino sherry of unparalleled excellence.

> 'Tio Pepe … Gonzalez, Byass, & Co., … London, E.C.; Wine and Spirit Merchants': *Trade Marks Journal*, p 953, 15th September 1886. 'Some of the finer kinds are really supernacular [to be drunk to the last drop] – the best Tip Pepe, for instance': George Saintsbury, *Notes on a Cellar-Book*, ii, p 18 (1920). 'Gonzalez Byass & Co. Limited … Tio Pepe … For Wines … First use 1905': *Official Gazette* (US Patent Office), p 16, 16th April 1968.

tilde/til *Tilde* is the Spanish name for the curly diacritical sign placed over the letter *n* to signify that the letter is palatalized. Pronounced /ˈtildə/. The result is that the sound of the letter becomes /ɲ/, as in *señor*, /səˈɲɔːr/. The combinations *Ñ* and *ñ* are treated as separate letters of the Spanish alphabet, as also are the combinations *LL* and *ll*, these latter being pronounced /ʎ/, the sound of *-lli-* as in the English word 'million'.

The identical Portuguese diacritical sign is known as the *til*, /til/. Both the Spanish and the Portuguese words derived from the Latin *titulus*, following much the same path as our 'tittle', as in 'jot and tittle' (*cf Mt* 5:18). However, it is important to note that the Portuguese *til* has a radically different function from the Spanish *tilde*, which, alone, makes it worthwhile to employ its Portuguese name rather than, as is customary in English-speaking circles, its Spanish name. The function of the *til* is to nasalize the letters *a* and *o*. Thus, *ã* as written and pronounced in Portuguese is realized by the same symbol and diacritical sign in the IPA, thus: /ã/. Similarly, the Portuguese õ is realized by /õ/. It is difficult to relate these two nasalized sounds as realized by their IPA symbols without first having heard a native speaker pronounce them. If we take the word *amanhã*, 'tomorrow', which in IPA is rendered /əmaˈɲã/, we might perhaps render it, in an approximate English-speaker's 'imitated pronunciation', tonic accent indicated by capitals, as 'uhmuhnyANG', but with this proviso: the final *G* is not pronounced as *g*. All the organs of speech are poised ready to articulate the English sound *ng* (/ŋ/, as in 'singer') but, at the last micro-second, the process of articulation ends abruptly with the emission of breath for the last vowel. (The vowel-sounds written *uh* in the 'imitated' pronunciation above are meant to represent the sort of neutral sound an English-speaker emits while he hesitates in speech.) Similarly with the very common word *não*, 'no', /não/, which might be imitated as follows: *NAH-oong*, again with the important proviso that the g is not sounded: it is there to prepare the mouth for the pronunciation of *-ng* – which never takes place. The two syllables in *NAH-oong* should be pronounced virtually as one.

The nasalized *o* of Portuguese, /õ/, is quite similar to the French nasalized o as in *on dit*.

Tirso de Molina Pseudonym of the Spanish priest, Gabriel Téllez (1571-1648). The first mention of him was in Andrés Claramonte y Corroy's *Letania Moral* as Padre Frey Gabriel Téllez of the Order of Nuestra Señora de le Merced. Almost all his entire adult life seems to have been spent in Holy Orders, latterly in positions of responsibility. Despite his exemplary life in religion, Tirso was extremely prolific in his output for the theatre. He is credited with having written four hundred plays, but only about eighty have survived. During his life his comedies were published in five parts, the first in Seville, 1627, the third in Tortosa, 1634, the second and fourth in Madrid, 1635, and the last in Madrid, 1636. These contain fifty-nine plays. The play that is now remembered, not for itself but for its progeny, is his *Burlador de Sevilla y Convidado de Piedras,* in which he created the immortal character *Don Juan.* (*Cf Calderón* and *Lope de Vega, above.*)

Tirso particularly excelled at writing for the stage, but his attainments in the field of narrative writing, in his *novelas,* is also significant. He is at his best in his comedies and his secular *novelas.* He excels in wit, originality of dialogue, and ingenuity of plot.

The *nom-de-guerre* 'Tirso de Molina' is perplexing, as is, one supposes, his lifelong life in religion coupled with an intensely active life in literature, particularly the high-profile life of the theatre. There is no suggestion that Padre Frey Gabriel Téllez hid behind the disguise of 'Tirso de Molina', since *both* names appear on the title-pages of his published works.

tomato Not strictly a Spanish word in this form. The word is a Mexican word, *tomatl.* 'Tomato' is an anglicization, perhaps modelled on 'potato'. There is evidence that other adaptations were tried at times: we see 'tomata', probably modelled on the Spanish form *patata,* 'potato'.

> 'You like potato and I like potahto
> You like tomato and I like tomahto
> Potato, potahto, Tomato, tomahto.
> Let's call the whole thing off': Ira Gershwin.

tonto 'Foolish, stupid'. How the Lone Ranger's trusted – sensible, level-headed – Indian scout attracted the name 'Tonto' is a perennial puzzle. For adaptations destined for Latin-American countries, the character's name was sometimes changed to Toro, 'bull'. At other times it was left unchanged, for reasons that have not appeared.

toreador A generic name for a bull-fighter, with a slight implication of a mounted bull-fighter. It is not a synonym for *matador,* as fans of Bizet's *Carmen* might imagine. *Cf torero, below.*

torero A generic name for a bull-fighter, with a slight implication of a bull-fighter on foot.

torista See quotations.

> 'The more solid Spanish *aficionados,* especially those known as *toristas* because their primary interest is in the Bull rather than the Bullfighter': A. MacNab, *The Bulls of Iberia,* p xii (1957). 'The torista exalts the toro over the torero to the point where he will ignore and despise the man's best achievements': McCormick & Mascareñas, *The Complete Aficionado,* ii, p 31 (1957)

tornado 'Several species of storm'. Neither a Spanish nor a Portuguese word. Both languages nowadays use the English invention 'tornado'. The derivation of 'tornado' is convoluted. Fundamentally, the word denoted a thunder-storm (French, *tonner,* 'to thunder'). Metathetically, it progressed to suggest some sort of derivation from the French *tourner,* 'to turn', no doubt influenced by mariners' experience of rotating storms such as cyclones.

tortilla A thin round cake made of maize-flour, baked on a flat plate of iron or earthenware and eaten hot. A staple of the diet in Mexico.

> 'One of our favourite luxuries is the tortilla (pronounced torteea)': Lees & Clutterbuck, *British Columbia 1887,* p xxii (1892).

Tudesco A term in Ladino (*q.v.*) denoting an Askenazi Jew. Also used attributively.

> 'They accentuated the superficial differences between them and the *tudescos*, from Germany and Poland, or even the *italianos* and *berberiscos* whose antecedents were nearer to their own': Cecil Roth, *A History of the Marranos*, viii, p 234 (1932). 'Not so long ago English Sephardic families used to sit in mourning if one of their members married, not a Goy (or non-Jew), but a Tedesco (or Ashkenazi Jew)': *The Spectator*, p 595/1, 4th November 1949. 'The intended union of Menasseh's daughter with a Polish Jew excites ... horror ... in the Mohamad [the governing body of a Sephardi synagogue]. A Tedesco did not pronounce Hebrew as they did, hence he was inferior': M. Wohlgelernter, *Israel Zangwill*, II, p vi (1964).

tuna A species of fish, *Orcynus*, especially the common tunny, *O. thynnus*. The fish grows to lengths of about 10 feet (about three metres) and is widely fished in the Mediterranean and the Atlantic. In the Mediterranean it has been fished since Antiquity, and was known to the Greeks as *θύννος*, whence French *thon*, the spelling influenced to some extent by Gallic antiquarianism. Though the English word 'tunny' or 'tunny-fish' is still found, the name for the fish at the retail stage is now irreversibly *tuna* in both England and the US.

ultraya A regular discussion group held by those supporting the *Cursillo* (*q.v., above*) movement, to encourage perseverance in the faith. The word *ultreya* is the name of the journal of the movement and is the first word of the hymn members sing on their pilgrimages to Compostela. It recalls the medieval cry (*E*)*ultreya*, 'onward!', 'forward!', and thus has some resemblance to the word 'Excelsior' in Longfellow's poem of that name.

> 'After each Sunday mass, ... the members gather in the church for the 'ultreya', a period to discuss personal matters, both secular and religious': *The New York Times*, p A1/1, 27th August 1984. 'More than 800 people gathered in the Washington Cathedral for the Fourth Annual Multi-Diocesan ultreya': *Washington Diocese*, p 4, February-March 1987.

vaquero In Spanish America: a cowboy or cowherd; a herdsman or cattle-driver. The Portuguese is *vaqueiro*.

Verdelho See *Madeira*, above.

vicuña A South American animal (*Auchenia vicunna*), closely related to the llama and alpaca, inhabiting the higher portions of the northern Andes and yielding a fine silky wool used for textile fabrics': *OED*.

vihuela There are two types of the early-music instrument known as the *vihuela*. The first, the *vihuela de mano*, is played with the fingers and thumb, as a guitar is played. The second, the *vihuela de arco*, is bowed in the manner a viol is bowed.

vin d'alho Portuguese: *vinho de alho*, 'wine of garlic' (i.e., garlic sauce'). Said to be the etymon of the word 'vindaloo', as in 'vindaloo curry'.

vinho verde 'Green wine'. A white wine that has not been allowed to mature

> 'There are, however, some wines such as the *pétillant* and *vinhos verdes* ('green wines'), which have a natural 'liveliness' or inclination to sparkle': P. V. Price, *Taste of Wine*, v, p 100/1 (1975).

yerba-maté 'Herb *maté*'. **See** *maté, above*.

zamarra A sheep-skin jacket.

zapateado The highly characteristic flamenco dance involving complex rhythmic syncopated stamping of the heels and toes in imitation of castanets.

Zapatista One who follows or followed the policies of Emiliano *Zapata* (1879-1919, the leader of the Mexican revolutionary *guerrillero* movement founded about 1910 by Zapata. The movement fought during the Mexican Revolution (1910) in order to achieve the redistribution of agricultural land. Among English-speakers, the name *Zapata* is known rather by virtue of the motion picture *Viva Zapata!*, released in 1952, featuring Marlon Brando as Zapata, than by any appreciation of the lasting effect Zapata had on Mexico's polity or well-being.

zócalo or **zocalo** A public square; a *plaza*.

zoco A market-place, from Arabic *sāk*, a marketplace.

zorro A fox-wolf, *Canis Azatae.*

zorino A species of skunk, *Mephitis patagonica*, unrelated to the *zorro.*

ACKNOWLEDGEMENT

I am deeply indebted to my friend Dr Günther Schmigalle, of Karlsruhe, the celebrated editor of the works of Rubén Darío and profound Hispanic scholar. His incomparable knowledge of Spanish-language culture and literature, coupled with his mastery of his own mother tongue and his no less notable *intimate* familiarity with French and English literature, have been of inestimable help in the compilation of this Lexicon, as, indeed, they have in the compilation of virtually every page in this publication.

LATIN

> In research the horizon recedes as we advance, and is no nearer at sixty than it was at twenty. As the power of endurance weakens with age, the urgency of the pursuit grows more intense … And research is always incomplete.
>
> Mark Pattison, *Isaac Casaubon.*

This Lexicon is the fifth in a series of relatively concise lists of words and phrases from foreign languages that have been adopted by reasonably well educated English-speakers.

A Latin Lexicon is a rather special case. In the first and most obvious place, Latin is a *dead* language. No one has spoken it as his mother tongue for some fifteen hundred years. In the second place, this dead Latin language is part of the common heritage of all of us, English-speakers and virtually everyone over the whole surface of the globe who has had the benefit of a liberal education. Dead though it is, *it lives.*

For what reasons it lives will perhaps become increasingly obvious as one reads through this Lexicon. Latin seems – at least to its many millions of mesmerized captives – to have been the medium by means of which the perennial wisdom of the ages has been *habitually* articulated. That is, in a nutshell, the *raison d'être* of this Lexicon.

The use of that phrase, *raison d'être,* reminds us that, during the Enlightenment, French bade fair to usurping the place of Latin as the medium for intellectual communication – as the international language – but was displaced by English in the last century. Despite that, Latin continues to live on in its own special ways, in ways too numerous and complex to epitomize. It is hoped, nevertheless, to *demonstrate* those ways in this Lexicon.

Any eulogy of this language, Latin, must start with a recognition of the immense debt civilization owes to the Roman Empire and to its language Latin as the transmitter and amplifier of Greek culture through the then known world. If it had not been for the influence of the Roman Empire, Greek-speaking outside Greece might well have been limited to the trading colonies founded by Greek-speaking *merchants,* not *scholars,* round the Eastern Mediterranean, and including Sicily and Southern Italy. Though there are notable specific instances of noble Greek architecture outside Greece, as, for example, the Temple of Poseidon at Paestum, Sicily, in the Doric Order, the world-wide dissemination of Greek culture that undoubtedly occurred was due to the imperialistic aspirations of the Romans, who, faithful acolytes of Greek culture, carried it with them wherever they went – to the extent that we can assuredly say, with Shelley, 'We are all Greeks now'.

But the role of the Roman Empire in history was not, of course, limited to its being a mere transmitter of what Edgar Allen Poe magnificently described as

> … the glory that was Greece
> And the grandeur that was Rome.

What accounts for the perennial claim that Latin has on our allegiance? Well, for one thing, one has to say that, however one feels about Coleridge's 'Poetry: the best words in the best order', one somehow feels that, once an eternal verity (or, it might be, a smart remark) has been recorded in Latin, it can never again have the same vitality in any other language, whether, in that other language, it is expressed in prose or poetry. In a million different instances, once a morsel of the bedrock of truth has been hacked out of the mother-lode *and expressed in Latin,* there is little chance that we shall ever hear it better put in any other language. It has been proverbial for centuries that *quidquid latine dictum sit, altum videtur:* 'Whatever is said in Latin seems profound'.

An amusing and memorable instance of a smart remark – smart remarks are not the normal exemplar of the wit and wisdom of the Romans – testifies to the enduring efficacy of their language long after they themselves were dead and gone. Giovanni Pico della Mirandola (1463-94) adopted a rather boastful motto, *De omni re scibili*: 'Concerning all things knowable': Voltaire long after the event but with great delicacy punctured Pico's vanity by adding *et quibusdam aliis:* 'and several other things'.

We are almost all of us English-speakers transfixed by Edward Gibbon's *Decline and Fall of the Roman Empire*, surely the most egregiously pessimistic book ever written. One senses that, contrary to probability, the first Duke of Gloucester somehow got it right on discovering the researching Edward Gibbon poring over a book in the Royal Library at Windsor: 'Another damned, thick, square book! Always scribble, scribble, scribble! Eh! Mr Gibbon?'. It is salutary to speculate what the ever-touchy Voltaire might have said in response to Gibbon's strictures, 'When I meet Voltaire on Grecian, Roman or Asiatic ground, I treat him with the indulgence he has so much occasion for, but we might have expected to have found him better acquainted with one of the finest writers of his own country ...' – that is, Pascal, on 'a sloppy reading of a passage in the Provinciales'. Voltaire's opinion of Gibbon would not have been augmented by an opinion that Gibbon expressed elsewhere on Voltaire, 'A bigot, an intolerable bigot'. One feels tempted to say, in one of the many, many clinching English phrases, 'It takes one to know one'. The nearest one can come to that sentiment in Latin is, perhaps, *Pares cum paribus facillime congregantur*, but, then, that sentiment is better expressed in native English by saying, 'Birds of a feather flock together'. Nevertheless, even if we allow for progress in its widest sense, the Latin language still harbours a myriad myriad unique locutions. Even after we have deducted from that hoard the nuggets of wisdom that, inevitably, have been overcome by events, there still remains an immense store of knowledge that has been preserved in Latin as flies are preserved in amber.

This Lexicon, one hopes, contains some of those apperceptions of the eternal verities that have withstood the erosion of the centuries. In the main, however, the entries in this Lexicon are more concerned with practicalities, as indeed the Romans themselves were, and for which their language was and is ideally suited. The permanence that surrounds the Latin component of the scholar's language is astonishing. It is of course perfectly true that the incursions of the Barbarians into the Roman Empire led to the decay of the language that was at the heart of the Roman Empire. The old *sermo urbanus*, literally 'the language of the town', meaning the speech of the most aristocratic of Romans, had early virtually disappeared: the simpler *sermo vulgaris*, 'vulgar speech', had made such immense inroads into the language that even purists had to concede room for the compromise *sermo cotidianus*, 'everyday speech'. But with wave after wave of Barbarian incursions, even that compromise speech became increasingly debased. No-one who has at heart what might be called the integrity of the Latin language can view with indifference, or, indeed, without the most profound emotion, the condition the language fell into as the Barbarian incursors eroded and degraded the *Romanitas* that had so signally characterized the Roman Empire for more than four centuries.

The extent and degree of this linguistic decline can best be discerned from an examination of the regions of the known world in which the linguistic decline was most noticeable. In parts of the Empire that had not been completely Romanized, the lingua franca of the Empire became increasingly foreign once the Imperial presence was diluted by the presence of powerful strangers. In 746 St Boniface, the Apostle of Germany (?-754), wrote to Pope St Zachary (?-752) to settle a question about the efficacy of the administration of the sacrament of Baptism by an illiterate priest – our inference is that he was Frankish – who had inadvertently introduced the notion of a Goddess by baptizing in the form '*Ego baptizo te in nomine Patria et Filia et Spiritus Sancta*'. Zachary responded:

> *Si ille qui baptizavit, non errorem introduces aut haeresim, sed pro sola ignorantia romanae locutionis, infringendo linguam, ut above fati dixisset, non possumus consentire ut denuobaptizentur*:
> 'If the man who [thus] baptized, not introducing error or heresy, but solely from ignorance of Roman speech, mistaking the language, used the words we have quoted above, we cannot consent that [those so baptized] should be baptized anew'.

Boniface's concern arose from the sacramental use of Latin by clerics who spoke as their mother tongues the languages of the many waves of invaders that had cascaded into the Empire. Increasingly a distinction is drawn between the languages of the incursors and the residual Latin of the Empire. Zachary's choice of words to designate 'Latin' stands alongside other terms such as *lingua latina rustica* and *lingua romana* that became standards on the Northerly borders of the Empire, where satisfactory Roman rule had never in general prevailed: that is, in the regions in which the 'Related Tribes', the Germani, ruled. As the *regnum Francorum* emerged – the empire of the Franks – these terms were necessary to distinguish Latin from the languages of the incursors, something that had not been necessary under the Empire, since Latin had effectively obliterated all indigenous languages. (It is salutary to recall that none of the languages indigenous to the parts of Europe subsequently occupied by Rome survived the conquest – except Welsh and Basque.)

Boniface's concern was that clerics in his mission-fields were misusing a language not their own. Elsewhere, in the regions of the Empire where Latin had completely extirpated the native languages, the situation was that clerics were misusing a language that was their own, but increasingly remotely their own. The decline in the day-to-day use of Latin was understandably less marked in these regions in which Latin had driven out the indigenous languages, but for that reason is was a more insidious threat to the continuity of Latin as a language. The peoples of what became, much later, Italy, France, Spain and Portugal were under the impression that they continued to speak the Latin of the old Empire, but, as Charlemagne realized, most of what was being preached to the people in Latin was such that they simply couldn't understand it, in that their 'Latin' had undergone such immense changes in vocabulary, syntax and pronunciation that even some of the most common Classical words were barely if at all recognizable. Many Classical words had been dropped because of confusion: *equus* had nothing to do with *equalitas* and so, by reviving a Celtic word that had survived in local Latin dialects, the speakers of *lingua latina rustica* acquired a simpler, unambiguous word *caballus*, which, losing its inflexions, became the word for 'a horse' in late Latin and the Romance languages. The Classical word for 'head', caput, had nothing to do with capture and so, in Gaul, the soldiers' slang *testa* ('cooking pot') became the word for 'head', hence tête. Dies, 'day', with its resemblance to Deus, 'God' and its tricky declension and shifts in gender, gave way to the adjective *diurnum*, 'daily', used as a substantive, hence *giorno, jour*. Charlemagne, the new, Frankish, Emperor, the first Holy Roman Emperor, on realizing that his people who were heirs to the Romanitas of old had ceased to understand their birthright, decreed in 813 that sermons should thenceforth be preached in *lingua latina rustica*, by which he meant the vernaculars that were developing from the older Latin of an earlier Empire. In that way the dialects of Late Latin that ultimately became Italian, French, Spanish and Portuguese were officially recognized. (Rumanian, also a Romance language, developed outside the influence of Charlemagne's empire, growing up under the wing of the Eastern Roman Empire and, later, under the Ottomans. It remains visibly quite clearly a Romance language, despite the importation of countless Slavic and other expressions and constructions.)

Latin in its integrity, though not the Latin of the Golden and Silver Ages, continued to be the language of scholarship and administration in the West, despite the fall of the Empire in the West. Learning certainly suffered greatly during 'the Dark Ages' as the fabric of the old Empire crumbled. Just as the majestic buildings of Classical Rome and the old Empire fell into disrepair and ruin, so also the language of the old Empire became ramshackle. Charlemagne's edicts effectively banning sermons in the Latin of the old Empire, far from weakening the hold Latin had on scholarship, greatly increased it. Curiously, though the Irish had never been colonized by the Romans, the restoration of 'pure' Latin was facilitated by Charlemagne's and his adviser Alcuin of York's reliance on Irish monks to guide the official efforts to purge Latin of its many accumulated blemishes. It is an arresting and dispiriting experience to read texts written during, for example, the seventh or eighth century in Italy, professedly in Latin, but in fact replete with gross mis-spellings, false concords, egregious syntactical errors and vocabularies drawn from who knows where, and then contrast them with the texts of limpid simplicity and purity produced by the Irish monks whom Charlemagne and Alcuin had laid under contribution.

Despite the disruption of almost the entire fabric of civilization consequent on the incursions into the Empire of wave after wave of barbarians, there appeared in the late fifth century a work of such stupendous significance that it truly deserved to be called a veritable beacon of Latinity throughout the entire Dark Ages. That was the translation of the Bible undertaken by St Jerome (340-420) and known to posterity as the Vulgate. Though it became fashionable, with 'the Revival of Learning', to disparage Jerome's Latin as falling short of the Latin of the Golden Age (approximately 75 BC - AD 14), it is increasingly difficult, in this present age, to accept the artificial standards of judgement that led to the deification of the authors of the Golden Age. Despite the almost universal veneration in which Dr Johnson is held by English-speakers today, and despite the undoubted elegance displayed in his periodic diction, no-one would recommend his prose style to working writers practising today. We should learn from that.

The belief current among biblical scholars nowadays contrasts with the beliefs current during the Revival of Learning. We tend, nowadays, to believe that a translator of the Old and the New Testaments is not to be blamed but probably to be complimented for retaining characteristics of Hebrew diction and of the idioms of *διαλεκτος*, the Greek from the end of the Classical Attic period until about 600 AD in which the New Testament is written. In consequence, Jerome ought not to be castigated for his putative failure to emulate the masters of the Golden Age in his epic Vulgate. Rather, perhaps, he ought to be judged, from a stylistic point of view, on, for example, his Prologues, or his Letters to Pope St Damasus (340-84), his 'patron'. Perhaps we need to break out of the confines of the Pantheon Erasmus (1466-1536) and so many others have erected. There is a directness and vitality – almost a 'businesslikeness' – in Jerome's prose, at least when it was written and revised by Jerome himself. (Most of his sermons were written down by his listeners, with the inevitable loss of authenticity.) Few can fail to be captivated by the directness and vigour of Jerome's style. Jerome's sparse diction derived in part from his schooling under Aelius Donatus, but in part, also, from his desire to communicate his message as directly as possible for the sake of souls. He said, '*Veneratione mihi semper fuit non verbosa rusticitas, sed sancta simplicitas.*' 'The object of my veneration has always been, not rustic verbosity, but holy simplicity.' He was too loyal a son of Classical rhetoric to admit the possibility of urban verbosity, and one suspects that it never crossed his mind that a major pitfall for the unlettered was the opposite node, the terrifying terseness of Classical Latin. To reduce our sustenance to the compass of a vitamin pill or two is hardly an appetizing prospect. Horace might well have had this thought in mind when he wrote, 'Brevis esse laboro / Obscurus fio'.

Jerome's Latin is a good bridge by which to pass from Imperial Rome to Papal Rome.

English-speakers have long been accustomed to recalling historical events and to marking periods in history by means of terse and pithy phrases. Examples are *1066 and all that* and, from that influential book, published in 1930, 'America was clearly top nation and history came to a full stop.' Regrettably, even epochs of immense moment to mankind are similarly encapsulated in this cavalier fashion and are committed to memory by a society fed on slogans and with a memory-span of seconds. A classic instance is found in Thomas Hobbes (1588-1679): 'The papacy is not other than the ghost of the deceased Roman Empire, sitting crowned upon the grave thereof.' A more measured and reasoned view is commonly met with today: 'The Church kept the flames of human culture alive in the West during the Dark Ages in the wake of the fall of Rome. It contributed some notable additions to the precious inheritance of Greco-Roman antiquity, including an emphasis on personhood, sympathy and forgiveness. With its monasteries and schools it sustained learning and a respect for truth'

The proportion of ecclesiastical Latin locutions included in this Lexicon is smaller than might be expected. The reason for that is that ecclesiastical Latin was used in a context that was itself Latin. This Lexicon is restricted to Latin words and phrases used in English. Thus, for example, though we refer to the two canticles used in the service of Evensong, in the Book of Common Prayer, as the Nunc Dimittis and the Magnificat, the rest of the two canticles, (that is, apart from their titles) is in English. So, also, we speak of the parts of Bach's Mass in B Minor as the Gloria, Sanctus, Osanna, Benedictus, Agnus Dei et Dona Nobis Pacem. The evidence of the continuing usage of ecclesiastical Latin represents only the very tip of the iceberg.

In the sphere of scholarship in general, the use of Latin remains widespread. Indeed, in ordinary conversation we use Latin more often than we realize. We all say vice versa, and, though the way in which most of us pronounce the phrase might dismay a Classical scholar, nevertheless we use Latin. It is true that the Latin we use is in the form of Latin tags, but there's no disgrace in that. Take the expression *argumentum ad hominem* as an example. Those who use it know what it means, and in most instances they will feel confident their audience, too, will know what it means. H. W. Fowler defined it as an argument 'calculated to appeal to the individual addressed more than to impartial reason'. It's undoubtedly useful to be able to express that notion in three words, but the utility of the expression is greatly enhanced by the fact that it is one of a battery of similar phrases – *argumentum ad absurdum* (an argument that depends on exposing the opponent's argument as absurd); *ad crumenum* (an appeal to 'the purse'); *ad baculum* (an argument implying resort to force, 'the stick'); *ad ignorantiam* (an argument depending on the audience's being ignorant of some essential element); *ad populum* (an argument appealing to popular passion); and *ad verecundiam* ('modesty', an argument depending on the audience's reticence, or, in Fowler's words, an argument 'to meet which requires the opponent to offend against decorum').

The art of logic has given the English language a considerable number of terse Latin expressions. Those vocations and avocations that depend on logic, such as philosophy, have greatly benefited from that open quarry. The Law, too, in a sense quite apart from its historical use of Latin as a language of record, makes much use of Latin tags in its argumentation. And, of course, theology relies heavily on Latin in its formulation and classification of abstruse ideas. The sciences depend on Latin as well as Greek as a quarry for the material from which to make up new words: the Linnaean System of Classification of Plants and Animals depends exclusively on the Latin language.

Not least among the advantages a knowledge of Latin conveys is that it constitutes a marvellous key to the Romance languages. Certainly a prior knowledge of Latin greatly facilitates the learning of French, Italian, Spanish, Portuguese and Rumanian. But perhaps the greatest boon Latin affords is that, learnt young, it shines a powerful light on one's own language. Even the slightest acquaintance with Latin grammar immensely improves one's grip on English grammar. Through the refracting glass of Latin, we see English with a startling, new, clarity. For example, alerted to the existence of the construction in Latin known as 'the accusative and infinitive', we are driven, if we have inquiring minds, to asking ourselves whether the accusative and infinitive is truly an English idiom, or is it, rather, an import from Latin. Is 'They believed him to be an imposter' English? Most of us would say, 'Of course it is!' But if we were to hold it up against 'They believed that he was an imposter', we might begin to see how a foreign construction can creep in by the back door. The other bugbear of every schoolboy, the ablative absolute, is not so easy to sneak into English: 'Me repentant, I wiped the slate clean' is simply not English, and never will be. The present compiler, having been transfixed by the gerund for many years, is beginning to have the same sort of nagging doubts that Aldous Huxley's timorous character Theodore Gumbril experienced. Was Otto Jespersen right, after all? Is the gerund nothing more than a fused participle?

As we have mentioned, a sphere that traditionally relied heavily on the use of Latin in an English-speaking context was the Law. Though English law remains Common Law, as distinct from Roman Law, a great deal of legal literature over the centuries, and much of the recording of judgements and the like, was reduced into writing in the Latin language. (See, too, the Law French Supplement to the French Lexicon.) In consequence, a great many Latin expressions have survived to this day, and, although in England in 2006 there is an express and determined effort by the Bench to suppress Latin expressions, as 'obfuscatory', they are likely to persist in use because they are normally more concise and accurate than their expansions in English. (As long ago as 1923, Lord Shaw of Dunfermline, a Lord of Appeal, said, 'The day for canonizing Latin phrases has gone past'. It appears that Lord Shaw, who was normally fearsomely right in his judgements, was wrong in this one. One hopes the anti-Latinists at present on the Bench will prove equally unprophetic.)

Whether learning Latin is the best way of learning to think, as so many proponents of Latin have avowed over the years, is a moot point. No doubt to teach formal logic would be a better way to induce pupils to think, but Latin is not a bad substitute, *pis aller*, for teaching formal logic, and it will be so for as long as our modern educational systems perversely neglect to teach formal logic at every stage from commencement of schooling onwards. The utter neglect of logic in the educational systems of the modern world is a truly anomalous and ostensibly indefensible position to take. One assumes that educationists must consciously take that position, otherwise this glaring lacuna in our educational system could not exist or persist. The failure to promote the teaching of logic is so widespread that all one can do is to be a voice crying in the wilderness. Truly, the utter neglect logic suffers at the hands of all our modern educational systems is to be wondered at: 'Lord, what fools these mortals be!'

However, one comforts oneself by concluding that Latin is a close second to logic as a means of teaching thinking. Why should that be so? For one reason above all others: its practice relies on reason in the unlocking of meaning from the delphic written word (translation) and in the fashioning of meaning from the seemingly intractable clay of 'a language not understanded of the people' (composition). Though the teaching of English grammar is (or ought to be) indispensable in English-speaking regions, it does not have nearly the same potential for squeezing out satisfactory solutions to problems by pure reason, by reason alone, that the teaching of Latin does. We all rely heavily on intuition when it comes to our own language. How do we rationalize the distinctions between yet, still and already? The answer is: we don't until we're asked to do so by a foreigner – and then we find ourselves stumped.

One thing we ought always to be aware of: learning Latin is not a chore. An illuminating lightning-flash comes from an unexpected quarter. Winston Churchill said of schoolboys: 'Naturally I am biased in favour of boys learning English. I would make them all learn English: and then I would let the clever ones learn Latin as an honour, and Greek as a treat.'

That seems a very good idea! (There is a slightly chilling counter-view to that inspiriting bit of uplift: the school Churchill went to, Harrow, had a reputation for one thing in particular: it imbued in its boys a profound belief in *the existence of* the Latin and Greek languages.)

Two salient impressions are made on the mind during one's earliest points of contact with the Latin language. The first is that one conceives the impression that one is looking at something as immense and overpowering as the Pont du Gard, near Nîmes. One senses that those Romans had something! The epic dimensions of their buildings! Their limitless vision in undertaking such feats as the building of the Coliseum and the Antique Theatre in Orange! Their indomitable courage in building and manning Hadrian's Wall! But it is not just the magnificence of Roman achievement that captivates one. It is the convenience of it! Think of the convenience of Roman life in Pompeii, Verulamium (St Albans) and Bath, Somerset, with their running water, their hypocausts, and their public baths. One begins to wonder whether civilization has really advanced so much as we perhaps naively assume.

And when we come to dip into the literature of the Roman Empire we are astonished at how contemporary with our own age the Classical scene seems to have been. If one ignores the poetry and drama of the Roman Empire and concentrates on the written remains of what one man wrote to another, in Horace's Epistles, for example, or in Cicero's Letters, one is immediately struck by the palpable fact that they were very much as we are! How often have we all said in our hearts precisely what Horace says, *Brevis esse laboro, obscurus fio*: 'I strive to be brief – and become obscure'! And when Cicero says, *Sed nescio quo modo nihil tam absurde dici potest quod non dicatur ab aliquot philosophorum*: 'I don't know in what way it is possible to say anything so absurd that it hasn't been said by some one of the philosophers', we nod wisely, in perfect agreement with him. And a phrase that strikes a truly, almost frighteningly, modern note is Horace's *Nos numerus sumus et fruges consumere nati*: 'We are just statistics, born to consume resources.'

A nice example of the community of spirit that exists between the ages can be demonstrated by a little excursion. Many know that St Jerome is credited with the saying, *Pereant qui ante nos nostra dixerunt*: 'May they perish who have said our things before we have.' We all know the feeling! We all recall hearing that when J. A. N. Whistler (1843-1903) made a witty remark, Oscar Wilde (1854-1900) said, 'I wish I'd said that!' Whistler replied, 'You will, Oscar! You will!' We all murmur, 'Just what I've thought of saying a million times!' We add, under our breath, 'Pereant qui ante nos nostra dixerunt!' And, no doubt, we've gone though life just waiting for someone to say, 'I wish I'd said that', so that we could come back with a lightning, Dorothy-Parker-like retort, 'You will, Jimmy! You will!'

Well, a Google search elicits no fewer than 811 references to *Pereant qui ante nos nostra dixerunt* and 1290 to *Pereant, inquit, qui ante nos nostra dixerunt*. The word inquit in the latter version reminds us that Jerome is himself quoting. He is commenting on the already widely quoted 'There is no new thing under the sun': as enshrined in *Ecclesiastes* 1:9 and 10:

> 9 Quid est quod fuit ipsum quod futurum est quid est quod factum est ipsum quod fiendum est.
> 10 Nihil sub sole novum nec valet quisquam dicere ecce hoc recens est iam enim praecessit in saeculis quae fuerunt ante nos.
> '9 What is it that hath been? The same thing that shall be. What is it that hath been done? The same that shall be done.
> 10 Nothing under the sun is new, neither is any man able to say: Behold this is new: for it hath already gone before in the ages that were before us.'

Jerome adds a note of additional practicality to *Ecclesiastes*. It is not just that in general there is nothing new under the sun; it's worse than that, for, specifically, even our own best bons mots about anticipatory plagiarism turn out to have been uttered already by others.

Jerome quotes from the Commentum Terenti, a commentary by his old master Aelius Donatus (fl 356, later to become 'Donat', the grammarian of the Middle Ages), on Terence (Publius Terentius Afer, 190-158 BC), hence the *inquit* that often crops up in this context. (Sometimes an uncritical use of the quotation by Googlers gives the impression that Aelius Donatus, a pagan, wrote a commentary on *Ecclesiastes*.)

The popularity of the quotation is, in its small way, an eloquent testimonial to the timelessness of human feelings.

A remarkable and much, much more influential indication of the timelessness of human feelings, and of the persistence of Latin as a vital force, can be found in the secular literature and, in particular, in the lyric poetry, of 'the Dark Ages'. The world of the Mediaeval scholar is wonderfully captured by Helen Waddell in her *The Wandering Scholars* (1927) and in the collection, *Mediaeval Latin Lyrics* (1929), of the material she enthused about so sympathetically in her earlier book. She understands how a Classically orientated posterity has seen the continuity of lyricism throughout her period as a 'hidden stream', breaking out again only with 'the Revival of Learning', but, in truth, her work posits a quite contrary thesis: it efficiently subverts the very notions of 'the Dark Ages' and 'the Revival of Learning'.

Only a little of the body of lyrics Waddell published and translated resides in the memory of English-speakers, but there has been a relatively recent flurry of interest in one of the major sources of Waddell's material, the Carmina (or Codex) Burana MS at the monastery of Benedictbeuern, Bad Tölz, Oberbayern (Bavaria), which represents the largest collection of twelfth- and thirteenth-century secular, Goliardic, lyrics extant. The reason for this relatively recent interest is that Carl Orff (1895-1982) took the lyrics of this manuscript as the libretto of a cycle of songs, which greatly increased interest in the collection of lyrics. The additional interest in these verses that Orff's work led to was greatly augmented by the use in an epic television commercial for a men's deodorant, Old Spice, of the first lyric in the manuscript, 'O Fortuna!', set by Orff as a chorus. It was used as the accompaniment to magnificent film of surfers breasting breakers of immense size. Perhaps rather more characteristic than O Fortuna of the robust, highly metrical verses of the Codex Burana is the following:

Fas et Nefas ambulant
pene [paene] passu pari;
prodigus non redimit
vitium avari;
virtus temperantia
quadam singulari
debet medium
ad utrumque vitium
caute contemplari.

Right and Wrong they go about
Cheek by jowl together
Avarice his brother.
Virtue, even in the most
Unusual moderation,
Seeking for the middle course,
Vice on either side it, must
Look about her with the most
Cautious contemplation.

Classical scholars who adhere to the belief that early Roman verse depended on accent, as our own does, rather than, as Classical Latin versification did, on quantity, will recognize the rumbustious rhythm of the metre (*versus Saturnius*) used in early Roman poetry, before the introduction of the Greek metres. The strong 'beat' that characterized Saturnian verse is certainly present in Goliardic versification. (Dryden, the 'classic' Classicist, wrote, 'The Romans had ... certain Young Men, who at their Festivals Danc'd and Sung after their uncouth manner, to a certain kind of verse, which they call'd Saturnian'.) It might well be that *per arsin et thesin* originally meant 'by the raising and lowering' of *the hand*, as in beating time to music, or in the tapping of *the foot* in sympathy with the rhythm in the music, either of which reaction is instinctive in accentual music and verse but not in quantitative verse. Indeed, the very word 'foot' itself, as a term of art in scansion, argues strongly for an accentual rather than a quantitative approach to native Latin poetry.

That raises the question: was there – *is there* – such a thing as *quantitative* music? One knows there was much music in the Roman Empire. We have no clear idea of what it was like, but it has to be said that it is extremely difficult to conceive of *quantitative* music. Perhaps the difficulty one experiences in conceiving of *quantitative* music might lead one ultimately to conclude that the *native* Latin versification continued to be *accentual*, despite the powerful influence of Greek practice. Is there any case to be made for assuming that the licentious, obscene, scurrilous and truly demotic Fescennine versification was ever quantitative?

It is of course perfectly possible that Greek and Latin in Antiquity were *tonal* languages. Tonal languages such as Swedish and Mandarin Chinese are worth considering in this context. The diacritical marks introduced into the writing of Greek by the Alexandrians are plausibly believed by some to be based on a *tonal* spoken language. Proponents of the idea point out that an acute accent could graphically have indicated a raising of the tone; a grave accent could have indicated a falling tone; and a circumflex accent a rising tone followed by a falling tone, particularly since many languages actually use the first two of those adjectives as adjectives meaning high and low in tone – *e.g.*, *les notes les plus aigües.*

The strongly accentual metre of almost all Goliardic verse is as irresistible as the metre Shakespeare used in:

> Heigh ho, sing heigh ho, unto the green holly; Most friendship is feigning, most loving mere folly: Then, heigh ho, the holly! This life is most jolly.

And the sentiments in those verses are very close to those that inform much Goliardic poetry.

Englishmen have a sneaking soft-spot for Latin. In the power-struggle after the end of the Second World War, Dean Acheson opined that 'Great Britain has lost an empire and has not yet found a role'. British prime ministers forsook their traditional role (Palmerston's 'Civis Romanus sum') and inculcated an attitude of mind on their constituents in which it was the *Americans* who were the Romans: the role of the *British* was to play the Greeks, guiding their apprentices, the callow Romans, in the right way. It did not cut any ice.

In the purely cultural sphere, the truth is that English Classical scholarship has been largely unscientific, in that it has relied most on the individual efforts (and genius) of men such as Richard Bentley (1662-1742) and Richard Porson (1759-1808), whereas German scholarship has been relentlessly methodical. The names Georges, Heinichen and Ingerslev, and Dinter, Hinzpeter, Kraner and Doberenz stud the pages of the literature, resembling more than anything else the shingles of the upper crust of New York corporate lawyers.

But German scholarship does have an immense claim on our gratitude for keeping brightly shining the light of Latin learning during the 19th century, at a time when the natural sciences were bidding fair to monopolizing the entire spectrum of higher education.

France, too, has an inherently Latin-based culture quite apart from the Romance character of its language. The incidence of Latin quotations in the conversation of educated Frenchmen is notable. The evidence of *les pages roses* in Larousse eminently testifies to that, but there is another source from which French draws its use of Latin, and that is the Vulgate. We are forcibly reminded of this by no less a personage than John Wilkes!

On Tuesday, 8 May 1781 the following conversation took place at Dr Johnson's bookseller Mr Dilly's house:

> The subject of quotation being introduced, Mr Wilkes censured it as pedantry. JOHNSON: 'No, sir, it is a good thing; there is a community of mind in it. Classical quotation is the *parole* of literary men all over the world.' WILKES. 'Upon the continent they all quote the vulgate bible. Shakespeare is chiefly quoted here; and we quote also Pope, Prior, Butler, Waller, and sometimes Cowley.'

The anti-clerical elements that fomented the Revolution appreciably emasculated the power of the Church to influence French minds in a Latinate direction, but it will not have escaped the acute ear that Wilkes's comment was not so far from the truth: every literate Frenchman still has at his command a respectable armoury of Latin quotations deriving from the Sacred Scriptures. English-speakers talk of 'casting pearls before swine' Frenchmen talk of strewing *ante porcos margaritas* (*Mt* 7:6). English-speakers say, 'Get thee behind me, Satan!' Frenchmen say, *Vade retro me, Satana!*: *Mk* 8:33.

The compiler remembers very clearly being told one day by a French businessman – *nota bene*, he was a businessman, not a scholar – that he, the compiler, had no reason to be puzzled by the lack of a word for 'Yes' and a word for 'No' in Latin, for, apart from his being, to the Frenchman's knowledge, a quarter Welsh – Welsh has no 'Yes' and no 'No' – the compiler ought to have known the verse from *Mt* 5 34-37, *Sit autem sermo vester est est non non:* 'Let your 'Yea' be 'Yea' and your 'Nay' be 'Nay''. It was a fair comment.

Many of the Latin tags we use have been altered from their originals for a variety of reasons. The major reason is that word order in Latin is not nearly so important as it is in English and most modern languages. Sometimes, therefore, we re-order the words to conform to what is natural to us. Moreover, many of our quotations come from Latin verse, in which word order is frequently further changed, *metri gratia*. Another relevant reason for departure from the original is that words separating the most important words are often omitted for the sake of brevity. In other instances of change, words that were in one grammatical case in the orginal have been put in another case for the purposes of the popular tag: Sallust's *Appius ait, fabrum esse suae quemque fortunae:* 'Appius says that each man is the maker of his own fate' becomes *faber fortunae suae,* and has led to some useful adaptations in English. For example, when English judges tend toward sententiousness, they are inclined to say of convicted persons that 'they are the authors of their own misfortune'.

Very often we face failure in our efforts correctly to attribute Latin tags to any particular author. There are several reasons for this. The two main ones are as follows. Many of the good, quotable things that exist in every language grew spontaneously from chance remarks that some hearers thought worthy of repeating and thus repeated them, and so put them into currency. The facility with which comedians' catch-phrases catch on is an indication of the power and speed of this word-of-mouth process. What English-speaking scholar can tell us who first had the happy thought of comparing a wet weekend with a long face? Even the expression 'a long face' was itself the happy invention of some nameless, faceless and unsung wordsmith.

The second consideration we ought always to have in mind when we review the vast storehouse of Latin locutions we are heirs to is this: that the immense accumulation of Latin tags is in some part the flotsam and jetsam of *the lost literature of Antiquity.* It is a truly mournful reflection that the bulk of Classical literature has been lost. For all we know, many of the unattributable sayings we encounter might well be fragments of the floating wreckage of, in Poe's words quoted above, 'the glory that was Greece / And the grandeur that was Rome.' We might sometimes imagine the literature of Antiquity to be *la Cathédrale engloutie*: the countless Latin tags we use are but the tips of the spires and finials of the submerged edifice. (See the entry *Amor ordinem nescit* in the Lexicon for a further discussion.)

Take as an instance of this phenomenon another of the locutions in this Lexicon, [*Ex*] *verbis ad verbera,* a neat little *jeu d'esprit.* It has been quoted and quoted a million times. In haste we might ascribe it to the humanist cleric Poggio, who certainly used it, as in *Ex verbis ad verbera devenerunt, ac unguium capillorumque certamen*: ('They went from words to blows, a battle of nails and hair'). We might also be tempted to ascribe the phrase to Christine de Pisan, who drops the Latin phrase into her *Lavision-Christine* with as little ceremony as we might say, in English, *et cetera*: *[E]t debas qui aucune fois tant moulteplioit entre eulx que de telz de chaude cole y avoit faisoient venir* de verbis ad verbera.

However, the alternative scenario is that both these authors, the first profoundly erudite and the second very much better educated than most women of her century – or of any century – were merely using a handy tag that was on the lips of many of the literate. These tags, which are extremely numerous (as the compiler of this Lexicon ruefully corroborates), are to some extent a rag-bag. They comprise the remnants of the spoken idiom of old Rome, favourite turns of phrase, hallowed and rendered timeless by usage, mixed with the memorable high-points of that part of the literature of Antiquity that was lost in the turmoil of 'the Dark Ages' – to which we must add the many felicitous inventions of the scholars of the one and a half millennia that have elapsed since the fall of the Roman Empire.

The life of Latin over two millennia has produced many anomalies. One is our distinguishing between the letters *i* and *j*, and the letters *u* and *v*. Practical users of Latin have, over the years, tended to ignore the Ancients' use of *i* to the exclusion of the (at that time) uninvented letter *j*, and have used *i* for the simple vowel and *j* for the consonant. That has seemed to most of us an aspect of progress. Likewise, European scholarship has introduced, over two millennia, a useful distinction between the written letter *u* (or *v*) in its solely vocalic function and in its consonantal function. Thus, we use *u* for the vocalic function and *v* for the consonantal function. In this Lexicon, we have tended to employ the *i* and *u* forms exclusively for all usages from Antiquity, and, for post-Classical usages, we have tended to use both the vocalic and consonantal forms. Thus, we have *eius* and *ejus*, *cuius* and *cujus* In references to the pronunciation(s) of Latin, we hear some of the reverberations associated with the powder-keg, *ueni, uidi, uici.* We have preserved a place in our hearts for *veni, vidi, vici* so spelt, as we all, in our *heart* of hearts, expect to see it written. Proponents of the Classical Pronunciation might regret this, but they might also, just for a moment, reflect that it was the insistence of the scholars at the time of the Renaissance on the use of a language utterly obsolete by that time that killed the international language from which our modern world might immensely have benefited – if Latin had been allowed to exist as the spoken and written language of all the clerks in Europe. A lost chance!

All this corroborates that new turns of phrase in Latin, the language of the literate in Western Europe, were being coined at all times. The Scholastics were particularly fecund in that respect. And lawyers, both generically and, in some cases, individually, were also prolific. Lord Coke alone generated scores of maxims. His Latinity was impeccable, but it is his knack of manufacturing, at will, locutions that have all the characteristics of time-worn but time-honoured nuggets of legal wisdom that has secured him such a large number of credits in the Law dictionaries of the Common-Law jurisdictions.

It has to be said that most of Lord Coke's Latin gems are uniquely his own, but they reflect to an uncanny extent the true spirit of the Common Law – hence their widespread acceptance by the profession in his own day and their continuing unquestioning acceptance ever since.

It needs to be pointed out that compilers of anthologies of proverbs, maxims and 'other men's flowers' are often remiss in not furnishing sources. To furnish sources is to give the reader the opportunity of looking at the context from which the quotation has been drawn, so that he can establish the true scope of the quotation. Frequently a glance at the context will completely alter the reader's conception of the nuances implicit in the quotation. Sometimes the context will elucidate what a quotation really means, completely contrary to our immediate inference – something of considerable value with the terser maxims that have come down to us.

Compilers of maxims such as Publilius Syrus, a writer of mimes of the first century, and Michael Apostolios (c.1422-1480) performed sterling service in preserving the wisdom of the ages, but in most cases they were not concerned to ascribe an extract to any specific work, and often they omitted to ascribe an extract to any named author. In consequence, it is very often extremely difficult to be sure that a given author was the actual 'onlie begetter' of a felicitous phrase. How can we be sure that the author credited with a quotation was not quoting an earlier author? Or how can we be sure that, by the time he was writing, he was not repeating something that was already proverbial, or at least already in the common stock? (See the entry *Amor ordinem nescit* in the Lexicon for a discussion of this issue.)

The adages compiled by Publilius from early Latin speech and literature provide us with a remarkable conspectus of early Roman life. Compilers such as Erasmus (c.1469-1536) bring Latin adages up to the Renaissance itself. Dictionaries of Latin tags abound during subsequent centuries. Macdonnel's *Dictionary of Quotations*, first published in 1811, ran into many editions. E. H. Michelson's *A Manual of Quotations*, published in 1856, is still to be seen on booksellers' shelves. Compilers of Greek adages include Joannes Stobaeus, Maximus Confessor, Antonius Melissa, Joannes Georgides, and Michael Apostolios, the last of whom (c.1422-80) efficiently draws on his predecessors and provides us with the most comprehensive compilation of Greek maxims that exists. It is of course a mistake to *ascribe* adages to him: he compiled maxims; he did not create maxims. His work *Paromiai* represents an immense quarry for the quotation-hunter. The same general caution applies to Publilius. Publilius and Apostolios were *indefatigable* compilers. If an earnest searcher for references in Antiquity fails to pin down his exact words in the works of original authors and has to resort to citing Publilius or Apostolios as the origin of a given saying, he is truly in the last ditch.

The task of verifying references is an arduous one, but it is one of immense importance to scholarship. A memorable anecdote encapsulates this notion. Dean Burgon (J. W. Burgon, 1813-88) asked 'the Last of the Non-Jurors', Martin Joseph Routh (1755-1854), for 'some axiom or precept' he thought of as being of special value 'after a long and thoughtful life'. Dr Routh, aged 92 at the time, had been President of Magdalen for almost 30 years! Routh 'looked thoughtful'. He 'presently brightened up and said, 'I think, sir, since you care for the advice of an old man, sir, you will find it a very good practice (here he looked me in the face) *always to verify your references, sir!*''

A word is necessary about the translations in this publication. They are the compiler's own except where another source is mentioned. The translations are almost always literal, intentionally. However, once in a while one needs to depart from the literal sense in order to convey the meaning. King Alfred knew that: he appreciated that he needed to translate *hwilum word be worde, hwilum andgiet of andgiete,* 'sometimes word for word, sometimes meaning for meaning'.

There is a statistic that dramatically bears on the compilation of a collection of Latin words and phrases that have been instrumental in shaping our thought and our language, and that is that, in the *Oxford English Dictionary* (still in the process of development), there are no fewer than 9,888 references in the text to 'Classical Latin'. Further to indicate the importance of Latin, albeit something as old *and obsolete* as Classical Latin, one might note that there are only 3,076 references to Anglo-Saxon and Old English combined, though that language is beyond doubt the *ur*-language of the entire English-speaking world.

We bring to a close this lengthy disquisition on the part that Latin continues to play in modern English-speaking culture. Readers might well say of it, as Dr Johnson said of Milton's *Paradise Lost*, 'None ever wished it longer than it is'. So be it. *Iacta alea est*: 'The die is cast'.

Nevertheless, we cannot finish without a further recourse to Dr Johnson, 'the Great Cham of Literature', as Smollett called him in a letter to Wilkes. Johnson's devoted dedication to the Classics shines through every activity he undertook in his eventful life. There are many, many illustrations of this in Boswell's *Life*, but none, I think, is so moving as this one:

> On Saturday, July 30 [1763] Dr Johnson and I took a sculler at the Temple-stairs, and set out for Greenwich. I asked him if he really thought that a knowledge of the Greek and Latin languages an essential requisite to a good education. JOHNSON. 'Most certainly, Sir; for those who know them have a very great advantage over those who do not. Nay, Sir, it is wonderful what a difference learning makes upon people even in the common intercourse of life, which does not appear to be much connected with it.' 'And yet', (said I) 'people go though the world very well , and carry on the business of life to good advantage, without learning.' JOHNSON. 'Why, Sir, that may be true in cases where learning cannot possibly be of any use; for example, this boy rows us as well without learning, as if he could sing the song of Orpheus to the Argonauts, who were the first sailors.' He then called to the boy, 'What would you give, my lad, to know about the Argonauts?' 'Sir, (said the boy), I would give what I have.' Johnson was much pleased with this answer, and we gave him a double fare.

A Note on the Enumeration of the Book of Psalms

The Book of Psalms is quoted extensively in this Lexicon, inasmuch as it played a profoundly important role in the dissemination of Latin among the Barbarian intruders who supplanted the Roman Empire, and thus also in the preservation of Latin. The significance of the Book of Psalms is testified to by the frequency of quotation and allusion we find throughout two entire millennia.

The Psalms come to us through two separate sources: the Hebrew Massoretic Text and the Greek text known as the Septuagint. The enumeration of the Psalms differs somewhat in the two versions. The Authorized Version (the King James Version) follows the Hebrew system, whereas the version we quote in this Lexicon, the Vulgate, translated by St Jerome, follows the Septuagint system of numeration. The following list gives outline details of the correspondence between the two systems.

Hebrew 1-8 > Septuagint/Vulgate 1-8
Hebrew 9 > Septuagint/Vulgate 9-10
Hebrew 10-112 > Septuagint/Vulgate 11-113
Hebrew 113 > Septuagint/Vulgate 114-115
Hebrew 114-115 > Septuagint/Vulgate 116
Hebrew 116-145 > Septuagint/Vulgate 117-146
Hebrew 146-147 > Septuagint/Vulgate 147
Hebrew 148-150 > Septuagint/Vulgate 148-150

Septuagint/Vulgate 1-8	> Hebrew 1-8
Septuagint/Vulgate 9-10	> Hebrew 9
Septuagint/Vulgate 11-113	> Hebrew 10-112
Septuagint/Vulgate 114-115	> Hebrew 113
Septuagint/Vulgate 116	> Hebrew114-115
Septuagint/Vulgate 117-146	> Hebrew116-145
Septuagint/Vulgate 147	> Hebrew146-147
Septuagint/Vulgate 148-150	> Hebrew148-150

The Lexicon

A bene placido 'At one's pleasure'.

A capillis usque ad ungues 'From the hair down to the nails.' From top to bottom. Petronius, *Satyricon*, 102:13.

A cantu avis dignoscitur 'A bird is known by its song.' Proverbial.

A capite ad calcem 'From head to heel'. St Augustine, *De Civitate Dei*, 15:26.

A capite bona valetudo 'Good health comes from the head'. Seneca, *De Clementia*, 2.2.1.

A contrario 'To [on] the contrary'.

A cruce salus 'From the cross comes salvation.'

A Deo et Rege 'From God and the King'.

A deo necesse est mundum regi 'God is needed to rule the world.' Cicero, *De Natura Deorum*, 2.77.

A gratia excidistis. 'Ye are fallen from grace.' *Gal* 5:4.

A lucis ortu 'From first light'. Apuleius, *Florida*, 6.

A fabulis ad facta veniamus 'From fables to facts may we come'. Cicero, *De Republica*, 2.4.

A fortiori 'With still stronger reasoning'.

A fronte praecipitium a tergo lupi 'A precipice in front, wolves behind'. To be between Scylla and Charybdis; to be between a rock and a hard place.

A fructibus eorum cognoscetis eos 'By their fruits shall ye know them.' *Mt* 7:16.

A latere 'From the side'. Said of a cardinal sent from the Pope's side, charged with a special mission, as in *Legatus a latere* or *Nuntius a latere*.

A mane ad vesperum 'From morning to evening'. Plautus, *Miles Gloriosus*, 503. *A mane usque ad vesperam. Ecclesiasticus (Sirach)*, 18.26.

A mari usque ad mare 'From sea to sea' (the motto of Canada).

A mensa et thoro 'From board [table] and bed', the operative words in a decree of judicial separation, not divorce, obtained from the ecclesiastical court. A decree of divorce granted for, say, nullity *ab initio*, is said to be *ab vincula matrimonii*, 'from the bonds of matrimony'.

> 'When the husband and wife are diuorced *à vinculo matrimonij*, as in case of precontract, consanguinitie, affinitie, etc. and not *à mensa & thoro* onely as for adulterie': *Co. Litt.* 36:32 (1628). 'The ecclesiastical court would only pass sentence of divorce *a mensa et thoro* (a divorce from bed and board), which had the effect of a modern judicial separation': O. R. McGregor, *Divorce in England*, 1:3 (1957).

A notis ad ignota 'From known things to unknown things'.

A novo 'Anew'. From scratch. More often, especially in the Law, *De novo*.

A pari ratione 'By parity of reasoning'. In discussions in English, the rather Latinate English phrase 'By parity of reasoning' is generally used in preference to more idiomatic expressions.

A pedibus usque ad caput 'From feet to head'.

A planta pedis usque ad verticem 'From the soles of his feet to the crown of his head'. In full, *Egressus igitur Satan a facie Domini percussit Iob ulcere pessimo a planta pedis usque ad verticem.* 'And going forth from the face of the LORD, Satan struck Job with grievous sores from the soles of his feet to the crown of his head' *Job* 2:7.

A posse ad esse 'From possibility to actuality'. In the Law the expressions *in posse* and *in esse* are frequently used attributively:

> 'A child *en ventre sa mére,* is a child *in posse,* but the law regards it as *in esse* for all purposes which are for its benefit: *Doe* dem *Clarke* v *Clarke,* 2 Bl H, 399.

The word *posse* as used in Western films is an abbreviation of *posse comitatus,* a legal expression meaning 'the strength or force or power of the county'. 'The force of the county'; the body of men above the age of fifteen in a county (exclusive of peers, clergymen, and infirm persons), whom the sheriff may summon or 'raise' to repress a riot or for other purposes; also, a body of men actually so raised and commanded by the sheriff': *OED.*

A posteriori 'From what comes after'. The phrase *a posteriori* denotes the essence of *inductive* reasoning, which is founded on observation and depends on arguing from effect to cause, as opposed to *deductive* reasoning, which in principle is founded on the contrary approach, that of arguing from cause to effect.

A primaevo flore iuventae 'In the first flower of youth'.

A priori 'From what comes before': see immediately above. The phrase *a priori* denotes *deductive* reasoning.

A pueritia usque ad hanc aetatem 'From childhood up to this present time'. Cicero, *Pro Balbo,* 1:3.

A puero 'As a boy'. There are many ways of saying this, including Horace's celebrated *Laudator temporis acti / Se puero,* 'A praiser of time past, when he was a boy.' Horace, *Ars Poetica,* line 173.

A quo 'From which place, time, circumstance, etc'. Very common in the phrase *Terminus a quo,* the reciprocal of *Terminus ad quem*: 'the point *from* which', 'to the point *to* which'. '*[T]erminus a quo, ad quem* are phrases originating in Scholastic L[atin]: 1250 in Albertus Magnus, *Phys.* 5. 2. 2; also in Aquinas, Roger Bacon, Duns Scotus, etc': *OED.*

A solis ortu usque ad occasum laudabile nomen Domini 'From the rising of the sun unto the going down thereof, the LORD's name is to be praised.' *Ps* 112.3. *AV Ps* 113:3.

A verbis ad verbera 'From words to blows'.

A verbis legis non recedendum 'The words of the law are not to be departed from.' Words in, for example, acts of the legislature should be construed as they stand and not interpreted as though the intention of the legislator were different from the intent of the words.

Ab asinis ad boves transcendere 'Move up from asses to oxen!' Plautus, *Aulularia,* 192.

Ab asino lanam 'Wool from an ass', an impossibility; *cf.* the English idiom, 'getting blood from a stone'.

Ab absurdo 'From the absurd'. A mode of argument depending on pointing out the absurdity of one opponent's case. See *argumentum ad absurdum, below.*

Ab aeterno 'From the beginning of time'.

Ab hinc 'From here on'.

Ab homine et flumine taciturno cave 'Beware of a still river and a still [silent] man.' Proverbial.

Ab homine homini cotidianum periculum 'Man's everyday peril comes from man.' Seneca, *Epistulae* 103.

Ab honesto [vir bonus] nulla re deterrebitur. 'By nothing will [the good man] be seduced from honesty'. Seneca, *Epistulae*, 76:18.

Ab imis unguibus ad verticem summum 'From the depths of his [toe] nails to the crown of his head'. Cicero, *Pro Roscio*, 7.20.

Ab imo pectore 'From the bottom of the breast [heart]'.

Ab impiis egredietur impietas In full, *Sicut et in proverbio antiquo dicitur ab impiis egredietur* 'As it is said in the old proverb, "From out of the wicked shall come forth wickedness"' 1 *Sam* 24:14. 'As saith the proverb of the ancients, Wickedness proceedeth from the wicked' *AV 1 Kings* 24:13. *Ab impiis egressa est iniquitas*. Erasmus, *Adagia*, 1:9:26.

Ab incunabulis 'From the cradle'. Livy, *Ab Urbe Condita,* 4:36:9. Erasmus, *Adagia,* 1:7:53.

Ab initio 'From the beginning'. Much used in legal contexts. A contract that is void *ab initio,* for some uncorrectable defect, is unenforceable. One that has defects that are capable of being remedied is said to be voidable.

Ab intestato A phrase describing circumstances arising from a person's having died without leaving a will.

Ab initio est ordiendus 'It is necessary to begin at the beginning.' Cornelius Nepos, *De Excellentibus Ducibus, Themistocles*, 1. This ostensible platitude was in fact a caution: a true understanding of the immensely influential role of Themistocles (523-460 BC) in Athenian history could not be acquired unless one went back to his earliest years as a child of an undistinguished family of the minor aristocracy. In general use, the saying acquired this slightly truistic reputation, but 'Let's begin at the beginning' has a good deal of sense to it, despite its seeming obviousness.

Ab invito 'Unwillingly'. This false friend–it suggests a voluntary implication, as in 'invited'–gained its currency from literary use, as in *Ab invito*, Cicero, *De Lege Agraria*, 1:14. *Invitus* is an adjective of uncertain etymology but certainly meaning 'unwilling': by extension, *[pecunia] coacta ab invitis*, Cicero, 2 *Verr* 2:153. In the Law, the expression *per invitos* is used sometimes to imply an element of coercion.

Ab ovo usque ad mala 'From the egg through to the apples': from start to finish. Horace, *Satires*, 1:3:6. Roman feasts started with eggs and finished with apples.

Ab scintilla una augetur ignis 'Of one spark cometh a great fire': *Ecclesiasticus (Sirach)* 11:34.

Ab urbe condita 'From the foundation of the city': the starting-point (753 BC) for the Roman way of expressing the year of the date, equivalent to our BC and AD.

Ab [Ex] uno disce omnes 'From one person, learn all people.' Altered from *Crimine ab uno/ Disce omnis*: 'From the one crime learn [to recognize] all [the others as criminals].' Virgil, *Aeneid*, 2:65.

Aberrare a fortuna tua non potes, obsidet te 'Thou canst not escape thy fate; it is all around thee'. Seneca, *De Clementia*, 1.8.2.

Abominatio est apud Dominum pondus et pondus; statera dolosa non est bona. 'Diverse weights are an abomination before the Lord: a deceitful balance is not good.' *Proverbs* 20:23.

Abeamus a fabulis, propiora videamus 'Let us depart from fables; let us look at things closer to us.' Cicero, *De Divinatione*, 2:9.

Abhorrent a vero principum aures 'Truth is abhorrent to the ears of princes.' Erasmus, *Encomium Moriae*, 36.

Abiecta omni cunctatione 'All hesitation aside'. Cicero, *De Officiis*, 1:72.

Ab origine 'From the origin'.

Abiit ad plures 'He has gone to join the majority', *i.e.*, he is dead. Petronius, *Satyricon*, 42:5.

Abiit, excessit, evasit, erupit 'He has left, absconded, escaped and disappeared.' Cicero, *Oratio in Catilinam II, In Populum,* 1.

Absente reo 'In the absence of the accused'.

Absentem laedit cum ebrio qui litigat 'Who argues with a drunken man wrongs someone who is absent.' Publilius Syrus, *Sententiae*, 6.

Absentem qui rodit amicum, hic niger est 'He who slanders an absent friend – he is black.' Horace, *Satires*, 1:4:81.

Absenti nemo non nocuisse velit 'No-one wishes not to speak ill of the absent.' Propertius, *Elegiae,* 2:19:32. The double negative here has immense force.

Absentia eius qui reipublicae causa abest, neque ei, neque aliis damnosa esse debet 'If absent to the public good, neither he not anyone else shall be disadvantaged.' Justinian, *Digest*, 50:17:140.

Absentia longa et mors aequiparantur 'Long absence is equivalent to death.' Law.

Absit invidia 'No offence intended.'

Absit omen 'May the omen be absent', *i.e.*, May this not be an omen! *Cf*, *Quod di omen avertant!*, Cicero, *Third Philippic*, 35.

Absoluta sententia expositore non indigent 'Plain words require no explanations'. Justinian, 2 *Institutes* 5:3:3.

Absolvere debet iudex potius in dubio, quam condemnare Law. 'If in doubt, the judge ought rather to acquit than convict.' Law.

Absolvere nocentem satius est quam condemnare innocentem 'Acquitting the guilty is better than convicting the innocent'.

Absum! 'I am leaving!'

Abundans cautela non nocet 'Great caution does no harm'. Haydon's case 11 *Co. Rep.* 5a at 6b.

Abusus non tollit usum 'Wrong use does not preclude proper use.' Proverbial, especially in the Law. Much copied and adapted, as in *Abusus non est usus, sed corruptela,* 'Abuse is not use but corruption':

> *Datur etiam abusus usuum, sed abusus non tollit usum, sicut falsificatio veri non tollit verum, nisi solum apud illos qui id faciunt*: 'It is a given that misuse of uses occurs, but wrong use does not preclude use, just as falsification of the truth does not take away truth except among those who practise falsification.' Emanuel Swedenborg (1688-1772), *De Divino Amore et de Divina Salientia, 1763,* ed John C. Ager (2005), no 331. *Ab abusu ad usum non valet consequentia*: 'No valid conclusion as to the use of a thing can be drawn from its abuse' Adverted to by Lord Denman CJCP in *Stockdale* v *Hansard* (1839) *9 Alolphus & Ellis Reports* 1, p 116.

Abyssus abyssum invocat In full, *Abyssus abyssum invocat in voce cataractarum tuarum omnia excelsa tua et fluctus tua super me transierunt*: *Ps* 41:8 in the Vulgate: 'Deep calleth unto deep at the noise of thy waterspouts: all thy waves and thy billows are gone over me': *Ps* 42:7 in the Authorized Version. It is extremely difficult to explain the meaning of this verse. Why *Abyssus abyssum invocat* or 'Deep calleth to deep' should have gained currency is inexplicable, unless the sheer rhetoric of the expression accounts for its popularity.

Accepti memores nos decet esse boni 'It becomes us to remember past favours.' Walter of England (Gualterius Anglicus), Archbishop of Palermo, *Aesop's Fables,* Fable 41, 'The Shepherd and the Lion'. The fable is of the shepherd who took a thorn out of a lion's paw.

Accessorium non ducit sed sequitur suum principale 'The accessory right does not lead but follows its principal.' *Co. Litt.* 152 a. Finch, *Law,* 128.

Accipere quam facere praestat injuriam 'Accept rather than do an injustice.' Cicero, *Tusculanae Disputationes*, V, 19.

Acta est fabula, plaudite! 'The play is over, applaud!' (Said to have been the Emperor Augustus's last words.)

Acta non verba 'Actions, not words'.

Acta sanctorum 'Deeds of the saints'.

Actus reus 'Wrongful act'. Many ostensibly wrongful acts require the proving of *mens rea*: literally, a 'wrongful mind' or wrongful intention.

Accusare nemo se debit, nisi coram Deo 'No-one need accuse himself unless before God.'

Ad absurdum 'To the point of absurdity'.

Ad acta 'To the archives or files'. Said of a (legal) matter no longer alive but of which a record might be needed.

Ad alta 'To the summit'.

Ad astra 'To the stars'.

Ad astra per aspera 'To the stars through difficulty'.

Ad augusta per angusta 'To high places by narrow roads', a punning saying much quoted.

Ad Kalendas Graecas 'At the Greek Kalends', Augustus (63BC-AD14). The Greeks did not use kalends in stating the date; hence, 'never'.

Ad captandum vulgus 'To capturing the crowd', a species of argument intended to appeal to popular sentiment rather than reason, etc.

Ad clerum 'To the clergy'. A pronouncement by an ecclesiastical authority addressed for the attention of the clergy, not the laity, such as a diocesan bishop's charges to his clergy.

Ad eundem gradum 'To the same level'.

Ad eundem More fully, *Ad eundem gradum.* 'To the same level.' A term used to convey that a graduate of one university is to be or has been admitted to the same degree at another university without examination.

Ad fontes 'To the sources', an abbreviation of *Redite ad fontes*, 'Go back to the sources', a slogan of Renaissance Humanism.

Ad fundum 'To the bottom', said when, after a toast, one drinks up; 'bottoms up'.

Ad hoc 'For a particular purpose', meaning improvised, made up in an instant.

Ad hominem 'To the man.' A species of argument intended to appeal rather to the opponent himself, as a person, than to abstract, dispassionate reasoning.

Ad honorem 'In honour of'. Sometimes the phrase means 'honorary', that is, without reward.

Ad idem To be 'Of the same mind'.

Ad infinitum 'To infinity; without end'.

Ad interim 'For the time being'.

Ad libitum 'At one's pleasure'. Said, very often, of an option given to a musical performer to do or refrain from doing something. Often used as a verb, 'to ad-lib', implying that an actor or presenter, for example, is speaking not from a script but extemporizing.

Ad limina apostolorum 'To the thresholds of the Apostles.' Bishops and Vicars Apostolic in the Catholic Church are required to visit Rome at periodical intervals (every five years if their responsibilities lie in Europe, every ten years otherwise) in order to give an account of their stewardship.

Ad litem 'For the purposes of suit or action'. A minor at Common Law is required to be represented by a 'guardian *ad litem*', an adult who acts on his behalf during the proceedings.

Ad locum 'At the place'.

Ad lucem 'Towards the light', the motto of the University of Lisbon.

Ad maiorem dei gloriam (AMDG) 'To the greater glory of God', a motto of the Society of Jesus.

Ad multos annos 'To many years!', 'Many happy returns!' Also *Da multos annos!*, shortened from Juvenal's *Da spatium vitae, multos da, Jupiter, annos:.* 'Grant a span of life, Jupiter! Grant many years' (*Satires*, IV, x 188). (The toast, *Ad multos annos*, is probably proverbial rather than an adaptation of Juvenal.)

Ad nauseam 'To the point of making one sick'.

Ad perpetuam rei memoriam 'For the perpetual remembrance of the thing'.

Ad praesens ova cras pullis sunt meliora 'Eggs today are better than chickens tomorrow'; the certainty of eggs today is better than the uncertainty of allowing the eggs to hatch for the sake of the grown birds. A Latinate way of saying, 'A bird in the hand is worth two in the bush'.

Ad referendum 'Subject to [further] reference [to others]'.

Ad rem 'To the thing'; to the point; relevant. A proverbial phrase is *Acu rem tetigisti*, 'Thou hast touched the thing with a needle', meaning with great precision and accuracy. Another idiom is *Rem acu tangere*, 'To touch the thing with a needle.'

Ad [in] usum Delphini 'For the use of the Dauphin'. Editions of books so called because the tutors of the eldest son of Louis XIV specially prepared them for his education, expurgating them to some extent.

Ad valorem 'By the value'. For example, a commission agent received his remuneration *ad valorem.*

Ad vitam aeternam 'For all time'.

Ad vitam 'For life'.

Addendum 'Something to be added'.

Adeste Fideles 'Be present, faithful ones!' The first line of a Christmas carol, *Adeste fideles, laeti triumphantes*, 'O come all ye faithful, joyful and triumphant!'

Adscriptus glebae 'Bound to the land'. In Feudal Law, the legal status of the serf.

Adsum 'Here! Present!'

Absque baculo ne ingreditor 'Without the stick, no progress will be made.' Erasmus, *Adages*, 3:4:61. *Cf., Qui parcit virgae suae odit filium suum qui autem diligit illum instanter erudit* 'He that spareth his rod hateth his son: but he that loveth him chasteneth him betimes.' *Proverbs* 13:24. That sentiment was popularized in English as the terse, 'Spare the rod and spoil the child.' The virtue of the expanded versions is that they preclude the false reading,' You are recommended to spare the rod and spoil the child – for violence breeds violence'. Another English adage, 'Stuff a cold and starve a fever', is open to the same charge of ambiguity, for it could mean, 'The best treatment for a cold is to stuff it (that is, eat well). The best treatment for a fever is to starve it (that is, eat sparingly.' Equally, the meaning might well be, 'Stuff a cold and you will end up starving a fever.' Very often brevity is a false friend.

Adversus incendia excubias nocturnas vigilesque commentus est 'Against the dangers of fires, he conceived the idea of night guards and watchmen': Suetonius, *Lives of the Roman Emperors: Augustus*, ch 30.

Adversus solem ne loquitor Proverbial. 'Do not speak against the sun.' That is, 'Do not argue against the existence of the obvious' or, simply, 'Don't waste your time arguing the obvious.'

Advocatus diaboli 'The devil's advocate'. In beatification and canonization proceedings, an ecclesiastic formerly (until 1983) charged with bringing to attention factors in the life of the candidate that would militate against beatification and sanctification.

Aegis 'Shield, protection'.

Aegrescit medendo 'The disease worsens with the treatment.' The remedy is worse than the disease.

Aegri somnia 'A sick man's dreams'. Abbreviated from *Credite, Pisones, isti tabulae fore librum persimilem, cuius, velut aegri somnia, vanae fingentur species, ut nec pes nec caput uni reddatur formae:* 'Believe me, dear Pisos, a book would be exactly like such pictures [an artist's impressions of a beautiful mermaid with a scaly, black tail] if idle fancies were to be formed like a sick man's dreams, in which neither head nor foot can be properly positioned.' Horace, *Ars Poetica*, line 6 *ff.*

Aegrotat 'In the Eng. Universities, a certificate that a student is too ill to attend at a lecture or examination. A degree or pass awarded to a candidate prevented from sitting an examination because of illness; also *N. Amer.*, a credit ... awarded for similar reasons': *OED*

Aegroto, dum anima est, spes esse dicitur 'It is said that for a sick man, there is hope as long as there is life'. Cicero, *Ad Atticum*, 9:10. 'Where there's life, there's hope.'

Aequam servare mentem Shortened from Horace's *Aequam memento rebus in arduis/ Servare mentem*: 'Remember in hard times to keep a calm mind' (*Odes*, 2:3:1-2).

Aequo animo 'With an impartial mind'.

Aes triplex 'Triple bronze'. An impenetrable defence. Cf. Horace, *Odes*, 1:3:9.

Aetatis ... 'Of age ...' *Aetatis suae* ... 'of his age ...'

Aeternum vale 'Farewell forever'.

Affidavit Literally, 'He has sworn.' The word has been a noun in English for centuries. It means a statement made in writing, confirmed by the maker's oath, and intended to be used as judicial proof. The *OED* says, 'In legal phrase [*sic*] the deponent *swears* an affidavit, the judge *takes* it; but in popular usage the deponent *makes* or *takes* it.' *Sed quaere*. Though everyone, lay and professional, nowadays tends to say 'swear' an affidavit, there are some who greatly fear tautology and thus, in their parlance, an older form of expression is used: *viz*, the deponent 'makes' an affidavit. The officer empowered to administer the form of oath, typically a Commissioner for Oaths, thus 'takes' the affidavit. The active verbal phrase 'sworn before me' is used in the procedure: the officer qualified to take the affidavit merely *attests* that the oath was sworn 'before me'. A distinction is drawn in practice between one who makes an affidavit (that is, he acts solely in writing) and one who makes a written statement as a result, say, of an appointment with his adversary's advisers. One who makes an affidavit was called, and is still called in the US, the 'affiant'. One who makes a deposition – who 'depones' – is called a 'deponent'. He 'deposes' to what he knows. In England one who makes an affidavit is also known simply as a 'deponent'.

As mentioned, in recent months the affidavit has given place, in England, to a 'Statement of Truth', which, for all practical purposes, serves the same ends as the affidavit, but does not require attestation in the presence of a Commissioner. The signature of the person making the Statement of Truth suffices to permit the document to be adduced in evidence.

Age quod agis 'Do what you do [well].'

Agenda 'Things to be done', strictly a plural, but widely used in English as a singular.

Agnus Dei 'The Lamb of God'. A part of the Mass, *Agnus Dei, qui tollis peccata mundi*: 'O Lamb of God, that takest away the sins of the world.'

Alea iacta est 'The die is cast', *i.e.*, the dice have been thrown. Attributed to Julius Caesar. The ascription is complex: see *The Oxford Dictionary of Quotations*, 4th edn (1992) *s.v. Caesar*, quotation no 19.

Alias 'Otherwise [known as]'.

Alibi 'Elsewhere'. A defence at Law relying on the provable fact that the accused person was elsewhere at the time the offence was alleged to have been committed. In slipshod use, employed to mean a defence of any kind.

Aliena nobis, nostra plus aliis placent 'Other people's things are more pleasing to us, and ours to other people.' Publilius Syrus, *Sententiae,* 28.

Aliquis non debet esse judex in propria causa 'A person ought not to be judge in his own case.' See *Nemo debet esse judex in propria causa, below.*

Aliquot 'Some, so many'. 'In phrase aliquot part: Contained in another a certain number of times without leaving any remainder; forming an exact measure of': *OED*.

> 'None of our coins are aliquot or even parts of our weights': Jos. Harris, *Money and Coins*, p 9 (1757).

Aliter 'Otherwise.' This Latin adverb is frequently interjected into legal argument and in judgements to indicate that matters, though they are as described in present circumstances, are otherwise in other circumstances. Another Latin adverb for 'otherwise', *secus*, is used in exactly the same circumstances, without differentiation. Cf. *Dis aliter visum*, 'The gods decided otherwise': Virgil, *Aeneid*, 2:428.

'Consequently only one action will lie, and in it full damages are recoverable for both the past and the future. *Aliter* if I have brought a heap of soil and left it on the plaintiff's land': J. W. Salmond, *The Law of Torts*, 5:162 (1907).

Alma Mater 'Nourishing mother'. One's old school or university.

Alter ego 'The other "I"' or one's other self.

Alter ipse amicus 'A friend is another self'.

Altissima quaeque flumina minimo sono labi 'The deepest rivers flow with the least sound.' *Cf.* 'Still waters run deep'.

Alumnus 'Nursling'. Used to denote a former pupil of a school or former undergraduate of a university. Feminine: *alumna*. The plurals are, respectively, *alumni* and *alumnae.*

Amanuensis 'One who writes from dictation or makes fair copies.'

'Caesar could dictate to three amanuenses together': Abraham Tucker, *The Light of Nature Pursued*, II, p 446 (1768).

Amantes sunt amentes 'Lovers are lunatics.' A good example of the punning element so characteristic of many Latin tags. The attraction of this sort of word-play has persisted until the present day: see, for example, *traddutore, traditore* in the Italian Section.

Amantium irae amoris integratio est 'The quarrels of lovers are the renewal of love.' Terence, *Andria*, 655.

Amare et sapere vix deo conceditur 'Even a god finds it hard to love and be wise at the same time.' Publilius Syrus, *Sententiae*, 22.

Amat victoria curam 'Victory favours those who take pains'. Erasmus, *Colloquia Familiaria*, *Lusus Pueriles* X, 'Pila'.

Ambo, ambones 'The pulpit[s] or reading desk[s] in early Christian churches.' They were often and increasingly found in pairs, one to the left of the altar and the other to the right. The word *ambo* also means 'both, two'; *cf. Arcades ambo, below.* One meaning seems to have influenced the other, though there is some etymological link in Antiquity. Generations of clerical schoolmasters have elicited a titter by aspirating the plural.

Amicitiae nostrae memoriam spero sempiternam fore 'I hope that the memory of our friendship will be everlasting.' Cicero, *Aelius de Amicitiae*, 4:13.

Amicus certus in re incerta cernitur 'A sure friend is discerned during unsure proceedings.' Cicero, *De Amicitia,* 34.

Amicus Curiae 'Friend of the Court'. In England, a lawyer appointed to assist the Court in cases where it is apprehended that the adversarial nature of Common-Law procedure will not furnish the Court with enough impartial material on which to arrive at a judgement. Since the publication of the (English) Civil Procedure Rules in 1999, the term *amicus curiae* has been 'phased out' in favour of the term 'Court Advocate'. Until fairly recently, the general understanding of the term *amicus curiae* was as in the 1959 quotation below. In the US the range of meanings, nounal, adjectival and adverbial, of the term *amicus curiae* is different from English usage; see the 2006 quotation below.

> '*Amicus curiae*, a friend of the court, that is to say, a person, whether a member of the Bar not engaged in the case or any other bystander, who calls the attention of the court to some decision, whether reported or unreported, or some point of law which would appear to have been overlooked': Jowett, *Dictionary of English Law*, I, p 114/1 (1959). 'A person, not a party to the litigation, who volunteers or is invited by the court to give advice upon some matter pending before it. Also called *friend of the court*': *Random House Unabridged Dictionary, s.v. amicus* (1997). 'Amicus curiae: Inflected Form(s): *plural amici curiae.* Etymology: New Latin, literally, friend of the court; one (as a professional person or organization) that is not a party to a particular litigation but that is permitted by the court to advise it in respect to some matter of law that directly affects the case in question': *Merriam-Webster On-line Dictionary, s.v. amicus* (2006).

Amicus humani generis 'A friend of the human race:' a philanthropist.

Amicus verus est rara avis 'A true friend is a rare bird'. For *rara avis,* see also Juvenal's use of the idiom, *below, s.v. rara avis.*

Amor animi arbitrio sumitur, non ponitur 'Love is embraced of our free will but is not freely cast away':Publilius Syrus, *Sententiae*, 5.

Amor caecus est 'Love is blind'. Proverbial in Antiquity. Jacobus de Cassolis OP, a thirteenth-century friar, incorporates the phrase in his *Ludus Scaccorum*, 'Game of Chess': *Attendant autem judices, ne amore privato vel odio in judicio moveantur. Nam omnis amor caecus est.* 'Judges should therefore take care not to be moved in their judgement by private love or hate. For all love is blind.'

Amor ordinem nescit 'Love knows no order.' St Jerome certainly wrote this saw: see the extract below. Nevertheless, this quotation exemplifies one of the major hazards in relying on the over-terse entries that characterize most compilations of quotations. In the first place, the tag *Amor ordinem nescit* was probably proverbial by St Jerome's time: he was doubtless no more the author of those words than Shakespeare was the author of 'All that glisters is not gold' (*Merchant of Venice*, 2:7). In the second place, the context of many of the recorded instances in literature of the use of this tag do not bear out the most popular interpretation placed on it – that love knows no rules [of conduct, of war, of fair play, etc]. Writers tend to use the tag as they please, and of course that means that, if they choose to use the tag to imply that 'All's fair in love and war', then they are entitled to do so. *But* ... is not the use of a Latin tag in that instance rather an admission that the thought itself is a little threadbare? In the third place, Latin tags gathered together in a word-list are very rarely given a proper reference, so that prospective users of the tags cannot easily verify exactly what they are quoting from. (The internet is choked with plagiaristic word-lists that are devoid of references: sometimes, only the author's name is supplied; very often, not even that. This clutter, which is utterly counter-productive, merely serves to provide a quarry for after-dinner speakers and adolescent essay-writers. Nevertheless, *Abusus non tollit usum.*

The following three case-studies demonstrate the substance of the remarks above.

St Jerome wrote:

> *Et miremini forsitan, quod in fine iam epistulae rursus exorsus sim. quid faciam? vocem pectori negare non valeo. epistulae brevitas conpellit tacere, desiderium vestri cogit loqui. Praeproperus sermo; confusa turbatur oratio; amor ordinem nescit.*
>
> 'You are surprised, perhaps, that, at the end of my letter, I should now make a new beginning. But what can I do? I cannot deny the voice in my breast. The brevity of a letter compels me to leave things unsaid; [and yet] my affection for you urges me to speak. Too hasty speech! My language is confused and ill-arranged; but love knows nothing of order.'

Michel de Montaigne (1533-92) wrote:

> *Plus courte possession nous luy donnons sur nostre vie, mieux nous en valons. Voyez son port. C'est un menton puerile, qui ne sçait en son eschole, combien on procede au rebours de tout ordre: L'estude, l'exercitation, l'usage, sont voyes à l'insuffisance: les novices y regentent.* Amor ordinem nescit? 'The shorter authority we give to love over our lives, 'tis so much the better for us. Do but observe his port; 'tis a beardless boy. Who knows not how, in his school they proceed contrary to all order; study, exercise, and usage are, there, ways for insufficiency; there, novices rule; *Amor ordinem nescit.*'

Another use of the tag, selected at random from the many extant, is a remarkable one.

> Dame Gertrude More OSB, a great-great-grand-daughter of Sir Thomas More and a member of a community of English Benedictine nuns in Paris, kept a note of

> her spiritual reflections. She entitled her manuscript *Amor Ordinem Nescit: an Ideot's Devotions.*

Amor patriae 'Love of one's country'.

Amor platonicus 'Platonic love'. Nowadays taken to mean a love that has no sexual ingredient. Its earlier meaning is well conveyed by a note in the *OED*:

> *Amor platonicus* was used synonymously with *amor socraticus* by Ficinus (the Florentine Marsilio Ficino, 1433-99), president of Cosimo de' Medici's *Accademia Platonica,* to denote the kind of interest in young men with which Socrates was credited: *cf.* the last few pages of Plato's *Symposium.* As thus originally used, it had no reference to women. (Prof. I. Bywater.)

Amor vincit omnia 'Love conquers all', altered from *Omnia vincit Amor: et nos cedamus Amori* 'Love conquers all: let us, too, give in to Love!': Virgil, *Eclogues*, 10: 69. This quotation demonstrates the supreme importance of word-order in modern languages. Our reliance on word-order radically affects our perception of how Latin tags should be formulated. It is futile for classicists to murmur that *Omnia vincit Amor* does not mean that 'All conquers love.' To *us* it seems to. To avoid any possible hesitation on the part of the lay reader, our ancestors have rearranged word-order to obviate misapprehension. English-speakers will recall the jewelry of Chaucer's Prioress:

And thereon heng a brooch of gold ful sheene/ On which ther was first write a crowned *A*/ And after *Amor vincit omnia.*

Amphiboly Greek αμφιβολια, 'ambiguity'. The slightly longer version, 'amphibology', is also in use. A rhetorical figure of speech or trope in which the words themselves are unambiguous yet the order in which they are placed gives a confused impression. In the mnemonic quoted below, a slogan used by the British government during the Second World War seems to urge two things as desirable: saving rags and wasting paper. Another example is, 'Spare the rod and spoil the child.' Are those two imperatives – that we should spare the rod and spoil the child, rather than that, if we spare the rod we shall spoil the child? A useful mnemonic might be:

> Amphibology? What a caper! 'Save rags and waste paper.'

An nescis, mi fili, quantilla sapientia mundus regatur? 'Dost thou not know then, my son, with how little wisdom the world is ruled?' A translation of a remark made by Axel Count Oxenstierna (1583-1654), counsellor to Gustavus Adolphus, in a letter to his son in 1648: 'Vet du icke, min son, med husu liten wishet verlden regeras?': see J. F. af Lundblad, *Svenska Plutark,* pt 2, p95 (1826). The fourth edition (1992) of the *Oxford Dictionary of Quotations* has a note: 'John Seldon, in *Table Talk* (1689) 'Pope' no. 2, quotes 'a certain pope' (possibly Julius III) saying 'Thou little thinkest what *a little foolery governs the whole world!*'

Anathema sit 'May he be accursed.' Words implying ecclesiastical censure, as used in the Athanasian Creed, that begin with the words *Quicunque vult.*

Angelus, The The prayer beginning *Angelus Domini annunciavit Mariae,* 'the angel of the Lord said unto Mary'. The prayer is recited three times a day, and the faithful are reminded of this by means of a bell, the Angelus Bell, rung at six o'clock in the morning, noon and six o'clock in the evening.

Anguis in herba 'A snake in the grass. A treacherous person'. Virgil, *Eclogues*, 3:93.

Angulus terrarum Altered from Horace's *Ille terrarum mihi praeter omnis / Angulus ridet:* 'That corner of the earth smiles for me more than all others' (*Odes*, 2:6:13-14). Hence, one's most favoured spot.

Animis opibusque parati 'Prepared in minds and resources'. One of the mottos of South Carolina. The other is *Dum spiro spero,* 'While I breathe I hope.'

Animus 'Mind, spirit, soul'. A special application of the word approximating to 'animosity, hostility, malevolence' has been in common use in English since the beginning of the 19th century. It is never used to denote an attitude of other than extreme hostility. See also, in general, *Aequo animo, above,* and *ex animo, below*'.

Animus facit nobilem 'The spirit makes noble.' Seneca the Younger, *Epistulae Morales*, 5:44:5.

Anno (an.) 'Year'.

Anno Domini (AD) 'In the year of the Lord'. In deference to non-Christian sensibilities, it is not unusual to use *CE*, for 'Common Era', as in '1066 CE'. (In place of BC it is not unusual to use *BCE*, 'before Common Era').

Anno Hegirae (AH) 'In the year of the Hijrah'. The Arabic system of dating relies for its starting date on the date of Mohamed's flight (*al hijrat*) from Mecca to Medina, 16 July 622.

Anno urbis conditae (AUC) 'From the year of founding of the city', Rome. Also *Ab urbe condita* the starting-point of the Roman system of dating and equivalent to 753 BC.

Annuit coeptis A motto of the United States; it appears on the dollar bill. Its translation is complicated. It is said to derive from a passage in Virgil's *Georgics*: *Da facilem cursum, atque audacibus annue coeptis,* 'Give [me] an easy course, and favour [my] daring undertakings': bk 1, line 40. The word *annue* is the imperative of the verb *annuo, annuere,* also spelt *adnuo, adnuĕre,* a word that first meant 'to nod the head', from which point it considerably increased its range of meanings, always implying approval. The Founding Fathers altered the imperative to the third person singular of the present indicative or the perfect indicative tenses, active voice (they are identical in form), so as to permit a translation as follows: 'He [or it] favours [or favoured] undertakings.' The word *coeptis* means, in essence, 'those things we have started'. The implied subject of the phrase is variously identified as *God* or *Providence*. The latter conforms quite closely to the deist *zeitgeist* of the later eighteenth century in what became the United States of America. There are strong suggestions of a Masonic influence in the choice of motto, which, in the light of the overt Masonic symbolism on the dollar bill and the Great Seal of the United States (the eye and the incomplete pyramid), seems an inescapable conclusion.

Annus bisextus 'A leap year'.

Annus horribilis 'A horrible year'. A judgement made by Queen Elizabeth II in 1992, alluding to a well known expression (see next). In that year a fire at Windsor Castle devastated St George's Hall and other parts of the castle. In the same year the marriages of her sons Prince Charles and Prince Andrew dissolved.

Annus mirabilis 'Year of wonders'.

Ante 'Before'.

Ante meridiem (a.m.) 'Before midday'.

Ante mortem 'Before death', the converse of *post mortem.*

Ante prandium (A.p.) 'Before a meal', a medical injunction occasionally found in prescriptions.

Ante bellum 'Before the war'. Much used adjectivally to denote the state of affairs in the Southern States of the US before the War between the States, 1861-5.

Aposiopesis Greek *αποσιωπησις*, 'keeping silent'. A rhetorical figure of speech or trope in which the speaker affects to be unable to complete what he is saying. In Greek, the word is accented on the fourth syllable, which ought, from precedent, mean that we, too, in English, should place the tonic accent on that same syllable, but the dictionaries place it on the fifth. A useful mnemonic might be:

> Aposiopesis? Thus Aposiopesis: 'You can ruddy well go to … '–the speaker ceases.

Apparatus criticus The range of materials needed for a critical examination of a text. Frequently a short, convenient way of saying 'Footnotes, index, appendices, and so on' – all the *petits soins* that the hard-pressed reader expects of a considerate author.

Aqua fortis 'Nitric acid'.

Aqua pura 'Pure water'.

Aqua regia 'Royal water', a mixture of nitric and hydrochloric acids, so called because it can dissolve the 'noble' metals, gold and platinum.

Aqua vitae 'Water of life'; brandy.

Aquila non captat muscas 'The eagle doesn't capture flies'; don't concern yourself with small things. Erasmus, *Adages*, bk 3, century 2, no 96.

Arbiter elegantiae 'The judge in matters of taste', an accolade bestowed by posterity on Petronius Arbiter (died AD 65). Tacitus has *elegantiae arbiter*: *Annals* 16:18.

Arbitrium 'Absolute authority' *Cf.* Horace's use of the word *s.v. Multa renescentur, below.*

Arboretum 'A plantation devoted to the cultivation of rare trees'.

Arcana imperii 'Secrets of the empire'; state secrets.

> 'The *disease* hath established a *Kingdome*, an *Empire* in mee, and will have certaine *Arcana Imperii, secrets of State*, by which it will proceed, and not be bound to *declare* them. But yet against those secret conspiracies in the State, the *Magistrate* hath the *rack*; and against the insensible diseases, *Phisicians* have their *examiners;* and those these employ now.'

It is difficult to discern Donne's drift here. Perhaps we ought not to intrude into people's devotions: no doubt they ought to remain private. William Blake's frothy imaginings are perhaps excused by the fumes from his etching procedures, but what excuse has Donne?

Arcades ambo 'Both Arcadians'. Said of two people having tastes in common. Cf, Virgil, *Eclogues* 7:4.

Arduum sane munus 'A truly arduous task', the title of an Encyclical Letter dated 19 March 1904 by which Pope Pius X announced his intention of appointing a

Commission to codify the Canon Law of the Church.

Arguendo Literally, 'arguing'. Thus, for the sake of argument; hypothetically. In Law Reports, used to include in the printed Report some comment or point made by Counsel in argument, and sometimes to mark an interjection by the Court during argument. In both cases, the comment is not included in the Court's judgement but is considered worthy of mention.

Argumentum ad hominem One of a collection of species of argument. In the prefatory note to this Lexicon there appears this summary:

> H. W. Fowler defined it as an argument 'calculated to appeal to the individual addressed more than to impartial reason'.

It is undoubtedly useful to be able to express that notion in three words, but the utility of the expression is greatly magnified by the fact that it is one of a powerful battery of similar phrases – *argumentum ad absurdum* (an argument that depends on exposing the opponent's argument as absurd); *ad crumenum* (an appeal to 'the purse'); *ad baculum* (an argument implying resort to force, 'the stick'); *ad ignorantiam* (an argument depending on the audience's being ignorant of some essential element); *ad populum* (an argument appealing to popular passion; and *ad verecundiam* ('modesty', an argument depending on the audience's reticence, or, in Fowler's words, an argument 'to meet which requires the opponent to offend against decorum').

Armis Exposcere Pacem 'They demanded peace by force of arms.' An inscription used on some military medals, execrable to the pacifist lobby. The sentiment is a corollary of the adage *Si vis pacem, parat bellum,* the wisdom of which has still to sink into countless thousands of minds enslaved by the fallacy that no defence is better than self-defence.

Ars est celare artem 'Art is to conceal art.' Proverbial.

Ars gratia artis 'Art for art's sake.' The motto of Metro Goldwyn Mayer.

Ars longa, vita brevis 'Art is long, life short', an aphorism attributed to Hippocrates of Chios (470-410 BC): *ο βιος βραχυς, η δε τεγνε μακρη*. The art he referred to was the practice of medicine. The sentiment has been widely disseminated. *Vita brevis est, longa ars*: Seneca, *De Brevitate Vitae* 1.

Artium baccalaureus 'Bachelor of Arts'; BA.

Artium magister 'Master of Arts'; MA.

Asinus asinum fricat 'The ass rubs the ass'; one ass rubs another. A complex adage. It can mean that one person praises another in the expectation that that other person will in turn praise him. It can also mean something like 'One hand washes another': that there's always reciprocity – 'There's no such thing as a free lunch'. The adage is not much used by English-speaking people, perhaps because of the existence of our native 'You scratch my back: I'll scratch yours'.

Assiduus usus uni rei deditus et ingenium et artem saepe vincit or **quod adsiduus usus uni rei deditus et ingenium et artem saepe vincit** 'Constant practice devoted to one subject often outdoes both intelligence and skill' (Cicero, *Pro L. Cornelio Balbo Oratio*, 20: 45). A maxim – or, rather, an astute comment on life – that neatly demonstrates that Cicero's reputation does not necessarily depend on his stylistic prowess.

Atque inter silvas Academi quaerere verum 'And seek the truth midst the groves of Academe.' Horace, *Epistles*, 2:2:45.

Atrium 'The central hall or court of a Roman house.' The modern architectural use implies a central open space extending from the ground up to a glazed ceiling, with floors round that area, which often has escalators and lifts (elevators) as a prominent feature.

Aude sapere 'Dare to know', from *Dimidium facti qui coepit habet: sapere aude*, 'A job half done is half the battle: dare to know!'

Audaces fortuna iuvat From *Audentis Fortuna iuvat*, 'Fortune helps the brave', Virgil, *Aeneid*, 10: 284. *Cf. Fortis fortuna adjuvant, below.*

Audi partem alteram 'Hear the other side.' St Augustine, *De Duabus Animabus contra Manicheos*,14:2.

Audio, video, disco 'I hear, I see, I learn.' This motto seems to have been brought into being by some nameless wit in the audio-visual business, no doubt specializing in the educational aspects of that industry.

Aurea mediocritas 'The golden mean'; the avoidance of excess in either direction. Horace, *Odes* 2:10: 5. In our day, a hazardous choice of quotation by which to praise something: 'mediocrity' has acquired so pejorative a meaning that the old meaning that Horace had in mind has long since disappeared.

Aurora australis 'The Southern Lights'.

Aurora borealis 'The Northern Lights'.

Aut Caesar aut nihil 'Caesar or nothing': to aspire to be all or nothing. A motto engraved on the sword of Caesar Borgia (1476-1507). The quotation is reminiscent of *Aut frugi hominem esse oportere dictitans, aut Caesarem,* '[Caligula] was always saying that a man had to be either frugal or Caesar': Suetonius, *Caligula*, 37.

Aut disce aut discede 'Either learn or leave.' There are several variants on this theme. Speaking of the first St Paul's School, founded by John Colet, Dean of St Paul's in 1512, 'Don Manoel Gonzales' (a pseudonym) tells us, 'Upon every window of the school was written, by the founder's direction: AUT DOCE, AUT DISCE, AUT DISCEDE–*i.e.*, Either teach, learn, or begone': *London in 1731*, (1745-6).

Aut insanit homo, aut versus facit 'The fellow is either mad or he is composing verses.' Horace, *Satires*, 2.7.117.

Aut tu es Morus When Erasmus met Thomas More first, in 1499, it was said to have been by accident. Hearing More speaking across the table at a Lord Mayor's Banquet, Erasmus exclaimed, *Aut tu es Morus, aut nullus!* 'Either you are More [or 'a fool'] or no-one!' More smartly responded by replying, *Aut tu es Erasmus, aut diabolus' 'Either you are Erasmus or the devil!* (Erasmus was of course to be the author of *Encomium Moriae*, 'Praise of Foolishness', 1509. This story, certainly apocryphal, we owe to More's great-grandson, Cresacre More, 1572-1649.)

Aut viam inveniam aut faciam 'I will either find a way or make one.' A proverbial motto or 'mission-statement'.

Aut vincere aut emori 'Either conquer or die.' Cicero, *De Officiis,* 3:32.

Auxilio ab alto 'By help from on high'. Proverbial. Sometimes simply *Auxilium ab alto*, 'Help from on high.'

Avarus animus nullo satiatur lucro 'A greedy mind is satisfied with no [amount of] gain':

> Nil nimis. Avarus animus nullo satiatur lucro. Ab alio expectes alteri quod feceris. Seneca, *Epistularum Moralium ad Lucilium*, liber XCIV, 42.

Seneca (c. 4BC-AD65) appears to be quoting from Publilius Syrus (a writer of mimes in the first century BC).

Ave atque vale 'Hail and farewell.' A formal way of addressing the dead, used by Catullus (84-54 BC) in *Atque in perpetuum, frater, ave atque vale*: 'And in perpetuity, brother, hail and farewell!', *Carmina*, 101:10.

Ave Caesar [Imperator]! Morituri te salutamus 'Hail Caesar! We who are about to die salute you.' Said by gladiators before the contests. Suetonius, *Lives of the Roman Emperors: Claudius,* ch 21.

Ave Maria 'Hail Mary.' The commencing salutation of the prayer of the church commonly known by this name. The first part of this three-part prayer, 'Hail [Mary] full of grace, the Lord is with thee, blessed art thou among women', embodies the words used by the Angel Gabriel in saluting the Blessed Virgin (*Lk*, 1: 28). The second part, 'and blessed is the fruit of thy womb [Jesus]', derives from the divinely inspired greeting of St Elizabeth (*Lk* 1:42). The words 'benedicta tu in mulieribus' (1: 28) or 'inter mulieres' (1: 42) link both salutations. The petition 'Holy Mary, Mother of God, pray for us sinners now and at the hour of our death. Amen' was added by the Church.

Ave verum corpus *Ave verum corpus / natum ex Maria Virgine* 'Hail true body, born of the Virgin Mary!' A fourteenth-century Eucharistic hymn, widely known today from Mozart's choral setting of the words.

Balbus balbum rectius intellegit 'One stammerer more correctly understands another.' Erasmus, *Adages*, 1:9:77. St Jerome had said, *Balbum melius balbi verba cognoscere*: *Epistulae* 50:4:7. A slight variation is *Barbarus barbaram orationem rectius intellegit.*

Ballista 'A siege weapon resembling a catapult in action.'

Banni nuptiarum The banns of marriage.

Barba non facit philosophum 'A beard does not make a philosopher.' This adage is typical of an entire species of adage. *Cucullus non facit monachum* 'A cowl does not make a monk.' Shakespeare, *Measure for Measure*, 5:1: 271. Others are *Non tonsura facit monachum* and *Vestimenta pium non faciunt monachum.*

Barbarus hic ego sum, quia non intellegor ulli 'I am a barbarian here [at Tomi], for I am not understood by anyone.' Ovid, *Tristia*, 5:10:37.

Beata aeternitas vel aeterna beatitude 'Blessed eternity or eternal blessedness.' St Augustine, *De Civitate Dei*, 9:13.

Beata morte nihil beatius 'Nothing is happier than a happy death'. Proverbial.

Beata simplicitas 'Blessed simplicity'. Thomas à Kempis, *De Imitatione Christi* 3:18:5. *Cf. O sancta simplicitas!, below.*

Beati misericordes, quoniam ipsi misericordiam consequentur 'Blessed are the merciful: for they shall obtain mercy.' *Mt* 5:7.

Beati mites quoniam ipsi possidebunt terram 'Blessed are the meek: for they shall possess the land.' *Mt* 5:4.

Beati monoculi in terra caecorum 'Blessed are the one-eyed in the land of the blind'. A mock Beatitude (see immediately above) that appears in many forms; *e.g.*, *Beatus monoculus in terra caecorum. Caecorum in patria luscus rex imperat omnis. In caecorum regno regnant strabones. In regione caecorum rex est luscus* (Erasmus, *Adages,* 3:4:96). *In terra caecorum monoculus rex. Inter caecos luscus rex. Inter caecos regnat luscus. Inter caecos regnat strabo. Inter caecos strabo rex est. Inter pygmaeos regnat nanus. Monoculus inter caecos rex.* This glossary might help. *Luscus,* 'one-eyed man'; *rex,* 'king'; *strabo,* 'squinter'; *pygmaeus,* 'pygmy'; *nanus,* 'dwarf'.

Beati mortui qui in Domino moriuntur 'Blessed are the dead who die in the Lord.' *Apocalypse (Revelation)* 14:13.

Beati mundo corde, quoniam ipsi Deum videbunt 'Blessed are the pure in heart, for they shall see God.' *Mt* 5:8.

Beati oculi qui vident quae vos videtis. 'Blessed are the eyes which see the things that ye see.' *Lk* 10:23.

Beati pacifici 'Blessed are the peacemakers.' *Mt* 5:9.

Beati pauperes spiritu, quoniam ipsorum est regnum caelorum 'Blessed are the poor in spirit: for theirs is the kingdom of heaven.' *Mt* 5:3.

Beati pauperes, quia vestrum est regnum Dei Blessed are ye poor, for yours is the kingdom of God.' *Lk* 6:20.

Beati possidentes 'Happy are those in possession.' Law.

Beati prorsus omnes esse volumus 'We all of us wish to be happy [or blest].' St Augustine, *Confessiones*, 10:21.

Beati qui custodiunt iudicium et faciunt iustitiam in omni tempore 'Blessed are they that keep judgement, and do justice at all times.' *Vulg Ps* 105:3. ('Blessed are they that keep judgement, and he that doeth righteousness at all times.' *AV Ps* 106:3 .)

Beati qui esuriunt et sitiunt iustitiam, quoniam ipsi saturabuntur 'Blessed are they which do hunger and thirst after righteousness: for they shall be filled'. *Mt* 5:6.

Beati qui lugent, quoniam ipsi consolabuntur 'Blessed are they that mourn, for they shall be comforted.' *Mt* 5:5 (*AV Mt* 5:4.)

Beati qui non viderunt, et crediderunt 'Blessed are they that have not seen, and [yet] have believed.' *Jn* 20:29.

Beati simplices, quoniam multam pacem habebunt 'Blessed are the simple, for they shall have much peace.' Thomas à Kempis, *De Imitatione Christi*, 1:11:3.

Beatitudo in excelso est; sed volenti penetrabilis 'Happiness is almost inaccessible, but it may be gained by those who are willing [to search].' Seneca, *Epistulae Morales,* 65.

Beatitudo non est virtutis praemium, sed ipsa virtus. 'Happiness is not the reward of virtue: virtue is its own reward.' Benedict Spinoza, *Ethics,* 5 (1677).

Beatius est magis dare quam accipere 'It is more blessed to give than to receive.' *Acts* 20:35.

Beatos esse omnes homines velle 'All men wish to be happy.' St Augustine, *De Civitate Dei*, 10:1:1.

Beatos puto, quibus deorum munere datum est aut facere scribenda, aut scribere legenda, beatissimos vero quibus utrumque 'Happy, I think, are those to whom, as a boon of the Gods, it is given to do something worth writing about or to write something worth reading: most happy, of course, are those to whom it is given to do both.' Pliny the Younger, *Epistulae* 6:16:3.

Beatus enim esse sine virtute nemo potest 'Without virtue, no-one can be happy.' Cicero, *De Natura Deorum*, 1:18. *Beatum autem sine virtute neminem esse: ibid,* 1:32.

Beatus est praesentibus, qualiacumque sunt, contentus 'Happy is he who, whatever his circumstances, is content.' Seneca, *De Vita Beata*, 6.

Beatus homo cui donatum est habere timorem Dei 'Blessed is the man to whom it is given to have the fear of the Lord.' *Eccles (Sirach)* 25:15.

Beatus homo qui corripitur a Domino 'Blessed is the man who is corrected by the LORD.' *Job* 5.17.

Beatus homo qui invenit sapientiam 'Blessed is the man who finds wisdom.' *Proverbs* 3.13.

Beatus ille qui procul negotiis, ut prisca gens mortalium, paterna rura bobus exercit suis 'Happy is he, far from his preoccupations, as were the primitive race of mortals, who tills in his fathers' fields with his own oxen.' Horace, *Epodes*, 2:1.

Beatus qui habitat cum muliere sensata. 'Blessed is he that liveth with a sensible woman.' *Eccles* 25:11.

Beatus qui intellegit super egenum et pauperem: in dei mala liberabit eum Dominus 'Blessed is he who looks after the needy and poor: the LORD will deliver him in the day of trouble.' *Ps* 40:1 in St Jerome, *Psalmi juxta LXX.* The slightly different version, *Beatus qui cogitat de paupere in die mala salvabit eum Dominus*, derives from St Jerome's alternative translation to the one he made from the (Greek) Septuagint, or rather, in many instances, adapted from existing versions depending on the Septuagint. This alternative version of St Jerome's, his *Liber Psalmorum iuxta Hebraicum Translatus,* was based on Hebrew texts surviving in his time, including Origen's *Hexapla*, most of which texts, including, lamentably, the Hexapla itself, no longer survive. (The verse is numbered 41.1 in the Authorized Version.)

Beatus vir qui non abiit in consilio impiorum et in via peccatorum non stetit: in cathedra derisorum non sedit 'Blessed is the man that hath not walked in the counsel of the ungodly, nor stood in the way of sinners, nor sat in the seat of the scornful': *Ps* 1 *Iuxta Hebraicum*. Ps 1:1 in *Iuxta LXX* concludes 'et in cathedra pestilentiae non sedit'.

Beatus vir qui timet Dominum: **in mandatis eius volet nimis** 'Blessed is the man who feareth the LORD: he shall delight exceedingly in his commandments': *Ps* 111:1 *iuxta LXX*. In *Ps iuxta Hebraicum*: *Aleph beatus vir qui timet Dominum: Beth in mandatis eius volet nimis*. In the *AV*: 'Praise ye the LORD. Blessed is the man that feareth the LORD, that delighteth greatly in his commandments': *Ps* 112:1.

Bella gerunt urbes septem de patria Homeri; nulla domus vivo, patria nulla fuit 'Seven cities waged war over Homer's fatherland; alive, he found neither home nor fatherland.' George Buchanan (1506-82), of whom Joseph Justus Scaliger (1540-1609) said, *Imperii fuerat Romani Scotia limes: Romani eloquii Scotia limes erit?* 'Scotland had been the ultimate extent of the Roman Empire: will he [Buchanan] be the ultimate extent of Roman eloquence?'

Bene decessit 'He has left well.' A testimonial said of someone leaving employment, indicating that he has not left under a cloud.

Bene esse 'Well-being'. Contrasted with *esse*, 'Mere existence'. *Cf. De bene esse, below.*

Benedicite, The *Benedicite omnia opera Domini Domino laudate et superexaltate eum in saecula* 'Bless the Lord, all ye works of the Lord: praise and exalt him above all for ever.' Daniel 3:57-90 in the Vulgate. The name given to the canticle sung by the Three Children, Shadrach, Meshach and Abednego, as they stood in 'the fiery furnace' in the presence of Nebuchadnezzar.

Benigne faciendae sunt interpretationes instrumenti, ut res magis valeat quam pereat 'Documents ought to be interpreted liberally, so that the thing should survive rather than perish.' Henry de Bracton (d 1268), cited by Staunford J. In *Throckmerton* v *Tracy* (1555) 1 *Plowd.* 145 at 160. See *Ut res magis, below.*

Bona fide 'In good faith'. Frequently used adjectivally: 'a bona-fide gift'. *Uberrime fidei*; 'In the greatest good faith'.

Bona fides 'Good faith'.

Bona vacantia 'Unclaimed goods', goods the legal ownership of which cannot be ascertained.

Boustrophedon Greek *βουστοΦεδον*, 'as the ox ploughs', denoting writing in which the first line is written and read in one direction and the next in the other direction, and so on. Several early scripts went through this stage of development.

Breviora 'Shorter'. A generic name for the shorter works of authors.

Brutum fulmen 'A weak or spent or pointless thunderbolt', said of, for example, an edict, enactment of Papal Bull that appears to have great force but that in fact is pointless or ineffectual for one reason or another. *Cf.* Pliny, *Natural History*, 2:43.

Cacoethes scribendi inania See *Tenet insanabile multos, below.*

Cadit quaestio Literally, 'the question falls': there is nothing left to discuss.

Caesura 'The division of a metrical foot between two words, especially in certain recognized places near the middle of the line': *OED.*

Caetera desunt 'The rest is missing', a phrase used to denote that what should be the remaining part of a manuscript or other work is not extant.

Caeteris paribus 'Other things being equal'.

Calculus 'A pebble, a stone'. In addition to its primary sense, the word is used for the medical condition known in English as 'the stone' and for the system or method of calculation generally depending on differentiation. The latter application stems from the primitive use of counting-stones for calculation.

Camera lucida 'Light room'. An optical device for projecting an image illuminated by daylight or artificial light through a prism onto another surface, so that an artist can copy it at whatever reasonable size of enlargement or reduction might be required. Owing to the clever conception of the device, the artist can see his own hand, pencil, brush, etc as well as the projected image, and can size the image as he needs to. Invented by Robert Hooke (1635-1703). *Cf. Camera obscura*, next.

Camera obscura 'Dark room'. An optical device or apparatus invented by Baptista Porta (1542-97) comprising of a darkened chamber or box, into which light is admitted, formerly through a pin-hole but more recently through a lens, the light thus admitted forming an image of external objects on a surface of paper. An artist is thus able to complete his work without the need for a preliminary sketch. *Cf. Camera lucida* above.

Cantabit vacuus coram latrone viator 'The traveller with empty pockets will sing in the thief's face.' Juvenal, *Satires*, 10:22.

Cantoris 'Of the precentor.' Said of the north side of the chancel of a cathedral or collegiate church, the left-hand side looking towards the communion table, that being the side of the chancel on which the precentor's reading-desk is placed. *Cf. Decani, below.*

Capax imperii nisi imperasset See *Omnium consensu, below.*

Caret 'It is lacking'. The name of the inverted letter *v* indicating in proof-reading that some matter needs to be inserted. The new matter is written in above the line or in the margin.

Carpe diem, quam minimum credula postero 'Seize today, and put as little trust as you can in the morrow.' Horace, *Odes*, 1:11:8. See, also, *Dum vivimus, vivamus, above.* In English, the sentiment has been poetically expressed in this form:

> Gather ye rosebuds while ye may,
> Old Time is still a-flying:
> And this same flower that smiles to-day
> To-morrow will be dying.

Casus omissus 'Omitted case'. A legal expression denoting a circumstance that has not been envisaged and, thus, has not been provided for.

Catena 'A chain'. Often used to denote a series of works arranged in chronological order with the object of demonstrating, for example, the development of a theological or legal doctrine.

Catharsis 'Purging'. A borrowing from Greek. Aristotle advocated a purifying or *καθαρσις* of the emotions and sentiments by means of, for example, tragic drama. During the 19th century, the desire to purify their language of foreign words reminiscent of Ottoman occupation led the newly liberated Greeks to develop a somewhat artificial language purged not only of Turkish and other alien words, but reintroducing many words that had dropped out of use since the fall of Constantinople, and, indeed, some that had not been used since Democritus. They called this archaizing language *καθαρευουσα*. The Greek generally *spoken* by the Greek people has the name *δεμοτικε*. Until recent years the purified language was the official language of Greece. However, there has been a general abandonment of it in favour of the popular speech, which is nowadays formally the official language of the Greek Republic.

Causa causans 'The causing cause'. In formal logic there are two *causae*: the *causa causans*, the cause that is immediately responsible for the existence of something; and the *causa causata*, 'the caused cause', something in the chain of causation produced by the *causa causans* that is necessary for the ultimate effect to be produced. To over-simplify somewhat, and applying the terms to the Law, it might be said that, in a characteristic railway accident, a defective set of points was the immediate cause of an accident. On analysis, it might be thought better to say that the defective points were not the *causa causans* of the accident, but were the *causa causata*, in that the points were defective because, by negligence, they had been improperly maintained. The *causa causans*, negligence of a party, had *caused* the points to fail, hence the past participle used adjectivally, *causata*.

Cave! 'Look out!' A schoolboy usage.

Caveat 'Let him beware.' A step in court borrowed from the Ecclesiastical Courts whereby proceedings are suspended: a party (the *caveator*) gives notice to the proper officer of his interest in the matter and moves that no further step be taken without his being heard. Also a notice ('a caution') filed at the Land Registry by a party with a legal interest in land, such notice to be exhibited to the file relative to the land in question to notify the public of such interest and to prevent dealing.

Caveat emptor 'Let the buyer beware.' A principle of the Common Law whereby the buyer is expected to satisfy himself of the quality, fitness for purpose and general suitability of goods offered for sale before he makes his purchase. The principle has been eroded by Statute Law in recent years. The increasing sophistication of life renders consumer protection ever more necessary, but there is nevertheless a part to play in modern life for the principle of *caveat emptor*.

Cedant arma togae Literally, 'Let arms give way to togas': let warfare give place to civil administration. Cicero, *De Officiis*, 1:22:82 and *In Pisonem*, 30:73.

Censor morum 'Censor of morals'.

Census 'A counting of population'.

Cento Literally, 'a patchwork'. A term used to denote a collection of pieces of literature by various authors.

Certiorari A writ formerly issuing from the Court of King's Bench requiring the recipient to cause the Court to be more fully informed of an indictment being heard by an inferior court. The method by which such a command was complied with was by removing the case from the inferior court to the High Court. The Writ of Certiorari was abolished in 1938, being replaced by the Prerogative Order of Certiorari. The Civil Procedure Rules of 1998 have replaced the Order of Certiorari by the Quashing Order.

Certum est quod certum reddi potest See *Id certum est, below.*

Certum est quod impossible est 'It is certain because it is impossible.' Adapted from Tertullian (AD160-225) In full, *Crucifixus est dei filius; non pudet, quia pudendum est. Et mortuus est dei filius; [prorsus] credibile est, quia ineptum est. Et sepultus resurrexit; certum est, quia impossibile.* 'The Son of God was crucified [born]: I am not ashamed – because it is shameful. The Son of God died: it is [immediately] credible – because it is absurd. He was buried, and rose again: it is certain – because it is impossible.' Tertullian's reasoning is hard to follow from the words quoted here. The extended context helps somewhat, but it has to be admitted that, in this case, Tertullian adopted a hazardous means of propagating his own notions – as the history of this passage demonstrates beyond doubt. It is pointless to say, as is no doubt perfectly true, that Tertullian was using ploys from Classical Rhetoric if the ultimate effect of his tactics is to leave posterity confused about his precise process of thought. What is certain is that he did not say *Credo quia impossible est,* 'I believe because it is impossible', as so many have carelessly assumed.

Chiasmus A rhetorical figure or trope in which the order of words in one of two parallel clauses is inverted in the other. So called because the 'X' configuration of the figure, if it is drawn for explanation purposes, resembles the Greek letter ς, chi. A useful mnemonic might be:

> Chiasmus means a cross of themes; A cross of themes chiasmus seems.

Chimaera A fantastic animal formed of parts of natural animals. A figment of the imagination.

Chommoda dicebat, si quando commoda vellet / Dicere, et insidias Arrius hinsidias, admirably translated in the *Oxford Dictionary of Quotations*, 4th edn (1992) thus: 'Arrius, if he wanted to say "amenities", used to say "hamenities", and for "intrigue" "hintrigue".' Catullus, *Carmina*, 84. This is one of the few clues Antiquity offers us about matters of *pronunciation*. Livy was charged by Asinius Pollio with *patavinitas* – the dialect of Padua, but no satisfactory instances were adduced. Infuriatingly, the few clues that *are* given turn out to be broken reeds: for instance, in this very entry, how should one differentiate in speech between the correct *commoda* and Arrius's incorrect *chommoda*? We have no reason at all to believe that the Romans – or any race but the English – ever changed the sound of the letter *c* by placing the letter *h* after it unless the following letter were an *e* or an *i*, which is certainly not the case with *commoda*. How, then, would Catullus have pronounced Arrius's mispronunciation? (The answer, purely speculative, is that Catullus intended to convey the information that Arrius pronounced the first sound of *commoda* as the Greek letter ϖ.)

Scansion gives us a few clues about how the Romans spoke. For example, a vowel at the end of a word was so lightly pronounced that, if the next word began with a vowel, then the first vowel was discounted for metrical purposes. The phenomenon is known as *elision,* or, if the syllable is obscured rather than suppressed, *synaloepha*. We hear both today in many Italian arias. Similarly, if the syllable *-um* preceded a vowel, it was suppressed, at least for metrical purposes, a process known as *ecthlipsis*. There has been much dispute about the extent to which these phonetic phenomena existed in day-to-day speech. Were they, like the elisions in Italian arias, largely a convention? Or did they mirror popular speech? The high probability is that they mirrored popular speech. For one thing, most Romance nouns derive from the accusative case of the original word, the declensional ending having been no match for the erosive power of common speech. With the ready acceptance of prepositions, the declensional system faded, the case-endings in general disappeared and the Romance languages ultimately developed as almost completely free from inflection.

'Livy was censured by Asinius for Patavinity in his writings, by which was meant that he had too much used the phrases or affectations of Padua, and neglected those of Rome': T. Blount, *Glossographia* s.v. *Glossographia* (1661). 'None of the critics could make out what Livy's Patavinity is': Horace Walpole, *Letters* (edn 1846), 2:54 (1747).

Ciborium A vessel for containing the consecrated hosts for distribution at Holy Communion, normally in the form of a chalice with a lid.

Circa 'About'. Used to indicate an approximate date, as in *circa* 100 BC. Normally abbreviated to 'c.'.

Civis Romanus sum 'I am a Roman citizen.' Cicero, *In Verrem,* 5:147. Lord Palmerston (1784-1864) alluded to this passage in the celebrated Don Pacifico debate (*Hansard*, 25 June 1850, col 444).

Clerici vagantes 'Wandering clerks'. More or less co-terminous with the term popularized by Helen Waddell (1889-1996), 'The Wandering Scholars'. See her *The Wandering Scholars* (1927) and the associated collection she made of their output, *Mediaeval Latin Lyrics* (1929). Alternative names for these wanderers were *gyrovagi* and, simply, *vagrantes.* The term *goliards* has been applied in a way that includes Waddell's subjects, though, strictly, it applies to all itinerant performers, though many of them were somewhat less scholarly than Waddell's. At the height of the Middle Ages, the goliards propagated the notion that they were inspired by one Golias, to whom some accorded the title 'bishop'. This imaginary figure was also called 'the Archipoeta.' Giraldus Cambrensis (c.1146-c.1223) certainly believed Golias had existed. The truth is more mundane. The word *goliard* derived from the Old French *gole*, in Modern French *gueule*, 'the mouth, the muzzle'.

Codex A word that has progressed in meaning. It derives from *caudex*, 'the trunk of a tree', through *codex*, 'a wooden tablet with wax applied (for scratch-writing)', to a book-form manuscript as distinct from a scroll-form manuscript.

Cognomen Originally, a nickname, in part a forerunner of our surname. The cognomen developed into the third component, the family name, of Roman citizens. The Romans had, first, a *praenomen*, designating the individual (similar to our Christian name); the second, or *nomen*, the name of the *gens* or tribe into which the individual was born; and the third, or *cognomen*, the family name. For example, Cicero's full name was Marcus Tullius Cicero. *Marcus* was his *praenomen*; *Tullius* indicated the name of his gens; and *Cicero* was his *cognomen*. The name *Cicero* derives from *cicer*, 'a chick pea'. Many *cognomina* are derived from nicknames of earlier members of the family. Allusive *cognomina* are *Strabo*, from *strabus*, 'squinter'; *Caecus*, 'blind'; and *Varro*, from *varrus*, 'knock-kneed'. Sometimes a fourth name, an *agnomen*, was added, usually as a mark of honour or distinction. For example, Scipio received the honorary *agnomen* of *Africanus* because of his military victories in Africa during the Second Punic War. Hence, his full name was Publius Cornelius Scipio Africanus. Quintius Fabius Maximus (275-203 BC) earned his *agnomen* of *Cunctator*, 'the Delayer', by reason of the success of his military delaying tactics. After the disaster of Trasimene (217 BC), he harried the Carthaginian army through Italy, monitoring their activities closely, but engaging only in sporadic guerilla warfare, thus wearing his enemy down rather than engaging him in open warfare.

The practice of nicknaming continued throughout the Middle Ages. Notker (840-912) was known as, and is still known as, *Babulus Notker*, 'Stutterer Notker'. Sometimes *cognomina* were complimentary in tone, as with Saxo Grammaticus (1150-1220), the historian of Denmark. Emperors of the Eastern Roman Empire acquired nicknames, some complimentary, other not so. Among the complimentary ones was *Porphyrogenitus* (*Πορφυπογεννητος*, 'born in the purple', stressing that the bearer of the title was of unquestionable legitimacy, born in the lying-in chamber of the Imperial Palace, which was panelled with porphyry. The actual etymology is disputed.) That cognomen is used particularly of Constantine VII (913-59).

Less complimentary names abound: perhaps the least complimentary was the *cognomen* given to another Emperor of Byzantium, *Copronymus*.

> So Constantine V was surnamed (718, 741-75). 'Kopros' is the Greek for dung, and Constantine V was called Copronymus: *Parce qu'il salit les fonts baptismaux lorsqu'on le baptisait.*

This explanation comes from the 1894 edition of *Brewer's Dictionary of Phrase and Fable*. It does not appear in more recent editions, is not ascribed to any author and is inexplicably partly in French. This coyness is as unexpected as Gibbon's own coyness. It comes as a surprise to read in his *Memoirs of My Life* 'My English text is chaste, and all licentious passages are left in the obscurity of a learned language.' (The word 'decent', which is so frequently attributed to Gibbon, was in fact inserted – 'decent obscurity' – into the authentic quotation by a lampoon in the Tory periodical, *The Anti-Jacobin*, 1797-8.)

Coitus 'Sexual intercourse'. The tonic accent falls on the first of three syllables.

Colophon from the Greek *κολοφων*, 'summit', 'finishing touch'. In the world of publishing, 'a colophon' orginally denoted a symbol, device or *rebus* identified with the printer. It was, as it were, the printer's trademark. Often the device resembled a printer's flower, and thus a loose usage of the word *colophon* crept in to mean a printer's flower at the end of the book, or at the end of a chapter or other section. Usage differs somewhat today. There are two tendencies in publishing affecting the identification of the publisher and the printer. The minimum identification required by the Common-Law jurisdictions has often been merely the publisher's name on the title-page and the printer's name at the foot of the last text page. The generic name for such a minimal identification is normally 'the imprint'. That modest gesture in the way of identifying whom to sue is virtually extinct. Modern principles and practices affecting copyright, legal responsibility, electronic identification of publications and so on have dictated a much more generous inclusion of information, which tends to be placed on the reverse side of the title page. There is a trend towards calling this deposit of information 'the colophon', which seems a good idea. The older and imprecise meaning of 'colophon' has outlived its usefulness, and the new requirement for an abundance of information about a given publication needs a name. The adoption by some forward-looking publisher of the word 'colophon' for these data seems to indicate that the word 'colophon' has acquired a new lease of life. In fact, the compilation of the matter that goes onto the verso of the title-page is probably the last stage in the production of the publication, so, in its original meaning, the word *colophon* is not inappropriate for its modern function.

Concordia discors 'Discordant harmony'. Horace, *Epistles*, 1:12:19.

Columbarium 'A dove-cote'. The word is worthy of note by reason of its transferred application: a chamber or building the walls of which are formed into niches or recesses for the deposit of cinerary urns. After centuries of disuse owing to the Christian distaste for, and active prohibition of, cremation, since cremation appeared to frustrate the Resurrection of the Dead, the word has come back into use to denote the same sort of things as in Antiquity: crematoria will often provide a columbarium for the retention of the ashes of those who have been cremated on the premises, as an analogue to a grave that people can visit, leave flowers at, and so on. Increasingly, in churches and churchyards where it is no longer permissible by law to bury people, columbaria are not infrequently provided for the lodging of urns containing the ashes of those who have some special connection with the church.

Contemporanea expositio est optima et fortissima in lege 'A contemporaneous exposition is best and most strong in Law.' 2 *Inst* 11.

Compendium 'Some work that professes to include or comprehend everything relevant to a certain matter.'

Compos mentis 'Of sound mind'. In possession of one's faculties. More common in the contrary, 'Non compos mentis'.

Confiteor 'I confess.' A prayer at the beginning of Mass, *Confiteor Deo omnipotenti...* 'I confess to Almighty God...'. Also, the prayer in isolation or the recitation of it as given as a penance during auricular confession.

Consensus 'Agreement of opinion'. Often mis-spelt 'concensus'. A mnemonic to ensure the correct spelling of the word is to remember that it relates to *consent,* not *concentrate.*

Consortium A word that has immensely increased its currency in the 20th century. Largely used by the most influential bankers, the word has (usefully) come to mean an association of business, banking, or manufacturing organizations devoted to a common business aim. An earlier legal acceptation of the word was '(The right of) association and fellowship between husband and wife'. The *OED* adds, laconically, 'The action for loss of consortium was abolished by the Administration of Justice Act, 1982 (c. 53) 2.'

Conspectus 'An over-view'. In many senses, by extension and figuratively, a bird's-eye view.

Continuum In essence, the word means some circumstance that continues to exist. The *OED* says, 'A continuous thing, quantity, or substance; a continuous series of elements passing into each other.' In specific contexts, the word has valid connotations. For example, it is used adjectivally in the expression *continuum hypothesis,* a mathematical hypothesis that there is no transfinite cardinal between the cardinal of the set of positive integers and that of the set of real numbers. More often, it seems the word is an archetypal buzz-word. For example, it is a commonplace to hear, in the context of discussions that adumbrate the Theory of Relativity, such grandiloquence as, 'We are imprisoned in the unexamined assumption or unconscious illusion of a homogeneous, forward-flowing space-time continuum'. In hands other than those of George Steiner, we might suspect that we are being treated to a display of verbal smoke and mirrors.

Contra bonos mores 'Contrary to proper codes of moral behaviour.'

Contra mundum 'Against the world'; denying everyone. The saying gained currency by reason of its application to St Athanasius (298-373), Bishop of Alexandria, *Athanasius contra Mundum.* He was five (some say seven) times driven out of his See. At all times he was an implacable opponent of heresy. He often found himself, as the *sobriquet* implies, pitted against the whole world, with the whole world in turn pitted against him.

Coram 'In the presence of'. Usages are, for example, ecclesiastical, as in *coram episcopo,* 'in the presence of a bishop', and legal, as in *coram judice,* 'before a judge; *coram nobis,* 'before us' (*i.e.*, the sovereign, meaning 'in our Court of King's Bench'); *coram non judice,* before one not the proper judge, or who cannot take legal cognizance of the matter'; and *coram paribus*, 'before one's peers.

> 'When a Cause is brought in a Court, whereof the Judges have not any Jurisdiction; there it is said to be *Coram non judice*': J. Cowell, *The Interpreter*, *s.v. Coram* ((1684).

Corrigendum 'Something to be corrected'. The plural is *corrigenda.*

Corruptio optimi pessima Corruption of the best leads to the worst. The sentiment was expressed by Shakespeare as follows:

> For sweetest things turn sourest by their deeds;
> Lilies that fester smell far worse than weeds.

The sheer magic of that second line blinds us to the possibility that, botanically speaking, it might be utter nonsense.

Cornucopia A late Latin form, written as one word, of the earlier *cornu copiæ* 'horn of plenty'; fabled to be the horn of the goat Amalthea by which the infant Zeus was suckled; the symbol of fruitfulness and plenty. In the arts, the horn of plenty is always represented as a goat's horn overflowing with flowers, fruit, and corn.

Corona 'Crown'. Used to denote a luminous halo surrounding a celestial body, especially that surrounding the sun that is visible during a total eclipse.

Corpus 'Body'. Used to denote the entirety or great bulk of an author's works. Also in the expression Corpus Christi, 'the body of Christ', as in the Oxford college and the feast-day decreed in the Church in 1311.

Corpus delicti This is a highly technical legal term. It might be well to say at the outset what it does *not* mean. It does not mean the body or corpse in a murder. It is succinctly defined by John Austin (1790-1859) thus:

> *Corpus delicti* (a phrase introduced by certain modern civilians) is a collective name for the sum or aggregate of the various ingredients which make a given fact a breach of a given law.

As Austin says, the term is a modern one devised by jurisconsults in the Civil Law. It might have been better to choose one that was less likely to mislead. A good summary of the essential implication of the term, perhaps even more succinct than Austin's, can be gleaned from:

> The *corpus delicti*, in murder, has two components, death as the result and the criminal agency of another as the means.

Readers of crime novels were well instructed by Julian Hawthorne (1846-1934):

> The term *corpus delicti* is technical, and means the body of the crime, or the substantial fact that a crime has been committed.

Corpus Juris Canonici 'Body of Canon Law'. A term used unofficially since the 12th century, and officially since the Council of Basle (1441) for the body of Canon Law that had grown up over the centuries. The *Corpus Juris Canonici* comprises Gratian's *Decretum* (1114-50); Raymund of Pennaforte's *Liber Extra* (otherwise known as the *Decretales Gregorii IX* or the *Liber Extra Decretum* (1234); the *Liber Sextus* of Boniface VIII (1298); the *Clementines* of Clement V (1313); and the *Extravagantes Joannis* XXII (1325) and the *Extravagantes Communes* (not formally published until 1499-1505). As one of the results of the Council of Trent (1545 to 1563), the Corpus was re-edited by a commission of cardinals and doctors and published in 1582 under its by-now official title, the *Corpus Juris Canonici*. Canonists refer to Canon Law prior to Gratian as *jus antiquum*, to the Codex Juris Canonici of 1582 with an addition called the *Appendix Pauli Lanceloti* as *jus novum*, and to subsequent legislation as *jus novissimus*. In 1917 Benedict XV promulgated a new Code of Canon Law.

As one of the *desiderata* emerging as a result of the Second Vatican Council, John XXIII announced, on 25 January 1959, his decision to institute a revision of the *Corpus Juris Canonici*. On 28 March 1963, he set up a commission of cardinals for that purpose. On 17 April1964, his successor, Paul VI, named the first consultants. Nineteen years later, the second *Codex Juris Canonici* was promulgated by Pope John Paul II, on 25 January 1983, and entered into effect on 27 November 1983. It remains in effect.

Corpus Juris Civilis 'Body of Civil Law'. The name now given to Justinian's works on the Roman Law. The name appears to date from only 1583, and was brought in, it seems, as the analogue of the *Corpus Juris Canonici (q.v., above)*. The *Corpus Juris Civilis* comprises five volumes: the *Digestum Vetus* (Bks 1-24.2); the *Infortiatum* Bks (24-3-38); the *Digestum Novum* (Bks 39-50), the *Codex* (Bks 1-9); and, in the fifth volume, the *Institutes*, the *Novels* (in the form of the *Authenticum)*, the remaining three books of the Code (*Tres Libri*); the *Libri Feudorum* and some imperial statutes. The last items are referred to as the *Volumen Parvum*.

Coryza 'The running at the nose which constitutes or accompanies a cold in the head; catarrh': *OED*. The Greek is *κορνζα*, 'running at the nose'...

Credat Iudaeus Apella, / Non ego 'Let Apella the Jew believe that, not I.' Horace, *Satires*, 1:5:100.

Credo 'I believe.' The first word of the Apostles' and the Nicene Creeds. Hence the creeds themselves. In modern use, any fairly formalized system of belief, as in 'Public ownership is an essential element in the credo of Socialism.'

Credo quia impossibile est 'I believe because it is impossible.' See *Certum est quia impossibile est, above*.

Crematorium 'Where one incinerates corpses'. Plural: *crematoria*.

Crisis From the Greek *κρισις*, 'a turning-point'.

Criterion From the Greek *κριτεριον*, 'a standard, norm, a principle by which one may judge', itself from *κριτης*, 'a judge'. When the Romans took into Latin Greek words ending -ιομ, they normally domesticated them by making them end in -*ium.* For example, εγκωνιον became *encomium.* The reason 'criterion' has remained in its Greek form is that it was borrowed into English directly from Greek, and, indeed, in the seventeenth century the word was normally written in Greek characters.

A very few other words were similarly directly imported, among which are *hubris*, of which the expected form would be *hybris*. Another is the completely anomalous phrase 'hoi polloi', in which the definite article is only very rarely recognized as such. Some importations are available to us in two forms: the adjective for peace-loving or peace-motivated may be spelt *eirenic* or *irenic*: there is a slight and growing preference for the former, no doubt owing to the popularity of the noun ειρηνικον, *eirenicon*, 'A proposal designed to promote peace, esp. in a church or between churches; a message of peace', though the noun, too, may be spelt *irenicon.* The second vowel is normally short, though academically minded people tend to pronounce it long, in recognition of the *eta* in the original.

There are a few technical terms that have recently been taken into English in a completely Greek form, one of which, 'kenosis', is discussed under *Depositum fidei, below*. Another two, again from theology, are the complementary words 'kerygma' and 'didache', meaning 'preaching' and 'teaching, the first from κηρυσσειν, 'to proclaim', and the second from the first word of the title of a sub-Apostolic treatise *Διδαχη των δωδεκα αποστολων*, 'Teaching of the Twelve Apostles'. A word that came and went was 'enosis', from Modern Greek usage of εωοσις, the watchword of Archbishop Makarios (1913-77), signifying union of Cyprus with Greece. Only a very few other Modern Greek words have entered English, among them *retsina, ouzo* and the trademark of a sweetened Greek brandy, *Metaxa*. Lamentably in the eyes of those who still espouse, words such as *baklava, dolma, halva* and *moussaka* persistently appear on the menus of Greek restaurants, though they are in fact words imported into Greece by the Ottoman oppressors.

Very occasionally words are introduced into English that have been directly derived from Greek. They are now thought of as English words, not Greek. An instance is *νοῦς, nous,* a contracted Attic-dialect form of the word *νόος*, 'the mind, the intellect; intelligence; intuitive apprehension', or, more generally, 'sound common sense.' In the latter sense, the English pronunciation of Greek makes the word rhyme with 'house' and 'mouse', and that has the effect of naturalizing the word beyond question. The celebrated character actor Tom Walls (1883-1949), a native of Northamptonshire, talked in an interview with the BBC, with evident relish, of. 'that grand old North-Country word "nous"'.

Instead of following the normal fiction that Greek words have come to us through Latin, even though the word is for a concept unknown to the Romans, the occasional word gets through by direct means. This occasional word retains its Greek mode of spelling. An instance of this is the word *stoicheiometry*, often spelt *stoichiometry*, which means (the study of) the quantitative relationship between the substances in a reaction or compound. The term was introduced by J. B. Richter (1762-1807) in his work *Anfangsgründe der Stöchiometrie, oder Messkunst chemischer Elemente* (1792), to denote the determination of the relative amounts in which acids and bases neutralize each other. The more regular formation would have been *stoechiometry* or *stechiometry*. Ernst Heinrich Haeckel (1834-1919), a scientist of uncritically evolutionary leanings, was a prolific inventor of scientific terms directly from the Greek. They *abounded* in his published works. Fortunately, his principles and his exuberant vocabulary did not appeal to his fellow scientists, and are of only historical interest nowadays.

Sometimes words supposedly derived from Greek manifest errors that we should be justified in calling schoolboy howlers. One of the Ages in Geology is known as the Miocene. W. Whewell (1794-1866) had proposed four terms to denote four ages in Geology, '1 *acene*, 2 *eocene*, 3 *miocene*, 4 *pliocene*'. H. W. Fowler says of the third:

> A typical example of the monstrosities with which scientific men in want of a label for something, and indifferent to all beyond their own province, defile the language. The elements of the word are Greek, but not the way they are put together, nor the meaning demanded of the compound.

The word *miocene* is tantamount to saying 'more newer'. The Second Edition of the *OED* (1989) warned readers that the word *miocene* was irregularly formed. The draft revision of March 2002 has suppressed all mention of irregularity. To introduce in the 21st century cautions about irregular etymologies might be seen as pedantic, but to *suppress* existing cautions there already set up in type seems to savour of dumbing-down.

The anomaly of anomalies is *eureka*, 'The exclamation ("I have found it") uttered by Archimedes when he discovered the means of determining (by specific gravity) the proportion of base metal in Hiero's golden crown. (See Vitruvius *Arch.* IX. iii, Plutarch *Mor.* (Didot) 1338.) Hence *allusively*, an exulting exclamation at having made a discovery': *OED*. The exclamation Archimedes let out was 'ευπηκα', the first person singular, perfect tense, of the verb ευρισκειν. It has an absolutely unmistakable rough breathing at its commencement. How a race accustomed from the cradle to aspirating with vigour could have dropped the initial aspirate of this word is 'a riddle wrapped in a mystery inside an enigma'. Certainly, one *never* sees or hears 'heureka'. How very curious!

Crux 'A cross'. In literary contexts, the word has a special technical meaning. It denotes a point or passage in a manuscript or other work that presents difficulty in interpretation, in deciphering, etc. In general use as in the phrase 'the crux of the argument', meaning the essential point in the argument. The word appears in its ordinary meaning in titles of hymns such as *Crux fidelis*, 'O faithful cross!', and in esoteric contexts such as the term *crux ansata*, 'a cross in the form of an ankh'.

Cucullus non facit monachum 'The cowl does not make the monk'. See, *above, Barba non fecit philosophum.*

Cui bono? 'To whose good?' *(i.e.,* Who benefits?) Cicero, *Pro Roscio Amerino* 84 and *Pro Milone*, 12:32, quoting L. Cassius Longinus Ravilla, 'L. Cassius quarere solebat, "Cui bono fuisset?"'.

Cujus regio, ejus religio 'In (a prince's) country, that (prince's) religion'. This watchword enshrined an interim solution to the confessional turmoil during the Reformation in Germany. By it, the religion of the ruler automatically became the religion of his subjects. The principle was adopted by the Diet of Augsburg in 1555. It is hard to see, *ex post facto*, how, except on shamefully Erastian grounds, such a compromise could have been perpetuated. Even in parts where princes were absent, as in the Swiss cantons, the principle gave rulers – often municipal authorities – the right to determine the religion of their subjects, so that, in, for example, Geneva, John Calvin (1509-64), a layman, became able to command the allegiance of all the inhabitants of the canton and republic to such an extent that he ultimately appropriated all church lands and all the eleemosynary charities such as the bequests for the saying of masses for the repose of souls and placed them at the service of the new *régime*. Gibbon testifies to the affluence of the canton of Berne until the turbulent events of 1798[6] Max Weber (1864-1920), *The Protestant Ethic and the Spirit of Capitalism* (1920) and R. H. Tawney (1880-1962), *Religion and the Rise of Capitalism; a Historical Study* (1926) supply much information about the connection between Calvinism and the management of money.

Cum ita dicunt accedere ad rem publicam plerumque homines nulla re bona dignos, cum quibus comparari sordidum 'Thus, they tell us that those who get mixed up in public affairs are in the main incapable of doing good, whom it is squalid to be coupled with' Cicero, *De Republica*, 1:5. Note that Cicero *reprobates* those who speak in this way.

Cum grano salis 'With a grain of salt'. With a pinch of salt – expressing doubt. Pliny had *addito salis grano*, 'a grain of salt added': *Natural History*, 23:8.

Cum laude 'With praise'. An additional mark of merit in the award of degrees gained by examination: *magna cum laude, maxima cum laude* and *summa cum laude*. Primarily awarded by American universities.

Cum privilegio 'With the privilege'. In full, *Cum privilegio ad imprimandum solum,* 'With sole printing rights'. The phrase frequently appears on title-pages of books published during the period when governments restricted the right to print.

Curiosa felicitas 'Careful felicity (of style)'. Petronius's compliment to Horace: *Horatii curiosa felicitas*, *Satyricon* 118:5.

Currente calamo 'With running pen'. Written at speed.

Curriculum A regular course of study, as at a school or university. Plural: *curricula*.

Curriculum vitae 'The course of one's life'. An account of one's academic attainments and subsequent career, most often a requirement in applying for employment. Often, *résumé* in the US, normally without accents or italics.

Cursus honorum 'The course of honours'. The course or sequence of honours (*quaestor, aedile, praetor*) passed through by a Roman official before he was eligible for the consulate. By extension, any similar progression.

Cursus litterarum 'Course of letters'. The primary meaning of the term is the progression of transcription that texts have undergone, a knowledge of which will frequently permit experts to anticipate scribal errors in newly discovered documents and correct them. A notorious source of corruption in, for example, mediaeval muniments occurred because of a confusion between the letters *m, n* and *u*. Texts copied from, say, manuscripts in Carolingian characters into a later form of lettering known informally as 'Gothic' often present considerable difficulty arising from those troublesome letters. The letters *u, m* and *n* are quite frequently indistinguishable, and have been responsible for many transcription errors. The phenomenon was not unknown in earlier times than the 'black letter' period:

it is at the root of the variant readings of a verse in the Te Deum that we sing as:

> We therefore pray thee, help thy servants: whom thou hast redeemed with thy precious blood.
> Make them to be numbered with thy Saints: in glory everlasting.

In the orginal Latin, it reads:

> *Te ergo quaesumus, tuis famulis subveni, quos pretioso sanguine redemisti.*
> *Aeterna fac cum Sanctis tuis in gloria*

Da mihi castitatem et continentiam, sed noli modo 'Give me chastity and continency – but not yet!' St Augustine, *Confessions*, 8:7.

Damnosa haereditas 'A ruinous inheritance'. In Roman Law an inheritance that brought loss rather than profit. Thus, a term applied to anything acquired by or devolving onto a person that is disadvantageous to that person. *Cf.* Gaius, *Institutes*, 2:163.

Damnum sine [or **absque**] **injuria** Approximately, 'Loss without damage'. In Law one might suffer loss for which relief is available but one might also suffer loss for which relief is *unavailable*. An old example runs: if my neighbour builds a mill upon his own land whereby I suffer a loss of profit from my own mill, no action will lie, for everyone may lawfully erect a mill on his own land. In modern times, it sometimes happens that a shop may open close to another and be in direct competition. No action will lie, since anyone may open a shop if there are no regulations prohibiting that. Of great contemporary relevance is the case of local shops threatened by supermarkets: that is a classic instance of *damnum sine injuria*. The concept of compensation in English law is somewhat clouded by the subtle shades of meaning attaching to the terms of art involved. 'Loss' is fairly simple, though its ambit is a little wider than might seem obvious: it includes not only loss by deprivation of something *in esse (q.v.)* but also the failure to gain something *in futuro (q.v.)*, as in the loss of a bargain. If an action is maintainable in relation to a loss, that loss is said to be *actionable*, and, if the action is successful, the claimant is eligible to be awarded damages by the Court. Damages may be defined as the pecuniary satisfaction awarded by a judge or jury in a civil action for a wrong suffered by the claimant. Note that a *loss* does not automatically entitle a claimant to damages, but, normally speaking, a *wrong* does. Relief may take forms other than pecuniary ones: an injunction restraining one's opponent from actionable conduct might well be of much greater value to a claimant than any monetary recompense. (The wording of the Latin maxim avoids the inevitable confusion that exists with the two shades of meaning implicit in the word *damage,* in the singular and in the plural.)

Dat veniam corvis, vexat censura columbas 'Censure acquits the raven, but pursues the dove.' Juvenal, *Satires*, 2:63.

Datum 'Something given'. Nowadays restricted to such things as information, in which usage the plural is far commoner than the singular. The singular is used attributively as in such expressions as 'datum-line'.

De bene esse A protean legal expression. Something may be done *de bene esse* in legal proceedings that is not demonstrably necessary but is nevertheless being done 'to be on the safe side'. Alternatively, the phrase can mean 'for what it is worth'. In other contexts, it might mean 'for the time being, in case a better occasion [*e.g.*, for taking evidence] does not arise'. This phrase is typical of a range of phrases in use in the Law that defy ready definition or explanation but that are replete with meaning to those who use them. Lay persons resent such phrases, but it should be borne in mind that phrases of this nature are not the exclusive preserve of the Bar. It is a salutary lesson to hear a darts expert discoursing on his skills.

De die in diem 'From day to day without intermission'. A court normally sits *de die in diem* since interruptions such as adjournments are viewed with disfavour.

De facto 'In fact'. Said of, for example, a government that lacks legal legitimacy but is 'in fact' in control. Jacobites eventually came to recognize the Hanoverian Dynasty as *de-facto* kings, but not *de-jure* kings until, perhaps, an event of some striking significance had taken place. The second son of James Francis Edward Stuart, the Old Pretender, Henry Benedict Maria Clement Stuart (1725-1807), was created Duke of York by his father, took Holy Orders and became a cardinal. He was known commonly as the Cardinal-Duke of York. As a consequence of the French Revolution, he lost the revenues from his benefices in France and then, as a result of the French invasion of the Papal States, he lost his estate at Frascati, of which see he was bishop. In an act of profound generosity, George III granted the cardinal a life-annuity until his estate at Frascati should be returned to him. In recognition of the benevolence of George III, the cardinal bequeathed the Stuart Crown Jewels to the then Prince of Wales, later the Prince Regent and then George IV. It was from the date of that bequest that many Jacobites have conceded the legitimacy of the Hanoverian Dynasty – now *de-jure* sovereigns rather than merely *de-facto* sovereigns.

De fide 'Concerning the faith'. Said of matters affecting the essential elements in Christian belief.

De gustibus non disputandum (est) 'There is no disputing tastes.' Proverbial.

De industria 'By industry', that is, deliberately, intentionally.

De jure See *De facto.*

De minimis non curat lex 'The law takes no account of trifles': *Cro. Eliz.* 148. In the Civil Law, *De minimis non curat praetor.*

De mortuis nil nisi bonum Of the dead, speak nothing unless it is good'. Proverbial.

De novo 'Anew'. Sometimes written *denuo.* This word is one of the little clues that enable the ordinary man in the street to see that, just as the proponents of the Classical pronunciation of Latin have persistently told us, the letters *u* and *v* were once a single letter in Latin. Moreover, that letter was a *vowel,* sounding as the letter *w* does in present-day English.

Another powerful indication that the Classical pronunciation was the pronunciation of Latin during the Golden and Silver Ages is the pronunciation of the title 'Emperor' in German, *Kaiser*. There are reasons for believing that the Germanic tribes took the word *Caesar* into their language with the pronunciation that was used by the Romans themselves. The most influential evidence, however, is the abundance of Roman names we find in Antiquity written in Greek characters. That the letter *h* was aspirated is beyond any doubt: one sees *Horatius* as *Ωραυατιος*. One sees the letter *c* as kappa consistently: the Greek *Καισαρ* corroborates the German evidence; and *Κικερον* speaks for itself as to the pronuciation of the letter *c* before the vowels *e,* and *i. Κολοσσαι* gives us the sound of the digraph *ae. Μενοιτιος* gives us the sound of the digraph *oe* and of the letter *t* before the vowel *i.* And, arguing in reverse, the transliteration into Latin of every single Greek word noun proper or common, adjective, adverb, preposition of verb that had ever occurred in Antiquity corroborates the case for the Classical pronunciation. It is a pity, as one caustic critic said, that the Classical pronunciation sounds like a German crossing-sweeper reciting an Italian sonnet.

De profundis 'From out of the depths'. The first words of Psalm 129 (Vg): *De profundis clamavi ad te Domine* 'From out of the depths I have cried to thee, O Lord.'

De propaganda fidei Short for *Congregatio de Propaganda Fidei* 'Congregation for the Propagation of the Faith', a department of the government of the Catholic Church instituted in 1622 by Pope Gregory XV and charged with the oversight of foreign missions. Re-named the 'Congregation for the Evangelization of the Peoples' by Pope John-Paul II in 1982.

Decani 'Of the dean'. Said of the south side of the chancel of a cathedral or collegiate church, the right-hand side looking towards the communion table, that being the side of the chancel on which the dean's reading-desk is placed. *Cf. Cantoris, above* [p323].

Decessit sine prole 'Died without issue'. With family trees and genealogy, often abbreviated to *d. s. p.*

Dei gratia 'By the grace of God'.

Deo gratias 'Thanks be to God'.

Deo Optimo Maximo 'For God, the Best and Greatest'. The motto of the Benedictines, adapted from the title accorded by the Romans to Jupiter, *Iuppiter Optimus Maximus.*

Deo volente 'God willing!' Often abbreviated to *D V.*

Dele Either the second person imperative of *delere*, 'to delete', or an abbreviation of the English 'delete', an instruction to the printer to delete the indicated matter. Various systems are followed for proof-correcting, but most depend on some means of marking the surplus or incorrect copy and then putting a lower-case delta in the margin, viz, δ.

Delenda est Carthago 'Carthage must be destroyed!' Cato the Elder, the Censor (234-149 BC), in Pliny the Elder, *Naturalis Historia*, 125:74. Carthage was razed to the ground and her fields sown with salt, a precaution as old as the hills: 'And Abimelech ... beat down the city [Sechem] and sowed it with salt': *Judges*, 9:45.

Delicatus debitor est odiosus in lege 'A luxurious debtor is odious in Law': 2 *Bultstr.*148.

Depositum fidei 'The deposit of the faith'. A term denoting the *corpus*, material and immaterial, of the faith or doctrine committed to the keeping of the Church. The Vulgate uses the term *depositum* in 1 *Tim* 6:20: *O Timothee depositum custodi devitans profanas vocum novitates et oppositiones falsi nominis scientiae*, a passage the *AV* (1611) renders (but directly from the Greek) as, 'O Timothy, keep that which is committed to thy trust, avoiding profane and vain babblings, and oppositions of science falsely so called.'

The very much more Latinate Rhemes version, published in 1582, had, 'O Timothee, keepe the depositum... , much to the indignation of William Fulke (1538-89), who with great passion expostulated about

> Affected novelties of terms, such as neither English nor Christian ears ever heard in the English tongue: Scandal, prepuce, neophyte, depositum, gratis, parasceve, paraclete.

Fulke was happy enough, though, to accept *doctrinal* neologisms from Geneva, such as *congregation* for 'church', *washing* (for 'baptism'), *overseer* (for 'bishop') and *elder* or *presbyter* (for 'priest'). Four of the words Fulke criticizes are now perfectly naturalized English words, in part and anomalously because Fulke chose to give the Rhemes Version great exposure by printing it, in 1589, in parallel columns with the Bishops' Bible, originally published in 1568.

One word in the Rhemes New Testament in particular excited much ridicule: *exinanite*, 'To reduce (a person) to emptiness; to empty (of dignity, power, etc.); to abase, humble; chiefly *refl.* said of Christ with reference to *Phil.* ii. 7': *OED*. The Vulgate has *Sed semet ipsum exinanivit formam servi accipiens in similitudinem hominum factus et habitu inventus ut homo*, literally 'But emptied himself taking the form of a servant being made in the likeness of men and in habit found as man'. The Authorized Version reads: 'But made himself of no reputation, and took upon him the form of a servant, and was made in the likeness of men'. The real point is this: that to translate the Greek as 'made himself of no reputation' does more violence to the literal meaning of the Greek than 'exinanite' does to the native genius of the English language. That is particularly so since theologians of all denominations are nowadays glad to use the anglicized 'kenosis' as a valued term of art.

The Revised Version (1911) of 1 *Tim* 6:20 reads 'emptied himself', wording used by Richard Challoner (1691-1781) in his eighteenth-century revisions of the Rhemes New Testament.

Desideratum 'Something desired'. Plural: *desiderata*.

Designatio unius personae est exclusio alterius et expressum facit cessare tacitum 'The naming of one is the exclusion of the other, and that which is express makes that which is implied to cease.' *Co. Litt.* 210 a.

Designatum 'The designated one'. A term from grammar denoting the noun antecedent of a pronoun.

Desunt caetera and **Desunt nonnulla** 'Some things are missing' and 'Not a few things are missing'. Annotations encountered in transcriptions of manuscripts to indicate *lacunae* (*q.v.*).

Detritus 'Fragments of rock detached by weathering.' Sometimes used for the figurative rubble and *débris* left after disputes.

Devitiis nostris scalam nobis facimus, si vitia ipsa calcamus 'Of our vices we make for ourselves a ladder, provided we tread the same underfoot.' St Augustine, *Sermon No 176* in J. P. Migne (ed), *Patrologia Latina* vol 38 (1845).

Deus absconditus 'Hidden God'. *Vere tu es Deus absconditus Deus Israhel salvator* 'Verily Thou art a hidden God, O God of Israel and Saviour.' *Is* 45:15. See *Praeteriens enim et videns simulacra vestra inveni et aram in qua scriptum erat ignoto deo quod ergo ignorantes colitis hoc ego adnuntio vobis,* 'For passing by and seeing your idols, I found an altar also, on which was written: To the Unknown God. What therefore you worship without knowing it, that I preach into you': *Acts* 17:24.

Deus ex machina 'A god from a machine'. 'A power, event, person, or thing that comes in the nick of time to solve a difficulty; providential interposition, esp. in a novel or play': *OED* From the Greek *θεος εκ μηχανης*. The reference to *machina* is to the stage machinery by which deities were presented at an elevated position on the stage during Greek theatrical productions. (In the English pronunciation, /'diːəs eks m'□ kɪnə/.)

Diaspora 'A dispersion or dispersal'. Specifically, 'The Dispersion; *i.e.* (among the Hellenistic Jews) the whole body of Jews living dispersed among the Gentiles after the Captivity (John vii. 35); (among the early Jewish Christians) the body of Jewish Christians outside of Palestine (*Jas.* i. 1, 1 *Pet.* i. 1)': *OED.* The word *diaspora* has come into modern European languages through Deut 28:25 in the Septuagint: *εση διασπορα εν πασαις βασιλειαις της γης* 'Thou shalt be a diaspora [or dispersion] in all kingdoms of the earth.' Nowadays, the word *diaspora* has come to mean the population of Jews not resident in the State of Israel, as, for example, in the phrase, 'Jews of the Diaspora' – almost always with a capital initial – but it ought to be kept in mind that the word also applied to the generations of Jews who were driven or taken from what became known later as Palestine, those who in English translations of the Bible are called 'captives' or 'exiles'. Moreover, there is an important secular sense of the word, to denote the extremely numerous body of Jews who populated the borders of the Mediterranean and beyond, and for whom the Septuagint was produced, translating Hebrew into Greek in recognition that they had forgotten Hebrew and probably Aramaic too, but were fluent in the *κοινε* Greek that was the common language of trade in the entire known world.

Dictum 'A saying'. A useful word meaning in general 'a wise saying, a saw, a proverb'. The plural is *dicta.* In the phrase *obiter dictum*, the meaning is 'a remark thrown out in the course of discussion, conversation, etc'. In legal parlance, the phrase *obiter dictum* indicates that a remark has been made by the Court but that it was not intended to be part of the formal judgement of the Court: rather, it was made as a remark in the course of the proceedings. Though *obiter dicta* are not part of the *rationes decidendi (q.v.)* of the case, they are accorded respect and quoted if they fall from the lips of eminent judges.

Dictum sapienti sat est 'A word to the wise is enough': Terence, *Phormio* 541. Normally quoted as *Verbum sapienti sat est* and abbreviated to *verb. sap.*

Dies irae 'O day of wrath!' The first words of a penitential and funerary sequence by Thomas of Celano O.F.M. (1190-*c.*1255) beginning:

> *Dies irae dies illa,*
> *Solvet saeclum in favilla:*
> *Teste David cum Sibylla*
> O day of wrath, that day!
> The world turns into ashes
> As David and the Sybil foretold!

Dies non (juridicus) A day on which no judicial business is or was done. These days did not count in cases where a time limit was in force.

Difficile est propria communia dicere 'It is difficult to utter common notions in an individual way.' Horace, *Ars Poetica*, 128.

Difficilis facilis, iucundus acerbus es idem: / Nec tecum possum vivere nec sine te 'Difficult, easy; agreeable or acerbic; thou art the same; I cannot live with thee, or without thee.' Martial, *Epigrammata*, 12:46.

Difficilis, querulus, laudator temporis acti / Se puero, castigator censorque minorum 'Difficult, querulous, a praiser of times past when he was a boy, a critic and nay-sayer of the young.' Horace, *Ars Poetica*, 173.

Difficilior lectio potior A maxim in palaeography and diplomatic whereby a less easy reading is given to a contested passage in preference to one that strikes the reader as more plausible. The reasoning behind the maxim is that scribal errors themselves tend to favour easier, more plausible readings than harder, less plausible readings. Therefore, if there are readings that comprise easier ones and harder ones, the probability is that the harder ones, being less susceptible to careless transcription are to be preferred. On the whole, the practice of preferring the more difficult readings has paid dividends.

Diffugere nives, redeunt iam gramina campis / Arboribusque comae 'The snows have fled; already the grass is returning to the fields and the leaves to the trees.' Horace, *Odes*, 4:7:1.

Dilemma Not strictly a Latin word but a Greek word, *διλημμα*. In modern usage, it implies a highly complex situation, but in practice the concept has been much simplified, to permit the word to perform a useful everyday function. A dilemma is a situation that arises in argument whereby one is faced with two (and, strictly, *only* two) choices, either of which is or seems equally unfavourable. These two alternatives are spoken of figuratively as the 'horns' of the dilemma. In the austere beauty of formal logic, a dilemma is defined as a hypothetical syllogism having a conjunctive or 'conditional' major premiss and a disjunctive minor (or, one premiss conjunctive and the other disjunctive).

Disiecta membra See *Etiam disiecti membra poetae, below.*

Doctor Originally, 'one who teaches', from *docēre*, 'to teach'. Over the centuries in England the title *doctor* has consistently implied that the bearers were Doctors of Divinity or, more rarely, Doctors of Law or Doctors of Music. Thus, when Dame Celia Fiennes, on her peregrinations round England, speaks of 'the doctors' houses' in cathedral closes, she means the houses of the chapter, of the dean and canons. A few personages have carried the title to beyond the grave. Dr Johnson, albeit a honorary doctor, is consistently referred to as *Doctor* Johnson. Those of a musico-historical bent will refer to Charles Burney (1726-1814) as Dr Burney, and, equally, especially if they have been schooled in the traditions of English cathedral and collegiate choral music, to William Croft (1678-1727) as Dr Croft.

Dogma Again, a Greek word, *δογμα*, adopted by the Romans but inflected as in Greek. It derives from the verb *δοκειν*. 'to seem, seem good, think, suppose, imagine.' It means a tenet, an article of belief as formulated by some authority, normally a religious authority. Plural: *δογματα*.

Domi procerum 'In the House of Lords [locative case]'. A legal phrase. More commonly, *in domo procerum*, abbreviated to *in dom. proc.* Hardly used these days.

Dominus illuminatio mea 'The Lord is my light.' *Ps* 26:1 *Vg*; 27:1 *AV*. The motto of Oxford University.

Donatio mortis causa 'A gift by reason of death.' A gift of personal property made by someone who apprehends that he is in peril of death.

Dono dedit 'He gave it as a gift'. An inscription often written on the beginning pages of a book, with the donor's name, as a memorial of the giving.

Dramatis personae 'Persons in the drama.' The caste of a theatrical performance.

Ductus litterarum 'Drawing of the letters'. A term used in palaeography, diplomatic and calligraphy to denote the technique and practices of the writer that go to give the written record its own recognizable characteristics. See also *Cursus litterarum, above.*

Dulce domum 'Sweet home'. The first words of a song sung at Winchester College.

Dulce et decorum est pro patria mori 'It is a fair and honourable thing to die for one's country.' Horace, *Odes*, 3:2:13.

Dum bene se gesserit 'For so long as he behaves himself.' See *Durante bene placito* and *Dum sola et casta* for similar conditional stipulations.

Dum sola et casta [vixerit] 'For so long as [she shall live] single and chaste.' This condition was included in many settlements and legacies: by it, the beneficiary was obliged to remain un-remarried and chaste. In legacies, the condition of chastity was much less often stipulated for than that of continuing widowhood. The stipulation for chastity, conversely, was very frequently inserted in deeds of separation between husband and wife. A *dum-casta* clause may still be inserted in a decree for the dissolution of marriage and also in an order for maintenance.

Dum spiro, spero 'While I breathe, I hope.' See *Animis opibusque parati, above.* Also the motto of the Clan MacLennan.

Dum vivimus, vivamus 'While we're alive, let us *live*!' See *Carpe diem, below.*

Dulce est disipere in loco 'It is pleasant to play the fool in due season.' See *Misce stultitiam, below.*

Durante bene placito 'During the good pleasure [of the Crown]'. The term of office of many Officers of State, contrasted with the more permanent status enjoyed by those, such as judges, who serve *dum bene se gesserint*, 'for so long as they behave themselves'. In the slightly different but essentially equally valuable form *quamdiu se bene gesserint*, as used in the Act of Settlement of 1701, the tenure of office of judges is guaranteed, to protect them against pressure from the Crown or Parliament.

E libris 'From the books of ...' An inscription often seen on bookplates. Sometimes *Ex libris,* though, strictly, *e* is used before a following consonant and *ex* before a following vowel.

E tenebris lux 'From darkness, light'. A Masonic motto.

Ecce homo 'Behold, the man!' Used as a name for paintings of Christ wearing the crown of thorns. The declaration comes from Jn 19:5:

> *Exiit iterum Pilatus foras et dicit eis ecce adduco vobis eum foras ut cognoscatis quia in eo nullam causam invenio.*
> *Exiit ergo Iesus portans spineam coronam et purpuream vestimentum et dicit eis ecce homo.*

> Pilate went forth again, and saith unto them, Behold, I bring him forth to you, that ye may know that I find no fault in him.
> Then came Jesus forth, wearing the crown of thorns, and the purple robe, and Pilate saith unto them, Behold the man!

Ego The personal pronoun *I*. Popularized by Sigmund Freud (1856-1939) as the name for the conscious, thinking part of the human being.

Ego et rex meus 'I and my king'. The phrase was said to have been used by Cardinal Wolsey (1475-1530) and has many times been cited as an instance of his egotism: cf. Shakespeare's *Henry VIII*, Act III, Sc ii. Though in fact in Latin that word order is normal and correct.

Edax rerum See *Tempus edax rerum, below.*

Eheu fugaces, Postume, Postume, / Labuntur anni 'Alas, O Postumus, Postumus! The fleeting years are slipping by!' Horace, *Odes*, 2:14:1

Eidolon Another Greek word, *ειδωλον*, that the Romans took and left as a Greek word, though often spelling it *idolon.* In its primary acceptation, it means a phantom, a phantasm, an unsubstantial image, a spectre. Later in Antiquity it came to mean, also, an image as in a painting and as in a statue. Owing to the influence of the Septuagint, the word came to mean an image worshipped as a god, and for many generations that was the meaning in English. At the Reformation, the iconoclasm of the Reformers impelled them to use the word 'image' in place of 'idol', and so many images that were by no stretch of fancy ever worshipped were effaced or destroyed. This mindless barbarism has been well chronicled by Eamonn Duffy in his *The Stripping of the Altars* (1992).

Francis Bacon (1561-1626) used the word 'idol' in a sense almost exclusively his own – a characteristic of much of his subtle, profound thinking. One of these terms has had a period of popularity, *idola fori*, 'the idols of the marketplace', but, alas, largely owing to a misunderstanding of the expression! Bacon postulates the existence of four species of fallacy, and he gives them what are peculiarly his own idiosyncratic names, using *idolon* as a synonym for 'fallacy': idols of 'the tribe', 'the cave', 'the marketplace' and 'the theatre'. The 'Idols of the Tribe'(*idola tribus*), are fallacies we share in common with other members of our society, race, or golf-club; 'Idols of the Cave' (*idola specus*), the fallacies that are peculiarly our own, which we mull over in the privacy of our den, our 'cave'; 'Idols of the Marketplace' (*idola fori*), which are fallacies stemming from the misuse of language we pick up in the hurly-burly of the market-place (the everyday world); and 'Idols of the Theatre'. (*idola theatri*), the fallacies that are the result of the latest fad or fancy in philosophy – whatever, at any given moment, is filling the house on Broadway or packing the Royal Court Theatre. Bacon's highly individualistic nomenclature disguises the profoundly direct approach he brings to philosophy.

Eiusdem generis or **Ejusdem generis** 'Of the same sort'. A 'shorthand' expression used chiefly in the law. See the quotations below. (*Cf Sui generis, below.*)

> 'Where in a statute, etc, particular classes are specified by name, followed by general words, the meaning of the general words is generally cut down by reference to the particular words, and the general words are taken to apply to those *ejusdem generis* with the particular classes': Mozley & Whiteley's *Law Dictionary,* 10th edn. "Other records" … had to be construed *eiusdem generis* with "ledgers, day books, cash books and

> account books" and unsorted bundles of cheques and paying-in slips were not "other records" within the meaning of the Act': *The Daily Telegraph*, p 13/6, 10th August 1987.

Elegantiae arbiter. See *Arbiter elegantiae, above.*

Elenchus One of the wealth of highly technical terms in logic that endow that discipline with its many virtues. In formal logic an elenchus is a syllogism in refutation of a proposition that has been syllogistically defended. In principle and in practice over the centuries, the word ελεγκος has implied minute 'cross-examination', a technique perfected by Socrates for establishing the truth by means of short questions and answers. In the Disputations or practical exercises in reasoning that characterized Mediaeval teaching and learning, an *ignoratio elenchi* was a logical fallacy that consisted in the apparent refutation of an opponent's contention, whereas in fact one had actually disproved some statement different from that advanced by him. By extension and less correctly, the term *ignoratio elenchi* is also used to stigmatize any argument that is really irrelevant to its professed purpose.

> 'The fallacy of *Ignoratio Elenchi*, ... also called by Archbishop Whately the Fallacy of Irrelevant Conclusion': J. S. Mill, *Logic*, 5:7:3 (1843). 'The fallacy of Irrelevancy (or, as it is sometimes called, shifting ground) is technically termed *Ignoratio Elenchi*, i.e. ignorance of the syllogism required for the refutation of an adversary ... this has now received a wider meaning. Whenever an argument is irrelevant to the object which a speaker or writer professes to have in view, it is called an ignoratio elenchi': Thos. Fowler, *The Elements of Deductive Logic*, 8:4 (1866).

Emeritus 'Merited'. A term originally applied to those who had ceased to be employed by reason of their having been discharged with honour, used especially of soldiers. Now used of retired professors.

The adjective is used before or after a singular; always after a plural (in the form *emeriti*). The feminine does not appear to be used.

Encaenia Greek *τα εγκαινια*. The annual commemoration of the founders and benefactors of Oxford University. The word was first used to denote the Feast of Renovation established by Judas Maccabaeus to commemorate the re-consecration of the Temple.

Encheiridion Greek *εγχειριδιον*, literally, 'a handbook'; a manual; 'a concise treatise serving as a guide or for reference': *OED*. The word may also be spelt *enchiridion*, though there is a tendency nowadays to transliterate closely in accordance with the original Greek spelling when there are other indications of a Greek origin, such as the termination *-ion*.

Encomium From Greek *εγκωνιον*, 'a formal or high-flown expression of praise; a eulogy, panegyric': *OED*. The *OED* says the plural *encomia* is rare and favours *encomiums*. However, it seems illogical to depart from Classical usage as regards making the plural since the word is in any event so singularly academic.

Enosis See *criterion, above.*

Entasis Greek *εντασις*. An architectural term to denote a slight swelling towards the mid-point of the height of a column and thereafter an equivalent reduction in the diameter of the column deliberately introduced by the Greeks to compensate for the undoubted optical impression created by a completely cylindrical column that it grows narrower towards its mid height and then swells again as it reaches its top.

Entia non sunt multiplicanda praeter necessitatem 'Entities ought not to be multiplied beyond necessity.' These words, known as 'Occam's Razor', enshrine the principle that, in explaining anything, no more assumptions ought to be made than are necessary. The principle is also known as the Law of Parsimony. The words in which the principle has become established are not found in William of Occam's works, though similar contentions are found in the works of other philosophers such as his master, Duns Scotus (1266-1308), and are in fact found in William of Occam's own works in the form *Pluralitas non est ponenda sine necessitate.* Sir Isaac Newton was of a similar parsimonious cast: *Hypotheses non fingo*. However, in the form quoted above, *Entia non sunt multiplicanda praeter necessitatem,* the principle has become known – and famous – as 'Occam's Razor'. William of Occam (or Ockham) (1285-1349), an English philosopher and Scholastic theologian who was the leading Nominalist philosopher 'of all time', was known as *Doctor Invincibilis*, 'Unconquerable Doctor', and *Venerabilis Inceptor.* 'Venerable Initiator'. His school of Scholastic Philosophy, the Nominalist School, was in essence a co-equal rival of the Thomist and Scotist schools.

The principle underlying Occam's Razor, as is the case with so many other aspects of Mediaeval philosophy, appeals directly to the bedrock of common sense that underlies the thinking of those of our contemporaries who choose to think.

The very word *ens,* the singular of *entia,* is emblematic of a louring problem that obscures our vision of the Middle Ages. We are taught by stiff-necked rigorists that, in the Golden and Silver Ages, 'the best periods', there was no present participle of the verb esse, 'to be'. There were, of course, words such as *absens* and *potens,* but there *never was* a present participle of *esse,* and thus, they say, there never *should be* one. There never should be a noun *ens.* It is hard to comprehend why there should be such opposition to the use of a word so necessary as *ens* – our 'entity'. One feels strongly tempted to expostulate, 'If *ens* had not existed, it would have been necessary to invent it!' It would not be so galling if the rigorist school were consistent and were to lumber themselves with all the manifest inconveniences of a return to Classical practice – to abandon the marks of punctuation, the use of capitals and italics, the very spacing of words, sentences and paragraphs, all of which were absent from the writing of Classical times, but these are sacrifices the rigorists are not prepared to make.

Episcopus vagans 'Wandering bishop'. From time to time, persons who have been consecrated bishops by episcopalian churches fall out of communion with those churches and hold themselves out as bishops 'with a roving commission'. Sometimes episcopal consecration is obtained from bishops of Eastern churches, and such consecrations have led to the formation of a small number of autonomous churches, commonly with extremely small numbers of adherents. Plural: *episcopi vagantes.*

Epithalamion 'A marriage song', an ode to the bride and groom. From the Greek επιθαλαμιον. Plural: *epithalamia.*

Epigram 'A short poem ending in a witty or ingenious turn of thought, to which the rest of the composition is intended to lead up': *OED.* Nowadays rarely in verse, and most often extremely short. H. W. Fowler says, 'Four distinct meanings, naturally enough developed. First, now obsolete, an inscription on a building, tomb, coin, etc. Secondly, (inscriptions being often in verse, and brief) a short poem, and especially one with a sting in the tail. Thirdly, any pungent saying. Fourthly, as style full of such sayings.'

> 'Even Rochester in his merciless epigram was forced to own that Charles [II] 'never said a foolish thing' [scil, 'and never did a wise one']': Green, *A Short History of the English People* , 9:3:617 (1874).

Epithet By origin, from the Greek *επιθετον*, a word the grammarians used for what we should now call an adjective. In a cautionary note, the *OED* says: 'The Greek word was used by grammarians for 'adjective', but they did not distinguish between adjectives and descriptive nouns in apposition with a name.' The definition *per se* in the *OED* reads: 'An adjective indicating some quality or attribute which the speaker or writer regards as characteristic of the person or thing described. A significant appellation': *OED*.

Into the second of those definitions, 'A significant appellation', falls a frequent application of the word *epithet*: the item in question – the item being examined – is a noun or noun clause being used as an adjective, *to describe*, as in 'A Daniel come to judgement! Yea, a Daniel!' We might go further and exclaim, 'A Solomon!'

It is in that context that complex word patterns can often be resolved by the use of the word *epithet*. In the phrase 'a Solomon-like judgement', the word *Solomon*, although primarily a proper noun, is used in an unambiguously adjectival sense, and is thus often, together with *like*, said to be used as a *transferred* or *epithet* adjective. It seems preferable to use the word *epithet* for this acceptation, rather than the less precise *transferred*. Perhaps it might be going too far to suggest that the term *epithet adjective* be restricted to nouns and noun clauses used adjectivally. There are other names already in place by which to denote other parts of speech.

The late R. W. Burchfield has an entry in his edition of *Fowler* that he entitles *Transferred Epithets*:

> A curiosity of our language is the way in which an adjective can be made to operate in such a way that it has merely an oblique relevance to the noun it immediately qualifies. Examples: 'It's not your stupid place' she says. 'It's anyone's stupid place' – P. Lively, 1987 (the person addressed, not the place, is stupid) …'

With the respect due to Dr Burchfield's eminence, it seems necessary to differ from him in this particular. He himself rightly concludes his entry by remarking, 'The traditional name for this phenomenon is 'transferred epithet' or 'hypallage'', but it needs to be said that all instances of hypallage are transferred epithets but not all instances of transferred epithets are hypallage. Hypallage is only one species of the transferred epithet. One of the quotations that support the *OED* entry for *transferred* reads:

> 'The *Transferred Epithet* is a common figure in Poetry. The shifting of an epithet from its proper subject to some allied subject … is seen in … "Hence to his *idle bed*"': A. Bain, *English Composition and Rhetoric*, p 24 (1866).

'Hence to his idle bed' is pure *hypallage*. So also, in translation, is 'The trumpet's Tuscan blare'. Shakespeare's 'His coward lips did from their colour fly' is a classic instance. Gray's 'The ploughman homeward plods his weary way' is, again, a classic. How many of us have echoed Gray's 'weary way'! (We have used *hypallage*! Many of us must feel as

Monsieur Jourdain felt when he learnt he spoke prose!)

The OED has an informative note on hypallage:

> A figure of speech in which there is an interchange of two elements of a proposition, the natural relations of these being reversed. Servius, in commenting on Virg. *Æn.* iii. 61, explains *dare classibus austros* [to give winds to the fleet] as a hypallage for *dare classes austris* [to give the fleet to the winds]. In Quintilian (VIII. vi. 23) the word (written as Greek) has the sense of METONYMY, and English authors have sometimes applied it loosely or incorrectly to other variations from natural forms of expression, esp. to the transference of attributes from their proper subjects to others (cf. quot. 1586 [below]). '*Hypallage*, when by change of property in application a thing is delivered, as to say...*the wicked wound thus given*, for having thus wickedly wounded him': Angel Day, *The English Secretorie*, edn 1625, 2:3 (1586). 'The phrase, "you also are become dead to the law" [Rm 7:4] … is a hypallage for "the law has become dead to you"': T. N. Harper, *Peace through the Truth*, 2:1:44 n (1974).

Hypallage derives from υπαλλαγη 'an exchange or interchange'. It is a quadrisyllabic word with the tonic accent on the second syllable, pronounced either /hɑɪpæləʤɪ/ or, with a hard *g*, /hɑɪpæləgɪ/. A useful mnemonic for hypallage is:

> Hypallage shunts epithet? 'The trumpet's Tuscan blare' we get.

The word *epithet* has a respectable history as a code-word (in some case perhaps as a euphemism) for 'an offensive or derogatory expression used of a person; an abusive term; a profanity': *OED*.

> 'Blockhead, Dunce, Ass, Coxcomb, were the best Epithets he gave poor John': John Arbuthnot, *Lewis Baboon turned Honest*, 1:2: [*Law is a Bottomless Pit. Exemplified in the case of the Lord Strutt, John Bull, Nicholas Frog, and Lewis Baboon* (in Arber, Eng. Garner VI) (1712).

Epitome 'A brief statement of the chief points in a literary work; an abridgement, abstract. Something that forms a condensed record or representation "in miniature"': *OED*. In a draft addition published by the *OED* in June 2005 the following very popular meaning is given: 'A person who or thing which is a perfect embodiment of a particular quality or type. Usu. in *the (very) epitome of*. From the Greek επιτομε. There has been only one plural ever possible in English: *epitomes,* a quadrisyllabic word.

Epopee Strictly, 'the making of epics'. The word is derived, though a French literary coining, *épopée*, from a 'New Latin' word *epopaeus*. There is some ground for suspecting that 'epopee' is often used in English as a longer and rarer word than the noun 'epic'.

Ergo 'Therefore'. Used to introduce the conclusion of a syllogism. By extension, used to introduce a conclusion in writing and speech.

Eripuit coelo fulmen, sceptrumque tyrannis 'He seized lightning from heaven and the sceptre from tyrants'. A. R. J. Turgot for an inscription on a bust of Benjamin Franklin (1706-90), the inventor of the lightning conductor.

Errare mehercule malo cum Platone … quam cum istis vera sentire! 'I would rather, by Hercules, err with Plato than believe correctly with these men [the Pythagoreans]!' Cicero, *Tusculanae Disputationes*, 1:39. Much imitated over the centuries. 'But one may say of him [Thomas Hobbes], as one says of Jos. Scaliger, that where he erres, he erres so ingeniosely, that one had rather erre with him then hitt the marke with Clavius.' Byron chimed in with: 'Better to err with Pope than shine with Pye.'

Erratum 'An error'. In printing, an error recognized as such. See *corrigendum, above*. Plural: *errata*.

Est modus in rebus 'There's moderation in all things.' Horace, *Satires*, 1:1:106.

Esto 'Let it be' An interjection used in earlier times in argument, in particular in the courts, to express the notion that, though a particular contention might be true, yet it does not affect one's own contention. The English-language equivalent is the silky response, 'Be that as it may.'

Esto perpetua 'May it last forever!' *Res*, 'the thing' is understood, and is feminine.

Et alia 'And other things'. *Et alii* means 'And other people'. The abbreviation *et al.* disguises the difference.

Et cetera 'And the rest'. Sometimes still spelt *et caetera*. Abbreviated to *etc* or *etc*.

Et hoc genus omne. See *Hoc genus omne, below.*

Et in Arcadia ego 'And I in Arcadia too'. An enigmatic tomb inscription, often depicted in classical paintings. For an indication of the literature on the inscription, see the *Oxford Dictionary of Quotations*, 4th edn (1992).

Et semel emissum volat irrevocabile verbum 'And, once sent out, the word takes wing beyond recall', as translated in the *Oxford Dictionary of Quotations*, 4th edn (1992).

Et sequentes and **et sequentia** 'And the following'. The first form is used for masculine and feminine subjects, the second for neuter subjects. Since the phrase as always abbreviated to *et seq* (and sometimes *et seqq* for plural numbers) the distinction scarcely matters.

Et tu, Brute? 'You too, Brutus?' Reputedly said by Julius Caesar at his assassination, on seeing Brutus, his friend (and possibly son), among the assassins. Suetonius tells us that, when Marcus Brutus rushed at him, Caesar exclaimed, in Greek, *'και συ, τεκνον'*, 'You too, my child?'

Etiam disiecti membra poetae 'Even though broken up, the limbs of a poet'. Horace, *Satires* 1:4:62. Horace's meaning is not entirely clear. He is referring to Quintus Ennius (239-169 BC). Not a single work by Ennius survives in its entirety. Much has perished completely. We know of those lost works only from the scattered fragments of them as quoted by other writers. Are those scattered fragments what Horace means by *disiecti membra poetae*, the limbs of a scattered poet, recognizable even though scattered? Much of earlier literature was lost *actually in Antiquity*, a thought that is not perhaps as influential in today's thinking as it ought to be. Is Horace lamenting those losses, appreciable even in his own time?

Alternatively, a more humdrum interpretation might be that Horace is saying, no doubt ironically: 'Even though all writers draw on a common stock of words, yet, however the words of, say, Ennius, are redistributed among other writers, yet a couplet from Ennius will nevertheless shine out with undiminished distinction.' Such an argument runs quite contrary to that favoured in Antiquity, which was broadly that if one re-marshalled the words of poetry so as to make them prose, the magic would be gone. The verses that Horace chose as an exemplar refer to the famous breaking open of the Gates of War in the First Punic War as recounted in Ennius's *Annales*.

One might find it hard to discern any particular merit in Ennius's words, whatever their order, but, as was proverbial in Horace's time, *De gustibus non disputandum est.*

Etymon From the Greek *ετυμον*, '(1) the "true" literal sense of a word according to its origin; (2) its "true" or original form; (3) hence, in post-classical grammatical writings, the root or primary word from which a derivative is formed': *OED*. Cicero renders the word by *veriloquium*. Its present-day use is virtually as a synonym for 'the beginnings of the etymology of a word'.

Euphoria 'A feeling of well-being', perhaps tinged with over-confidence or over-optimism. From the Greek *ευφορια*, 'well bearing'.

Euthanasia 'Good death'.

Ex abundanti cautela 'From abundant caution'. Also *ex abundanti cautelae*, 'from an abundance of caution', and *ob majorem cautelam*, 'by reason of greater caution', all phrases used in the law to invoke the principle of leaving nothing to chance, one of the motives for periphrasis in the Law that makes the lay client so impatient – until he experiences a lack of caution.

Ex animo Literally, 'from the spirit or soul'. In a typical usage, the expression means 'from the heart; without equivocation or mental reservation'.

'As to the Church of England, I am hers, ex animo'. 'Therefore, in order to give them full satisfaction, if I can, I do hereby profess *ex animo*, with an absolute internal assent and consent, that Protestantism is the dreariest of possible religions; that the thought of the Anglican service makes me shiver, and the thought of the Thirty-nine Articles makes me shudder. Return to the Church of England! No; "the net is broken and we are delivered". I should be a consummate fool (to use a mild term) if in my old age I left "the land flowing with milk and honey" for the city of confusion and the house of bondage.'

Ex antecedentibus et consequentibus est optima interpretatio 'The best interpretation [of a part of a document] is gained from what goes before and what follows.' A maxim in *Shep. Touch.* 87. It is associated with a number of other maxims, among which the more important are *Turpis est pars quae cum suo toto non convenit* 'That part is bad that does not agree [is inconsistent] with its total', and *Maledicta expositio quae corrumpit textum* 'Cursed is the interpretation that corrupts the text.'

Ex cathedra 'From the throne'. Said of an authoritative pronouncement, especially one of the Pope delivered in Consistory or in the definition of dogma in matters of faith or morals and intended to be binding on the whole Church.

Ex debito justitiae 'Out of a debt to justice'. An expression in the Law conveying the notion that, regardless of any other (perhaps technical) considerations, a judgement is merited as a simple matter of justice. A judgement that is not *ex gratia*, *q.v.*, or delivered in the exercise of judicial discretion.

Ex delicto 'Arising out of a crime'.

Ex gratia 'As an act of grace', that is, something done not as a duty or obligation but a favour. See *ex debito justiciae, above*.

Ex hypothesi 'From the hypothesis'. Said of any conclusion that is legitimately drawn from a hypothesis.

Ex nihilo nihil fit 'Nothing comes of nothing.' Persius (AD 34-62) has *de nihilo nihil*, quoting Lucretius (99-55 BC), *Nil posse creari / De nilo*, 'Nothing can be created out of nothing.'

Ex officio 'By virtue of office'. A phrase used to explain the presence of individuals on committees, etc, as in 'The Club Secretary shall *ex officio* be a permanent member of the Committee.'

Ex opera operato A concept from Scholastic theology whereby the efficacy of the sacraments is independent of the merit of the minister, though the dispositions of the recipient are of course material. The phrase, literally translated, means 'operated by the operation': that is, sacramental grace is efficaciously conveyed provided the *matter* and *form* of the sacrament are validly observed. Technically, the administration of the sacrament is analysed and sub-divided: the *opus operatum* is 'the act done', which is distinguished from the *opus operans*, 'the [actual] doing of the act' and the *opus operantis*, 'the act of the doer'. 'To say, therefore, that a sacrament confers grace "ex opere operato" is to assert in effect that the sacrament itself is an instrument of God, and that so long as the conditions of its institution are validly fulfilled, irrespective of the qualities or merits of the person administering or receiving it, grace is conferred ... The doctrine, which does not deny that right dispositions are necessary if grace is to be really effectual, was formally approved by the Council of Trent (sess. 7, *de sacramentis in genere*, can. 8).'

Ex parte 'Of the one part; one-sided'. An *ex-parte* statement is a statement by one party of its own case. A step in legal proceedings may be taken, with the Court's permission, by one party alone, in the absence of other interested parties: these steps are known as a *ex-parte* applications and, if successful, result in, *e.g.*, *ex-parte* injunctions restraining, on a temporary footing, the other party/ies, until, *e.g*, the other party/ies can be heard. Such 'emergency' applications are frequently made to preserve property and, in general, to maintain the *status quo* (*q.v.*) pending formal proceedings.

Ex pede Herculem 'From the foot of Hercules'. In fact, a literal translation of the phrase is impossible, since, as Professor A. J. Bliss points out, the fact that the name *Hercules* is in the accusative case, not the genitive case, argues for a lost verb in the accusative-and-infinitive construction. He argues, inferentially, for the earlier existence of a locution, now lost, such as (but probably pithier and more idiomatic) *Ex pede Herculem proceritatis immensae fuisse credenda est*, 'From the foot of Hercules it might be believed that he was of immense height.' When once it is postulated that we are talking of a *statue* of Hercules, of which only the foot is now left, can we infer that the maxim means, 'We can judge the size of the whole from the size of the part.' See *ex ungue leonem, below.*

Ex post facto 'After the event'.

Ex professo 'From profession'. The phrase means, in practical use, 'based on a declaration or avowal of the person in consideration.'

Ex silentio '"From silence": a phrase used to designate an argument or conclusion based on lack of contrary evidence. Freq. in phr. argumentum *ex* (or *e*) *silentio*': *OED*.

> 'The only supportable concentrations of power or wealth are those that are at the direct disposal of the state (an exception in the case of trade unions being implied *ex silentio*)': *The Times*, 2 October 1961, p 13/2 1.

Ex tempore Literally, 'out of time' but meaning 'on the spur of the moment'. Cicero uses the phrase in *De Oratore*, 3:50, but it seems to have been a common-stock phrase.

Ex ungue leonem An abbreviated form of an expression that nowadays irritatingly lacks a verb. It was originally probably *ex ungue leonem agnoscere* (or some similar verb, perhaps *pingere*), 'You can tell [or paint] the lion by his claw.' The expression *εξ ονυχοςτον λεντα γραφειν*, attributed by Plutarch (c.AD 46-119) to Alcaeus (620-? BC) and by Lucian of Samosata (AD ?-165) to Pheidias (c.490-c430 BC), no doubt involves considerable play on words, in that the verb *γραφειν* meant original 'to scratch', something that claws do, and then, later, 'to draw', and, later still, 'to indict (in a court of law)'. In a number of senses the saying can be made to furnish sense. It is similar to *ex pede Herculem* (*q.v., above*), and has been widely understood to mean that it is possible, as some say Pheidias could, to sculpt the entire lion from the evidence of a single nail. In consequence of that interpretation, the maxim has come to mean that one can tell the whole from the part, or derive much information from an examination of the part.

The tag *ex ungue leonem* occurs in a letter the abashed Johann Bernoulli (1667-1748) wrote to Jacques Basnage de Beauval (1653-1723), effectively owning that he had failed to goad Sir Isaac Newton into admitting defeat over the Brachistochrone Problem: in fact, Bernoulli says he now knows that 'the anonymous Englishman' who had solved the problem was Newton, but, in any event, he says it was clear *ex ungue leonem* that the author of the solution was Newton.

Exceptio probat regulam 'The exception proves the rule.' A useful means of proof. H. W. Fowler says 'Special leave is given for men to be out of barracks tonight until 11.00 p.m.'; *the exception proves the rule* means that this special leave implies a rule requiring men, except when an exception is made, to be in earlier. The value of this in interpreting statutes is plain.' To be precise, 'Special leave is given for men to be out of barracks tonight till 11.0 p.m.' proves the existence of *a* rule. If the wording had been 'Special leave is given for men to be out of barracks for an extra hour (*i.e.*, till 11.0 p.m.), that would prove the existence of *the* rule. A form of the maxim sometimes quoted at Law is *Exceptio probat regulam de rebus non exceptis* – 'concerning things not excepted': (11 *Rep*. 41).

The maxim certainly does not mean that an exception to a rule proves the validity, force, or authenticity of a rule. To say, 'It always rains on St Swithun's Day. This year it didn't. The exception proves the rule' is *absurd*.

Exceptis excipiendis 'With the exception of the exceptions', or 'When [all] exceptions have been made.' Approximately equivalent to *mutatis mutandis, q.v., below.*

Excursus 'Something out of the way, or off course'. Said of a digression in a discussion. Sometimes used to denote a supplement or appendix devoted to a subject not conveniently dealt with in the text.

Exeat 'Let him go out.' A permission or leave of absence given by a school or college.

There was for many years a writ, *Ne exeat regnum*, prohibiting the named person from leaving the realm.

Exegesis 'Explanation, interpretation'. From the Greek, normally implying a word-by-word grammatical exposition of the meaning of the language of, *e.g.*, Sacred Scripture. Sometimes contrasted with *hermeneutics*, a word that has a tendency, nowadays, to imply not the study of the language involved by means of a painstaking analysis of vocabulary and syntax but the desire to explore the hidden, perhaps allegorical, figurative, or mystical, meaning of the text. The word was used in the early days of the Church to mean an interpreter who translated the Divine Service for the benefit of those who spoke a language different from the liturgical language. Though it might sound *pii auribus offensis* (*q.v*), there is some warrantable suspicion that the word *hermeneutics* has been contaminated by a confusion with the ill-formed adjective *hermetic* in its particular application to Hermes Trismegistus and the theosophic writings ascribed to him.

Exegi monumentum aere perennius 'I have erected a monument more lasting than bronze.' Horace, *Odes*, 3:30:1. The succeeding verses capture this man's charming lack of modesty. He knew he was good!

> *Exegi monumentum aere perennius regalique situ pyramidum altius, quod non imber edax, non Aquilo impotens possit diruere aut innumerabilis annorum series et fuga temporum. non omnis moriar, multaque pars mei vitabit Libitinam: usque ego postera crescam laude recens, dum Capitolium scandet cum tacita virgine pontifex. Dicar, qua violens obstrepit Aufidus et qua pauper aquae Daunus agrestium regnavit populorum, ex humili potens princeps Aeolium carmen ad Italos deduxisse modos. Sume superbiam quaesitam meritis et mihi Delphica lauro cinge volens, Melpomene, comam.*
> I have wrought a monument more lasting than bronze and loftier than the royal sites of pyramids, that gnawing rain nor headstrong northern winds can raze, nor yet the numberless course of years, erase, not e'en the fleetful flight of time efface. Not all of me shall die! The greater part of me shall slip the grasp of Death. With silent Vestal let the Pontiff silent scale the steps of Rome! My fame shall bloom anew. From where the ample Aufid river runs, to parchèd plains where once the thirsty Daunus ruled, I shall be spoken of as one of humble stock–but first to make the Grecian metres go, and fit them out to make th'Italian lyrics flow. To you, Melpomene, let the honour go to know these virtues and the crown bestow! *On me!*

Exit 'He leaves [the stage].'

Exodus Greek *εξηγησις*, 'going out'. The title of the book of the Old Testament that narrates the departure of the Israelites out of Egypt. The fuller title in English Bibles is 'The Second Book of Moses, called Exodus'. The Greek name derives from the Septuagint.

Exordium 'The beginning of anything; *esp.* the introductory part of a discourse, treatise, etc.; "the proemial part of a composition" (J.)': *OED*. As the mention of Dr Johnson reminds us, there is a Greek noun *προοιμιον*, meaning 'beginning' or 'prelude', borrowed by the Roman with the spelling *prooemium*. The awkward appearance of that word is one of the few reasons for using the digraph *œ* in Latin, rather than the better practice of printing the two letters *o* and *e* separately. The close proximity of two letters *o* is a temptation to English speakers to make the sound /u/–that is, the sound in the word 'two' (During the struggle for Cypriot independence from

Britain in the 20th century, much reporting of military activities in the Troodos Mountains was marred by the pronunciation /'trudos/ rather than /tro'odos/ or /tro'oðos/.)

Expedit esse deos, et, ut expedit, esse putemus 'It is expedient that there should be gods, so, since it is expedient, let us assume it.' Ovid, *Ars Amatoria* 1:637.

Experentia docet 'Experience teaches.' Adapted from Tacitus, *The Histories* 5:6: *Experientia docuit*, 'Experience has taught.' Mrs Micawber in *David Copperfield* (1850), ch 11, says, 'Experientia does it – as papa used to say.' In his *Saturnalia*, 7:5, Macrobius, who flourished at the end of the fourth century and the beginning of the fifth century AD, has *Experientia docebit*, 'Experience will teach.'

Experto credite 'Believe ye one who has been through it!' Virgil, *Aeneid*, 11:283. For 'expert' in the modern sense, see *Peritus in arte, below*. The maxim *Experto credite* is often quoted as *Experto crede*, 'Believe thou.' In Mediaeval times, there was a shadowy figure, Robertus, who appears only in the saw *Experto crede Roberto*. Why this should be is quite unknown.

Exeunt 'They leave [the stage].' *Exeunt omnes* 'They all leave.'

Experimentum crucis An experiment the result of which will determine the course of all future experiments in that discipline. The literally meaning 'Experiment of the cross' is misleading. One has to remember the implications of the adjective 'crucial'.

Explicit '[Here] ends.' An addition by the scribe to the effect that a section of a manuscript had come to an end. The analogue – of when a section began – was *Implicit*. In the days before our present elaborate system of dividing the text into words, sentences, paragraphs and chapters, any help afforded by the scribe was welcome. For instance, St Jerome in the Vulgate marks the transition from the Book of Joshua to the Book of Judges in this way:

EXPLICIT LIBER IOSUE BENNUN
ID EST IESU NAVE
INCIPIT LIBER SOPTHIM
ID EST IUDICUM.

Extra metrum 'Outside the meter'; said of feet or syllables in excess of those required for the purposes of correct scansion. Verses that lack the necessary number are called *catalectic*, and those that do not are called *acatalectic* (An acatalectic verse is defined by Dr Johnson as, 'A verse, which has the complete number of syllables, without defect or superfluity.')

Faber fortunae suae Shortened from Sallust's *Appius ait, fabrum esse suae quemque fortunae,* 'Appius says that each man is the maker of his own fate': *Ad Caesarem Senem Publica Oratio,* 1:1:2. Appius is Appius Claudius Caecus, fl 312-279 BC.

Facetiae 'Facetious things; pleasantries'. H. W. Fowler tells us that booksellers in his day were wont to call obscene publications *facetiae* in their catalogues, hiding them in Gibbon's 'obscurity of a dead language'. He says, 'The following extract is vouched for by the *Westminster Gazette*: – FACETIAE. 340 – Kingsley (C.) Phaethon; or *Loose Thought for Loose Thinkers*, 2nd ed., 8vo, boards, 1s., 1854.'

When the Public Libraries of the Metropolitan Borough of Chelsea were in the throes of introducing the Dewey Decimal System, a senior librarian noted that an assistant had temporarily entered a title, *Hints for Young Mothers*, in the classification 632:7, 'Entomology'.

Facile princeps 'Easily the first'. The acknowledged leader.

Facilis descensus Averno 'Easy the descent to Avernus [the Underworld]'. Virgil, *Aeneid*, 6:126. Sometimes quoted as *facilis descensus Averni*, using the genitive.

Facsimile 'Make alike.'

Factotum 'Do everything.' A Jack-of-all-Trades; a general servant who can turn his hand to everything.

Falsa demonstratio non nocet 'A false description does no harm.' 6 *Term Rep.*, 676. The implication of this legal maxim is that an erroneous description of something the identity of which is not in doubt does not vitiate proceedings.

Falsa orthographia sive falsa grammatica non vitiat concessionem 'False spelling or false grammar does not vitiate a grant.' 9 *Co. Rep.* 48.

Fas est et ab hoste doceri 'It is right to learn even from the enemy.' Ovid, *Metamorphoses*, 4:428.

Fasciculus Literally, 'A small bundle [of sticks]'. Used in printing and publishing to mean a gathering of pages as it were in the form of pamphlets, for convenience in circulating the printed matter, for proof-reading, to permit subscribers to have the work at intervals rather than wait until the entire work is printed, or for other purposes for which it is desired to split the publication into parts. Also used for the individual sections from which case-bound and other books are made up, clearly visible if the spine of the books is inspected. Often abbreviated: the most common abbreviation is *fascicule*, but *fascicle* is also found.

Fatetur facinus qui judicium fugit 'He who flees judgement confesses his guilt.' 3 *Inst.* 14.

Favete linguis! 'Be courteous with your tongues!' A decorous way of securing silence. Horace, *Odes*, 3:1:2.

Fecit 'He made it.' Followed by the name of the creator. More specific usages are *caelavit, delineavit, pinxit* and *sculpsit,* for 'to engrave', 'to draw', 'to paint' and 'to sculpt'. Very often abbreviated to the first syllables.

Felix qui potuit rerum cognoscere causas 'Happy is he who can know the cause of things!' Virgil, *Georgics*, 2:490. Quoted by Lord Coke, *Co. Litt.*, 231 b.

Felo de se 'Felon of the self'. 'One who "deliberately puts an end to his own existence, or commits any unlawful malicious act, the consequence of which is his own death" (Blackstone)': *OED.*

Ferae naturae 'Of a wild nature'. A term of art of the Law, applied to animals that are generally found at liberty, though it might happen that they are 'tamed and confined by the art and industry of man'. They are regarded as 'property' but cannot be stolen within the meaning of the word unless it can be demonstrated that they had first been 'reduced into possession'. Domesticated animals within the meaning of the word 'domesticated' are said to be *mansuetae naturae*, 'tamed', or, by a seven-league etymological leap, 'house-trained'.

Ferula Originally, merely (a stem or rod of) the fennel. The fennel provided a cane with which pedagogues administered punishment. Hence, *ferula* became a metonym for punishment or discipline. The word *ferula* frequently appears in the sempiternal denigrations of the Jesuits, who have a reputation for over-use of the *ferula*. It is tempting to speculate that these critics believe that the word *ferula* derives in some way from *ferrum*, 'iron', as in *Et reget illas in virga ferrea tamquam vas figuli confringentur*, 'And he shall rule them with a rod of iron; as the vessels of a potter shall they be broken to shivers.' In fact, over the long history of Latin the word *virga* became the predominant one for the rod in the sense, 'Spare the rod and spoil the child':

> *Noli subtrahere a puero disciplinam si enim percusseris eum virga non morietur.*
> *tu virga percuties eum et animam eius de inferno liberabis.*
> Withhold not correction from a child: for if thou strike him with the rod, he shall not die.
> Thou shalt beat him with the rod, and deliver his soul from hell.

Festina lente 'Hasten slowly'; more haste, less speed. Augustus (63 BC - AD 14). In Suetonius, *Lives of the Caesars*: *Divus Augustus*, 25:4. Augustus in fact said *σπευδε βραδεως*.

Fetus See *foetus, below.*

Fiat 'Let it de done.' An order or command that something should imperatively be done. In English Law, a *fiat* was a short order or warrant for permitting certain proceedings. Nowadays, the word is in practice restricted to an endorsement by the Lord Chancellor or the Attorney-General on a petition in any matter in which the consent of the Crown is needed before steps may be taken.

Fiat justitia ruat coelum 'Let justice be done, though the heavens fall!'

Fiat experimentum in corpore vili 'Let the experiment be carried out on something worthless.' The *OED* definition of *corpus vile* is: 'A living or dead body that is of so little value that it can be used for experiment without regard for the outcome; *transf.*, experimental material of any kind, or something which has no value except as the object of experimentation': *OED*.

Fiat lux 'Let there be light.' *Genesis* 1:3, *Vg.*

Fibula The word has two relevant meanings. It means an ancient form of brooch or clasp, and also the long or splint bone on the outer side of the leg, so called from its apparent resemblance to the tongue of a clasp, of which the *tibia* forms the other part. The word *tibia* itself means 'flute' or 'pipe'. Both words are instances of how words are extended in meaning over the course of the years, to the extent, in fact, that the transferred senses become words in their own right, often taking over the primary meaning. Who, nowadays, *first* thinks of 'brooch' when the word *fibula* is mentioned?

Fidus Achates 'Faithful Achates'. A trusted friend of Aeneas. Virgil, *Aeneid*, 6:158 and *passim*.

Fieri facias 'Cause to be done.' The name, from its first two words, of a writ of execution available to a litigant who has recovered judgement in an action of debt or damages. It commands the sheriff to levy the debt or damages from the goods of the party against whom judgement is recovered. Abbreviated 'fi. fa.', rhyming with 'I say'.

Filioque 'And from the Son'. A clause in the Creed referring to the Holy Spirit reads, according to the Western Church, 'Who proceeds from the Father and the Son.' The Eastern Church omits 'and the Son'. This divergence on doctrine continues to separate the Churches.

Filius nullius 'Son of no-one'. A term used in place of 'bastard'. Sometimes *filius populi*, 'son of the people.'

Filum aquae medium 'The middle thread of water'. Riparian proprietors possess the bed of a river *usque ad medium filum.*

Finis 'The end'. Often printed at the ends of books.

Flagrante delicto 'During the flagrant commission of a crime'. More often *in flagrante delicto.* Colloquially expressed as 'catching someone red-handed'.

Flora 'The flower population of an area', often linked with *fauna*, the animal equivalent.

Floreat Etona! 'May Eton [College] flourish!' The motto of Eton.

Florilegium. 'A collection of flowers [normally 'the flowers of literature']'. The exact Greek equivalent is ανθολογια, 'anthology', much the more common term in English.

Floruit 'He flourished.' A means whereby writers can convey the notion that the person or school referred to was working at a time or during a period that cannot be precisely defined. Normally abbreviated to *fl.*

Foederatus An ally of the Romans. The Romans made a point of converting the last tribe conquered on the borders of the Empire into an ally, so that the Imperial troops were better able to overcome the next tribe. Plural: *foederati.*

Foetus 'The young of any animal while still in the womb'. The better spelling *fetus* has been used by Americans since Noah Webster (1758-1843) compiled his *Dictionary* in 1806.

Fons et origo 'The fount and origin'. A commonplace expression even in Antiquity.

Forsitan et nostrum nomen miscebitur istis 'Perhaps our name, also, will mingle with these.' Ovid, *Ars Amatoria* 3:339. This quotation occurs in Boswell's *Life of Johnson,* Friday, 30 April 1773.

> JOHNSON. 'I remember once being with Goldsmith in Westminster-abbey. While we surveyed the Poets' Corner, I said to him,

'Forsitan et nostrum nomen miscebitur istis.'

> When we got to Temple-bar he stopped me, pointed to the heads upon it, and slily whispered me, 'Forsitan et nostrum nomen miscebitur ISTIS.' [Boswell's note appended to the incident reads, 'In allusion to Dr. Johnson's supposed political principles, and perhaps his own.' The heads upon Temple Bar were the heads of some executed Jacobites.]

Forsan et haec olim meminisse iuvabit 'Perhaps one day it will be joyous to remember even these things.' Virgil, *Aeneid,* 1:203.

Fortis fortuna adiuvat 'Fortune favours the brave.' Terence, *Phormio,* 203. Virgil nods to Terence in *Audentis Fortuna iuvat, Aeneid,* 10:284. *Cf. Audaces fortuna iuvat, above.*

Forum The market-place of a Roman town and, thus, the focal point of municipal affairs. From that to the tribunal that determined legal issues between the state and the citizen, and between citizen and citizen. From that to the modern use, a discussion-group or a discussion-point on the internet.

Frigidarium 'The cold room in a Roman bath.'

Frustum A word meaning, originally, 'a remnant, something left over' – and, *n.b.*, not *frustrum* (that is, without the second letter *r*). The development of meaning associated with this word is a marvellous exemplar of the proficiency of our ancestors in adapting old words to new meanings. In the field of plane and solid geometry this propensity shows itself to its fullest effect, and in particular in the province of solid geometry known as *conic sections*.

In solid geometry the term of art *frustum* means the portion of a regular solid left after cutting off the upper part, the *apex*, in a plane parallel to the base – giving us a truncated cone, the shape of cut being a circle – a useful concept, but hardly earth-shattering. However, as one goes further and slices the cone in different ways, one suddenly discovers that the surfaces exposed as a result of our sections (our cuttings) have – already – names that ring bells. If we angle our cuts so that they are *not* parallel to the base, the exposed surfaces we get are a series of *ellipses*. If we angle our sections more steeply, so that they cut the base and one side of the cone, the exposed sections are called *parabolas*. Variations on this theme produce *hyperbolas*.

> 'If the inclination of the cutting plane to the axis of the cone be greater than that of the edge of the cone, the section is an ELLIPSE (with the *circle* as a particular case when the plane is perpendicular to the axis; if less, a HYPERBOLA; if the plane be parallel to the edge, a PARABOLA. (The pair of intersecting straight lines formed by a section through the vertex – strictly a particular case of the hyperbola – is not usually reckoned as a conic section.)': Note in *OED, s.v. conic.*

Fulcrum 'A prop or support; now only *spec.* in *Mech.* the point against which a lever is placed to get purchase or upon which it turns or is supported': *OED.* The word as now used is an adaptation of the Classical Latin *fulcrum*, which meant 'the foot of a couch'. In principle, the word ought to be pronounced so that the first syllable rhymes with 'mull' and not 'full'. Certainly, until Edward Smith's Supplement (1857) to John Walker's *A Critical Pronouncing Dictionary* (1791), only that pronunciation is given. From that time on, murmurings were heard from Continental Europe that no-one was trying to speak as Caesar spoke, which was on the whole a contention that was sympathetically received. Scholars in general recognized that the letter *u* as a vowel probably rhymed with the vowel in 'full', but it was not until the widespread introduction into schools of the Classical Pronunciation, persuasively advocated in England by the Classical Association and formally adopted in 1906, that the normative English value or pronunciation was given to the first vowel in *fulcrum.* Thus, the pronunciation /fulkrəm/ crept in among the scholars, and, even in the last bastion of the 'vice-versa' school of pronunciation – the lawyers – that pronunciation predominates.

Among the half-educated, the story was somewhat different. They had never been able to ignore the attraction of the precedent of 'full': it was too strong to resist. The further ostensible precedent of 'fulsome' has also had a powerful influence.

For the word *fulcrum*, the Second Edition of the *OED* (1989) gives pride of place to the pronunciation embodying the sound that rhymes with 'mull', relegating the 'full' sound to second place. With the word 'fulsome', however, the *Dictionary* gives pride of place to the 'full' rhyme and brands the 'mull' rhyme 'older' – which is *the kiss of death*.

Fumum et opes strepitumque Romae 'The smoke and wealth and din at Rome'. Horace, *Odes*, 3:29;12.

Functus officio 'Having ceased to perform an office'. A judge who has completely disposed of a case or matter is said to be *functus officio*: he no longer has jurisdiction, since there is no longer a *lis* (*q.v., below).*

Ganglion Strictly, a Greek word, *γαγγλιον*, meaning an enlargement or knot of a nerve from which nerve-fibres radiate. Most of the everyday words derived from Greek that are used in medicine today are derived from the seminal works of Galen (AD 129-c216).

It is fashionable to deride the Mediaeval surgeons and physicians for their slavish adherence to what they considered Galen had taught, but it is fatally easy to be wise after the event. Many readers of this Dictionary will remember the cult of sunshine that, under the influence of Dr Robert Ley (see *Kraft durch Freude* in the German Section) dominated the 1930s. They will contrast that progressive optimism with the conclusions of the present generation of medical experts on the topic of skin cancer caused by the actinic properties of sunlight. *Experientia docet.*

Grammatici certant at adhuc sub iudice lis est. 'The scholars dispute: as yet, the case is still before the court.' Horace, *Ars Poetica*, 78.

Gaudeamus igitur 'Let us therefore rejoice!' A German students' drinking song:

Gaudeamus igitur
Juvenes dum sumus
Post jucundam juventutem,
Post molestam senectutem
Nos habebit humus!
Nos habebit humus!

Let us therefore rejoice!
For we are young!
After a merry youth.
And a troublesome old age.
The earth will have us!
The earth will have us!

Gaudium certaminis 'The joy of the victory [in a contest both physical and figurative]'. The satisfaction of having come out best from a contest, discussion, argument, lawsuit, election, etc. The concept is taken up in a hymn attributed to Venatius Fortunatus (530-609), which begins:

Pange lingua gloriosi / Lauream certaminis.

St Thomas Aquinas (1225-74) incorporated the theme in his own hymn:

Pange, lingua, gloriosi Corporis mysterium.

Generalia 'Things in general'.

Genesis The first book in the Bible. The word Genesis is a Greek word, *λενεσις* 'origin'. It was the name given to that book in the Septuagint, the theme of which book is the creation of the universe. St Jerome commences his translation of the first chapter of the book with these words: *Incipit Liber Bresith id est Genesis.* In the common modern transliteration of Hebrew, *Bresith* is rendered *Bereshit* or *Bereshith.*

> 'The Bereshith of Moses bears a triple meaning . . viz. Ethico-political, Physico-theosophical, and Literal': Henry More, *Divine Dialogues*, 1668, 565 (1713).

Genius domus 'The spirit of the house', adapted from *genius loci*, 'the spirit of the place', meaning the effect or influence a house or place is thought to have on its inhabitants. How the word *genius* came to mean 'native intellectual power of an exalted type' and how the word was affected by 'the spirit in the bottle' is recounted in some detail in the *OED*.

Gloria in excelsis Deo 'Glory be to God on high.' The opening words of a prayer in the Mass.

Gnomon 'The 'finger' of a sun-dial; the part of a sun-dial that casts a shadow in the surface.' Greek γνωμων, 'a carpenter's square'.

Gnosis A supposed special understanding or knowledge of spiritual mysteries. Greek χμ(ρι, 'investigation' or 'knowledge'.

Gnothi seauton A transliteration of the Greek χμ(ηι ρεατσ–μ, 'know thyself'. The Latin is *nosce teipsum*.

Gradatim 'By steps'.

Gradus ad Parnassum 'A step towards Parnassus', the Latin title of a dictionary of prosody until recently used in English public schools, intended as an aid in Latin versification, both by giving the quantities (the short or long values of vowels) of words and by suggesting poetical epithets and phraseology. Hence applied to later works of similar plan and object; also extended to other languages, as in *Greek gradus*. The earliest edition of the *Gradus* in the British Museum is that of Cologne 1687; there was a London edition in 1691.

Gravamen 'A grievance'. The weightiest part of a case or argument. In Ecclesiastical Law, the word is applied to a grievance alleged by the clergy and addressed to the archbishop and bishops in Convocation. Plural *gravamina*. See quotation for an application from the Civil Law.

> 'In an Appeal, whether from a Gravamen or the Sentence, an Inhibition is issued from the Superior Court to the Inferior, to stop Proceedings': S. Hallifax, *Roman Civil Law*, 126 (1775).

Gravitas 'Gravity of demeanour, thought, etc'.

Gutta percha The thickened juice of various trees found chiefly in the Malayan archipelago, chiefly the *Isonandra* (or *Dichopsia*) *Gutta* (N.O. *Euphorbiaceæ*), formerly much used for the insulation of electrical wiring. Not in fact Latin: the Malay expression *getah percha* fortuitously means 'gum of [the] percha [tree]'.

Gutta cavat lapidem, consumitur anulus usu 'Drips of water hollow out a stone: a ring is worn away with use': Ovid, *Epistulae: Ex Ponto*, 2:9:47.

Habeas corpus Historically, the most important writ issuing from English courts, itself divided into a number of forms depending on the object desired, all directed at the person detaining the 'corpus' or defendant in custody. (This entry is cast in a mixture of the present and the past tenses. There have been numerous statutory developments over the years that have rendered obsolete some of the consequences of the issue of writs of habeas corpus. Nevertheless, the salient *desiderata* underlying the writ remain intact, though accomplished by other means. Moreover, legislation over the years has closed up loopholes whereby the authorities have attempted to circumvent the intentions of the writ.)

The words *Habeas corpus* are the first two in all forms of the writ and mean, literally, 'Thou shalt have the body [brought before the Court].' The most important of the writs is the *Habeas corpus ad subjiciendum*, or, more fully, *Habeas corpus ad faciendum, subjiciendum et recipiendum*, 'to do, to submit to and to receive [whatever the judge or Court awarding the writ would direct]'. Other forms are *ad respondendum*, 'to bring up to a superior court a prisoner confined by the process of an inferior court so that he might be examined and if necessary charged with a fresh offence in that superior court'. The writ *ad satisfaciendum*. requires the bringing up of a prisoner already in custody by reason of the jurisdiction of a superior court so that a judgement of the inferior court might be implemented. The writ *ad faciendum et recipiendum*, otherwise known as a *habeas corpus cum causa* because it particularizes to some extent the subject-matter, requires the recipient 'to do and receive what the King's court shall deliver in that cause'. A further variation on the writ was the *Habeas corpus ad prosequendum, testificandum at deliberandum*, which was issued to secure the bringing up of the prisoner so that he could give evidence in any court, or be tried in the proper jurisdiction.

Haec olim meminisse See, *above*, *Forsan et haec olim meminisse iuvabit.*

Habitat 'He lives.' Now widely used as a noun to denote the area in which an animal (or, less often, a plant) flourishes.

Halitus 'Vapour, exhalation'. *Halitosis*, meaning 'bad breath', was almost the creation of dentifrice-advertising copywriters in the twenties and thirties of the last century. It has been said that the word *halitosis* stands to 'bad breath' as 'coryza' stands to 'the common cold'.

'Thus *halitosis*, the happy discovery of purveyors of mouth-washes, has found a wider usefulness, and *bad breath* is taboo': S. Robertson, *The Development of Modern Engineering*, 11:447 (1934).

Hamartia Greek *αμαρτια*, 'Fault, failure, guilt'. Aristotle, in his *Poetics*, propounds the principle of *αμαρτια*, by which he means the undoing of a hero by reason of some personal fault or error.

Hapax legomenon Greek *απαζ λεγομενον*: 'read only once'. This technical term denotes the sole instance of the appearance of a word or phase in the surviving records of a language or the surviving works of an author. The plural is *hapax legomina.* In the light of the great number of *hapax legomina* in Classical literature, it might be thought that their low incidence is more easily ascribed to the immense loss of literature during the decline and fall of the Roman Empire than to the idiosyncrasy of individual authors, with the problematical implications of that hypothesis – that authors had their fad words that other authors eschewed. It is inherently much more likely that these *hapax legomina* were survivors of the wreckage of Classical literature than that they were the nonce-words of surviving authors.

The implications of that thought are prodigious. The fixation of Classical scholars with the pressing need to lock us into the Golden Age of Latin literature has meant they are all too ready to write off *hapax legomina* as foibles of individuals, rather than see them as probable survivors of the ship-wreck, desperately clinging to life-rafts for all they are worth.

The further implication of all this is even more significant. The scholars will let in *hapax legomina* but only as *oddities*. If these *hapax legomina* are respectably evidenced, then the scholars cannot realistically ignore them. But what if *every written instance* of a word or phrase has been drowned in the shipwreck of Classical literature? What then? Why, the scholars say the words never existed – at least, never existed in the utterly artificial construct of Classical Latin, the *καθαπευουσα* that ignores any writer not in the club: Caesar, Cicero, Horace, Juvenal, Livy, Ovid, Sallust, Tacitus, Terence and Virgil.

What a waste of words!

Has praesentes litteras 'These present letters'. The origin of the abbreviated 'these presents' in leases and other deeds, meaning the document itself.

Haud facile emergunt quorum virtutibus obstat / Res angusta domi 'It is not at all easy to emerge from obscurity if one's qualities are thwarted by narrow means at home.' Juvenal, *Satires*, 3:164.

Hendiadys A late Greek word derived from *εν δια δυοιν*, 'one by means of two'. A rhetorical trope or figure of speech in which a single but complex idea is expressed by two words connected by a conjunction, normally two substantives with 'and' between them, rather than with some adjectival form that the listener or reader might expect. A useful mnemonic might be:

Hendiadys? Hendiadys
Says 'bliss and youth' for 'youthful bliss'.

Hiatus 'A (largish) hole'. Apart from specialist usages (in medicine, grammar, prosody, geology, phonetics, etc.) the word is a grand word for 'gap', as in someone's genealogy, in someone's narrative of events or in a chain of deductive reasoning. It derives from the Latin *hiare*, 'to gape'. The word is a fourth-declension noun, so in principle we ought to say *hiātūs* for the plural. In the English 'vice-versa' pronunciation, that would be to rhyme it with 'juice'. In the Classical Latin and Church pronunciations, it would rhyme with 'noose'. There is authority for saying 'hiatuses', but it sounds and looks clumsy. *Lacuna*, 'a hole, a pit', is likewise a grand word used in much the same way as *hiatus*. Its plural is more obvious: *lacunae*. The word 'gap' is probably a serviceable word for use in place of these two Latin words; it also has the merit of making a perfectly ordinary plural.

Hic jacet 'Here lies.'

Hic vivimus ambitiosa / Paupertate omnes 'Here we all live in ambitious poverty.' Juvenal, *Satires*, 3:182

Hinc illae lacrimae 'Hence those tears' (Terence, *Andria* 1:26.).

Hinc lucem et pocula sacra Literally, 'From here light and sacred draughts'. The motto of Cambridge University.

Hoc genus omne 'All that lot!' Horace, *Satires*, 1:2:2.

Hoc volo, sic iubeo, sit pro ratione voluntas 'I wish it, I so command it. Let my will take the place of reason.' Juvenal, *Satires*, 6:223.

Homoeoteleuton Greek *ομοιοτελευτον*, 'like ending.' A rhetorical figure or trope consisting in the use of a series of words with the same or similar endings. Also used to denote a common scribal error whereby lines with the same ending as the previous line are inadvertently omitted. Sometimes spelt in a transliteration closer to the Greek, *homoioteleuton*. The tonic accent sometimes follows the Greek, but more often follows the Latin and is placed on the penultimate syllable. The quantity of the first vowel is short if the Greek precedent is followed; otherwise, it is long as spoken in English.

Homo sum; humani nil a me alienum puto 'I am a man; I count nothing alien to me that is human.' Terence, *Ηεαυτοντιμορουμενος*, *Heauton Timorumenos* 77.

Homo ludens 'A 'jokey' man'. **Homo sapiens** 'Thinking man'. The species to which mankind belongs.

Homo trium litterarum 'Man of three letters'. The letters were *f, u* and *r*, spelling the Latin for 'thief'. The allusion is from Plautus's *Aulularia*, 2:4:46. The turn of phrase is similar to our present-day 'four-letter word'.

Homo unius libri 'Man of one book'. A characterization employed to suggest that a man who knows one book thoroughly knows no other. The saying is attributed to St Thomas Aquinas by Robert Southey (1774-1843), *The Doctor*, 1:164. (The tonic accent in *unius* falls on the middle syllable.)

Homoiousion Greek *ομοουσιαν*, neuter, denoting the doctrine that the Father and the Son are of like, not identical, substance. See *Homoousian,* next.

Homoousian Greek *ομοουσιαν*. The word used in, for example, the formula promulgated at the Council of Nicaea in AD 325 whereby the Son is declared to be 'of one substance' with the Father (that is, 'consubstantial with the Father'). In Gibbon's immortal jibe, Christendom was divided by a diphthong.

Honorarium 'A professional man's fee', so termed because it was not considered a debt that could be enforced at Law but was owing in honour only. The English Bar still abides by this principle.

Honoris causa 'For the cause of honour'. A type of university degree awarded in recognition of public service rather than of success in an examination.

Horresco referens 'I shudder to mention it!' A parenthetic exclamation: Virgil, *Aeneid*, 2:204.

Hypallage See *Epithet, above.*

Hyperbole Greek, *υπερβολη* 'Over-shooting; exaggeration.' A rhetorical figure or trope depending on deliberate exaggeration, used to express strong feeling or produce a strong impression, and not intended to be taken literally. The word is a four-syllable one, with the tonic accent on the second syllable. A useful mnemonic might be:

> Hyperbole? Hyperbole
> Says 'millions', meaning two or three.

Hypotheses non fingo 'I do not invent hypotheses': Sir Isaac Newton: see *Entia non sunt multiplicanda, above.*

Hysteron proteron Greek *υστερον προτερον*, 'the latter placed as the former'. A rhetorical figure of speech or trope in which the position of elements is the contrary of what the listener or reader might expect. A useful mnemonic might be:

> Hysteron proteron, skilfully versed:
> 'Carts before horses' and 'Last before first'.

Ibidem 'In the same place'. Used in publications to indicate that another reference is being made to the 'same place' (that is, in some published work or other source) as has just been mentioned. Abbreviated to *ibid.* In the full word the tonic accent falls on the middle syllable.

Idem 'The same'. Used in a similar fashion to *ibidem*, above, to avoid repetition when referring to a person already mentioned. Usually reserved for the conventional lingo of the scholarly *apparatus criticus (q.v. above).*

Id certum est quod certum reddi potest; sed id magis certum est quod de semet ipso est certum 'It *is* certain that which can be *made certain*; but that is most certain which is certain in itself [on the face of it].' 9 *Rep.* 47.

Ignis fatuus 'Foolish fire'. Marsh gas in the phosphorescent form known as Will-o'-the-Wisp. Figuratively, 'a thing (rarely a person) that deludes or misleads by means of fugitive appearances': *OED.*

Ignoramus 'We do not know.' By origin, not a noun but a verb, the endorsement by means of which a grand jury signified that they were unable to bring in a true bill of indictment. Hence, an ignorant lawyer, and from that to any ignorant person. The plural is 'ignoramuses'.

Ignorantia juris haud [neminem] excusat 'Ignorance of the Law excuses nothing [no-one].'

Ignoratio elenchi See *elenchus, above.*

Ignotum per ignotius The explaining of something unknown by reference to something even less known.

Impedimenta 'Encumbrances', such as Caesar's baggage-trains. Every schoolboy knows the *locus classicus* (*q.v.*) of the use of the gerund coupled with ablative absolute: *Binis cohortibus ad impedimenta tuenda relictis:* 'Two cohorts being left behind to look after the *impedimenta*': *De Bello Gallico, 8:2.*

Imprimatur 'Let it be printed'. The formal certificate given by a bishop to a book testifying that the work contains nothing contrary to the religion. It is not intended to convey approval, much less to imply that the subject-matter is correct in any other sense. The bishop will almost always appoint a *censor deputatus* ('deputed censor') to examine the work in detail. If the author is a member of a religious order, the appropriate superior will give his permission for publication by endorsing the work with the phrase *imprimi potest*, 'it can be printed'.

Impromptu For *in promptu*, 'In readiness'. Something spontaneous. The early etymology appears to indicate a usage contrary to the present-day one: an impromptu speech, for example, is not normally considered to be one that is 'in readiness'.

In absentia 'In the absence [of someone]'.

In articulo mortis 'In the grip of death'. See *In extremis, below.*

In camera 'Behind closed doors'. Said of trials from which the public is excluded. Though *camera* means 'chamber', proceedings 'in chambers' are not proceedings *in camera*; they are discussions during which a judge may discuss matters with Counsel in his chambers (his 'office') in a less formal manner than is possible in court. (An alternative expression for *in camera* is *januis clausis*, 'closed doors': *cf. Jn* 20:26.)

In commendam Said of an ecclesiastical benefice that has been filled by a cleric who, though in receipt of the income of the benefice, will not be expected to perform the duties associated with the benefice. In former times, the appointment of clerics to livings to be held *in commendam* was a convenient means, from the Papacy's point of view, of staffing and paying for an 'international civil service'.

In custodia legis 'In the custody of the Law', said of goods seized in execution by the sheriff and thus exempt from distress for rent.

In esse In the Law, a thing is sometimes said to be *in esse* when it actually exists, and *in posse* when it might exist at some time in the future. These two phrases are characteristic of the useful, time-saving 'shorthand' expressions in Latin and Law French that abound even today.

In extenso 'At length, in full'.

In extremis 'On the point of death'. See also *In articulo mortis, above.*

In forma pauperis 'In the form of a pauper'. Formerly, if a litigant was without the means to retain the services of lawyers, he was permitted to appear *in forma pauperis*. Legal Aid considerably diminished the incidence of the phenomenon. Now that Legal Aid in England is extremely hard to obtain, there might be a recrudescence of the practice of appearing *in forma pauperis*. One of the most significant and important characteristics of the status of pauper is that one suing *in forma pauperis* was exempt from paying the other side's costs if he, the pauper, were unsuccessful.

In invitum 'Against one's wish'. See *Ab invito, above.*

In jure non remota causa, sed proxima spectatur 'In the Law, it is not the remote cause but the proximate cause that is to be regarded.' Bacon, *Max. Leg.* 1.

In limine 'On the threshold'. In the Law, said of a matter at its commencement. An objection *in limine* is a preliminary objection. If a case is brought in a court that lacks the jurisdiction to try issues of the nature propounded, the action is said to fail *in limine*.

In loco parentis 'In the place of the parent'. Said of schoolteachers and others in charge of children, implying that such persons have the same rights and duties as those whose place they take.

In medias res 'In the middle of things'. See *Semper ad eventum, below.*

In odium spoliatoris omnia praesumuntur 'All things are presumed against a wrongdoer.' 1 *Vern.* 19.

In pari causa possessor potior haberi debet 'When the rights of the parties are equal, the party in possession ought to be allowed to have the stronger claim.' *D*, 59:17:128.

In pari delicto, potior est conditio possidentis [or defendentis] 'When both parties are equally at fault, the condition of the possessor [or defendant] is the stronger.' 4 *T. R.* 564. Also *In aequali iure melior est conditio possidentis* 'With equal rights, the position of the possessor is better.' (*Plowd.* 296). *Melior est conditio possidentis, ubi neuter ius habet* 'The position of the possessor is better, when neither has the right.' Jenkins, *Cent.* 118. These maxims derive from a precept of Justinian, *Melior est conditio possidentis et rei quam actoris* 'The position of the possessor [often the defendant] is better than that of the plaintiff.' 4 *Institutes*, 180.

In pari materia 'In the same circumstances', 'With the same facts', 'in an analogous case'. An expression in the Law that permits comparisons to be made and inferences to be drawn from one case to another, though always controlled by well established canons of construction.

In partibus infidelium 'In the parts of the unbelievers'. Officials of the Catholic Church are frequently appointed bishops and archbishops of purely titular sees – sees that were once active but have been swept away by, most frequently, the invasions in the Near East and on the North African coast by Arabs professing Islam, but also by the extinction of the Eastern Empire by the Seljuk Turks and, more recently, by the Ottomans in Turkey in Europe.

In personam A term of art in the Law. An action *in personam* is one directed against a named person. 'A proceeding *in personam* is one in which relief is sought against, or punishment sought to be inflicted on, a specific person': *Mozley & Whiteley's Law Dictionary*, 10th ed Ivamy (1988). Prosecutors are in general concerned to bring charges against known persons because they are *ejusdem generis* with known and defined categories of wrongdoers: prosecutors proceed against *known* persons because they are suspected of being members of a body of wrongdoers, all of whom will be proceeded against if they are apprehended. An action *in personam* is directed specifically against a defendant precisely because he is who he is.

In posse See *in esse, above.*

In propria persona 'In his own person' – that is, in a suit or action, not represented by a proxy.

In re 'In the matter of'. A shorthand phrase used to identify an action or matter, as in 'In re *Blenkinsop* v *Carruthers*'. Used also in the title of cases concerning the winding up of estates or companies. Very occasionally some purist will use the plural form *In rebus,* 'in the *things* of such and such a one'.

In rem Literally, 'Into the thing'. Broadly, a proceeding *in rem* is one that is concerned with relief against a thing, not against a person or persons. Actions *in rem* are generally instituted to try claims to some specific property, title or status, as, for example, where it is sought to condemn a ship in the Admiralty Court, or to recover land in an action of ejectment.

In silvam ... ligna feras insanias 'It's insane to carry wood into a wood.' Horace, *Satires*, 1:10:34. In the days when children knew what coal looked like, there was a saying in England, 'You don't carry coals to Newcastle [a primary mining area].'

In statu pupillari 'In the status of a pupil'. In the capacity of a ward of court or other person under the protection or tutelage of a guardian, but nowadays more commonly intended to imply that the subject is under some type of scholastic or academic discipline. *Cf sui juris, below.*

In terrorem Minatory provisions are sometimes incorporated in instruments that are such that the law will not enforce them but are inserted by the *proferens* to cow the other party. An instance of this might be a sum mentioned in a bond as a penalty to be forfeit if the obligee fails to comply with the condition of the bond. The Court will ignore the penalty and direct that the actual damages the claimant has sustained shall be awarded in lieu of the penalty. Notwithstanding the nugatory nature of conditions *in terrorem*, they are commonly met with, a token that it is not only wolves that huff and puff.

In transitu 'In transit'.

In vitro 'In glass'. As in the phrase 'in vitro fertilization', used to mean artificial insemination. In popular usage, the term 'test-tube babies' had a long currency but seems now to be obsolete.

Incipit See *explicit, above.*

Incunabula Literally, 'swaddling-clothes' but widely used to mean early printed books, with some tendency to restrict the word to books printed before 1500. The singular, rarely met with, is *incunabulum*. The singular means only a single early book; it is not a singular meaning a swaddling-cloth.

Index expurgatorius 'Guide to purging'. An ecclesiastically compiled list of passages in books to be deleted or revised so as to render those works suitable for reading by the faithful.

Index librorum prohibitorum 'Guide to prohibited books'. A list of books forbidden by ecclesiastical authority to be read by the faithful unless specific permission has been given. Abolished in 1966.

Indicium In general, 'an indicator'. In trademark law the plural *indicia* is much used as a generic term for the characteristics that associate a product with any name or other appellation protected by registration of a trademark (such as colour and shape), and, in the elegant term of trademark attorneys, the 'get-up' that distinguishes such a product from its competitors when it is on sale.

Indignor quandoque bonus dormitat Homerus, verum operi longo fas est obrepere somnum 'I am aggrieved when sometimes good Homer nods off, but, with a long work, sleep rightly steals up on one' [or 'on it']. Horace, *Ars Poetica*, 359. Most often quoted as *Bonus dormitat Homerus,* '[Even] Homer sometimes nods.'

Indocilis pauperiam pari 'Untaught to bear poverty'. Horace, *Odes*, 1:1:18.

Infra 'Below'. Used, as in this book, to direct the reader to a point below the point at which the word *below* occurs (that is, later in the book), 'the book' always being regarded as a succession of pages and thus things that have gone are 'up', *above*, and things that are to come are 'down', *below.*

Infra dignitatem 'Beneath one's dignity'. Commonly abbreviated to 'below dig'. Professor A. J. Bliss has a sage comment on *below dignitatem*: 'The abbreviated form is now only *facet* [facetious].'

Inopem me copia fecit 'Plenty has made me poor.' Ovid, *Metamorphoses*, 3:466.

Inopi beneficium bis dat qui dat celeriter 'He gives double to the poor man who gives quickly.' Publilius Syrus, *Sententiae*, 274 in J. And A. Duff, *Minor Latin Poets* (1934). The sentiment has been adapted and adopted proverbially as *Bis dat qui cito dat* 'He gives twice who gives quickly.'

Instanter 'At once, instantly'. Originally a purely legal term, but often encountered in more general parlance.

Inter pocula 'In one's cups'; drinking. Persius (AD 34-62), *Satires*, 1:30. Common idioms are *In poculo*, (Cicero, *Cato Maior*, 46) and *Inter pocula laeti* (Virgil, Georgics, 2:383). St Jerome uses the phrase *Inter epulas et pocula*, 'amid feastings and drinking' *(Judges* 9:27), a phrase used also by, for example, Justin (M. Junianius Justinus) in his *Epitome* of Gnaeus Pompeius Trogus (*Epitome*, 12:6:6).

Innuendo 'By intimating'. A term originally in use in the Law of Slander. Where the words complained of were not overtly defamatory, Counsel would interpolate what he contended would be the inference of the average hearer.

Inter vivos 'Between living persons.' A phrase much used in history in the context of testamentary dispositions, and, in our own times, as an essential ingredient of the tax-planning vocabulary. A gift made before death but not in anticipation of imminent death was always deemed to be a valid disposition. (See *donatio mortis causa, above.*) A consequence of that was that it was not subject to the rules of inheritance, and, more recently, it did not fall under the ban of what we still talk of as 'death duties'. Modern legislation has severely restricted the right of a person freely to dispose of his assets without incurring, to the detriment of his estate, a tax obligation, and that can mean, at the worst, that seven years must elapse before the entirety of the gift becomes truly tax-free.

Interest respublicae ut sit finis litium 'It is in the interest of the common good that there should be an end to litigation.' *Hynde's Case* (1591) 4 *Co. Rep*. 70b at 71a.

Interregnum 'An interval between two reigns'. In English history, the period known euphemistically as 'the Commonwealth' (1649-60). Sometimes extended in meaning to comprise any interval.

Ipse dixit 'He himself said it'. 'An unproved assertion resting on the bare authority of some speaker; a dogmatic statement; a dictum': *OED*. From being an endorsement of a statement, the phrase has become a caustic condemnation of a statement. No school of philosophy held its founder in such high esteem as the Pythagoreans, who relied heavily on the authority of 'the Master.' Their constant cry was *ipse dixit*: 'He said it.'

Ipsissima verba 'In the very words'.

Ipso facto 'By that very fact'.

Item 'Also, likewise'. This Latin word was used very frequently in lists, to signify 'Next', and sometimes to avoid repetition: see *Ditto*, in the Italian Section. The words as the noun 'item', has become a completely naturalized English word.

Ira furor brevis est 'Anger is brief madness.' Horace, *Epistles*, 1:2:62. Cynics have adapted the maxim to read *Amor furor brevis est*, 'Love is brief madness.'

Iuppiter ex alto periuria ridet amantium 'Jupiter from on high laughs at lovers' perjuries.' Ovid, *Ars Amatoria*, 1:633.

Iure sit gloriatus marmoream se relinquere, quam latericiam accepisset 'He [Augustus, 63 BC - AD 14] could surely say he found it brick and left it marble.' Suetonius, *Lives of the Roman Emperors: Augustus*, ch 28 (said of the city of Rome).

Judex est lex loquens 'The judge is the law speaking.' Coke, *Reports*, 7:4.

Judicia sunt tamquam juris dicta, et pro veritate accipiuntur 'Judgements are as it were sayings of the law, and are received as truth.' Justinian, *Institutes*, 537.

Judicis est judicare secundum allegata et probata 'The judge must give judgement according to the things alleged and proved.' (*Dyer*, 12).

> 'Nay, Mr Attorney [Sir Edward Coke] ... [y]ou should speak *secundum allegata et probata*': Sir Walter Raleigh, 2 *State Trials*, 25.

Jus gentium (ius gentium) 'The Law of the Nations'; loosely, International Law.

Jus primae noctis See *Droit de Seigneur* in the French Section.

Juvenilia 'Young things'. Works produced by a writer, artist, etc, during his youth.

Kerygma 'Preaching'. See a reference to *kerygma* in *Criterion, above.*

Laborare est orare 'Working is praying.'

Lacrimae rerum 'The tears of things'. The cryptic sentiment of Virgil is more fully expressed as, *Sunt lacrimae rerum, et mentem mortalia tangunt,* 'There are tears in the things [of life] and [the things of] death afflict the soul': *Aeneid,* 1:462.

Lacuna See *hiatus, above.*

Lapsus calami 'A slip of the pen'.

Lapsus linguae 'A slip of the tongue'.

Lares et Penates The household gods of the Romans.

Latet anguis in herba 'There is a snake hiding in the grass.' Virgil, *Eclogues*, 3:93.

Laudant illa sed ista legunt 'They praise these [books] but read those.' Martial, *Epigrammata*, 4:49.

Laudator temporis acti See *A puero, above.*

Laus Deo semper 'Praise God always', a motto of the Society of Jesus and often abbreviated to *LDS*.

Lavabo 'I shall wash.' *Ps* 25:6 *Vg*, 25; 26:6 *AV*. Hence, a washing facility of various descriptions; now a word in some modern languages for a wash-basin.

Legatus a latere See *A latere, above.*

Lemma The head-word of an entry in a dictionary, glossary or lexicon. Plural: *lemmata* or *lemmas*. (The English word for this function – as used by Dr J. A. H. Murray in soliciting submissions from readers for the *New English Dictionary*, now the *OED* – was 'catchword'.)

> 'The pages are pleasingly uncluttered . . , with just enough contrast between the boldface lemmas and the lightface commentaries': *American Speech*, 1976, 51:1381 (1979).

Lex fori The law of the place in which a lawsuit is in progress or due to take place.

Lex non scripta 'Unwritten law'. The common law of a country, as distinct from its statute law. 'Unwritten' is of course a relic of the earliest days of law-giving: the written records of the *lex non scripta* nowadays fill *volumes.*

Lex talionis 'The law of retaliation in kind.' The saying 'An eye for an eye; a tooth for a tooth' (*Mt* 5:38) precisely epitomizes the *lex talionis.*

Lignum vitae 'Wood of life'. Species of trees, *Guiaiacum officinale and G. Sanctum,* indigenous to the West Indies, the wood of which is extremely dense and durable. The name *lignum vitae* is due to the medicinal properties the trees, through their timber and resins, were thought to possess.

Limae labor 'The work of the file [the tool]'. The final polishing of a work of literature: Horace, *Ars Poetica*, 292.

Limbo Strictly, the ablative of *limbus,* 'a region supposed to exist on the border of Hell as the abode of the just who died before Christ's coming, and of unbaptized infants': *OED*. In full, *[in] limbo patrum,* '[in] the limbo of the fathers', and *[in] limbo infantum,* '[in] the limbo of the infants'. In English, 'limbo' is the only form used and is considered exactly as though it were a nominative, etc.

Limes The boundaries or frontiers of the Roman Empire, a string of forts connected by a military road.

Linctus A medicinal syrup, from *linctum*, the supine of *lingere*, 'to lick'.

Lis 'A lawsuit'. *Lis mota*, a lawsuit in motion. *Lis pendens*, 'a lawsuit in motion.' Also in inflected use, as in *pendente lite*, 'the lawsuit pending'. (In this usage, 'pending' does not mean 'imminent' but 'in existence'.)

Lis alibi pendens An old plea to the effect that a lawsuit in the same matter and between the same parties was pending elsewhere.

Litera scripta manet 'The written word remains.' Proverbial in Antiquity.

Literati 'Men of letters'.

Literatim or **litteratim** 'Literally'.

Litis contestatio In Roman law, a stage by which both parties had stated their pleas to the praetor. By what was in essence a contract, the parties would abide by the decision of the praetor. In Scots Law a similar procedure is followed, generally known by the English word, 'litiscontestation'; it is constituted by lodging defences and any decree granted thereafter is not a decree in absence. In the Ecclesiastical Courts, one of the older meanings of the phrase has been preserved: that is, the formal entry of a suit in a court of law, the procedural means by which the suit is instituted.

Litotes Greek *λιτοτης*, 'smooth,' plain, small, meagre'. A rhetorical figure of speech or trope in which an affirmative is expressed by the negative of the contrary. The tonic accent falls on the first syllable. A useful mnemonic might be:

> Litotes? Litotes 'Not small' means 'great', 'stays not' means 'flees'.

Examples are given in the quotations.

> 'But Paul said, I am a man which am a Jew of Tarsus, a city in Cilicia, a citizen of no mean city: and, I beseech thee, suffer me to speak unto the people': *Acts* 21:39. 'And when neither sun nor stars in many days appeared, and no small tempest lay on us, all hope that we should be saved was then taken away': *Acts* 27:20.

Loco citato 'In the place cited', a scholarly way of referring the reader to the last place at which a given authority was cited in full. Abbreviated to *loc cit*. Cf *opere citato*, *below*.

Locum tenens 'Place holding.' The generic name for one who stands in for another. Nowadays almost exclusively restricted to medical practitioners who stand in for other medical practitioners while the latter are sick, on holiday or otherwise absent.

Locus 'A place'. For technical senses used in mathematics, the reader is referred to specialist works. In the Law, the *locus in quo* is 'the scene of the crime', where it happened, etc.

Locus classicus 'The classical place', otherwise the perfect place at which to find an example of the subject under consideration. For example, for Christians, the scriptural quotation under *Lex talionis, above*, is the *locus classicus* of the concept.

Locus communis The habitual reference-point for a given reference, allusion, authority, etc. The reference of St Paul to himself as 'a citizen of no mean city' (*cf litotes, above*) is both a *locus classicus* and a *locus communis*.

Locus poenitentiae 'A place of repentance'. In Law, a provision in an agreement whereby a party might in specified circumstances reconsider his obligation. *Cf.* also *Heb 12:17.*

Locus standi 'A place for standing'. A term in the Law to denote a person's right to litigate. Some interest, albeit very generously interpreted today, must be present before a prospective litigant is permitted to trouble his peers. Often abbreviated to *locus*, and frequently substituted by the noun 'standing'.

Lucus a non lucendo 'A copse because it does not light up', or 'because there is no light there.' This extremely useful locution, sometimes ascribed to Quintilian, comes from the profoundly learned Maurus Servius Honoratus, who flourished at the end of the fourth century. He ridicules the amateur etymologizers who pronounce on the derivation of words without furnishing themselves in advance with any pretense of scholarship. In particular, he derides those who invent etymologies by contradiction, '*sicut lucus a non lucendo, bellum a nulla re bella*', 'as, for instance, "a wooded grove because there is no light in it", and "war because it is not a beautiful thing."'(In fact, an earlier form of *lux, lucis* was *lucus*. One of the salient features of the development of the Romance languages was the gradual elimination of misleading homophones.)

Dr E. C. Brewer, in his *Dictionary of Phrase and Fable* (1870), or his continuators, include among those words attracting a mistaken etymology the word *ludus,* 'a primary or elementary school'. They doubt its deriving from *ludere*, 'to play', but that seems an unjustified stricture. Our modern word 'play-school' surely gives the lie to *Brewer's* condemnation.

It is fair to say that the editors of *Brewer* have drastically cut down the number of etymologies that fall under this ban. In the edition of Brewer's of 1894 there were no fewer than 17 instances of ostensibly bogus derivations. Now (1989) there are only three.

Though we are grateful to authorities that draw our attention to fictitious etymologies, we have to keep an open mind on the subject. If we keep an open and vigilant mind as to etymologies, we might one day stumble across the etymology of the common French verb *aller*, for which, astonishingly, the scholars have been unable, so far, to discover any origin.

Lupum auribus tenere 'To hold a wolf by the ears'. Varro, *De Lingua Latina,* 7:21:4; Suetonius, *Lives of the Roman Emperors*: *Tiberius*, 26). As graphic and popular as our 'To have a tiger by the tail'.

Lupus in fabula 'The wolf in the tale'. Cicero's way of saying, 'Talk of the Devil'. The phrase denotes a person who suddenly appears as he is being spoken of: *Ad Atticum* 13:33.

Lusisti satis, edisti satis atque bibisti: / Tempus abire tibi est 'You have played enough; you have eaten and drunk enough. Now it is time for you to depart.' Horace, *Epistles*, 2:2:214.

Lustrum 'A period of five years'. So called because, every five years, the Romans performed an expiatory sacrifice or a purificatory rite (*e.g.* by washing with water) so as to purify a place or thing.

Lusus naturae 'A joke of nature'. A freak of nature.

> 'The wild turkey is invariably black: although it is possible that by some *lusus naturæ*, there may be white': Henry M.

Brackeridge, *Journal of a Voyage up the Missouri*, p 46 (1816).

Macron 'Long'. The horizontal bar placed over a vowel to signify that its quantity is long, as with ō. The sign for a short vowel is a *micron*, as with ŏ.

Macte nova virtute, puer, sic itur ad astra 'Good for you and your young courage, boy – the way to the stars!' Virgil, *Aeneid*, 9:641.

Magisterium 'The teaching authority of the Church'.

Magna Carta 'The Great Charter', the great charter of English liberties sealed by King John at Runnymede in 1215. The Mediaeval spelling is commonly *Charta.*

Magna est veritas at praevalebit 'Truth is great and shall prevail.' 'Magna veritas et praevalet': 'Great [is] truth and it prevails': 3 *Ezras*, 4:41.

Mandamus 'We command'. See *sub judice, below.*

Magnas inter opes inops 'A pauper in the midst of wealth. 'Horace, *Odes*, 3:16:28.

Magnificat *Magnificat animam meam Dominum*, 'My soul doth magnify the Lord'; *Lk* 1:46. The prayer so named: specifically, when set to music.

Magnum opus: 'Great work'.

Mala fide 'Bad faith'.

Manes 'The spirits of the departed'.

Mansuetae naturae See *ferae naturae, above.*

Manus manum lavat 'One hand washes another.' Proverbial. *Cf. Asinus asinum fricat.*

Mare clausum 'A closed sea': a sea closed to international navigation by action of some riparian power. Hugo Grotius (1583-1645) wrote a powerful argument against such practices, *Mare Liberum*, but acquiesced in embargoes, blockades and other restraints of trade if they benefited his own trading nation, the United Provinces.

Mare nostrum 'Our sea', the Roman name for the Mediterranean. For a note of recent usage of the term, see *Fascism* in the Italian Section.

Marginalia 'Margin [notes]'. The generic plural for the notes frequently written in the margins of ancient and other manuscripts. The fairly rare singular is *marginalium.*

Mater familias See *pater familias.*

Materia medica 'The medical materials'. The entire range of medical knowledge to date.

Maxima debetur puero reverentia 'The greatest reverence is due to a child.' Juvenal's penetrating insight into human conduct ('behaviour'): *Satires*, 5:14:47. One must at all cost avoid shocking a child with grossness or indecency.

Mea culpa 'Through my fault'. The operative part of the *Confiteor*, 'I confess', as embodied in the Tridentine Mass: *Mea culpa, mea culpa, mea maxima culpa*, 'Through my fault, through my fault, through my most grievous fault'. Nowadays often used in general for an admission of fault.

Medium 'A means.' The fundamental notion behind the Latin word is the occupation of a position between two or more *datum* points (*cf. datum, above*). Hence the expression 'the media of communication', which has been worn down to 'the media', without more. The word 'media' is now very frequently taken to be a singular. The matter is aggravated by the presence in the language of the word 'medium', meaning one who professes to be an intermediary between this sublunary world and some supposed spirit world. The plural of that sort of medium is 'mediums'.

Megalomania 'Folly of greatness', illusions of grandeur. From the Greek *μεγαλομανια*, signifying precisely that.

Medio tutissimus ibis 'Thou wilt go safest by the middle way.' Ovid, *Metamorphoses*, 2:137.

Mediocribus esse poetis / Non homines, non di, non concessere columnae 'Nor men nor gods nor bookstalls allow poets to be mediocre'. Horace, *Ars Poetica*, 372.

Meiosis 'Lessening'. A rhetorical figure of speech or trope that uses a diminishing of the importance, stature, relevance, etc, of a subject in order to enhance the effect a statement so modified has on the listener or the reader. Instances of *meiosis* abound in English! 'Rather jolly!' means 'Very jolly!' 'Pretty awful!' means 'Really awful'. Even the word 'awful' in these examples is an instance of *meiosis* 'in reverse', for the subjects are only very rarely truly 'awe-inspiring' or 'awesome'. The trope *litotes* (*q.v., above*) is a species of this protean figure of speech. Fuller, below, speaks oceans about the impact of these figures of speech.

> 'Some condemne Rhetorick as the mother of lies, speaking more than the truth in Hyperboles, lesse in her Miosis,' T. Fuller, *Holy State*, 2:7:73 (1642).

Memento mori 'Remember death.' A maxim of general acceptance, but particularly applied to the depiction of a skull as a reminder of death. A skull was often seen sculpted into the lintel of the porch at the entrance to a graveyard, as with Pepys's graveyard at All Hallows, Hart Street, in London.

Memorabilia 'Memorable things'. A word very popular in present-day society as a catch-all word for knick-knacks that evoke reminiscences of former days. Owing no doubt to the influence of balladeers' singing ditties such as César Franck's *Panis Angelicus,* the pronunciation 'memorabeelia' (in the International Phonetic Association system, /memәra'biːlia/) has gained currency.

Mens rea 'Guilty mind'. A complex concept in the Law. It fundamentally means one of the elements that must be proved if someone who has ostensibly committed a crime is to be convicted. It must be shown that he *intended* to commit what constitutes the *essence* of that crime. However, it is an over-simplification to assert that *mens rea* means the *intention* to commit the crime, since the accused person might well not know what constitutes the *essence* of that crime. In any event, as a matter of proof, a man's intention can remain locked up in his bosom until the end of time. Though the matter is still, mercifully, open to the widest discussion, much useful guidance can be gleaned from the Law Reports, as, for instance, from *DPP v Smith.* The test that emerged from that decision (ultimately of the House of Lords) was that a man was taken to foresee and intend the natural and probable consequences of his acts. An extremely strong House of Lords, comprising Lord Denning, before he 'moved downstairs' to become Master of the Rolls, gave a good account of itself, an account that has attracted an implacable barrage of dissent from the Academy but has, it seems, withstood that attack. One might justifiably say, 'The jury is out.'

Mens sana in corpore sano 'A healthy mind in a healthy body.' Once again, Juvenal says it all, in *Satires* 4:10:536.

Metempsychosis 'The transmigration of souls'.

Metri causa 'Because of the metre.' Used by scholars to explain that an emendation has been made so as to correct a fault in the metre of verse, or that the original author has departed from a rule so as to preserve the metre of his verse.

Metri gratia 'For the sake of the metre.' A comment often made to explain an aberration from the normal or expected syntax of a passage of verse, indicating that a quantity has been altered or a syllable suppressed or elided in order to permit the verse to conform in other respects to the norms of versification.

Micron See *macron, above.*

Mimesis Greek μιμησις, 'imitation.' Sometimes the word means a literal mimicking of a person. At other times it is the name of a rhetorical trope that relies on mimicking in a figurative sense. So, for example, in a direct, representational sense, a young character might, in a drama, mimic an old person, or a forthright, determinate character might imitate an indecisive, hesitant character, by deploying and perhaps exaggerating the major characteristics of the other *persona*. In rhetoric, the word applies to much less obvious instances of mimicry, sometimes almost indiscernible instances.

A mnemonic for *mimesis* might be:

> *Mimesis* is as though to say? The ass's brazen bray.

Minutia 'A little thing'. The plural *minitiae* is much more common than the singular. It means the fiddling little bits that busy people ought to ignore – but there is an equal and opposite caution implicit in the warning that 'The devil is in the detail'.

Misce stultitiam consiliis brevem: / Dulce est desipere in loco 'Mingle some brief folly with thy wisdom. To play the fool in due place is sweet'. Horace, *Odes*, 4:12:27.

Multa fero, ut placem genus irritabile vatum 'I put up with much, that I might pacify the touchy tribe of poets.' Horace, *Epistles*, 2:2:102.

Mirabile dictu 'Wonderful to say!' An exclamation immortalized by Virgil, *Georgics*, 2:20.

Miserere *Miserere me Deus secundum misericordiam tuam*, 'Have pity on me, O God, according to thy mercy' : *Ps* 50:3 *Vg.*, *AV* 51:3. The polyphonic setting of this psalm by Gregorio Allegri (1582-1652) was *de industria* never published but, on the contrary, was restricted to performance in the Sistine Chapel every Holy Week. On one occasion, W. A. Mozart was a member of the congregation. After the service, he transcribed from memory the entire psalm, and it is generally his recension that we hear nowadays.

Modicum 'A small amount'. A modest amount.

Modulus A word meaning variously, by origin, a standard unit of measurement, a rhythmic measure, a pipe for controlling flow of water, etc. In present-day usage, this omnifunctional word has acquired a number of *crucial* meanings. No lexicographer ought ever to tussle with the actual users of words if those users can give an account of their stewardship. Only one instance of such an occasion needs to be cited, as a model exemplar of how consummately the *users* of words can justify the existence of those words. A prime example of that is the term of art on which the entire conspectus of modern industry depends – Young's Modulus of Elasticity. See the quotation below for some indication of what the layman ought to be about in technical terms. They are emphatically *not* being introduced to bamboozle the lay public.

> 'Young's modulus [for Thomas Young, 1773-1829], [a] number representing (in pounds per square inch or dynes per square centimeter) the ratio of stress to strain for a wire or bar of a given substance. According to Hooke's law the strain is proportional to stress, and therefore the ratio of the two is a constant that is commonly used to indicate the elasticity of the substance. Young's modulus is the elastic modulus for tension, or tensile stress, and is the force per unit cross section of the material divided by the fractional increase in length resulting from the stretching of a standard rod or wire of the material.'

Modus operandi and **Modus vivendi** 'Way of working' and 'Way of living'.

Monstrum horrendum, informe, ingens, cui lumen ademptum 'A monster horrendous, shapeless, huge, deprived of sight.' Virgil, *Aeneid*, 3:658. See *Chommoda dicebat, above.*

Monumentum aere perennius See *exegi monumentum, above.*

Moratorium 'Delay'. A legal authorization to suspend payment for a certain time; the period of such a postponement.

Mores The manner and customs of a period or place.

Morituri te salutant 'Those about to die salute thee.' The traditional greeting to the Emperor given by the gladiators. Suetonius, *Lives of the Emperors: Divus Claudius*, 21.

Motu proprio 'Of [one's] own motion'; of one's own wish. Used as a quasi-noun for messages from the Pope to the clergy.

Mula docet muleculam A *sgraffito* found at Pompeii. The word *mulecula* was not in any dictionary at that time. G. B. De Rossi (1822-94) thought the word was a barbarous word for a fly. Subsequent palaeographic work coincidentally established that the word was demotic Latin for a young mule. Thus, the *sgraffito* meant 'The [old] mule teaches the young.'

Multa renescentur quae iam cecidere, cadentque / Quae nunc sunt in honore vocabula, si volet usus / Quem penes arbitrium est et ius et norma loquendi 'Many terms shall be reborn that are now dead, and others shall fall that are now held in high esteem if usage so wills it – usage, to which belongs the final judgement as to what is right and proper speech.' Horace, *Ars Poetica*, 70. Elsewhere in *Ars Poetica* Horace makes out an excellent case for the judicious invention of new words. He stresses that one should look to Greek for the ingredients. His intention was of course to restrict the manufacture of new words so that only those deriving from respectable Greek roots would be admitted, but his words are nonetheless astonishingly prescient, as a glance at the scientific vocabulary of the last two hundred years will amply demonstrate.

Multi quidem facilius se abstinent ut non utantur, quam temperent ut bene utantur

'To many it is easier to be abstinent than to be temperate.' St Augustine, *On the Good of Marriage*, 21. Boswell alludes to this characteristic in Dr Johnson.

Mutatis mutandis 'Changing those things that need to be changed.' *Cf exceptis excipiendis, above.*

Nam risu inepto res ineptior nulla est 'Than a silly laugh there is noting sillier.' Catullus, *Carmina*, 39.

Nam tua res agitur, paries cum proximus ardet 'When your neighbour's wall is on fire, it becomes your business'. Horace, *Epistles*, 1:18:84.

Natura non facit saltum 'Nature does not make a leap.' Nature works gradually. Proverbial.

Naturam expellas furca, tamen usque recurret 'Thou mayest drive Nature out with a pitchfork, yet for all that she will still find her way back.' Horace, *Epistles*, 1:10:24.

Ne plus ultra 'No more beyond'. The utmost limit, normally of a search for perfection.

Ne varietur 'Not to be varied'. Said of what is intended to be the final version of a document.

Negatio destruit negationem, et ambo faciunt affirmativum 'A negative destroys a negative, and both make an affirmative.' A maxim that needs careful handling. In Latin and in French Law, Lord Coke himself would have admitted many ostensible double negatives.

Neminem oportet esse sapientiorem legibus 'No-one ought to be wiser than the laws.' *Co. Litt.*, 97b.

Nemesis Greek *Νεμεσις*. The goddess of vengeance.

Nemine contradicente 'No-one dissenting.' Abbreviated to *nem. con.*

Nemo aliquam partem recte intelligere potest antequam totum perlegit 'No-one can rightly understand a part until he has read the whole.' Coke, 3 *Rep* 59.

Nemo dat quod non habet 'No-one gives what he does not have': *Jenk. Cent* 250. In the Law: no-one gives a better title (to, for example, land) than he himself has.

Nemo debet bis vexari, si constat curiae quod sit pro una et eadem causa 'No one ought to be twice harassed, if it is demonstrated to the court that it is for one and the same cause.' Coke, 5 *Rep*, 61.

Nemo debet bis puniri pro uno delicto 'No-one ought to be twice punished for the same offence.' Coke, 4 *Rep*, 43.

Nemo debet esse judex in propria causa 'No-one ought to be judge in his own case.' Coke, 13 *Rep*. 113.

Nemo me impune lacessit 'No-one provokes me with impunity.' Motto of the Crown of Scotland and of all Scotch regiments.

Nemo repente venit turpissimus 'No-one suddenly became extremely wicked.' Juvenal, *Satires*, 2:83.

Nec audiendi qui solent dicere, Vox populi, vox Dei, quum tumultuositas vulgi semper insaniae proxima sit 'They ought not to be listened to who are accustomed to saying "The voice of the people, the voice of God", since the tumults of the crowd are always very close to madness.' Alcuin of York (*c*735-804), Letter 164 in *Works*, vol 1, p 438 (1863).

Nihil ad rem 'Nothing to the point'. Said in order to point out an irrelevance.

Nihil obstat See *imprimatur, above.*

Nil desperandum Teucro duce et auspice Teucro 'With Teucer as leader and under Teucer's star, never despair'. Horace, *Odes*, 1:7:27.

Nil habet infelix paupertas durius in se / Quam quod ridiculos homines facit 'Nothing in poverty is more grievous than this: that it makes men ridiculous.' Juvenal, *Satires*, 3:152.

Nisi 'Unless'.

Nolens volens 'Willy-nilly'.

Noli me tangere 'Do not touch me'. Words used by Christ to St Mary Magdalene (*Jn* 20:17 *Vg*). Used as a generic name for paintings depicting Christ appearing to St Mary Magdalene at the Sepulchre.

Nolle prosequi A plea by a prosecutor that he is 'unwilling to proceed'; the case against the defendant is thus dismissed.

Nolo episcopari 'I do not wish to be a bishop.' The formula by which a bishopric is declined. Sometimes used in relation to other refusals, and sometimes used to suggest false modesty. (It is said that a bishop refuses twice and, at the third request, he modestly acquiesces.)

Non amo te, Sabidi, nec possum dicere quare: / Hoc tantum possum dire, non amo te 'I do not love thee, Sabidus, but cannot tell thee why: as much as I can say is, I do not love thee.' Martial, *Epigrammata*, 1:32. Dr John Fell (1625-86) was Dean of Christ Church, Oxford from 1660 (later, 1676, Bishop of Oxford). Thomas Brown (1663-1704), while an undergraduate at Christ Church, wrote the following clever parody on Martial:

I do not love thee, Dr Fell. The reason why I cannot tell. But this I know and know full well, I do not love thee, Dr Fell.

Non Angli sed Angeli 'Not Angles but Angels'.

> *Responsum est, quod Angle vocarentur. At ille: Bene, inquit; nam et angelicam habent faciem, et tales angelorum in caelis decet esse coheredes.* 'They answered that they were called Angles. "It is well", he said, 'for they have the faces of angels and such should be the co-heirs of the angels of heaven.' Gregory the Great (AD 540-604) on seeing young Angles on sale as slaves at Rome. Bede's *Ecclesiastical History*, 2:1.

Non compos mentis See *Compos mentis, above.*

Non est vivere, sed valere vita est 'Life is not just living but being in good health.' Martial, *Epigrammata*, 5:20.

Non fumum ex fulgore, sed ex fuma dare lucem cogitat 'He thinks, instead of flame producing smoke, that smoke might produce light.' Horace, *Ars Poetica*, 143. The subject is the poetaster in *Semper ad eventum, below,* who is also the subject of Horace's withering scorn in *Parturient montes, below.* Horace's meaning is no doubt that this unskilled writer whom he castigates has chosen, instead of following the natural order whereby flame produces smoke, to use smoke, figuratively, to conceal the growth of his narrative so that he might present his event with a factitious element of surprise.

Non nobis Domine 'Not unto us, O Lord' (*Ps* 113:9 *Vg*). The opening words of this verse are sometimes sung as a glee or part-song on festive occasions.

Non omnis moriar 'I shall not altogether die.' Horace, *Odes*, 3:30:6. See *Exegi monumentum, above.*

Non placet 'It does not please me.' A formula for expressing dissent in ecclesiastical and academic meetings: a 'No' vote in those circumstances.

Non sequitur 'It does not follow.' Frequently used as a noun.

Nondum amabam, et amare amabam ...querebam quid amarem, amans amare 'I loved not yet, yet I loved to love ... I sought that which I might love, loving to love.' St Augustine, *Confessions*, 3:1. The sheer and utter openness of this sentiment might lead us to miss the rhetorical force of his repetition. The Ancients are said to have disliked 'jingles'. That inveterate Classicist Addison said, 'Milton ... often affects a kind of Jingle in his Words, as in the following Passages ... "And brought into the World a World of Woe."' The innate genius of *Latinitas*, however, seems to make much use of repetition, and one must add that the Greek rhetoricians, too, relied on aspects of repetition, to the extent that they bequeathed an entire vocabulary to that end: *anadiplosis, anaphora, antimetabole, antistnophe*, and *polyptoton*, all of which schemes depend on repetition of one variety or another. And alliteration and assonance are species of jingle.

Can anything beat that product of one who is usually credited with being dismissive of the Romans' own 'native wood-notes wild', Ennius? He wrote: *O Tite tute Tati tibi tanta tyranne tulisti*! Is that not the classic instance in Latin of the rhetorical vice the Greeks called *Ομοιοπροφερον?* A close runner-up is again from Ennius: *At tuba terribile sonitu taratantara dixit.*

Nosce teipsum See *Gnothi seauton, above.*

Nota bene 'Note well'. Abbreviated to *n.b.*

Nous See a reference to this word in *Criterion, above.*

Nulla fere causa est, in qua non femina litem moverit 'There is hardly a case in which femininity did not promote it.' Juvenal, *Satires*, 6:242.

Nulla injuria est, quae in volentem fiat 'No injustice is done to someone who wants that thing done.' Ulpian (d. AD 228), *Corpus Juris Civilis* Digests, 47:10:1.

Nulli secundus 'Second to none'.

Nullum quod tetigit non ornavit 'Nothing that he touched he did not adorn.' Dr Johnson's epitaph on Oliver Goldsmith (1728-74): Boswell, *Life*, 22 June 1776.

Nullumst iam dictum quod non dictum sit prius 'Nothing now said has not been said before.' Terence, *Eunuchus*, Prologue, 1:41. Quoted as *Nihil dictum quod non prius dictum* in Lord Chesterfield's letter to his son.

Nunc est bibendum, nunc pede libero / Pulsanda tellus 'Now is the time for drinking, now the time to beat the earth with unfettered foot.' Horace, *Odes*, 1:37:1.

Numerus clausus 'Closed number'. 'A fixed (maximum) number of entrants admissible to an academic institution. Also: a restricted number of educational places allocated to a particular (esp. racial or ethnic) group': *OED*.

Nunc dimittis 'Now thou dost dismiss'. The first words of the Song of Simeon (*Lk* 2:29 *Vg.*). The Latin words are, as with the *Magnificat,* the normal way of referring to these two passages from Sacred Scripture when they are said or sung in English during Divine Service.

Nux vomica 'Emetic nut'. The seed of an Eastern plant from which strychnine is obtained.

O altitudo! An exclamation of exultation, religious or other. See *O altitudo divitiarum sapientiae et scientiae Dei,* 'O the depths of the riches of the wisdom and knowledge of God!'*: Rom* 11:33 (*Vg.*).

O mihi praeteritos referat si Iuppiter annos 'O, that Jupiter might give me back my past years!' Virgil, *Aeneid,* 8:560.

O sancta simplicitas! 'O holy simplicity!' 'John Huss c 1372-1415. Bohemian preacher and reformer. At the stake, seeing an aged peasant bringing a bundle of twigs to throw on the pile; in J. W. Zincgref and J. L. Weidner, *Apophthegmata* (Amsterdam, 1653) pt 3, p 383': *Oxford Dictionary of Quotations,* 4th edn, p 357/1, 3 (1992). *Cf Beata simplicitas!, above.*

O imitatores, servum pecus 'O imitators, ye slavish herd!' Horace, *Epistles,* 1:19:19.

O si sic omnes! O si sic omnia! 'Oh, if only all things and all people [had been or were to be so]!' A proverbial wish for perfection.

O tempora, o mores! 'Oh, the times! Oh, the manners!' Cicero, *In Catilinam* 1:1:2.

Obelus Greek *οβελος*, 'a roasting spit'. The typographic symbol †, otherwise known as the 'dagger', used in old-fashioned footnoting schemes and also to signalize in a text what is probably a spurious or suspect reading, and also to indicate that a person is now dead. Sometimes anglicized as 'obelisk', from the Greek diminutive.

Obiit 'He or she died', followed by a date. Abbreviated to *ob.*

Obiter dictum 'A remark made in passing.' Said of a comment thrown into a discussion or conversation that is not a necessary ingredient of that discussion or conversation. 'A throw-away line.' In the Law, observations or comments made by the Court during the proceedings that are not intended to be part of the formal judgement of the Court are called *obiter dicta,* and are accorded the respect the reputation of the judge warrants. Many penetrating apperceptions of the Law have been supplied by *obiter dicta* over the years. *Cf. Dictum, above.*

Obscurata diu populo bonus eruet atque / Proferet in lucem speciosa vocabula rerum, / Quae priscis memorata Catonibus atque Cethegis / Nunc situs informis premit et deserta vetustas 'Terms long lost in darkness the good poet will unearth for the people's use and bring into the light – picturesque terms which, though once spoken by a Cato and a Cathegus of old, now lie low through unseemly neglect and dreary age.' Horace, *Epistles,* 2:2:114: tr H. T. Fairclough, *Loeb Classical Library.*

Occidit miseros crambe repetita magistros 'Warmed up cabbage kills off the poor master.' Juvenal, *Satires,* 7:154.

Oderint dum metuant 'Let them hate, so long as they fear': quoted by Cicero, *Philippic,* 1:14 and elsewhere, and by Suetonius, *Lives, Divus Caligula,* 30.

Odi profanum vulgus et arceo; / Favete linguis; carmina non prius / Audita Musarum sacerdos / Virginibus puerisque

canto 'I hate the uninitiated crowd and keep them at bay. Kindly listen! I, the Muses' priest, sing for girls and boys songs never heard before'. Horace, *Odes*, 3:1:1.

Oedema Greek *οιδημα*, 'dropsy'. A medical term for the localized or generalized accumulation of excessive fluid in tissues or body cavities. Frequently used with a distinguishing word indicating the site, nature, etc, of the *oedema* (*e.g.*, ankle *oedema*, for 'swollen ankles').

Olim quos volpes aegroto cauta leoni / Respondit referam: 'Quia me vestigia terrent, / Omnia te adversum spectantia, nulla retorsum' 'Once a wary fox made answer to a sick lion: "[I decline your invitation to enter your den] because all the footprints are directed inwards, and none back again"'. Horace, *Epistles* 1:1:73.

Omne ignotum pro magnifico 'Everything about what is unknown is taken to be marvellous': Tacitus, *Agricola*, 30.

Omnia praesumuntur rite et solennitur esse acta. 'Everything is presumed to have been done properly and solemnly.' The maxim is often prefixed by, *Ex diuturnitate temporis,* 'After a lapse of time', the entire maxim implying that the Law will not allow obligations entered into years before and so far undisturbed to be impugned by allegations of some irregularity. The Law does not prohibit *ex post facto* correction of error but will not encourage what it suspects might be the common-law offence of barratry, 'The offence of habitually exciting quarrels, or moving or maintaining law-suits; vexatious persistence in, or incitement to, litigation.' Traditionally, the Law has been particularly on guard against those who have made a living from searching out weaknesses in persons' titles to land.

Omnia Romae / Cum pretio Everything at Rome / at a price. Juvenal, *Satires*, No 3:183.

Omnium consensu, capax imperii nisi imperasset 'Everyone thought him [Galba] capable of being emperor until he tried being emperor': Tacitus, *Histories*, 1:49.

Onomatopoeia Greek *ονοματοποα*, 'name-making'. 'The formation of a word from a sound associated with the thing or action being named; the formation of words imitative of sounds': *OED*. H. W. Fowler, *op. cit,* quotes 'babble', 'cuckoo' and 'croak' as probable instances of this phenomenon. Dr J. A. H. Murray (Sir James Murray, 1837-1915) suggested a group of words derived from *echo* so as to particularize this phenomenon, but only 'echoic', for the awkward 'onomatopoeiic' and the very slightly misleading 'onomatopoetic', seems to have caught on.

Onus probandi 'The burden of proof'. He who alleges must prove his allegation. The claimant has the duty of proving his case: the defendant has no initial obligation to do anything.

Opaco / Pelion imposuisse Olympo 'To pile Pelion on umbrageous Olympus'. Horace, *Odes*, 3:4:52. See *Ter sunt conati, below.*

Opere citato 'In the work [already] cited'. Abbreviated to *op. cit. Cf loco citato, above.*

Opus Dei 'God's work.' Primarily, a way of describing the recitation of the Divine Offices, seen as the most important part of the monastic life. Secondarily, the name of a politico-religious movement operating in Spain and elsewhere.

Opus operans See *ex opera operato, above.*

Orandum est ut sit mens sana in corpore sano 'One's prayer must be for a sound mind in a sound body.' Juvenal, *Satires*, 10:356.

Oratio obliqua 'Reported speech', as in 'The speaker said he was honoured to be invited.'

Oratio recta 'Quoted speech', as in 'The speaker said, "I am honoured to be invited"'.

Otium cum dignitatem 'Ease with dignity'. Cicero's phrase for an honourable retirement: *Pro Sestio* 45:98.

Pabulum 'Food, fodder, fuel for fire, food for thought'. The last Classical Latin meaning above, 'food for thought', is the only surviving application, and, on the whole, in a pejorative sense. The *OED* suggests that the word has acquired its somewhat derogatory sense from its similarity to the registered trademark of an American breakfast-food, Pablum, which seems to have the reputation of being bland. No doubt the meaning of the word has been influenced, also, by 'pap', 'Semi-liquid food, such as that considered suitable for babies or invalids, usually made from bread, meal, etc., moistened with water or milk; bland soft or moist food', and 'Something easily acquired or understood but lacking in value or substance; light intellectual or spiritual fare (in early use occas. in neutral contexts; later almost always *depreciative*. Now usually: *spec.* trivial or unsophisticated reading matter, etc.; undemanding (esp. commercial) entertainment.': both *OED*).

Pallida Mors aequo pulsat pede pauperum tabernas / Regumque turris 'Pale death, with impartial step, knocks at the huts of the poor and the towers of kings.' Horace, *Odes*, 1:4:13.

Pallium Originally a rectangular cloak favoured by Greek philosophers and adopted to some extent by the Romans. The pallium was preferred by Christians to the toga. In more recent times, the pallium has come to mean a woollen collar-like vestment bestowed by the Pope on archbishops as an emblem of their office. It is represented in heraldry by the charge resembling the letter *Y*.

Palmam qui meruit ferat. 'Let him who merits the palm wear it.' Proverbial in antiquity.

Pendente lite This phrase does not mean 'Pending the trial'. It means 'while the trial is taking place', or, in the more formal language of the Law, 'during the pendency of the trial'.

Panem et circenses From Juvenal's *Duas tantum res anxious optat / Panem et circenses* 'Two things only he anxiously wishes for, bread and circuses.' *Satires*, 10: 80. Juvenal speaks of the typical Roman as being one who is content with his ruler provided his ruler can ensure a continuous supply of bread and a continuous display of public entertainments.

Paraphernalia Strictly, the possessions of a wife over which, under Roman law, the husband had no control unless by the wife's consent. The word came into Latin from the Greek *παραφερνα*, 'outside the dowry'. The development of the word, so that it now means to most people only 'bits and pieces' is indeed a strange one.

Pares cum paribus facillime congregantur 'Like with like easily mix.' Birds of a feather flock together.

Pari passu 'In step'. Said of, for example, shares in a limited company that, though they may be differently denominated, yet they rank equally as to voting rights.

Parturient montes, nascetur ridiculus mus 'Mountains will be in labour, and give birth to a ridiculous mouse.' Horace, *Ars Poetica*, 139. The sentiment approximates to, 'Much ado about nothing'.

Passer mortuus est meae puellae / Passer, deliciae meae puellae 'My lady's sparrow has passed away. The sparrow, that was the delight of my lady.' Catullus, *Carmina*, 3.

Pater familias 'The father of the family'. *Familias* is an old genitive.

Pater noster 'Our Father.' The first words of the Lord's Prayer.

Passim 'Here and there.' Used in scholarly publications to indicate that a given word, expression, topic, etc, occurs in several or numerous places in the work in question.

Peccavi 'I have sinned.' Sometimes used as a light-hearted admission of guilt.

In a singularly odd combination of factors, one of the best puns in circulation revolves round this word *peccavi.* Catherine Winkworth (1827-78), known only for her hymn-writing, is credited with the pun. The Oxford *Dictionary of Quotations* reads as follows:

> *Peccavi* – I have Sindh. Of Sir Charles Napier's conquest of Sindh, 1843 (*peccavi* I have Sindh); printed in *Punch*, vol 6, p. 209 (18 May 1844,) supposedly sent by Napier to Lord Ellenborough.

There is also another story, about the capture of Oudh in which a message *Vovi,* ('I have vowed') is reputed to have been sent – but that's another story.

Pecuniam non olet 'Money doesn't stink.' Traditional summary of Suetonius, *Lives of the Caesars*, 'Vespasian', 23:3.

> Vespasian replying to Titus's objection to his tax on public lavatories; holding a coin to Titus's nose and being told it didn't smell, he replied, *Atque e lotio est* 'Yes, that's made from urine.' *ODQ* (1992).

Per ardua ad astra 'Through struggle to the stars.' The motto of the Royal Air Force.

Per capita Strictly, the phrase means 'by heads' – that is, in the plural – but it is almost always used as though it meant 'per head'. The phrase 'per caput' hardly exists in English speech and writing.

Per contra 'On the other hand'; said in, *e.g.*, putting the opposite side of an argument, in contrast to the side already put. It does not mean 'on the contrary'.

Per diem 'Per day', said of fee-earning.

Per impossible A phrase used in a species of argument that depends on the supposition that something impossible can be assumed possible: 'Supposing it were possible, but it is not, then the following would be the consequence ...'. (There are five syllables in *impossibile.*)

Per incuriam 'Through lack of care.' A phrase used in the Law to signify that an error has been made in, for example, a judgement. Courts often give decisions in extempore judgements ('unreserved' judgements); the convention whereby errors are gently treated is a wholesome one. (If a judgement of a court comprising more than one judge is given on behalf of all the judges trying the case, then it is said to be made *per Curiam*, which is not the opposite of *per incuriam.* The phrase *per Curiam* means 'by the Court'.)

Per mensem 'Per month'.

Per procurationem In effect, though not strictly true, the phrase or its much more common abbreviation *per pro.*, is equivalent to 'for and on behalf of,' which is a better expression if the user is able to make a choice. Those to whom the phrase *per procurationem* is legally important will know the ramifications of the Law of Agency.

Per saltum 'By a leap'. See *Natura non facit saltum, above.*

Per se 'Of or in itself'.

Periphrasis Greek *πειφρασις*, 'speaking periphrastically.' A rhetorical figure of speech or trope in which a notion is expressed in several words rather than few; circumlocution. The tonic accent falls on the second syllable. A useful mnemonic might be:

> Periphrasis? Periphrasis Says 'Taste my lips' instead of 'Kiss.'

Peritus in arte 'Skilled in the art.' The preferred neo-Latin way of expressing the notion of 'expert'. *Cf experto crede, above.*

Persona designata An individual as distinct from or opposed to a member of a class.

Persona non grata A term primarily confined to diplomatic usage. It denotes a person whose presence in the country in which he is *en poste* is or has become unacceptable to the host country. His ambassador would then withdraw him and he would return to his own country. The expression *persona grata*, once common, has virtually disappeared.

Petitio principii A phrase in logic that equates to 'begging the question', but, since that English phrase is very frequently misused, it might be well to explain that 'to beg the question' does not mean 'to raise the question' but 'to ask or beg your opponent to grant your contention' – to concede your point, unargued.

Pietas 'Dutiful affection'. The sense of the Latin word is better conveyed by its use in 'filial piety' than in the modern English acceptation of 'piety', but *pietas* is also used in neo-Latin for 'piety' in the religious sense. See the next entry.

Pii auribus offensis 'Offensive to pious ears'.

Placet 'It pleases me'. A formula for expressing assent in ecclesiastical and academic meetings: a 'Yes' vote in those circumstances.

Plethora From the Greek πκεηθα, 'fullness, repletion'. 'Over-fullness in any respect, superabundance; any unhealthy repletion or excess': *OED.*

Plus uni maneat perenne saeclo 'May it live and last more than a century!' Catullus, *Carmina* 1, of his own *Carmina.*

Posse comitatus See *a posse ad esse, above.*

Post coitum omne animal triste 'After coition every animal is sad.' A saying attributed to Aristotle, but apparently post-Classical.

Post hoc, ergo propter hoc 'Later than that, therefore because of that.' A pithy exposition of the fallacy that temporal succession implies causality.

Prima est haec ultio quod se / judice nemo nocens absolvitur 'The most fearsome punishment is that no guilty man is acquitted by his own judgement.' Juvenal, *Satires,* 13:2.

Prima facie 'On the face of it', at first sight. In legal use, the term means 'sufficient to warrant prosecution, or to found an action'.

Primus inter pares 'First among equals'.

Principibus placuisse viris non ultima laus est. / Non cuivis homini contingit adire Corinthum 'To please the leaders of men is not the meanest glory. It is not given to everyone to go to Corinth.' Horace, *Epistles*, 1:17:35.

Prisco si credis, Maecenas docte, Cratino, nulla placere diu nec vivere carmina possunt / Quae scribuntur aquae potoribus 'Learned Maecenas, if thou believest venerable Cratinus, no poems can please for long or live that are written by water-drinkers.' Horace, *Epistles*, 1:19:1.

Pro bono publico 'For the public good.' In recent years the phrase has acquired a good deal of publicity in England in that, since access to legal aid is increasingly restricted, members of the English Bar and other legal professionals have increasingly volunteered their services in the interest of those who do not qualify for legal aid and who are unable to afford after-the-event legal-expenses insurance. Increasingly, the phrase is reduced to *pro bono*, and is much used adjectivally, as in '*pro-bono* work'.

Pro forma 'For the sake of formality'. Nowadays, almost completely restricted to an adjectival use in the expression '*pro-forma* invoice'. The implication is that an invoice is not necessary since payment is not sought, as with a free supply or a trade sample (particularly if destined for overseas) but the *pro-forma* invoice sufficiently warrants that no payment is due.

Pro hac vice '[Solely] for this purpose'; an exception is being made in this case and is not to be taken as a precedent.

Pro rata 'In proportion, proportionally'. There is an extremely rarely used adjective and adverbial couplet, 'rateable/rateably.' Its virtual demise is no doubt due to the extreme convenience of *pro rata.*

Pro tanto 'To such an extent'. Extremely useful in the construction, '*Pro tanto* the rate of tax was raised, *pro tanto* the "take" was diminished'.

Probitas laudatur et alget 'Honesty is praised and is left out in the cold.' Juvenal, *Satires*, 1:74.

Procul omen abesto! 'May that fate be far off!' Ovid, *Amores* 1:14:41.

Procul hinc, procul este, severae! 'Go far from here, go far away, ye grim women!' Ovid, *Amores*, 2:1:3.

Procul, o procul este, profani 'Far off'. O stay far off, ye profane!' Virgil, *Aeneid*, 6:2568.

Proferens 'The one who proffers [a contract, an agreement, a lease].'

Proicit ampullas et sesquipedalia verba 'He tosses aside his bombast and his words a foot and a half long.' Horace, *Ars Poetica*, 97.

Prolepsis Greek *πρόληπσις*, 'a preconception'. In rhetoric, an 'anticipation'. In diplomatic and palaeography, a dating that is too early. In logic, an anticipation of an opponent's argument. In rhetoric, a figure of speech or trope as exemplified in the mnemonic below:

> Prolepsis looks a step ahead:
> 'Their murder'd man' is not yet dead.

Propaganda See *de Propaganda Fidei, above.*

Proviso 'Provided [that]'. Strictly, a past participle, but nowadays, in English, a noun denoting something that must be 'provided' or put in place before some other thing can be accomplished.

Proxime accessit 'He or she came next.' A comfort offered to the second in the race (and applied figuratively).

Punica fide 'With Punic [Carthaginian] faith'. Sallust, *Jugurtha*, 108:3. *Scil*, 'treachery'.

Purpureus pannus 'A purple patch' (in a written work). Horace, *Ars Poetica*, 15-16.

Quadriga A chariot drawn by four horses in line abreast. Specifically, in England, the sculpture on the Monumental Arch in sight of Apsley House.

Quadrivium The four-part upper division of the seven liberal arts in Mediaeval times, comprising arithmetic, geometry, astronomy and music. *Cf trivium, below.*

Quaere See *Sed quaere, below.*

Quaestio subtillissima, utrum chimaera in vacuo bombinans possit comedere secundas intentiones 'A most subtle question: whether a chimaera buzzing in a vacuum can devour second intentions.' Rabelais, *Pantagruel*, 2:7. As a sharp jab at Scholasticism, Rabelais invents what he conceives is a typical arid, nonsensical topic for disputation by Schoolmen. If Rabelais (1483-1553) had chosen to look at the disputations of his Humanist Reformer contemporaries, he might have found a field more fecund by far for his browsing, with the embattled Scholastic *transubstantiation*, Luther's *consubstantiation*, Osiander's *impanation*, the Bohemians' *utraquism* and a myriad other subtleties that make Aquinas look like Joe Blunt.

Quantum meruit 'As much as he deserves.' If no specific fee or charge has been agreed for work done and the matter is referred to some impartial person, the decision will in most cases depend on an analysis of what work has been done and what expenses incurred. On the basis of all the known facts, the independent assessor will arrive at a conclusion based on what the claimant deserves. If specific provisions in a contract for services fail for unavoidable reasons, a court will generally assess the value of the claim on a *quantum-meruit* footing.

Quem Deus vult perdere, prius dementat 'Whom God wishes to destroy he first sends mad.' Adapted proverbially from Publilius Syrus, *Aphorisms*, 490: *Stultum facit Fortuna quem vult perdere*, 'Fortune makes foolish whom she wishes to destroy.'

Qui desiderat pacem, praeparet bellum 'Let him who desires peace prepare for war.' Vegetius (AD 379-95), *Epitoma Rei Militaris*, bk 3, Prologue, usually quoted as *Si vis pacem, para bellum* 'If you wish for peace, prepare for war.' See also *πολεμουμεν ιν ειρηνην αγωμεν* 'We wage war so that we might live in peace': Aristotle, *Nicomachean Ethics*, 10:1177b 5-6.

Qui facit per alium facit per se 'Who does it through another does it himself.' Proverbial in the Law of Agency.

Qui iure suo utitur neminem laedit 'He who exercises his right injures no-one.' *D.*50:17:151.

Quid non mortalia pectora cogis / Auri sacra fame! 'To what lengths do you not drive human hearts, cursed craving for gold!' Virgil, *Aeneid*, 3:56.

Quis custodiet ipsos / Custodes? 'Who is to guard the guards themselves?' Juvenal, *Satires*, 6:347.

Quid pro quo 'A tit for tat.' The term may also mean a fair bargain: something of value for something of value, but this usage is perhaps obsolescent.

Quidquid agunt homines, votum timor ira voluptas / Gaudia discursus nostri farrago libelli est 'Whatever moves men – their wishes, fears, anger, pleasures, joys, and miscellaneous pursuits – is the hotchpotch of our little book.' Juvenal, *Satires*, 1:85.

Quidquid delirant reges, plectuntur Achivi 'For every folly of their kings, the Greeks feel the lash.' Horace, *Epistles*, 1:2:14.

Quicunque vult [salvus esse] 'Whosoever wishes [to be saved].' The first words of the third Creed of the Church, the Athanasian Creed.

Quieta non movere Literally, 'quiet things not to move'; 'Let sleeping dogs lie.'

Quietus 'A discharge from a debt', short for *quietus est.* Figuratively, death.

> 'When he himselfe might his quietus make / With a bare bodkin': Shakespeare, *Hamlet*, 3:1:75. (1602).

Quo vadis? 'Whither goest thou?' Cf *Jn* 13:36 *Vg.*

Quod erat demonstrandum 'What was to be demonstrated.' From *οπερ εδει δειξαι* 'Which was to be proved', added at the end of a proof of a theorem. Euclid, *Elementa*, 1:5 and *passim*.

Quod est inconveniens, aut contra rationem, non permissum est in lege 'What is "inconvenient" or against reason is not permissible in Law.' *Co. Litt.* 178 a. The word *inconveniens* is not well translated by 'inconvenient'. The word implies some undesirable potential in a decision or judgement, or in any step in an action, that is likely to produce results that are contrary to the interests of the Law.

Quod scripsi, scripsi 'What I have written, I have written.' See *Jn* 19:21-2.

> *Dicebant ergo Pilato pontifices Iudaeorum noli scribere rex Iudaeorum sed quia ipse dixit rex sum Iudaeorum: respondit Pilatus quod scripsi scripsi.*
>
> 'Then the chief priests of the Jews said to Pilate: Write not: The King of the Jews. But that he said: I am the King of the Jews.
>
> Pilate answered: What I have written, I have written.'

Quod semper, quod ubique, quod ab omnibus credenda est 'What has always, what has everywhere, what by everyone has been believed': St Vincent of Lérins, *Commonitorium*, 2.

Quod vide 'Which see', a direction to the reader to refer to the item specified. Abbreviated to *q.v.* The plural is *quae vide* but the abbreviated way of displaying that is *qq.v.*

Quodsi me lyricis vatibus inseres, / Sublimi feriam sidera vertice 'But if thou should'st place me among the lyric bards, I shall touch the stars with my exalted head.' Horace, *Odes*, 1:1:35.

Quondam 'Former', as in '*quondam* Provost of King's College, Cambridge'.

Quorum 'Of which'. The specified number of members of, *e.g.*, a committee necessary to effectuate business. The wording of old charters and such specified the number of members of governing bodies, etc, and stipulated that *quorum*, 'of them', such-and-such a number was necessary for the proper conduct of business.

Quot homines, tot sententiae 'As many men, so many opinions.' Terence, *Phormio* 454; quoted by Cicero, *De Finibus*, 1:5:15.

Quota Mediaeval Latin *quota (pars)*, 'How many'. 'The part or share which is, or ought to be, paid or contributed by one to a total sum or amount; in early use chiefly with ref. to contributions of men, money, or supplies, from a particular town, district, or country': *OED*.

Quousque tandem abutere, Catilina, patientia nostra? 'For how long, O Catiline, will you abuse our patience?' Cicero, *In Catilinam*, 1:1. The beginning of a passage much used by English typefounders as a demonstration of their type-faces.

Radix malorum est cupiditas Quoted by Chaucer in the Prologue to *The Pardoner's Tale*. Abbreviated from *Radix enim omnium malorum est cupiditas*, 'For the love of money is the root of all evil': *Tim* 6:10 *Vg*.

Rara avis in terris nigroque simillima cycno 'A rare bird upon the earth, and very like a black swan'. Juvenal, *Satires*, 6:165, a translation used by Henry Fielding in *Tom Jones*, 4:0:1 (1749).

Ratio decidendi 'The reason for deciding'. The reason for a judge's decision. Plural: *rationes decidendi.* Judges may make a number of decisions during the course of a hearing, not all of which are decisive as to settling the case. The reason that ultimately prompts the judge's decision is his *ratio decidendi*: other decisions, made, for example, on preliminary issues, or on an interim footing, are not. (Of course, a judge might well have more than one *ratio decidendi* in determining a given action.)

Rebus Literally, 'By, with or from the things'. A term used in heraldry and elsewhere to denote a graphic device or design that plays on words, most often on the name of a person, often by incorporating pictorial elements that allude to syllables in the name. The etymology is complex. See the *OED s.v. rebus*.

Rebus sic stantibus 'With things as they stand.' An instance of the use of this expression is the standard stipulation in Law that, in valuations of, for example, landed property, the assessment must be made *rebus sic stantibus* and not with reservations such as 'if the property were in good repair' or 'if the property were untenanted'.

Recipe 'Take thou.' The first words of early prescriptions given by medical men to their patients. Later used jointly with *receipt* for directions in cooking; now predominant in cookery.

Reductio ad absurdum 'A reduction to absurdity'. A mode of argument that proceeds by way of demonstrating that, if an opponent's argument is developed as he appears to wish, it would end in absurdity.

Rem acu tetigisti 'Thou hast touched the thing with a needle.' 'You have hit the nail on the head.'

Res gestae Facts in a case that are material to its presentation and to its disposal by the Court.

Res integra In Law, a case that raises legal issues that have not arisen before. An almost alternative phrase is 'a case of first impression'.

Res judicata 'Things that have already been adjudicated'. It is contrary to public policy to allow matters to be re-litigated.

Requiescat [requiescant] in pace 'May he/she [or they] rest in peace.'

Res inter alios acta 'Things agreed to between other parties.' Though very frequently used by itself, this phrase is strictly an abbreviation of *Res inter alios acta alteri nocere non debet,* 'Things agreed to between two parties ought not to damage a third party.' *Cf. Codex Juris Civilis,* Cod 7:60.

Res ipsa loquitur 'The thing speaks for itself.' This maxim is not quite so simple and straightforward as it seems, but it may properly be explained in this way: in actions for damage occasioned by negligence, it is frequently the case that the facts – the *circumstances* of the accident – are so unambiguous that the accident *itself* proves negligence.

Rictus A gaping mouth. A wide grin.

Rigor A medical condition characterized by a chill and violent shivering. Most medical men use the English pronunciation of Latin, so that this term is distinguished from the English word 'rigour' by its *long* first vowel.

Rigor mortis Stiffening of a body after death. The English pronunciation of *rigor* (see above) is still quite common among medical men, but modern police dramas have tended to blur the distinction between *rigor* and 'rigour'.

Roma locuta est; causa finita est 'Rome has spoken; the case is decided.' St Augustine of Hippo (AD 354-430). The maxim is not strictly a quotation from St Augustine but a summary of a passage in *Sermons*, Antwerp, 1702, no 131, sect 10. The maxim had, of course, been a by-word for centuries before 1702, and at all times had been associated with St Augustine.

Rota By origin, 'a wheel', but now a roster or list of duties. Also the Supreme Court of the Holy See, charged with dealing with matrimonial and secular causes.

Ruat coelum! 'Let the heavens fall!' See also *Fiat justicia, above.*

Rus in urbe 'The countryside in town'. Martial, *Epigrammata*, 12:57:21.

Saeva indignatio 'Fierce indignation'. From Jonathan Swift's epitaph, *Ubi saeva indignatio ulterius cor lacerare nequit,* 'Where fierce indignation can no longer lacerate the heart.'

Sal Atticus 'Attic salt'. Said of Athenian wit; Athens was the capital of Attica. From Pliny, *Natural History*, 31:87.

Sal volatile 'Volatile salt'. A solution of ammonium carbonate used as a restorative in fainting fits.

Salus populi suprema lex 'The well-being of the people is the supreme law': Cicero, *De Legibus*, 3:3:8.

Sancta simplicitas! See *O sancta simplicitas, above.*

Satura quidem tota nostra est '[Verse] satire is something entirely ours.' Quintilian, *Instititio Oratoria,* 10:1:93. Quintilian is pointing out that verse satire owed nothing to Greece.

Scibimus indocti doctique poemata passim 'Unskilled, skilled, we scribble poems all over.' Horace, *Epistles*, 2:1:117.

Scholium Greek *σχολιον*, a gloss or explanatory note; specifically, an ancient exegetical note or comment on a passage in a Greek or Latin author. The plural is *scholia.*

Scilict A Latin contraction of the Latin phrase *scire licet*, 'it is permitted to know'. The word is inserted before an explanatory or amplifying passage. The word is similar in meaning to *id est*, 'that is', but it is less a means of introducing an explanation and more a means of supplying a sort of list. Abbreviated to *scil.*

Securus judicat orbis terrarum 'The judgement of the entire world is conclusive': St Augustine, *Contra Epistolam Parmenidis,* 3:24.

Sed quaere 'But a doubt'. An interjection calling into question something stated or postulated; a note of caution.

Semper ad eventum festinat et in medias res / Non secus ac notas auditorem rapit 'He [some boastful, unskilled writer] always hastens to the event, carrying off his listener into the middle of things as though they already knew all about it.' Horace, *Ars Poetica*, 148. Horace speaks of what the unskilled writer will commonly do – drag his readers into the midst of things. This is an instance of 'motion towards' with the accusative case. The phrase does not mean 'in the static middle of things', which would need the ablative case.

Semper eadem 'Always the same'. The motto of Queen Elizabeth I and of Queen Anne. Since *eadem* is feminine, the motto ought not to be used if men are implied. The masculine would be *semper idem.*

Semper expressum facit cessare tacitum 'That which is express makes that which is implied to cease.' *Co. Litt.* 183 b.

Servus servorum Dei 'Servant of the servants of God'. One of the Pope's titles.

Si foret in terris, rideret Democritus 'If he were on earth, Democritus would laugh.' Horace, *Epistles* 2:1:194. One of the many brilliant (and memorable) verbatim examples of Latin grammar chosen by the Rev. Dr. Benjamin Hall Kennedy to pin-point the practice of skilled writers. With his accustomed facility with his own mother-tongue, Kennedy says, 'The Imperfect or Pluperfect Subjunctive is used if the condition is represented as contrary to known fact.'

In 1869, Lord Acton contributed an article to *The North British Review,* October1869, p131, in which he wrote:

> Bellarmine asserted that if a Pope should prescribe vice and prohibit virtue, the Church must believe him – 'Si autem papa erraret praecipiendo vitia, vel prohibendo virtutes, teneretur Ecclesia credere vitia esse bona et virtutes mala, nisi vellet contra conscientiam peccare.'

If Acton had recalled his Horace, he might have avoided what was a cardinal grammatical error. But correct grammar, crucial though it is, is not enough to preserve a man from stark, insensate Febronianism.

Si monumentum requiris, circumspice 'If you require a monument, look about you': Sir Christopher Wren's epitaph in St Paul's Cathedral.

Si possis recte, si non, quocumque modo rem 'By right means, if thou canst, but, if not, by any means make money.' Horace, *Epistles*, 1:1:66.

Si quid tamen olim scripseris, nonumque prematur in annum 'If thou shouldst ever write something, let it not be published until the ninth year.' Horace, *Ars Poetica*, 386-7.

Si vis pacem, para bellum 'If thou wishest for peace, prepare for war.' See *Armis Exposcere Pacem, above.*

Sic 'Thus [in the original]'. A note to warn the reader that the text as printed is faithful to whatever is being published, however wrong or improbable that might appear.

Sic itur ad astra 'This is the way to the stars!': Virgil, *Aeneid*, 9:641.

Sic transit gloria mundi 'Thus passes the glory of the world!' *O quam cito transit gloria mundi*, 'Oh, how quickly passeth the glory of the world!': Thomas à Kempis, *Imitatio Christi*, 1:5:6.

Silent leges inter arma 'Laws are silenced in time of war': Cicero, *Pro Milone*, 4:11.

Simplex munditiis 'Simple neatness'. Horace, *Odes*, 1:5:5.

Sine die 'Postponed without a new date's having been fixed'. Mainly a term in the Law.

Solatium 'Consolation'. A sum of money paid, over and above the actual damages awarded in litigation, intended as a solace for injured feelings. Curiously, the spelling of this word is properly *solacium*: almost every transcript or photograph of a Mediaeval manuscript one sees spells words with *-ti-* in them as *-ci-*: *initium* is spelt *inicium*, *refutatio* is spelt *refutacio*, and so on. Here we have a word rightly having a *c* rather than a *t* – and, perversely, we go and spell it with a *t*! Probably we are so conditioned to correcting the Mediaeval *c* that we obtrude the letter *t* unconsciously.

Sorites In formal logic, a series of propositions in which the *predicate* of each proposition is the *subject* of the next proposition, the *conclusion* being formed of the *first subject* and the *last predicate*. In the form of *Sorites* first formulated by Rudolf Goclenius (1547-1628), the Goclenian Sorites (otherwise called the *descending sorites*, contrasted with the *Aristotelian* or *ascending sorites*) the *subject* of each proposition is the *predicate* of the next, the *conclusion* being formed of the *last subject* and the *first predicate.* A characteristic of this species of reasoning is that all the conclusions in the chain, whether in an Aristotelian series or a Goclenian series, are omitted except the last.

The word *sorites* derives from the Greek *σωρειτης*, which itself derives from *σωρος*, 'a heap or pile'. There is another logical 'stratagem' that is called *sorites*, whether correctly or not, and that is the celebrated ploy by which one's opponent is forced into the predicament of saying, for example, how many grains of corn constitute a heap – a semantically impossible task. Questions such as 'How many handfuls of corn constitute a pile' can be asked but they simply cannot be answered.

Splendide mendax et in omne virgo / Nobilis aevum 'Splendidly untruthful and a virgin renowned for ever [of the Danaid Hypermestra],' Horace, *Odes*, 3:11:35. The concept has crystalized that Horace was applauding lying in an honourable cause.

Spondet peritiam artis, et imperitia culpae adnumeratur 'He holds himself out as skilled in the art and [thus] lack of skill is charged as a fault.' A maxim summing up the Law of Professional Negligence that derives from various sources. Cicero has, *Si quis quod spopondit, qua in re verbo se uno obligavit, id non facit, maturo iudicio sine ulla religione iudicis condemnatur* 'If one holds himself out whereby, in the matter [in hand], he engages himself to someone, and then does not perform, then the judges, with mature consideration and without scruple, will condemn him.' *Pro Caecino*, 7. The contemporary situation in England is still as expressed by Sir Nicholas Tindal, Chief Justice of the Common Pleas, in the case of *Lanphier* v *Phipos*:

> Every person who enters into a learned profession undertakes to bring to the exercise of it a reasonable degree of skill and care.

Stare decisis 'Stand by the decisions!' In other words, 'Abide by precedent!'

Stat magni nominis umbra 'There stands the shade of a great name': Lucan (AD 39-65), *Pharsalia*, 1:135, of Pompey.

Status quo 'The situation as it is' or 'as it was at a certain time'. Often with the added words *ante bellum,* no doubt in recognition that the ultimate outcome of many wars has been a return to the situation as before.

Stet 'Let it stand.' An instruction to the printer to ignore a correction and to 'let the original stand.'

Stet processus An entry on the roll (that is, in the legal records) to the effect that the parties have agreed to withdraw their pleadings and agreed to a stay of the proceedings. This step can be taken only with the consent of all parties.

Stratum A layer, especially of rock. Some times used figuratively for anything resembling a layer. Plural: *strata.*

Stria 'Ridge'. This word has several rather technical meanings. In a sense that has for some reason emerged in the last decade or so, it means ridges on a surface, and is sometimes expanded to 'striations'. The verb is 'to striate.' The plural of the Latin noun is *striae.*

Suaviter in modo, fortiter in re Approximately 'Suave in manner, strong when it comes to it.' It seems that the maxim first appeared with the two clauses reversed in order, *Fortiter in re, suaviter in modo*, in *Industriae ad Curandos Animae Morbos* by Rudolfo Aquaviva (1543-1615), the fourth General of the Society of Jesus.

Sub judice Said of matters already under judicial review – that is, already before the Court. There has been a shift in the meaning of 'judicial review' since the (English) Civil Procedure Rules of 1998 have replaced the former Prerogative Orders of Certiorari, Mandamus, and Prohibition by newer orders. The procedure in place for the obtaining of these new Orders is known as Judicial Review.

Sub rosa 'Under the rose'. Secretly, silently. No-one has postulated an explanation for this curious idiom, which is used in Latin and in Dutch, German and English conversation and writing.

Sub silentio 'Under silence'. Said of some part of, for example, a religious or other ceremony, that is said in a voice inaudible to the assembly in general.

Sub voce 'Under the voice'. An expression used by lexicographers and other harmless drudges to direct the reader to an entry, usually abbreviated to *s.v*, as in, 'See Lewis, *Latin Dictionary for Schools, s.v. fero.*'

Subpoena A thoroughly anglicized form. The word comprises two Latin elements, *sub* and *poena*, which mean 'under penalty'. A subpoena is a summons to attend court under penalty for non-appearance. It is both noun and verb: the verb conjugates as an English verb and forms two past participles, either of which is acceptable: subpoenaed and subpoena'd.

Suggestio falsi 'Suggestion of the false'. A heinous offence in polite argumentation. A kindred offense is *suppressio veri*, 'suppression of the truth'.

Sui generis 'Of its own kind'; the only such. Frequently used in the Law. *Cf eiusdem generis, above.*

Sui juris Said of persons who are legally of full age and capacity, able to manage their own affairs. *Cf*, in general, *in statu pupillari, above.*

Supra 'Above'. See *below, above.*

Suppressio veri See *suggestio falsi, above.*

Syllepsis See *zeugma, below.*

Symbiosis Greek συνβιωσις 'living together.' A new, figurative, use of the word symbiosis, increasingly present in our lives today – the concept that organisms can co-exist without one robbing the other, with both sides benefiting – seems to have caught on.

Synecdoche A rhetorical figure or trope in which a more comprehensive term is used in place of a less comprehensive one, and vice versa. So, 'a fleet of fifty sail', where 'sail' stands for 'ships'. A useful mnemonic might be:

> Synecdoche? Synecdoche gives part for whole, as 'waves' for 'sea'.

Tabula rasa 'A blank page.' Strictly, the phrase means a tablet coated with wax that the Ancients used for note-writing, but, in this idiom, skimmed to make the surface capable of taking new writing. The expression is widely used figuratively to convey the notion of a mind or a situation ready for a new lease of life, without preconditions and without the residue of former usage.

Tantum Ergo The first two words of the last two stanzas of a hymn written by St Thomas Aquinas (1225-74); the musical settings, plainsong and other, of those words.

Te Deum laudamus, te Dominum confitemur 'We praise Thee, O God: we acknowledge Thee to be the Lord.' A hymn of the Church, traditionally ascribed to St Ambrose and St Augustine, but more recently to Nicetas of Remesiana (c.335-c.414).

Tempora mutantur, et nos mutamur in illis 'Times change, and we change with them.' The *ODQ*, 4th edn (1992), says, 'In William Harrison, *Description of Britain* (1577), bk 3, ch 3, attributed to the Emperor Lothar I (795-855) in the form, '*Omnia mutantur, nos et mutamur in illis*' [All things change, and we change with them].'

Tempus edax rerum 'Time, the devourer of all things'. Ovid, *Metamorphoses*, 15:234.

Tempus fugit Altered slightly from Virgil's *Fugit irreparabile tempus:* 'Time flies irretrievably' (*Georgics* 3:284).

Tenebrae 'Darkness[es].' The names of the Offices of Mattins and Lauds for the Wednesday of Holy Week, Maundy Thursday and Good Friday that were sung in penitential mode and at which the candles lighted at the beginning of the service were extinguished one by one after each psalm, in memory of the darkness at the time of the crucifixion.

Tenet insanabile multos / Scribendi cacoethes et aegro in corde senescit 'An inveterate and incurable itch for writing besets many and grows old with their sick hearts.' Juvenal, *Satires*, 7:1. The word *cacoethes* demonstrates with what facility the Romans borrowed Greek words: it is the Greek for 'a bad habit.' *κακοηθης*.

Ter sunt conati imponere Pelio Ossam / Scilicet atque Ossae frondosum involvere Olympum; / Ter pater exstructos disiecit fulmine montis 'Three times it was attempted to pile Ossa on Pelion – that is, to roll leafy Olympus on top of Ossa; three times our father shattered the towering mountains with a bolt.' Virgil, *Georgics*, 1:281. See *Opaco Pelion imposuisse Olympo, above*. In English, the word-order is always, 'To pile Pelion on Ossa'. No doubt that inversion springs from the word order in the Latin rather than from the sense of the Latin, which is unambiguous.

Terminus ad quem and **Terminus a quo** Two points in time, at which, respectively, an action starts and an action finishes. The terms denote the starting-point and the finishing point of an activity, with a strong emphasis on the *purposefulness* of moving from one to the other.

Textus Receptus The accepted text of an ancient work, specifically the second edition of the Greek New Testament published by Elzevier (Elzevir, Elsevier) in 1633.

Timeo Danaos et dona ferentes In full, *Equo ne credite, Teucri / Quidquid id est, timeo Danaos et dona ferentes*. 'Do not trust the horse, Trojans! Whatever it is, I fear the Greeks even when they bear gifts.' Virgil, *Aeneid*, 2:48.

Tolle lege, tolle lege 'Take, read; take, read.' St Augustine, *Confessions*, 8:12. The 'story-line' that culminates in this passage is characteristic of the profoundly *human* appeal of Augustine, in that he tells us *everything*, he tells us *all*. He was sitting in his walled garden at Cassiciacium. He heard a child outside the wall playing some sort of game. The child cried out, *Tolle, lege! Tolle, lege*!, Take up and read! Take up and read! Augustine had a pagan father and a Christian mother. Until this point in his life, the turning-point in his garden in Cassiciacium, he had followed his father's bent, but, at the moment the child cried out *Tolle, lege! Tolle, lege*!, Augustine happened to have had the Sacred Scriptures at his elbow. He took up the codex and opened it, haphazardly, and read, *Sed induite Dominum Iesum Christum et carnis curam ne feceritis in desideriis* 'But put ye on the Lord Jesus Christ, and make not provision for the flesh, to fulfil the lusts thereof': *Rom* 13:12. He counted his conversion from that point.

Toties quoties 'As often as may be required.' A direction used on prescriptions.

Trivium The three-part lower division of the seven liberal arts in Mediaeval times, comprising grammar, rhetoric and logic. See *quadrivium, above*.

Uberrime fidei 'In the greatest good faith'. *Cf bona fide, above.*

Ubi jus, ibi remedium 'Where the law is, there is a remedy.' Proverbial in the Law.

Ubi Petrus, ibi ergo ecclesiam 'Where Peter is, there, therefore, is the church.' St Ambrose (*c.*339-97), 'Explanatio Psalmi 40' in *Corpus Scriptorum Ecclesiasticorum Latinorum*, 64:250 (1919).

Urbi et orbi An annual Papal Blessing 'To the city [Rome] and the World'.

Ut desint vires, tamen est laudanda voluntas 'Though the strength is lacking, the will is nonetheless praiseworthy.' Ovid, *Epistulae: Ex Ponto*, 3:4:79. Cf *Spiritus quidem promptus est caro autem infirma* 'The spirit indeed is willing but the flesh is weak.' *Mt* 26:41.

Ut res magis valeat quam pereat 'That the thing should survive rather than perish.' Noy, *Max.*, 50. The Law ensures as far as possible that instruments should have effect rather than be made void.

Vade retro me, Satana 'Get thou behind me, Satan': *Mk* 8:33 *Vg.*

Vae victis 'Woe to the vanquished!'. Death to the defeated! Livy, *Ab Urbe Condita,* 5:48, reporting an already proverbial use of the expression put into the mouth of Brennus, the Gaulish chieftain who occupied all Rome except the Capitol. According to legend, the guard on the Capitoline Hill was roused from sleep by the noise of the geese kept by the garrison and, thus alerted, they were able to prevent the capture of the Capitol. Hence, Rome was not entirely occupied.

Vanitas vanitatum *Vanitas vanitatum, et omnia vanitas* 'Vanity of vanities, and all is vanity': *Eccl* 1:2 *Vg.*

Varia lectio A variant reading in a manuscript. Plural: *variae lectiones.*

Variorum An edition of a work with which are included the notes and commentaries of other scholars.

Varium et mutabile semper / femina 'Fickle and changeable always! Woman!' Virgil, *Aeneid*, 4:569. *La donna è mobile*. See *Chommoda dicebat* for a note about elision.

Veneratione mihi semper fuit non verbosa rusticitas, sed sancta simplicitas 'The object of my veneration has always been, not rustic verbosity, but holy simplicity': St Jerome, Letter 'Ad Pammachium', Migne, *Patrologia Latina*, 22:579.

Veni, vidi, vici 'I came, I saw, I conquered.' This saying, attributed to Julius Caesar, comes to us from two sources. Suetonius, in his *Lives of the Caesars*, 'Divus Iulius', 37, tells us that the phrase was the inscription on Caesar's Pontic triumph. Plutarch, in his *Parallel Lives*, 'Iulius Caesar,' 50:2, tells us it was in a letter to Rome written by Caesar announcing his victory at Zela on 2 August, 47 BC, which concluded the Pontic campaign.

Venite, The *Venite exultemus* 'O come let us sing unto the Lord.' *Ps* 94 *Vg*, *Ps* 95 *AV.*

Verba cartarum fortius accipiuntur contra proferentem 'The words of contracts should be interpreted most forcibly against him who adduces them.' *Co. Litt* 36 a; Bacon, *Elem. Common Lawes Eng*. (1630), 1:11; Blackstone, Comm. 2:23:380. The reasoning behind this maxim is twofold. In the first place, it is for the plaintiff or claimant, the *dominus litis* ('lord of the action'), to make out his right: the defendant is under no obligation to help him. The second reason is that the *proferens* is adducing his own document, and in almost every case the *proferens* had control of the wording of the document. It was up to him or his predecessor in title to make sure his words mirrored his or their intention. In *Taylor* v *St Helen's Corporation* (1877) 6 Ch. D. 264 at 270, Jessel M. R. doubted the continuing applicability of the maxim but it has continued to be applied.

Verbum sapienti sat est See *Dictum sapienti sat est, above.*

Via media 'The middle way'.

Vitae summa brevis spem nos vetat incohare longam 'Life's short span forbids our embarking on far-reaching hopes.' Horace, *Odes*, 1:4:15.

Volenti non fit injuria Ulpian, *Ad Edictum*, 56. The meaning of this maxim is that one cannot consent to something and later contend that such was an actionable injury; one cannot agree to something and then, subsequently, bring an action upon that same something, claiming damages. See *Nulla injuria est, above.*

Vos exemplaria Graeca / Nocturna versate manu, versate diurna 'As for you, turn over the pages of the Greeks, as exemplars, by night and by day.' Horace, *Ars Poetica*, 268.

Zeugma Greek *ζευγμα*, 'a yoke [for beasts].' A rhetorical figure of speech or trope in which a single word is made to refer to two or more words in the sentence; especially when properly applying in sense to only one of them, or applying to them in different senses. There is another figure of speech, *syllepsis*, that is very close to zeugma in meaning. In general, the confusion implicit in zeugma is owing to a *misuse* of words; in *syllepsis* the confusion does not depend of error. An instance of zeugma is 'See Pan with flocks / With fruits Pomona crowned' – the error there being that Pan was not 'crowned' with flocks: the one verb, *crowned*, will not do for both the subjects. An instance of *syllepsis* is 'Miss Bolo went home in a flood of tears and a sedan chair'. In that case the preposition *in* serves perfectly well for both notions, '*in* a flood of tears' and '*in* a sedan chair'.

Index

K

L

M

N

O

P